Surviving in the Field of International Arbitration

Surviving in the Field of International Arbitration

War Stories and Lessons Learned

Edited by

José María de la Jara
Carolina Arroyo
Álvaro Awad

Wolters Kluwer

Published by:
Kluwer Law International B.V.
PO Box 316
2400 AH Alphen aan den Rijn
The Netherlands
E-mail: international-sales@wolterskluwer.com
Website: lrus.wolterskluwer.com

Sold and distributed in North, Central and South America by:
Wolters Kluwer Legal & Regulatory U.S.
7201 McKinney Circle
Frederick, MD 21704
United States of America
Email: customer.service@wolterskluwer.com

Sold and distributed in all other countries by:
Air Business Subscriptions
Rockwood House
Haywards Heath
West Sussex
RH16 3DH
United Kingdom
Email: international-customerservice@wolterskluwer.com

ISBN 978-94-035-1760-5

e-Book: ISBN 978-94-035-1811-4
web-PDF: ISBN 978-94-035-1855-8

To Alfredo Bullard,
for all our Friday afternoon talks.
José María de la Jara

To Lucas and Sven.
Carolina Arroyo

To my mentor, Óscar Contreras,
for trusting in me since the very beginning of my career.
Álvaro Awad

Editors

José María de la Jara is a Peruvian arbitration attorney working as a global visiting lawyer at Covington & Burling LLP in Washington, D.C. He holds a J.D. from Pontificia Universidad Católica del Perú and an L.L.M. from Columbia Law School. He currently serves as an Ambassador for Arbitrator Intelligence. Previously he acted as Training Coordinator at the American Bar Association Rule of Law Initiative and worked for eight years as an arbitration associate at Bullard Falla Ezcurra in Lima, Peru. He founded PsychoLAWgy and has authored more than fifty articles at the intersection of dispute resolution, behavioral sciences, and technology.

Carolina Arroyo is a senior associate at Andrade Veloz in Quito, Ecuador, where she directs the Dispute Resolution and Complex Litigation Department. Carolina holds an L.L.M from Bucerius Law School and Otto Beisheim School of Management in Germany. She lectures as a professor at the Universidad San Francisco de Quito and acts as secretary for arbitral tribunals in the Arbitration and Mediation Center of Quito's Chamber of Commerce. Carolina is an Ambassador for Arbitrator Intelligence as well as a member of the Committee of Young Practitioners of the Ecuadorian Arbitration Institute. In addition, she has cofounded different Internet platforms for the construction and art industries of Latin America.

Álvaro Awad is a partner at Contreras Velozo, a dispute resolution boutique law firm in Santiago, Chile. He holds an L.L.M. from The University of Chicago Law School, where he studied with both a Fulbright and Chile Scholarship. He currently lectures as Professor of Civil Law, Arbitration, and Oral Advocacy at Pontificia Universidad Católica de Chile, the university where he earned his J.D. *summa cum laude*. Álvaro is an Ambassador for Arbitrator Intelligence in Chile as well as a reporter for the *Bulletin of International Commercial and Investment Arbitration* in Latin America. He founded the Santiago Very Young Arbitration Practitioners group. He is also listed as Arbitrator of the Santiago Court of Appeals' Official Roster.

Contributors

Ricardo Ampuero is the President of the Special Commission which represents the Republic of Peru in international investment disputes at the Ministry of Finances and Economy. He received his L.L.M. from Columbia University.

Félix Antolín is Director of Civil Litigation and Arbitration at Albagli Zaliasnik, in Santiago, Chile. He received his L.L.M. from New York University.

Crina Baltag is Senior Lecturer in International Arbitration at Stockholm University. She received her Ph.D. from the Queen Mary University of London.

Gary Born is Chair of the International Arbitration Practice Group at Wilmer Cutler Pickering Hale and Dorr LLP. He also serves as President of the Singapore International Arbitration Centre (SIAC) Court of Arbitration and authored *International Commercial Arbitration* (2nd ed. 2014), the preeminent treatise in the field, and *International Arbitration: Law and Practice* (2nd ed. 2015) as well as other notable works on international arbitration.

Alfredo Bullard is Partner at Bullard, Falla, Ezcurra + in Lima, Peru. He received his L.L.M. from Yale Law School.

María Angélica Burgos is a lawyer from the Pontificia Universidad Javeriana in Bogotá. She received her L.L.M in International Business Regulation, Litigation, and Arbitration from the University of New York.

Roque Caivano is a professor at the University of Buenos Aires and Cofounder of the UBA-Universidad del Rosario International Arbitration Moot. He received his Doctorate Degree in Juridical Sciences from Universidad del Salvador.

Briana Canorio is Director of the Administrative Arbitration Direction of Peru Government's Supervisory Agency and Sub Manager of Contracts of the Legal Corporate Management of PETROPERÚ S.A. in Lima. She formerly served as ICC YAF Representative. She received her L.L.B. from the University of Lima.

Manuel Casas is Counsel at WilmerHale's Litigation Department in London. Prior to joining WilmerHale, he worked as a law clerk (U.T.) at the International Court of Justice in The Hague. He received his L.L.M. from Yale Law School.

Manuel Conthe is an arbitrator as well as Chairman of the Advisory Board of the Spanish business newspaper *Expansión*.

Diana Correa is founder of Diana Correa International SAS in Bogotá, Colombia. She received her Ph.D. from Université Panthéon Assas (Paris II).

Daniel Cuentas is an associate at Osterling Lawyers in Lima as well as Arbitrator Intelligence Ambassador. He received his L.L.B. from the Peruvian University of Applied Sciences in Lima.

Juliana de Valdenebro works as Foreign Law Clerk for Hogan Lovells in Miami. She received her L.L.M. at Harvard Law School.

Christopher R. Drahozal teaches as John M. Rounds Professor at the University of Kansas School of Law. He also serves on the Board of Directors for Arbitrator Intelligence, Inc.

Mauricio Duarte is an international associate at ASJ Tech Store. He received his L.L.M. from the University of St. Thomas in St. Paul.

Valeria Galíndez is an arbitrator and founder of Galíndez Arbitragem, a boutique law firm in Brazil. She received her J.D. from Pontifícia Universidade Católica de Sao Paolo.

Diana Gárate is the Senior Manager at EY Law in Lima, Peru. She received her L.L.M. from Columbia Law School.

José Ignacio García Cueto is the special legal consultant of Clifford Chance US LLP in Washington D.C. He received his L.L.M. from Georgetown University.

Francisco González de Cossío is an arbitrator. He received his Doctorate Degree in Law and Economics and L.L.M from the University of Chicago as well as his OPM in Finance from Harvard Business School.

Clifford J. Hendel is an arbitrator and founder of the Madrid law firm HENDEL IDR.

René Irra is Partner at Cuatrecasas in Mexico City. He received his L.L.M. from the Université Versailles Saint-Quentint-en-Yvelines.

Rafael Llano is Partner at White & Case LLP in México City. He formerly served as National Consultant for the Unit for the Promotion of Democracy of the Organization of American States in Asunción, Paraguay. He received his L.L.M. from Harvard Law School.

Edson López is Partner of the Integrum Office which is in charge of the practice of Arbitration and Educational Law in Guatemala. He is also CEO of the Latin-American Group of Educational Advisors (GLAE).

Lucas Loviscek is an associate at Quinn Emanuel, Urquhart & Sullivan, LLP. He received his L.L.M. from Georgetown University.

Juan Felipe Merizalde is a special legal consultant for Dechert's LLP in Washington D.C. He received his L.L.M. from New York University and the Master 1 in International Law from Université Paris 2 Panthéon-Assas.

Caterina Miró Quesada is an international associate at White & Case LLP. She received her L.L.M. with a Certificate in Energy Law from the University of Lima.

Francisco Muñoz is the regional manager of Dispute Resolution at Mercado Libre in Buenos Aires, Argentina. He received his L.L.M. from New York University.

Rachel Ong is an advocate and solicitor for the Supreme Court of Singapore as well as solicitor for the Senior Courts of England and Wales. She received her L.L.B from the University of Southampton and her L.L.M from Columbia University.

Arturo Oropeza is Visiting Attorney at King & Spalding LLP in New York and Cofounder of Mexico City Very Young Arbitration Practitioners. He received his L.L.B. from Instituto Autónomo de México and his L.L.M. from Stanford Law School.

Daniela Páez-Salgado is an associate at Herbert Smith Freehills in New York. He received his L.L.M. from Harvard Law School.

Frank Ramos is Managing Partner at Clarke Silverglate in Miami. He received his J.D. from the University of Miami School of Law.

Juan M. Rey is an associate at Philippi, Prietocarrizosa & Uría in Santiago, Chile as well as ICC YAF Representative. He received his L.L.M. from Columbia Law School.

Aníbal Sabater is Partner at Chaffetz Lindsey LLP in New York. He also serves as Chair of the International Law Committee of the Association of the Bar of the City of New York as well as Director of the New York International Arbitration Center.

Cristóbal Sarralde is the principal associate at Garrigues in Santiago, Chile. He received his L.L.M. from the University of California, Berkley School of Law.

Robert H. Smit is an adjunct professor of law at Columbia Law School.

Cedric Soule is a senior associate at King & Spalding LLP in New York. He received his L.L.B. from McGill University and M.A. (Oxon) in Philosophy, Politics, and Economics from St. Hugh's College of the University of Oxford in the United Kingdom.

Clovis Trevino is Special Counsel for Covington & Burling's international arbitration practice in Washington D.C.

Luis Miguel Velarde is Senior Associate in the International Arbitration Department at Dechert LLP in Paris. He received his L.L.B. from Pontificia Universidad Católica del Perú (PUCP) and L.L.M. from Harvard University.

Patricia Vera is the Director of the Arbitration and Mediation Center of the Ecuadorian-American Chamber of Commerce in Quito, Ecuador. She received her L.L.M. from the Universidad San Francisco de Quito.

Shoschana Zusman is a senior professor at the Pontificia Universidad Católica del Perú (PUCP) Law School and partner at Estudio Zusman in Lima, Peru. She is also a member of the Administrative Tribunal of the Inter-American Development Bank.

The opinions expressed herein are those of the authors and do not necessarily reflect those opinions of other attorneys on their firm or their clients.

Summary of Contents

Foreword

Surviving in the Field of International Arbitration: War Stories and Lessons Learned is an extraordinary compilation about what happens behind the scenes in the international arbitration market.

This book, published from the outset in a convenient English-Spanish bilingual edition, analyzes the reality of counsels and arbitrators from a refreshing and pragmatic perspective.

José María, Carolina and Álvaro, three very prominent young Latin-American practitioners, have managed to coordinate the experiences and advice of some of the most renowned names of arbitration worldwide in a single publication. Their teachings alternate between many episodes, sometimes personal and even tragicomic, inherent to arbitration practice. Thus, these stories from different jurisdictions combine all the experiences at different stages of a career in arbitration, ranging from the beginnings of a law career to the challenges faced by seasoned arbitrators.

The text wisely advises on the work itself, for example how to work with a cocounsel, how to participate in a deliberation, or how to write that first arbitral award. It also touches on the personal and professional development of lawyers and arbitrators, such as how to balance motherhood with work, how to develop a personal brand, and even what conferences to attend.

In this context, it is becoming increasingly important to give space to those professionals who propose best practices and, likewise, have experienced the new problems emerging in the market.

Without a doubt, this book is a fundamental contribution to anyone who intends to enter the world of arbitration. It is likely that, in a short time, this compilation will turn into an inescapable consultation text to anyone who wants to dedicate themselves to this very interesting area of law.

Alexis Mourre
President of the ICC International Court of Arbitration
Paris, February 2020

Preface

What could I possibly do to become a better arbitration practitioner? How could I become a respected arbitrator? What is it like to work at an international firm? How should I conduct myself in a team? How important are social events for my career in arbitration? Is creativity rewarded in arbitration? How can I get clients? And how should I treat them? How do I transfer from one area of law to arbitration? Can I thrive in arbitration if I also like academia?

This book aims to engage its audience with fun-to-read confessions, useful lessons and reflections about life as an arbitration practitioner. We expect this book to become the go-to guide to thrive in the arbitration market. It features forty arbitration practitioners and their intimate stories about critical issues such as their first oral pleading, discussing hot topics such as discrimination, and providing hands-on experience with arbitral litigation, decision-making, and academic work.

Difficult questions had to be asked, such as facing the rat race within firms, burnout, and bullying and reflecting on the balance between work and life.

Surviving in the Field of International Arbitration: War Stories and Lessons Learned features some of the *crème de la crème* in arbitration. These contributors come from different jurisdictions and touch upon very different and creative topics.

It was about time to compile—in a book—the experiences and tips of some of the main participants in this complex market.

List of Abbreviations

AAA	American Arbitration Association
ABA	American Bar Association
BITs	Bilateral Investment Treaties
CAD	Columbia Arbitration Day
CEA	Spanish Arbitration Club
CIAR	Iberoamerican Arbitration Centre
CIETAC	China International Economic and Trade Arbitration Commission
CoLAP	Commission on Lawyer Assistance Programs
CONSUCODE	Peru's Superior Council for State Contracting
DNA	Deoxyribonucleic Acid
GAR	Global Arbitration Review
HKIAC	Hong Kong International Arbitration Centre
IBA	International Bar Association
ICC	International Chamber of Commerce
ICC YAF	International Chamber of Commerce Young Arbitrator Forum
ICCA	International Council for Commercial Arbitration
ICDR	International Centre for Dispute Resolution
ICSID	International Centre for Settlement of Investment Disputes
ICTs	Information and Communication Technologies
INTA	International Trademark Association
ISDS	Investor-State Dispute Settlement
LOI	Letter of Intent
MOU	Memorandum of Understanding
NDA	Nondisclosure Agreement
NGO	Nongovernmental Organization

OSCE	Peru Government's Supervisory Agency
OBOR	One Belt One Road
SHA	Shareholders' Agreement
SIAC	Singapore International Arbitration Centre
SPA	Sale and Purchase Agreement
SRA	Solicitors Regulation Authority
SWOT	Strengths, Weaknesses, Opportunities, and Threats Analysis
UNCITRAL	United Nations Commission on International Trade Law
US	United States of America
VCLT	Vienna Convention on the Law of Treaties
WWA	Women Way in Arbitration

Part I War Stories and Lessons about Working as a Counsel

CHAPTER 1

What Makes an Excellent International Arbitration Lawyer

Gary Born & Manuel Casas

This chapter addresses how to be an excellent international arbitration lawyer. It focuses on four essential characteristics that distinguish an *excellent* international arbitration lawyer from those professionals who are *good* or even *very good*.

The four characteristics are simultaneously obvious and counterintuitive. They are obvious because they are the type of advice you would get from a wise grandmother; however, they are counterintuitive because they are not the typical characteristics you would associate with a litigator. We describe these characteristics below and provide some examples of their application in practice.

The first characteristic is to work hard, very hard, very, very hard. Excellence requires exertion. There are no shortcuts or magic formulas that substitute a substantial amount of effort. Not even geniuses are exempt from working hard. As an actual genius once stated, being a genius is 99 % hard work and 1 % talent. This concept also applies to international arbitration. In fact, the nature of the job finds that it is not uncommon for a medium-skilled, but hardworking lawyer to defeat a more talented, but lazy opponent.

All aspects of practice require hard work *all* the time. It is not enough to work extremely hard a few weeks before a submission is due or in the run-up to a hearing. Excellent international arbitration lawyers work hard in all stages of a case and generally, in all their professional activities. Hard work usually means dedicating a little more time than absolutely necessary for each task, editing a submission a few more times, and spending additional hours to adjust a presentation.

It also means being overprepared, be it for a cross-examination, client meeting, or procedural hearing. This surplus preparation usually pays just as effort—when channeled properly—tends to be reflected in the work product. For example, the submission drafted in 200 hours tends to be better than the one drafted in 20 hours. But preparation also builds your own skills—it teaches you how to be a better arbitration lawyer in future cases.

The second characteristic is to know how to listen. Listening instead of talking is perhaps one of the most undervalued skills of a litigator and advocate. Perhaps it is because the skill most people tend to associate with a litigator is eloquence. The emphasis tends to be more on how a lawyer talks and what s/he says instead of *how* s/he listens and to *what* s/he listens.

However, the main task of an advocate is persuading someone (i.e., the sole arbitrator or the tribunal president) to do something. The advocate must understand what is important for the person s/he wants to persuade and accordingly determine which points to address and how. This scenario is particularly true for international arbitration lawyers. They often must persuade people from different cultural backgrounds and legal traditions, and different persons almost always approach cases from different angles. The excellent international arbitration lawyer must be able to identify that specific angle and adjust his or her strategy accordingly. To create a successful strategy, it is crucial to understand the tribunal's concerns: What points are interesting to the arbitrators? What parts of the case are troubling them? Which arguments are having traction? The only way to determine the answers to these questions is by listening to the tribunal.

Here, listening is used broadly. It is not limited to listening to the tribunal's questions—although it is probably a good place to start. Listening also includes observing and analyzing the tribunal's attitude, body language, and interactions throughout the proceedings. When a certain issue is being discussed, are the arbitrators interested, immersed, and engaged? Or are they distracted, aloof, and uninterested? Are they perhaps looking at their phones or computers or even taking a nap?

Knowing how to listen is not a skill limited to the hearing room. Listening to clients is also crucial. The excellent international arbitration lawyer must understand his or her client's priorities in a case and determine whether there are commercial considerations that, despite being legally irrelevant, are crucial to the client. Again, it is usually impossible to take these considerations on board without carefully listening to the client.

Similarly, it is also important to listen to other team members. In large cases, it tends to be difficult—perhaps even impossible—to understand all aspects of a case in detail. Thus there will usually be a team member who will have a better grasp of some aspects of the case, be it a stream of documents or an expert witness, or who may have more useful insight on certain issues.

The third characteristic is to always be honest with oneself, and it implies several things. Mainly the excellent international arbitration lawyer is humble. He or she does not fool himself or herself but instead admits when s/he does not know something. Of course, it is easier said than done. There is an expectation, sometimes quite culturally ingrained, that a litigator must always give the impression of being very sure of what s/he is saying. The classic example of this mindset is the renowned law professor who quipped that he was "often in error, but never in doubt." Yet this stance of purported infallibility not only is a *cliché* but also tends to be an obstacle for doing the best work possible. It is much more productive to admit not understanding something—and taking the necessary steps to solve it—than to continue acting as a know-it-all and persist in error.

Professional practice offers many opportunities for self-deception. For instance, it is common to think that we have found a perfect argument, the one that will automatically win the case, without having critically considered whether it is compatible with the other given arguments of the case or whether it is supported by the evidence on record. This attitude does not help win a case. In contrast, approaching work from a perspective of humility does, as it allows oneself to detect weaknesses and areas for improvement.

The fourth characteristic is honing one's communication skills, both written and oral, which is the flip side of knowing how to listen. Being able to precisely detect what arguments would persuade the tribunal is insufficient if the arbitrator cannot articulate those points effectively. These communication skills must be exhibited throughout the arbitration. An excellently drafted memorial loses credibility if the prior procedural correspondence is mediocre, just as an eloquent oral argument is undermined if the written submissions are deficient. Indeed, an excellent advocate must see every interaction with the tribunal as an opportunity for persuasion—and approach them as such.

For Latin-American international arbitration lawyers, it is also important to develop communication skills in English, a considerable challenge for those persons who are not native speakers. However, given the position of English as the lingua franca of international business, developing these skills is indispensable. It especially applies to those professionals that plan on focusing their practice exclusively in Latin America. The international aspect of arbitration means it is highly likely that a fair number of cases will have elements in English. The language of the arbitration may be in Spanish or Portuguese, but at one point there will probably be a client, witness, or expert that can only speak English or a critical document that is written only in English. After all, exchanges between a Chinese company investing in an infrastructure project in Brazil with funding provided by a German bank will most likely be in English.

Making a list of characteristics for aspiring excellent international arbitration lawyers is difficult. After all, like most attributions of quality, there is an inherent degree of subjectivity involved. Litigation is more of an art than science, and personal preferences play a significant role, even more so in international arbitration as there is a confluence of practitioners from different legal traditions. The expansion of international arbitration has contributed to the development of a more *international* style of advocacy that is influenced by domestic practice but that also adopts a more transnational flavor. Nevertheless, some practitioners may still prefer the assertiveness of US-style litigators, whereas others will favor the collegial approach adopted by some civil law practitioners.

By proposing these four characteristics, we are not aiming to give a categorical answer to what constitutes excellence in international arbitration. Our objective is more modest. It is to share a series of observations, developed throughout the years, that could help someone starting their career to focus on harnessing some skills that may be overlooked but will definitely be helpful in their path toward excellence in international arbitration.

CHAPTER 2

The Decalogue to Work with Cocounsel

Aníbal Sabater[*]

In international arbitration a party is often represented by two or more law firms. Sometimes both firms have similar profiles and experience, and other times they are different but complement one other. For example, one firm provides knowledge that the other does not have about a specific law or industry. The following Decalogue is a guide to help firms work together efficiently on behalf of their client. Although some of its contents may be extended by analogy, this Decalogue is not intended for situations where the client is represented by a single firm, but there is another firm providing "shadow counsel."

First Commandment:	Both firms' teams shall do their best to meet each other in person or, failing that, by videoconference or telephone. Even if the lawyers already know each other before working on the case, they will arrange a new meeting as soon as possible.
Second Commandment:	Both firms' teams shall agree beforehand—and certainly without waiting for crises or emergencies to arise—on which firm will work on which substantive and procedural areas of the case. The client must know at all times which firm is responsible for which area. Example: Depending on the circumstances of the case, one firm may be responsible for the analysis and preparation of arguments subject to local law, while the other may be responsible for the rest of the strategy.

[*] The opinions expressed herein are those of the author and do not necessarily reflect those opinions of other attorneys in his firm or the firm's clients.

Third Commandment:	Both firms' teams shall quickly become familiar with their respective areas of work and faithfully exchange information about them.
Fourth Commandment:	Both firms' teams shall agree beforehand—and certainly without waiting for crises or emergencies to arise—on how to report to the client. In matters where both firms can and should have an opinion, both will try to agree on their recommendation to the client beforehand. If a firm gives an opinion directly to the client, then a copy of that opinion will also be given to the other firm. What protocol will be followed when the firms do not agree on the recommendation to the client?
Fifth Commandment:	Both firms' teams shall work together from the outset to identify witnesses and experts who can support the client's position and will coordinate their activities to contact, interview, and work with them.
Sixth Commandment:	As soon as there is an established procedural calendar, the firms shall agree on the procedure, deadlines, and division of tasks that they will follow for the preparation of briefs. The deadlines agreed upon by the firms shall be long enough to give the client time to review the drafts to avoid delays in the submission of the briefs.
Seventh Commandment:	The firms shall agree sufficiently in advance on each one's role at hearings and their preparation. This agreement includes determining: (1) which firm and, specifically, what attorney will lead the client's representation at the hearing; (2) which firm will prepare each witness and expert for the hearing; (3) which firm(s) will do opening and closing arguments (and if there is more than one firm, the issues that each of them will address); and (4) which firm will examine each witness or expert.
Eighth Commandment:	Both firms' teams shall be respectful and polite to each other while remaining aware that they belong to different organizations. Their legal cultures, experiences, and roles in the dispute may be different, but both are expected to work hard to bolster the case.
Ninth Commandment:	While remaining aware that they are working together in just one particular case, both firms' teams shall behave as if they had to work together for years to come. For this reason, if their relationship is effective, they will try to find more cases to work on together.
Tenth Commandment:	Everything shall be done and in consultation with the client. Any of the foregoing commandments shall yield before an instruction of the client to the contrary.

Chapter 3

Building Instructions for a Second Chair

Cedric Soule & Arturo Oropeza[*]

§3.01 INITIAL DESCRIPTION OF THE PRODUCT

Let us begin with terminology. What is a second chair? An ordinal number followed by a noun? If these instructions were not a guide for attorneys, it might as well be a furniture catalog. We consulted the dictionary of the Spanish Royal Academy and did not find any results, not even in the specialized linguistics section. What a pity!

If our chair is second, it is because there must be a first chair. Sound and impeccable reasoning, no? This reasoning is the first element in our quest to understand the meaning of the second chair. But what or who is the first chair? English-language dictionaries define the first chair as the lead attorney in court. The second chair is defined as the attorney who assists the first chair. In other words, our character seems to have been born in the shadows of a law firm, or any other location where attorneys commonly meet. Moreover, our character has a supporting role in the context of a legal proceeding that contemplates some type of oral presentation before a judge.

Arbitration, as it often does, has borrowed the term and adapted it for its own purposes. The second chair is the attorney who usually sits next to the lead attorney who pleads the case before the arbitral tribunal during a hearing. At the same time, the role of a second chair in arbitration is more flexible. It is not uncommon for a second chair to plead at the hearing as well, particularly if the scope or complexity of a case requires the involvement of multiple attorneys.

Perhaps in Spanish we could dare to be more inventive. Even if we are prohibited in our language from forming compound nouns or using hyphens to link words together, let us try nonetheless: the taker of (illegible) notes; s/he who stares at

* This chapter does not reflect the views of King & Spalding, its clients and/or its attorneys.

witnesses and fills them with awe; s/he who knows the confines of the lists of exhibits and legal authorities; the provider of highlighters and facts. All of these descriptions do more justice to the role of a second chair than the term in English, particularly when these tasks are usually lost in the anonymity of a hearing room or amidst nervous whispers while the court reporter types up the hearing transcript.

However, beyond definitions, what is clear is that the second chair is not in the limelight. Recognition—the ovation, the applause—will go entirely to the first chair. Most likely everyone at the firm will discuss the first chair's mastery and skill; how the tribunal agreed with him/her with a gesture; how a witness finally caved after a barrage of clever questions. Our second chair will remain unnoticed. Perhaps s/he will receive a pat on the back or a drink after work, but nothing more.

History has always known how to keep supporting roles to the side; for example, Sancho is not Don Quixote. Soccer, the true gospel of Hispanic culture, more so than Cervantes himself, offers clearer examples. A midfielder or a defender will never be as popular as the striker. Everything being said, it is now time to be more generous with these unsung heroes. It would be unfair to underestimate the importance of the second chair. Just like a kitchen loses its focus without a good sous-chef to supervise it, any attorney who has been involved in a hearing knows that success does not depend on a single person. The path to a favorable award goes through the participation of numerous actors, not just the talent of a good pleader. Without a trustworthy and diligent aide-de-camp, years of work can fall to pieces and jeopardize the final result.

§3.02 ASSEMBLY INSTRUCTIONS

An arbitration hearing is a complex occurrence where hundreds of elements unfold simultaneously. The pleadings represent a clash not only of legal arguments but also of personalities, psychologies, and strategies. In this context, the best performance depends on the efficient and coordinated efforts of a group of individuals. The second chair gravitates toward the center of this proceeding—a crucial, yet at times passive element. The most important skills that a good second chair must possess are knowledge of the case, communication management, and meticulous organization.

It is not possible to overemphasize the importance of knowing the underlying case. This knowledge encompasses mastering the entire record, including briefs, exhibits and legal authorities, and all other relevant materials, but this task is not about ingesting and then repeating countless lines of text. The second chair must identify the strengths and weaknesses of any argument that is pleaded and must determine when it is necessary to send a message to the first chair or require information from another member of the team. The second chair must also be aware of the opposing counsel's virtues and shortcomings, must follow closely the contentions pleaded by the other side, and must be alert to any stumble or fall. Furthermore, the second chair must anticipate controversial issues as well as any questions that the tribunal may ask. All will be well so long as the second chair has studied the case rigorously and intelligently. When you know the case perfectly, you narrow down the chances of the unexpected.

Communication with the first chair is also essential. Weeks before the case, the first and second chairs should discuss expectations, methodologies, and synergies. They should also talk about required tasks and obligations for the second chair in order to avoid coordination mistakes. The relationship between chairs should be as smooth as clockwork and is only achievable so long as the chairs know each other and agree to a relationship that fosters trust and mutual support. The second chair should not only pay particular attention to the first chair, but s/he must also constantly coordinate (or be prepared to coordinate) with other team members, arbitrators, and hearing participants (court reporters, interpreters, etc.) as well as any officers representing the arbitral institution. As for the relationship with the other side, it should always be diplomatic and courteous. The second chair should nevertheless always remain vigilant and take note of reactions, slips, and mistakes.

Finally, let us not forget organizational skills, such as the ability to determine the order and priority of the tasks that need to be accomplished during the hearing. In that regard, the second chair must know how to lead and manage the rest of the team; s/he must take control and command the field of legal arguments. Part of this role includes knowing when and how to delegate tasks and functions, filtering the information that is received as a result, and then distilling it to the first chair. Categorization of relevant information becomes an essential task to take advantage of one's strengths and resolve any issues in an efficient manner.

In any case and despite the long list of responsibilities, being a second chair also has its perks. Perhaps the greatest one is the learning experience. To be able to observe, up close, the thousands of patterns and details of a hearing is one of the most valuable experiences that an arbitration attorney can have. Each tribunal, pleading, and intervention has its own rhythm, and as with any other craft, one's ability is molded by the passage of time. Being a second chair allows you to witness and assimilate these continuous lessons on a firsthand basis.

§3.03 NECESSARY TOOLS

We do not wish to ignore practical matters. At the end of the day, this book is a professional survival guide. Thus, we have compiled advice gleaned from the good and the bad days. This advice is the result of rebukes as well as celebrations and emotions found in the professional universe in which we live. The list below is not exhaustive, but we hope that it will provide some assistance to the inexperienced second chairs. We urge our readers to keep things in perspective and to take into account our own subjectivity.

[A] Study, Study, and Then Continue Studying

The better you know the case, the calmer and more confident you will be. These two elements are fundamental in a hearing. In addition, you should never trust the knowledge of others, particularly the knowledge of the first chair. You must never think the first chair knows the case better than you because it is rarely true.

[B] Know How to Make Decisions and Delegate Tasks in Relation to the Case

When the second chair has these skills, it allows the first chair to focus on the substance and form of his/her pleadings.

[C] Never Lose Sight of Your Role

Let us be clear. The second chair is not and should not be the first chair. You cannot make important decisions without authorization, and you cannot lose your focus or patience with the rest of the team. At the end of the day, the second chair remains, in general, a less-experienced attorney. In this respect, the second chair must lead in a subtler way through tact and consensus-building.

[D] Be Prepared for the Unexpected

Being prepared means being ready to intervene and taking on a more prominent role if necessary. Knowing the case, as well as being calm and confident, will help you to excel in these situations.

[E] And of Course, Smile at All Times

It is important that the other side does not perceive what you may be thinking or feeling during the hearing. Moreover, never forget that it is only a hearing with its inherent theatrics. At the end of the day, we all know that an arbitration is much more than a hearing, and the post-hearing brief can be just as important and sometimes even more than the hearing itself.

We conclude with a directive. In every structure, there is the will to progress and to improve. The selection of a second chair generally means rewarding talent and securing positive exposure. With the passing of time, our second chairs gradually become first chairs, but the wait need not be undeservedly long. We want more young attorneys acting as first chairs as well as more women and minorities too. As an old carpenter once said: "*The chair belongs to those who work on it.*"

Chapter 4

My First Oral Pleading

Rafael Llano

Hearings, especially hearings on merits, are the peak phase of an arbitration. At this time, the parties have already exchanged briefs containing their positions. It is when the oral argument takes on special importance as it allows us to verbally explain our client's case to the Arbitral Tribunal for the first time. Similarly, it is an opportunity to test the arguments of our counterparty.

My first oral argument was an opening statement made during the hearing on the merits at the International Centre for Settlement of Investment Disputes (ICSID) in a case against a Latin-American state while I was still an associate. I remember when the partner in charge told me that I would be responsible for setting and presenting a portion of the fact section of the oral argument I felt simultaneously exhilarated and apprehensive. I had spent my fair share of time observing partners with whom I had worked make oral presentations and now the time had come for me to do the same. When one prepares to make his or her first oral argument, it is common to want to emulate what one has seen. It was certainly my case, and I used the good examples of my partners.

As a starting point, I printed the briefs that our side had presented and manually annotated and highlighted the main points I wanted to make during my presentation. As I read our arguments, I pictured the best way to introduce them to the tribunal. Gradually, I began listing slides through the briefs, numbering the different points, and including references to legal authorities, documents, and witness statements. It was my first draft which I still have as a souvenir to date.

Once I had prepared the slides I would be presenting, I focused on preparing the oral argument itself. Once again, I remembered the more effective examples I had seen in past hearings. Until that point, I had encountered three categories of speakers.

The first category of speakers I will call "the master of preparation." These persons take many weeks before the hearing to prepare their oral presentation. They write and practice it over and over again. They also organize team meetings and exercise the argument to see their colleagues' reactions. They polish and gradually improve their presentation. They rehearse it so many times that when they finally present the argument at the hearing, it would appear as though they are speaking impromptu when in reality they know the speech by heart.

The second category of speakers I will call "the master of improvisation." These lawyers prepare beforehand and master the law and facts of the case. When the time comes to present their oral argument, they are able to improvise much of the presentation, adapting to the tribunals' questions and reactions. In this way they mold their argument to speak about points of concern to the tribunal which are key to their client's position.

Finally, the third type of speakers I will call "the master orator." These persons have prepared a script where every word has been meticulously chosen. They use slides to guide their presentation, but they only contain general references to the themes being addressed. The carefully written script drives the argument, not the slides.

When preparing my first oral argument, I chose to take the best of each of these approaches. I prepared slides containing the key arguments I wanted to convey. I memorized my speech almost entirely, and I also had written out sections of my argument.

While I believe that my first oral argument fulfilled its mission, in hindsight I believe that today I give higher value to being flexible when making an argument. It is of course normal to be nervous before making such a presentation, even when it is not the first one, but I believe that the combination of the three different categories of "masters" did not provide the natural, smooth result that I was hoping.

To achieve a successful oral presentation, it is important to find one's own style and cultivate it through practice, progressively gaining confidence. To develop the ability to present an oral argument is like gradually sharpening a pencil. One learns from the experience, and like a sharp pencil becomes more precise in what one wants to express. Moreover, one learns to read the tribunal and to adapt the oral argument on the spot depending on the tribunal's reaction. Preparation is key but so is flexibility. Preparation will take weeks, multiple practice runs, and minute refinement of the slides. Flexibility will require knowing the record and the law most thoroughly.

Ultimately, things can always go wrong. Nevertheless, preparation and experience will provide the tools that are necessary to know how to react to scenarios, for instance that tricky question by a member of the tribunal or a technical glitch. These situations might distract an unprepared attorney who is not sufficiently knowledgeable of the supporting material to continue.

Today, more than ten years after my first oral argument, I can say that my style has evolved. I continue to think that intensive preparation is key. Although I admit that my drafts are no longer fully written on paper, I always allocate considerable time to think and structure my arguments. It is important to give enough time to review both sides' pleadings, the exhibits, and relevant legal authorities as well as the witness statements and expert reports. I give much importance to the structure and sequence of the points I want to make. Also, I strive to balance between being exhaustive and being selective as to which points to allocate the usually limited time available during an oral argument.

I no longer memorize a script and instead seek to be more conversational in my style. I still use slides, but only as a guide, and I do not allow the slides to impede spontaneity as needed. The slides are a useful tool as they allow me to convey key documents, phrases, and testimony to the tribunal. I find that graphics make the presentation more didactic and easier to follow, and timelines help to place the listener within the story. Images of the documents make them more real, almost tangible.

Finally, it is important to know your audience. To this effect, it is key to research the members of the tribunal from their relevant experiences with respect to the dispute to their own personalities and preferences. Listening is a skill as important as speaking. Listening to what the tribunal has to say is of utmost importance. Many mistakes are made by not listening. Being overly focused on a script prevents us from listening effectively to the tribunal's questions and comments, which can lead to missing an opportunity to help the members of the tribunal get the information which they ask and need. Questions should be perceived as windows of opportunity. Do not leave them unanswered. If you have the answer, give it. Otherwise, make sure to give the required information at a later point in time. By preparing yourself adequately and by being flexible, you will be more efficient in making your presentation and in providing the tribunal with the necessary tools to understand your case, best points, and evidence. At the same time, it is also important to know your counterparty. It will also help you prepare to be able to anticipate counterarguments or reactions and not let them take you by surprise.

The experience of my first oral argument gave me multiple lessons. As I mentioned, it allowed me to find my own style and to become the kind of presenter I am today. However, we must not forget that, as lawyers, ultimately we are the voice of our clients, and oral arguments are the key to advance our clients' cases. These arguments give us the opportunity to tell our clients' stories in a straightforward manner and to reduce big concepts to a simple narrative that requires the application of justice by the tribunal.

CHAPTER 5

Writing Tips for Arbitration Practitioners

Caterina Miró Quesada

Although it is important not to lose track of the big picture of your case, let us not forget that the devil is in the details. I remember that once while preparing a request for arbitration based on a treaty, I identified that the English and Spanish versions did not coincide in relevant information for the notification of the dispute. This opportunity taught me the importance of reviewing even the smallest detail since something that seems irrelevant could affect your briefs and your position before the arbitral tribunal.

The saying goes that anything and everything can be said on paper. Nevertheless, it is not the most effective way when trying to be persuasive in our memorials or writings directed toward an arbitral tribunal. In international arbitration, it is not odd to find writings full of qualifiers, hundreds of pages saying nothing and everything at the same time or only managing to have the reader finish reading without them having a clear idea of what the parties intended to convey. As counsel, our job consists in preventing that the arbitrators, after reading our memorial, think: "*I still do not know what happened*" or "*I have not been given the arguments that I need to resolve this case.*"

Before starting writing we should come up with an action plan as a preliminary matter. The process that should be executed before translating our ideas to paper is key for the effectiveness of our writings. They should be organized in such a way that they reflect exactly what we want to transmit to the tribunal. To this effect, it is advisable to take into consideration the following.

§5.01 KNOW YOUR CASE

Identify what are the relevant facts and the legal theory in play. It is only once all details are known that you will be able to formulate your position for each and every single one of them. Put your arguments to the test, imagining if they would pass the scrutiny of a counter interrogatory or questions by the tribunal and looking at how they can be enhanced or clarified. Additionally, anticipate what could be the arguments of the opposing party to know how to answer them. It is always best to anticipate than to react.

§5.02 KNOW THE STORY YOU WANT TO CONVEY

It is important to identify the story one wants to tell. To that end, you should be able to answer the following questions: (1) What is the principal idea of your case? (2) What are the relevant facts of your case? and (3) What is your position regarding each of your claims? With this information, you will be able to start building your theory of the case.

[A] Summary of Your Position

Think about one or two sentences that reflect your position in the case. In other words, identify what will be the guiding thread in the writings that will allow you to transmit your position in a clear way to the arbitral tribunal.

[B] Document Support and Legal Basis

The facts tend to be at the heart of our writings. Identify the documents that support your position as well as the witnesses and experts on which you can rely to back up your contentions. Likewise, identify the legal sources that support your arguments and take into consideration dissenting positions that will help you anticipate counterarguments.

[C] The Writing's Outline

Broadly speaking, put every idea that comes to mind into every argument that you want to make. To that end, and I insist, it is of the utmost importance to have a clear idea of what it is that we wish to convey before starting to write.

Once the above steps are completed, you will be under the right conditions to start writing your memorial. Writing is no easy task. It is a skill that requires thorough practice. One way to better oneself, especially when we are new to a task, is to observe what other people with more experience and practice do, to learn from them, and to put aside what is not effective for yourself. For instance, having a notepad, a file in the computer, or even a "note" on your phone where you write down sentences you have read or approaches and strategies that have caught your attention will come in handy when the time to write comes. In order to be persuasive, the following advice can be used when writing a memorial.

[1] Know Your Audience

Look into who the members of the tribunal are, their experience in the field or in areas present in your case, their capacities in the language of your case, etc. This could influence your strategy and focus. For instance, this information will tell you whether or not you should include a chapter that will broadly introduce technical information in a very basic way in your writing.

[2] *Write in a Clear, Simple, and Straightforward Manner*

When writing in Spanish, we are used to using a plethora of words to describe our ideas. However, we should avoid that temptation and write our memorials and writings in a clear and simple manner. That way we can ensure that the tribunal will understand our position and incidentally read everything. Be straightforward. No arbitrator will think, *"I wish the memorial would have been longer."*

[3] *Every Fact Has to Be Relevant*

We often forget that the tribunal does not have the same knowledge of the facts as we do. When one reads a summary of facts for the first time, one cannot distinguish with certainty which fact is important and which one is not. Hence, it is important that the facts that are included serve a purpose and are part of the story we are trying to tell. You will only manage to confuse the reader by adding unnecessary details or facts that have nothing to do with your arguments and make them lose the idea that you were trying to convey. On the other hand, sometimes it is necessary to take the time to explain the background with detail to avoid missing the point.

[4] *Do Not Avoid Unfavorable Facts*

You would rather have the tribunal hear unfavorable facts from you than from the opposing counsel. Hiding facts is never a good idea. More likely than not, they will be revealed at some point during the arbitration, which will make it more complicated to deal with them later. For that reason, it is crucial to know what to do with unfavorable documentation, even more so when it is likely that they will be required to be committed as an exhibit or given during document production. It might be useful to put those documents on the table from the beginning and to be able to control the message being conveyed. Additionally, it will help establish your trustworthiness in front of the tribunal.

[5] *Avoid Being Repetitive or Aggressive*

Presenting an idea repeatedly will not make it truer. The same applies to aggressive adjectives. Let facts and arguments speak for themselves.

[6] Introduction

Add an introduction that will give your audience a clear idea of what they will find in the memorial and what the conclusion of it will be. It is a good opportunity to highlight key aspects of your arguments in a favorable way.

[7] Include Persuasive Titles and Divide Your Writing in Sections

Divide your memorial into logical sections in such a way that it supports your theory about the case. At the beginning of each section, include an introductory paragraph where you summarize the points, allowing you to give context on what is to come. Likewise, it is particularly important to take the time to think thoroughly for a persuasive title for each section; it should properly reflect the content of each of them.

[8] Evidentiary Support

Make certain that every factual claim has documental or witness support, always linking it to a footnote indicating the source of the evidence. Of course, the same goes for legal arguments. It is frustrating to read a writing that does not help the reader find a document or evidence on which the argument finds support. This practice will also help you ensure that you are not exaggerating or overevaluating the weight of each piece of evidentiary support.

[9] Editing

Finally, review and correct the document. Preferably, print it more than once. Some errors are unnoticed on screen. It is important that your memorial is free of typographical errors.

Following these practical tips will help you find your own style of writing and at the same time identify what works for you and what does not, so you can learn from your mistakes. Good writing is an art that develops over time.

CHAPTER 6

How to Arbitrate for the State

Ricardo Ampuero

I had the opportunity to participate in an event with the purpose of presenting different perspectives of international arbitration, and I was able to share my viewpoint of working in the defense of a State in international investment disputes. One of the attendees asked what I enjoyed most about my work. My response as defined from the first day I started working for the State was the satisfaction and pride generated by being able to defend and represent my country in an international forum. With sincerity, I can say that it is something that I consider a true privilege and an honor.

I strongly believe that the essential starting point to address what it means to work on arbitration issues from the State is public service vocation. A true sense of public service generates the indispensable level of commitment necessary to advance the objectives of a country's public policy. An adequate system of coordination and response of the State in international investment disputes is an important part of any serious policy of attracting foreign direct investment.

A lawyer who litigates for the State must "live" his or her case and commit to doing the best possible work for its client. At the risk of sounding romantic, the client is all the citizens of the country since the job implies protecting public funds and the defense of sovereign decisions. Therefore, although rewarding, it is a task that involves a very important responsibility of which it is indispensable to be aware.

The work pace may be different from the work of a law firm or the legal department of a company, but it does not mean that it is less intense. It is necessary to deal with certain aspects that are surely not present in the private sector, and there are relevant matters related to the international responsibility of the State to be taken into consideration.

In disputes between States and investors, it may happen that the company making an investment changes its legal status in the course of its operations. It can be dissolved, merged, absorbed by another company, or make any other changes in its corporate structure as it sees fit. In the same way, although the number of investment arbitrations maintains a sustained growth rate in recent years, not all companies that make a direct foreign investment initiate an international investment arbitration process in relation to each project. A State, on the other hand, endures. Considering the increase in the flow of foreign direct investment and the opening of markets and globalization, a State can face several international investment arbitrations which generates the need to protect the consistency and coherence of the State's positions over time.

The State is large and complex. It is comprised of different agencies and political subdivisions on different levels, each with its own objectives, responsibilities and legal mandates. The actions and decisions of these agencies can generate claims that may trigger the international responsibility of the State.

An adequate coordination between public entities involved in an international dispute is crucial for the orderly development of the case and the presentation of a solid sovereign position. This coordination allows the centralization of all relevant information and documents, avoids public statements that could be used against the State itself, and articulates the developed work in general.

It is a significant challenge because this coordination must be present when the arbitration begins and must be maintained throughout the entire process. Therefore, state agencies must adequately internalize the contingencies faced by the State, establish what their role will be in that context, and find ways to work harmoniously with each other within the framework of their own objectives and priorities and within the pursuit of an effective and organized defense.

Depending on the system implemented by the State to deal with international investment disputes, another challenge is to adequately manage and supervise the work of international firms in charge of the State's defense in every case. Each one can have very different teams, styles, and practices, but it is important to ensure that the strong defense of the interests of the State is the main priority. The defense in each case must also be aligned with the objectives set.

In the case of Peru, since the time it faced its first international investment arbitration process in 2003 (a first case in 1998 culminated in an agreement that ended the dispute), crucial elements were identified as necessary for an adequate defense of the State. Based on these elements and in line with its policy of attracting foreign direct investment, the State Coordination and Response System for International Investment Disputes was created in 2006.

As part of the system, the Special Commission representing the State in international investment disputes was created. It is the interinstitutional collegiate body whose purpose is to represent the State in all stages of an investment dispute. It is important to note that the Special Commission has permanent members and nonpermanent members. The nonpermanent members include each public entity involved in the specific dispute, and, of course, it may include more than one entity. In this way, the system is based on an ad hoc composition for each case, ensuring that all necessary stakeholders participate in the deliberation and adoption of the main decisions of the case.

The Special Commission is responsible for evaluating the settlement possibilities in the negotiation phase and for carrying out the steps necessary to implement the

State's strategy. These steps include requesting reports and information from entities involved in the dispute and selecting legal counsel and other professionals and experts who are necessary for a specific case. In addition, it includes appointing arbitrators, assisting with the work of the law firms, and determining the level of responsibility of the Public Entity involved in the dispute as this agency will be responsible for the execution of an award.

State officials are deeply involved in the development and implementation of the legal strategy for each case through the Special Commission. For example, public officials identify the relevant documents of the case, prepare the witnesses, and participate in the hearings. Based on this accumulated experience of several cases, the Peruvian State has managed to successfully design and implement strategies aimed at reaching a negotiated solution of some claims—sometimes without outside counsel—thus avoiding the need to go through an arbitration process.

To successfully arbitrate from the State, it is crucial to previously implement dispute prevention policies. These policies can range in a number of goals. For example, they can define early warning mechanisms which allow the timely identification of potential controversies and the prevention of situations escalating into litigation processes. They can focus on developing training workshops for public officials with the purpose of raising awareness of the existence of investment protection standards and the knowledge of State commitments. They may also provide useful tools for the decision-making process, such as risk assessment.

One of the most important lessons in working with the State is to learn how to deal with the bureaucracy. It can be difficult to process at first, particularly if you are coming into public service from private practice. Although it is associated with a frustrating element, bureaucracy is not negative per se. Administrative procedures respond to a hierarchical and organized structure which divides responsibilities within the State. Therefore, they are necessary in public administration.

Along these lines, another element to consider is public officials' relationships with comptrollers and their subjected responsibilities. Under the principle of legality, public officials are only authorized to carry out the actions that the laws and regulations allow. Their decisions must be duly motivated, meaning they must be reasoned and have legal support.

Likewise, when planning and organizing the work, it is important to consider the inevitable fact that, generally, the State is not as agile in its reactions as a private entity. It is not only because of its procedures, double checks, prior authorizations, and control mechanisms. There are compliance regulations that must be observed in every step, even in the context of the State's legal defense in an international investment dispute. In addition, the centralization of documents and identification of the relevant information can be an arduous task that may require considerable time depending on the complexity of the facts and the number of public entities involved.

It is also important to consider that it is usual for States to act as respondents in the Investor-State dispute resolution system, meaning that States face various types of contingencies. Mainly there is the economic contingency since this type of dispute generally includes large compensation claims. It can have a direct impact on the management of public finances and the structuring of the budget of the entities involved. However, an adverse decision can also lead to other contingencies. Some decisions can generate public discussions in the press, so it will be important to coordinate and manage an efficient communication plan by political actors. There are cases where States seek to protect certain aspects of the legal framework or affirm certain positions in a regulated sector, and in such cases an unfavorable award may represent a negative precedent beyond the economic impact. In this way, there is a lot at stake when an arbitration process is triggered, and the State is forced to take steps to face it.

The fact that States are generally respondents also means that in many occasions a sovereign will only begin to organize its defense upon the formal notification that a dispute exists, which in turn may trigger certain procedural deadlines at the outset. This process differs greatly from the process of the investor. Because the investor is usually the claimant, it has control of the moment in which the formal notification is presented and the arbitration begins. This circumstance gives the claimant the opportunity to have more time to organize all relevant documents and background, develop a legal strategy, and even organize the work of experts and witnesses to be presented in the arbitration.

Because of the measures that are potentially under review, international investment disputes may also involve sensitive aspects of a State and political implications in many cases. These implications cause involvement of high levels of government where there is usually limited time to devote to a single issue because of the responsibilities they hold. It is therefore critical to be able to identify the essential information in each matter and be able to prepare executive documents or transmit crucial information efficiently within a very short time frame.

There is a popular metaphor to exemplify the synthesis capacity needed in these situations. It is known as the "elevator test." One must be able to summarize in less than a minute what would normally require a meeting to explain and discuss. Ultimately it is the duration of an elevator ride. My version of this test is what I have called the *Desamparados* test.

On one occasion, prior to a meeting at the Government Palace of Peru, I was summoned by the top management of the Ministry of Economy and Finance. The idea was to first have an internal discussion of what would later be addressed in the meeting. I prepared a short presentation with slides that addressed the relevant background, the main points under discussion, and even possible future scenarios, considering certain variables in the decision-making process.

I arrived on time and began to study the most important points while waiting. It had been a challenge to summarize so much information in such a short presentation. As the waiting time continued, passed the agreed meeting time, I found myself cutting more and more out the presentation, calculating what information I would get to discuss with the time that was available.

An unforeseen circumstance had required top management to extend a previous appointment. This last-minute change, which is not unusual, consumed almost all the time set for our discussion. I found myself then in the need to synthesize the essential points of the presentation in the time it took us to walk from the Ministry to the

Government Palace.[1] It was not the only time that a similar situation occurred, and since this meeting, I do not consider myself ready for a meeting unless the subject to be treated passes the *Desamparados* test.

The coordination of arbitration issues from the State presents many challenges, but it also comes with a satisfaction that I think is difficult to find in any other job. Sometimes it is only possible to appreciate certain intangibles when a case is litigated from a particular perspective. It is a position that will hardly fall into monotony since it encompasses very different situations, regulations, and decisions in various sectors and industries and involves agencies of all levels. The breadth and depth of topics make it a truly unique experience. It is, after all, an enriching and rewarding position that certainly allows a better understanding of the challenges that States must face when making decisions. It can ultimately generate a change in the perspective and approach under which the Investor-State dispute resolution system is addressed.

1. I call it the *Desamparados* test in honor of the path we walked on that occasion. The distance between the Government Palace of Peru and the Ministry of Economy and Finance is short. It requires going one block along *Jirón Lampa* until the Church of San Francisco de Asís and then turning left and advancing one more block along the boulevard of *Jirón Ancash* to the *Desamparados* Station—an old train station in Lima now transformed into the House of Literature—where the entrance to the Government Palace is just a few meters away.

CHAPTER 7

An Uncomfortable Ex Parte Arbitrator Interview

Robert H. Smit

It was the early 1990s, and I was a mid-level litigation associate in a large international law firm based in New York City. International commercial arbitration was still relatively young in the United States. I had interned at the International Chamber of Commerce (ICC) International Court of Arbitration and was hoping to help my law firm develop an international arbitration practice. I was excited when a senior partner in the firm's litigation department told me that one of the firm's long-standing clients had retained us to represent it in a large ICC arbitration in which the client had been named as respondent. The senior partner told me that he wanted me to work with him on the arbitration because I was the only lawyer at the firm who knew anything about what he called "*Ick*" arbitration.

The contract giving rise to the dispute called for the arbitration to be conducted by a three-member tribunal, with each of the parties nominating one member of the tribunal and the two party-nominated arbitrators nominating a chairperson. The claimant had already nominated a well-respected professor of international law at a leading US law school as its party-nominated arbitrator. Without seeking my input, the senior partner told me that he wanted to appoint a former US judge as our client's party-nominated arbitrator and that he had already invited what he described as "the perfect candidate"—a former federal judge that he knew well—to our offices for an interview. I had never heard of the candidate, who was not well known in international arbitration circles, although he had served as an arbitrator in a few domestic insurance arbitrations since retiring from the bench.

On the morning of the interview, the senior partner instructed me to bring the case files to the conference room where the interview was to begin at 10 A.M., to arrange for lunch for six people (the candidate, the senior partner, the client representative, two junior associates, and me) to be delivered to the conference room, and to make dinner reservations at a nearby restaurant in the event that it might please the candidate. *Why do we need so much time with the candidate just to confirm his suitability and availability to serve as arbitrator? And dinner?* I thought these questions to myself, having read the relevant International Bar Association (IBA) and other guidelines on permissible ex parte interviews with prospective party-appointed arbitrators.

The interview started innocuously with the usual introductions and greetings. The candidate then asked about the case, and the senior partner proceeded to tell him. He described the key background facts, the major issues that were likely to arise, and the parties' respective positions on the issues. I worried: *Was this a "general description of the dispute" that the relevant guidelines say are appropriate, or a description of "facts and positions giving rise to the dispute" that they identify as inappropriate?* The guidelines were unclear to me, but I was quickly becoming uncomfortable.

"*Why don't you take a look at these documents to better understand the case,*" the senior partner told the candidate, passing him a copy of claimant's Request for Arbitration and our client's Answer. While he read the pleadings, I thought to myself: *Is this ok? Have we agreed with the claimant's counsel to share the pleadings with prospective arbitrator candidates?* On the one hand, the parties' pleadings clearly went to the merits of the dispute where ex parte communications are not supposed to go. On the other hand, there was no risk that the candidate would learn anything from the pleadings that all three arbitrators would not learn in due course since they too would be supplied with those same pleadings. Therefore, showing the candidate the pleadings should not infect the integrity of the proceedings. But still my discomfort level rose.

After our catered lunch, the senior partner asked the candidate: "*So, now that you've read the parties' initial pleadings, is there any reason our client should hesitate to nominate you as its arbitrator?*" *What did he just ask? He did not directly ask whether the candidate would rule in our client's favor, but it sounded like a "wink wink" type of question.* Then the client spoke for the first time and asked the candidate: "*Our case is strong, don't you think?*"

Oh no, that statement clearly crossed the line! What do I do? This was the senior partner's case—his primary responsibility, not mine—and the candidate, the client, and he were all clearly comfortable with what was being said. The senior partner and the client obviously wanted to win the case, and choosing a favorable party-nominated arbitrator was key to that objective. I did not know what the candidate was thinking, but he was used to US-style insurance arbitrations where party-appointed arbitrators are expected to be partisan and ex parte communications are not unusual. I also did not want to say anything—voice any objection—that would annoy or alienate the senior partner and the client on whom my future at the firm depended. I did not believe that anything said during this prenomination interview would actually really matter once the arbitral tribunal was appointed, and the arbitration was underway.

But it did not feel right to sit there and say nothing. My silence made me complicit in ex parte communications that I felt were improper in international arbitration. I wanted to build a career in international arbitration, and participating in this interview without objection felt like a bad way to start that career. I had to do something, and I had to do it quickly before the candidate answered the client's question about the strength of our case.

So I excused myself from the conference room to go to the bathroom. I then emailed the senior partner that I was not feeling well and would not return to the meeting. Not my proudest moment.

CHAPTER 8

My First Cross-Examination

Cristóbal Sarralde

Participating in an international arbitration is not the same as taking part in domestic arbitration or litigation. It is a completely different experience. Since a diversity of cultures and legal systems are involved, the parties produce evidence in a much more flexible way and know the evidence much more in advance to the corresponding hearing, allowing both the parties and the arbitral tribunal to have plenty of time for preparing the hearings. This diversity of traditions is the first thing that you need to consider when an associate has to face the examination of witnesses or experts, especially when it is a cross-examination. It is much more relevant when kept in mind that many associates in international arbitration have started gaining experience in domestic arbitration or directly in litigation. In addition, Latin-American associates are not so familiar with cross-examination since it is not common in the civil law systems as opposed to the common law ones. Actually, it is something that happened to me when I first had to face an international arbitration case.

At the beginning of my professional career, I was more linked to litigation and afterward to domestic arbitration. Thus, when I had to face my first international arbitration experience, particularly my first cross-examination, I personally realized that the way to face international arbitration was profoundly different from my previous experience. Fortunately, I was a member of an experienced international arbitration team which allowed me to take due note of practical knowledge which I did not have in my background. In addition, because of having a counterpart without much knowledge about how to conduct an international arbitration and a cross-examination, I was able to recognize with higher precision what lawyers should not do under these circumstances. Therefore, what I will try to convey in this chapter is part of that first experience and my experience afterward.

A number of skills are required in order to face an examination and especially a cross-examination, whether one is the member of the team in charge of the relevant documents or questions or in charge of conducting the questioning itself. At this moment, these skills are systematized and able to be taught and learned, notwithstanding it is probable that the best way to learn them is the experience itself: watching, trial, and error.

Some good advice is to attend cross-examination hearings as soon as possible, even if the attendance is—at a first moment—as an associate in charge of managing the relevant documents and delivering them to the witnesses and the tribunal. In fact, when conducting a cross-examination, it is highly appreciated to have attended hearings and to have seen live and firsthand the momentum generated at them.

As an introduction to the first cross-examination that an associate might face in international arbitration without being exhaustive, I would like to focus on four points, which from my point of view are crucial to face it successfully: (1) preparedness; (2) clarity on the purpose; (3) flexibility; and (4) credibility. Even though most of these aspects might be applicable to all kind of arbitration and litigation, there are some elements which belong and characterize international arbitration. The following is a description of each one of them.

§8.01 PREPAREDNESS

Without this aspect, there is no possibility of a successful cross-examination. Probably this element subsumes and relates to all the other aspects we are reviewing. There can be no room for mere improvisation. When the international arbitration hearing is taking place, the parties have already presented their positions and both factual and legal grounds as well as submitted all the evidence in order to support those grounds as opposed to a domestic arbitration or litigation. In addition, the date of the hearing is scheduled with months of anticipation. Therefore, both the arbitral tribunal and parties have reasonable time to know about the dispute and the more technical facts and aspects to be discussed, particularly when the experts' reports have been presented and those experts can be cross-examined.

First, an associate who is facing a cross-examination must have a deep and detailed knowledge and understanding of all the facts related to the dispute, comprising all the parties' memorials, produced evidence, written statements of factual witnesses and experts, and expert reports as well. If those facts are not fully known, it will be very difficult for the associate conducting the examination to go smoothly from one issue to another in order to persuade the tribunal. In addition, the associate might not have enough sensibility to realize, by listening to a witness' answer, when it is the precise moment to go deeper into a specific issue which might be crucial to support his or her client's position, or to suspend the interrogatory.

Second, preparedness must consider the audience the associate will face when cross-examining, namely the associate must have as much information as possible regarding the arbitral tribunal's background, style, and way of approach to the cases. The same information is required regarding the counterparty's attorneys, witnesses, and experts.

Third, preparedness also implies assessing and deciding which factual or expert witnesses presented by the counterparty are worthy of summoning to the hearing in order to be cross-examined. Obviously, a known strong witness could generate a big risk for the party summoning him or her. Nevertheless, an arbitral tribunal might also consider it as inappropriate or a bad strategy for not summoning a certain witness of the counterparty which might be crucial for the case.

Lastly, being properly prepared requires clarity about which specific questions might undermine the credibility of a witness. Specific topics for the cross-examination should be considered, including specific questions and information regarding documents where witnesses are involved and are relevant to confront the witnesses.

§8.02 CLARITY IN THE SCOPE

An associate who has clarity in the desired outcome for a cross-examination will be able to conduct the questions directly to the point, supporting his or her party's position and/or undermine the counterparty's credibility or reasonableness.

The starting point to define this scope will be the witness statement or report, depending on whether it is a witness of facts or an expert. However, the statement or the report must not limit the questioning. On the one hand, the associate might have additional information about other circumstances where the witness could have been involved, yet these circumstances were not included either in the statement or in the report. On the other hand, bear in mind that, as a rule, arbitral tribunals are not inclined to limit cross-examinations to the statements' and reports' content. This rule usually triggers when some questions are relevant to the case, considering any applicable procedural rules agreed by the parties or stated by the tribunal.

Second, it is worthy to determine the specific outcome you want to obtain from cross-examining some witness. It is probable that a cross-examination loses its focus and also its strength—and the attention of the arbitral tribunal—either if the associate determines many and very diverse outcomes, or a generic outcome, or if the outcome is trying to affirm the whole position of a party.

Third, being clear about the scope of a certain witness' cross-examination will be much easier if you can be efficient in the time it will take you. Trying to question the witness regarding several topics already well defined, issues already confirmed by other witnesses, or explanations of certain documents that have no relevance or that the witness did not participate directly makes no sense at all and is counterproductive. Due to the latter, it is advisable to focus cross-examination only in those issues related to the particular and previously defined scope as well as the documents directly related to the specific witness. In this way, it will be easier for the associate conducting the cross-examination to smoothly take the questioning to the desired outcome.

§8.03 FLEXIBILITY

Although it is relevant to focus on the aim of the cross-examination, the capacity of the leading person to adapt to the course of the cross-examination or to the particular audience and their given feedback is just as important. You might think that this capacity resembles more of improvisation rather than preparation; however, it is not quite true. On the contrary, the higher the preparation of the associate, the easier it is for him or her to develop and adapt the focus within the course of the audience and the witnesses' answers.

Thus, the first suggestion is preparing topics on which the witness will be cross-examined, rather than creating specific questions. Having the issues supported by a set of possible questions grants more space when conducting the interrogation to ask questions with regards to how the witness is going to answer. Notwithstanding the foregoing, you can also prepare some questions by subject, especially when you are interrogating in a language other than your native one.

A second suggestion is not to ask a witness about all the issues, nor to ask all the questions that were prepared. Conducting a cross-examination is not about covering all the issues planned for a witness, or asking all the prepared questions. Many times, less is more. It may be that a fact that supports the position of the party conducting the interrogation has been confirmed by virtue of an answer to a previous question. Therefore, it is not necessary to request further explanations or reasons about this fact from the witness. Sometimes it could even jeopardize the point already established. In the same way, if a witness is declaring an extremely damaging fact to the party conducting the cross-examination, it may be better to not allow the witness to continue strengthening the position of the opposing party and to consequently terminate the interrogation early.

Finally, whoever cross-interrogates has to adapt to the way in which the arbitral tribunal has approached the facts, witness, or counterpart. Indeed, it is possible that the arbitral tribunal gave much importance to a particular event, either during the hearing prior to the interrogation or during such interrogation, in which case, it might be desirable to introduce that subject in the cross-examination, if the witness might have something to say about it. On the contrary, if the arbitral tribunal has shown that there is a certain fact to which it has not given any relevance, it may be preferable to omit certain questions. The same is true in the case that the opposing party challenges certain questions or tries to downplay them. It could be a serious sign of the importance of the point, or the witness could respond in a manner contrary to his/her position which motivates the one who leads the question to refocus it toward that fact.

§8.04 CREDIBILITY

Finally, we must never forget that the exercise of cross-examining is not only to give an idea to the arbitral tribunal of which witness is credible and which is not. It is also about what position and party shall prevail. It allows the arbitrator to understand the lawyers representing each of the parties and to determine if the lawyers seem credible and serious in their position.

Cross-examination is an essential opportunity to persuade the arbitral tribunal. If it is directed in an orderly, logical, and efficient manner, and the established points support the party's position represented by the person making the interrogation, it will grant greater credit before the arbitral tribunal.

In the same vein, if the witness of the opposing party has been confused, hesitant, contradictory or rightly lost credibility before the arbitral tribunal, it is likely that the position of the party that has been successful in his or her cross-examination will gain appreciation of the arbitral tribunal.

Therefore, it is advisable to avoid situations of hostility vis-à-vis witnesses or to start irrelevant discussions with the arbitral tribunal. Also, it is not best practice to insist on questions that do not have a clear objective or that refer to facts without major consequences in the decision of the final award by the arbitral tribunal.

With consideration of all the above-described elements, it may not be possible to validate or confirm all the relevant points of the position of one of the parties in the cross-examination. However, if it is possible to validate or confirm some of them, then the foregoing allows plausibility to be granted to that position. It may even constitute a more effective tool than hundreds of documents and allegations made in the memorials exchanged by the parties. On the contrary, a poorly conducted cross-examination without preparation, clarity of the objective, flexibility, or credibility before the court could have fatal repercussions not only on the position of the party being represented but also on the costs of the arbitration.

CHAPTER 9

Arbitrating under the Bangladesh Accord

Clovis Trevino[*]

Back in 2015, global trade union federations IndustriALL Global Union and UNI Global Union engaged my firm, Covington & Burling, to represent them in potential arbitrations under Bangladesh Accord on Fire and Building Safety.

"What is the Bangladesh Accord?" I was intrigued.

I soon learned that in the aftermath of the 2013 Rana Plaza building collapse—the deadliest garment industry disaster in modern history—the Unions and approximately 200 clothing brands from over twenty countries entered into a five-year legally binding agreement to make garment factories in Bangladesh safe workplaces.

In an unprecedented model of accountability, the Accord established independent inspection and safety training systems covering more than 1,600 garment factories and two million workers in Bangladesh. Signatory brands agreed to require their supplier factories to implement lifesaving corrective actions in a timely manner and to ensure the financial feasibility of their supplier's implementation of these corrective actions.

In what was a watershed development for business and human rights, the Bangladesh Accord provides that a party may "appeal" decisions by the Accord's internal governing body in binding arbitration. The idea that international labor unions and a large number of global fashion brands would agree to arbitrate disputes over business-related human rights commitments was groundbreaking. It highlighted the promise of arbitration as a means to enforce human rights obligations and improve the living conditions of thousands of Bangladeshi garment workers. I was excited to be a part of this.

In July and October 2016, the Unions triggered the Accord's groundbreaking dispute resolution mechanism by initiating arbitration against two global fashion

[*] The views expressed in this chapter are the author's and do not necessarily reflect the views of Covington & Burling or its clients.

brands. On behalf of the Unions, we brought the case to the Permanent Court of Arbitration in The Hague, arguing that the brands had failed to require their supplier factories to remediate workplace safety hazards in a timely manner—leaving thousands of workers at risk—and to ensure the financial feasibility of such remediation, in violation of their Accord commitments.

The stakes could not be higher. The uncorrected safety hazards ranged from defective fire alarm systems, smoke detection systems, lack of sprinklers, exit doors, exit signs and other fire, electrical, as well as structural hazards that increased the risk of another building collapse like Rana Plaza. The Bangladesh Accord arbitrations gave me a rare opportunity to contribute to the protection of thousands of garment workers as intended third-party beneficiaries of the Accord.

In September 2017, we had our first win. An arbitral tribunal seated in The Hague found that the Unions' claims were admissible and within its jurisdiction—paving the way for the first arbitrations under a business and human rights agreement. In its decision, the tribunal acknowledged the unique, hybrid nature of the Bangladesh Accord, sitting somewhere between public law, private law, and labor law. The tribunal also recognized "the public nature of the Accord" and the "public interest" at stake in its interpretation and enforcement.

The tribunal struck a balance on confidentiality. Although the brand names would not be revealed and proceedings would be held in private to protect the brands' reputations, the tribunal ordered that certain case documents would be released in redacted form in recognition of the public interest in the dispute.

The Unions settled the first arbitration in December 2017, reaching an agreement that would ensure that the supplier factories associated with the respondent fashion brand are remediated and that substantial funds are available for that remediation work, consistent with the Bangladesh Accord.

The second arbitration was settled at the end of January 2018, when we helped secure one of the largest payments made by a brand to remedy workplace dangers in its supply chain, which would ensure the remediation of over 150 supplier factories. As part of the settlement, the fashion brand also agreed to contribute funds to the Unions' joint Supply Chain Worker Support Fund, established to support the work of the Unions to improve pay and conditions for workers in global supply chains.

More importantly, the threat of arbitration under the Bangladesh Accord triggered industry-wide change, with signatory companies ramping up their efforts to bring their supplier factories into compliance with Accord obligations.

Beyond the Bangladeshi ready-made garment industry, the Bangladesh Accord arbitrations signal a new frontier for the resolution of business and human rights disputes, with meaningful, broader participation of public and private stakeholders interested in the creation and enforcement of business and human right norms that cut across national borders.

I am proud to have been at the forefront of this new frontier in arbitration as a means to protect and enforce human rights.

PART II War Stories and Lessons about Arbitrating Disputes

CHAPTER 10

Awkward Conversations with Three Arbitrators

Roque Caivano, Valeria Galíndez & Francisco González de Cossío

§10.01 CAREER AS AN ARBITRATOR

[A] What Has Been the Most Unpleasant Episode in Your Career as an Arbitrator?

Roque: In this regard I can identify two: (1) having been challenged by the same party that appointed me on grounds that the party was fully aware from day one and (2) having to deal, as president of the tribunal, with an ostensibly partial arbitrator, who quite cheekily (and with some ignorance) did not even look after appearances.

[B] What Has Been the Most Satisfying Moment in Your Career as an Arbitrator?

Valeria: Without a doubt, it was at the end of a week-long hearing in an arbitration in which I was the sole arbitrator when both parties and their attorneys applauded and congratulated me on the conduction of the proceedings. The opinion of these parties, who are the true users of arbitration, is finally the most important one.

§10.02 REGRETS

[A] If You Could Change Something in Your Career, What Would It Be?

Roque: Not too much. Maybe I would be a little more selective in the activities in which I get involved because sometimes I find myself doing things that I probably should not have accepted.

[B] Do You Regret One or More Awards You Have Issued?

Valeria: No. All of my awards have been the result of an attentive analysis of all the arguments and evidence and are true to my conviction. Fortunately, to this day, I have not experienced any situation of dissent among the members of the tribunal or complicated situations in the deliberation. Some awards have obviously been more difficult than others, either because of the complexity of the case or due to doubts during the formation of my conviction. However, in those cases, I was always lucky to work with experienced arbitrators with whom the exchange of opinions was as open as possible. This exchange allowed me to learn and to be calm with the decision made at the end.

[C] Do You Regret One or More Cases That You Have Assumed?

Francisco: No. I have had some cases that have taken away my sleep, or in which I have seen very unfortunate things, but I do not regret anything. This feeling arises when I consider that I have made a mistake, and it is not the case.

§10.03 PERSONAL LIFE

[A] Do You Think It Is Easy to Make Friends in the World of Arbitration?

Roque: No, it is not easy. The world of arbitration is a very competitive environment where vanities abound, and actions are not always sincere. Fortunately, I have reaped many, very good friends in my career.

[B] What Are Your Hobbies? How Much Time Do You Devote to Activities Other than Law or Arbitration?

Valeria: I recently returned to practicing classical ballet. I was a dancer when I was 6-15 years old. Now I try to devote two hours a week. I cannot always practice due to trips and hearings, but I have always liked to exercise and try to do something (even in hotel gyms) at least three times a week. On top of exercising, I love movies, and I am always reading something unrelated to arbitration. I like novels and always try reading in different languages.

[C] Do You Think You Have Sacrificed Other Aspects of Your Personal Life to Have a Successful Career as an Arbitrator? What?

Francisco: Yes, leisure.

§10.04 COMPETITION AND MENTORS

[A] Do You Compete with Yourself or with Other Arbitrators?

Roque: Definitely, I am my main critic. I try overcoming myself and not disappointing others' expectations. Although I do not seek to compete with other arbitrators, in the end we are quite a lot of people trying to gain space in a relatively small world.
Valeria: Always with myself.
Francisco: With myself. He who stops improving stops being good.

[B] Who Was Your Mentor or Role Model?

Roque: I did not have a particular mentor, but I have arbitrated with many colleagues from whom I have received many good things and have learned a lot (even from their mistakes).
Valeria: My mentor and the person responsible for introducing me to arbitration was the Brazilian Professor Arnoldo Wald with whom I learned law, professionalism, and discipline as well as how to interact with colleagues and clients. There were almost ten years of hard work with him, and they were some of the most interesting and challenging years for me. At a time when Brazil was just entering the world of arbitration, I was also fortunate to have the support and advice of other admirable professionals such as José Emilio Nunes Pinto, Juan Fernández-Armesto, and Julie Bédard (whom I particularly consider a professional female role model in international arbitration).
Francisco: José Luis Siqueiros and Jan Paulsson.

§10.05 ARBITRATORS' PERFORMANCE

[A] What Do You Think Is the Biggest Challenge for an Arbitrator?

Roque: In a rather dizzying activity, the biggest challenge is to give yourself the necessary time to devote to each case the attention that the parties deserve.
Valeria: To never forget what it is like to be on the other side (acting as a party representative).

[B] What Makes a Good Arbitrator?

Roque: Above all things, honesty (including intellectual honesty), dedication, and a good base of legal training, which allows you to capture the essence of each controversy and not get lost in intricacies or details.

[C] Have You Refused to Participate as an Arbitrator Due to Availability Issues? How Often?

Valeria: Yes, twice.

[D] Do You Actively Work to Mitigate the Cognitive Biases You May Face When Ruling?

Francisco: Yes, a lot. Sometimes I feel I do it too much—something in itself a cognitive bias.

[E] How Many Simultaneous Cases Do You Feel Capable of Handling?

Francisco: It is impossible to answer this question with a simple number as cases vary. There are times when a single case saturates the veins of my team, and there are other times that a couple of dozen does. It depends on the size, complexity, and, above all, the laboriousness of the case.

§10.06 RELATIONSHIP WITH OTHER ARBITRATORS

[A] Have You Ever Had to Face a Tyrant President?

Roque: Not as much a tyrant, but I have had presidents unwilling to listen. In these cases, the challenge is to earn your place as a co-arbitrator without confronting the president. I have also had "comfortable" presidents (some, even, bordering on indolence). I was able to get around this difficulty achieving a good chemistry with the other co-arbitrator, to get off the case.

[B] Has Your Professional Relationship with Other Arbitrators Ever Been Affected by the Approach to Any Case?

Roque: Not directly, but in a case where several very important arbitrations were consolidated into one, and the other tribunals were unaffected, I felt that the other arbitrators did not see with much sympathy the tribunal that finally concentrated the entire case.
Valeria: No.

Francisco: Yes. Unfortunately, unethical behavior is no exception, and it sometimes requires confrontation and always requires no tolerance.

[C] What Qualities Do You Seek in a Co-arbitrator?

Francisco: A technical lawyer who knows the law, is intelligent, and works hard. Someone who has an open mind. Above all, a decent person.

§10.07 YOUNG ARBITRATORS

[A] What Advice Would You Give to Professionals Starting Their Career as an Arbitrator?

Roque: They should prepare technically for acting as an arbitrator, and they should seek to become known in the "market" so the parties or co-arbitrators will take them into account when they need to appoint arbitrators.
Valeria: To have a lot of humility. There is nothing worse than believing that one knows everything. There will always be something new to learn.

[B] What Kind of Cases Do You Think Young Arbitrators Should Accept?

Francisco: Simple and small cases that *in crescendo* enter the young practitioner into the complexities of the process of the law and judging. It is dangerous to start "from the top." What at first might seem like a blessing ends up being a curse (for the young practitioner's career). Be patient: good things *sometimes* take time.

§10.08 WOMEN AND ARBITRATION

[A] Do You Perceive Any Difference Between Teams of Lawyers Made up Mostly of Men Than Teams with an Equivalent or Higher Number of Women?

Roque: In general, in the cases in which I have intervened with female lawyers I have perceived a greater degree of dedication to the case and a more methodical and neat way (argumentatively speaking) to present the case.

[B] As a Woman, Have You Ever Felt Any Disadvantage in the Practice as an Arbitrator? If So, which One?

Valeria: I have never felt a disadvantage for being a woman. But I am aware that I have been fortunate for it.

[C] What Is Your Perception of the Active Participation of Women and Minorities in Arbitration?

Francisco: I do not know if I understood correctly, but I anticipate that this question has to do with the gender efforts that exist in the international arbitration environment. My perception is the problem exists, but it is less than what is often heard. It is true that we must open doors to women (in fact, to everyone). It is also true that there is a male preponderance. It is not so true that quotas should be forced as they can cause problems (which have already occurred). In my opinion, women have been playing an important role for some time. Prominent female arbitrators are not few. I have shared tribunals with many, and I have chosen many as well. The criterion to follow is not different from the criterion of men. Again, I want a technical attorney who knows the law and is intelligent and hardworking as well as someone who has an open mind and above all is a decent person. In my opinion, this process should be the approach.

§10.09 OPINION ON ATTORNEYS

[A] What Style Do You Prefer in Attorneys? Openly Aggressive, Passive, or Passive-Aggressive?

Roque: I prefer attorneys who behave loyally and with correction toward the tribunal and their counterpart colleagues. These attorneys avoid making notoriously inadmissible statements or raising objections that are not well founded. They use vehemence in the defense of the interests of their client without being detrimental. This way of behaving does not signify a strategic disadvantage but represents a benefit for the represented party. In the eyes of the tribunal, the credibility of the lawyer reflects the credibility of the party.
Valeria: A good attorney is the one who knows how to adapt to situations (not just to the client). The attorney must know how to identify when you should be more aggressive and when it is not convenient for the case. Emotional intelligence is essential.
Francisco: Smart, prepared, decent. The styles cited in the above question include variables that may or may not be necessary.

[B] What Attitudes Do You Consider Annoying or Inappropriate?

Roque: It is similar to those indicated attitudes when answering the previous question. Other attitudes include the multiplication of incidents, oppositions, or statements that are ostensibly inadmissible.
Valeria: Lack of objectivity and irony.
Francisco: To be rude or to make the controversy a personal problem.

§10.10 CONFIDENTIALITY AND EVALUATION OF ARBITRATORS

[A] Would You Feel Uncomfortable under Scrutiny If the Parties Could Disclose Your Name in Any Forum and Assess Your Handling of the Proceedings and the Issued Award, Maintaining the Confidentiality of the Parties?

Roque: It has not happened to me, but I would feel uncomfortable surely. A "forum" (understood as a public sphere) is not the appropriate place to express criticism about the performance of an arbitrator, given the impossibility of delving into the many nuances that a case may have had. The arbitrator explains his decisions in the same award, and my way of dealing with that aspect is to motivate every decision, sometimes even in an overabundant way. It is even less appropriate if the arbitrators do not have the opportunity to refute the opinions made about them.

§10.11 BEFORE BEING APPOINTED AS ARBITRATOR

[A] Do You Feel Comfortable with Interviews Conducted by the Parties Prior to an Appointment? Are they Useful?

Roque: I think they are useful for the parties who often have to "validate" their attorney's suggestion and to appoint someone they probably have never seen. I have felt uncomfortable sometimes because the party did not understand clearly the purpose or limits of this interview and sought to venture into the merits of the case. From that experience, when attorneys contact me to arrange an interview with their client, I ask them to warn the client about the "rules of the game" of this interview to avoid awkward situations.
Francisco: Yes, there must be guidelines.

[B] Do You Worry about Ex Parte Communications?

Valeria: No, I have never had problems with ex parte communications.

§10.12 STATEMENT OF IMPARTIALITY AND INDEPENDENCE

[A] If the Arbitrator Recognizes His or Her Impartiality and Independence, Is That Statement Sufficient? What Is the Purpose of Revealing Past Information That in the Eyes of the Arbitrator Does Not Affect His or Her Ability to Decide the Dispute?

Roque: In my opinion, the arbitrator's look on his or her own independence and impartiality is not entirely relevant. I absolutely agree with the rules that require disclosure to be made taking the parties' gaze into account. The purpose of revealing specific information is to "level out" the information that the arbitrator has about possible conflicts of interest and that the party probably does not have. A timely, detailed, and complete disclosure generates confidence and ultimately avoids doubts and future challenges.

[B] How Do You Know to What Extent Financial, Professional, and Personal Relationships Should Be Disclosed with the Parties, Their Representatives, Attorneys, or Related Parties?

Valeria: There is no precise answer. Actually, I think there will never be an exact answer because relationships and the way people relate constantly change, with great speed. The basis is the use of common sense.

§10.13 REPETITIVE APPOINTMENTS

[A] Do You Consider That the Repetitive Appointment of an Arbitrator Causes Reasonable Doubts?

Roque: It depends on the circumstance: fundamentally the frequency with which the arbitrator is appointed, the lapse of time between appointments, and the "market size" where such arbitration takes place (understood as the number of cases that the party has and the ones the arbitrator has).

[B] Would You Refuse to Be Appointed More than Once by the Same Party?

Valeria: Everything would depend on the specific situation. I would take several elements into consideration before deciding whether to accept the appointment or not, such as when was the first appointment, who are the attorneys, and what is the subject matter. In any case, I would make a revelation.

[C] Do You Feel Comfortable or Are You Worried about Being Named Repeatedly by the Same Party?

Francisco: No, because I am impartial. But it has never happened to me.

§10.14 ROLE OF THE ARBITRAL SECRETARY

[A] Do You Consider Hypocritical the Critic to the Arbitral Secretary Participates in the Drafting Tasks of the Award?

Roque: It depends on the degree of intervention allowed to the secretary. One thing is to write the "procedural history," and another very different thing is the secretary interferes in the decision-making, which is proper to the arbitrators. I know they exist,

but in my experience, I have not personally known many cases of secretaries that supplant the role of the arbitrators or exceed what they are expected to do.
Valeria: Totally. There are tasks that can perfectly be delegated and that do not interfere in any way in the process of deliberation of the arbitrators.
Francisco: Yes!

§10.15 DOUBLE-HATTING

[A] Has the Double Quality of Arbitrator and Party-Attorney Generated Any Kind of Conflict for You?

Valeria: No.

[B] Is It Common to Participate as an Arbitrator and as a Party-Attorney in International Arbitration?

Roque: As seen in practice, the majority are part-time arbitrators. Most of the time, they act as party-attorneys and occasionally as arbitrators. It is not particularly my case since I almost always act as an arbitrator, and I am occasionally hired as an attorney (not to lead a case but to assist the attorney who does). But I understand that situations like mine are the minority.

CHAPTER 11

Jumping in the Pool: How to Write Your First Arbitral Award

Álvaro Awad

Every arbitrator had his or her *debut*. Gary Born, Gabrielle Kaufmann-Kohler, Yves Derains, Bernardo Cremades, and so many other arbitration experts once faced the challenge of drafting their first award.

In this regard, training new arbitrators is essential to diversify the arbitration community. It is known that the excessive concentration of cases in a handful of specialists causes unnecessary delays in the resolution of disputes both locally and internationally. Hence, the initiation guide for those professionals who have the opportunity to act as arbitrators for the first time is beneficial.

While the mere idea of settling a dispute—in a virtually final way—is daunting for most, this deference to the task of dispensing justice is perhaps the first step to becoming an excellent arbitrator. The preparation of a well-reasoned and enforceable award is a great responsibility. Accordingly, it must be taken seriously from the very beginning of a career in the world of arbitration.

What better than receiving a couple of tips for that special occasion?

Though there are surely many—and seriously, many—more experienced arbitrators who could share their strategies, I present in this chapter a compilation of advice that I would have wished to have in hand when I (enthusiastically) drafted my first award.

The first thing to know is there is no universal standard or approach. Each arbitrator has his or her own style. Yet there are certain virtues that are shared by every effective decision. Features such as clarity, precision, and consistency in the used terms[1] are indispensable in any kind of legal writing, including an arbitral award.

1. International Bar Association Arb40 Subcommittee, *Toolkit for Award Writing*, section 5 (2016).

It is usually suggested to title the document as an award, so there are no doubts about its nature.[2] If the case allows many types of awards—such as "interim," "provisional," "partial," "final," etc.—it is convenient to set down which one it is. The number of pages will depend on the particular case, quantity of discussed issues, and magnitude of the parties' pleadings and evidence.

Sarcasm is inappropriate,[3] and in general a respectful approach toward the most debatable issues makes the award more acceptable for everyone involved. Wherever possible, the use of plain language is preferable to legalese or technical terminology. Abbreviations can be useful, but too many might make the text complicated.

On the other hand, the applicable procedural rules must be taken into account at all times. These are found in the parties' agreement, the respective rules of the arbitral institution—in case of an institutional arbitration—[4] and the seat of arbitration's laws. Should you want to be more exhaustive, it would be worth reviewing the legislation of the place where the award will probably be executed (if different from the seat). Issuing a satisfactory award entails including all the information that these rules require; for example, the complete details about the parties, the seat of arbitration, and the date of the award. Maybe the latter needs to be signed in a specific way.

A central aspect in which I would like to dwell on is the structure of the decision. The document must contain as many sections as necessary with clear and logical formatting. Dividing the document into duly organized sections eases its reading and comprehension. Thus, after explaining the story of the tribunal's composition, the subject matter of the arbitration, the most relevant procedural events, and the issues related to the tribunal's jurisdiction, the award should summarize the parties' main submissions, pointing out the facts, arguments, and claims that are to be decided by the tribunal.[5] Afterward, it should describe the evidence and the tribunal's reasoning on the applicable law (or, in the case of an *amiable compositeur*, the general notions of fairness and equity applied). Finally, it will conclude with one or more decisions.

If the case has only a few points in discussion, it may be sufficient to explain—in brief—all the requests of one party before moving onto mentioning the petitions of the others, as is customary. Instead when faced with more complex cases (e.g., multiparty arbitrations with a myriad of issues to be solved), an alternative is to separate the sections of the award by topics, distinguishing in each of them the claims of each party with respect to a specific point. This second option is convenient when the determination of some issues depends on the determination of others.[6] Indeed, it will serve as a guide for the reasoning and will orient both the tribunal and the future reader.

2. Chartered Institute of Arbitrators, *International Arbitration Practice Guideline—Drafting Arbitral Awards*, Part I (2016).
3. International Bar Association Arb40 Subcommittee, *Toolkit for Award Writing*, section 5.1 (2016).
4. Many institutions, such as the ICC International Court of Arbitration, provide very helpful award-checklists.
5. The award solves a substantive issue. If the decision concerns only a procedural matter, it is really a procedural order.
6. International Bar Association Arb40 Subcommittee, *Toolkit for Award Writing*, section 4.8 (2016).

When considering the facts, it is crucial to clarify whether they were disputed or not. Likewise, the tribunal must respect the rules on the burden of proof. Each time the tribunal deems an event as proven, it must lay down its reasons and refer to the supportive evidence. The tribunal should cite the latter as precisely as possible and then evaluate it according to the applicable system.

In each debated matter, it will be necessary to show how the law instructs to decide on the basis of the facts that were verified in the process. Explicitly stating the complete reasoning of the tribunal is, undoubtedly, the best guarantee that the award will overcome a possible challenge due to lack of reasoning since it will allow the examining court to understand the position of the arbitrators.

Occasionally, it is helpful to include alternative reasonings of the following type: "*Even if … the claim should still be accepted/rejected, because … .*" These reflections are known as obiter dicta, for they are complementary arguments that are "said in passing."

In the operative part, every statement needs to be especially clear. It is recommended not to include in such part any defined terms nor references to other sections of the award. It must be self-sufficient in order to simplify its enforcement.

For instance, if the tribunal orders the payment of a sum of money, it is critical to indicate the amount and currency in which it must be paid, its inflation-adjustment, and interest, as appropriate (with its parameters and the dates from and until which they apply) as well as who should pay whom and any other payment terms.

Concerning payments, arbitrators must not forget the decision on the costs of the procedure, which should be—at least succinctly—justified.

After ruling on the parties' claims in a final award, it is advisable to include at the end a general decision such as "*Any other claim submitted to the present arbitration is dismissed,*"[7]in order to avoid any loose ends.

For the sake of issuing the award in a timely manner, always save enough space in your schedule. One of the virtues of arbitration vis-à-vis court litigation is that, due to the specialization and commitment of the tribunal, a more expeditious resolution of disputes can be reached. Therefore, it is imperative that the arbitrator—even if s/he is a beginner—meets this efficiency expectation by planning the stages of the case.

A useful technique is to prepare a confidential draft of the award in advance, including all the information related to the parties, their allegations during the discussion period, and the various steps as they are taking place in the proceeding. Keeping an updated draft helps with the identification of the key issues that the tribunal must solve once all the means of evidence have been weighed. This technique allows the arbitrator to think beforehand about the problems involved in the case and their possible solution scenarios.

In the case of a panel of arbitrators, it is of the utmost importance to have a deliberation procedure established by the president. Each co-arbitrator should participate in it with freedom to exchange ideas and to generate an enriching debate.[8]

---

7. *Ibid.*, section 4.11.
8. *See* Chapter 13: *Franklin, Rubin or de Bono: How to Face the First Deliberation* (Manuel Conthe).

When preparing the draft, the arbitrator must bear in mind who will study the award. In other words, to whom is s/he writing?[9] The losing party will thoroughly review the grounds for the decision. On the other hand, the winning party will want a particularly clear award in its operative part. Lastly, the courts before which the decision might be enforced or challenged will review the operative part, procedural history, and respect of due process.

An arbitrator ought to make the exercise of thinking about the possible grounds for challenging the award, not only when signing it but also throughout the course of the arbitration process until its end. In this respect—without falling into the extreme of the so-called due process paranoia—the tribunal must take into consideration that its conduct during the arbitration could have repercussions in the subsequent annulment or nonenforcement of its decision.

For example, if the arbitrator prevents one of the parties from presenting its arguments during the proceeding, the award will hardly be able to correct this violation to the principle of *audi alteram partem*. In this field, it is wise for the arbitrator to protect the award by expressly stating the manner in which s/he was appointed as well as the notices made and phases of the procedure, showing how the procedural guarantees were observed.

Another example: if the arbitrator ultimately decides on issues that were not submitted to the arbitration or if the tribunal grants more than what was requested, the affected party may challenge the award with a high likelihood of success. A good recommendation to circumvent this risk is to reproduce the complete text of the arbitration agreement, the parties' requests for relief as stated in their main submissions, the precise points to be resolved by the tribunal, and the decisions that were made on them.

Arbitral justice, however expert, remains human, meaning that awards may contain errors of all kinds from omissions to ambiguities. Consequently, the arbitrator—especially if s/he is inexperienced—should carefully review the product of his or her work, avoiding the need to clarify or rectify later what was decided. Before its issuing, it is recommended to perform a double—and even triple—check of the references and calculations contained in the award.

Finally, a question that is being greatly discussed in the international arbitration community is how much work can be done by arbitral tribunal secretaries.[10] Although it is unlikely that a young arbitrator will have an assistant in his or her first case, it is important to highlight that the mandate to the arbitrator is *intuitu personæ*. Put differently, s/he cannot delegate to a secretary—or anyone else—the duty to decide the case. Certainly, the arbitrator can ask for the secretary's assistance during the proceeding and when outlining the formal aspects of the award, but in no way should an arbitrator stop determining—for himself or herself—the substantive points of the dispute.[11]

---

9. *Ibid.*, section 5.1.
10. Arguably the best school to become an arbitrator.
11. *See* Chapter 12: *Guide for the Arbitral Secretary* (Lucas Loviscek).

In summary, the drafting of the first award is a fascinating challenge. As can be seen, the job of an arbitrator demands thoroughness and commitment. I hope these guidelines come in handy for those practitioners who are starting their arbitration career.

Over time, the experience improves the method and allows to deal with increasingly complex disputes, letting the arbitrator acquire his or her unique style. As in all things, practice makes perfect.

CHAPTER 12
Guide for the Arbitral Secretary

Lucas Loviscek

§12.01 INTRODUCTION

This chapter aims to share my gratifying and fruitful experience and lessons learned serving as secretary of arbitral tribunals in ad hoc and institutional arbitrations and to provide some recommendations in the hope that they will be helpful to young practitioners, as well as those not so young professionals, who are opening their way through the fascinating practice of arbitration and who are interested in serving as arbitral secretaries.

To that effect, it is first necessary to understand the role and implication of the secretary[1] in the conduct and development of the arbitral proceedings. The main function of the secretary is to assist the arbitrators in fulfilling their mandate. The mandate of the arbitrators is to analyze and weigh the arguments of the parties and the evidence submitted in the proceedings and decide the dispute.[2] The secretary then must not replace, supplement, or perform functions that correspond to the arbitrators' personal mandate,[3] but its role is very important as it assists the tribunal in fulfilling its mandate of conducting the arbitral proceedings and resolving the case in an efficient and effective manner.

The secretary performs case management and administration tasks (e.g., organizing documents and evidence, preparing procedural calendars, handling

1. When I refer to the figure of the "secretary," I mean both female and male.
2. It is appropriate to remember the famous quote commonly attributed to the Greek philosopher Socrates (470 AC-399 AC) on the functions of the judge, equally descriptive of arbitrator as for its jurisdictional powers without entering into any disquisitions as to the nature and prerogatives of one and the other: "*Four characteristics correspond to the judge: Listen politely, respond wisely, ponder prudently and decide impartially.*"
3. The parties' choice of the arbitrators is personal as they select these arbitrators (and not others) to resolve their dispute.

notifications and communications between the tribunal and the parties, and ensuring the parties' compliance with formalities, deadlines, and procedural orders). On the need and directions of the tribunal—and always under the tribunal's supervision—the secretary may also prepare drafts of procedural orders or even some sections of the award, conduct research and analyze legal issues, and assist the deliberations of the arbitrators.[4] These types of functions give those professionals who serve as secretaries the invaluable experience of: (1) understanding and coordinating the interactions and synergies among the parties, counsel, experts, and tribunal and administering the institution of the arbitration where appropriate; (2) developing interpersonal skills by interacting with the different actors in the arbitration proceedings and addressing their needs; (3) managing deadlines efficiently; (4) managing and organizing documents, calendars, and important procedural and case management aspects for the efficient conduct of the arbitration proceedings; and depending on the circumstances and the arbitral tribunals, (5) attending the arbitrators' deliberations and understanding how the arbitrators think, identifying relevant evidence and arguments, assisting with legal research and analysis of specific legal issues, as well as preparing drafts of procedural orders, and in some cases, drafting sections of the award. All of these, of course, occur under the proper instruction and supervision of the arbitrators.

The above denotes the reasons why more and more professionals aspire to serve as arbitral secretaries, as it is an unbeatable opportunity to get involved in the practice of arbitration and to develop the necessary tools to serve in that role, or as counsel to the parties, or, eventually, as arbitrators. Below, I share some lessons learned and recommendations for persons who are working toward becoming an arbitral secretary or who are already serving as one.

§12.02 GUIDELINES AND RECOMMENDATIONS TO SERVE AS AN ARBITRAL SECRETARY

Much has been discussed about the role of the secretary and, in some cases, its role has been criticized for excessive involvement, in what is known in the arbitration community as the paranoia of the "Fourth Arbitrator."[5] It is not the purpose of this

4. It should be noted that I am referring here to arbitral secretaries appointed in institutional and ad hoc arbitrations for the specific case and not to secretaries of permanent arbitral tribunals or to the Secretariat of arbitral institutions. The latter, which is more akin to the clerk of a court, may have broader functions as to the conduct of the arbitral proceedings, such as issuing interlocutory resolutions, although their specific duties vary depending on the jurisdiction, the institution and corresponding regulations. As we will see next, the trend in practice is to grant greater responsibilities to the secretary, but this will depend on each tribunal, after consultation with the parties and on the experience that the secretary may have.
5. *See* Constantine Partasides. *The Fourth Arbitrator? The Role of Secretaries to Tribunals in International Arbitration*, 18 Arb. Int'l 147 (2002). The discussion was reactivated with *Yukos Universal Limited v. The Russian Federation* (PCA Case No. AA227), where Russia requested the annulment of the award alleging that by virtue of the hours worked and the fees billed by the secretary, the secretary had played a significant role in the deliberations and the drafting of the award and that, therefore, the arbitrators did not fulfill their mandate personally. For more on this, *see* Dmytro Galagan. *The Challenge of the Yukos Award: An Award Written by Someone Else—A Violation of the Tribunal's Mandate?*, Kluwer Arb. Blog (February 27, 2015).

chapter to delve into this controversial issue, but it is important to take it into account in order to provide recommendations and guidelines to professionals who want to serve as arbitral secretaries.

[A] First Recommendation

It is important to have experience in litigation and arbitration, or the training of an arbitral secretary, in order to be considered and appointed as an arbitral secretary and to serve and perform well in that role.

In the first case that I acted as an arbitral secretary, the parties considered several facts for my appointment. I had three years of experience in litigation, and I had acted as counsel for the parties in several cases. In addition, I provided references from the president of the arbitral tribunal. At that time, these three years of experience in litigation and arbitration was certainly not much, but it was very helpful.

The arbitral community is aware of the need for well-trained arbitral secretaries, especially due to the increasing number of arbitration proceedings and the complexity of the cases submitted to arbitration. Usually, the arbitration proceedings involve many parties, as well as a large volume of documents and evidence which require the arbitrators to issue detailed and thorough awards to avoid nullities.[6]

There are training programs for arbitral secretaries that have been created to address this trend and are very useful. One of them is implemented by the ICC, which provides training to secretaries through the conferences it organizes. It should also be noted that currently there are no lists of secretaries, and therefore in order to serve as a secretary, the candidate is not required to be part of a list or to undergo a selection process by an arbitral institution. For this reason, the training that the candidate has as well as the prior knowledge that the arbitrator or the presiding arbitrator of the tribunal has of the candidate's working experience are important to be proposed and appointed as arbitral secretary.

[B] Second Recommendation

The candidate's resume should include case management skills, such as the ability to identify and organize relevant documents, to prepare chronologies of facts and positions of the parties, to handle deadlines and notifications, etc. It is important since the tribunal usually proposes the use of a secretary to the parties and the parties must provide their agreement with the proposed candidate.

It is common practice for the tribunal or the presiding arbitrator to provide the parties with copies of the candidate's resume and declaration of availability, independence, and impartiality before appointing him or her as the arbitral secretary so

6. International Council for Commercial Arbitration, *The ICCA Reports No. 1: Young ICCA Guide on Arbitral Secretaries* 1, 26, 27, 43 (2014) (hereinafter "Young ICCA Guide").

that the parties can interview the candidate[7] if they wish. This type of interview is aimed at getting to know the candidate's background further, and, of course, the interviews should not discuss opinions on the underlying issues of the controversy. The interviews facilitate the process for appointing the secretary in an appropriate manner and grant greater legitimacy and confidence of the parties in the appointed secretary, all of which contributes to the transparency and efficiency of the arbitral proceedings.

[C] Third Recommendation

It is essential that the secretary responds at all times to the instructions and supervision of the tribunal or the presiding arbitrator. In matters on which there is no precise instruction, the secretary should always consult with the tribunal. The arbitrator's mandate is *intuitu personæ*.[8] Therefore, it cannot delegate the functions that are essential for the performance of its duty to weigh the parties' claims and arguments and decide the dispute. While the arbitrator should not delegate these decision-making functions and is required to supervise and control what the secretary does, the secretary should simultaneously make sure not to cross the limits of its duties when assisting the tribunal in the analysis of the parties' claims and the evidence produced, as the arbitrators are generally very busy people who will focus their attention on substantive legal issues.[9]

The secretary must keep the tribunal informed at all times about the progress of his or her work, as well as the procedural developments of the arbitration, including reporting to the tribunal the parties' compliance with deadlines and procedural orders. To preserve the transparency and efficiency of the proceedings, it is crucial that the secretary properly handle the procedural calendar (and the set calendar for internal use among the members of the tribunal and the secretary) by sending alerts or reminders to the arbitrators and informing the tribunal (or the president, if applicable) of any communication that the parties or their counsel have with the secretary.

7. Notification and the agreement of the parties in the appointment of the secretary is part of the practices and guidelines proposed by the majority of the arbitration institutions. *See*, e.g., ICC, *Note on the Appointment, Duties and Remuneration of Administrative Secretaries*, August 1, 2012, at 1, https://actuarbitragealtana.files.wordpress.com/2015/04/note-on-administrative-secretaries-icc.pdf; SIAC, *Administered Cases: On the Appointment of Administrative Secretaries*, Practice Note (PN-01/15), February 2, 2015; JAMS International, *Guidelines for Use of Clerks and Tribunal Secretaries in Arbitrations*, https://www.jamsadr.com/files/Uploads/Documents/JAMS-International-Guidelines-for-Use-of-Clerks-and-Tribunal-Secretaries-in-Arbitrations.pdf; *LCIA Notes for Arbitrators 2017*, section 8.3; SCC, *Arbitrator's Guidelines*, January 2017, at 6, 7, https://sccinstitute.com/media/171486/guidelines-january-2017.pdf.
8. It is a fundamental principle of the arbitration process since the parties choose the arbitrators based on their profile, experience, and background, and after an arduous due diligence process, select that person, and not anyone else, to ponder the parties' claims and decide the dispute.
9. In no way does it exempt the arbitrator from the responsibility to personally review the record of the case, but the secretary's job can help review more efficiently.

[D] Fourth Recommendation

The secretary should not give information to the parties or their counsel regarding the proceedings, apart from information on deadlines and formalities for the filings as required and notified to the parties by the tribunal. He or she should only give information unless the tribunal instructs or authorizes it.

As secretary, I have experienced situations in which a party's counsel approached me with unilateral queries, for example asking about the order in which the tribunal would resolve different pending issues, about the criteria the tribunal would apply to certain provisions of the applicable arbitration rules, or about the timeframes for the tribunal's resolutions. In these situations, it is extremely important that the secretary states that it cannot answer these questions, or in any event, states that it will consult with the tribunal. Depending on the kind and extent of the information requested, the tribunal may order the secretary to respond to the requesting party or to send a notification to the parties with some clarification.

It is recommended that the secretary discusses its specific functions with the tribunal and the kind of information that can be provided to the parties. For example, it would be reasonable for the secretary to answer the parties' questions on whether a memorial has been received by the tribunal's office, on when the tribunal estimates to issue its resolution, or to share other matters concerning logistics and formalities of the filings. If for these issues the parties would need to speak directly with the tribunal or the presiding arbitrator, the communication between them would be slow and tedious. The secretary can facilitate the communication in procedural matters, thus making the proceeding more efficient and effective. But again, when in doubt, the secretary should always consult with the tribunal, and the tribunal should direct the steps to follow.

[E] Fifth Recommendation

The secretary should know well the applicable arbitration rules, procedural orders and calendars set by the tribunal in the proceedings. The secretary must have full knowledge of the rules applicable to the procedure, whether they are the rules of an institution, of the United Nations Commission on International Trade Law (UNCITRAL) rules if it is an ad hoc arbitration, or of the tribunal. The secretary must also have a thorough knowledge of the procedural orders issued by the tribunal and the respective procedural calendars and properly handle them.

Under the supervision of the tribunal, the secretary will take due account of the development of the different procedural stages and the deadlines for filings and resolutions to be issued. It is good practice for the secretary to schedule and send reminders of deadlines to the arbitrators in a timely manner. It is usually done through the common virtual calendar created for this purpose. Also, the secretary must alert the tribunal of the parties' compliance or noncompliance with deadlines as well as other formalities required under the applicable rules and procedural orders regarding the filing of memorials, such as their content, presentation of annexes and legal authorities, translations and page limits, or formatting if applicable. It also contributes to the celerity of the proceedings, since the tribunal may require clarification or amendments to the submissions before analyzing the substantive arguments. In this regard, the secretary must fulfill its duties impartially and treat the parties equally.

As an example, in a commercial arbitration under the UNCITRAL Rules in which I served as a secretary, the tribunal had entrusted me to make a preliminary scrutiny of the parties' compliance with deadlines and formalities in their submissions and to report the findings to the arbitrators.[10] On that occasion, the scrutiny involved an analysis of the notice of arbitration, confirmation that the submissions met the requirements set forth in the UNCITRAL Rules, and then a review of the final allegations that the arbitral tribunal had limited to thirty pages. Based on my preliminary scrutiny, the tribunal requested the claimant to clarify the contracts upon which the claims were based pursuant to Article 3.3(d) of the UNCITRAL Rules of 2010.[11]

[F] Sixth Recommendation

The secretary should keep a complete record of the case file for consultation of the parties and the tribunal. It is not so much a recommended practice but an obligation of the arbitral secretary.

The secretary must keep a complete record of the proceedings in chronological order, including all the communications between the parties and the tribunal, memorials and accompanying documents, expert reports, procedural orders, and resolutions. It is common practice to create a virtual document-exchange platform where the parties and the tribunal can upload, store, and download all the filings, documents, and communications of the proceedings. This platform helps to maintain a virtual record of the case file and allows access to it at any time. Usually, in the first procedural order, the tribunal instructs the parties to submit the memorials and documents via email, with hard copies to follow, and also to upload them to the virtual platform. In any case, it is advisable to keep a physical record of the case file, which must be available to the parties and the tribunal.

[G] Seventh Recommendation

The secretary must know well and efficiently handle the case file to better assist the tribunal and, eventually, the parties. The primary duty of the secretary is to assist the tribunal in resolving the dispute effectively and efficiently, and as I mentioned above, depending on the tribunal and always under the direction and supervision of the arbitrators, the role of the secretary can go beyond its administrative and

10. It may be the case that the findings report is first sent to the president of the tribunal and then shared with the co-arbitrators. It is important to discuss with the president the logistics for the communications with the other arbitrators.
11. Article 3.3 of the UNCITRAL Rules of 2010 provides, "The notice of arbitration shall include the following: (...) (d) Identification of any contract or other legal instrument out of or in relation to which the dispute arises ... ."

organizational tasks to include, for example, analyzing evidence for the arbitrators' review, researching and examining specific legal issues, and preparing drafts of procedural orders, resolutions, or even parts of the award.[12]

I had the opportunity to be a secretary of the tribunal in an ICC arbitration where the presiding arbitrator was in charge of preparing the first draft of the decisions, which he then discussed with the other arbitrators. In that case, the presiding arbitrator instructed me to analyze legal issues and prepare draft resolutions. These drafts were reviewed and revised by him and then sent to the other members of the tribunal for approval or comments. I also had the opportunity to participate in the arbitrators' deliberations. The participation in the deliberations is also governed and limited by the guiding principle that the secretary's role is to assist the tribunal. The secretary cannot perform any decision-making functions nor has the power to act on behalf of any of the arbitrators in the deliberations. Given the tasks I had performed and my knowledge of the proceeding, the tribunal entrusted me to prepare the drafts of certain parts of the award, subject to the supervision and review of the arbitrators. It was a very interesting and enriching experience because I also had the opportunity to observe the ICC's scrutiny of the draft award. Since I also assisted the tribunal in the preparation of the final version of the award, I could see where the arbitrators incorporated the comments of the ICC.

[H] Eighth Recommendation

The secretary should report any possible conflict of interest. It is a matter of obligation, more than a recommendation. The secretary must inform the arbitral tribunal of any event that may affect its impartiality or independence or of any actual or potential conflict of interest so that the tribunal can inform the parties accordingly. It is the tribunal's responsibility to select the appropriate secretary and supervise him or her. However, it is very difficult for the arbitrator to identify any possible conflict of interest of the secretary, so the latter must be alert and report any circumstances to the arbitrator.

§12.03 CONCLUSION

Serving as an arbitral secretary is undoubtedly an arduous task. The role of the arbitral secretary is very important for the efficient conduct and management of the arbitration proceedings and to help the arbitrators to fulfill their mandate.

It is also a great opportunity for young attorneys to get involved in the practice of international arbitration, to learn from interacting with the arbitrators, parties and their

12. The practice indicates that most arbitrators delegate certain functions to the secretaries and that the arbitration community and most of the arbitration institutions accept this practice, subject to the proper instruction and supervision of the tribunal. In this regard, ICCA has done a formidable job conducting surveys confirming the above and preparing a document of good practices for the appointment and use of arbitration secretaries. *See* Young ICCA Guide, *supra* note 6, Annex A, p. 28; Annex B, p. 62; Annex C, pp. 76-80; Annex D.

counsel, and arbitral institutions, and to develop their career in this practice while facilitating efficient and expeditious arbitration proceedings. The secretary must be aware of the limits, responsibilities, and requirements to duly and fully comply with its role, so it does not intrude upon the arbitrators' personal mandate to decide the dispute, and always act under the consultation, direction, and supervision of the arbitrators. The recommendations given in this chapter are intended to provide some helpful tools to perform the role of arbitral secretary in order to preserve the legitimacy, integrity, and transparency of the arbitration proceedings.

CHAPTER 13

Franklin, Rubin, or de Bono: How to Face the First Deliberation

Manuel Conthe

A good president of an arbitral tribunal must ensure a climate of cordiality between the three arbitrators from the outset. Thus, their possible discrepancies may be expressed freely in an environment of mutual respect and resolved in a friendly manner, appealing to the majority rule if necessary. To favor this climate, when I am appointed president, and the three arbitrators do not know each other personally, I usually invite my colleagues to eat to get to know each other without addressing any significant question of the arbitration. That early informal meeting will be difficult if the arbitrators live in distant places. Then it will be convenient to maintain a first teleconference to avoid the coldness and dangers of using email as a means of communication between strangers, especially, if in matters of courtesy, any of the arbitrators does not follow the advice of Don Quixote according to which "in civilities it is better to lose by a card too many than a card too few."

Once that climate of collaboration and respect is created, unless the tribunal has to decide soon on procedural issues (such as a request for bifurcation of proceedings, discovery of documents, or interim injunctions), the first substantive deliberation should await that, with the counter-memorial or rejoinder (according to the chosen procedure), the parties conclude the presentation of their main submissions.

During the hearing, a good president should reserve sufficient time for the tribunal to ask questions, and not obstruct any questions of an arbitrator, as they will be useful not only to the parties but also to the president of the court, to identify primary issues that concern their colleagues and should be addressed in the award.

Before, during, or normally after the hearing will be the ideal time for the tribunal to have a first substantive deliberation, which in many cases will allow it to send parties a list of questions, on matters of fact or law, that it would like the parties to address in their final submissions. On occasion, I have heard that this list should include some "distracting" questions, so it does not appear that the tribunal has already taken a firm position on the capital issues of the arbitration. But honestly, I do not think that trick is necessary. At this stage of the arbitration, it is natural for the arbitrators to have already formed themselves a preliminary opinion. The essential thing will be that the parties have the opportunity to refute it and make them change their minds. The minds of the arbitrators, although not empty, should be kept open.

After the written conclusions, it will be convenient for the president to prepare an orderly and complete list of the essential issues on which the award must decide and invite his colleagues to complete and correct it.

Once these issues have been identified, the time will come to inquire about the preliminary position of the arbitrators on each one of them. It will be the most delicate trance because as human beings we are reluctant to change our minds once we have expressed our opinions (especially if we have expressed them in writing). Who, then, shall be the first to "show the cards" and express his or her opinion?

In my experience, many presidents invite their co-arbitrators to be the first to express their criteria, in order to reserve for themselves the leading role of *umpire* in case of discrepancies. Sometimes it will put the co-arbitrators in a predicament as they will naturally tend to share many of the views of the parties that designated them. Those "doctrinal predispositions" might be precisely what motivated their designation; however, they would not like to give arguments to where they are believed to be biased. Because of this frequent reluctance to express themselves clearly and their recurrent circumlocutions and ambiguities, it is sometimes difficult to facilitate an effective deliberation.

Therefore, it seems more productive to me if the president, free of that suspicion or presumption of bias that will inevitably fly over the co-arbitrators, is the first one to "jump into the ring." Before giving his or her opinion, he or she can follow the method to solve difficult cases that Benjamin Franklin described in his famous letter to the British scientist and theologian Joseph Priestley: divide a sheet of paper into two columns, match the arguments for and against each issue, and ponder their weight before reaching the final decision. Irrespective of following or not following this comparative procedure, the president should emphasize with a broad view that he or she will accept any point of view which is different but better justified than his or her own. That will allow the co-arbitrator who disagrees with any of the president's preliminary opinions to explain the reasons for his or her discrepancy.

If such discrepancies arise, a good president should not silence them nor refute them prematurely, but on the contrary, follow the method that Robert Rubin, Secretary of the Treasury at the Clinton Administration, describes in his memoirs about those years (*In an Uncertain World*, 2003):

> The meetings [in the Treasury] produced the best results when those who disagreed with the dominant opinion were encouraged to express themselves. Therefore, if a consensus was emerging at a meeting, I insisted that those who disagreed speak. Disagreeing with me was socially well regarded and not discouraged. If no one disagreed, I asked someone to act as the devil's lawyer. I said, for example: "We are reaching this conclusion, but we need to know the

> opposite point of view, in order to analyse it." And then, myself or another person, would defend that point of view.

This "Rubin method" to avoid premature decisions or consensus is related to the "hat method" or the "parallel thinking method" that in 1985 was proposed by Edward de Bono, the famous Maltese consultant. This method requires that the president of a committee, instead of letting its members express themselves freely, structures the debate in phases, each symbolically characterized by the color of an imaginary hat: the white or the cold fact-finding; the black or the critical and pessimistic attitude; the yellow or the positive and optimistic attitude; the red or the visceral or passionate attitude; the green or the innovative, creative and iconoclastic attitude; and the blue or the organization of the debate while obtaining conclusions. In each phase all members must intervene in the direction set by the president. Thus, if he or she has asked them to "wear the black hat," everyone should strive to discover the weaknesses or risks of the idea under discussion, without anyone being able to come out in its defense, a thing which everyone without exception should do when the president orders to "put on the yellow hat." By requiring all members to think in parallel, the system will avoid personal antagonisms and dialectical duels. By forcing everyone to wear the different hats, it will prevent them from getting into partial positions and will force them to analyze the issue from different perspectives. And, in the end, it will allow the group to conduct a thorough analysis of the matter within a reasonable time.

I confess that I have never seen a tribunal applying the de Bono method, and I have not even tried it myself as president. I usually follow Rubin's approach of trying to truly understand the reasons for the dissent and, when they are not clear, ask him or her to clarify them. It allows the eventual majority to explain in the award why they have not accepted the point of view of the dissenting arbitrator and will make the opinion of the latter, if he or she acts in good faith, be very brief and calm, without any surprise or new affirmation that the award has not weighted.

Whether you follow or not the advice of Franklin, Rubin, or de Bono, in my opinion, a good president should not start writing a single word of the legal basis of the award before agreeing on the list of issues to be addressed and discerning the majority feeling of the tribunal over each of them.

CHAPTER 14
Dissenting Opinions in Commercial Arbitration

Clifford J. Hendel

§14.01 INTRODUCTION

International commercial arbitration is an area of practice in which there is an abundance (if not to say, an excess) of literature and discourse on a myriad of topics. Certain topics, truth be told, may not be of compelling interest and importance, while others may very well be. All or virtually all that can be said about them has already been said.

Some would say the result is that literature is comprised largely of discussions of topics of limited relevance or of essentially repetitious treatment of more important issues. The recent avalanche of articles and conferences on the Prague Rules may be a good example.

Occasionally, one finds an area which seems of real importance and about which precious little has been written or said.

The question of dissenting opinions in international commercial arbitration may be one such example.[1] Different issues are raised in the area of investment arbitration due to the issues of policy and precedent which are essentially inapplicable in

1. The classic piece in the area is Alan Redfern's "Dissenting Opinions in International Commercial Arbitration: The Good, the Bad and the Ugly," *Arbitration International*, Vol. 20, No. 3, LCIA, 2004, pp. 223-242. Other, more recent, articles include Peter Rees' and Patrick Rohn's "Dissenting Opinions: Can They Fulfil a Beneficial Role?," *Arbitration International*, Vol. 25, No. 3, LCIA, 2009, pp. 329-346 and Mark Baker's and Lucy Greenwood's "Dissent-But Only If You Really Feel You Must: Why Dissenting Opinions in International Commercial Arbitration Should Only Appear in Exceptional Circumstances," *Dispute Resolution International*, Vol. 7, No. 1, 2013, pp. 31-40.

commercial arbitration. The literature in the area of investment arbitration is both abundant and lively.[2]

§14.02 THE ORIGINS OF MY INTEREST IN THE AREA

My active involvement in international commercial arbitration dates back some fifteen years. In the dozens of cases in which I have sat as arbitrator, there were two in which the possibility (and one in which the reality) of penning a dissenting opinion arose. Both sent me digging into literature and reflecting on the pros and cons and the dos and do nots.

The first was a case which I chaired and which I disagreed with my two wing arbitrators on the proper resolution of a dispositive issue as I considered it an issue of principle. A series of deliberation sessions on the tricky issue commenced a period of weeks where memos and drafts were exchanged and debated. In the end, these deliberations revealed that we were at real loggerheads.

The situation was hardly optimal. On the one hand, I as Chair might have felt compelled to issue an opinion dissenting from the majority view of my wings, an unusual situation to say the least, and one which might put into question my abilities as Chair. On the other hand, my dissent (whether embodied in an actual opinion or in a dissenting vote) would reveal that one of the wings had sided with the "opposing party's position, which might put him in a delicate position with the party that appointed him.

Ultimately, we found a solution. We were able to agree unanimously on another dispositive issue, leaving the trickier issue (as to which we also, finally, reached unanimity) reduced to mere obiter dictum by our resolution of the other issue.

In the end, there was no dissenting opinion and no dissenting vote.

My second experience, in which I was wing arbitrator named by the administering institution in the absence of the respondent making a nomination within the allotted time, resulted in the issuance of my first and only dissenting opinion.

Again, the issue (as I saw it) that divided me and the majority was one of principle, and I felt I owed it to my principles, to the parties, and to the institution that appointed me, not only to vote in dissent but also to reflect in a few pages the reasons for my discrepancy. Before voting, I consulted the above literature and tried to follow the sound suggestions that it contained.

2. *See*, e.g., Jan A. Van Den Berg's "Dissenting Opinions by Party-Appointed Arbitrators in Investments Arbitration," in *Looking to the Future: Essays on International Law in Honor of W: Michael Reisman*, Martinus Nijhoff Publishers, 2011, pp. 821-843, Charlie Brower's and Chip Rosenberg's "The Death of the Two-Headed Nightingale: Why the Paulsson-Van den Berg Presumption That Party-Appointed Arbitrators Are Untrustworthy Is Wrongheaded," *Arbitration International*, Vol. 29, No. 1, LCIA, 2013, pp. 7-44, and Professor Van den Berg's response in "Charlie Brower's Problem with 100 Per cent-Dissenting Opinions by Party-Appointed Arbitrators in Investment Arbitration," *Arbitration International*, Vol 31, No. 3, LCIA, 2015, pp. 381-391.

§14.03 LESSONS LEARNED

Reflecting on the past, I have no regrets about either of these two experiences.

Naturally, reaching unanimity—even if it involves a certain amount of "horse-trading" and might result in an award which may not be 100% cohesive—must be considered in almost all cases a supreme aim of any self-respecting arbitral tribunal and its Chair. It took weeks for my tribunal to find this solution in the first case mentioned, but I was and remain very glad that we did.

Similarly, wherein the second case unanimity proved impossible, but I believed that the matter separating the tribunal was one of principle, and managed to craft a short and respectful dissent, I again have slept comfortably ever since. More comfortably, probably, than if I had resisted the temptation to issue a dissent.

So, what lessons have I learned from these experiences? I would say that the literature, albeit limited, is right on point in this area and provides good guidance on the "when" and the "how" of dissents in international commercial arbitration.

As a first lesson, I would agree fully with Baker and Greenwood that one should dissent in commercial arbitrations only in exceptional circumstances:

> The arbitrator's fundamental right to hold a dissenting opinion should not be confused with a right or indeed a responsibility to publish that dissenting opinion. It would be invidious to seek to prohibit dissents as no one would wish to be seen as stifling an arbitrator's right of expression, but their use should both be exceptional and published in such a way as to minimise as far as possible the negative impacts such a dissent could have (...).[3]

As to what constitutes "exceptional circumstances," let your conscience be your guide:

> What, then, are the exceptional circumstances in which an arbitrator could, and should dissent in writing? We believe that this is a matter of conscience for the arbitrator; namely in the extremely rare situation in which an arbitrator, acting fairly and impartially between the parties, simply cannot stay silent and does not feel that he or she could address the issue by refusing to sign the award. In 20 years of acting as an arbitrator in commercial arbitrations, one of the authors has only felt compelled to issue a written dissent in one case: on a dispositive legal issue, which, in the author's view, the majority simply preferred to ignore in the interests of achieving a "just" result. There is no shame in a majority opinion without a dissent. There will always be panels where agreement cannot be reached. The question is whether or not the disagreement should be publicised as a dissent in the majority of international commercial cases. Our view is that the answer to this should be no, unless the arbitrator really feels they must.[4]

And as a second lesson, I would agree fully with Redfern that when an arbitrator feels him/herself to be in those exceptional circumstances in which a dissenting opinion is appropriate, care should be taken so that the dissent is not of the "ugly" or "bad" varieties, but of the "good" variety. It is short, focused, and respectful, rather

3. Baker and Greenwood, *supra.*, p. 40.
4. *Ibid.*

than scathing and disrespectful or, worse, questioning the process of the deliberations and setting out a roadmap for an eventual annulment action.

§14.04 CONCLUSIONS

In light of these conclusions, my best recommendation to the interested arbitrator or counsel—rather than reinventing the wheel or lowering the level of the existing discourse—would be to read the excellent literature available on the topic and cited in this chapter.

Part III War Stories and Lessons about Big Law and Alternative Paths to Arbitration

CHAPTER 15

Challenges of a Global Practice

Juliana de Valdenebro

The word "global" is an intrinsic element in the practice of international arbitration. By definition, our field is inclusive of the entire globe, encompassing every nationality, culture, legal tradition and language, as there is no way to limit the international component of arbitration.

In fact, this element is evident not only in the parties or the disputes but also in the "players" that make up this global practice. Arbitrators, lawyers, law firms, partners, associates, clients and experts play in the field of international arbitration without being divided by boundary lines. It is where a "global" practice really consolidates since it is its players that potentiate it.

It undoubtedly makes it an interesting practice and places it in line with the globalized world in which we now live. Nevertheless, it is those same components that also bring about great challenges. This work intends to analyze some of the main challenges that arise from this legal world without borders. It aims to cover both practical and theoretical aspects which all international arbitration associates should consider.

To analyze these challenges, one should start by considering that the rules of this playing field are dictated by its own players. Since it is a globalized practice, there is no central body that can control the creation of new rules. To analyze this point further, it is useful to turn to the categories of "players" of a legal system as identified by Marc Galanter. According to this author, the players of a legal system are divided between "repeated players" and "one-shotters." In defining "repeated players," Galanter explains that they are the players who have multiple opportunities to interact in the legal system. This category includes all of the repetitive users and comprises the clients as much as the lawyers who participate actively in the same field.[1]

1. Galanter, Marc, 1974-1975, *Why the Haves Come Out Ahead: Speculations on the Limits of Legal Change*. The Law and Society Review, Vol. 9, pp. 97, 114.

In the case of international arbitration, the "repeated players" of this legal system would be all the common users who are part of this practice, including the institutions, arbitrators, firms, lawyers and now the "third party funders." According to Galanter, all have a comparative advantage, since, in their condition as repeated players, they have the capacity to influence the creation and modification of the applicable rules in their field.[2]

From this characteristic derives the first challenge of international arbitration as a global practice. Namely, this global practice has its own rules and its own language. If you are not a repeated player, if it is the first time you enter this playing field, if you are a first-time user or a "one-shotter," then you need to understand and abide by the rules created by others. Moreover, the first-time player not only needs to learn a new system of legal rules or soft-law that can define its role in the game but also learn a new language full of words that only make sense to those who have previously practiced in this field.

The new player should start by understanding the legal components of the system and then overcome the slang barrier that repeated players have imposed. The first-time user must learn what is a memorial and procedural order as well as terms such as the "chess-clock" system; the "cooling off period"; the "terms of reference"; the traffic lights of the green, orange, and red lists; the "hot-tubbing"; and a "Redfern." The newcomer must understand what an international arbitral tribunal is, what an award is (or is not), and what bifurcation is. Plus, the new player needs to decipher the various acronyms that are used daily (ICC, ICSID, AAA, ICDR, IBA, VCLT, BITs, and ISDS). In sum, to understand this global practice, you should learn and relearn a new language and, like all languages, only with daily practice will you be able to master it. This barrier of rules and language created by the repeated players is, therefore, the first challenge imposed by the global practice of international arbitration.

But the challenges do not end there. Since the players of this field are scattered throughout the world, a global practice also faces global competition. Unlike local practices, the global practice implies that a competitor of different origin with a completely different country or culture may displace another player. It is true both for the search for clients and for associates' professional advancement.

With respect to business development, two fundamental premises should be considered: (1) one must comply with certain minimum requirements to compete in the field, to be recognized as a repeated player, and to have mastery of the rules and language; and (2) simultaneously, one must have certain added value or differentiating element. As a law firm or as an arbitrator, a player should have experience in the field, be duly recognized as a player by his peers, and have a trained team and infrastructure that allows him to meet the necessities of the case. However, all these items are not sufficient as they are only the minimum requirement. All competitors bring exactly the same to the table and, thus, a distinctive element is required—which, in a global world, is increasingly more difficult to achieve. That element may be language skills, although almost all teams already have this capacity, as they include multilingual associates

2. *Ibid.*, p. 100.

from diverse origins. It could also be experience in a specific sector, although almost all global firms can form teams by expertise in certain sectors.

Therefore, in a global practice, the differentiating element should be identified and tailor-made to each client, dispute, or context in which the legal advice is being provided, as it may be the only way to offer an added value that is different from what the rest of the players can offer. For example, a client recently expressed that upon having interviewed various peer law firms, the client opted to pick the one that had concrete experience in an arbitration against its counterpart. Knowing the modus operandi of the eventual counterpart was key to the client's selection of that particular law firm.

After finding the differentiating element, one must convey to the client that he or she can "trust" in the team, so the client feels that he or she is passing along his or her problem to expert's hands. That trust can only be gained "face to face" as there is no virtual medium in this technological world that replaces direct interaction with the client. The same applies in the case of arbitrators, which is why the pre-appointment interview is fundamental before trusting that arbitrator with the dispute.

However, global competition is not only between law firms looking for new clients or cases. Every young lawyer that works or seeks to work in this field faces global competition which is why it is more difficult each day for young lawyers to create differentiating values to bring to a new team. Nowadays, it is not enough to be a lawyer of a single jurisdiction, nor is it enough to have studied a single legal system. No, in this global practice, young lawyers assume the challenge of being lawyers prepared to resolve disputes under any law, in multiple languages, and with the capacity to identify a legal or factual problem independent of their country or legal tradition of origin.

It implies that every young lawyer at least competes with all of his or her generation who want to practice in international arbitration in his or her region. Participating as an interviewee or interviewer in the New York job fair that is organized every year for the L.L.M. students of American universities is sufficient proof of what it feels like to compete in a globalized market.

After overcoming the sensation of "speed dating" in fifteen-minute interviews at this fair, interviewees must sell all their potential and explain what makes them different from all of his or her peers. In this global practice, that differentiating element is more difficult to identify, since many candidates have the same language capabilities, similar experiences, and normally the same enthusiasm to join a multinational firm. For this reason, associates are to differentiate themselves based on their skills as a lawyer, their training, and in some manner their knowledge of the rules of the game in this global practice. Accordingly, a young lawyer facing this global practice should focus his or her efforts on acquiring concrete experience that could distinguish them from his or her peers.

Now, some of those professionals who have practiced outside their jurisdiction will have found that global practice has limits that have not yet been overcome. For example, one may find limits in certain jurisdictions with respect to who can practice law in a certain state or country. Even though this practice is not tied to one particular place, certain associates are still required to seek admission to additional bar associations or to even pursue additional studies. It evidences that in the end, the global system must deal with local limitations in one way or another.

Moreover, sometimes these local limitations are necessary. Given that there are no regulatory or supervisory entities in this global practice, it is thus a "self-governed" practice where, as we have already seen, the players define their own rules and supervise compliance with the same. But these players do not have sanctioning power, so the practice has no ability to control unethical behavior. In fact, despite it being an international and modern practice, there is still not sufficient transparency that allows players to learn of others' faults or to punish them.

Therefore, another challenge of the global practice is to define the ethical minimums that govern every player and to find a way to put them into practice. However, the reality is little to nothing can be done to sanction violations of these ethical standards if there is no central, global entity that can ensure compliance. For this reason, the local component is inevitable because it is the only way to guarantee that the players of the globalized world abide by minimum standards of behavior in some form or another and can be sanctioned.

In general, if it were necessary to define the challenges of the global practice in a single line, it would be summarized by stating that the very benefits of a lack of borders are itself the challenges in international arbitration. Common language barriers, global competition, legacies that bind us to certain jurisdictions, and lack of control or sanction over questionable ethics are direct consequences of a global practice and little to nothing can be done to mitigate them.

Perhaps, the key to success (if there is one) may be in navigating within this world without borders without forgetting that one has to first be an excellent lawyer with integrity before anything. Everything else, the language, the added value, and the opportunities, will come as an addition.

CHAPTER 16

How to Advance Your Career in an International Law Firm

Luis Miguel Velarde

The training and development of a lawyer with proclivity to work in an international law firm (which is not the case with everyone) has several stages. For simplicity, it is possible to identify three general stages: (1) pursue a career in law, (2) position yourself in a good international law firm (which can take some time in view of the strong competition that exists today), and (3) develop as a lawyer (both academically and professionally).

The idea of "advancing in an international law firm" is part of item (3). Once hired by an international law firm, the lawyer will seek to settle into his or her position and be promoted over time. This process is not easy. It requires hard work and development of a series of soft skills that unfortunately are not taught at law school.

In this chapter, I will comment on three skills which are essential in my opinion for advancing professionally in an international law firm. Some of these skills are general and therefore necessary to ascend professionally in a local law firm. Others are specific or at least more commonly used in international law firms. The three skills I will discuss are: (1) to delegate work and give feedback, (2) to work as a team and maintain a good relationship, and (3) to develop the personal brand and sell the business.

§16.01 DELEGATE WORK AND GIVE FEEDBACK

Learning to delegate work is critical for advancing in your career in a law firm. This skill is particularly important for mid-level or senior associates, whose hourly rates are higher and who are required, as their careers progress, to work on more cases and more efficiently.

A lawyer who does not delegate work ultimately does all the work himself or herself. It is more expensive for the firm (the hourly rate of a mid-level or senior associate is higher than a junior associate who could do part of the job) and may end up being problematic. In large commercial or investment arbitrations, the client often requires that the law firm sets a fee cap, and if such fee cap is surpassed because the mid-level or senior associate spends too many hours working on the case, it tends to be problematic for the firm. In addition, an associate who bills too many hours in the same case could be perceived as inefficient and be criticized for it in the periodic firm evaluations and may even cause senior associates and partners to be reluctant to work with him or her. As the senior associates and partners are responsible for the case, they may prefer not having to justify why the number of billed hours exceeds the fee cap agreed with the client.

A mid-level or senior associate who delegates has more time to perform other activities that are expected of his or her standing at the firm, such as academic activities (e.g., writing and/or speaking at conferences) and business development (e.g., participating in business meetings and organizing training workshops on topics relevant to international arbitration). The mid-level or senior associate can also organize training on the more technical/economic issues that arise in arbitrations within the firm for the benefit of his or her colleagues.

Delegating work appropriately requires: (1) knowing to whom to delegate and (2) giving feedback well.

Knowing to whom to delegate a task requires reflection. One must take into account the complexity of the task in order to decide who can perform it. Some tasks may be delegated to interns or to junior associates, and other tasks simply *cannot* be delegated. Therefore, delegating work to someone requires previous analysis, and in turn it will provide clear and precise instructions on the expected work product.

Once the delegated task has been performed, the delegating lawyer should allow himself or herself time to give feedback. Feedback is necessary for a simple reason. Through feedback, the delegating lawyer makes sure to convey what was well done and what was not as well as to indicate the points of improvement for future assignments. It will improve the quality of future work and bring it closer to the expectations of the delegating lawyer. A lawyer who does not give feedback leaves the associate who did the task in the dark. The associate may think that he or she did the assignment well, and there is nothing on which to improve. In this case, the next time a task is assigned to that lawyer, it is highly likely that the same mistakes will be made, and it will not be the associate's fault.

Those professionals who do not give feedback undermine the very purpose of delegating a task. If someone does not perform a task properly and is not given feedback on how to improve, that person will make the same mistakes in the future. The work will have to be corrected (if not done again from scratch) by the delegating lawyer, increasing the latter's billing in the case and risking the latter being perceived as inefficient.

Giving feedback is also fair. Just as a mid-level or senior associate has been trained to become the lawyer and to reach the position where he or she is, he or she also has the duty to train the younger lawyers with whom he or she works so that they can advance professionally.

Beyond good intentions, those professionals who give feedback must always be aware of cultural differences. The same feedback can be received very differently between a European, Asian, or Latin American lawyer. It is difficult to generalize, but one must be careful and prudent in the way one gives feedback. The golden rule is to always start with the positive aspects and make the receiver understand why such feedback is important. Reasons include contributing to the lawyer's learning and professional development, allowing coworkers to align expectations, etc.

Although all these characteristics may seem evident, a problem for some international law firms in my experience is delegating lawyers often lack time to give feedback. If they do not like the work of an intern or junior associate, then they simply prefer working with someone else (who typically does not require much feedback). In my opinion, it is a malpractice that can be very frustrating for the intern or junior associate.

§16.02 WORK AS A TEAM AND MAINTAIN A GOOD RELATIONSHIP

A second skill that is fundamental in order to develop and advance one's career in an international law firm is teamwork. Teamwork is essential to do a good job and to be efficient.

The teams are inclusive of people, each with different personalities, interests, and tolerance levels. It is normal to get along better with those persons with whom we have more in common than those persons with whom we do not have much in common.

However, beyond these differences, one must learn to integrate into the "group" (at least, in the professional context). More or less equal, they are all ultimately part of the same team and their objectives point to the same direction.

As time passes and one gains maturity, one also learns the importance of having a good relationship with other team members. A good relationship does not mean becoming best friends. On the contrary, it means being respectful of the ideas of others, knowing how to conduct a conversation despite having different points of view, and knowing how to recognize the virtues of others and good work. It is essential to build both mutual respect and a good and healthy relationship.

A mid-level associate who does not have a good relationship with his or her peers or junior colleagues will have trouble working with them as a team. It could pose a challenge to advance in an international law firm.

In arbitration, these firms normally conduct large international commercial and/or investment cases which require continuous and fluid contact between the various members of the team working on the case. Continuous contact fosters the exchange of ideas, arguments, and relevant evidence and ensures adequate coordination between the various sections of the brief on which each team member is working. All of which results in a better final product.

A lawyer who does not have a good relationship with his or her team may feel deterred from consulting with a colleague or proposing an internal brainstorming meeting which may lead him or her to work in isolation. This isolation has a negative impact on his or her work and at the end of the day can lead him or her to have to work harder, thereby increasing his or her billing hours and creating the perception that he or she is inefficient (as well as unskilled in interpersonal relationships).

To be able to work in a team, it is therefore essential to have a good relationship with the members of the team.

This good relationship is also very important for the evaluations that the firm performs periodically (which mark the progress of the lawyer and are paramount for his or her promotion in an international law firm). Beyond the traditional downward review where the partner or senior associate evaluates the younger associates, many international law firms also have upward review processes where the junior associates evaluate the more senior associates. A bad relationship with the team will surely be reflected in the upward review with the resulting harm to the lawyer trying to be promoted in the firm.

§16.03 DEVELOP THE PERSONAL BRAND AND SELL THE BUSINESS

In addition to being capable and responsible, a lawyer must develop his or her personal brand and learn to sell the business to advance in an international law firm.

Sometimes, I have heard the phrase "*who is he or she?*" or "*nobody knows him or her.*" Beyond the inappropriateness (or not?) of these phrases, they draw attention to an important point. The lawyer must make a name for himself or herself in the marketplace.

There are several activities that should be natural for a lawyer and that contribute to the development of his or her personal brand. These activities include being a professor, publishing, giving lectures and/or trainings, etc. They are important for the development of the personal brand and should be of interest to the law firm because they give good publicity. In addition, they allow the mid-level or senior associate to have greater self-confidence and to speak more comfortably about topics that he or she might otherwise not have felt comfortable.

It is essential that a mid-level associate gives himself or herself the time to carry out these activities and that he or she also advertises them without exaggerating. The better your reputation in the marketplace is, the better your chances of being promoted in your firm.

In addition to developing your personal brand, a mid-level associate, or above all, a senior associate, must learn how to sell the business. This skill is certainly less natural for a lawyer than the previous ones although it is equally (or more) important. To sell the business, a lawyer must first learn to engage naturally with others and to have fluent conversations. Being congenial is a big plus, but not everyone has the same flair. In addition to knowing the business well, the lawyer must have a clear mind and be able to express a legal opinion in a clear, simple way (without entering into complex formulations that scare off the prospective client). A lawyer perceived as sympathetic, capable, and knowledgeable creates the trust sought by a client. A client will hire the lawyer with whom the client gets along well and trusts. Therefore, selling the business requires developing different skills.

The best way to learn how to sell the business is to learn from more experienced lawyers which is achieved by participating in business dinners, pitch meetings with prospective clients, and work meetings with clients and their teams. A less effective way to learn (in my opinion) is by participating in training on how to sell a business.

CHAPTER 17

A Law Firm's Rat Race

Manuel Casas

It is no secret that law firms are competitive places, and litigation departments are usually the most competitive places within them. Litigation is a contest, and litigators like to win. It is also not a secret that progression at a law firm is a zero-sum game. The number of opportunities is fixed, be it making partner or carrying out advocacy at a hearing. Therefore, granting an opportunity to one person implies denying it to another.

It seems like the perfect setup for a toxic workplace, and, sadly, sometimes it is. When these toxic workplaces form, relationships between associates tend to be pathologically negative. The overriding mentality is a fight to the death, where every dispute requires some knifing and where all opportunities to make someone look bad must be taken. These types of places are akin to a Hobbesian state of nature, where *advocatusadvocato lupus* is the rule.

My advice on how to deal with the rat race in this type of place is simple: flee! I mean it. When you are trapped in a hostile and toxic workplace, the best path is usually to find another job. The benefits in terms of professional satisfaction, not to mention physical and mental well-being, are substantial. Fleeing a toxic workplace is not cowardice. It is common sense.

These types of places usually cannot be fixed from the inside. Indeed, I dare to say that in a good deal of them, there is no desire for change. It may be either because the individuals who lead the practice are toxic themselves (and thus the hostile environment is a reflection of their personalities) or because they subscribe to the mistaken (and stupid) belief that recreating the *Hunger Games* brings out the best of people and wins more cases.

Nevertheless, I believe these places are not representative of the majority of law firms. This chapter will focus on what I consider to be the average law firm, a place that is only *moderately* dysfunctional. It is a place where people with strong personalities work under constant stress and where not everyone is a villain, but there are a few lurking. No one will wantonly harm you, but people may to improve their standing. You might not get a knife in the back, but you may get an elbow to the chin.

My best piece of advice for dealing with internal competition in such a place is also simple: read, memorize, and apply all the advice provided in *The Art of Worldly Wisdom*, by Balthasar Gracián. In my view, there is no better guide to deal with the complexities of modern legal practice (or, for what it is worth, any other professional setting) than this collection of aphorisms written by a Jesuit priest almost four hundred years ago.

To show the relevance of *The Art of Worldly Wisdom* today, I will apply two of its aphorisms to situations that may well arise in an international arbitration practice.

The first aphorism is the most important one:

> Wage War Honourably: you may be obliged to wage war, but not to use poisoned arrows. Everyone must act as he is, not as others would make him to be. Gallantry in the battle of life wins all men's praise: one should fight so as to conquer, not alone by force but by the way it is used ... An honourable man never uses forbidden weapons.[1]

Unless there is a radical change in the way we practice law, competition at a law firm cannot be avoided. It is just the nature of the legal profession. But the fact that there is competition does not mean that it should be no holds barred, or that one should leave aside all ethical considerations. It is exactly the opposite: success or failure, when product of a clean fight, is either more enjoyable or less painful.

There are two key reasons to play fair. One is ethical, the other pragmatic. The ethical reason does not require much explanation. It is just the right thing to do. Personal ethics or professional integrity at least should be a sufficient incentive to avoid being a scoundrel.

The second, pragmatic reason, does not require much explanation either. The practical benefits of playing fair are obvious. However, these benefits are particularly more important for practitioners of international arbitration.

In all professional settings, there is the possibility that today's rival will be in a position of power tomorrow, but this possibility is even higher in the world of international arbitration. For example, there is a high risk that our former rival could be deciding our case as an arbitrator. Of course, no serious arbitrator would allow a personal grudge to affect how he or she approaches and decides a dispute. Nevertheless, human beings are subject to cognitive biases, and prior experiences can negatively predispose someone.

On the other hand, the international arbitration community is small and, given its global character, is more intertwined than other practice areas. People know each other, and people talk. Therefore, the negative consequences of not playing fair are more severe. Foul play against a rival may not only turn the rival but also his close friends into an enemy.

Even minor instances of foul play can have negative consequences. Losing opportunities is easier than getting them. For instance, when composing the list of

1. Balthasar Gracián, *The Art of Worldly Wisdom* (J. Jacobs trans.) (1892), aphorism 165.

speakers for a panel, the shortlist for a tribunal, or potential counsel for a case, it usually suffices for someone to say "I'm not sure about this person" for said person to be discarded. Not playing fair exponentially increases the possibility of being the person for which people are not sure.

In other words, not playing fair to "win" a (probably irrelevant) competition is a typical short-term thinking error. It is better to take a long view, one that keeps in mind that today's purported rival is tomorrow's tribunal president, general counsel, or minister of justice. Or less cynically, it may just be someone that is irrelevant professionally but exceptional on a personal level. Risking alienating people by engaging in foul play is not worth it.

The second aphorism is more defensive:

> Watch him that acts on Second Thoughts. It is a device of business men to put the opponent off his guard before attacking him ... Prudence can discern the artifices which such a man uses, and notices the pretexts he puts forward to gain his ends. He aims at one thing to get another: then he turns round smartly and fires straight at his target. It is well to know what you grant him, and at times it is desirable to give him to understand that you understand.[2]

Not everyone will play fair. At some point, we will all likely have to deal with a competitor that is not sincere, whose true intentions differ radically from what they appear. A pinch of litigator's shrewdness is useful to detect this conduct and avoid any pitfalls.

Nonetheless, the problem with ulterior motives is precisely that they are hard to detect. Let us consider a hypothetical situation: someone above you says that you should be the one to inform the client about a recent development "because you where the person who worked the most on it." At first glance, it looks like something positive, a reward for your effort and an opportunity to have visibility with the client. Perhaps it was the actual reason, and the suggestion was made in good faith. In that case, great. But it is always worth wondering whether there is something else at hand. For instance, if the information is negative, and the client will likely be upset, perhaps the actual reason for this suggestion was because your superior wanted to avoid being the bearer of bad news and subsequently passed that burden onto you.

Or, consider the scenario where during a team meeting, someone proposes that you handle issue X in the case. Issue X, of course, is impossible to solve, not only because it is incomprehensible but also because there is no book nor case addressing it. Again, the suggestion could have been made in good faith, based on your talent and legal acumen, yet it is also possible that the person who suggested you handle issue X had understood that the issue was impossible or problematic and is thus trying to see you fail.

Dealing with underlying motives requires caution. There is a fine line between prudence and paranoia. Moreover, dealing with situations in which you suspect someone is acting with ulterior motives requires a good deal of tact. The best answer is perhaps oblique. It is usually easier to avoid the trap by stepping to the side than by

2. Balthasar Gracián, *The Art of Worldly Wisdom* (J. Jacobs trans.) (1892), aphorism 215.

accusing a coworker of creating a scenario of failure for us, as it implies accusing someone of dishonesty. It is not only a declaration of war, but it is usually a pointless one, particularly if the other person was skillful as the setup usually involves a half-truth rather than a complete lie.

In sum, competition and rivalry within law firms are impossible to avoid. It is outside anyone's control. However, what is under our control is the attitude that we assume that competition and whether that competition is healthy or toxic—of the type that motivates us to become better lawyers or better schemers.

The two abovementioned aphorisms should guide us down the first alternative. This mix of ethics and prudence is a good guide to overcome complicated scenarios. There is perhaps an easier option: finding good colleagues who are focused on collaborating rather than competing and are even more focused on beating opposing counsel than beating you. It has been my experience so far, and I am grateful for it.

CHAPTER 18

Bullying and Other Coexistence Challenges in Law Firms

Edson López

During my professional career, I have met partners and associates of different levels from many American, European, and Asian law firms, who have kindly shared with me their personal experiences from their organizations, which has allowed me to learn about their dynamics, organization models, compensation structures, career paths, and expansion strategies. After several conversations in different contexts, I can conclude without a doubt that, in one way or another, every lawyer faces essentially the same challenges, regardless of our nationality, place where we practice, or culture in which we have received our personal and professional education.

I have had the opportunity of learning from firms that are completely based on a corporative vision and from others that rather base their commercial strategy on academia. I perceive that every firm, either consciously or unconsciously, has its own vision regarding their business and has a unique internal dynamic, regardless of its size or areas of practice.

As Jaime Fernandez Madero puts it,[1] the main asset of professional services firms—which include lawyers and auditors—is human talent, which is comprised by people who work in "*a work dynamic resistant to the traditional models*" and whose work "*is based on the application of their knowledge in a creative way, not subject to controls or narrow rules.*"

It is precisely why putting together an efficient team with high technical skills and a great capacity for interaction has become more and more crucial in firms that operate in the era of information and communication technologies (ICTs).

It is not a secret that the most successful organizations have been able to identify the big challenges that they face and have implemented the necessary actions to turn

1. J Fernández Madero, *Organizando Firmas de Servicios Profesionales. El Caso de los Abogados*, p. 31.

those challenges into opportunities from the beginning. These organizations undoubtedly have a competitive advantage: vision.

As explained in the following paragraphs, it is not a secret that one of the biggest challenges faced by professional service firms is the clash between senior partners and associates and their younger generations, mainly regarding the different ways of envisioning the profession or getting things done, the use of technology, and from my perspective one of the most conflictive aspects, the largely criticized unwillingness of millennials—who today represent the vast majority of associates globally—[2] to wait for long periods of time in order to climb up their way to partnership.

In many forums by regional or global organizations of lawyers, I have witnessed heated discussions—often superficial and sometimes even desperate—about the challenges that law firms face when dealing with millennials. The common denominator of the vast majority of these forums is to assume that the millennial generation is a "problem" which I view as a big mistake. This stance clearly evidences an absolute lack of understanding and need to break paradigms and adapt to the current world. The current world is steadily becoming a more globalized, technological one that has a generation with particular characteristics and behaviors taken from their homes, schools and other such influences. Ironically, the ones who "created" the millennial generation are the ones who complain about them the most: parents and educators.

§18.01 HYPER-PARENTING AND BULLYING

As a general premise, the parents of the millennial generation focused their efforts on preventing their children from "suffering what they suffered in their time," in providing "better things than they had at their age," and "making their life easier." When these efforts reached an unsustainable level and awareness of what they, as parents, were doing got lost, a phenomenon that the expert Eva Millet later referred to as hyper-parenting[3] was born.

In sum, hyper-parenting translates into overprotection which results in excessive involvement of parents in the lives of their children, which in some cases reaches irrational levels. This new model of parenting resulted, in turn, in hyper-children[4] whose lives were handled in many ways—including the emotional side—by their parents, turning them into selfish and less respectful humans with less and less reverence toward authority figures. In addition, this whole phenomenon took place during the boom of ICTs, which provided hyper-children with fast and unlimited access to information and the necessary tools in order to openly question the authorities and their dogmas. To make it worse, it created a parallel universe that is still unknown to previous generations: the virtual world.

2. According to Deloitte's Millennial Survey 2014, millennials will represent 75% of the global workforce in 2025.
3. E Millet, *Hiperpaternidad. Del modelo mueble al modelo altar*, Barcelona, Plataforma Editorial, 2015, p. 5.
4. E Millet, *Hiperniños ¿Hijos perfectos o hipohijos?*, Barcelona, Plataforma Editorial, 2018, p. 28.

So, what happened when these hyper-children started coexisting in society? Many things. The creation of new technology-based markets radically changed the world—a millennial achievement that is often dismissed—and behaviors that were previously irrelevant became accentuated and strengthened, especially of bullying.

In accordance with the US Health and Human Services Department, bullying is "*unwanted, aggressive behavior among school aged children that involves a real or perceived power imbalance. The behavior is repeated, or has the potential to be repeated, over time. Both kids who are bullied and who bully others may have serious, lasting problems.*"[5]

Bullying is a scourge that consists of learned behaviors from the bully, who sees the behavior as normal and harmless, as much as from the bullied, who suffers without knowing how to handle the situation. Further, it is also true for witnesses, who assume a passive position of not reporting what they see. These behaviors are usually learned during school, a time in which these behaviors take root in children. They often persist into the different stages and aspects of life, including the professional aspect and the workspace of lawyers, even if we tend to think of ourselves as a "superior human race" in comparison to the rest of professionals. The correct term for these behaviors in the workplace is *mobbing*.[6] *Mobbing* is when the behavior generates among peers and *bossing* is when the behavior comes from bosses. This chapter will continue to use bullying in order to refer to these behaviors.

The phenomenon is present at different degrees in practically every educative center in the world, save for specific examples like Finland and Sweden, where very successful anti-bullying methods have been put into place. The same occurs in many companies around the world and even more in professional service firms, whose primary sources of production are the individuals who ought to work together while competing against themselves, sometimes in unfair manners.

Millennials are stressed with the idea of waiting for the same professional growth process as their predecessors did. Therefore, they are inclined to rely on certain behaviors, such as bullying, which were learned during their time in school as a reaction to the need to grow faster than their competing peers. These practices may also be triggered by their bosses, who fearing the possibility of being displaced often harass their potential successors in response to that fear. All in all, bullying results in chain effects that may affect everyone involved as well as the organization to which they all belong.

In other words, bullying is present in law firms, and it is possible to compare it with a cancer that, little by little and one by one, kills each organ of a working team and eventually affects the global functioning of the bigger organization.

---

5. Stopbullying.org. Available at: https://espanol.stopbullying.gov/qu%C3%A9-es-el acoso/346k/%C3%ADndice.html.

6. "*[M]eans bullying of an individual by a group, in any context, such as a family, peer group, school, workplace, neighborhood, community, or online. When it occurs as physical and emotional abuse in the workplace, such as 'ganging up' by co-workers, subordinates or superiors, to force someone out the workplace through rumor, innuendo, intimidation, humiliation, discrediting, and isolation, it is also referred to as malicious, nonsexual, non-racial/racial, general harassment.*" Available at: https://en.wikipedia.org/wiki/Mobbing.

§18.02 REALITY OR FICTION?

Currently, most states in the United States have some kind of confidential assistance program for lawyers, judges, and students who struggle against stress, anxiety, depression, substance abuse, and addictions on a daily basis as a consequence of their practice.

The American Bar Association's (ABA's) Commission on Lawyer Assistance Programs (CoLAP) was created specifically for the development of programs that provide that kind of assistance. It aims to improve the system by providing personal training, diffuses information, and creates platforms for communication among lawyers.

As a result of the Commission's 2016 and 2017 research on the impact of alcohol, abuse of substances, and mental diseases in lawyers and law students, it was determined that students were reluctant to ask for help and to recognize their problems. This reluctance seriously impacted their insertion into the market, just as a quality control test casts aside a defective product without even trying to improve or fix it in any way.

The Commission and the Hazelden Betty Ford Foundation conducted research as well, and the results were shared in the article *The Prevalence of Substance Use and Other Mental Health Concerns Among American Attorneys*. The study concluded that the levels of depression, anxiety, and stress in lawyers, especially among the younger ones, were significant with at least 28% of them suffering from depression, 19% from anxiety, and 23% from stress.

For us, as litigators and arbitrators, anxiety and stress are inherent to the job. The preparation of a hearing, filing of a submission, or cross-examination of a reluctant witness are naturally stressful situations, even more if we consider the fact that these tasks often have deadlines that may completely change the course of a case if missed.

This is confirmed by colleagues in the field who contribute with specific details:

> International arbitration can be very stressful. The stress can be increased as a result of working for difficult clients and difficult bosses. It is also easy to overload yourself, particularly if you are too focused or too ambitious. But if your health is affected you must change things[7] (Ben Giarreta).
>
> I was given responsibility and tasks that were more akin to mid-level associates in more established groups. For example, I got to do my first cross examination in international arbitration in my second month as a second-year associate. While I initially felt like I was drowning, I would not have wanted it any other way[8] (Nora Fredstie).

The *Iberian Lawyer* magazine conducted a survey in 2018 aimed at lawyers of big law firms in Spain and Portugal. The results identified that anxiety and stress are the most repeated symptoms, followed by depression and alcohol consumption. Eighty

7. https://www.linkedin.com/pulse/how-succeed-international-arbitration-associate-ben-giaretta.
8. http://www.youngicca-blog.com/tips-from-the-top-young-icca-interviews-nora-fredstie/.

percent of the participants considered that solutions to these problems must come from the profession itself.[9]

Year after year, more persons from different disciplines join these projects, creating institutions such as the Instituto de Salud Mental de la Abogacía, the Dave Nee Foundation (created after the suicide of Dave Nee, recently graduated and studying for his ABA exams), the Treatment Advocacy Center and many others. Thousands of psychologists, medical therapists, and other professionals are together with one objective: to improve the quality of life and the well-being of lawyers.

This objective takes us to an unavoidable question: Bullying in law firms? As if there were not enough adverse factors already.

The freedom, health, projects, family, aspirations, and lives of our clients often depend on our intellect, abilities, and willpower. Lawyers solve problems by analyzing legal precedents, successful experiences, and failures, and by turning them into prevention or correction measures for future or present situations. As we share the same challenges and problems and the same sense of aspiration to become a society capable of solving disputes—and therefore capable of focusing on creation and development—what is it that divides us? Why are we competing so hard?

As I showed in the previous paragraphs, the typical structure of a law firm follows a vertical hierarchy comprised of senior partners, junior partners, senior associates, junior associates, assistants, and paralegals. Junior associates from the millennial generation are typically the ones who either instigate or suffer from bullying.

The average age of junior and senior partners in law firms is between 35 and 60 years, respectively, setting them in the category of either Generation X or baby boomers. Baby boomers are characterized for dedicating their lives to work and lacking flexibility. Remember, this generation is the one who raised the divorce rate. Generation X—the children of the baby boomers—are characterized for their organization and administration skills, independence, and appreciation of responsibility. Most of Generation X rejected the baby boomers' lack of attention to family, and therefore they improved the quality and quantity of time spent with their children, the millennials.

In general, the average age of a junior associate is between 23 and 30 years old which means that law firm associates belong to the millennial generation, one characterized for their need of acknowledgement, collaborative work, global vision, instant gratification and constant search for meaning. This generation wants to use their work to make a difference and has an impulse to break traditional hierarchical structures. In the absence of any of these elements, they typically lack motivation.

As a consequence, law firms face a clash of generations in which millennials seek to shine, accomplish goals, and earn good money. They want to have untraditional experiences and leave a mark in their studies. Meanwhile, Generation X and the baby boomers fight to keep the traditional structure of a law firm with its rigid hierarchical structures and client orientation, especially since this structure has proven to be successful in preserving the financial health of their firms for years.

---

9. *Iberian Lawyer*. Available at: http://www.iberianlawyer.com/news/news-focus/7698-the-secret-terror.

§18.03 WHY IS THERE BULLYING? WHAT CAN BE DONE?

It would be irresponsible to state there is only one cause for bullying in law firms, or there is only one group of people responsible for it. In order to illustrate some bullying situations that may take place in law firms, let us look at the example of partners and senior associates that do not want to be outpaced by junior associates. Since these professionals do not want to outpaced, junior associates find their self-esteem attacked with verbal, psychological and, in some of the worst cases, physical abuse. This bullying takes form as giving them tasks for which they are not prepared or irrationally flooding them with work beyond the nights or weeks without sleep that are already included in the job description. It is a clear application of the etymological concept of bullying bull, not necessarily for its physical strength, but for the power granted by authority. This scenario is even more stressed with the clash of millennials, a generation generally more prepared and greatly educated in academia. In contrast, Generation X and baby boomers are better prepared for the practical application of knowledge.[10]

In addition to the personal or generational characteristics, there are many factors inherent to the international arbitration industry, like the excessive workload, the urgent deadlines, the need to verify a case in detail, the narrow margin of tolerance for errors, and the constant and repetitive presence of some subjects. These factors create situations that are difficult to handle at an emotional and professional level, resulting in stress, anger, and hostility toward coworkers.

Bullying in law firms is a problem that is influenced by both internal and external factors, and therefore it is a problem that screams for an integral solution.

Our names and reputation usually make our clients look for us in order to settle their disputes. Hence, the first step toward eradicating bullying is to accept that while we are able to solve other persons' problems, we might actually need someone else to help solve ours.

The second step is to acknowledge that there is a problem and to identify whether the problem originates from the person suffering from bullying or the one instigating it. The assistance programs for lawyers around the world are confidential, and confidentiality is essential for lawyers and law students to be able to accept the existence of a problem (be it as a victim or as an instigator). We must face the fact that we are not as perfect as we seek perfection in our cases for our clients. We must sometimes be bothered or bother someone else as a consequence of situations which remove us from our comfort zones. Of course, it is difficult to accept as they typically cause feelings of shame and guilt in front of those persons who see us as great bosses, parents, or lifelong friends.

The third step is to establish official communication channels available to lawyers in case they have a problem. It is a difficult task as the receiving end of the communication channel might be the very people who are the bullies or are friends with the bullies.

10. MP McQueen, *The American Lawyer. Here Come the Big Law Millennials*, 2016.

Bullying is a reality, and it is not sufficient to only report the situation to the human resources manager or other responsible person at the firm. Moreover, it is necessary to create an environment of trust among all the members of the firm, especially among bosses and their subordinates. In addition, diverse alternatives of communication and solutions to the problem must be established in order for the problem to be minimized.

On August 2017, the US National Task Force on Lawyer Well-Being conducted a report named *The Path to Lawyer Well-Being: Practical Recommendations for Positive Change*. It recommended practical tools to manage issues related to the well-being of lawyers. In accordance with the report, well-being includes the emotional, occupational, intellectual, social, physical, and spiritual dimensions of the human being.

This definition reaffirms the relevance of approaching bullying from the internal side of the human being and the importance of seeking improvement for the quality of life in general for lawyers. Not taking the necessary steps to prevent bullying will eventually result in the detriment not only of the workplace but also of the clients.

The concept of collaborative learning—which emerged during the twentieth century—consists of the acquisition of skills and attitudes that occur as a result of group interaction and cooperation. In order to achieve collaborative learning, it is required for the group to achieve symmetry of knowledge, to establish a common goal, and to set an appropriate division of labor. Bullying may often come as a symptom of a defect in one of these factors. Thus, the improvement of collaborative learning—embraced by millennials—is key to preventing and correcting bullying.

The technological revolution, online education, and prevalence of social interest above particular other interests have broken the paradigms of learning. If we can act collectively to gather "likes," increase the views of a video, or create a trending topic, why are we waiting to put our common efforts together? Why are we not highlighting our strengths instead of our weaknesses?

Law firm bullying exists, and it severely and adversely affects lawyers and their productivity, emotional health, money, and reputation. There is an advantage for those professionals who are aware of this reality. There is importance of great coexistence among case management teams in the diverse areas in which we work and of proper management by those persons in charge of arbitration teams. Arbitration teams need to work like a Swiss watch in order to properly deliver results, regardless of their size. This advantage translates into a significantly bigger chance of success and positive learning in the managed cases. If not aware of bullying, in contrast, these lawyers usually bear the weight of a hidden cost, the size of which remains unknown until it is too late.

CHAPTER 19

Balancing Work and Life: Arbitration, Ego, and Golf

René Irra

You cut and shape your hair, but most of the times you forget to cut and shape the Ego.

*Albert Einstein**

Balancing work and personal life is one of the greatest dilemmas of our society, particularly in the field of international arbitration. Some of the reasons that led us to dedicate almost a lifetime to this activity include the numerous study hours to understand, prepare, and present a case, the high demands that an increasingly competitive market imposes on us and, at some point, the need to attend hearings, conferences, and activities of business development in other cities and countries.

Even though we cannot properly establish a balance (which would mean resting an hour for each hour of work), the question to pose is how to prevent our work from affecting other areas of our life (which are actually the most important) or at least how to find mechanisms to mitigate said impact.

Excess work may give the false illusion that with that high level of commitment, we are more productive and therefore more successful and appreciated in our professional environment. We strive for this level in our pursuit for a successful life, presumably with great satisfiers of material nature and consequently with the achievement of happiness. However, the opposite actually happens.

Such regime in the long-term is not sustainable. The only thing we get with excess work is to be increasingly unproductive and to run the risk of failing seriously in our activity, to say the least. Clearly, the most important effects are the damage that we generate to ourselves in terms of health and our emotional state.

* https://exploringyourmind.com/ego-wont-go-away-send-go-buy-humility/.

In a more thoughtful analysis, we realize that *excess work is not the real problem, but the symptom of a deeper problem. The deeper problem is the true origin of said behavior*. The nerve point revolves around *the intention of why we do things, which is the real problem.*

To find the true intention of our behavior and the driving force that motivates us to decide whether to incur any kind of excess, it is necessary to do a thorough exercise of personal honesty and to determine the true "why" of my "abuse of work."

Although there is surely more than one answer to this question, I will only focus on two that seem the most relevant in this brief reflection.

In a first consideration, we can understand the work is not an end in itself but is a means to achieve higher objectives within our personal scale of priorities. Hence, work may be perceived as what allows us to guarantee material satisfactions for personal and/or family benefit and what lets us have the means to do what is essential to us in life. By means of this conception, work only serves to achieve something superior and nothing more. If we deem our work only as a vehicle, it may be less complicated to set the necessary limits for ourselves. These limits help to set what is priority and not negotiable for us in our lives, whether it is time for our family or oneself, fun, rest, hobbies, or any other activity that represents well-being to us.

Notwithstanding this reflection could work as the answer to the question searching for our intentions and reasons as to why we work. For some of us, it is necessary to make a greater exercise in honesty. A second deeper reflection leads us to discover the underlying intention of why we work and carries a very important burden of satisfaction of our own uncontrolled ego. In general, this uncontrolled ego is the mechanism that we often use to compensate for our emotional deficiencies, such as low self-esteem, for the continual need of acceptance and recognition, and for the constant reinforcement of our own value against the world around us.

At this point, we realize that the *true intention of our actions is to obtain self-gratification, applause, and public recognition*, which may be translated into being the one who works the most, has the most recognition, shines in all rankings, or is the star of the team/practice/office/country/world/universe.

Said considerations guide us to a constant leading attitude or conducts that seek perfectionism. An example of how perverse the uncontrolled ego can be is portrayed in each memorial or hearing that we prepare with excessive perfectionism. It is different to put our greatest effort so that our submission is sufficiently strong to successfully defend the interests of our client as expected of a professional versus pretending that our submission is perfect and hoping that everyone who reads it thinks how extraordinarily bright we are.

These excessive manners will inevitably lead us to disregard what is really important in life. My belief in this analysis is that it is essential to understand that external stimuli (power, economic position, recognition, and professional success) can never compensate for internal needs (happiness, spiritual peace, and fulfilling life). If we intend to satisfy our internal needs through the above external stimuli, then our needs will never be truly satisfied. The search for satisfaction will be limitless and therefore infinite. Here we will find ourselves working without stopping our entire life to settle the true intention that underlies our behavior and wasting our lives to achieve a success that will be proved to be an illusion.

One of the reflections that has given me most clarity on this subject is about the search for false gold:

> Pride is the primary source of difficulties for human beings and the main obstacle to all progress. Pride induces us to impose on ourselves, or others, demands that cannot be met without violating or abusing our instincts. When the satisfaction of our security and society's instincts become the primary objective of our lives, pride appears to justify our excesses.[1]

There are many lessons that I have learned after these reflections and, above all, after several very important disasters. My summary of these lessons is as follows:

- Professional success can never remedy the emotional lack of self-esteem and self-love.
- Everything in life is temporary, including life itself. The professional position we have will end one day, and at one point we will stop being. Because everything is temporary, it is dangerous to devote our entire energies to our personal value in our professional position.
- Nothing is so important that it is worth the cost of our own life.
- Having the uncontrolled ego as our main intention will never lead us to a positive result.
- Understanding these lessons will give us more tools to set our own limits. No one places our limits for us.

With these reflections, it is not my intention to encourage the disregard of our professional obligation by leaving the office for a round of golf course and living the *dolce vita*. My only proposition is to discover the true intention with which we perform our work which then allows us to define a correct scale of priorities. Second, once we have greater clarity, it is important to firmly establish the limits that are convenient for us. Thus, we can aspire to live a useful and happy life.

And as not to slight golf, which gets along very well with arbitration, I conclude with a phrase attributed to Ben Hogan's disciple, the professional golfer Gardner Dickinson: *"They say golf is like life, but do not believe them, golf is much more complicated than that."*

1. Grapevine, W. Bill, June 1961.

CHAPTER 20

Empathic Leadership for Associates in "Big Law"

Daniela Páez-Salgado

Empathy is the ability to understand other people's emotions and feelings as if they were our own. It is the ability to put yourself "in someone else's shoes." Empathy allows us to understand the frustrations and reactions of others and—taking it one step further—it also allows us to help others with their personal and professional development. Empathy, combined with a desire to motivate the growth of one's teammates, constitutes the "empathic leadership" qualities that this chapter discusses.

Being "empathetic" or having the ability to understand others in any degree is usually not one of the characteristics that candidates advertise in a job interview. It is even possible that they have not spent more than five minutes thinking about the importance of empathy while completing their law school studies. In fact, it would seem that empathy is not part of the relevant skills sought in candidates when starting to work in "big law." Concerns are usually focused on the quality and sophistication of the work, billable hours, and commitment to the cases as the core considerations.

For example, my international arbitration practice began with a team that had just been formed in the New York office of Herbert Smith Freehills. I worked with two senior associates, and because of the size of my group, I was not formally assigned a "mentor." As a result, I found myself a bit nervous to ask the natural questions that arise in every new associate's day-to-day tasks because I did not want to appear impertinent or to interrupt the work of my teammates.

This experience, although enriching, made me develop a lot of empathy for my colleagues who joined our growing team after me. Our team is now comprised of more than fifteen associates. I now realize how priceless it is to know that you can count on someone who is willing to stop their own work to answer questions—no matter how basic they may be—in an environment of openness and trust. In the legal profession, we all start from similar beginnings. We all learn to prepare memoranda, deal with demanding clients, and communicate to the team when a mistake is made.

The practice of international arbitration is increasingly sophisticated and requires the participation of groups of people who feel comfortable to raise their voices and know that they will be heard. As I have progressed in my career, I have come to understand that my ability to understand other people's emotions and reactions is a natural result of having previously experienced situations that my more junior colleagues are facing now. My past experiences have allowed me to feel empathy because I have previously "been in their shoes" and can genuinely understand what they are experiencing.

As to the leadership component, it is not enough to have had good grades, multiple master's degrees or a doctorate, or many years of local or international experience to be noticed in the world of "big law." It is also important that skills are developed from the beginning and throughout one's professional career. Therefore, this chapter goes beyond any intellectual qualification and focuses on certain skills that are developed in the practice. For example, the idea of "acting like a leader" should not be reserved only for partners. Leadership qualities should be put into practice from the beginning of one's professional career as an associate and should grow as one grows professionally.

After four years of working for Herbert Smith Freehills, I share with you my views on the qualities and responsibilities of an "empathic leader" within an international arbitration team.

§20.01 OPEN COMMUNICATION

One of the most common mistakes I have seen in my years of practice is that associates do not have the confidence to say there is a problem. It is usually because either they think they will have to take personal responsibility for the mistake or they do not want to add an additional problem to the case. They fear being a nuisance, knowing the whole team is busy.

My recommendation is that it is always better to talk through the problem and look for ways to address it rather than putting it to the side or waiting for it to resolve on its own. Even if part of the problem is the result of a mistake made by the associate, it is essential that it be raised so it can be addressed.

On the other hand, to assume "the partner is the one who must realize that there is a problem" is fatal. Our reality is one where partners are very busy. They are managing their teams, dealing with current clients, and bringing in new clients as well as living their own personal lives. Therefore, if there is a problem or situation that deserves the attention of the partner, the associate must inform the rest of the team and not wait for it to "just happen" in its own time. Failure to bring attention to problems could lead to situations of extended discomfort over time (and sometimes render the problem irremediable) when it could have instead been resolved with a simple conversation with the team. Associates must not assume that the partner "notices everything," because it is often not the case.

For example, suppose an associate is in charge of conducting the review of documents for the preparation of a risk assessment memorandum for a new case. If the associate realizes that the task is taking more time than expected and will not be able to meet the deadline, he or she has the obligation to immediately inform the rest of the team. While the associate's first inclination might be to stay quiet and to worry that others think that he or she is inefficient, the reality is a problem has been identified. Once identified, it is essential that the associate has enough confidence to alert the team. In some instances, the amount of work is disproportionate to the allocated time, and it does not necessarily mean that an associate has not fulfilled his or her duties. Perhaps, simply, a reassessment of deadlines is needed. It is important that there is enough confidence on the part of the associate to raise the point in time to allow for a solution.

On the other hand, it is understandable that an associate who has just started working is afraid to ask questions because he or she does not want to appear to lack knowledge or skills. In those cases, it is always advisable for the junior associate to ask questions to the more senior associates who supervise him or her if there are any doubts of the expectations, or if there is a need to reanalyze the assigned tasks. At the end of the day, this practice can surely save all of the associates working on a case many hours spent correcting mistakes, which could have been solved with an *ex ante* conversation.

Finally, another strategy for working on a team is to talk with the other associates about a problem before going to the partner. Thus, you can think of a common solution that can be offered to the partner and reach an efficient solution to the problem together. It is all possible when an open communication channel is encouraged within the team.

§20.02 FEEDBACK

Feedback is a factor related to open communication that must also exist in the workplace. The responsibility usually falls on the partner and associates who supervise the work of others. Feedback is very important to train new associates and to ensure that job expectations are known, understood, and eventually reached. There is usually an annual evaluation of the performance of an associate that is done by collecting feedback from team members and partners. However, this annual exercise may not be sufficient for everyone. The passage of time could lead to certain situations being forgotten, or it could create a situation where the associate has lost the opportunity to start improving his or her performance earlier in the year.

For example, at Herbert Smith Freehills, we have feedback sessions every time we finish a filing, academic project, or hearing. In these meetings, we evaluate with total honesty what was done well and what can be improved. In addition, we ensure that all team members know how their performance is being perceived and that they all understand what needs to be improved and what they are doing well.

Timing: When things do not go as expected, it is advisable to not provide feedback immediately. In those moments of increased stress or pressure, feedback can actually be counterproductive. Waiting for the "waters to calm" can help the feedback to be objective and processed in a better way. Thus, waiting (e.g., one or two weeks) helps both parties to convey their opinions more concretely and objectively. It also helps to improve the perception of the person who is giving the feedback, so they can focus on being calm and objective instead of influenced by the emotions of a situation that just occurred.

§20.03 PROFILE RAISING: NOT EVERYTHING IS BILLABLE HOURS!

One of the most important goals of every associate is to achieve, or exceed, the minimum billable hours required by the firm. Sometimes the concern to show that we are "profitable" means that the activities of "business development" and "profile raising," which are fundamental for an associate's professional development in international arbitration, are put to the side. However, participating in these types of activities improves team spirit and motivates the rest of the team to get involved with other people or organizations that are also interested in international arbitration.

How to do it?

The world of international arbitration is full of events and conferences for young practitioners who are taught by highly respected lawyers and arbitrators. Sometimes these events are attended by potential clients, and informative conversations about the firm, the practice, and the team can be initiated. In no way is business development reserved exclusively for partners. For example, it is always a good idea to assist with the organization of an event in which a colleague is participating or to get involved with events the firm is sponsoring—as these activities ultimately benefit the whole team.

Second, propose and write publications. Joint publications have the advantage to cultivate interpersonal relationships because they are projects in which, as authors, people become more personally involved. For example, if you have worked on a case that required extensive research that is worth sharing, team members can prepare a public document which allows direct interaction with colleagues in a separate environment from the "billable work" one in addition to helping your profile raising.

For the partners and business development teams in a firm, it should always be a priority that their associates be active in raising their profile in the legal market and training them on their responsibility as a "business developer." It does not have to be boring! The truth is associates are not work machines that are always researching in an office and typing on a computer all the time. An important part of professional development is learning how to develop one's profile, regardless of whether you are a fifth-year or first-year associate. Working on these types of activities with fellow team members can change the perspective and role that associates have in a firm and even motivate them to continue their professional development in the future.

§20.04 AVAILABILITY AND ACCESSIBILITY

Presenting yourself as a person who is open to listening and sharing an interest with your colleagues is important to keeping a team motivated. Sometimes, levels of work and stress can make us forget that we work with other *people* and that a practice grows, thanks to the efforts of each team member. My recommendation is to avoid being the person that people are afraid to approach or to ask a question. Be open and try to inspire confidence in the rest.

In addition to availability which is always dependent on work and personal commitments, being accessible to the people in your team is also important. In other words, knowing how their day is going, how they feel or what cases in which they are working are small things that contribute to a good work environment. In this sense, participating in the events and programs organized by one's firm (from a lunch or talk or external event) not only helps people to get to know you but it is also an opportunity for you to get to know others. It shows that you care about what happens in the organization, and you are interested in what your colleagues do. Additionally, these events which in general are more "relaxed" allow for opportunities to expand your day-to-day relationships that are usually otherwise limited to work-related subjects.

§20.05 CONTROL, ORGANIZATION, AND DISCIPLINE

Leadership entails responsibility over a team and implies control, organization, and discipline. It has been one of the most important missions I have personally undertaken at Herbert Smith Freehills. It is crucial for the associate leading a case to know exactly what is the status of each assigned workstream and its coordination with the responsible person throughout the development of the entire arbitration. We usually use a "case management tracker" where we identify the tasks and responsibilities of each person as well as the status of each task, allowing us to keep the partner informed of the overall progress of a case.

For example:

Task	*Responsible*	*Status*	*Deadline*

It is a great way for identifying which tasks are in progress and monitoring each phase of the case. It also helps keep the whole team informed. The frequency of preparing and sending the case management tracker certainly depends on the particular case, but in general terms, once a week is ideal.

The organization of work is not a skill that is necessarily learned at university but is instead developed and adapted through practice. It is particularly important in complex arbitrations where there are usually several partners involved, various witnesses and experts, multiple parties and claims, voluminous documentation, and/or parallel proceedings. The coordination of all those factors can become difficult, so it is vital to maintain a detailed organization of all workstreams.

This method is also useful for the associate in charge of coordinating matters with local counsel or experts appointed for the arbitration. In both instances, it is vital to have a clear record of the communications and requests for information and documentation that have been circulated between the parties. For example, in the preparation of an expert report, there are always many documents that the expert requires from the client, and it is usually the partner's responsibility to ensure that there is a record of all such documentation. In the same way, it is always good to propose deadlines with local counsel and to clarify the expectations of the desired work product.

Finally, no one should feel ashamed or nervous when following up on the tasks of each team member, experts, and/or local counsel. Sometimes it might seem "too intense" or "repetitive," but it is vital for the proper handling of the case. The truth is, a client will expect to be able to contact any of the team members and to receive an answer about the pending tasks, their status, and deadlines. Certainly, it is the expectations of a client that engage an international firm for its representation in an arbitration. For example, if the partner in charge is traveling or in a hearing, and the client wants to know the status of the financial proposal that the damages expert had to submit for the client's consideration, the associate can go to the tracker and provide the client with a quick and accurate response.

Something that definitely generates empathy and "good vibes" in a team is being in a good mood. Having fun on the cases you are working, enjoying a good relationship with the client or experts, and sharing activities with your team outside the office contributes to enjoying the legal profession and lightens the long hours that international arbitration associates often face.

CHAPTER 21

Starting a Career in Arbitration: The Case of an In-House Lawyer at a State Enterprise

Briana Canorio

Since I am writing about my personal experience, I am going to share as if I were writing in my diary or journal. It is there where I began to write some of my personal and professional achievements with the support of my family, especially with my mother's guidance and intercession from heaven, as well as with the good advice of some people that life has put in my way, mainly teachers and lawyers from my university and professional stages.

I was about to finish high school. One of the things I longed to do was study at a university that would give me a solid academic background to become a good professional as well as complement and strengthen the formation of the principles and ethical values that I learned from my parents.

And fortunately my wish came true! At the University of Lima, they not only gave me the knowledge to develop in the professional field but also gave me the opportunity to meet excellent professionals who performed their positions and functions with a high degree of responsibility, commitment, principles, and ethical values. To the professionals that I met throughout my university career and accompany me still today with their advice and support, I can only thank them.[1]

I have learned that gratitude is a feeling of the highest value, and we should be especially grateful to those persons who selflessly share their knowledge and experiences with us to be better people and professionals.

To tell you about my beginnings in arbitration, I am going back in time and placing you in my penultimate year of law school.

1. Among them, my special thanks to Elvira Martínez Coco and Roxana Jiménez Vargas-Machuca.

In one of the many conversations I had that year with the Academic Director César Augusto Mansilla Novella,[2] he challenged me to always think about giving a quota of knowledge for the service of my country. Dr. Mansilla was a wonderful person well known for his intellectual qualities and enormous generosity. He thought that the most outstanding professionals of the universities should work for their country, acting in public positions, being political leaders, and working for the benefit of society with professionalism, responsibility, prudence, respect, and generosity.

While it was no easy task, I had to decide whether to continue doing my internship at Muñiz Law Firm where I had the possibility of a career or to do the Civil Service of Graduates (SECIGRA). SECIGRA is a program administered by the Ministry of Justice of Peru and created so law students can legally practice in an entity or institution of the State for one year.

At the end of that academic year, I visited Dr. Mansilla to tell him my thoughts about doing SECIGRA and to discuss making that difficult decision. From this conversation, I learned that sometimes it is necessary to renounce some securities to continue advancing because there is always more to learn everywhere. If one has the possibility of contributing with knowledge in this new place, our permanence would be all the more significant. It was one of the first decisions that would later set the tone for my professional career.

I decided to apply to Petróleos del Perú (PETROPERÚ S.A., a hydrocarbon company owned by the Peruvian State). In the last year of my law degree, I did my preprofessional internship with this company, which was an experience I can summarize in two words: enriching and gratifying.

It was enriching because I had the opportunity to learn about the hydrocarbon sector (oil and gas) and to discover the norms of public contracting and other quite specialized subjects that are taught in postgraduate courses. It was also gratifying because I was able to contribute my acquired knowledge from the University and preprofessional practice in the cases assigned to me. In this way, I risked and renounced my eventual assurances in order to continue advancing on the path of learning.

In PETROPERÚ S.A., I helped with the arbitration cases that were in the Arbitration Center of the Lima Chamber of Commerce and the Arbitration Direction of the Government's Contracting Supervisory Agency (OSCE).

Once again, a dream was becoming true! When I took the subject "Dispute Settlement" at the University, a concern and desire rooted inside me to know more about the functioning of arbitration jurisdiction that my professor spoke so much. It

2. In my opinion, Dr. César Augusto Mansilla Novella was a brilliant professor at the Faculty of Law of the University of Lima, an excellent professional, magistrate and jurist of the country. For those who were not fortunate to meet him, I invite you to search for him on the Internet and read the articles he wrote on various subjects of procedural law and others; likewise, you will find beautiful portraits that many prominent Peruvian lawyers wrote about him, and several of them conclude that he was an outstanding judge, noble jurist and wonderful person. Now that I remember him, Dr. Mansilla was one of the first arbitrators I met in my university career because after having dedicated himself to the judicial career, he developed an arbitral and academic career.

was a jurisdiction characterized by administering justice quickly and efficiently and in resolving very specialized issues. Not even two years had passed since I took this subject, and I was already putting my knowledge into practice and participating in arbitration jurisdiction.

While I was finishing the year of civil service in PETROPERÚ., I received a proposal to continue working for that company. Thus, I began my professional career in the business world.

During the first three years working as a lawyer in PETROPERÚ S.A., I provided legal advice on a corporate level. Another lawyer and I were in charge of defending the arbitration processes that the company had, and these years were intense work. On the one hand, I loved advising and resolving the legal issues of the different operations of the company, and I dedicated a good number of working hours a day to it. On the other hand, I had to take the company's arbitral cases. My invested personal time was rewarded at the end of the process when I received the first arbitration awards that embraced our positions and claims. It was the result of joint work by the technical areas of the company. I cannot deny that there were also cases where despite all the effort we put, the main purpose of the defense was to prevent the other party from obtaining more than it really deserved.

The first successful arbitral case always remains in each one's memory. Mine was a case in public procurement arbitration. We remember everything we did and everything that happened in the case was not in vain. This first case is the one that motivates us each time we assume a new arbitration process. With each added case, we obtain more experience.

Those years were also years of learning about various technical issues in the hydrocarbon sector. I learned about the uses and customs of the international hydrocarbons market in which the company's technicians spoke so much. I began to speak their language and to understand them, and therefore I was able to build a good defense in arbitration cases.

Before starting the fourth year at PETROPERÚ S.A., I received an offer to work in the Head of the Office of Conciliation and Administrative Arbitration of the Superior Council for State Contracting and Acquisitions, an institution that later became known as the Directorate of Administrative Arbitration of the OSCE. I accepted because I wanted more knowledge and professional training on arbitration in public procurement. With this opportunity, the context became clearer. My primary purpose was to understand how an "arbitral institution" worked, especially one that administered about 500 arbitration files at that time. It was a rewarding experience because of everything I learned from public administration.

During that period I was in charge of the Administrative Arbitration Directorate of the OSCE. I was able to learn more about the work of arbitrators, and I personally verified that idea that "arbitration is worth what the arbitrator is worth." I was indeed able to observe the responsible and dedicated work of some very outstanding arbitrators and learn a great deal from them. After a year and a half of trying to make some changes to improve the public procurement arbitration system, I saw that some changes could not be made due to the limitations of the public sector. Before this limitation frustrated me, I decided to resign.

At the end of 2009, I was appointed as arbitral secretary by two very outstanding arbitrators (Fernando Cantuarias and Elvira Martínez Coco), whom I thank for the trust and opportunity they gave me for working and learning from them. It had only been a few months since I began as an arbitral secretary when I received a new proposal from PETROPERÚ S.A. to support and integrate the team of specialists that would evaluate one of the most important projects of the company and the country. Once again, the decision I had to make was not easy. The prevailing factor for my decision was knowing that this project of PETROPERÚ S.A. was a once in a lifetime opportunity, and I wanted to be part of it.

Almost nine years have passed since I returned to PETROPERÚ S.A. In this period of time, I have continued advancing and learning by advising on corporate issues that are transcendental for the company and the country. In addition, in some cases I have had the opportunity to work together with law firms that are very well known internationally. Several of the corporate issues in which I have worked in recent years were closely linked to the project for which I decided to return to PETROPERÚ S.A. Some achievements were very satisfactory, including the issuance of bonds in the international financial market. This bond issuance was granted the Project & Infrastructure Finance Awards 2018 in the Best Oil & Gas Financing Category by *LatinFinance* magazine. Also, the operation of an USD 300 million syndicated loan with CESCE guarantee recently received the Latin American Downstream Oil & Gas Transaction of the Year Award from *IJGlobal Project Finance & Infrastructure* Journal.

This period has been very interesting and enriching for my arbitration experience because we had our first cases administered under the Rules of Arbitration of the ICC. In these cases, I appreciated the responsible and prudent conduct of the Court and its Secretariat. In complex and specialized arbitration cases, we relied on international law firms to work as a single team with our technicians, combining synergies and providing the knowledge and case experience.

Everything that I could observe, learn, and obtain from my experience as an in-house lawyer working together with the hired law firms for the defense of certain cases I was able to share in the 2016 panel "Experience in International Arbitration Between External Lawyers and Internal Lawyers" at the XIV Annual Conference of the ICC, an event held annually in Miami that brings together all Latin American lawyers dedicated to international arbitration. I was also invited by the Court of Arbitration of the ICC to speak about my experience in "Arbitration in State Enterprises" for the Meeting of the Latin American Group of the National Committees of the ICC in 2017.

Another dream came true! I have always felt that any knowledge that can help others should be shared. Likewise, it is rewarding to share the knowledge gained with students in the classroom setting, since it is an opportunity to encourage new generations to follow new paths, to innovate, and to achieve their own goals. I had the opportunity to be a part-time teacher of the subjects of Legal Act and Contracts at the University that formed me. Subsequently, I taught the subjects of dispute resolution mechanisms conciliation and arbitration in public procurement, thanks to the experience I had acquired in the OSCE. Currently, as an arbitrator for the Lima Chamber of Commerce and the Center for Analysis and Resolution of Conflicts at

Pontificia Universidad Católica del Perú, I participate as a speaker in national and international arbitration events.

And like everything else in life, if you dedicate effort and perseverance to something in which you are passionate, the results you obtain are wonderful and extremely rewarding. Those small moments of satisfaction that occurred at the beginning of my arbitration career motivated me to apply to be a representative of the Young Arbitrators Forum of the International Chamber of Commerce (ICC YAF). During the 2017-2019 period as ICC YAF representative for Latin America, I can say that I met great and talented young lawyers who continue to advance in their arbitration career like me.

Finally, I would like to conclude by saying that perseverance is the perfect ally to achieve our goals. Let us maintain our eternal curiosity and concern to always learn something new, either by updating ourselves or by consulting the arbitrators who have more experience and whom we admire. When we have the opportunity, we are prepared and able to develop our arbitration practice in which we are so passionate.

CHAPTER 22

On Being Irreplaceable: Alternative Paths in the Arbitration Market

*José María de la Jara**

§22.01 LEGAL VIRUS VERSUS DIABOLICAL MACHINES

In 1945, two farmers pled their case before the United States Supreme Court. They were devastated about the massification of a new technology now known as the plane. When this diabolical device first crossed their sky, their chickens tried to follow it and ended up crashing into the farm walls.

To support their claim, the cunning farmers relied on an unquestionable property right at the time. "*From the time of Lord Blackstone*," they argued, "*property rights extend down to the center of the earth, and up, as far as the eye can see.*"[1] Based on this definition, they concluded that airplanes had to request permission to fly over their farm, or they would be invading their property. This example is used by Larry Lessig to explain how the law can be used to stifle creativity, and arbitration departments are not safe from this characterization either.

First, arbitration teams often use the billable time system. This system prevents young associates from having the necessary time to learn other "languages" such as legal design, project management, economics, or psychology. It perpetuates the cycle of ignorance and discourages innovation. An associate who must spend thirty hours reviewing thousands of documents in a discovery prefers to exchange his or her time for billable hours. The associate has no stimulus to stop to think about a tool that could automate the process and reduce inefficiencies.

* The opinions expressed herein are those of the author and do not necessarily reflect those opinions of other attorneys on their firm or their clients.

1. L. Lessig. "Free culture." Available at: https://www.researchgate.net/publication/28802969_Free_Culture/link/00b7d5187a44bd9f38000000/download.

Second, the vast majority of arbitration departments follow the structure of the Cravath model. Partners make the decisions, and the remuneration of the associates does not depend on how efficient their productivity is (lockstep). Again, it stifles innovation. An older partner does not find it attractive or necessary to invest time and energy into rethinking the business model. The easiest option is to continue providing the services in the same way as the model endures. It is business as usual.

Also, the dispute resolution culture suffocates collaboration and creativity to innovate. The associate quickly sees how this virus attacks his or her ability to communicate, increasing the use of phrases loaded with adverbs ("it has been clearly tested") and complex linguistic constructions to protect himself ("my understanding is that"). It is more difficult to innovate without clear communication. The virus then affects the ear. The associate believes it is acceptable that he or she interrupts the client, that he or she finishes another's sentence, and that he or she can jump to conclusions. Cognitive flexibility is also compromised. The associate quickly realizes that focusing on problems instead of solutions is rewarded. It pays to assume the worst without giving the benefit of the doubt. Again, it undermines collaboration. Finally, the lawyer's immune system is compromised, leading the virus carrier to always act defensively, to reject criticism, and to not recover from disappointment (low resilience).

These symptoms explain why law in general and arbitration departments in particular are reluctant to innovation.

§22.02 THE WORLD HAS ALREADY CHANGED, BUT LAWYERS DO NOT WANT TO REALIZE IT

Three hundred thousand years ago, *Homo sapiens* discovered fire. This new technology marked a milestone for our survival. It allowed us to cook food and use fire to scare away predators, but it also became the favorite space to tell stories. Although the only evidence was the biased memory of the protagonists, these stories had an adaptive benefit and allowed the organization of the tribe's cooperation.[2]

In the year 2020, it is difficult to find an arbitral tribunal that feels comfortable with an opening statement told next to a campfire. It is why lawyers have opted for another type of technology to (1) communicate with the counterpart and the court; (2) collect, analyze, and produce the evidence; and (3) persuade the tribunal.

These innovations range from the classic Skype and Zoom to have video conferences with the tribunal to programs such as Everlaw and Nextpoint to expedite the production of documents in discovery. We can even hire consultants, such as A2L, for the preparation of these new virtual reality environments.

We have also changed the way we work. We use task management systems like Trello and store documents in shared cloud repositories like Google Drive. Some law firms have even dared to take these digital changes to the physical field, choosing to

2. Smith, D., Schlaepfer, P., Major, K. et al., *Cooperation and the evolution of hunter-gatherer storytelling. Nat Commun* 8, 1853 (2017).

move their offices to co-working spaces with an open-door policy. The objective of these transformations is not only aesthetic. It responds to a demand for greater flexibility and collaboration.[3]

This process of removing physical and digital barriers has revealed the differences between baby boomers, Generation X, and millennials.[4] Compared to other generations, millennials demand greater flexibility. They prefer work centers that allow telework or grant paid parental leave. They are the generation that is more willing by far to make sacrifices to find a balance between work and family.[5]

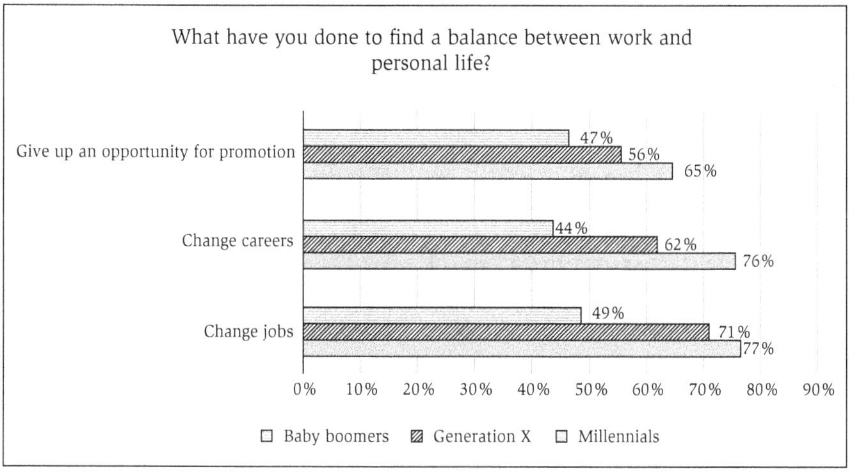

Source: Global generations: a global study on work-life challenges across generations.

The results of the EY Report coincide with the results that the editors Carolina, Álvaro and I found when surveying thirty-five of the most recognized young arbitration professionals in Latin America. Specifically, we found that 53.6% of respondents missed a really important family event due to work and 37% spent less than five hours a week at leisure. A total of 34.3% of the respondents want to establish their own firm, and 46.9% would be willing to receive less money for more free time.[6]

Market players have also changed, including the international recognition of boutique firms such as Chaffetz Lindsey and Three Crowns, the incursion of the Big Four, the growing prominence of dispute financiers, and the strengthening of different arbitration centers such as SIAC and HKIAC.[7] It remains to be seen if Latin-American

3. DeStefano, M., *Legal upheaval: A guide to creativity, collaboration, and innovation in Law*. Chicago: American Bar Association (2018).
4. Baby boomers are usually identified as those born between 1946 and 1964; Generation X includes those born between 1967 and 1980; and millennials are those born between 1981 and 1996.
5. *Ibid*., p. 15.
6. De la Jara, J.M., Arroyo, C., Awad, A. *How do arbitration associates survive in Latin America?*.
7. 2018 International Arbitration Survey: *The evolution of international arbitration*. Available at: https://www.ey.com/Publication/vwLUAssets/Global_generations_study/$FILE/EY-global-generations-a-global-study-on-work-life-challenges-across-generations.pdf.

firms can convince customers that just because they are cheaper does not make them less sophisticated.

Finally, since the economic crisis of 2008, customers have taken control of the market. They are focused on finding greater value in their legal representation spending, that is greater predictability and efficiency without compromising the quality of services. The 2018 Queen Mary survey confirms it. Costs continue to occupy first place in the worst characteristics of arbitration (67%), and lack of speed as fourth (34%). The lack of information regarding the efficiency of the arbitrators, the selection of arbitrators by the arbitration centers, and the efficiency of these institutions are also considered 30%, 15% and 11%, respectively.[8]

The world has already changed. And as Jordan Furlong says, it is useless to think about the future. There is only the present, and every day that a law firm anticipates "the future" is an additional day in which it lags behind its competitors moving forward.[9]

§22.03 THE DELTA MODEL

The Delta Model focuses on three crucial areas for the success of a lawyer in the twenty-first century: Law, Business & Operations and Personal Effectiveness skills. This model highlights the importance of knowledge of technological tools and customer service when providing legal services.

DELTA MODEL V.3

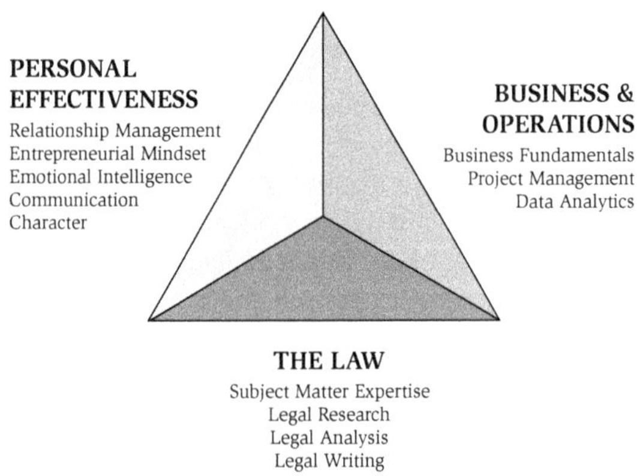

Source: Natalie Runyon and Alyson Carre—Adapting for 21st Century Success: the Delta Lawyer Competency Model.[10]

---

8. 2018 International Arbitration Survey: *The Evolution of International Arbitration*, p. 8.
9. HighQ. *SmartLaw 2.0: expert insights for the future of law*, p. 9.
10. N. Runyon, A. Carre. *Adapting for 21st century success: the Delta Lawyer Competency Model*. Available at: https://legal.thomsonreuters.com/content/dam/ewp-m/documents/legal/en/pdf/white-papers/delta-lawyer-competency.pdf.

These below roles have recently emerged in the arbitration market and show the importance of the Delta Model.

[A] Knowledge Attorney

It is not necessary to reinvent the wheel when preparing a memorial or writing a report. The firm where you work probably has a model that you can use. The larger the office, however, there is a greater chance that knowledge will be lost in a virtual folder in which nobody knows. Therefore, the role of the knowledge attorney focuses on creating content, automating precedents, leading training workshops, developing friendly platforms that allow access to knowledge to the team, and encouraging a culture of collaboration and data-driven decision-making.

[B] Discovery Specialist

Discovery document production is an expensive procedure, in money for the client and in time and energy for the lawyers. Despite the cost, only 8% of those surveyed by Berwin Leighton Paisner indicated that the production of documents had contributed significantly to a favorable outcome.[11] In addition, the costs of a document production procedure are divided into approximately 8% in data collection, 19% in processing and a gigantic 73% in document review.[12] These costs can be dramatically reduced with the use of software such as eDiscovery Point, accompanied by outsourcing to a discovery specialist. This new role is responsible for identifying, preserving, collecting, processing, reviewing, and producing documents relevant to disputes. The discovery specialist usually has an education in information science and law. Thus, his knowledge of technological and legal language makes him a valuable resource for lawyers without technical skills or those who understandably prefer to invest their time in more creative tasks.

[C] Trial Advocacy Consultant

Arbitration is increasingly sophisticated. However, most counsels do their jobs without knowing the scientifically proven grounds of persuasion. This space has been occupied by dispute consultants who are professionals with legal and psychological knowledge working hand in hand with the team to increase their chances of winning the case. The consultant's work focuses on developing a persuasive narrative of the case that includes storytelling techniques; directing simulations of opening and closing statements to detect opportunities for improvement; designing graphics, animations,

11. *Berwin Leighton Paisner International Arbitration researched report on the perception of document production in the arbitration process.*
12. N. Pace, L. Zakaras. *Where the money goes. Understand litigant expenditures for producing electronic discovery.* Available at: https://www.rand.org/content/dam/rand/pubs/monographs/2012/RAND_MG1208.pdf.

and models that help arbitrators understand the case; and facilitate the process of persuasion as well as providing technical assistance during the hearing.

§22.04 AND NOW, WHAT?

As David Halliwell points out, the forecasts for lawyers always seem obvious. Learn to program in computer code. Become a design thinker. Build an app. Use social networks. Learn a new language. Be mindful. Play the flute.[13]

In short, it is no longer adequate to just be a lawyer. Use the Delta Model to find your own path, without having to cover all fields. Focus on what you are passionate and has utility for your career. Find a human group guided by empathy, a tribe. Make it grow. Connect with a mentor. Take a risk. Use technology to customize your life but do not let it deprive you of having meaningful conversations. Make everyone's brain explode. Be irreplaceable.

13. HighQ. *SmartLaw 2.0: expert insights for the future of law*, p. 16.

CHAPTER 23
Challenge Accepted! From the Corporate World to the Arbitral World

Diana Gárate

For almost ten years I had focused my professional career in the corporate field, particularly in project finance and infrastructure. In my day to day, I worked in bid tenders, joint ventures, consortiums, loan agreements and a bit of SPAs, SHAs, NDAs, LOIs, MOUs, and all the Anglo-Saxon acronyms that one can imagine. However, through it all, I discovered the adrenaline and passion for arbitration.

My life took an unexpected turn. By that time, I had already completed an LL.M. with a specialization in corporate finance in New York. I felt changing my career path was not the convenient thing to do. I was afraid it was too late to start in a new law field. I did not know how or where to start. For me, it seemed like a big risk with much to lose. However, thanks to the advice of my bosses and my mentor, I decided to fully enter into the arbitral world.

If at this moment you are thinking of making the "big change," or to learn more about arbitration and dedicate yourself to it too, take a chance! When you discover your true calling, there is no turning back. I took courage. I risked starting from scratch in a new field, and I said: challenge accepted!

I must say that I am still learning a lot and discovering new challenges within the arbitration field. When my friends asked me to share the twist in my career in this chapter, my first thought was to focus on tips and advice that I received when I decided to change. These tips greatly helped me during that time.

§23.01 READY, SET, GO!

My first approach to arbitration was in a BigLaw in New York five years ago. It was my first day of work at the department of Project Finance, and a partner called me to ask me if I had ever seen an arbitration process. "*I have never seen an arbitration case in my life*," I said to which he replied, "*Well, this will be your first case.*"

Afterward, I was on a plane flying to Peru to take witness statements and seek evidence for one of the most important arbitrations against a Peruvian state entity at that time.

Despite the long hours of work and the need to "learn on the go," the experience was very rewarding. The first case in which I worked was related to a Peruvian concession. "*It's my field*!" I thought, and I was able to get fully involved in the case because the substance of the controversy was my expertise (infrastructure). However, at that time, I lacked theoretical knowledge about the arbitration process and the hard and soft skills of a litigator.

At that point of my professional career, I spent long nights reading books of Jan Paulsson and Gary Born for the first time and thought it was too late to dedicate myself to arbitration. I remember that a very good friend gave me excellent advice: "*Diana, you don't have to put aside your experience in corporate, projects, and infrastructure, and you don't have to put aside arbitration if you like it. Why don't you merge both fields?*"

The majority of arbitrations in Latin America come from disputes related to public infrastructure and private projects; for example, construction or operation, controversies on project financing, and investor disputes with the State. By that time, I already felt comfortable and adequately experienced in such matters. However, the problem is these disputes are usually referred to an arbitration lawyer. I thought, "Why do I not work these cases with my team and arbitration specialists instead of referring them to an arbitration lawyer?" If we know and handle the underlying issue of the dispute, we can—with a team made up of corporate and litigation specialists—take the case. This question led me to pursue a career in the arbitral world without neglecting my corporate/infrastructure experience.

It was not an easy nor a smooth transition, but luckily, I had great mentors and bosses who helped me through it. Hence, I want to share with you some of the tips that they gave me that made my transition from the corporate world to the arbitration world easier.

[A] Win-Win? Prepare to Lose

One of the situations that cost me the most was learning and accepting to lose a case. It is not that easy. When you get involved in a case, and you work hard on it (even years), there is nothing sadder than losing. I would have also wanted someone to warn me about how it feels to lose. I never felt the sense of losing in the corporate world, because in corporate deals, there is hardly a "loser." If two parties execute an M&A deal, project or corporate finance, both parties win.

Although a party is selling the company because it is perhaps bankrupt, it is not a loss because the bankrupt company is recovering part of its investment, or at least obtaining resources to liquidate its business. In a financing project, both parties also win. One party gets the facility it needs to develop a project, and the other party earns interest, commissions, etc.

On the contrary, there will never be two equally happy parties in an arbitration process. There will always be a winner and a loser to a greater or lesser extent. Also, what happens if the parties settle during arbitration? Is this a win-win scenario? It is possible for one of the parties to prefer to save the costs of time and money involved in seeking an arbitration, even if the resulting settlement is not the ideal scenario? I am still not sure what the answer is.

In a nutshell, it is important to keep in mind that this winner-loser situation is expected, and it is better to be prepared sometimes for defeat, especially when you know you have a weak case.

[B] "It's a Man World"

Another surprise was to discover that, unlike the corporate law world, there is a majority presence of men in the arbitration community, not only as practitioners and litigators but also mainly in arbitral tribunals.

During the last years, I had hearings before tribunals formed solely by men. I also had a team of only men lawyers as counterpart. I also faced certain occasions when I experienced discrimination and "mansplaining" because of being a young woman.

For this reason, I began to investigate more on gender, diversity, and inclusion in arbitration and discovered ArbitralWomen Nongovernmental Organization (NGO), an international organization that encourages the greater participation of women in dispute resolution worldwide. The NGO promotes women in dispute resolution through events, social gatherings, and mentoring and by sponsoring female law students in moot court competitions. I immediately fell in love with this initiative and became an actively involved member.

Being a young woman and coming from Latin America brought me some opportunities, but they also brought several obstacles in the domestic and international arbitration community. ArbitralWomen mentorship and great network helped me to address these arising challenges in the early stages of my practice.

[C] Some Tips and Advice

To conclude, I would like to share with you some useful tips and suggestions so you can make your arbitral practice compatible with your former practice (in corporate or any other area of law), as well as to make a smooth transition to the arbitral world:

- Do not abandon or change your transactional and corporate expertise, rather complement it with arbitration.
- Always keep updated with the latest news from the arbitration community, especially with regards to important cases and awards. You can subscribe to Wolters Kluwer, the Global Arbitration Review, and CIAR Global as well as read the news from ICC, ICSID, and other national newspapers.

- Become an active member of a young arbitration association in order to expand your network. Recommendations include ICC YAF, young associations by country, Spanish Arbitration Club (CEA) under 40, Young ITA, Young ICCA, Young Arbitral Women, and WWA.
- Create your own niche in the arbitral community. Choose an academic subject or specialty within arbitration and focus and prepare yourself on it, for example legal tech, sports, start-ups, fashion, infrastructure, M&A, real estate, insurance, etc. There are so many options!
- Take litigation and persuasion and advocacy skills courses in addition to theoretical courses and lectures. It is also advisable to take courses in psychology and theater. They will be very useful to learn how to persuade the tribunal.
- Add value to your former expertise. Apply your hard and soft skills in dispute litigation and your new *litigator mindset* in the field of your expertise. For example, if you also work in corporate law, at the time of drafting an agreement, letter, or any document in the context of a corporate deal, always write it as if it were to be eventually read by an arbitral tribunal or give it a potential conflict prevention approach. This technique adds value to your counseling.
- Commercial tip: *Cross-selling* applies! If you have clients from your corporate practice, they will be your first clients for your arbitration practice. Do not worry at first to "go out to get customers." First, try to approach those you already have as clients.

And finally, I can only say, take the risk and enjoy the ride!

CHAPTER 24

Empirical Legal Research and Arbitration Associates

Christopher R. Drahozal

§24.01 INTRODUCTION

Broadly speaking, empirical research is research "originating in or based on observation or experience."[1] By that definition, much legal research is empirical (which is distinct from the theoretical) because it is based on observation or experience with what happens in the legal system. In common usage, empirical research refers to research that collects information based on observation or experience using some systematic methodology. Under this narrower definition, a study examining a single court case or arbitration case in detail would not be empirical, but a study examining data on a sample of similar cases would be.

While empirical research is often considered and commonly is quantitative in nature, it can also be qualitative. In this regard, "quantitative research methods involve the collection and analysis of numerical data, while qualitative methods involve the collection and analysis of nonnumeric data."[2] One of the best known empirical studies about international arbitration is a qualitative one: *Dealing in Virtue* by Yves Dezalay and Bryant Garth.[3] Because my experience is with quantitative rather than qualitative empirical studies, the rest of this chapter will focus on quantitative empirical research.

1. *Empirical,* Meriam-Webster Dictionary, https://www.merriam-webster.com/dictionary/empirical (last visited February 22, 2019).
2. Towards a Science of International Arbitration: Collected Empirical Research 4 (Christopher R. Drahozal & Richard W. Naimark eds. 2005).
3. Yves Dezalay & Bryant G. Garth, Dealing in Virtue: International Commercial Arbitration and the Construction of a Transnational Legal Order (1996).

§24.02 TYPES OF QUANTITATIVE EMPIRICAL RESEARCH

Lee Epstein and Gary King describe the three aims of empirical research as "*amassing data* for use by the researcher or others; *summarizing data* so they are easier to comprehend; and *making descriptive or causal inferences*, which entails using data we have observed to learn about data we would like to gather."[4] The most common methods empirical researchers use to collect data are surveys, observational studies, and experiments.

Surveys (including interviews) collect data by asking people questions and are what most people consider as empirical research. Observational studies collect data by observation of actual cases and contracts, examining what people actually do rather than what they say they do. Experiments collect data by having participants in the study respond or analyze hypothetical situations. Social science experiments are obviously different from experiments in the natural sciences.

The burgeoning body of empirical research on international arbitration uses all these methodologies. Of course, this short chapter is not the place for a detailed description or analysis of those studies. Suffice it to say that empirical studies examine all aspects of the international arbitration process to some degree at least. These aspects include the use of arbitration clauses in international contracts, procedures in international arbitral proceedings (including their cost and length, appointment and challenge of arbitrators, interim measures, emergency arbitrators, multiparty proceedings, and mediation), arbitrator demographics, decision-making, arbitral proceedings outcomes, and enforcement of the international arbitral awards.[5]

§24.03 BENEFITS OF EMPIRICAL RESEARCH

Empirical research can benefit arbitration associates by providing a broader perspective on what the legal world looks like and how it works.

For example, a lawyer drafting an arbitration clause often starts with a clause from a prior contract he or she prepared or a form clause drafted by another lawyer in the firm, an arbitral institution model clause, or a published book of forms. Perhaps the lawyer has read an article on clause drafting by an expert in the field or attended a class addressing the topic. An empirical study examining the provisions of international arbitration clauses provides additional and more systematic information about how other lawyers draft arbitration clauses.[6] The study can highlight issues or approaches identified by other drafters, enabling the arbitration associate to learn not just from his

4. Lee Epstein & Gary King, The Rules of Inference, 69 U. Chi. L. Rev. 1, 19-20 (2002) (emphasis added).
5. *See* generally Christopher R. Drahozal, Empirical Findings on International Arbitration: An Overview, in Oxford Handbook on International Arbitration (forthcoming 2019) (draft available at, www.ssrn.com).
6. For example, John F. Coyle & Christopher R. Drahozal, Dispute Resolution Clauses in International Supply Contracts, 52 Vand. J. Transnat'l L. (forthcoming 2019) (draft available at www.ssrn.com).

or her own experience but from the experience (or at least behavior) of numerous others.

In addition, empirical research can help lawyers in crafting policy arguments directed to legal decision-makers, such as judges, arbitrators, regulators, or legislators. Often lawyers will know of the practices of their client or the facts of the case in dispute. But the individual case or contract provision is simply an anecdote; it may not be typical of all cases or contracts. A well-constructed empirical study provides a broader and more representative perspective and may reveal that the apparently egregious case is, or is not, particularly common.

Finally, empirical research can provide insights into aspects of the arbitration process that otherwise are difficult to observe. For example, recent experimental research suggests that arbitrators use the same decisional heuristics and are susceptible to the same decision-making biases as the rest of us.[7] These sorts of psychological insights can assist lawyers in making arguments to the tribunal or predicting the outcomes of cases. In addition, the growing availability of legal analytics—such as Arbitrator Intelligence which is collecting data and making it available for arbitrator case management practices and decision-making—[8] will help in evaluating cases and selecting decision-makers.

Empirical research is by no means the solution to all the challenges facing arbitration associates. But using and understanding empirical research is another tool that a good lawyer can use to represent clients effectively.

§24.04 LIMITATIONS OF EMPIRICAL RESEARCH

All empirical research methods have limitations.[9] Understanding those limitations is essential to being a knowledgeable user of empirical research.

For example, survey results provide information on how those responding to the survey answered the questions asked. But survey respondents, either consciously or unconsciously, might provide answers that reflect what the respondents wish they did rather than what they actually do. Moreover, the administration of surveys raises questions of representativeness. Are the respondents representative of the entire population, or are the survey results biased by overrepresentation or underrepresentation of some portion of the population?

Observational studies raise similar concerns about representativeness. For example, a study that examines a sample of arbitration awards must take into account that many cases settle before an award is issued. There is every reason to believe that settled cases differ systematically from cases resolved by an award. The fact that the

7. *See* Susan D. Franck et al., Inside the Arbitrator's Mind, 66 Emory L.J. 1115 (2017); Rebecca Helm et al., Are Arbitrators Human?, 13 J. Emp. Legal Stud. 666 (2016).
8. For more information on Arbitrator Intelligence (AI), *see* the AI web page at www.arbitratorintelligence.org.
9. *See*, e.g., Christopher R. Drahozal, Arbitration Innumeracy, YB. Arb. Med. 89 (2012); Drahozal & Naimark, *supra* note 2, at 8-11. *See* generally An Introduction to Empirical Legal Research (Lee Epstein & Andrew D. Martin 2014); Oxford Handbook of Empirical Legal Research (Peter Cane & Herbert M. Kritzer eds. 2012).

case settled is a pretty good indicator if nothing else. As a result, the settlement of cases may mask (or embellish) the effect in which the researcher is interested. A related point is the difficulty to control the strength of a claimant's case in studies of court or arbitration outcomes. Unless the researcher is able to evaluate objectively the credibility of the witnesses' testimony, for example, it is extremely difficult to conclude that outcomes differ because of, say, the forum, rather than differences in the merits of the claim.

Experimental studies provide a possible way to lessen or avoid that problem because they use hypothetical cases or scenarios that hold constant the strength of the claim.[10] But extrapolating experimental results from laboratory to real-world settings is difficult. Hypothetical cases necessarily involve simplified (if not highly simplified) facts with little or no real money at stake. The subjects might be college students studying psychology or judges or arbitrators at conferences who might not take the experiment as seriously as they would a real case. While experiments avoid some of the limitations of empirical research, they come with limitations of their own.

§24.05 CONCLUSION

I conclude with a few general comments for the arbitration associate about using empirical research:

- Empirical studies can provide important and useful insights into real-world practices, going beyond mere anecdotes to more systematic data.
- All empirical studies have limitations. Good empirical studies identify and discuss those limitations.
- Be aware of pop advertising and pseudoscience. Do not rely only on press releases and media reports of empirical studies. Such reports can help you find the existence of empirical research, but they should not be the only source on which you rely.
- Do not just read the results of an empirical study. Be sure to read the methodology section of the study as well. You cannot understand what the study found without understanding what the study did.

10. Another way to deal with the issue is to assign cases randomly among the forums being studied. Not surprisingly, such studies are difficult to conduct.

CHAPTER 25

Disruptive Innovation in Arbitration

Mauricio Duarte

If in the first half of the nineties someone would have asked us about the possible impacts of the Internet in arbitration, many of us would not have been able to answer the question. Now, we face the same question but with technologies that have even a larger disruptive capacity and with the ability to change the world as we understand it.

I still remember my professor of Disruptive Innovation and Coding for Lawyers constantly asserting:

> We are currently living the fourth industrial revolution driven by technology's accelerating changes. You will witness how the roll of the old-fashioned attorney will drift ... attorneys will have to innovate and evolve with technology.

It was impossible to ignore an alumnus of The University of Chicago who was well known by everybody for generating debates at the World Economic Forum regarding the impact of blockchain in economics and law.

The subject was so complex that it pushed me to be curious about it and to do some research. On the outset, I looked up this new technology of "blockchain" and its possible impacts on law. It is how I stumbled upon my first book about the topic, written by Dan Tapscott. I still remember this fascinating quote I discovered in the book:

> The first generation of the digital revolution brought us the Internet of information. The second generation—powered by blockchain technology—is bringing us the Internet of value: a new platform to reshape the world of business and transform the old order of human affairs for the better.[1]

That statement made me think about the way in which we, attorneys, could evolve at hand with technology.

1. Tapscott, D., & Tapscott, A. (2016). *Blockchain Revolution: How the Technology Behind Bitcoin Is Changing Money, Business and the World*. Toronto: Portfolio/Penguin.

I still recall when I was sitting in front of a computer while writing the entry for my blog on LinkedIn. Without further platforms for writing, I spent hours thinking about the ways in which arbitration could be disrupted. I started by writing small texts which I would send to a few acquaintances of mine. I even got to the point of asking my girlfriend—who is an electrical engineer—if the topic was interesting for her.

Despite humble beginnings, in the process, I learned how artificial intelligence, smart contracts, blockchain, and cybersecurity protocols have the potential of simplifying all of the arbitration processes.

I must admit that it would take me up to one or two weeks to deliver an article of 1,000 words. However, I understood that there was no rush in getting there. Without leaving aside the technical foundations of technology, I was led by both imagination and creativity to explore unprecedented (for some people) and wonderful (to others) ideas.

I am no superhuman and I have been, indeed, criticized by my ideas of the relationship between arbitration and technology. I still look back at the conversation I had with an attorney who insisted that I should "stop wasting my time over these science fiction dreams." Other colleagues of mine would overemphasize that my ideas would not thrive in the actual arbitration system. Of course, I thought about stopping my writing about technology and just reviewing the existing rules of procedure for arbitration, the regulation for arbitration in Guatemala, or an outstanding award.

However, ideas such as: (1) the use of blockchain to make the acknowledgment and enforcement of awards processes more efficient in accordance with the New York Convention;[2] and (2) the use of crypto security mechanisms in arbitration,[3] were

2. One of the central objectives of the New York Convention was to eliminate the "double exequatur," meaning that the award needed the confirmation in the place of the arbitration before it could be recognized internationally. If either court denied exequatur, the award could not be recognized and enforced. This process made the recognition and enforcement of arbitral awards difficult, unreliable and slow. The New York Convention eliminated the double exequatur requirement, with the objective of making foreign awards efficiently enforceable and subject to fewer opportunities for judicial challenges.

If we want foreign awards efficiently enforceable, could blockchain, the technology behind Bitcoin, provide another perspective to this issue? Blockchain can best be described as a digital platform or a distributed and immutable ledger that stores records, known as blocks. Blocks can store various kinds of information; in the case of Bitcoin, blocks store information about financial transactions. These blocks, which collectively form a "blockchain," are stored on various nodes ("computers"), which ensure that no single person or entity can manipulate the ledger without everyone else knowing.

A key property of blockchain technology, which distinguishes it from traditional database technology, is that it is publicly verifiable, supported by integrity and transparency of the system. In other words, it would be practically impossible to change an entry in the database, because it would require changing all of the data that comes before, on every single node.

With this mechanism, it is possible to store a duly rendered award in an arbitration proceeding. By having this information in the blockchain, the competent authority could verify the existence of the award and avoid additional costs, judicial proceedings and the traditional method of doing things. Forget about having the "burden of proof" to show the existence of the award that is duly certified. The blockchain can do the task in its own. Further reading: Duarte, M. (March 15, 2018). *Could Blockchain Help the Recognition of International Arbitration Awards?*, available at: http://arbitrationblog.kluwerarbitration.com/2018/04/20/blockchain-help-recognition-international-arbitration-awards/.

appealing, passionate and interesting notions. Finally, I had ideas that could be explored along with software developers, technology geeks and futurists.[4]

Despite my excitement, I understood that law practitioners, and especially arbitration practitioners, have been reluctant to incorporate new technologies into practice since historically attorneys have been very conservative about their profession. Moreover, the resistance to these new technologies still exists due to a deep concern that technology may alter the traditional "roll" of the attorney.[5] For example, Dana Remus, professor at the School of Law at the University of North Carolina, conducted a study regarding the threat of digital automatization in the attorneys' work.[6] The report concluded that the implementation of new technologies would reduce billable hours for attorneys by 13%.

Once I realized I was part of the problem (but part of the solution as well), I started to see more clearly the win-win relationship between arbitration and new technologies.

§25.01 MILLENNIAL ADVICE

Nowadays, any practitioner interested in technology can use a dozen platforms that generate digital mechanisms for dispute resolution. For instance, JUR,[7] Jury.Online,[8] Confideal,[9] and Kleros[10] seek to generate automatization in dispute resolution through blockchain.

3. As a result of many cyber security incidents, the United States National Institute of Standards and Technology (*NIST*) issued a Framework for Improving Critical Infrastructure Cyber security. The framework defined high-level goals of any cyber security risk management program. *Identify, Protect, Detect, Respond, and Recover* are the five main goals for any successful cyber security program which could be considered in international arbitration. In 2018, ICCA, the New York Bar Association and the International Institute for Conflict Prevention and Resolution released a draft of the Cybersecurity Protocol for International Arbitration ("Cybersecurity Protocol"). The Cybersecurity Protocol originated as an acknowledgement from practitioners that arbitration proceedings are not immune to increasingly pervasive cyberattacks. This also meant that attention to cyber security is required and essential to ensure that international arbitration maintains the confidentiality of the dispute resolution process. In a digital era, a variety of factors must be considered when adopting security protocols for the transfer of sensitive information. However, with the new Cybersecurity Protocol, arbitral institutions and arbitrators will have some principles and guidelines to *Identify, Protect, Detect, Respond, and Recover* data from cyber security incidents that might take place in the arbitration proceedings. Further reading: Duarte, M. (February 6, 2019). *Essential Tips on Cybersecurity for Arbitrators: Identify, Protect, Detect, Respond and Recover,* available at: http://arbitrationblog.kluwerarbitration.com/2019/02/06/essential-tips-on-cybersecurity-for-arbitrators-identify-protect-detect-respond-and-recover/.
4. Duarte, M. (November 22, 2018). *High Technology Arbitration, Legal Business World,* available at: https://www.legalbusinessworld.com/single-post/2018/11/22/High-Technology-Arbitration.
5. Jones, R., & Moore, R. (2013). *Information Technology and Traditional Legal Concepts*. London: Taylor and Francis.
6. Remus, D., & Levy, F. (December 11, 2015). *Can Robots Be Lawyers? Computers, Lawyers, and the Practice of Law,* available at: https://papers.ssrn.com/sol3/Papers.cfm?abstract_id=2701092.
7. https://jur.io/.
8. https://jury.online/.
9. https://confideal.io/.
10. https://kleros.io/.

New technologies can improve efficiency and transparency and reduce the costs of arbitrations. Nonetheless, arbitration must innovate more and become a reliable mechanism to solve a new type of disputes, the disputes within a digital ecosystem.

Since you are aware of the challenges of arbitration but are eager to know the benefits of technology to solve them, I hereby share with you some tips to become part of the millennial generation of the arbitration world.

[A] #BeCurious

It all starts with being curious, well informed, and critical regarding the technology trends. An active participant must immerse himself or herself with the technological "doctrine." Reading, studying, questioning, and participating are mandatory in order to participate in technological matters aimed to build new ideas.

In the digital world, one of the best sources of information is another human being as human beings happen to be software developers or software engineers. Being able to discuss with colleagues and complete strangers through social media has pushed forward my knowledge of technology topics.

I invite any curious person to participate in the active discussion of Medium[11] with attorneys, economists, and experts over the limitations of blockchain or artificial intelligence.

[B] #ProfessionalPractice

Learning is not everything. To implement knowledge with people and to put ideas into practice are also needed. We demand spaces with other professionals for creativity to bloom.

To find a way in society has always been key to every aspect of work and life. But now the approach is focused on establishing improbable partnerships and multidisciplinary collaborations that allow us to create and enhance ideas. Amidst the digital era, we must work with software developers, nerds, economists, mathematicians, and other professionals in order to implement ideas in a digital ecosystem. Only through professional practice you can get a solid idea ready to implement new products, services, and strategies.

[C] #ComplexProblemSolutions

A legal syllogism implies the creative settlement of problems with very complex factual patterns. That process requires critical thinking, analysis, and application. We attorneys are trained to think with sophisticated concepts, and it is a highly praised ability in order to solve the unbeknownst challenges of the future.

11. https://medium.com/.

Once you have a solid idea, this idea has to solve highly complex problems. Diversity in the designation of arbitrators, transparency in the procedures and the reduction of costs in arbitrations are "highly complex" topics that technology can partly solve.

It is these reasons as to why the attorney is needed to identify problems and adapt possible (legal) solutions with digital tools. Thus, the attorneys will be crucial for "Adapting a New Global Architecture for the 4th Industrial Revolution" (the topic of last year's World Economic Forum). Think of solving complex topics. Do not limit yourselves to innovate by buying a new printer for your office.

[D] #ConstructionAndImplementation

We must not try to predict and prepare ourselves for the future. We must design it. Build it. First, we must change our ways of thinking regarding the roll of the attorney in the future.

Attorneys will become important partners for software developers and engineers. They will have leading roles in the construction of a decentralized digital architecture.

In spite of what I just stated, attorneys will have to learn and understand the foundations of technology to build and implement digital solutions. To accomplish this feat, the attorney must not work on his or her own. He or she must work with software developers and engineers, and specialists in artificial intelligence.

For instance, Clifford Chance has implemented the *Tech Academy* initiative for partners and associates to learn about artificial intelligence, blockchain, and smart contracts.[12] *Tech Academy* is the living proof that as technology is massively implemented, the demand for legal services will increase.

[E] #Perseverance

When people talk about the millennials, many think that said generation just wants everything to work out immediately. Unfortunately, it is not how it is. The results are not immediate. I do not believe that being a millennial is related with the epoch where you were born and have a need for immediate results. Being a millennial resembles a mentality and an attitude of openness toward the digital era.

Perseverance and adaptation are qualities that everybody needs to remain relevant. If an idea does not work, perhaps it is time to think of a new one. If a solution has flaws, perhaps it is time to question your methods. Reinventing notions, ideas, and solutions is not a synonym for failure. It is alright to savor success, but it is far more important to learn what failure teaches us.

Irrespective of our generation, we attorneys must promote a socially responsible and free self-expression and entrepreneurial culture with the tools that technology provides us with. All we need is an open, ambitious, and creative mind.

---

12. Clifford Chance. (2018). *Clifford Chance Launches Tech Academy*, available at: https://www.cliffordchance.com/news/news/2018/04/clifford-chance-launches-tech-academy.html.

[F] #StayBold

Do not be indulgent with the previous procedures and proceedings. Very often, the existing proceedings are the ones stopping industries' evolution. Blockbuster disappeared due to its lack of innovation and its idea that nobody would be willing to get their digital content through Netflix.

In the same line of thought, arbitration practitioners must think, create, and implement innovating ideas for arbitration. We must be the boost for a new generation of arbitrators. To be a millennial and young creates an unprecedented energy-momentum. Nonetheless, in order to enter into this new era, we need more open-minded, ambitious and creative millennials for innovating arbitration.

[G] #BeYourself

The above steps will be useless if you do not have a personal conviction regarding the possible impacts of technology in arbitration. Just by being yourself, you will be able to have a true passion for this topic. This passion will turn into creative expression and thinking. I get a lot of "here comes the blockchain guy!" comments which started as a joke. However, I take it as a description for somebody who is aware that technology lives among us.

§25.02 BUILD THE DIGITAL FUTURE

Many of us have been scolded in the same way by our mothers: "*Technology distracts! Where is your privacy? Technology is addictive! That screen is going to make you blind!*" However, technology, as any other tool, can be useful if we think through its purposes to resolve complex topics.

The digital era allows us to feed our curiosity. Especially for the ones loving arbitration, we are before the chance of building new solutions to preserve its excellence. But to build the future, we must do it with passion.

It does not matter how many people we follow on Twitter nor the number of followers on Instagram. To be successful in the digital future, we must question, innovate, and build future solutions. Let us think periodically about how to improve arbitration (including technology or not). Most of all, the successful ideas started sounding hasty, stupid, and futureless.

If we understand technology, we can dream. We will be part of the new generation that will build the future. Let us remember that in the future the legal services will have to be compatible with the digital world.

I am deeply concerned with the future of arbitration, and I hope that you are as well. The future of arbitration belongs to all of us who are willing to implement a "tradition of innovation." May we see beyond the problem and build the future. An automated machine can do the work that a human once did, but no technology can do the work of extraordinary human beings who are willing to build ideas for the sake of arbitration.

Part IV War Stories and Lessons about the Arbitration Market

CHAPTER 26

Preparing for a Job Interview

Frank Ramos

Do you have a job interview? Congratulations!

Many law students and young lawyers struggle to land interviews. If you want more interviews, spend time networking and meeting and developing relationships with those professionals in a position to hire you or with those connections who know people in a position to hire you. The adage "it is not what you know, it is who you know" applies to landing a job. You do not have to come from a family with connections to land a good job. You can make your own connections through networking at voluntary bar associations or nonprofits where you could volunteer alongside attorneys who may one day be your boss.

Once you land the interview, do the following:

- Study the law firm's website and the profiles of the attorneys you will be meeting and may possibly meet.
- Study the firm's mission, vision, and values. Think about how you can support the firm's mission and vision and how your values complement the firm's values.
- Review the firm's social media postings and online presence.
- Research the firm and read everything you can about the firm that is in the public domain.
- Dress conservatively and professionally.
- Work on your body language. Convey confidence by keeping and holding eye contact, having good posture, setting your shoulders, giving a firm handshake that you hold for a few seconds, projecting your voice, and creating a presence with your body. Own your space.
- Check your nerves at the door. Firms do not hire anxious candidates. Yes, I know you need the job. Yes, I know you really need it. But desperation has a scent, and its musk is repellant. Practice some mock interviews with lawyers

or other professionals you know so you become comfortable with sitting across the table from someone and answering his or her questions.
- Have answers ready to common interview questions. Why did you become a lawyer? Why do you want to work here? Why do you want to leave your current job? What can you do for us? Where do you see yourself in ten years? There are dozens of common interview questions. Research them and be ready with thoughtful answers.
- Be prepared to discuss how you can serve the firm. The firm is interviewing you because they are evaluating whether you are a good fit for the firm. Keep your focus on how your skills, interests, and passions can serve the firm and its goals.
- Be on guard for different interviewing styles. Some interviewers will be serious. Some will try to test you, and some will just have a friendly chat. Follow the interviewer's lead and communicate on his or her terms.

On the day of the interview, do the following:

- Arrive early. You can always wait in your car if you arrive too early. Arriving late, even a minute late, is unforgivable. Bad traffic is not an excuse. I cannot tell you how many candidates are rejected for arriving late.
- Bring extra copies of your resume and writing samples.
- Treat everyone with politeness and respect. Whether it is the receptionist, security guard, or legal assistant, treat everyone the same way you would treat the firm's managing partner.
- Keep your answers focused and, where appropriate, brief.
- Listen and answer only the questions asked.
- Do not bad mouth your current firm or former firms.
- Do not bad mouth other attorneys or judges.
- Do not take the bait to gossip.
- Everything you do and say is being watched, dissected, and evaluated. You are under a microscope. Be on your best behavior at all times.
- Try to schedule interviews in the evening, so you are not preoccupied with arriving late to your current office.
- Do not ask about salary. If they are interested, they will call you and let you know what it is.
- Sometimes you will get inappropriate questions. Politely state you do not feel comfortable answering the question and change the subject.
- If you meet with different people, you will likely get the same questions. Be prepared to give the same answers multiple times.

After the interview, do the following:

- Send handwritten thank-you notes to everyone who interviewed you.
- Wait, and if you do not hear anything, then follow up.
- Wash, rinse and repeat. Keep persisting until you land a job you want. Best of luck!

CHAPTER 27

Rankings of Arbitrators and Counsels: Do They Matter?

Francisco Muñoz

I have been tasked with analyzing whether the various rankings and surveys of arbitration lawyers and arbitrators that we observe today are useful and matter.

The reality is that they do matter.

The rankings and opinions in magazines or legal publications have relevance in the professional activity when it comes to both attracting new clients to work as counsel and being appointed as arbitrator in a case.

To address this issue, we need to do some preliminary clarifications. First of all, we will talk about the rankings and opinions of international publications of a certain reputation and credibility. Second, we will analyze the importance of these rankings for both academic and professional activities. Finally, we will give the explanations from an empirical face, although without being able to count on statistical data in the real level of influence in results.

We consider that the usefulness of these rankings is true, although not necessarily essential for the academic or practical exercise of the profession.

The career and success of a lawyer in any area of law, but especially in arbitration, should be based primarily on the seriousness, conduct, rigor, and behavior of the lawyer. The credibility of the lawyer/arbitrator plays a preponderant role. Rankings are not necessarily the reflection of it.

§27.01 THE MOST RELEVANT RANKINGS IN INTERNATIONAL ARBITRATION

The journals and specialized publications have created various rankings or opinion sections on lawyers practicing arbitration, arbitrators, and law firms participating in this area.

Several rankings can be named as a way of example, including: (1) Global Arbitration Review (GAR); (2) The Legal 500 Arbitration; and (3) Chambers & Partners sections on Dispute Resolution and Arbitration.

The rankings of these prestigious publications are characterized by having the opinion of specialists in the area and selected clients. The rankings are not based solely on personal assessments or payments. The work that publishers do is essential for the credibility of these rankings.

The editors contact specialists or referents in the area to learn about the ranked or potentially ranked professionals. In addition, the editors investigate the selected ones and consult with the main clients referred by the legal study to know how the behavior of the candidate is.

The classifications of lawyers are made considering arbitration in a generic way, although some publications classify professionals according to the subject, whether commercial or investment arbitration (even, some are divided by specific industries) and also to their qualities as counsel or arbitrator. These more specialized rankings—like GAR—allow us to obtain information with greater precision regarding the quality of the professional and his or her real area of experience.

Likewise, these publications also evaluate and rank the different law firms, mostly classifying them by "bands." The most prominent law firms, due to the magnitude of the cases and their professionals, are classified as "band 1" until usually "band 4."

As already mentioned, the credibility of these publications is mainly given by the research work they perform. Despite being initiated on many occasions by direct application or through the respective law firm, if an individual does not have the merits to be selected, he or she is not ranked.

Consequently, the prestige of the publication guarantees the fidelity of the data. The prestige of the publication is maintained with the research done by the editors, which focuses on the experience of the classified person during the year, according to both peers and clients. It allows us to consider that the result would be impartial.

§27.02 ARE THERE REALLY BENEFITS TO BEING RANKED?

After briefly explaining how the most prestigious rankings work, it is appropriate to analyze what are the benefits, if any, that emerge from them.

We start from the ground that being ranked matters because it brings more benefits than costs to the lawyers who are part of those rankings. In addition, rankings are also beneficial for companies in search of lawyers or arbitrators.

[A] Professionals as the Main Beneficiaries

Both ranked counsel and arbitrators get important benefits from being included in those rankings.

To the best of our knowledge, the main beneficiaries are young associates or young partners and arbitrators who take their first steps as such. These rankings allow them to be better known. Renowned partners and experienced arbitrators generally do not get great benefits because they already have a proper name and reputation that makes them notorious in the market.

We consider that the benefits of being ranked are: (1) the academic prestige; (2) the professional recognition; and (3) the exposure of ranked professionals to potential clients.

First of all, we mention academic prestige as a benefit for the ranked professional, since the lawyer who is included is generally considered a specialist in the field, with a solid knowledge of arbitration.

It causes the ranked professional to raise his or her academic profile and opens the possibility of participating as a speaker in courses, conferences, or events. It also gives the ranked professional contacts and academic opportunities of different types. Event organizers, career directors, and book editors look for this kind of profiles to participate in their activities.

Also, the ranked lawyer is benefited by the professional recognition that comes with being named in this kind of publications. The professional recognition from peers and clients who elected the professional demonstrates his or her abilities as counsel or arbitrator.

Furthermore, the ranked professional is benefited by the "marketing" that the ranking brings. It is known that potential clients, particularly large companies or multinationals, tend to observe the most prestigious rankings to have a prior knowledge of the potential counsels to be hired or the potential arbitrators to be chosen.

[B] Rankings also Benefit Customers

First, the ranking often serves as a letter of introduction from lawyers. Potential clients can see what is the opinion of their peers and colleagues, as well as what type of clients they advise. Customers can also see what kind of cases in which the professional usually participates. Finally, clients can search through these rankings for lawyers in countries where they may not have great experience or contacts. This ranking helps to know if it is convenient to hire a certain professional and if that professional will be the right one to assist them.

Second, the ranking is useful for clients to know what kind of arbitrator they can name or who is the arbitrator already participating in a case. The experience, the cases in which he or she participated, and the knowledge he or she has are of the utmost relevance when appointing an arbitrator.

The rankings allow the customer to realize if an arbitrator is very busy or if he or she has enough time to devote to the specific case. It is due to the fact that rankings generally include the latest cases in which the arbitrator participated.

§27.03 COROLLARY

In conclusion, we believe that rankings are a good tool for young associates and partners, as well as for newly started arbitrators. Rankings are useful as advertising because they demonstrate the highlights of the included professionals. Rankings bring as benefit the appointment in academic activities, as counsel and as arbitrator. There is a fairly proven relationship between inclusion in rankings and new opportunities as counsels or arbitrators.

The renowned lawyers and arbitrators, who generally appear in these rankings, do not obtain important benefits for being included in them since they are already known by clients as well as by law firms. Hence, they are hired or appointed by their own weight.

CHAPTER 28

Events: When, Where, How, and Why

Félix Antolín

Certainly the life of young associates engaged in international arbitration is not an easy one, and most of the time is spent *inside* the offices where they work. From spending our hours performing activities, such as case law analysis, photocopying, and writing memorials, the tasks are varied. It is up to young practitioners to learn, albeit by force, how to develop successful multitasking skills without dying in the attempt.

However, no one explains to associates who are beginning their journey that there is a world *outside* their offices and that, sooner rather than later, leaving for that world becomes an indispensable task for advancing on the path of international arbitration. It is precisely here where it is necessary to stop and observe the phenomenon known as *conferences*.

Conferences in the legal industry are a complex figure, with multiple variables. If we were talking about the animal kingdom, conferences would be like a platypus, because they have parts and functionalities of different animals, without having a really defined characteristic of their own. In other words, conferences can be molded to the taste of the consumer, and therefore it is imperative to know what objectives we intend to achieve by participating in a conference. This brief chapter is intended to be a guide that allows young practitioners to dominate international arbitration events in order to get what they want from them and not to attend as mere spectators or bystanders.

§28.01 WHEN TO ATTEND EVENTS?

This question, to be fully answered, must be considered from two perspectives: first, at what point in a career it is appropriate to attend events; and second, what opportunities or periods of a calendar year one should choose to participate in them.

With regards to the first perspective, and as with all things, it is best to learn from a young age. There is no doubt that early exposure to conferences will allow practitioners to progressively obtain more benefits from them. In this sense, and although it may seem counterintuitive for law firms, the investment in sending their young practitioners to events will bring them greater future returns than sending associates for the first time who have not left their offices for years. As we will see below, an essential factor for getting the most of events is consistency in participation. In any case, this circumstance in no way prevents more experienced associates from beginning to attend to events, not only because of the added value they obtain but also because they can set different objectives for themselves, such as taking a break from their daily work to refresh and refine their skills and knowledge ("Sharpen the Saw").[1]

As for the latter perspective, although it is not possible to define exactly at what times of the year it is more convenient to attend conferences, there are certain guidelines to take into consideration. A good criterion is to be looking at the market, to determine which conferences are being attended by the people with whom you want to interact. Another parameter is to choose date ranges in which several events, or a large conference and several side events, are happening simultaneously in the same place. This way it is possible to maximize the resources involved in attending an event and thus make it more profitable in the eyes of oneself and, especially, the partners.

§28.02 WHERE TO ATTEND EVENTS?

The place where different events occur is clearly relevant from various perspectives. The geographic area in which the city of the respective event or conference is located should be considered in light of the areas of influence that the office in which the practitioner works has, or seeks to have. In other words, although an event in Sofia, Romania, may sound very interesting, it does not make much sense to attend from an office in Bogotá, whose client portfolio is mostly Latin American. On the other hand, logistical considerations are also very important when choosing events. It does not seem a good idea, for example, to undertake a trip of more than forty-eight hours to a city, with three stopovers, to attend an event that does not last more than one morning.

Finally on this issue, the importance that a given city has for international arbitration, whether as a venue or from the point of view of the practitioners who practice there, can also make it attractive to attend events there.[2] We must not forget that an event has value not only in itself but also in terms of the different activities that can be developed around it. We will come back to this idea later.

§28.03 HOW TO ATTEND EVENTS?

This question relates to two very relevant practical topics: the financing for attending an event and preparation prior to the event. In terms of budgeting, it is undeniable that

1. *12 reasons you should attend conferences* (May 28, 2020), https://www.takeflyte.com/reasons-to-attend-conferences#.
2. For example, the ICC points out the relevance of Miami in its promotional material related to the *ICC Miami Conference on International Arbitration* (May 28, 2020), https://iccwbo.org/media-wall/news-speeches/12-highlights-to-get-geared-up-for-icc-miami-conference/.

office support for its associates is important. However, it is the job of young practitioners to explain—or actually *persuade*—the partners of the benefits that their involvement in a given event will bring to their office. Usually a coherent and responsible plan, in line with the office's arbitration practice, will allow young practitioners to open doors in this regard. Additionally, office funding is not the only option for attending an event. Several conferences have scholarships for young lawyers that can be attractive, and ultimately a practitioner's direct investment can have positive externalities, such as demonstrating the determination and interest that exists for developing one's own career internally in the office.

When it comes to preparing for an event, it is a task that young practitioners cannot leave to chance. Attending a conference without preparation may even resemble simply not attending. For these purposes, it is very relevant to review the list of attendees for the event (do not be afraid to ask for it if it has not been published) and previously contact practitioners with whom it may be useful to meet or get to know. We must always remember that others attending an event are probably doing the same thing; therefore these practitioners will not be surprised or upset if a stranger sends them an email. In the same way, it is also useful to contact law firms in the city of the event to schedule meetings, even if those attorneys would not attend the event in question. Time is money, and the more you can take advantage of the trip, the better. To this end, my suggestion is the young associate informs its respective office that they will participate in a particular event and obtain feedback and data from other lawyers who work in it. This announcement also produces useful internal publicity. Finally, it is also convenient to have promotional material available from the office where you work (even if it is in digital format), and most importantly, never but never forget to carry business cards!

§28.04 WHY ATTEND EVENTS?

Saving the best for last, probably we get to the most important question of all: what reasons or motives justify attending an international arbitration event?

The truth is there are multiple reasons to attend an event. In the legal industry, there is a number of general benefits that can be obtained from events, as well as specific profits and returns that certain events provide within specific areas of the legal practice. For example, in the world of Intellectual Property, the annual conference of the International Trademark Association (INTA) is massive and attracts the attention of the entire industry. In this regard, a survey was recently conducted with respect to this specific conference. Ninety-five percent of respondents said it was "very likely" that during the conference they would have meetings with known clients or contacts. Eighty-one percent indicated that it was "very likely" that they would have meetings with potential clients or contacts at the conference. Finally, 87% stated that it was "very likely" that they would attend receptions and social gatherings organized by law firms and companies.[3] Likewise, the benefits commonly reported in different publications are related to "networking":[4] with the possibility of having access to experts in the fields covered by the respective conference;[5] acquiring knowledge about the latest technological advances in the subject matter of the event;[6] and just having a good time.[7]

In this sense, the events offered in the international arbitration industry also share the abovementioned benefits, although with certain peculiarities. First, in the conferences of this practice, the attorney-client relationship is much scarcer. With a few exceptions,[8] seeking clients at an international arbitration event could even be a mistake. The participation of in-house counsel in these instances is not only infrequent but also when they attend, they have leading roles such as panelists, making it difficult for young associates to reach them. Hence, the attraction of clients might happen in an indirect way due to the visibility that law firms gain by participating in events.

Second, on the contrary, international arbitration events are a great opportunity for lawyers to meet with different service providers and actors who, although not necessarily lawyers, play an essential role in arbitration proceedings. I am referring to court reporters, stenographers, and especially experts. It is very frequent to see the participation of experts belonging to different industries in international arbitration conferences. In these cases, it is they who are selling their services, and associates can return home with interesting information from professionals who can be extremely useful for the presentation of their cases, for example drafting damages reports or the like.

Third, international arbitration conferences can also be tremendously useful instances for acquiring knowledge and keeping abreast of the latest industry trends and practices. We must remember that despite being largely globalized, the international arbitration community is still relatively small. This small community helps the constant participation of the big players in different conferences, providing important learning opportunities.

Finally, and without attempting to make an exhaustive list (surely to more experienced practitioners, other advantages not mentioned here may come to mind), in general, international arbitration events summon diverse practitioners from different generations. Thus, in the same conference, the litigators and arbitrators leading the industry today coexist with young associates who will probably "take the baton" tomorrow. It presents a unique opportunity because it allows beginning practitioners to

3. Michael Loney, *Survey: the truth about conferences* (May 28, 2020), http://www.managingip.com/Article/3719378/Survey-The-truth-about-conferences.html.
4. *So … why do you attend the IBA Conference?* (May 28, 2020), https://www.tamimi.com/law-update-articles/so-why-do-you-attend-the-iba-conference/.
5. Lisa Pansini, *5 benefits of attending legal conferences* (May 28, 2020), https://www.rocketmatter.com/general/5-benefits-attending-legal-conference-infographic/.
6. *5 reasons why every attorney should attend legal conferences* (May 28, 2020), https://www.google.com/amp/s/www.practicepanther.com/blog/top-five-reasons-every-attorney-attend-legal-conferences/.
7. Michael Loney, *Survey: the truth about conferences* (May 28, 2020), https://www.takeflyte.com/reasons-to-attend-conferences#.
8. Such as the conferences organized by the *Corporate Counsel International Arbitration Group*.

develop long-term relationships with their *peers*. In my experience, the search to shine in front of a consolidated lawyer in an event is often quite difficult, and sometimes even useless, because the young and experienced in all sorts of things tend not to share the same objectives or interests. On the contrary, the confluence of young people from different places and backgrounds, but with similar objectives, allows associates to relate to each other and build networks. These networks will be useful to them not only today but also in the future and will also forge friendships that endure over time.

After having tried to explain the main guidelines to be able to navigate the world of events with some success, I would like to close this contribution with a reminder to young associates and practitioners of international arbitration. At the end of the day, the most relevant thing when attending a conference or similar event is to know beforehand what are the objectives you want to achieve with your participation in the short, medium, and long term. In order to try to implement that plan, be yourself and be the one who molds the event to your needs. With time, patience, and motivation, everyone will know exactly when, where, how, and why to participate in an international arbitration event.

CHAPTER 29

COVID-19 Wreaking Havoc at My Doorstep

Rachel Ong

This is my war story about how a global health pandemic upended my experience in planning Columbia Arbitration Day 2020 (CAD). CAD is Columbia Law School's annual conference on international arbitration. As the University's flagship event and indeed a premier arbitration conference, it has successfully brought together scholars, practitioners and students across various jurisdictions to engage in spirited discussions about challenges facing the international arbitration community. As of September 2019, this year did not seem any different and the planning committee had high hopes for the conference—in fact, we even decided to cover more ground by increasing the number of panel discussions.

As one of the cochairs, I was tasked with putting together a panel of speakers to discuss dispute resolution arising out of the One Belt One Road (OBOR) initiative. Naturally, practitioners in Hong Kong and China, who were familiar with the jurisdiction, were prime candidates for this discussion. By the middle of January 2020, we had secured our speakers. I managed to secure the attendance of a few speakers from China—a partner in Beijing who used to serve as deputy director of the China International Economic and Trade Arbitration Commission (CIETAC) prior to private practice, and another who served as a judge in China's International Commercial Court, among others. In Hong Kong, I managed to secure a speaker who used to serve as the Secretary-General of a major arbitral institution and currently works as an independent arbitrator and is a member of the ICC Belt and Road Initiative Commission. In New York, we secured the attendance of a law professor specializing in CIS jurisdictions who could provide a unique perspective, and, in London, we secured the attendance of the moderator who had participated in multiple panel discussions on the One Belt and Road initiative. At this point, the prospects seemed promising and optimistic. Alas, it was all about to go downhill from there.

Sometime in early January, I had heard news reports of a mysterious novel strain of coronavirus emanating from the city of Wuhan and the greater Hubei province in

China which had already reached the shores of Hong Kong, Taiwan and Singapore. Like many others at that time, I did not think that it would have a significant impact in the US, much less on a university conference, and I believed this virus was geographically limited. About a week later, I received news that the Chinese government had locked down the Hubei province such that nobody could enter or leave. Airports, trains and roads were shut down and heavily policed to enforce the lockdown. Such draconian measures attract equal measures of praise and criticism, but I still did not think that the outbreak would impact CAD since my speakers were based in the relatively unscathed capital of Beijing. Governments around the world were chartering flights to airlift their citizens out of the locked-down city of Wuhan. Less than ten days later, the Trump administration announced on January 31, 2020, that foreigners who had been in mainland China (excluding Hong Kong and Macau) for the past fourteen days would not be allowed into the US. This ban dealt a devastating blow to the panel as half of our speakers would not be allowed to enter the US.

The affected speakers themselves were unsure of whether and when the travel ban would be lifted. For the sake of planning, I was in a dilemma as to whether it was difficult to determine whether the ban would be lifted by the end of February such that all three speakers could participate in CAD or if I should start looking for speakers outside of China. If we started looking for speakers outside of China and the travel ban got lifted before CAD, we could potentially have a panel of eight to nine speakers. As the days went on, it became clear that the COVID-19 was becoming more and more widespread with various cities across China shutting down and the workforce working from home. Other nearby countries such as Singapore and Hong Kong were stepping up measures and public panic was sweeping through these countries. It became apparent that the hope of a travel ban lift looked more idealistic than realistic.

In early February, the planning committee had to decide whether we should look for speakers who were based outside of China and who were likewise able to discuss this topic, or choose to abandon this panel completely. If we chose the first option, were we going to attach a deadline to this search? Would it be prudent to continue inviting speakers from Asia in the light of the ban? If we could not fill the panel by the deadline, were we going to reshuffle our remaining three speakers onto the other panels? If so, then they would need time to prepare to discuss another topic. These were considerations that crossed my mind.

It was decided that we would no longer hope on a lift of the travel ban, and I would start looking for speakers based outside of China who were likewise able to discuss this topic. I gave myself a deadline of mid-February and all timelines were expedited from then. While speakers would usually have two weeks to respond before we sent a polite chaser email, potential speakers now only had two days to respond. During these two weeks, we received a handful of rejections for various reasons but we also managed to secure the attendance of two speakers who were based in New York. By mid-February, the equilibrium was restored on the OBOR panel and CAD was firming up. LinkedIn flyers of respective panels were advertised, the brochure was being designed, our confirmed CAD schedule was being printed, tickets were selling, lunch and evening reception menus were being confirmed.

This calm was, however, short-lived and COVID-19 was in the meantime ravaging through Asia and Europe. By this time, several major international arbitration events were postponed and law firms were issuing advisories against nonessential travel. A week before CAD, my Hong Kong-based speaker wrote to inquire if there were any concerns by the University regarding her attendance at CAD as she wanted to be sensitive to the sentiments of attendees toward a speaker coming from a COVID-19 affected region. At this time, some of my other colleagues in the planning committee were getting inquiries from the Europe-based speakers on their respective panels as to whether CAD was still happening while others were receiving notice from speakers, who after weighing the pros and cons of traveling decided they would not attend CAD. At this time, the University which was aware of the upcoming CAD did not voice any concerns about the event and we took that to mean that CAD would proceed as planned. The planning committee proceeded to confirm the event by email with all the involved speakers. Throughout the week, there was a considerable amount of movement and reshuffling within almost all the remaining five panels, but we had already foreseen this and were therefore mentally prepared that the configuration of panels would inevitably change. The week of CAD was also a busy one as the Columbia International Arbitration Association would be advertising CAD in school. We managed to get a little table at the lobby of the Law School, and we presented our confirmed CAD schedule which included all the confirmed speakers, and the Columbia International Arbitration Association's board members were taking turns to man the table and advertise CAD to the student body.

On the morning of March 3 (three days before the event), the Dean of Student Services verbally informed the organizers that my Hong Kong-based speaker would not be allowed to speak inside campus, let alone attend. Apparently, it was communicated to us that anyone arriving from China (including Hong Kong), South Korea and Italy would not be allowed inside campus. I immediately wrote to the Dean of Student Services to request a meeting, only to receive a reply stating that her earliest available slot was Thursday, a day before CAD. Given that the speaker in question was about to board a twenty-hour flight in less than twenty-four hours, I felt that it was only fair to share the latest development with her. Given the patent uncertainty at that moment, we agreed that it would not be sensible to travel such a substantial distance all the way to New York just to be barred from entering the campus. I can only remain grateful that she was so understanding and gracious under those circumstances. I was, however, not ready to exclude her participation completely as she had invaluable insight on the topic and her exclusion would have disrupted the agreed flow of the discussion. The next option was to skype her into the discussion. However, one disappointment led to another, and I was informed by the IT team that there would not be an available venue with the appropriate equipment to support videoconferencing.

I called the remaining speakers the next morning to explain the development and seek their opinion on whether they were confident of carrying the discussion on their own. However, it was almost unanimous that the panel discussion was severely handicapped without our Hong Kong-based speaker's participation. It also came to light that another New York-based speaker had just returned from Singapore that same morning and was met with a new firm policy that he should stay home, which also meant that he would not be able to attend CAD. This latest development dealt a death blow to the panel. It was not possible for the panel discussion to carry on with only three speakers, and likewise unfeasible to secure the attendance of replacement speakers two days before CAD. Eventually, the painful decision was made to pull the plug on this panel.

Up until today, I am sure that questions surrounding dispute resolution arising out of OBOR remain an exciting topic worth discussing. While economists have welcomed the OBOR initiative as a steady step toward growth in world trade and political scientists viewing it as a sturdy anchor against anti-globalization sentiment, members of the legal profession are in a more pensive mood because they are thinking about the capacity of the law at all levels—national, transnational and international—to facilitate the resolution of commercial disputes between enterprises that may arise in the course of the implementation of the OBOR initiative. What dispute resolution options do contracting parties have when their cross-border transactions turn sour? And which of these options best guarantee that the winning party gets his money back?

It is indeed ironic that the reason behind the last-minute changes to the OBOR panel has made this discussion even more relevant. The COVID-19 has seen a new term being coined—"Health Silk Road"—which is an extension of the One Belt and Road trade-and-infrastructure initiative. It has been widely reported that China has been extending medical aid to multiple European cities, including Italy, Spain, France, Bulgaria and Slovenia. With the intertwining of the global economy and further cooperation with China by an increasing number of countries, the OBOR takes on an enlarged dimension and dispute resolution features all the more prominently.

CHAPTER 30

Dealing with Difficult Conversations: How to Work at a Firm, Raise a Family and Not Die Trying

Daniel Cuentas

Sometimes your personal and work life move at different frequencies. It is common for family or personal matters to interfere or even collide with work responsibilities. In order to solve this issue, you may need to resort to difficult conversations.

Perhaps your personal expenses have increased, and you need a raise. Maybe you need more time to focus on additional projects, and you require a change in your work conditions or even a new job. Possibly you need personal leave or a sabbatical. These situations show daily examples that cause you to have a difficult conversation.

In my case, after working in an arbitral institution for a long time, my professional life needed a change. After a round of negotiations, my incorporation to a law firm was imminent. Thereon, I gave my resignation letter to the arbitration center. I knew it would have an impact on the workload assigned to my colleagues, and I would no longer be part of their future plans. At that same time, my personal life was going through some radical changes. I was getting married and had just discovered that I would be a father.

After having the difficult conversation about quitting a job where I was comfortable, I had to ask the partner of the firm in which I was incorporating for some time to focus on my new family and civil status. Naturally, it was hard to tell the senior partner that his most recent associate had plans that may temporarily keep him from his desk. I had just incorporated into the firm! What would they think about my commitment to work, my attention levels, and my productivity? These questions came to mind immediately. I thought that revealing these personal matters would make him regret hiring me. Surely the leader of a law firm expects his associates—especially the new ones—to turn into real terminators or hounds ready for hunting. At least, it would be my expectation as the leader.

As you can imagine, it was necessary to have these conversations with my new employer. When there comes time to have difficult conversations, it comes with many doubts about what the person will think and what you think about yourself. It is what Douglas Stone and Bruce Patton call *Feelings Conversation* and *Identity Conversation*.[1]

§30.01 HOW TO DEAL WITH A DIFFICULT CONVERSATION?

What makes a conversation turn difficult is the fear that the result may not be as expected or even worse than expected. In other words, a difficult conversation is one where you cannot predict the consequences with certainty, and you put your expectations about the result or even the relationship with the other person at risk.

A difficult conversation has two very clear ways of approaching it: avoiding it or dealing with it. Avoiding a difficult conversation can sometimes be tempting. At first glance, it can be a practical way to save you some trouble. However, from my point of view, this option leaves the person with the never-ending feeling of *what if*.

On the other hand, a more difficult way but perhaps more satisfactory way—if you know how to address it—is dealing with the conversation.

From my experience, there are at least five key points to consider in order to deal with a difficult conversation successfully. The following five hints may help.

[A] You Already Have the "No"

It could be that you have a dilemma as to whether or not to deal with a complicated conversation. Perhaps you want a raise yet think it is not a good time to request one. Maybe it will occur on its own later. Perhaps it is not the right time for the company to pay attention to matters that are urgent for you. However, in all these situations, avoiding the conversation will only leave you in the same position as if you had gotten a "no" for an answer.

Objectively, the worst thing that can happen to you is that you indeed get a "no." In this case, you will be in almost the same situation you were before you started the conversation. On the other hand, if you deal with the conversation and know how to deliver your message, things can go perfectly well. So you can decide to stick with a "no" that you already have, or you can plan your conversation to try and get the results you want. It seems to me that having the conversation will always bring more benefits than avoiding it.

It is normal to think that if you get a "no" for an answer, the other person will have a bad perception of you. Following the previous example, your boss will think you are not happy with the salary you earn, or you are not committed to the company's interests. It all depends on how the situation is presented and how to avoid creating these perceptions that you are afraid of causing.

1. Douglas Stone, Bruce Patton and Sheila Heen. *Difficult conversations: How to discuss what matters most* (Penguin Books, 2000).

[B] Do Not Improvise, Unless It Is Absolutely Necessary

No lawyer will think about going to an audience of opening or closing statements without carefully preparing what to say. The same occurs when dealing with a difficult conversation.

Difficult conversations, as paradoxical as it may seem, start a lot earlier than when you start to speak. First, the difficult conversation takes place on the inner side, when you imagine what you will say and when you imagine what will happen when you say it. For this reason, you have to think very well what ideas you want to communicate and avoid going in circles. It does not mean you have to write a script and act as if it was a theater play. It means clearly stating what the main ideas for your conversation are and what goals you want to achieve.

Like every rule, there is an exception. We cannot always predict the course of a conversation or event, and about this matter, the theory of probability explains that in every situation there are at least four scenarios: what you know can happen, what others know will happen, what everybody (including you) knows, and what no one knows, the uncertain. This last scenario, which represents 25% of any situation, is what philosophers call destiny or luck. Only when you are in this last scenario, where the conversation has gone somewhere no one could predict, are you allowed to improvise. However, when improvising, always take into consideration the goals you previously set.

[C] Keep It Real

Sometimes when preparing for a difficult conversation, we can fall in argumentative fallacies, or we may bring information to the table that we cannot necessarily prove, or even worse, false information. For example, when asking for a raise, you could be tempted to say that lawyers in other companies or in other firms earn a higher salary than you when you cannot prove this information and/or do not have specific data about it. In the same situation, in order to get that raise, you may feel tempted to cover the truth about the reasons why you are asking for such raise, creating stories that may make your argument sound more "dramatic."

If the other person with whom you are having this difficult conversation is your boss or partner, it means this person probably has more seniority or experience than you. It may not be very strategic to address him or her with information that you cannot prove or have not verified. If this person finds out that the information you are using to support the reasons for your raise is not certain or false, then your request will lose credibility. All your effort would have been in vain. It is even worse to lie to give strength to your request for a raise because the consequences of a detected lie lead to an immediate loss of trust.

A similar situation may occur in the scenario of quitting a job. Perhaps you want to avoid confrontation and not reveal the true reasons on why you are leaving. In some cases where your former employer does not know the reasons you quit, he or she may imagine what the motivations were, and these motivations can sometimes give him or her the wrong idea about you. While being honest, it can give the boss the opportunity to take action, so valuable assets do not feel the need to leave their jobs.

In any case, being honest with the reasons that motivate your decision to ask for a raise, quit a job or any other circumstance is a useful tool because it avoids the other person making the wrong conclusions about you and your motivations. Also, honesty in a difficult conversation is well appreciated when you know how to address the topic with common sense and respect. Therefore, it is necessary to develop this skill for the conversation not to turn uncomfortable.

[D] Empathy and Timing

Empathy is a very important skill because it implies putting yourself in the other person's shoes. Even though you will never get to know everything the other person thinks or feels in regards to a specific matter, you can certainly foresee some scenarios.

In this sense, being empathic involves asking yourself the following question before or during a difficult conversation: What would I do if things were reversed? This type of question may seem obvious, but it can help foresee some scenarios and avoid taking the conversation to a dead-end street.

On the other hand, timing is a key element that can go together with empathy in some cases. The following situations may show a complete lack of good sense: letting your boss know that you are quitting when he has just given you an important task or a promotion, asking for a raise when strategic clients have just left the firm, or even worse, pretending to start a difficult conversation when the other person has just finished having a very stressful meeting about a different matter. Without considering your motivations, your conversation will most likely not be successful and may also create a negative perception about you.

From my experience, good opportunities to have a difficult conversation are at the beginning of the day or at the end of the day. At any of those times, people tend to be more willing to listen and exchange ideas.

[E] Be Ready to Get a "No"

As it was mentioned, a conversation may not necessarily end favorably for you. It is possible that the raise you requested is denied or that the personal leave is not granted. In other words, getting a negative answer or an answer that does not fulfill your expectations is a perfectly possible scenario. Therefore, it cannot be ignored.

During negotiations—without a doubt, these are also difficult conversations—the term BATNA *(Best Alternative to a Negotiated Agreement)* is commonly used which is basically Plan B or the backup plan. The need to have a Plan B is that, sometimes, even though you have taken the risk of having a difficult conversation, preparing your best arguments, being honest and empathic, and choosing the best time to deal with this conversation, it is not possible to obtain your expected result. In that case, it will be important to know what are your options for the situation not to produce more anxiety than needed.

Thus, starting a difficult conversation must include the "No" as a possible scenario. If this fear is finally confirmed, we can consider a Plan B that you created or we can simply address the issue on a future conversation which will probably be more uncomfortable and will require new preparation, according to the guidelines previously stated.

§30.02 CONCLUSION

A difficult conversation can take place at any level, and it turns more difficult if the other person has a higher position than you in the company's hierarchy. In any given circumstance, a difficult conversation has two possible scenarios: avoiding it or dealing with it. In this short chapter, we have summarized why dealing with it is better than avoiding it and what are the techniques that can contribute to deal with a difficult conversation in a successful way. To summarize, if you have decided to deal with a difficult conversation without improvising while telling the truth in a timely and emphatic way and assuming that you could still get a negative response, you are likely to deal with it and eventually get a positive result.

In my case, the story I started telling had a happy ending. I was able to quit my previous job on very good terms. I was able to talk to my new boss about letting me have the time I needed to get married and to prepare for the birth of my child. Currently, I am still an associate of the law firm that accepted me in the middle of these changes, and I can keep the work balance with my new family. Naturally, none of these results would have been possible if my choice had been to avoid difficult conversations, or if I had dealt with it without considering the five key aspects mentioned in this chapter.

CHAPTER 31

How to Create and Develop Your Personal Brand in International Arbitration: From Pawn to Bishop

José Ignacio García Cueto[*]

§31.01 INTRODUCTION: DEFINITION, CHARACTERISTICS, AND IMPORTANCE OF BUILDING YOUR OWN BRAND

> It is not enough to be good. In order to be found, you have to be findable.[1]
>
> *Dr. Austin Kleon*

The *curriculum vitae* has died. The personal brand is the new *curriculum vitae*. It has multiple features.

It is *unique*. It identifies and differentiates us from the rest. It allows a lawyer to shine in a homogeneous and competitive environment. It is something that one develops and will accompany him throughout his professional career like his shadow. It will define the perception that most people have of us in the market.

It *evolves*. The personal brand is evolving over time, so the development strategy must adapt to the lawyer's profile.

It is *fragile*. It takes years to build a personal brand but seconds to destroy it.

It is *complex*. The level of competitiveness and specialization in our profession is increasing, which means that having your own brand is increasingly difficult.

It is *complementary*. Our own personal brand is compatible with the brand of the place where we work. Both brands can be developed at the same time. However,

---

* The opinions expressed in this chapter do not represent the opinions of the firm in any way but are the opinions and considerations solely attributable to the author. The author would like to thank Julieta Monteroni for her assistance in finding information and reviewing the chapter.

1. The quote is attributed to Dr. Austin Kleon.

having our own brand allows an internal projection within our workplace and external projection toward clients and colleagues.

It is *usually forgotten in a drawer*. Despite being such an important asset, personal brands are neglected in the legal sector. Lawyers focus more on their internal relationship with clients than on the external one with the market.

In conclusion, personal branding is one of the cornerstones of a modern lawyer's success. There is no single formula to create and develop it. Each person applies what he or she has considered most suitable. In this case, I share the methodology I applied to develop my own, for its simplicity. The process consists of two simple steps and is based on a method of economic analysis.

§31.02 HOW TO TURN FROM PAWN TO BISHOP? STEPS TO CREATE AND DEVELOP YOUR PERSONAL BRAND

The formation and development of a personal brand should be tackled like any other business decision. When doing business, we focus on selling a product. A personal brand allows arbitration practitioners to sell themselves. The formation and development of the brand should follow a strategic business vision; therefore, the lawyer must analyze the feasibility and strategy to be implemented through a 'SWOT' analysis of Strengths, Weaknesses, Opportunities, and Threats, of oneself and of the market in which he operates. The purpose of the SWOT analysis is to determine the competitive advantages and disadvantages of the lawyer's profile and the relevant market through an objective analysis. This analysis decides the optimal strategy for the formation and development of the personal brand.

The SWOT analysis is divided into two: an internal analysis of the lawyer and an external analysis of the market. Strengths and weaknesses are part of the internal analysis, while opportunities and threats are part of the external analysis. The success of this analysis depends on how honest you are with yourself in the internal analysis and the amount of knowledge you have about the market in which you operate.

[A] The Internal Analysis: What Is Your Brand?

The internal analysis must start from a premise: honesty and objectivity about what strengths and weaknesses the lawyer under analysis has. A good starting point may be to answer the following two questions: (1) Why me? and (2) What do I need to improve with respect to my competence?

[1] Strengths: Why Me? What Can You Offer That Distinguishes You, or How Can You Improve to Offer It?

It is essential to identify what your competitive advantages are. What you can offer or contribute is what differentiates you or makes you more interesting than your colleagues in the field. Some parameters that a lawyer should take into account are: (1) the previous experience related to the matter; (2) the undergraduate and graduate degrees that you hold; (3) the expertise in an area of law or in a particular industry sector; (4) the languages you speak; (5) the availability and flexibility you have and the ease of communicating with colleagues and third parties; and (6) the price for your services versus the market price.

Once you know your advantages and contributions, you can define what you offer and start positioning yourself as a reference.

[2] Weaknesses: What Do You Not Have? In What Is Your Competition Better than You?

An honest analysis of the weaknesses must be done in order to know the competitive advantages/disadvantages.

Weaknesses are knowledge and skills we do not have or areas where others are better than us. In this exercise, there is typically a "fight of titans" between the lawyer's ego and reality. However, we must not forget that building a brand is a business decision, so feelings should have no place in the analysis. The variables to consider for this exercise are mostly the same as the strengths but "in reverse." It includes the lack of experience in the sector, the titles we have, the languages, etc. We may find weaknesses depending on which objectives we have chosen and the players of the targeted market.

Experience and expertise in the relevant market are fundamental. A new operator in the market with no experience and/or expertise is clearly at a disadvantage compared to the other operators. He or she will have to find a way to compensate for those shortcomings. However, having experience and/or expertise does not rule out weaknesses in the relevant market. For example, it may be the case that our competitors have more expertise. In this sense, the Gauss' bell principle applies. *We are as good or bad as our competitors.*

Other aspects that could be considered as weaknesses are: (1) our geographical location; (2) the lack of established personal brand in an already mature market, such as law; (3) a higher price than our competitors; or (4) a very small market in which we have no contacts.

[B] The External Analysis: Now That I Know I Am Worth It, How Do I Develop My Personal Brand?

Once the internal analysis is done, it is time to carry out an external analysis of opportunities and threats presented by the relevant market and thus know how to develop your personal brand.

[1] Opportunities: Identifying Your Market and Occasions for Growth

We must identify what our relevant market is and our prospective audience or pool. The development of a brand is typically aimed at being able to "sell" services to someone—in this case, legal services.

Knowing who your audience is and knowing why they may be interested in you can help to determine the content and the way you will communicate. On the other hand, if you do not identify your market and try to attract everyone, you might end up achieving the opposite: not attracting anyone.

You must first identify the legal and geographical area you want to enter or position yourself. Once defined, you must analyze the basic characteristics of the market: (1) who are the prospective customers; (2) who are your competitors; (3) what is the standard market price for services, etc. It will allow you to identify where the market opportunities are and optimize the chances that your brand is positioned correctly with the relevant audience.

Once you have the market and needs defined, expand your network. There are many ways to make new contacts: (1) request meetings; (2) publicize your ideas through publications or lectures; (3) participate in specialized social networks; (4) create or join specialized groups or associations; and (5) have a good relationship with your competition and/or other market operators. These interactions will give you more exposure to third parties and will help you create your personal brand through the opinion of third parties.

Nowadays, social networks or other media have special importance in this exercise as instruments to build a personal brand. We live in a digitalized world in which social networks and the media occupy an important part of our lives. Many employers conduct their job searches through the Internet. Colleagues are informed through digital platforms, and customers typically seek information about pressing issues, such as which attorney they will hire.

Being available and visible on the web is necessary, so people who want to meet or communicate with us can do it easily. This online availability will lead to new opportunities.

[2] Threats: What Threats Do the Market Present?

After defining our relevant market, we should aim at identifying the threats it could present, allowing us to avoid them completely or at least to mitigate their disruptive impact.

Typically, the biggest threats regarding the relevant market are: (1) price; (2) strong competition; (3) "commoditized" market in which the type of service does not require much experience or expertise; or (4) "hyper-populated" market.

[C] The SWOT Output

The previous exercise allows lawyers to think about the variables to optimize their personal brand and develop it. The exercise should be redone every two or three years since "everything flows, nothing remains." The lawyer's profile, the market and its operators evolve over time. The variables that will typically be (in one table or another) in the result are the following:

Internal Variables	*External Variables*
Strengths	*Opportunities*
- Experience in previous matters - Expertise in a particular market - Education level - Availability - Languages - Easy communication with third parties/colleagues - Competitive price	- New legal markets - Areas where there is a "natural barrier to entry" (e.g., technical knowledge) - Growing geographical areas - Geographical areas with little competition
Weaknesses	*Threats*
- Less experience or expertise than other competitors - Inconvenient geographic location - Absence of an established personal brand in a mature market	- Market competition and legal services increasingly being considered as a "commodity" - Price of competitors (quality/price) - Too many competitors

§31.03 CONCLUSION

Creating and constantly developing your personal brand should be a priority. Having a good brand is also not sufficient if the market does not know it or does not know how to find you. Therefore, creating and developing a brand requires us to consider our competitive advantage and to highlight that differentiation within the market. Some examples of exposure can be lecturing, writing articles, or participating in specialized groups. Our brand will grow or die depending on the decisions that each one adopts. To preserve it, it is essential to apply long-term and non-short-term strategies. Finally, the SWOT exercise must be performed at least once every three years as markets, competition, and operators change.

CHAPTER 32

Motherhood and International Arbitration

Diana Correa

"If I were a man." This scenario has been a recurring question during the last few years of my life. It circulates less frequently each time, but it returned to roam around my head in a very strong way when I was asked to write this chapter about motherhood and international arbitration. Now, the time has come to find catharsis.

I am not going to talk about the initial "if I were a man" that came with my first pregnancy when becoming a mother and building a career in international arbitration were all still new to me. It was a time when I criticized incessantly what an "easy" situation I thought men had. A man goes through no physical, psychological, or hormonal changes (my version of hormonal changes situate itself in a gray area between the physical and the psychological). He does not give birth, and right after it, he does not have to heal his body or take care of someone else's body who is completely dependent. He will not have to deal with never being able to sleep soundly again, where he is in a sort of light dream or waking state at least during the first days after the baby's birth. He is not connected in a strange and inexplicable way with this little person who has come to life. Because in reality, once the umbilical cord has been physically cut, it transforms into something stronger that defies science.

No. I will not speak about the "if I were a man" clause because, among other things, time has shown me that not everything I believed at that time is correct. And if it is, at least in part, men also live their own experiences with paternity and their careers in arbitration. It is a topic about which we should speak more often.

I will focus on the best version of "if I were a man," a more evolved, more cathartic version to which I have arrived today. "If I were a man," I would miss the wonder simply and plainly that I now will describe to you.

My name is Diana Correa. I am a jurist specialized in international law, arbitrator, legal counsel, university professor, and mother to three girls: Eva, who is 5 years old; Victoria, who is 3 years old; and Olivia, who is 1.5 years at the time I am writing this chapter. It seems like a lot of titles at the same time, irreconcilable for some people and difficult to manage for others. Well, it is my reality as it is of many other women. Although this road has not been easy, I can say that it is possible, and I will tell you how I have accomplished it.

§32.01 ME, A MOM? WHAT FOR? WHAT ABOUT MY CAREER? I AM THE BEST AUNT IN THE WORLD!

It was my point of view before becoming a mom, and I had many reasons for it. The world is overpopulated. I could adopt a dog. I can spend my money on myself. I can travel, have a night on the town, or spoil my nieces and nephews, whether biological or my friends' children. I get them all to call me "aunt" without really being their aunt. Above all, I am pursuing my career in international arbitration which I love so much.

This point of view lasted so long that I almost "missed the (biological) boat" for being a mom. I always thought motherhood would drastically sever my career. I thought I would have to choose between it (career) and them (children).[1]

To think about a balance between a family life with children and a professional life in international arbitration seemed impossible.[2]

1. "Even if minority women only faced the same obstacles as white women, they would still confront a number of daunting barriers to success ranging from disproportionate responsibility for child care (not to mention sole responsibility for childbirth), to exclusion from the 'old boys club,' to sexual harassment." David Wilkins, Diversity in Law Firms in the Legal Profession, Diversity and Inclusion Speaker Series, Inaugural Event, Center on Race, Law and Justice, February 21, 2018, p. 13, available at https://www.fordham.edu/download/downloads/id/10095/course_materials.pdf. *See also*: "The generally accepted issue is the choice many women face between partnership—on call 24/7 and under pressure to generate business—or starting a family. [...] For example, partners looking to build a team to work on a deal may assume a mother will not want a demanding client calling at 2am, or to travel frequently for work. These assumptions are not made about fathers. Firms seeking to improve diversity at the top need to make alterations to their processes, says Ms Bi. The problem is exacerbated by pressure to bring work into the firm, says Sarah Chilton, a partner at CM Murray, which specialises in partnership and employment law." Madison Darbyshire y Barney Thompson, Can You Be a Mother and a Senior Law Firm Partner?, Work and Carriers, Financial Times, April 16, 2019, p. 1, available at https://www.ft.com/content/8e70eb40-5a12-11e9-9dde-7aedca0a081a. *See also*: "Perceptions about motherhood and its compatibility with the life of a professional also seem to inhibit mobility. There seems to be an expectation that women will drop back or drop out after bearing children, and not be as professionally committed once they have family obligations. But-because they often unconsciously accept stereotypical views of themselves-many women lawyers do not ask for, or insist on, the treatment and assistance that would make them truly equal to men at all stages of professional development. Women lawyers themselves share that expectation and many simply assume that they will not be accepted as full professional colleagues after they have children. There is a perception on the part of women with children that they are not getting the same work opportunities they enjoyed B.C. (Before Children)." Cynthia Fuchs Epstein, Robert Sauté, Bonnie Oglensky y Martha Gever, Glass Ceilings and Open Doors: Women's Advancement in the Legal Profession, Fordham Law Review, Vol. 64, Issue 2, 1995, p. 298, available at https://ir.lawnet.fordham.edu/cgi/viewcontent.cgi?referer=https://www.google.com/&httpsredir=1&article=3203&context=flr.
2. In a survey done in the United States, with a sample of 222 law firms—without the motherhood mattered being discussed directly—certain pessimism was shown among women regarding their ability to have a balance in their life between their career and a personal (family) life. Apparently, this leads women to want to be promoted in their careers, but not to the point where they become partners: "Only 44 percent of women believe that they can have both, compared with 60 percent

Clearly, my decision had been made. "I want to have professional success, so I only have time for work." And this idea lasted until—as I have made public in many of my conferences—something happened to me. It is what I most feared at the time. I became a mom, and I say something happened to me because it was not in my plans. Because I became a mom, I am a self-proclaimed fortunate person by destiny, luck, alea, or whatever you want to call it.

Well, I was very wrong about the supposed irreconcilable nature of maternal and professional life, which had been my creed for years. I do not mean to say it has been easy. What I do admit, without any problem, is "if I were a man," I would not be narrating these experiences which though difficult are the best of my life.

§32.02 BUSTING MYTHS: MOTHERHOOD DOES NOT PREVENT YOU FROM HAVING A CAREER IN INTERNATIONAL ARBITRATION

Motherhood has made me incredibly strong, and I know the same has happened to a lot of other women. For this reason, one after the other, myths in relation to the loss of capacity to lead an arbitration career being a mother started falling as the best domino effect.[3]

[A] Myth about Loss of Work When You Are a Mom

When I became pregnant with my first daughter, I worked at a law firm dedicated to the practice of international arbitration. Although it took me a little over three months to tell my boss about my state for fear that I would get fired or overlooked for new cases, it never happened. Everything stayed the same. The trust was never lost. I continued working on the same cases and more as soon as they arrived at our offices.

Very quickly, my self-confidence was boosted which had been lost among the nausea, fear, and prejudice.

of men who do (versus 61 percent of women and 67 percent of men across the overall sample). Almost half of female attorneys call prioritizing work–life balance one of the greatest challenges to their professional success, on par with undermining peers. The difficulty of balancing work and family is the number-one reason that women do not want to make partner (61 percent), followed by inadequate benefits for the personal costs (54 percent) as the number two cited reason. Men cite the same top two reasons, but in reverse order, ranking the personal costs first (56 percent) and the difficulty of balance second (51 percent)." Marc Brodherson Laura McGee Mariana Pires dos Reis, Women in Law Firms, October 2017, pp. 5-6, available at https://www.mckinsey.com/~/media/mckinsey/featured%20insights/gender%20equality/women%20in%20law%20firms/women-in-law-firms-final-103017.ashx.

3. This general statement I am making is based on my own experience as well as in a few other working mothers I know. I am not claiming that it is this way in all industries and jobs. For instance, the related myth of losing jobs because of a pregnancy sadly seems to be a real issue to the point where the USA Congress has created a bill to protect pregnant women in the workplace. It is called the Pregnant Workers Fairness Act and it is available at https://www.congress.gov/bill/116th-congress/house-bill/2694?q=%7B%22search%22%3A%5B%22Pregnant+Workers+Fairness+Act%22%5D%7D&s=1&r=1.

[B] Myth about Loss of Interest in the Professional Life for a Mother

After the job I had at the law firm in which I was working when my first daughter was born, I not only changed countries, but I changed jobs and customs. Upon my return to Colombia—which was strictly due to personal and familial reasons—I not only found my job as an international law professor but also enjoyed the trust of my peers and arbitral institutions. In that way, I have been able to develop my career as an arbitrator and as legal counsel in international arbitrations, without the slightest effect from the fact that I am also a mother.

In fact, the execution of two important contracts in my professional life came along with considerably swollen bellies from my second and third pregnancies, respectively. Neither my pregnant state nor role as mother with three girls has made me lose credibility or professionalism before my colleagues or my clients.

[C] Myth about the Lack of Time for Moms to Work

This myth leads to think that motherhood is a full-time job which turns incompatible with any other job. This myth is also complemented by a historic element where for centuries a woman's role as a "homemaker" made her exclusively responsible for the children, while the man acted as "provider" for his family's material needs and assumed the role of "worker." However, ever since a few decades ago, these social roles started to be defied by thousands of working women[4] and by hundreds of male homemakers or simply by all of us fathers and mothers working in our professions without neglecting activities associated with our children.

My current situation fits within the contemporary reality of sharing the pleasures and difficulties of motherhood with the father of my daughters who—in turn, just as much as me—has had to reconcile the joys and stumbles of paternity with his job. The difference is that social questioning is done to women and not to men because of mere social stigmas that have no place in today's world. Today's world presents technology, specialty, efficiency, and equality which impacts the professional life of prepared and capable people, whether they be men or women.

Now, clearly time reduces because it is necessary to distribute it between more activities. Nonetheless, as activities multiply, proportionally so does work organization in a new, more efficient way. What is lost is idle time—a pause for coffee, procrastinating in front of your computer every morning while you get used to the rhythm of your work, and taking long pauses for lunch. It is because you know that this

4. Here, I would like to clarify what I mean by "working" women. I refer to mothers who work for a salary in consideration for a job that does not consist of taking care of children. It does not mean that I believe workhouse—which, among other things is not remunerated—is not a job. To this regard, a study in 2011 indicated that a mother who takes care of home should be paid USD 115,000 annually. "According to a new survey by Salary.com, a division of human resources consultant Kenexa, moms should be charging $115,000 per year for their work," Jenna Goudreau, Forbes, May 2, 2011, searchable in https://www.forbes.com/sites/jennagoudreau/2011/05/02/why-stay-at-home-moms-should-earn-a-115000-salary/#5220854b75f4.

idle time means you take time from your children and work until late hours of the night, or until early morning to comply with your job requirements.

It is completely false that mothers do not have the time to work. On the contrary, surveys show that mothers tend to be much more efficient than any other worker. It has even been suggested that the more children we have, the more productive we become.[5]

[D] Myth about Moms' Low Motivation to Work

Well, this myth has some truth to it, but it applies to both women and men. When children are born, at least for a considerable number of women, there is a joining bond which makes women want to spend more time with these little defenseless, dependent, and innocent creatures. They awake in you the noblest, pure, and charming feelings.

However, as weeks pass, one realizes that it is necessary to establish independence. Being a mother is not synonymous with a sort of slavery toward the child. It is necessary and satisfactory to return to professional life, to arbitrate, to write legal statements, and to participate in hearings because it also gives meaning to your professional and personal life, apart from being a source of income.

It is important that we do not confuse the motivation to keep working with the aspiration of climbing the arbitral ladder, wherever it may be. Some studies suggest that not all women (including mothers and non-mothers) working in the legal industry—inclusive of international arbitration practitioners—would have the professional aspiration to hold higher positions in their respective careers, such as partners at their law firms, directors at private companies, or in-house practitioner or professors of public entities.[6]

Apparently, and according to those studies, many of the women who are mothers, especially of little children, wish to spend more time with their children to enjoy their role as mothers. It is why they are not really interested in climbing in their respective careers, but rather keeping their intermediary positions without taking the risk to have a new role that demands more time and responsibility from them.[7] What is more, those who are not mothers, and even some men, also seem to enjoy having

5. "Mothers of at least two children are, on average, more productive than mothers of only one child, and mothers in general are more productive than childless women." Matthias Krapf, Heinrich W. Ursprung y Christian Zimmermann, Parenthood and Productivity of Highly Skilled Labor: Evidence from the Groves of Academe, Working Paper 2014-001A, Research Division Working Paper Series, Federal Reserve Bank of St. Louis, p. 15, available at https://s3.amazonaws.com/real.stlouisfed.org/wp/2014/2014-001.pdf.

6. Cynthia Fuchs Epstein, Robert Sauté, Bonnie Oglensky y Martha Gever, *supra*, 359 and on, available at https://ir.lawnet.fordham.edu/cgi/viewcontent.cgi?referer=https://www.google.com/&httpsredir=1&article=3203&context=flr.

7. "As expected, women associates were more likely to express negative feelings regarding partnership, citing the conflict between firm and family responsibilities. One female associate, who placed herself off-track, suggested that the work and life-style of partnership did not fit into her future: It was just that I didn't want to be involved in the bureaucracy of a large firm. I didn't want the stress. There's so much stress, pressure, and emphasis on hours. When you're a partner, there is stress in getting clients and doing huge deals. I just didn't want that kind of pressure on my life. I ... really enjoy being with family and friends and pursuing outside interests, and I just didn't want that to be 80% of my life. Even if I didn't have children, I would have wanted some

more time for leisure as well as personal and family time.[8] It is clear that in any case, it is not about a loss of interest in continuing to work. It is rather the honesty in not wishing to make extra efforts to climb in their careers because they prefer to use that time to spend with family. It responds to a legitimate need that some women experience when trying to balance their respective roles of being practitioners of international arbitration and being mothers.

If all of these beliefs can be placed around motherhood and international arbitration—most of them being myths—carrying out both activities requires organization and discipline to avoid these myths from becoming reality.

§32.03 DAY-TO-DAY OF INTERNATIONAL ARBITRATION PRACTICE AND MOTHERHOOD

The message that I want to leave with this chapter is clearly positive because it genuinely corresponds to what I feel and live. Nevertheless, and sadly, it does not mean that all international arbitration practitioners see pregnancy and children as something positive. It is why the above myths continue to disseminate. On the flip side of the coin, it means that there must be women who feel pressure and guilt for being mothers, and their career aspirations are frustrated.

In fact, it would seem that statistics do not help, and, in any case, for a woman (even more as a mother) to become a partner at a law firm is a truly epic mission. It even leads some people to propose a quota system to increase the number of women (and mothers) who can arrive at partner positions.[9]

It is for this reason that I want to finish this short chapter with my day-to-day routine in my double role as a mom and international arbitration practitioner: (1) I join the voices that have already begun to speak about the topic, (2) I convey words of encouragement to those women who doubt and think too much about the possibility of being a mother due to career fears, and (3) I try to persuade those professionals who see motherhood as an impediment for the career in international arbitration and prefer to hire men, women with older children, or women without interests of having children. I tell them that there is really nothing to fear.

With the exception of having bad moments, which is normal for any person, I can say that my day-to-day, when I am at home and not traveling, is really marvelous. I get organized in such a way that I can move forward with my job while I spend as much

sort of balance where it was more of a … nine to six, nine to seven sort of job, and I didn't have to work weekends, and I had my nights free, and I could just enjoy my life." *Ibid.*, p. 360.

8. *Ibid.*, p. 359.
9. Ms Chilton agrees. "The statistics are so awful that quotas are not a bad thing," she says. "Having quotas would encourage firms to make sure females achieved what they need to achieve to make partnership." Targets of 20%-25% are "depressing," adds Ms Chilton. "If you only have a target of 25 percent, you're never going to exceed it, and it is so out of kilter with the number of associates. Most leading firms have a roughly 50:50 gender split at associate level, or a slight female majority. That makes the partnership statistics all the more shocking." Madison Darbyshire y Barney Thompson, Can You Be a Mother and a Senior Law Firm Partner?, Work and Carriers, Financial Times, April 16, 2019, p. 1, available at https://www.ft.com/content/8e70eb40-5a12-11e9-9dde-7aedca0a081a.

time with my daughters as possible. However, all of it depends on how I manage my time. For this reason, learning and becoming an expert in this fine technique is vital to comply with responsibilities on all family and professional fronts.

Here is my advice.

[A] I Work from Home and Have Flexibility in the Distribution of My Work Hours

I know it is not for everyone, and many people with or without children cannot work from home. However, being independent, having one's own structure, and working with the team "in the cloud" without a schedule, without commuting, and without traffic congestions have been the key to being able to reconcile it all. When I refer to working from home, it does not mean that I take care of my daughters all the time. First, they go to their respective schools and kindergarten. My husband works from home, but I also rely on the help of a nanny. It simply means that the time I would spend commuting I dedicate to my daughters. Most of the times, I have breakfast with them, prepare them for school, carpool them after school, have dinner with them, and get them ready for bed.

The time I gain is not only from commuting. It is also the time to settle into the office, say hello and spend time with friends and colleagues, drink coffee, have lunch, answer the phone, etc. I do not deny that apart from answering the phone, I feel deprived of these nice moments at the office. But given the choice to find balance, I recognize the need to make sacrifices in this moment of my life to have more time with little girls. I am much happier and more appeased when I am looking after them than I am taking breaks, having coffee, and going to lunch with my colleagues every day.

Although it might sound exaggerated, it is incredible how much time is gained by not going into an office on a daily basis. It can range between one and three hours depending on the days. You can do your own calculations in your mind.

For those professionals who work in offices or law firms, I have heard a lot about many of the bigger structures allowing mothers to telework. Maybe not every day, but many. If they are in-house lawyers, teleworking is perhaps less easy, but it is my understanding from some colleagues' stories that they manage to get to work very early and sacrifice coffee breaks and lunch hour (they eat something fast) so they can go home earlier and share quality time with their children. University work also allows working mothers to manage their time a little better.

If we take law firms as an example, studies show that they make more efforts to achieve balance between family and professional lives. As an example, they promote work from home or reduce working hours.[10] Even though these achievements are not

10. "On the whole, part-time schedules and flex-time arrangements have been implemented to accommodate the needs of mothers. As we have seen, the formal policy at one firm explicitly limits part-time arrangements to women seeking a temporary solution to the conflicts between work and child care responsibilities. [...] Fax machines, cellular telephones, computer networks, and other forms of new communications technology are frequently cited as instruments that enable decentralized approaches to work. Attorneys seeking greater scheduling

completely significant, they must be strongly acknowledged, thanked, and encouraged so that firms continue to achieve a natural balance between personal and family life on the one side and professional life on the other side (Figure 32.1).[11]

Figure 32.1 What Law Firms and Companies Report to Offer

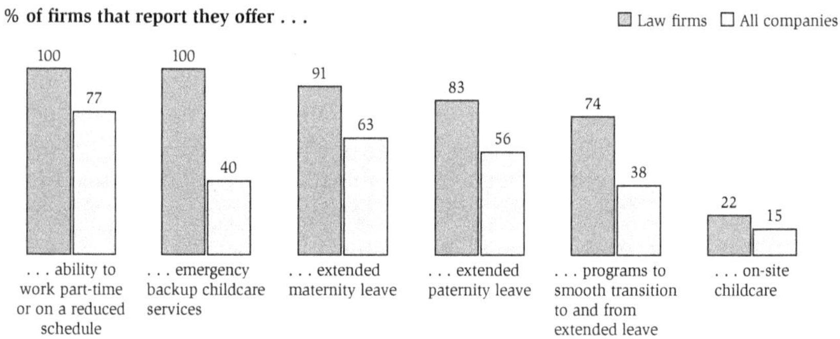

In any case, whatever the model each firm wants or can adopt, the truth is these women—including myself—turn on the computer after putting their children to bed. They do not watch Desperate Housewives (something I would like very much) but rather continue writing arbitral awards, memorials, or articles.

[B] I Work More Efficiently

As I know that every second wrongly spent means ten less seconds with my daughters, time is precious, I try not to waste it. It means that I have an almost military routine for work with mini-breaks for active rest, stretching, and resting my eyes. I try to get

flexibility might benefit from these developments. Surprisingly few of those interviewed, however, described taking full advantage of communications technology, although several acknowledged that firms should explore this solution to the work/home conflict. Indeed, a former associate at one of the firms in the sample recommended this solution as one way the firms could remove whatever 'glass ceiling' is imposed on working mothers by traditional work structures." Cynthia Fuchs Epstein, Robert Sauté, Bonnie Oglensky y Martha Gever, *supra*, pp. 409-410 and 412, available at https://ir.lawnet.fordham.edu/cgi/viewcontent.cgi?referer=https://www.google.com/&httpsredir=1&article=3203&context=flr.

11. "All the law firms surveyed offer the option of working part-time or on a reduced schedule (versus 77% across the overall sample). Most law firms allow telecommuting (versus 75% across the overall sample). Most law firms (91%) offer maternity leave that exceeds government requirements, and most (83%) offer paternity leave that also exceeds those requirements (versus 63% and 56% across the overall sample). All of the law firms surveyed provide emergency backup childcare services (versus 40% across the overall sample). But only 22% of law firms have on-site childcare, and none subsidize regular childcare (versus 15% and 18% of organizations across the overall sample)," Marc Brodherson Laura McGee Mariana Pires dos Reis, *supra*, p. 10, searchable at https://www.mckinsey.com/~/media/mckinsey/featured%20insights/gender%20equality/women%20in%20law%20firms/women-in-law-firms-final-103017.ashx.

directly to the point with different matters, and honestly, time and experience develop these abilities to optimize work to the maximum.

Whenever I am too tired or have low concentration, I see my daughters for ten minutes, or I organize papers I never want to see (particularly, invoices for preparing my finances) instead of procrastinating in the wide Internet world where one can lose oneself for hours. These short pauses take me again on a path to concentration. If the tiredness and lack of concentration continue, I try to take fifteen-minute naps, which are really effective.

[C] I Work Trying to Have a Healthier Life

Far from citing stereotypes or condemning any practice, who does not remember the long and sedentary nights of prefiling, prehearing, or hearing while ordering pizza or hamburgers or eating snacks all night as well as drinking lots of coffee and sodas? At some point in our lives, I believe many of us have experienced it. Although I have to admit, ever since sushi became fashionable it feels like one is eating healthier.

The phrase "sound mind in a sound body" is not *cliché*, and it is definitely true. I would even say it is the reverse "sound body in a sound mind," because it is necessary to have understood the importance of the body in the realization of everything, including professional aspirations. Although I have failed this premise many times, I do my best to integrate a correct healthy life to my day-to-day. It is definitely true that a healthy body works better than one that is ill and tired. Additionally, I must be well in order to meet my professional aspirations, as well as my family dreams. It implies many material things: to sleep and eat as well as possible without forgetting to practice a sport.

Sleeping is a pleasure for many, but in any case, it is a necessity. Some need to sleep a lot while others only a little. It depends on each person. In my case, I recognize that I sleep less than average, but my sleep hours are deep which is just what my body needs. Anecdotally, working a little during the night or early morning when being a mother (especially of small children) constitutes many benefits for all. Indeed, if you are working until late, and your children cry, you will be awake to console them and put them back to sleep without cutting your sleep cycle. You can return to work and let your husband sleep, something he will greatly appreciate. When it is your turn to sleep, it will be your husband who will console the children. In this way, your sleep hours are very effective and, above all, uninterrupted.

Eating is also a pleasure for many, and it is a necessity for everyone. Clearly, I am not in a legitimate position to give lessons at this level, but lately, I have understood the importance of eating well and healthy. It is why my only piece of advice is to consult with a specialized doctor who will help you adopt better-eating habits. I have recognized that being a mother made me change this aspect of my life in a positive way because you always want your children to eat as well as possible, and it reminds you that you should too.

In my opinion, to practice a sport is the best not only for the body and the mind but also for the spirit. It is a moment in which I finally meet with myself, and both arbitration and my daughters leave my mind. In effect, between twice and three times a week, I try to do some sport. I also practice short active pauses daily. Sports take time, but paradoxically, it is a great investment of your time because an active body works from two to three times faster than a tired and sedentary one. Again, being a mother of little girls has trained me physically, and I can say that my physical condition is even better than the one I had when I was not a mom and only worked in international arbitration. Now, I not only run after planes to not miss flights, but I also run behind my daughters to be present in their lives as well as preventing them from falling.

[D] I Work Happier

It is not that I was not happy, but being a mother has honestly turned me into a kinder, more sympathetic, and happier human being. I have always believed that happy people work better, and I am proof of it.

To stick all of my daughters' drawings on the wall in front of my desk; to use the colorful and original bookmarks that they make for me; and to find their little letters filled with hearts, stars, and unicorns on my desk—these small treasures turn into memories which draw a smile on my face even when I am facing current difficulties from my profession. To me, it is like sorting out the problems with an extra shield of family happiness. It makes me believe that everything is possible and worth it. I can think about my daughters and their future as well as endeavoring to achieve the best possible professional results.

[E] I Work with a Support Team

Everyone knows it, and it is truly not a myth. The practice of international arbitration is as exciting as demanding, and the lack of emergencies does not feature this area of the law. It is also well known and not a myth that children naturally demand a lot of time. In addition, there is no lack of unforeseen situations, such as falls or illnesses, or emergencies either. In order not to feel trapped in the middle of these two situations, and assuming that professional colleagues are always available as a Plan B at the working place, the best remedy is to have a support team.

My team is led by my own husband, a liberal and completely supportive man. He believes in my career and even encourages it, sometimes (many times), above his own. With him, I share the care of our daughters on equal terms. I also rely on my family nanny, and I have at least one more person who could potentially be ready to help me. Not to mention family support which for some people will be their own parents, parents-in-law, siblings, nieces, nephews, or even good neighbors. For me, these people are my dear nieces, who are also lawyers but always have a great willingness to help. Also, my fabulous friends from school, of whom the majority are also mothers, workers, and entrepreneurs at the highest levels are absolutely supportive.

[F] I Work Without Feeling Embarrassed about Saying I Am a Mother

Embarrassment or, at least, the sense of feeling "less professional" and "less competitive" for being a mother exists. It means feeling embarrassed for taking advantage of the options to extend the motherhood period, for working from home, or taking any other benefit that law firms or companies offer to its employees who are parents (men and women). It makes many people—both mothers and fathers—not want to use these benefits, or they feel bad for using them. Because of these feelings, they prefer to keep sacrificing their personal (family) and professional balance.[12]

Conquering the fear of facing the competitive world of arbitration, still dominated by older, male figures, I have learned that being pregnant and having children is nothing in which to be embarrassed.

I speak about my daughters and show photos of them. If I have the option of rescheduling a meeting due to family matters, I do it without lying or creating excuses. Also, being a mom does not prevent me from taking care of emergencies or continuing my professional day-to-day. In fact, I have responded to e-mails in delivery rooms. I have participated in hearings where my husband brought my baby after only a few weeks of being born, so I could feed her during the breaks. I have had team meetings with my baby in a carrier on my chest. I have also revised master's dissertations and read PhD thesis in my maternity leaves. I have organized and executed arbitration events being pregnant and very close to term. I have given a lecture with my oldest daughter coloring in silence in one of the room's desks next to my students.

In another sense—although I do not always manage to do it which is why having a supporting team is vital—I have taken one of my daughters on a Tuesday at 3 P.M. to her ballet class and the other to her taek won do class on a Friday at 2 P.M. I have taken the other one to physical therapy to stimulate her growth on a Monday at 11 A.M. I have also taken my daughters to kindergarten at 9 A.M., and I have taken them to the pediatrician at different times during the day.

None of it makes me less of a mom or less of a professional. It also does not make me a woman with superpowers. It only exemplifies a very courageous and organized woman, passionate for her family and professional life. I am only trying to be as present as possible as a mom without neglecting my profession at all.

[G] I Work and Believe in Education

Lastly, my professor soul has led me to educate my daughters from an early age on the values of hard work, effort, and love for what one does as well as the satisfaction of a job well done and money deservedly earned. They know that when mom is working, the study door (which is the room in my house that functions as an office) does not

12. "While most law firms offer flexible—work programs, many attorneys still fear that participating in these programs will damage their careers. More needs to be done to make these a viable option." Marc Brodherson Laura McGee Mariana Pires dos Reis, *supra*, available at https://www.mckinsey.com/~/media/mckinsey/featured%20insights/gender%20equality/women%20in%20law%20firms/women-in-law-firms-final-103017.ashx.

open. With time, they have invented all sorts of excuses to try to enter the place that is only reserved for mom. When they say, "Mom, we also have to work," they enter with coloring books and a box of colored pencils. Sometimes, I set up working tables for them next to mine, and each of us does their own work. Sometimes, the studio door remains closed.

§32.04 CONCLUSIONS

These are my most relevant experiences as to how I managed to reconcile my professional life in the practice of international arbitration with my family life as the mother of three little girls. It is not a magical formula, not a model, but it is what works for me.

In fact, I was having lunch with a colleague a few days ago (she is very famous in the international arbitration world), and I asked her what I am sometimes asked: "How did you manage to achieve it all?" to which she answered, "I see my children very little during the week, but I dedicate the weekends, almost exclusively, to them." It is completely valid. Every person finds his or her own formula[13] as is not wanting children and remaining unaffected in that life decision.

Out of everything said, it is important to remember that being a mother, as well as being a father, should not frustrate the dreams of international arbitration practitioners. It should also not continue to be perceived as something negative by other practitioners. The question for the international arbitration industry retaining legal services is as follows: Is it worth it to hire a woman and make her partner or manager? Is it worth it to understand the compatibility between her professional capacity and brilliance with her responsibilities as a mother? Or is it simply better to choose a man who can do the same "without" such responsibility? The answer to this question should be based on a fundamental premise consisting in the fact that family responsibilities belong to everyone, both men and women. In this up-and-coming generations, it will be unsustainable and archaic to think otherwise. It is why I clarify that it is worth hiring a woman as much as hiring a man, without the fact of having children being a concern whatsoever.

The companies and structures that survive will be those companies who see a man and a woman as equals in both their professional and family lives. Those adapted structures will make room to offer professional conditions for inclusion from conviction, in which diversity, gender equality, motherhood, and paternity are key elements in the equation for corporate success. In the legal world, this process has been slower than in other sectors. Maybe it is because the legal industry, especially

13. "Further, there are many different styles of mothering and variation in the use of surrogate care, as well as participation of fathers and other family members. Women also differ with regard to their ability to handle multiple roles that include motherhood, their relative interest in their various roles, and allocation of their priorities." Cynthia Fuchs Epstein, Robert Sauté, Bonnie Oglensky y Martha Gever, *supra*, pp. 409-410, 412, available at https://ir.lawnet.fordham.edu/cgi/viewcontent.cgi?referer=https://www.google.com/&httpsredir=1&article=3203&context=flr.

arbitration, was a world ruled exclusively by men for a long time.[14] However, it is important to remark on the evolution toward inclusion of women (mothers or not) in the arbitral world. It is real and each time greater. Hopefully soon, diversity, gender equality, and maternity/paternity will become normal to the professional arbitral market. There will no longer be a need to speak about it anymore.

14. It is also necessary to remember that women, mothers or not, have been plowing a long way in the world of arbitration for many decades. Let us not forget Jean McKelvey's words who would tell the story about her first arbitration. She entered a room in which there were only men, to which someone stated, "Oh, you're the secretary," and she said, "No, I'm the arbitrator," Jean McKelvey, Cornell University Memorial Statement, searchable at https://www.ilr.cornell.edu/about-ilr/founding-faculty/jean-mckelvey.

CHAPTER 33

What I Wish I Had Known Before Beginning a Career in Arbitration

Crina Baltag

I wish I had known that every dispute has its appropriate dispute resolution mechanism.

Reflecting on the beginning of my career in dispute resolution, the information available to both lawyers and users was scarce. Undoubtedly, there were some materials about dispute resolution mechanisms other than litigation and arbitration, but sixteen years ago,[1] few of us would have understood how mediation worked, how the disclosed information in the process was privileged and confidential,[2] or how courts could, in fact, sanction the party who was unreasonably refusing to participate in the process.[3] Users were not as aware as they are today. Previously in-house counsel was barely involved in the process and most often limited to gathering the evidence of the case.

Nowadays, when information is readily available to lawyers, as well as to users, it has become much easier to assess the suitability of a particular dispute resolution mechanism for a dispute at hand. Further, with the increased role of in-house counsel in case management,[4] lawyers and in-house counsel are in a better position to determine whether a suggested dispute resolution mechanism is the best alternative in the context of the specific business and of the underlying relationship.

1. Especially in an Eastern European country.
2. *See Unilever PLC v. Proctor and Gamble* [2000] 1 WLR 2436. But *see Brown v. Patel* [2007] EWHC 625 (Ch) and *Cattley and another v. Pollard* [2006] *EWHC 3130* (Ch).
3. *See Halsey v. Milton Keynes General NHS Trust* [2004] 1 WLR 3002.
4. *See* Ugo Draetta, *The Role of In-House Counsel in International Arbitration*, 75 *Arbitration* (2009) 470; Philippe Cavalieros, *In-House Counsel Costs and Other Internal Party Costs in International Commercial Arbitration*, 30(1) *Arbitration International* (2014) 201; Jean-Claude Najar, *A Pro Domo Pleading: Of In-House Counsel, and Their Necessary Participation in International Commercial Arbitration*, 25 *Journal of International Arbitration* (2008) 623.

A multitude of processes unfold before us: negotiation, adjudication,[5] early neutral evaluation,[6] mediation, arbitration, litigation, etc. They are all here to serve the dispute and users. Certainly, some dispute resolution mechanisms have distinct features that would be preferred to others for the dispute at hand. In general, the distinction is made between adjudicatory mechanisms—where a third party, be it a judge or arbitrator, is requested to decide the dispute—and non-adjudicatory mechanisms—where the parties are in full control and decide on the best solution to their dispute. Most certainly, adjudicatory mechanisms put an end to the dispute and prove more suitable for complex disputes. Further, entrusting the decision to a third party might advance the resolution of the dispute. At the same time, adjudicatory mechanisms would not provide the best outcome to both parties. Real interests of the parties are rarely uncovered in adjudicatory processes, as they are usually confined to what the applicable law provides for the specific legal relationship and are focused on positions.

By not addressing the real interests of the parties, it is generally considered that adjudicatory mechanisms fail to encourage the parties to maintain their business relationship and even tend to escalate the dispute, given their adversarial nature. Non-adjudicatory mechanisms, such as mediation and negotiation, are often regarded as providing for superior outcomes to the disputes between parties as the parties retain control of the process. By favoring the real interest of the parties, they encourage the parties to explore the best solutions that would satisfy their interests, without being confined to what the law provides. However, non-adjudicatory mechanisms cannot be employed without the consent of the parties in dispute.[7] Even when they are mandatory by law,[8] the effectiveness of these mechanisms is not possible if the parties are not truly engaged in the process.

The discussion is not without relevance when considering the role and duties of lawyers toward their clients in the context of the resolution of disputes. In their seminal work on transformation of disputes, Felstiner, Abel, and Sarat highlight that:

> Critics of professionals argue that they "create" at least some of the needs they satisfy ... Lawyers exercise considerable power over their clients. They maintain control over the course of litigation ... and discourage clients from seeking a second opinion or taking their business elsewhere ... There is evidence that lawyers often shape disputes to fit their own interests rather than those of their clients.[9]

---

5. *See* The Scheme for Construction Contracts (England and Wales) Regulations 1998 (SI 1998/649).
6. *See* UK Civil Procedure Rules and Direction, Rule 3.1(2)(m) and Civil Procedure Rules and Practice Direction—Pre-Action Conduct and Protocols, para. 1.10(c).
7. With the draft United Nations Convention on International Settlement Agreements Resulting from Mediation (also known as the Singapore Convention), the enforceability of mediated settlement agreements should no longer be seen as a disadvantage of mediation, https://www.uncitral.org/pdf/english/commissionsessions/51st-session/Annex_I.pdf (last visited, April 22, 2019).
8. *See* the position of the Court of Justice of the European Union on mandatory mediation in Case C-75/16, *LivioMenini, Maria Antonia Rampanelli v. Banco Popolare—Società Cooperativa*, Judgment of June 14, 2017.
9. William L. F. Felstiner, Richard L. Abel and Austin Sarat, *The Emergence and Transformation of Disputes: Naming, Blaming, Claiming ...*, 15 *Law and Society Review* (1980) 631, 646.

In face of this criticism, the relevance of a proper choice of a dispute resolution mechanism as a result of an exchange of information between lawyer and client is evident. Felstiner, Abel, and Sarat recognize that:

> Lawyers also produce transformations about which we may be more enthusiastic. They furnish information about choices and consequences unknown to clients; offer a forum for testing the reality of the client's perspective; help clients identify, explore, organize, and negotiate their problems; and give emotional and social support to clients who are unsure of themselves or their objectives.[10]

Further, lawyers also have an ethical obligation of presenting all these options to the client. For example, the 2018 Handbook of the England and Wales Solicitors Regulation Authority (SRA) lists for solicitors the following obligations: to uphold the rule of law and the proper administration of justice; to act with integrity; to act in the best interests of each client; to provide a proper standard of service to the clients; and to protect client money and assets.[11] The SRA Code of Conduct 2011 provides in Chapter 1 that a proper standard of service must be achieved and it:

> takes into account the individual needs and circumstances of each client. It includes providing clients with the information they need to make informed decisions about the services they need, how these will be delivered and how much they will cost.[12]

The following outcomes must be achieved:

> *O(1.12)*—clients are in a position to make informed decisions about the services they need, how their matter will be handled and the options available to them; and *O(1.13)*—clients receive the best possible information, both at the time of engagement and when appropriate as their matter progresses, about the likely overall cost of their matter (emphasis added).

In selecting the appropriate dispute resolution mechanism, Sander and Rozdeiczer suggest that lawyers and users respond to the following three questions: (1) What are my goals? This question is a way of advising clients to focus on their interests rather than on their positions; (2) Which process will capitalize on the best features of the dispute? As mentioned above, each dispute resolution mechanism comes with advantages and disadvantages which become more evident in the context of a specific dispute; (3) Which process will best overcome barriers to resolution? The authors

10. William L. F. Felstiner, Richard L. Abel and Austin Sarat, *supra*, p. 646. *See also*, Robert H. Mnookin and Lewis Kornhauser, *Bargaining in the Shadow of the Law: The Case of Divorce*, 88 *Yale Law Journal* (1979) 950, 985: "*Lawyers can provide the basic information about each spouse's bargaining endowment-the applicable legal norms and the probable outcome in court if the case is litigated. Indeed, as noted earlier, imprecision in the applicable legal standards increases one's need for legal advice. A rational client will want an accurate assessment of the possible costs of alternative modes of dispute settlement. Lawyers are also an important source of information about transaction costs, a major element of which will be legal fees.*"
11. *See* https://www.sra.org.uk/solicitors/handbook/code/content.page (last visited, April 22, 2019).
12. *See* https://www.sra.org.uk/solicitors/handbook/code/content.page (last visited, April 22, 2019).

mention that some disputes might disagree on the applicable law to the merits of the case, in which case, a judge or arbitral tribunal may be the preferred option.[13]

We are entering the age of Artificial Intelligence. With decisions to be made in the near future by using predictive tools, I trust my colleagues will be in a better position in assessing the best interests of their clients and in choosing the appropriate processes for the resolution of disputes.

13. Frank E.A. Sander and Lukasz Rozdeiczer, *Selecting an Appropriate Dispute Resolution Procedure: Detailed Analysis and Simplified Solution*, in Michael L. Moffitt and Robert C. Bordone (eds.), *The Handbook of Dispute Resolution* (Jossey-Bass, 2005), 386.

CHAPTER 34

Own Power and Derived Power

Alfredo Bullard

It's easy to run to others.

It's so hard to stand on one's own record.

The Fountainhead by *Ayn Rand*

§34.01 OWN POWER AND DERIVED POWER

Those professionals who have own power rely on their ability to do what needs to be done. They do what they believe and are consistent with that belief. They not only define what they have to do but also do it. Their conviction is the source of their behavior. They do not expect to gain power from others. They are the source of their own power.

In contrast, those professionals who own derived power make decisions based on what others think needs to be done. To move forward, they decide to do what others want them to do. According to the situation in which they find themselves, they borrow the conviction of others. In other words, they derive their power from others. When the one they follow loses power or stops deriving them, they also lose that power.

Many politicians are derived powers. They do not act based on what they believe but on what a group of voters wants them to do. It does not matter if they believe that giving certain regulations is bad. They will issue them as long as that lands them supporting votes. On the other hand, people with their own power support what they believe, even if it costs them not to be reelected.

Many people are derived powers in their work. They propose or do not necessarily do what is best for their function or duty, but what their bosses believe is best. They do not even raise the alternative. The decision being made by a superior (a firm partner telling an associate what to do) is no excuse not to make someone realize that he or she might be wrong.

Let us imagine that a lawyer has to decide what strategy a potential client should follow in a possible case. He or she listens to the facts raised by the client and comes to the conviction that the appropriate strategy includes requesting the termination of the contract for breach and damages. The conclusion is derived from his/her knowledge, experience, and convictions to determine what is good for the case.

But the client proposes a different strategy. The client wants to go beyond the nullity of the contract and the sought damages and to personally sue the other party's managers. He or she wants revenge from those persons who made certain decisions that hurt him or her.

The lawyer believes that suing the managers is not legally correct and will make his/her lose credibility in front of the arbitrators. His/her choice lies between what he or she thinks is appropriate or what his/her client thinks is appropriate. He or she knows that posing what he or she thinks puts his/her at risk of being pushed to the side by the client and replaced by another lawyer. If the lawyer has own power, he or she will defend the position. Derived power assumes the client's position without arguing to prevent the case from going elsewhere.

Those professionals who have own power act by their own conviction. They would tell the client that the proposed strategy is not the best. A derived power would change the way they act to derive power from the client, following not their conviction but of the client. We all want to derive power from our clients. It is sometimes difficult to give up that power. But to have your own power, sometimes you must.

Let us imagine now that a potential client calls the lawyer for a meeting to explain a case in order to make an offer for an arbitration representation. The client tells the lawyer that two other firms are also competing for the position.

The potential client does not have a bad case. Most of the claims have a very good basis. The rest is very debatable. But looking at the total amount under discussion, it is not clear that the costs of arbitrating the dispute are justified. The lawyer discovers it quickly and has the conviction that it is best to accept the settlement that was offered to the client. The dilemma is if he or she should tell the client to accept the settlement or if he or she keeps quiet and makes an offer to be hired.

The lawyer decides to share the true conviction. A few weeks later (and without having received a penny of fees), the potential client sends an email thanking him/her for the advice. It was because of that advice that the client decided to accept the settlement offer. The client thanks the lawyer for his/her honesty and clear advice. The lawyer lost a case but won the respect of someone. That respect can generate confidence to be sought in the future, but it is not what is really important. The important thing is the lawyer exercised his/her own power, even if it meant assuming a cost.

You are a young arbitrator, and it is your first case. You have been appointed by a prestigious law firm with many arbitrations. You have to issue the award. If the study stays happy with the award, they may reappoint you. You decide that your conviction should be the source of your power and not the transmission of power derived from new appointments. You remember what your conviction tells you, and you refuse to follow the convictions or wishes of the firm who appointed you.

It is difficult to rely on your own power because the path of derived power is more attractive and easier. Finally, the power is already there. All you have to do is take it. Instead, own power must be built. When you are young, your own power is seen as distant and unattainable, and derived power is right at your fingertips.

Building your own power is difficult. It involves sacrificing the short term to bet on the long. It implies frustration to see that others, perhaps with less merit, gain derived power quickly and climb more rapidly. To consolidate one's own power requires patience. It implies accepting the initial failure while being consistent with doing what one believes one has to do.

However, I do not want to be misunderstood. I am not saying that own-powered people always act correctly, and those professionals who derive their power from others always choose wrong. Own power can be misused. The leaders of criminal gangs usually have own power. Also, if a derived power follows the right people, he or she may act correctly.

Having own power does not necessarily have to do with correct behavior. It has to do with the conviction with which we act. It has to do with the engine of action and the path that we follow to grow and position ourselves in the world.

I do not use the term "derived power" pejoratively. It is legitimate to choose to be a derived power. You can be an excellent lawyer, but it is a different kind of success. It is different from own power, but it does not mean that you will be a bad lawyer. It is just that maybe you have given up being an even better one.

One is at risk of deriving power from those persons who do not act correctly. Then you will be vulnerable to mistakes committed, and they will become your own. At least own-powered people assume the consequences of their own mistakes and also the consequences of their successes.

Think of a person of any activity you admire, or more precisely in a lawyer or arbitrator. You will discover that he or she is usually own-powered. It does not mean that all famous or prominent people have their own power, but usually what we admire in a person is their ability to achieve what they achieved by their own conviction.

Usually, own-powered professionals are authentic (authentically bad or authentically good). They are what they are because of their decisions. Consistent and coherent performance with conviction makes them predictable and reliable. Some will not like it, and others will. But own-powered people do not act to please others. They do what they think they have to do.

§34.02 EMPATHY

Own power does not mean moving away from others. On the contrary, it means understanding them and putting yourself in their place. We always work for others: lawyers for their clients, arbitrators for parties, or teachers for their students. If you want to do things well, you have to understand them and put yourself in their place. It does not necessarily mean doing what they want you to do. It is doing what is best for them according to your conviction, even when they do not like it.

You have to be clear and direct. Do not create false expectations. Do not sell what you do not have or make them believe that your case is different from what it is. To be consistent, own-powered attorneys speak with coherence and explain in detail their conviction.

It is a mistake to move away from others to do things right. One does things well so others can reach their goals. If you do not think about them, you will get away from what you want.

But empathy is not limited to them. It includes your co-arbitrators, your counterparty, and your work team. Own power may (and should) need from others. Having power of your own is not living in a bubble. Although it implies defining your individuality, it is an individuality open to others. You cannot develop your own power if you do not trust and help develop the own power of others. Unlike the derived power that comes from others, own power builds with others.

A non-empathic lawyer will not be persuasive with the tribunal. A non-empathic arbitrator will move away from his co-arbitrators.

§34.03 DO THINGS RIGHT

The goal of an own-powered attorney is not to win but to do things well. It is not the same. They are different. Whoever does things well will have a better chance of winning. But many times, wanting to win does not let us do things right.

You have to lose your fear of losing. And to lose this fear, your goal should be not to win. It is very difficult to understand and execute it. The temptation to seek to win by ceasing to do what you think you should do is an important distraction. The client or your boss may not understand and ask you for other things. It is why you must be clear. You learn more from losing than winning. Wanting to win can keep away your goal.

There are many ways to win by doing things wrong.

To do things right is to prepare your case, to study it, to use your intelligence, and to be loyal. You can improve the chances of winning by having ex parte communications with the arbitrators, misrepresenting the facts, or destroying a witness in an interrogation without justification. But you would not be doing things right. I do not mean just acting ethically. I mean doing your job well.

If you do things right you will not be distracted from what you have to do. The line to do things right is easier to identify, but harder to follow. The best way not to reach your goal is to take shortcuts. They reflect doubts about your ability to do things right.

When I have trained moot teams in arbitration competitions, the members of a team are authorized by the rules to enter other hearings to hear the arguments of other teams and thus be able to incorporate them into their own arguments in subsequent hearings. However, proceeding this way is not unethical. It is allowed.

But in the real world one cannot do it this way because the possibility does not exist. There are no similar audiences to go hunting arguments for your case. It seems a disadvantage, but it really forces you to develop your own research and arguments in a similar way to what happens in the real world. That ability helps to make things better without taking shortcuts.

Perhaps an argument heard in another hearing could help you win. But it restricts the development of your ability to do things right. Deep down, listening to other teams is a form of derived power. You trust more in what others do than in what your team can do. Instead, trust that you have the power to develop your own abilities.

Reaching one's own power means precisely not looking for shortcuts.

In the same way an own-powered arbitrator does not seek to obtain appointments by taking shortcuts. What he or she seeks is to be a good arbitrator: independent, impartial, hardworking, studious, intelligent, and empathetic. A good arbitrator does not get caught by laziness. He or she knows that his or her authority depends on the parties and is due to both. If things are done right, he or she may receive more appointments although it may take longer than choosing the shortcut to favor whoever appointed him or her. You should never give up doing things right.

A good indicator that you are doing things right is that they start looking for you in more cases to preside over a tribunal. It can be a good symptom that you are developing your own power.

§34.04 THERE IS NO EXCELLENCE WITHOUT HUMILITY

Excellence, without humility, does not shine. Own power is easily diluted if you weigh it with pride. To act with conviction, you have to be aware of your limitations, and humility is a clear sign of empathy.

It is important not to confuse humility with passivity or lack of conviction. Own-powered attorneys are not scared of their ideas. They say what they think and sustain it decisively. But in turn, they also listen. Do not confuse conviction with stubbornness. Conviction is open to change, showing that own power has humility.

If a lawyer at a hearing structures a plea and does not persuade the tribunal that his/her client is right, he or she is moving from doing things right. Humility allows us to see more clearly how to achieve an objective because it eliminates arrogance as a tool of action. Arrogance usually obscures your objective, and humility replaces it with visibility. It always hides some insecurity.

Curiously, own-powered attorneys do not seek to prove who they are. They seek to demonstrate consistency in their behavior by doing things right.

It does not mean not believing in yourself. Precisely because you believe in yourself, you do not have to show others who you are. It is a characteristic of derived power because you are looking for the appreciation and admiration of others to feel good. It is easier to do it by not showing what you are but by demonstrating what you do.

For example, some lawyers believe that citing a lot of doctrine or many cases is an example of scholarship and wisdom. They see it as a form of showdown. But as

Dyke says, “scholarship is piracy redeemed by footnotes,” and piracy is a form of derived power.

It does not mean that others should not be cited. It only means that you should quote to reinforce the end you seek to do things right and not to show how much you know. It is why quotes should help your case and your award or the article you have written to be understood. The best way to achieve admiration is not to organize your behavior to seek such admiration. People do not admire those professionals who brag but who do things well.

Own power does not mean ignoring the experience and capabilities of people who may know more than us. Having convictions does not mean to stop listening to others or recognizing their intellectual superiority or knowledge. Respect for the experience of others is essential to be empathetic. On the other hand, pride is the most important obstacle to learning. Humility can be defined as the best way to open yourself to learn.

§34.05 THE STRENGTH OF SELF-ESTEEM

Own power is built on self-esteem. You cannot feel the power you have if you do not generate faith in yourself. Being humble does not mean not trusting oneself. It is quite the opposite. Self-esteem means that you do not need outside recognition to know what you can do. And therefore we should not focus on generating recognition from others, but recognizing it within ourselves. The recognition of others is possibly a consequence of our ability to believe in ourselves. Recognition is good, but it is not your goal. Your goal is to do things right.

Self-esteem generates confidence, and confidence conveys professionalism and the ability to persuade. You should know that you are focused on doing things right and that you have the skills to do it.

I have seen many young lawyers taking their first steps in arbitration. I have seen them in their first participation in hearings. I must say that what matters most to make a difference is usually not knowledge, preparation, or intelligence (which are also important). What makes a person stand out the most is the self-esteem with which he or she develops.

Sometimes I have seen young lawyers feel they have to do everything possible to win, and they take unnecessary risks or do not focus on what they have to do. The fear of losing is a very bad advisor. It is why if you concentrate on doing things well, by definition, you are thinking about your ability to do them. It is the basis for building your self-esteem. Own power is not afraid of losing. Its value comes from knowing itself with the ability to achieve its goal: to do things well.

In an arbitrator, self-esteem gives you the security that the parties seek. The arbitrator must convey that he or she is able to handle the case. Without the self-esteem of the members of the tribunal, the parties feel confused and filled with doubts. The parties look at the young arbitrators with particular suspicion. One cannot change his or her age, but the perception of conveyed security can be. Empathic self-esteem gives the parties the feeling that the tribunal knows what it is doing. It transmits maturity and security.

§34.06 AND FINALLY, LIKE WHAT YOU DO

You can hardly develop your own power if you do not enjoy what you are doing. If in the morning, when you wake up, you go happy to your work or the hearing, you are making an important step in your happiness. If not, there is something you have to change: your job, your profession, your boss, or maybe the way you do things. If you do not enjoy what you do, it will be hard for you to do things well.

Of all the elements necessary to do things right, the most important is the emotional one. Without balance in emotions, everything else is broken. If your work unbalances you emotionally, then you are in the wrong job.

It does not mean that there are no bad times or stressful situations, but it cannot be the constant state in which you live. As Guido Calabresi once told me, happiness depends on two things. The first is to have a job where you get paid to do something you would pay to do. The second is to have someone with whom you enjoy spending the rest of your life. Without that balance your own power will not flow. Taking care of your family life and friendships will give you more stability at work, and job stability will give you a better family life.

And always remember that what you do is defined from yourself and your ability to achieve what you want to do, and you cannot do these things if you do not love yourself.

As Ayn Rand said, "To say: 'I love you', one must first know how to pronounce 'I'."

CHAPTER 35

If I Had Been a Male Lawyer

Shoschana Zusman

I do not know whether I am a feminist, an anti-feminist, or just plain indifferent. Truth be told, I never stopped to think about the discrimination of women while trying to make it as a more or less respectable lawyer. I even thought that I had never been discriminated, and all it took to be successful in this profession was to study and work hard. I firmly believed in meritocracy, and any explicit attempt to change things seemed unnecessary.

Now that I think about it, my relatively uneventful experience as a law professor in the eighties prevented me from noticing what was already evident to "the rest" (of the women). I had to say it. The practicing lawyer was always a second-rate professional, usually relegated to Family Law or forced to work as a dim bureaucrat in some obscure ministry. She had no contact with Property Law or the possibility to join a law firm as a partner, but she would not aspire to those fields. The female lawyer had a salary way below her male colleagues. She lacked leadership, and she was always behind the male lawyer speaking at hearings, presentations, or business meetings. Women were limited to whispering in his ear.

To me, it was meant to be my role. It is how it was and how it should be. And—most important—I did not care anyway because I was a scholar, not a lawyer.

Later driven by the disastrous financial effect of a (poorly negotiated) divorce, I decided to foray into the profession. It was a time when law firms were starting to lift the barriers to admitting women in their staff—an unwritten rule but standard procedure during the seventies—although access was still not easy. Law firms preferred men for the same reason an illustrious Liberal Arts teacher used to say about the admission of women to the university. It should be restricted. He thought it was a waste of time and money to train a woman, for she would soon abandon the profession to take care of her children.

And—as I already said—to me, it was normal and therefore was not challenged as such marked inequality is at present. It was the ethics of "reserve," "femininity," "gentleness," and "discretion" at work typical of those years and now overcome.

At present, the larger numbers of women in all areas of the legal profession are remarkable. It was not the case during my years as a law student at Pontificia Universidad Católica de Perú, where women were a minority (ten women for every eighty men) or when I decided to foray into the profession where—again—a certain resistance persisted. I tried to join a couple of law firms, but they politely closed their doors to me. My profile arose no interest, something I still do not understand, even though at this point in time I would not trade being self-employed for anything.

I must acknowledge the resourcefulness of women to make a place for themselves in this profession. They delved into subjects that were "exotic" in the nineties, such as regulation. Regulation was not interesting to lawyers because the development of this area was just beginning and the required knowledge of how regulated industries operated included tedious (or rather gruesome) and technical, hard-to-understand matters. As we can see, this market was still uncharted territory and almost the only area in which women could venture and sometimes excel. Of course, currently regulation arouses the same interest in lawyers of both genders.

As I am unable to hypothesize about something on which much has been written and discussed, this modest contribution is an account of some incidents in which—I now realize—*machismo* "shone in all its brilliance." The question that needs to be asked is if the same would have happened if I had been a man. I have selected ten absolutely trivial anecdotes that call us to reflect on what is known as *machismo* which certainly still pervades the legal practice.

§35.01 "ASSIST THE SECRETARY"

At a hearing in an arbitration case concluded some years ago, I noticed that the court president seemed to be uncomfortable—I do not know why—because of my active participation in finding the solution to a minor procedural problem. Upon completion of this matter, the president told me, loud and clear and with a slight touch of irony: "Doctora,[1] *since you have been so active in seeking the solution to the problem, do me a favor and dictate to the secretary the text as it has been corrected.*"

It was as if, because he was the president—but most of all a man—he was hierarchically superior to me. Well, even though I noticed his attempt to belittle me, I obediently approached the secretary to dictate him the text. I did it to prevent any friction, as the case was "loaded."

I ask: Would the president have acted as he did with a male arbitrator? I do not think he would.

1. *Doctor* (or *doctora*) is a title of respect for lawyers in Peru.

§35.02 I ONLY SPEAK WITH MEN

In an arbitration process that concluded years ago, I realized that the arbitrator appointed by the other party would not talk to me. As a matter of fact, sometimes he did not even say hello to me. He only talked to the presiding arbitrator and always in a low voice.

I attributed that attitude to the fact that such arbitrator, I do not know to what effect, thought that it was best to ignore me, making the decision a "matter of men." Well, I gathered up my courage and talked to the presiding arbitrator, expressing how uncomfortable I felt with this mistreatment which was beyond comprehension. Although the president asked the arbitrator for "tolerance," things did not change. At that time, I did not perceive it as pure and simple *machismo* but as manipulative behavior. Now that I think about it, *machismo* is not incompatible with manipulation. Rather, it is a strategy. The arbitrator who spoke only with men did not prevail.

I ask: Would this odd arbitrator treat a male colleague the same way? I do not think he would.

§35.03 THE IMPORTANCE OF DRESSING PROPERLY

I will not deny that there were times when I rebelled against the establishment, especially with regards to "dressing properly," a must in the legal environment of the seventies.

I started teaching at the Law School dressed casually when it was uncommon. None of the Law School authorities criticized my attire. Sometime later, I was invited to a meeting of teachers who had worked in the drafting of the Peruvian Civil Code of 1984, and I had no better idea than to wear jeans to the meeting. A Civil Law professor came toward me disapprovingly and blatantly told me "*you can't be dressed like this.*"

I ask: Would he make this comment to a man? Probably if the lawyer had been a younger one, but making such a remark to a lawyer of his generation as I was, no way!

§35.04 CRISTÓBAL'S YELLS

In the hard road to advising a client in the brink of declaring bankrupt, I decided that I would not attend a meeting called to arrive to a settlement. I remember fully well that it was because I was very insecure and overwhelmed with fear of doing a bad job.

Hours later, I received a telephone call from the attorney of the other party. This guy named Cristóbal—who was yelling at me—told me that I had not attended the meeting to frustrate the settlement which according to him was in the best interest of my client. He accused me of everything, from being a treacherous, irresponsible liar to a malicious person of dubious behavior. And to think I had not attended because I lacked self-confidence!

Interestingly, no explanation was sufficient, and he would not stop yelling. It was an odd case of male hysteria. Today, of course, I would stop him in his tracks. But at that time, I did not have the nerve to do it.

Once again, I ask: Would Cristóbal have treated a man like he treated me? Honestly, I do not think he would have.

§35.05 THE QUOTA

Years ago, when some international organizations were trying to introduce arbitration in Peru, I was invited to a discussion panel with foreign arbitrators, and I went. There, a Peruvian officer who was supposedly a friend of mine told me that I was there to fill a female quota which those entities promoted.

And I had thought it was due to the recognition of my work, not my gender. How wrong I was!

I ask: Would this officer have made the same poisonous remark to a male colleague who is part of a discriminated minority? I do not believe it!

§35.06 GO BACK TO COLLEGE!

In an arbitration where I was the arbitrator appointed by one of the parties, and the president was a woman, we discussed the case with a third arbitrator (a man, of course). The two of us female arbitrators agreed on the direction that the award should have, but he was against it. As we shared our views, I noticed that this gentleman was increasingly losing his temper. Finally, he told us: *"You two have to go back to college! You don't have a clue!"*

I ask: What if I had been a man? And if the court had been presided by a man? Would he send them back to college? Frankly, I do not think he would.

Women can take it. Later, I realized that this arbitrator had ceased to be on speaking terms with me. I hope he gets over it.

§35.07 I CANNOT SEE A DAMSEL IN DISTRESS

This is one of the few cases—if not the only one—in which I thanked having been born a woman. In my beginnings as a lawyer, I had to talk with the legal counsel of a ministry who had communicated to me that his legal report would be contrary to the interest of my client.

Surprised and amazed, all I could tell him is "*oh,* doctor *how can this be.*" And, to my amazement, he told me: "doctora, *I am going to reverse my opinion because I can't see a damsel in distress.*"

I ask: Would he have made this response if the lawyer "in distress" had been a man? Of course not.

§35.08 THE VETO

As a member of an administrative court and due to the customary rotation in the position of president, I was to hold the position of president that upcoming year. My name was proposed, and, to my surprise, one of the court members ferociously opposed my designation without any convincing explanation at all.

His arguments were that "he did not agree," that I was "not prepared to represent the court," that "in any case it should be Juan," or similar platitudes with which he tried to conceal his true reasons. Now I know that the main reason was he felt awkward "submitting" to a female president.

To the above, I replied that if he did not agree, then I would decline. It was not because I was unworthy of the position but because I had always avoided presidencies and similar positions. These positions usually added a bureaucratic load to the already difficult task of analyzing and writing.

I ask: Would he have opposed if I had been a man? Certainly not, because we elected a man as president to which he wholeheartedly acquiesced.

§35.09 SPEAKING OF MACHISMO, ENTER THE WOMEN

What I am about to describe does not pertain to a concrete situation, but to the observation of how some female lawyers behave in arbitrations, negotiations, meetings with clients. For instance, insecure female lawyers think that by interrupting another female (not male) lawyer, they will score some points in a court consisting basically of men. It is a mistake because it frustrates the possibility of arriving to a solution, whatever it may be. Keeping respectfully silent is the right thing to do. A female lawyer will not be diminished by it.

The above story reminds me that once while discussing a case with a young female lawyer, she would put her head between her hands and tell me: "Well, once again, I will explain it again. Let us see if you understand what I am saying this time!" I did understand what she was saying; it is just that she was wrong.

Another common behavior among *machista* women is to exploit "feminism" by making it a privilege that men do not have, and not a right, to be equally heard. The strategy here is to state that the opposing party's lawyer is being disrespectful toward her as a woman, thus leading others to admonish the "disrespectful" lawyer. Big mistake. Equal opportunity is not the same as privilege, and until it is well understood, we women will be the worst enablers of *machismo*.

Lastly, the attitude of some female lawyers who will not say hello or goodbye to me or who look at me with hate (if I am the opposing party or a member of the court) is really beyond comprehension. It is they who increase discrimination.

§35.10 LISTEN, MAMITA!

Last but not least, a lawyer already elderly at the time, who I like very much and with whom I shared quite a few arbitration tribunals, used the following phrases when he addressed me: "Listen, *mamita*! Listen, *hijita*! You do not understand what the parties are trying to say! You do not get it, sweetheart! Let me explain it to you: You are not streetwise enough!" I cannot think of him being this "affectionate" with a man or would he?

CHAPTER 36

How to Make a Significant Impact with a Career in Dispute Resolution

*María Angélica Burgos**

The so-called *millennial* generation broke and challenged companies and professional culture. In the case of the legal market, law firms continue to ask themselves what are the appropriate strategies to retain them, given that they seem to be a difficult generation to satisfy. In most cases, strategies are in vain. At the end of the year, millennial lawyers continue to abandon their corporate jobs.

Among the challenges proposed by *millennials*, a question touching upon the DNA of our profession remains to be answered: How do we generate a positive impact through the practice of law? What exactly do we understand by *positive* impact?

According to a recent Deloitte survey, "*millennials*" are looking for companies that are not only focused on income but also strive for balanced objectives, which include: (1) generating a positive impact on society and environment; (2) designing innovative ideas, products, and services; (3) creating jobs, developing careers, and improving people's lives; and (4) promoting diversity and inclusion at work.[1] These aspirations seem to be concrete and achievable in the professional day-to-day. However, the interviewed professionals noted that their companies did not prioritize these areas but instead focused their attention on income generation, efficiency, and commercial aspects.[2] In the case of lawyers, Susan Smith Blakely recently observed

* The author thanks María Marulanda and María Cristina Martínez for their comments on this writing.

1. Deloitte. Deloitte 2018 *Millennial Survey. Millennials Dissappointed in business, unprepared for industry* 4.0. Available at: https://www2.deloitte.com/co/es/pages/about-deloitte/articles/millennialsurvey2018.html.
2. Deloitte. Deloitte 2018 *Millennial Survey. Millennials Dissappointed in business, unprepared for industry* 4.0. Available at: https://www2.deloitte.com/co/es/pages/about-deloitte/articles/millennialsurvey2018.html.

that the younger professionals look for a purpose and meaning in their work that goes beyond generating money. They want to feel that their work is making a difference.[3]

The desire to contribute to society and to generate a positive impact is not exclusive to *millennial* lawyers. On the contrary, it would seem that people who have chosen a profession that serves justice and the rule of law strive for the realization of collective values that ultimately result in an improvement for their entire society. It can be said that all lawyers, to a greater or lesser extent, have an interest in making an impact in our society.

And it is, without a doubt, the case for dispute resolution lawyers. By solving controversies through adjudication instead of weapons, we are prioritizing rule of law. Not surprisingly, a colleague who I deeply admire recently told me that for this reason, she believed we had the best job in the world. Law, as imperfect as it is, provides us with a solution that—at least in theory—is available to all people on equal terms. I have no doubt that through the achievement of this objective, lawyers generate a significant impact on our societies.

However, it is an ideal that may seem intangible and distant from the activities we do on a daily basis. In the context of a rapidly evolving legal world that is demanding, confronts us with aggressive competition, and faces enormous challenges, such as changes in the market, technology and the liberalization of the profession,[4] it would seem very distant—if not naïve—that we could focus on generating positive impact and at the same time be successful professionals. I am reluctant to believe that the only possibility is to leave our corporate jobs to seek a profession in the nonprofit sector or in the public sector.

So, the question that remains is: How do we generate a significant positive impact in our society? In our environment? From our work within an arbitration team? How do we achieve what the *millennials* so articulately described as generating positive impact, innovating, creating careers, improving people's lives, and promoting diversity and inclusion at work?

In my opinion, we can generate positive impact on several fronts: in our society, in our community, and in the legal organizations to which we belong as well as in our profession, in our work teams, and in the people with whom we interact. On all these fronts, the impact may involve the creation of well-being, innovation, growth, diversity, and inclusion in the workplace. We can also generate positive impact individually or collectively, either as work teams or as legal organizations.

And in practice, how do we do it?

Below I summarize some ideas about the ways in which as lawyers for dispute resolution we can generate this impact, from either our individual or collective actions. Naturally, these ideas are not intended to be exhaustive or comprehensive.

---

3. Susan Smith Blakely, *What Millennial Lawyers Want*, Wolters Kluwer, 2019 (Kindle Edition).
4. Richard Susskind, *Tomorrow's Lawyers. An Introduction to Your Future*, Second Edition, Oxford University Press, 2017 (Kindle Edition).

§36.01 FIRST, REAFFIRMING OUR ETHICAL COMMITMENT

Dispute resolution attorneys have a superlative commitment to ethics. Our profession demands behavior standards that generate confidence in the work we do, not only because of the quality of the work but also because we act correctly. Specifically in terms of ethics, we have several instruments in both domestic law and international soft law. In my opinion, this commitment involves not only strictly following our ethical and professional duties but also requiring compliance from our colleagues and rejecting bad practices. Only in this way can we contribute to the generation of a culture of ethics in arbitration practice.

§36.02 SECOND, RESPECTING HUMAN RIGHTS

Lawyer organizations, like companies, have a responsibility to respect human rights, regardless of their size.[5] This translates into four main actions, arising from the Guiding Principles on Business and Human Rights, adopted by the Human Rights Council in 2011: (1) adopt political commitments to assume its responsibility to respect human rights; (2) refrain from infringing human rights of third parties; (3) face the adverse consequences generated by its activities in which they have any participation, including reparation, wherever it may proceed; and (4) carry out due diligence processes that allow them to identify, prevent, mitigate, and account for their impact on human rights.[6] The IBA Practical Guide on Business and Human Rights for Commercial Lawyers clarified that the responsibility to respect the human rights of law firms is applicable to aspects of their business that are not the provision of legal services since they must be provided independently.[7] Thus, one way in which we can generate impact is by understanding these responsibilities and incorporating them into our practices.

In the case of legal organizations, there are important human rights challenges, for example discrimination and harassment. Recently, an IBA survey found that a significant percentage of men and women had experienced *bullying* and intimidation in

5. Guiding Principles for Business and Human Rights: Implementing the United Nations "Protect, Respect and Remedy" Framework, adopted by the Human Rights Council through resolution 17/4 of June 16, 2011, Principle 14.
6. Guiding Principles for Business and Human Rights: Implementing the United Nations "Protect, Respect and Remedy" Framework, adopted by the Human Rights Council through resolution 17/4 of June 16, 2011, Principles 11-24.
7. IBA Practical Guide on Business and Human Rights for Business Lawyers, adopted by a resolution of the IBA Council, May 28, 2016, p. 36.

the course of their careers.[8] Furthermore, this survey found that there are levels of gender discrimination and bullying practices that are worrisome.[9]

As lawyers we have the possibility of promoting the discussion of these problems in our organizations and being leaders of their solution. There are several ways to do it, including creating and participating in discussion groups within the organization, raising awareness of the existence of these difficulties, looking for alternatives to combat them, and promoting direct conversations regarding these challenges. Changing our collective attitude toward these challenges and working on our unconscious perceptions will lead us to build more inclusive and diverse law firms that provide legal services to the expectations of today's world. It is also important that those leaders of the firms generate the ability to listen and be self-critical in relation to the aspects where there is work to be done and dare to promote the necessary changes, so organizations really progress in these aspects.

§36.03 THIRD, SUPPORTING OUR CLIENTS IN UNDERSTANDING THEIR HUMAN RIGHTS RESPONSIBILITIES

Like legal companies, our clients have human rights responsibilities as companies. As their advisors, we have a duty to offer our independent advice and to adhere to the ethical standards that govern our profession. However, we are in a privileged position to support our clients in understanding their human rights and responsibilities. The IBA Practical Guide has named this role as the trusted advisor, which is accomplished through different measures that would allow the lawyer to become a specialist advisor on business and human rights issues, namely: offering training on companies and human rights to clients, providing advice on a pro bono basis, conducting information sessions for clients, etc. I believe that as dispute resolution attorneys, we could fulfill this role for our clients, without exceeding the mandate conferred on us.

§36.04 FOURTH, COMMITTING OURSELVES TO VALUES

As attorneys, we can commit ourselves voluntarily to the values in which we believe. In recent years, a series of initiatives have emerged that invite lawyers to take a step forward in self-regulation and to commit to taking specific actions in favor of specific values, such as inclusion, diversity, transparency, nondiscrimination and good treatment. In some cases, commitment to values can be interrelated with political commitments that human rights legal organizations can make. An example is the *Equal*

8. "*The findings of our survey include responses that suggest that some lawyers experience alarming levels of bullying and intimidation. These findings suggest that significant percentages of both women and men—women almost 50 percent and men 30 per cent—have been subject to bullying and intimidating conduct during the course of their careers.*" IBA Legal Policy and Research Unit, *Women in Commercial Legal Practice*, December 2017, p. 16. Available at: https://www.ibanet.org/LPRU/Women-business-Lawyers-Initiative-Front-page.aspx.
9. IBA Legal Policy and Research Unit, *Women in Commercial Legal Practice*, December 2017, p. 34 Available at: https://www.ibanet.org/LPRU/Women-business-Lawyers-Initiative-Front-page.aspx.

Representation in Arbitration Pledge, which to date has been signed by around 3,500 organizations and individuals.[10] Through the Pledge, as it has been called, the signatories undertake to take reasonable steps within their power to improve the profile and representation of women in arbitration. The Pledge has impacted the field of arbitration and was even recognized by the *Global Arbitration Review* as one of the most outstanding developments in arbitration. There are also other important initiatives that promote greater diversity in the field of international dispute resolution, such as the *Alliance for Equality in Dispute Resolution*.

When it comes to commitment to values, it must be remembered that efforts must also be oriented to actions, since inactive public commitments do not generate the intended impact. We must generate a collective vision that allows us to demand the fulfillment of those values from those professionals who commit to them and to be self-critical in those situations in which said commitments are not being sufficient.

For example, regarding diversity, the latest Queen Mary University and White & Case International Arbitration survey recognizes that although there is no consensus on the causal link between diversity and the quality of decisions, most of the interviewees agreed that diversity should be promoted.[11] This study showed that regarding arbitration appointments there is a very positive perception among arbitration users about the progress in gender diversity, but at the same time, it highlighted that the discussion on diversity should be broadened to include ethnic and cultural groups, increase geographic diversity, and include other generations.[12] It shows us that a significant impact has been achieved in bringing the gender discussion to the table, but at the same time, it invites us to consider diversity in a more holistic and global way. By betting on diversity as a value, we must be aware that political commitments and actions are not enough to increase the participation of women in arbitration since there are other minority groups whose participation in dispute resolution would contribute enormously.

§36.05 FIFTH, PROVIDING PRO BONO LEGAL SERVICES

Pro bono legal service delivery is one of the clearest ways to generate a significant positive impact.

Pro bono services can adopt different modalities from the attention of individual cases and consultancy in high-impact or social interest litigation to investigations that allow developing a specific topic for civil, cultural, or educational institutions. As provided in the Pro-Bono Work Declaration for the American Continent, pro bono work is free but must be provided with the same quality and professional (and ethical) standards with which paid legal services are provided.[13] It is a concrete commitment of lawyers to the realization of one of the values of our profession: access to legal advice.

10. *See*: http://www.arbitrationpledge.com/ (Last accessed March 29, 2019).
11. Queen Mary University, White & Case, *2018 International Arbitration Survey: The Evolution of International Arbitration*, p. 17.
12. *Ibid.*, pp. 17-18.
13. Pro Bono Work Statement for the American Continent.

Pro bono projects are an excellent opportunity to lend the knowledge and experience we have serving an impactful cause. I know of several dispute resolution attorneys who have participated in high-impact pro bono litigation projects, representing parties in international human rights forums and reconciling differences between two small businessmen by using the skills acquired in their daily chores.

Pro bono work also allows us to innovate in law and pursue interests other than our practice area. In my experience, I have been able to participate in legal investigations of issues of public interest for civil associations and in the care of particular cases that have generated a significant change in people's lives. I remember with great appreciation the case of a mother who went to pro bono services because her daughter was denied the provision of health services due to an error in the civil registry, and thanks to that advice she was able to normalize the situation.

I am convinced that the positive impact is not generated exclusively in large events or in the most visible nor is it measured in results, ranking positions, success commissions, statistics, or press releases. The positive impact is caused by those actions that make the lives of others better and that generate feelings of well-being and progress. This impact is just as important when it is deployed to our coworkers, colleagues, and our legal organizations, as it is when it drives a specific community or our clients. We also leave a definitive mark when we work under the highest ethical standards and defend the right in a decent way over force, dishonesty, and cheating.

In her TED Talk "*Being Young and Generating Impact*," Natalie Warne tells the story of a social organization which, with the support of a large number of interns and volunteers, managed to drive the approval of a US bill to take action against the recruitment of minors by Joseph Kony. In that talk, the young woman described the "anonymous extraordinaires" as those people who promote the movements and who work in a disinterested and vigorous way for those causes in which they believe. In closing, Natalie highlighted: "*In the small anonymous monotonous every single day acts, I have to remind myself to be extraordinary*." I believe that it is the philosophy that arbitration attorneys can adopt to generate a positive impact: to be anonymous extraordinaires in our daily tasks and activities.

CHAPTER 37

What Do Women Want in Arbitration?

*Carolina Arroyo**

In the movie *What Women Want*, Nick Marshall, the character played by Mel Gibson, acquires a supernatural power to listen to what he thinks are the wishes, thoughts, feelings, and desires of women. Marshall, who is a middle-aged chauvinist who thought he knew everything about women, discovers a very basic stereotype about them: apparently, women do not always say what they think, nor do they think everything they say.

In the field of law, much has been written describing what is the state of the legal profession for women, what obstacles they face when being promoted, and what are the diversity initiatives necessary for a greater and more active participation of women in arbitration. However, a deeper study has not been done to discover how young women live their profession, what are their desires, and if these aspirations differ from what men want.

In this chapter, I will try to examine the experiences and aspirations of young women who litigate in arbitration regarding some aspects of their profession. Is it true that women litigators prefer their profession over the development of their family? Are male litigators more ambitious or less emotional than women? Are women more willing to give up money for more leisure time?

I will try to answer these and other questions, based on a survey[1] sent via email to the associates in firms with arbitration practices who answered the survey anonymously. The sample is composed of thirty-five international arbitration practitioners who are residents in twenty-one countries of the world with an age between 24 and 40 years. In this sample, 31.4% of the participants were women.[2]

* The opinions expressed herein are those of the author and do not necessarily reflect those opinions of other attorneys on their firm or their clients.

1. The survey was designed by José María de la Jara, Carolina Arroyo and Álvaro Awad, editors of this book, and it is in Appendix I.
2. The results of the questions of the survey that are analyzed in this chapter are in Appendix II.

The survey had different sections with questions addressed to know the following information about the participants: (1) demographic information; (2) experience as a litigator; (3) experience as an arbitrator or administrative secretary; (4) work-life balance; (5) expectations about their professional future; (6) experiences, among others.

This chapter is written based on a general qualitative and quantitative analysis of the answers. A thorough and detailed statistical analysis has not been made due to the size of the sample. We will focus on certain questions where we considered those answers to be more relevant in understanding how true are some stereotypes about the thoughts and expectations of young women in their profession: (1) how they value themselves in the workplace; (2) how prepared they feel to face great professional challenges; (3) what are their expectations on the future; (4) how they perceive their benefits at work, among others.

I will now refer to the answers to some of the survey questions and what these results suggest.

§37.01 DO YOU FEEL AN IMPORTANT MEMBER AT YOUR JOB?

This question was aimed at knowing how participants perceive themselves or feel valued in their jobs, specifically, if they think they are important members of their teams. Of the twenty-four men surveyed, 42% said they "strongly agreed" with that statement while 37% said they "agreed," meaning 79% considered themselves as important members of their teams. Only 17% said they were neutral with that statement while a residual percentage of 4% said they "disagreed" or did not feel they were important members of their team. In the case of women, 45% of the participants said they "strongly agreed" while 55% said they "agreed."

Although the data would seem to suggest that there are no relevant differences between the responses of men and women, it is striking that in the case of men 4% answered that they did not feel important members of their team, while none of the women answered the same. The answers could indicate that women do not remain in jobs where they do not feel important or that men remain in teams despite not feeling important for the tasks they perform.

§37.02 HOW PREPARED DO YOU FEEL TO BE A SOLE ARBITRATOR IN A CASE?

In this question, 50% of men said they felt sufficiently prepared to assume a case as sole arbitrator while 8% said they were not prepared at all. A total of 29% acknowledged that they still needed preparation, and only 13% said they felt "overly prepared"; that is, their abilities were above the requirements to handle a case as a sole arbitrator. On the contrary, in the case of the surveyed women, 46% said they lacked the preparation required to take on a case as sole arbitrator, 18% said they did not feel "prepared at all," and 27% said they were "sufficiently prepared" leaving 9% who answered they were "more than prepared."

These responses suggest that women appear to be more cautious when assessing their readiness to face new challenges as arbitrators. In the case of men, the majority answered they at least felt sufficiently prepared, while in the case of women, the majority replied that they needed more preparation in order to act as sole arbitrator. The answers to this question seem to suggest that men feel more confident about their abilities when facing a new professional challenge, while women seem to assess themselves more critically.

§37.03 WHAT DO YOU EXPECT TO ACHIEVE IN THE NEXT 10 YEARS?

In this case, the majority of men and women surveyed stated that their main objective for the next ten years was to become partners of the firms in which they currently work. Therefore, it does not appear to be an obvious difference between genders regarding future expectations between arbitration practitioners.

It is interesting that 16% of the men and 45% of the women in the sample want to be arbitrators but also consider other options, such as dedicating themselves to academia and their family or completing a Ph.D. On the other hand, 18.18% of women and 8.33% of men expect to dedicate themselves exclusively to being arbitrators, and 16.67% of men and 9.09% of women want to establish their own firms.

§37.04 IF YOU WERE LOOKING FOR A NEW JOB, YOU WOULD LOOK FOR A PLACE THAT OFFERS ...

Participants were asked to choose one or more alternatives on what they want in their next job. The alternatives included the following: a higher salary, more free time, more exposure (in the market), more learning opportunities, greater recognition of their achievements, and more pro bono work.

Most men (58.33%) would seek a higher salary, accompanied in certain cases, by more learning opportunities, greater exposure, and greater recognition of their achievements. On the contrary, only 27.27% of women would seek a higher salary, accompanied by more opportunities for learning and pro bono work.

The majority of women (36.36%) and only 20.83% of men recognized the need for a job that offers more free time as well as more learning opportunities, greater exposure, and greater recognition of their achievements.

Finally, only 12.5% of the men and 27.27% of the women would look for more learning opportunities, greater exposure, and greater recognition of their achievements without considering a higher salary.

§37.05 DO YOU THINK IT IS POSSIBLE TO HAVE THE SAME SALARY AND PRESTIGE, WITH FEWER HOURS OF WORK?

A total of 59% of the men and 80% of the women surveyed consider that it is possible to have the same salary and prestige with fewer hours of work. If we evaluate the answer to this question with what was previously answered by women, it would seem that they think that it is possible to work less and have the same benefits. In any case, they would prefer a job that gives more free time than more money.

On the other hand, the survey also included statements about certain circumstances that could have arisen in the lives of the participants in order to understand their well-being as associates in arbitration practice. The statements refer to mental and physical health, among others. In the following paragraphs we will analyze the answers of the participants.

§37.06 I HAVE ATTENDED A MEDICAL CONSULTATION FOR SUFFERING FROM WORK-RELATED ANXIETY

A total of 25% of men and 36% of women recognized having attended a medical consultation because they suffer from work-related anxiety at least once. These results suggest that women seem to suffer more work-related anxiety or that they seem to seek more help than men in order to deal with work-related anxiety problems.

§37.07 I HAVE CRIED OVER WORK-RELATED ISSUES

A total of 82% of women and 25% of men claimed having cried at least once for work-related matters. These results suggest that women express their emotions regarding work issues more openly than men or that work matters affect women in a more personal way.

§37.08 I HAVE MISSED A REALLY IMPORTANT FAMILY EVENT TO FULFILL WORK COMMITMENTS

A total of 75% of the men and 73% of the women surveyed answered they have missed at least one really important family event due to work commitments. This answer suggests that men and women in principle maintain the same level of commitment to their work, even if it affects their family sphere. The data shows that contrary to what is frequently thought, women in the demographic group of the sample do not prioritize their family more than men do.

§37.09 I HAVE PANICKED ABOUT FACING MY BOSS FOR A DISAGREEMENT

A total of 25% of men and 45% of women said they felt "panic" about facing their boss for something in which they disagreed. According to this answer, women seem to suffer more emotionally when confronting their superiors. We do not know whether this answer would have varied depending on whether the "boss" is the same sex or not.

§37.10 I HAVE SERIOUSLY FEARED LOSING MY JOB

A total of 64% of women and 50% of men have never feared losing their job. It is striking that although women seem to suffer more about confrontations at work, they fear losing their jobs to a lesser extent than men.

§37.11 I HAVE MAINTAINED A VISIBLE ANIMOSITY TOWARD SOMEONE AT WORK

A total of 45% of women and 33% of men said they have maintained a visible animosity toward someone at work. Although it is impossible to know the different reasons for animosities in the workplace, it is interesting to know that women express their emotions regarding their colleagues more than men do.

§37.12 I HAVE FELT DEEP ENVY FOR A COWORKER'S ACHIEVEMENT

A total of 83% of men and 73% of women said they have never felt deep envy for the achievement of a coworker. These results suggest that envy and other negative emotions among members of arbitration teams are not experienced in greater extents.

§37.13 I HAVE FELT GENUINE HAPPINESS FOR THE SUCCESS OF A COWORKER

A total of 82% of women and 92% of men have felt at least once genuine happiness for the success of a colleague, which suggests that relationships between colleagues and associates in the arbitration practice are healthy.

§37.14 WHAT IS THE NUMBER OF HOURS YOU WORK ON AVERAGE PER WEEK? AND HOW MUCH TIME DO YOU SPEND ON LEISURE ACTIVITIES?

A total of 38% of men and 18% of women work between fifty-five and sixty-five hours per week on average which translates to eleven and thirteen hour workdays without considering weekends. A total of 55% of women and 33% of men work between forty-five and fifty-five hours per week on average or between nine and eleven hours daily. This data suggest that men work longer hours.

However, it is interesting that women, who seem to devote less work hours than men, also devote less time to leisure. A total of 73% of women dedicate less than five hours to leisure per week compared to 42% of men with the same amount of leisure time. It suggests that while women spend less hours than men at work per week, those remaining hours are not necessarily for leisure. Unfortunately, the survey did not include questions to learn what other activities women dedicate their extra time outside of work and leisure.

§37.15 WOULD YOU BE WILLING TO RECEIVE LESS MONEY FOR MORE FREE TIME?

A total of 73% of women and 29% of men would be willing to receive less money for more free time. This answer is perhaps one of the main differences found between the aspirations of men and women who work as associates in the arbitration practice.

Most women would be willing to give up money for more free time while most men would not be willing.

§37.16 ARE YOU SATISFIED WITH THE SALARY YOU RECEIVE?

A total of 54% of men and 73% of women are satisfied with the salary they receive for their work. Nonetheless, it is interesting to know that 29% of men in the sample said they disagree with the salary they receive, but no woman answered the same. These results again could mean that women do not remain in workplaces if they are not satisfied with working conditions or that for women the salary is not the main criteria while evaluating their well-being.

§37.17 ARE YOU SATISFIED WITH THE EFFORTS OF YOUR WORK TO GENERATE A WORK-LIFE BALANCE?

Finally, the survey participants were asked if they were satisfied with the efforts made by their law firms to generate a balance between work and personal life. A total of 73% of women and 54% of men responded that they agreed with their firms' efforts to reach this balance, while 29% of men said they disagreed with those efforts.

The answers to the survey allow us to know certain differences in general terms between the aspirations and experiences of women and men associates in arbitration practices. Men seem to feel more prepared than women to face new professional challenges, such as being a sole arbitrator in a case.

One of the most striking differences is the availability of women willing to give up part of their salary for more free hours. It is surprising that although a significant percentage of the men surveyed did not agree with the efforts of their firms to generate an adequate balance between work and personal life and work on average more hours per week than women, most of them would not quit their job for more free time. Yet most of the men would not give up part of their salary for more free time.

In short, it would seem that women are more critical when valuing their skills but feel they are important members of their teams to a greater extent than men. They are more afraid to confront their bosses which nonetheless does not increase their fear to lose their jobs. Likewise, women cry more than men for work reasons and attend medical consultations to a greater extent for work-related anxiety problems. Men, on the other hand, seem to have greater self-esteem when valuing their skills, feel less fear about facing their bosses, but unlike women, they seem to experience more fear about losing their job.

I must admit that as I experienced motherhood while writing this chapter, I sometimes struggled to carry this project and others forward. I discovered that some of my answers to the survey questions would have changed had I participated in it after becoming a mother. Now I know that your needs and expectations change with the arrival of a child, so it is very difficult to establish what a women in arbitration wants in general terms.

While the assessment of my abilities has not been modified, my aspirations and needs in practical terms have been altered. I still hope that in ten years I will become a partner of the firm where I am currently working, but now I know that I would not be willing to miss an important family event for work.

This chapter was intended to determine what women in arbitration want. I do not know whether it was accomplished or if it is even possible. What I know is that, at least in my case, writing this piece allowed me to clearly visualize what I, as a woman, aspire to have in a career in arbitration: having the chance to take care of my family and devoting enough time and attention to them without stopping my professional development to the best of my possibilities.

APPENDIX I HOW DO ARBITRATION ASSOCIATES SURVIVE?

Identification

1. Optional Description
2. Gender
    - Female
    - Male
    - Other
    - I prefer not to respond
3. Country of Residence
4. Age

Experience as a Litigator

5. How long have you been in your current job?
    - 1-2 years
    - 3-4 years
    - 5-7 years
    - 8-10 years
    - More than 10 years
    - Other
6. Do you feel like you are an important member at your work?
    - Strongly Agree
    - Agree
    - Neither Agree Nor Disagree
    - Disagree
    - Strongly Disagree
    - Unknown
7. Did your workplace invest training you in the necessary hearing skills?
    - Strongly Agree
    - Agree
    - Neither Agree Nor Disagree
    - Disagree
    - Strongly Disagree
    - Unknown
8. In the past two years, have you had any of the following responsibilities? You can mark more than one answer:
    - Assisted another lawyer in the execution of an interrogation/examination
    - Been in control of the evidence to be shown in the statement/to the witness
    - Been responsible for the PowerPoint presentation
    - Delivered an opening statement
    - Executed a direct examination of a witness
    - Executed a cross-examination of a witness

- Executed direct questioning of a legal expert
- Executed cross-examination of a legal expert
- Executed a direct examination of an expert witness
- Executed a cross-examination of an expert witness
- Delivered a closing statement
- I have not had the opportunity to directly execute any of these activities.

9. Tell us a horror story you have witnessed or suffered with an audience.

Arbitrator, Academy and Ranking

10. In the past two years, have you been appointed as an arbitrator?
    - Yes
    - No
11. In the past two years, have you been appointed as administrative clerk of court?
    - Yes
    - No
12. How prepared do you feel to participate in a case as sole arbitrator?
    - More than prepared
    - Sufficiently prepared
    - Less prepared
    - Not prepared at all
13. How many papers or articles did you publish in 2018?
    - 0
    - 1
    - 2
    - 3
    - 4
    - 5+
14. At how many conferences did you give a presentation in 2018?
    - 0
    - 1
    - 2
    - 3
    - 4
    - 5
    - 6
    - 7
    - 8
    - 9
    - 10+
15. Have you ever been featured in a guide like Chambers or Partners?
    - Yes
    - No

16. Do you feel you should have already been featured?
    - Yes
    - No
17. What is your position at your current job?
    - Associate at a law firm
    - Senior associate at a law firm
    - Partner at a law firm
    - Of-counsel at a law firm
    - Founder of my own firm
    - Government lawyer
    - In-house lawyer of a company
    - Legal manager of a company
    - Other

Your Future

18. What do you hope to achieve in the next 10 years?
    - Be a partner in the firm where I currently work
    - Found my own firm/business/consultant company
    - Work for the state
    - Dedicate myself to being an arbitrator
    - Dedicate myself to the academy
    - Dedicate myself to my family
    - Other
19. What is the main challenge in achieving the professional future you want?
    - Obtaining the approval of the partners at the firm in which I work
    - Getting noticed in the market (arbitration)
    - Finding more time to publish
    - Achieving a better direct relationship with clients
    - Receiving more training and education
    - Transitioning to a culture of greater flexibility
    - Getting clients
    - Finding balance
    - Other
20. In the event that you were looking for a new job, you would look for a place that offers:
    - Higher salary
    - More free time
    - More pro bono work
    - More learning opportunities
    - Greater exposure
    - Greater recognition of achievements
21. Do you think it is possible to have the same salary and prestige with fewer hours of work?

- Yes
- No

22. Think about the associates of the next 5 years. How essential do you think the following skills and knowledge will be for them?

	Most Essential	*Essential*	*Neutral*	*Not so Essential*	*Not Essential*
Book writing					
Knowledge about techlaw					
Understanding programming language					
Ability to program code					
Specialization in a specific branch of law					
Management of design techniques and thinking					
Ph.D.					
Lecturer at a university					
Knowledge of deliberation and persuasion					
Networking					
Good award writing					
Pro bono work					

Work-Life Balance

23. How would you rate the environment in your workplace?

Relaxed	1	2	3	4	5	6	7	Stressful

24. In my entire associate career …

	Yes	*Yes, More Than Once*	*No*
I have scheduled a medical consultation due to suffering from work-related anxiety.			
I have cried over work-related issues.			

	Yes	Yes, More Than Once	No
I have been unfairly angry at a coworker.			
I have missed a really important family event due to work commitments.			
I have panicked about confronting my boss about something in which we disagreed.			
I have seriously feared losing my job.			
I have had visible enmity with someone at work.			
I have been deeply envious of an achieving coworker.			
I have been frustrated by my performance at a hearing.			
I have felt genuine happiness at the success of a coworker.			

25. Who is primarily responsible for setting the tone of the work environment?
    - Partners
    - Associates
    - Practitioners or legal assistants
    - Administration
    - Customers
    - Myself
26. What is the average number of hours you work per week?
    - Less than 35 hours per week
    - Between 35 and 45 hours per week
    - Between 45 and 55 hours per week
    - Between 55 and 65 hours per week
    - More than 65 hours per week
27. In a working week (Monday-Friday), how much time do you spend in leisure?
    - Less than 5 hours
    - 5-8 hours
    - 9-10 hours
    - 11-14 hours
    - 15-20 hours
    - More than 20 hours
28. Do you play sports? Please indicate how many hours per week.
    - 0
    - 1
    - 2
    - 3
    - 4
    - 5

- 6
- 7
- 8
- 9
- 10+

29. Would you be willing to receive less money for more free time?
    - Yes
    - No
30. Currently, where do you rank on the below money-free time scale?

Maximum remuneration Minimum free time	1	2	3	4	5	6	7	Minimum remuneration Maximum free time

31. How many cups of coffee do you drink per day?
    - 0 cups
    - 1 cup
    - 2 cups
    - 3 cups
    - 4 cups
    - 5+ cups
32. Do you feel that engaging in arbitration has led you to an unhealthy lifestyle?
    - Yes
    - No
33. In the last 12 months, have you consumed any of the following:

	Yes	*No*
Tobacco		
Alcohol		
Marihuana		
Adderall, modafinil or any other "smart drug"		
Antidepressants		
Anxiolytics		
MDMA or any other "party drug"		
Cocaine		

34. Please indicate how satisfied you are with the following:

	Greatly Satisfied	*Satisfied*	*Neutral*	*Dissatisfied*	*Greatly Dissatisfied*
Your salary					

	Greatly Satisfied	*Satisfied*	*Neutral*	*Dissatisfied*	*Greatly Dissatisfied*
The relationship with your direct boss					
The relationship with the partners in your practice area					
The relationship with the associates in your practice area					
Your opportunity for pro bono work					
The freedom to deal with your clients					
The freedom to manage processes					
Your ability to attract customers					
Your firm's efforts to promote work-life balance					
Your professional development					

35. In your opinion, what is the greatest virtue of the lawyers that are 50-70 years of age in your country?
36. And the biggest flaw?

Tribe and Mentoring

37. Do you find it important …

	Strongly Agree	*Agree*	*Neutral*	*Disagree*	*Strongly Disagree*
Having someone with whom you can talk about work problems					
Having a mentor who can guide you					
Having an emotional support group					

38. Do you admire any young professional from Latin-American arbitration? Please share his or her story and why you admire him or her.

39. Do you have a caring mentor who helps you evolve professionally?
40. If you would like, tell us who your mentor is and something you admire about him/her.
41. Thank you very much for your support. Do you want to appear on the list of people who answered this survey?
    - Yes
    - No

APPENDIX II SURVEY RESULTS

1. Do you feel like you are an important member at your work?
   - Strongly Agree
   - Agree
   - Neither Agree Nor Disagree
   - Disagree
   - Strongly Disagree
   - Unknown

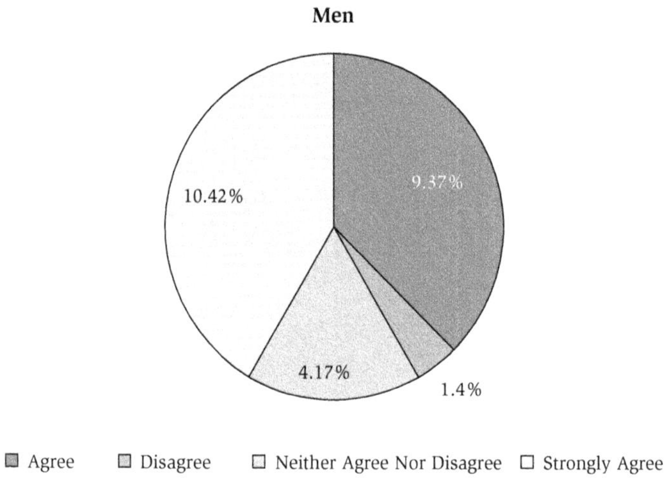

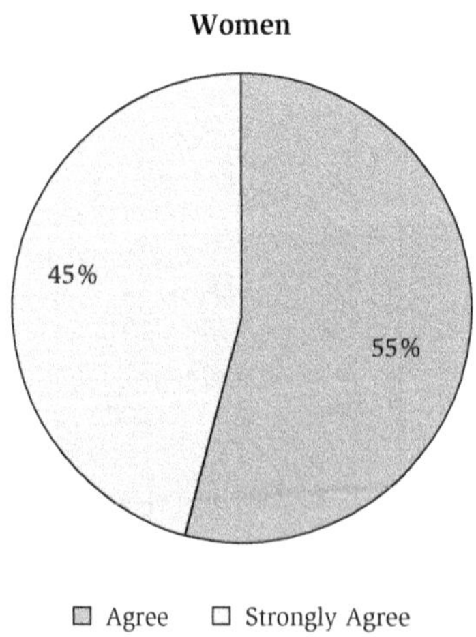

2. How prepared do you feel to participate in a case as sole arbitrator?
   - More than prepared
   - Sufficiently prepared
   - Less prepared
   - Not prepared at all

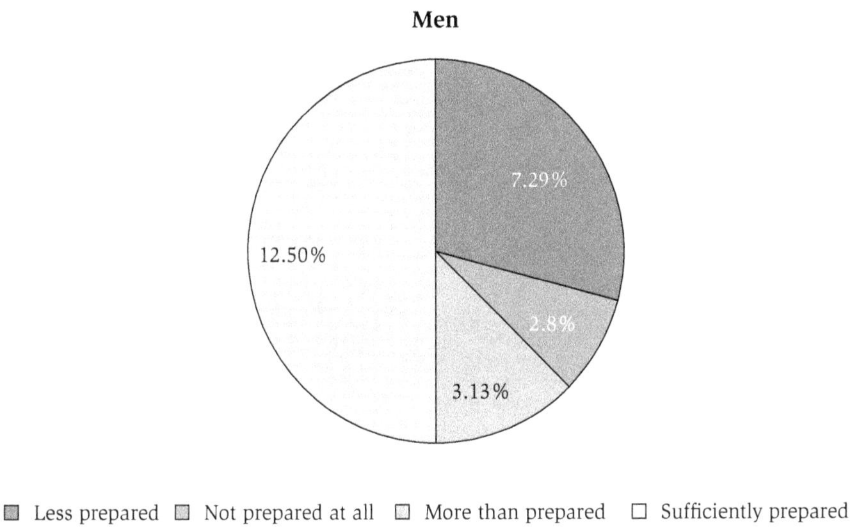

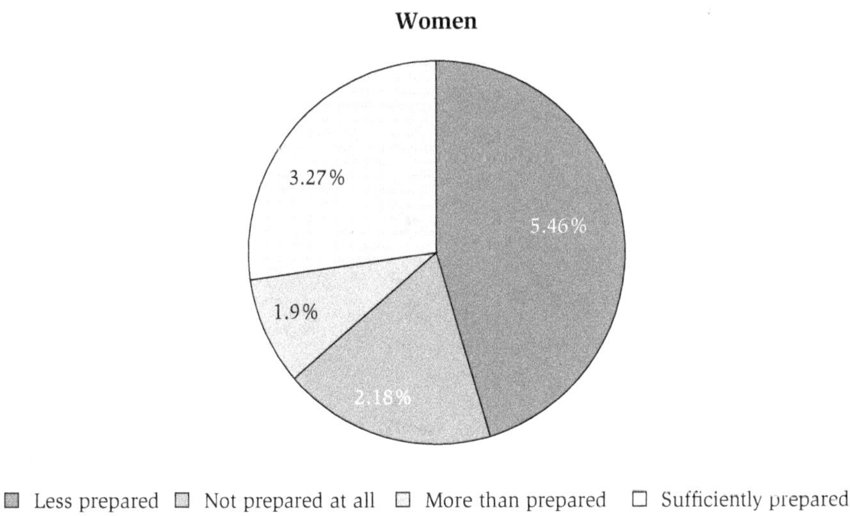

3. What do you hope to achieve in the next 10 years?
    - Be a partner in the firm where I currently work
    - Found my own firm/business/consultant company
    - Work for the state
    - Dedicate myself to being an arbitrator
    - Dedicate myself to the academy
    - Dedicate myself to my family
    - Other

Men

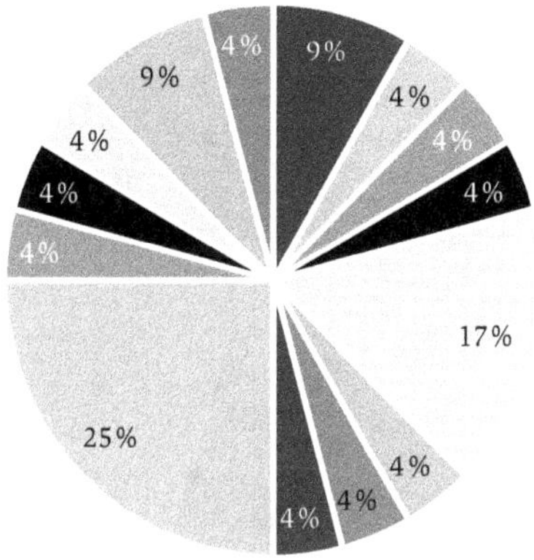

- Dedicate myself to being an arbitrator.
- Dedicate myself to being an arbitrator. Dedicate myself to the academy. Dedicate myself to my family.
- Dedicate myself to being an arbitrator. Dedicate myself to the academy. PhD in a third language.
- Dedicate myself to the academy.
- Found my own firm/business/consultant company.
- Found my own firm/business/consultant company. Dedicate myself to the academy. Dedicate myself to my family.
- Found my own firm/business/consultant company. Dedicate myself to my family.
- Found my own firm/business/consultant company. Work for the State.
- Be a partner in the firm where I currently work.
- Be a partner in the firm where I currently work. Dedicate myself to being an arbitrator. Dedicate myself to the academy.
- Be a partner in the firm where I currently work. Dedicate myself to the academy.
- Be a partner in the firm where I currently work. Dedicate myself to my family.
- Be a partner in the firm where I currently work. Found my own firm/business/consultant company.
- Be a partner in the firm where I currently work. Be the main reference of international arbitration in my country.

Woman

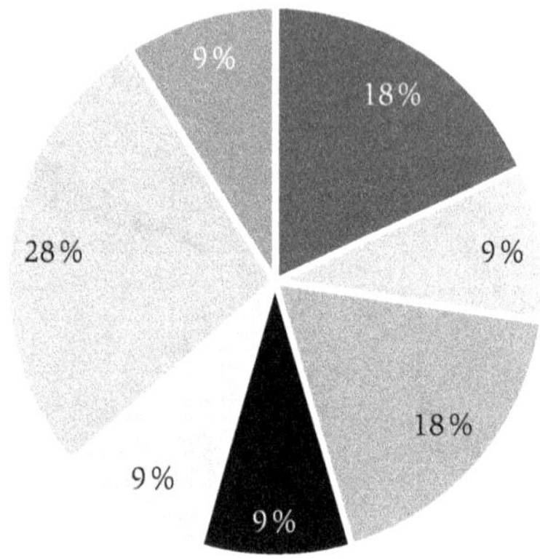

Dedicate myself to being an arbitrator.

Dedicate myself to being an arbitrator. Dedicate myself to the academy.

Dedicate myself to being an arbitrator. Dedicate myself to the academy. Dedicate myself to my family.

Found my own firm/business/consultant company.

Found my own firm/business/consultant company. Dedicate myself to being an arbitrator. Dedicate myself to the academy.

Be a partner in the firm where I currently work.

Be a partner in the firm where I currently work. Found my own firm/business/consultant company. Dedicate myself to being an arbitrator.

4. In the event that you were looking for a new job, you would look for a place that offers:
   - Higher salary
   - More free time
   - More pro bono work
   - More learning opportunities
   - Greater exposure
   - Greater recognition of achievements

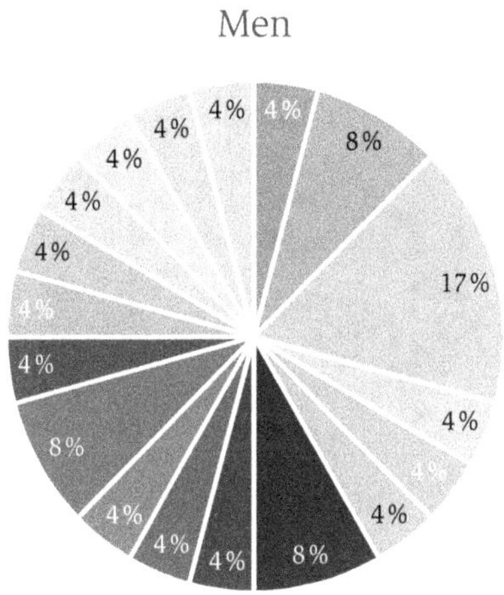

- More learning opportunities.
- More learning opportunities. Greater exposure.
- More free time.
- More free time. More learning opportunities.
- Greater exposure.
- Greater exposure. Greater recognition of achievements.
- Higher salary.
- Higher salary. More learning opportunities.
- Higher salary. More learning opportunities. Greater exposure.
- Higher salary. More learning opportunities. Greater exposure. Greater recognition of achievements.
- Higher salary. More free time.
- Higher salary. More free time. More learning opportunities. Greater exposure.
- Higher salary. More free time. More pro bono work. Greater exposure. Greater recognition of achievements.
- Higher salary. More free time. Greater exposure.
- Higher salary. More free time. Greater recognition of achievements.
- Higher salary. Greater exposure.
- Higher salary. Greater exposure. Greater recognition of achievements.
- Higher salary. Greater recognition of achievements.

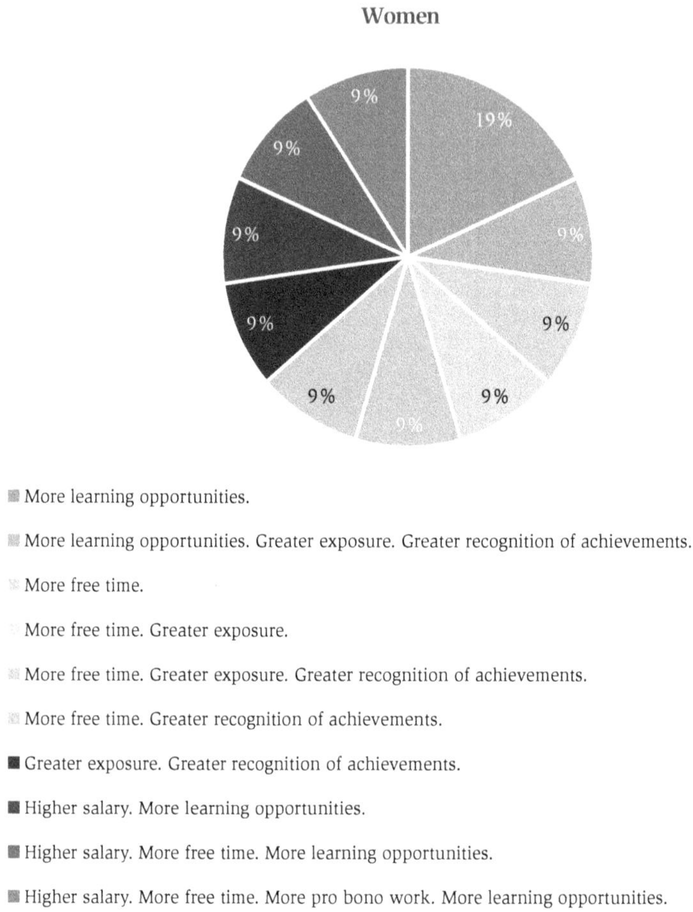

5. Do you think it is possible to have the same salary and prestige with fewer hours of work?
   - Yes
   - No

Men

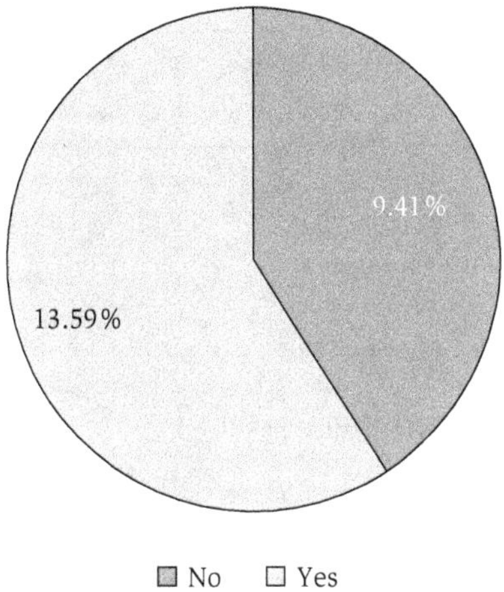

Women

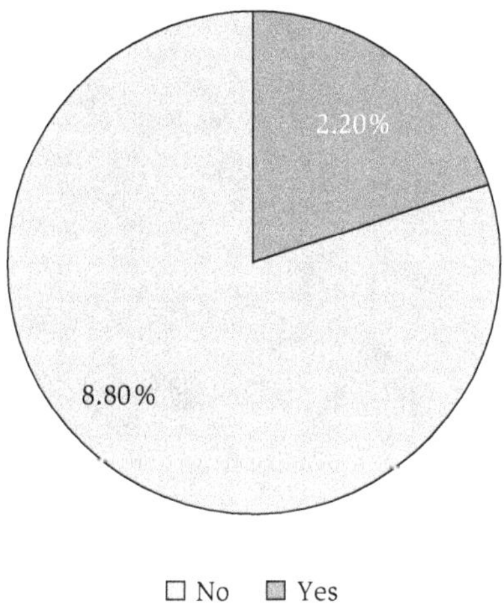

6. In my entire associate career ...

	Yes	*Yes, More Than Once*	*No*
I have scheduled a medical consultation due to suffering from work-related anxiety.			
I have cried over work-related issues.			
I have been unfairly angry at a coworker.			

	Yes	*Yes, More Than Once*	*No*
I have missed a really important family event due to work commitments.			
I have panicked about confronting my boss about something in which we disagreed.			
I have seriously feared losing my job.			
I have had visible enmity with someone at work.			
I have been deeply envious of an achieving coworker.			
I have been frustrated by my performance at a hearing.			
I have felt genuine happiness at the success of a coworker.			

I have scheduled a medical consultation due to suffering from work-related anxiety.

Men

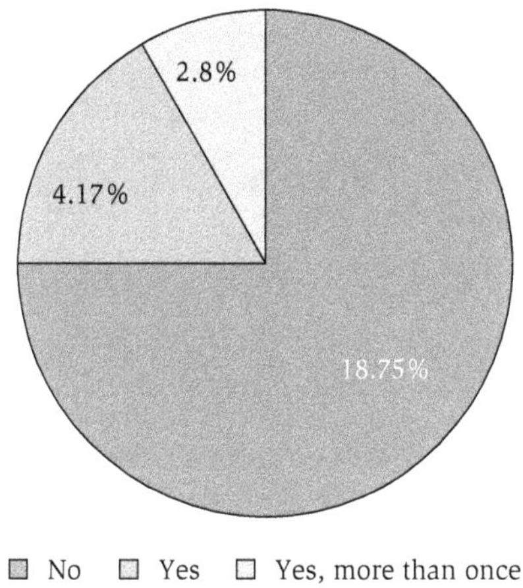

Women

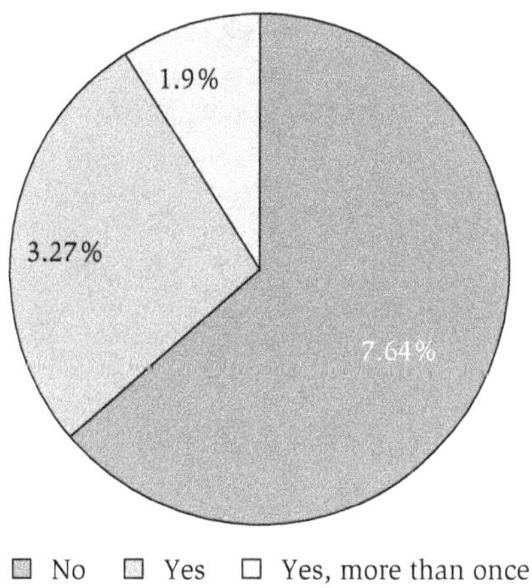

I have cried over work-related issues.

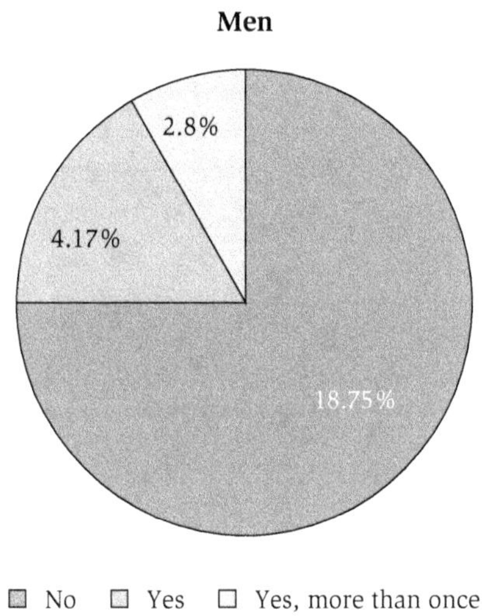

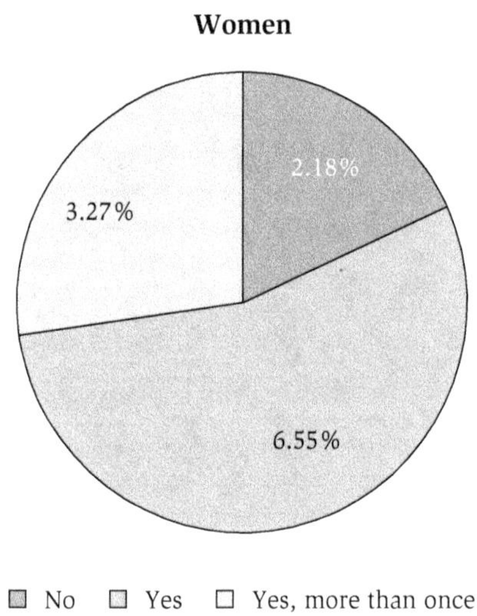

I have missed a really important family event due to work commitments.

Men

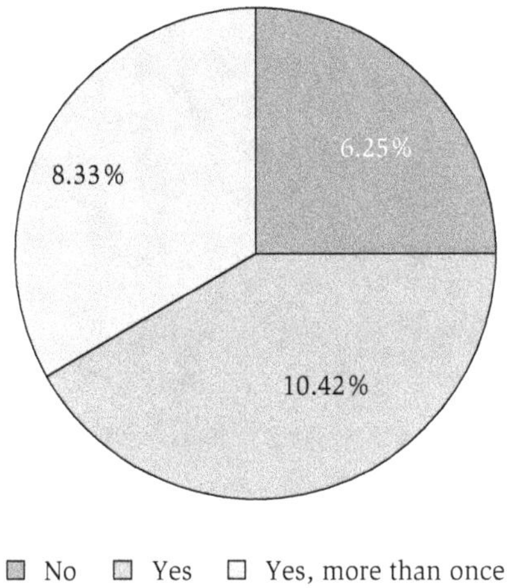

Women

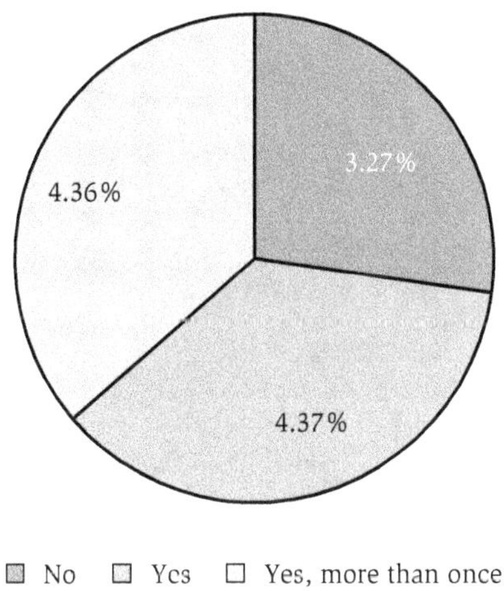

I have panicked about confronting my boss about something in which we disagreed.

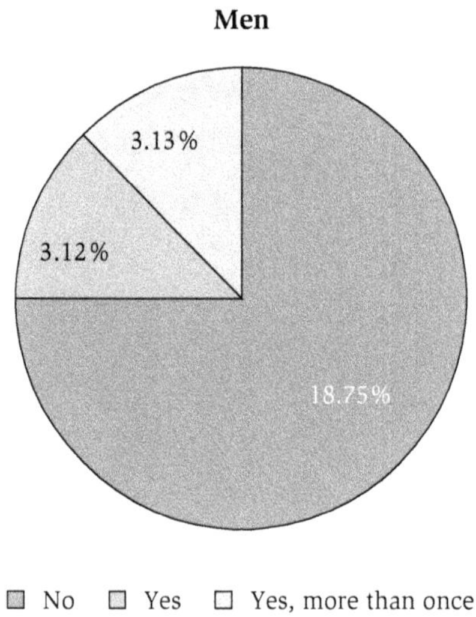

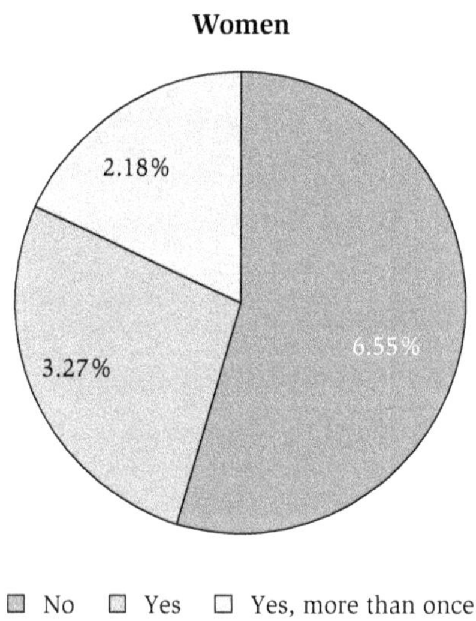

I have seriously feared losing my job.

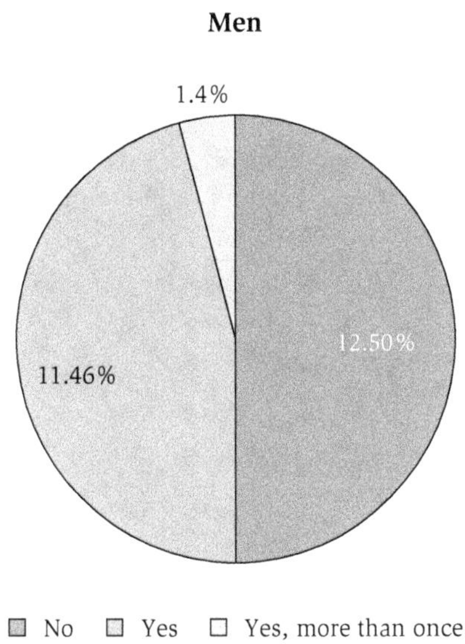

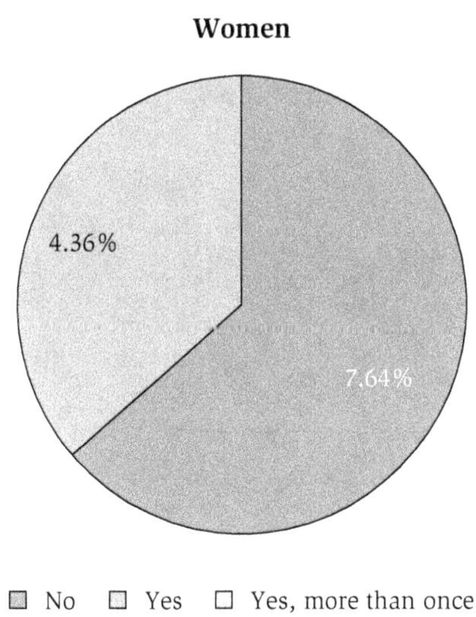

I have had visible enmity with someone at work.

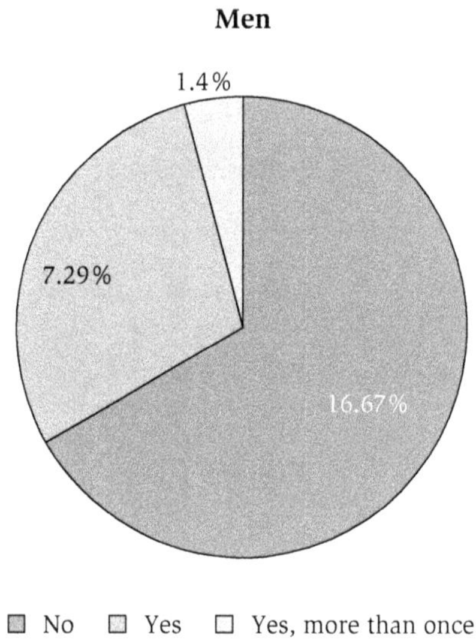

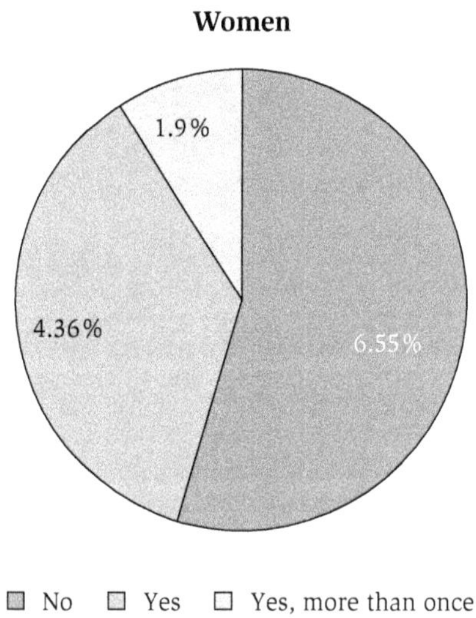

I have been deeply envious of an achieving coworker.

Men

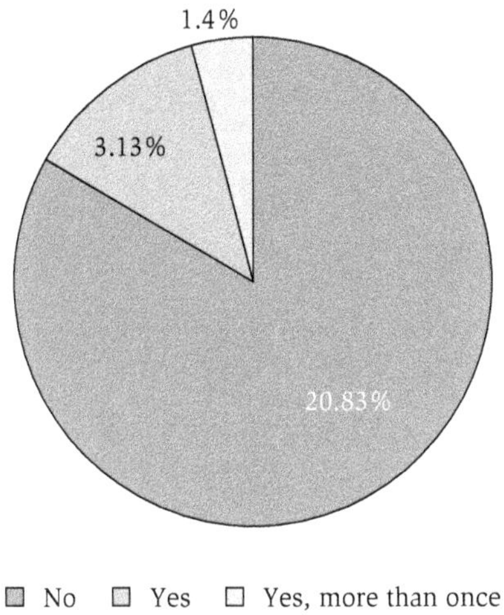

Women

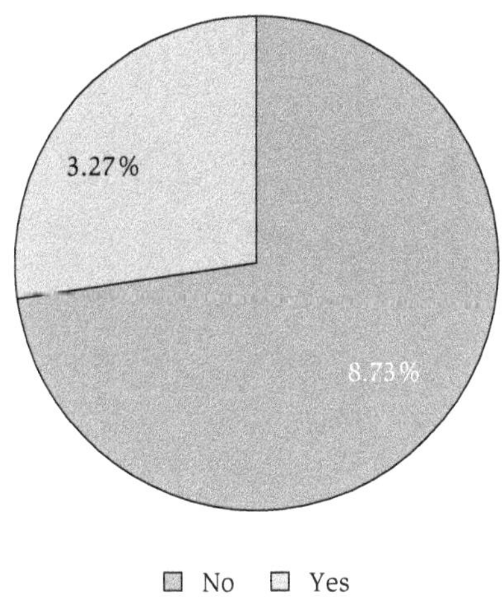

I have felt genuine happiness at the success of a coworker.

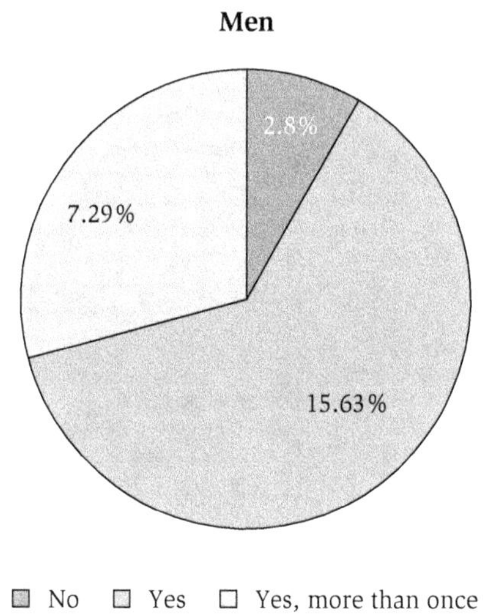

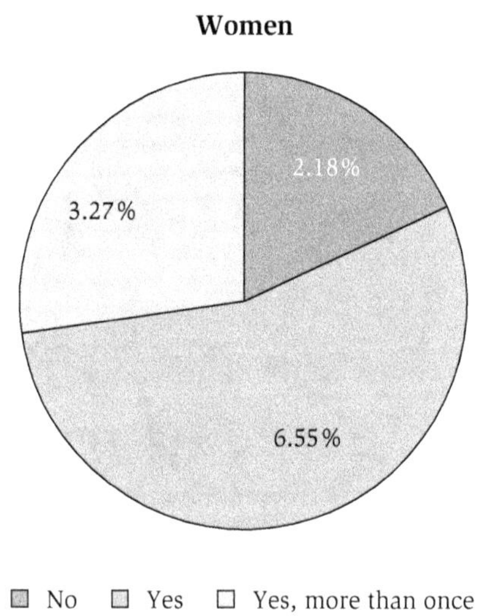

7. What is the average number of hours you work per week?
   - Less than 35 hours per week
   - Between 35 and 45 hours per week
   - Between 45 and 55 hours per week
   - Between 55 and 65 hours per week
   - More than 65 hours per week

Men

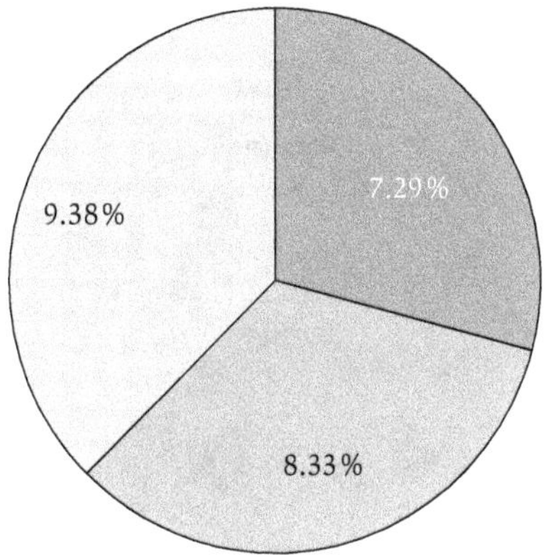

Between 35 and 45 hours per week. Between 45 and 55 hours per week.

Between 55 and 65 hours per week.

Women

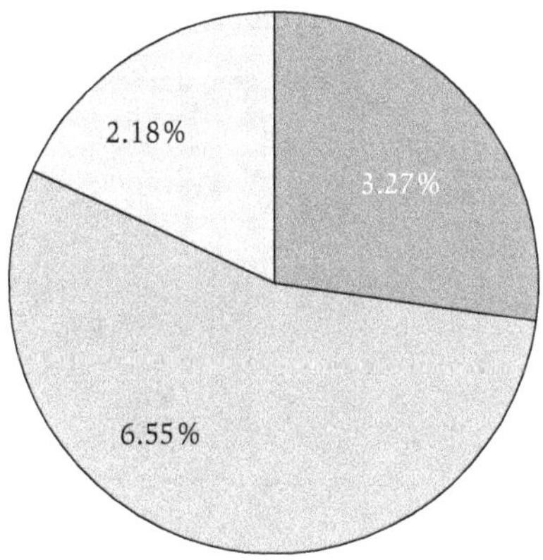

Between 35 and 45 hours per week. Between 45 and 55 hours per week.

Between 55 and 65 hours per week.

8. In a working week (Monday-Friday), how much time do you spend in leisure?
   - Less than 5 hours
   - 5-8 hours
   - 9-10 hours
   - 11-14 hours

- 15-20 hours
- More than 20 hours

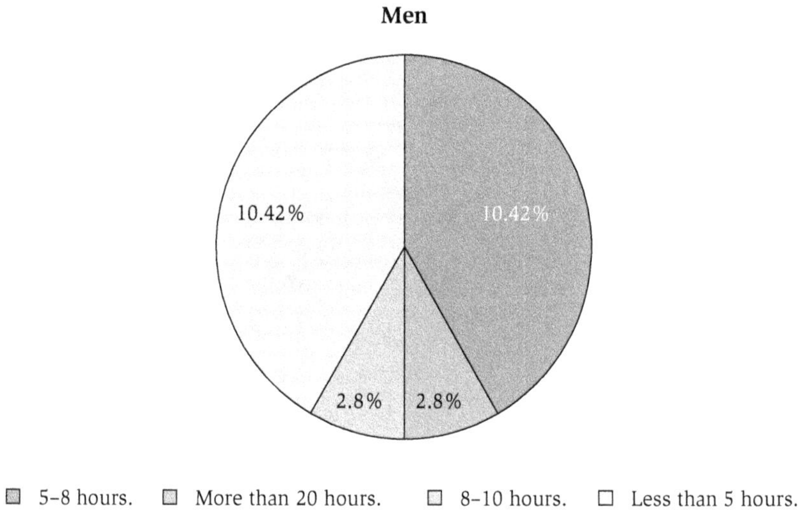

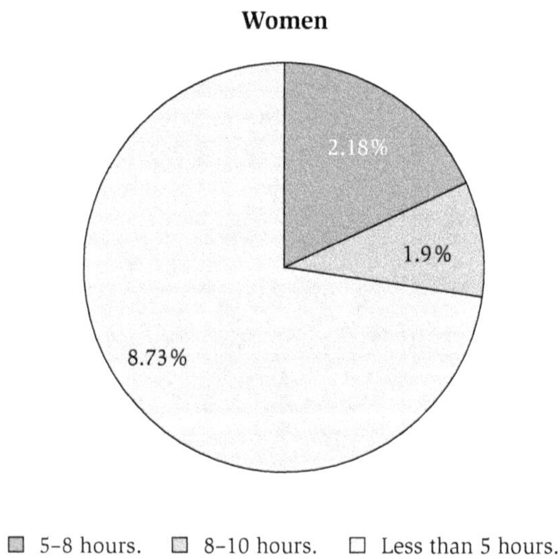

9. Would you be willing to receive less money for more free time?
    - Yes
    - No

Men

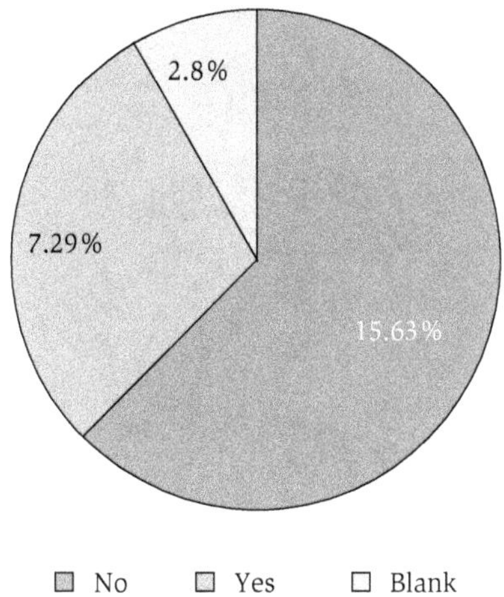

Women

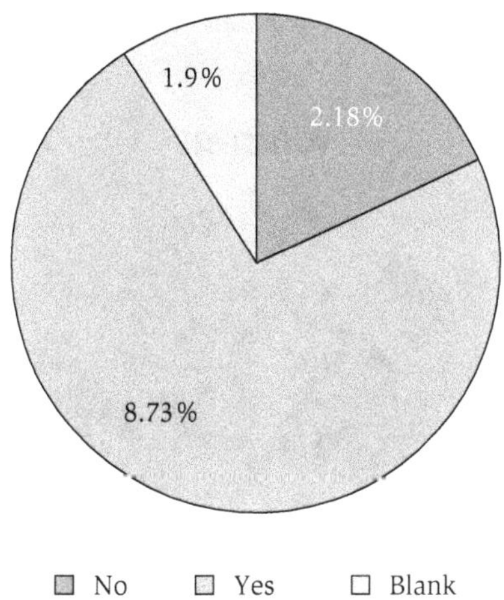

10. Please indicate how satisfied you are with the following:

	Greatly Satisfied	*Satisfied*	*Neutral*	*Dissatisfied*	*Greatly Dissatisfied*
Your salary					
Your firm's efforts to promote work-life balance					

Your salary

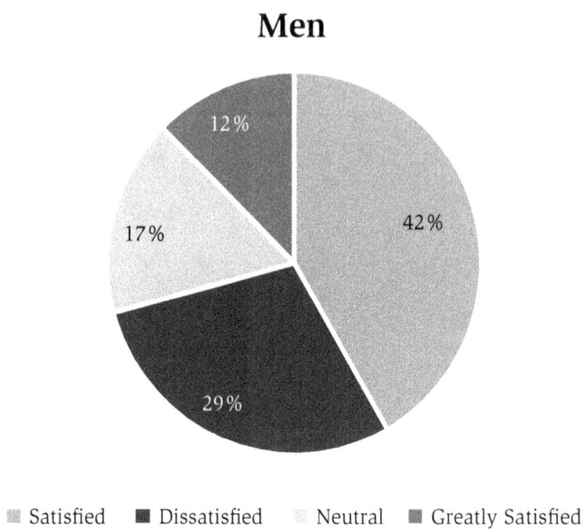
Men
12%
17%
42%
29%
Satisfied
Dissatisfied
Neutral
Greatly Satisfied

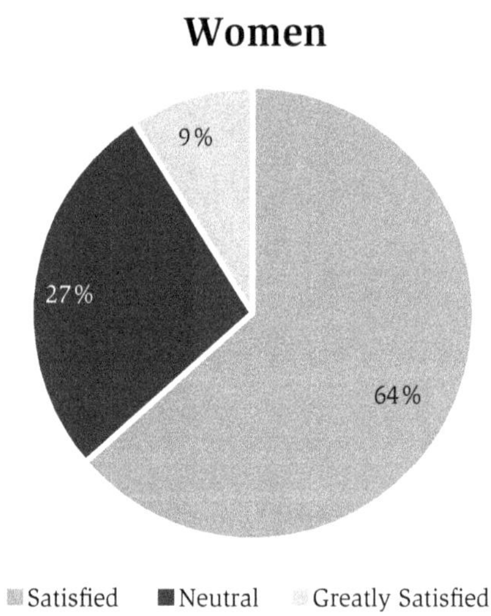
Women
9%
27%
64%
Satisfied
Neutral
Greatly Satisfied

Your firm's efforts to promote work-life balance

Men

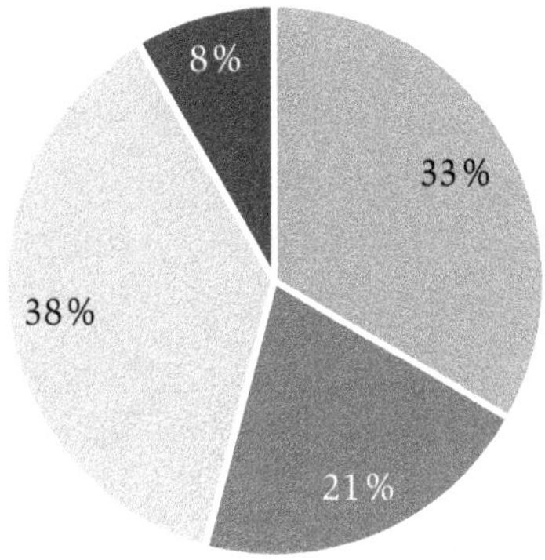

Women

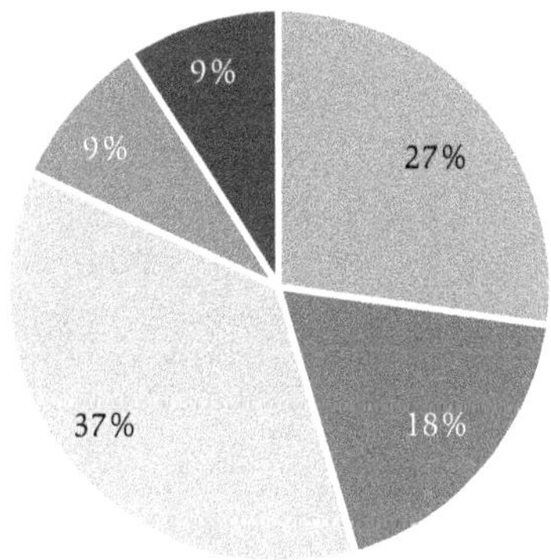

CHAPTER 38
Diversity in Arbitration

Patricia Vera

Without a doubt, the advantages of arbitration, including confidentiality of the proceedings and the possibility of choosing the arbitrators that will solve the dispute, have made arbitration a more attractive and reliable system. However, while disputes in arbitration are increasingly diverse, the participation of women in arbitration remains limited, including low percentages of their participation as arbitrators in different arbitral institutions.

This issue has been dealt with in several articles and statistical analyzes by some arbitral institutions in their annual reports. It is striking that notwithstanding the growth of international arbitration and the addition of important active participation of women lawyers, there is a greater number of cases in which the parties or the other members of the arbitral tribunal appoint men over women. These appointments are made despite the creation of groups that aim to promote parity in the designations of arbitrators and to generate a wide network of contacts with an active participation of women.

The data and information collected by the different arbitration institutions worldwide show a low percentage of women's participation. According to the ICC, only 16.7% of arbitrators are women with an average participation of women at 18% in 2017. Likewise, the Arbitration Institute of the Stockholm Chamber of Commerce, which handles a large number of arbitrations, has an average of 18% of participation of female arbitrators. This reality does not distance itself from the situation in Ecuador, where the participation of women as arbitrators is very low, and the reason why arbitral institutions are working to increase the number of women arbitrators in their lists.

It gives rise to the necessity to understand the reasons why this percentage of women participation in arbitration as arbitrators is so low in relation to arbitration activity and the number of cases. In an article written by Caroline dos Santos, called

"Diversity in International Arbitration: A No-Woman's Land?"[1] the author makes an interesting analysis of the unconscious biases that exist when appointing arbitrators. Biases that come along with us over time and that, implicitly, led to the appointment of arbitrators of the following category: white older men.

Biases go back to customs and traditions that unconsciously led us to have certain inclinations or to create stereotypes. At the beginning of my law career, when I thought of a judge, the first image that came to mind was an elderly man, representing the male figure of respect and recognition.

Today, the participation of women as arbitrators is still low in relation to the appointments of male arbitrators. Also, there is particularly little participation of young women as arbitrators due to the various limitations that the system itself has unconsciously generated.

Nowadays, two women who are great representatives of female arbitrators and who hold the most important designations are Brigitte Stern and Gabrielle Kaufmann-Kohler. Both have marked the difference in the history of female designations as arbitrators through their career and professional excellence.

It is important to note that the increase in the participation of women in arbitral tribunals, as well as the designations of male arbitrators, must be made in consideration of the professional and human qualities of each person. Under no circumstances, women should be solely appointed because they are women, and there is a need to meet a preestablished quota. On the contrary, equal opportunities should be provided considering merits and efforts.

Being aware of the existence of biases and patterns that are culturally repeating has both a negative and a positive side (as with everything). The negative side is realizing that despite the development and growth of international arbitration, there is currently a large difference in the number of appointments of male and female arbitrators. However, the positive side is the generating awakened interest of women to change a reality that has unconsciously been a limit to them. Likewise, being aware that changes must come from women have motivated many professionals to be more prepared and to join new spaces that seek to strengthen an international network of professional women. Different roles in the arbitration community encourage the participation of women in arbitral tribunals and academic activities, such as speakers at conferences about arbitration.

Several organizations and groups have emerged with the desire to create spaces in which professional women interested in arbitration can generate contacts and have a starting point. Among the most relevant organizations for this purpose are Arbitral Women since 1993, The Pledge since 2015, and CEA Women of the Spanish Arbitration Club since 2017.

One way to spread and encourage the participation of women in arbitration that comes from women themselves has been sharing their experiences and professional knowledge, the challenges they have faced throughout their careers, and the way they

1. Caroline dos Santos. "Diversity in International Arbitration: A No—Woman's Land." https://www.lalive.law/wp-content/uploads/2018/12/Diversity-in-international-arbitration_dos-Santos.pdf, May 2006.

were climbing in their professional lives. These experiences motivate other young female lawyers who on many occasions want to venture into the arbitral world but do not know how to do it.

Currently, there are also mentoring programs for women who want to know more about arbitration, allowing them to have personalized contact with a mentor who can guide them according to their expectations and challenges they wish to face.

Having knowledge about the low percentage of women's participation in arbitration has generated a lot of interest in the international arbitration community and has raised awareness when choosing an arbitrator, inviting a speaker, or suggesting a woman's name.

An important step to increase the participation of women in arbitration also comes from the side of the arbitral institutions since they have begun to include recognized and outstanding women with professional experience in their lists. Most arbitration institutions conduct a thorough analysis when including an arbitrator in their lists, so being part of one of them generates great support and trust in attendants of the arbitration process. Recently one of the most recognized European arbitration courts, the Court of Arbitration of Madrid, reached parity in the appointment of arbitrators.[2]

Finally, true changes in diversity will be seen to the extent that each of the different actors is aware and commits to consider and designate more women as arbitrators. Again, these women should be chosen based on their experience and capabilities and not simply on their gender, leaving prejudices or biases that unconsciously have accompanied humanity for a long time.

2. http://www.arbitramadrid.com/documents/20181/26618/180907 + Nota + de + prensa.pdf/36b867-4eac-4e81-ae45-4d0a897c2e72.

CHAPTER 39

Three Mentors, Three Lessons*

Juan M. Rey

Sometimes litigation is a craft. Like a carpenter who starts being an apprentice and turns into a master after some years, litigants usually start as paralegals until we finally reach the long-desired position of *first chair*. Experience does matter.

What we read in books is great information. It is a necessary requirement to be a good litigant. But experience and "grey hair" share some weight. There is worth in experience and in repetition, although the academic stage undoubtedly provides greater value. However, litigants do not work—yet—convincing robots. We work convincing humans: beings with their own past, emotions, and backgrounds. And it is mainly learnt while playing in the field.

In the arbitration world, nobody earns that experience for free. Given the intellectual attractiveness of the subject and a misunderstood "glamour" in what we do in arbitration,[1] experience is literally a commodity in which we pay. There are plenty of unpaid internships and job offers for interns to which graduates from the best master and doctorate degrees apply willing to work in exchange for *"a hotdog and a coke."*[2]

To sail the unreliable waters of arbitration and to acquire the relevant amount of grey hair, it is important to have a good mentor to help us. I would like to introduce three examples of mentors I enjoyed throughout the years—anonymously, of course—in the hope that it encourages some readers to seek mentors of their own.

---

* This chapter is about professional mentors rather than personal mentors. In connection to the latter, I keep those stories to myself.

1. Any person working as an associate in a hearing at Paris, New York or any other "glamorous" city knows that (i) Domino's pizza (the basic sustenance of every junior associate) tastes the same in every city, regardless of how glamorous the city is; (ii) after two or three nights without any sleep, the floor of a *war room* provides a better rest than the best bed of the available Plaza Hotel; and (iii) after a hearing concludes the only thing one desires is to lock oneself at a hotel and sleep. The only ones that enjoy the areas of the hearing are usually the arbitrators, partners, and clients. I say everything with some healthy envy and a pinch of the other one.
2. Phrase adopted from my Argentine Mentor as defined below.

I will call my first mentor the "Uruguayan Mentor." From my Uruguayan Mentor I learned to litigate.

My Uruguayan Mentor is the partner in charge of the contentious area at the first law firm in which I worked. For some unknown reasons, this partner—who has a great amount of grey hair—appreciated me and allowed me to be his shadow for a significant length of time.[3] In fact, being aware that the mentoring process at big firms is a nice story not always reflected in reality, this partner decided to train me by showing me—live and direct—how he destroyed my written documents one by one.

Therefore, as a paralegal[4] and then as a first- and second-year lawyer, this partner asked me to work directly for him in many opportunities, and I delivered my best effort. After I sent him my writings, I sat behind his chair and observed how he corrected my words, and my Uruguayan Mentor really corrected. Whole written texts expressed with the most flowery language would be reduced to a big red spot of track changes.

I did not learn by writing but by seeing how my Uruguayan Mentor wrote. One could say I learned to write by reading.

I will call my second mentor the "Argentinean Mentor." From my Argentinean Mentor, I learnt to trust myself.

I obtained my L.L.M. as a 25-year-old working in Washington D.C. I still remember my first day at that firm. I had no idea what I was going to do, how I was going to do it, and how much my tasks would cost me.[5] I started on a Monday, June 2. I did not have an apartment, given that I was asked to start earlier than planned. I arrived at a hotel and began to look for a place to live. On the first day, the Senior Associate of the firm—to whom I owe my life and sanity—let me know that we had to file a rejoinder for an UNCITRAL arbitration before the period of expiration. Then, at the end of July, we had to file a submission in connection to provisional measures of a process within the ICSID and hold a hearing. All of these tasks had to be done in two months.

As usual, one survives these work shocks. My baptism by fire had been quite accelerated with two filings and a hearing during my first two months, but I somehow managed. However, sometime after these initial months, the Senior Associate who had protected me from the beginning decided to change jobs. My workmate and I, both newbies,[6] were left there under the direct orders of our boss, who during his young age of 30 years old had been the lawyer in charge of litigating the most relevant cases of investment arbitrations of the twenty-first century's first decade. And at that time, I felt all I knew was how to tie my shoes.

3. My Uruguayan Mentor is about two meters tall. I am clearly not. Needless to say, as I walked behind him around the streets of the old city in my beloved Montevideo carrying the files of the hearings, many compared us with Don Quixote and Sancho Panza.
4. Depending on the country, paralegal means a worker at a law firm, legal practitioner, intern, and of course, paralegal.
5. Of course, I did not ask him what he—who would become my boss—expected from me. Between the exams to qualify for the firm and the stress of the situation, we spoke about *Real Hervido*—an amateur team from Fray Bentos, department of Río Negro, Uruguay—instead of asking him the questions I should have during my interview.
6. Brotherhood bonds are forged in war. As a first-year associate, even stronger bonds are forged.

I had never seen anyone work as my Argentinean Mentor. If my workmate and I did not sleep at night, he also stayed awake through the night. During hearings, he prepared cross-examinations and then executed them without having slept a wink. Anything we delivered was improved—sometimes even fully modified—after he corrected it. All happened without losing faith in the arbitral proceeding. Within that frame of admiration, he allowed my workmate and me, at 26 and 28 years old, respectively, to carry out our first examinations.[7]

I could not believe it. This partner from an international law firm, who had litigated the cases that one reads in books, had trusted me to carry out a cross-examination hearing. This fact—of little importance according to him, who until this day still gets mad when I tell I owe him my small career because he *"does not want to be anybody's mentor"*—provided me with more trust in myself than the best grade obtained at the most difficult exam from any university. This trust accompanies me to this date, and I still call him to seek advice about my professional decisions.

I will call my third mentor the "Chilean Mentor." From my Chilean Mentor, I am learning to live from arbitration without dying in the attempt.

I arrived to Santiago from Chile from Washington D.C. during the Southern winter peak. In the first days at my new office, I had lunch at noon sharp while working at my desk. On the sixth day, a partner at the office passed to see if I was doing well and encouraged me to go have lunch, saying "*You are not in D.C. anymore.*" After having spent many years in the United States, landing in a culture very similar to my own, without being my own culture, was itself a learning process. I wanted everything immediately. I could not understand how anyone could *join a call* four minutes late. I became desperate at meetings that could have been a team e-mail. I was undergoing a process of adaptation.

"*Easy Gordo, each day requires a different effort.*" My Chilean Mentor acted more as a psychologist than a mentor with my return to Latin America. Eventually, it became more difficult to continue carrying this nervous energy, as my boss, who was just 31 years old and an ICC arbitrator, always remained calm and trusted the process.

Litigation entails a commonsense practical requirement, and I believe that with each grey hair, you gain more common sense. When someone like my Chilean Mentor (who has seen many filings during his fifteen-year span) tells his senior associate not to worry for a filing when he faces an important health issue, you see this practical requirement in action. "*Gordo, no one is indispensable, health is always first.*"

In the turmoil of a case, sometimes you cannot see the forest. Obviously, if you need to work during the entire night, you work throughout the night. However, my Chilean Mentor taught me that an excellent exhausted lawyer is a bad lawyer.

7. I remember mine until this day. It was a short direct and redirect examination at a hearing performed pursuant to UNCITRAL rules in Paris. The other party's lawyer performing the cross-examination was one of those lawyers whose articles I had read and whom I profoundly admired. I objected his cross-examination twice and won once. I called my girlfriend (current wife) to tell her I had won an objection. She was happy for me but confessed she could not completely understand my thrill.

Sometimes, the search for perfection is the enemy of results. When one becomes a parent, missed birthdays are never repeated, and being happy and being *Band 1 in Chambers* are actually compatible.

CHAPTER 40

How to Survive a Decade at Dechert LLP

Juan Felipe Merizalde

"*I am going to get fired,*" I thought as I walked down Rue des Courcelles toward the corner of Avenue de la Messine. It was 23:45 and the last bus of Route 80—in the direction to Jules Joffrin—would pass at any time. But this cold winter night was different from any of the other four or five nights a week in which I had to run to reach the last bus.

"*Why did I do that? How will I pay the rent at the end of the month?*" I kept thinking. In 2008, my monthly salary of EUR 1,800 covered my expenses, a few nights on the town, and savings of EUR 100 or 200 to travel to see my mother in December. I will never forget that day. Eduardo—my boss, my mentor, and yet my friend—discovered that I was responsible for a wrongdoing that could have and should have represented the end of my days in the arbitral world.

We had just finished the hearing on damages in *Oxy*. *Oxy* was a unicorn for many. On the last day, with a mixture of tiredness, pride, and satisfaction, we ordered pizza for everyone, including expert witnesses, witnesses, attorneys, and clients. After a fun time remembering the anecdotes from the hearing, someone suggested the plan that would mark my future: "*Let's keep the empty pizza boxes. When Eduardo comes on his scooter, we will paste them on its back (the motorcycle's back, not Eduardo's back) so he has to distribute them.*" The plan was perfect. However, nobody imagined that the pizza smell would escape from the closet and mixed with the smell of two young attorneys who had spent so many nights in an eight square meter space would implicate us.

Eleven years after this instance, while reflecting on the kind invitation to write about the difficult issue of surviving a decade at Dechert, I thought this story would summarize my time, and these five circumstances account for it.

§40.01 YOU WILL GROW FROM BELOW

First, because in Dechert, as in many other firms in Paris, the driveway will be long and full of Laestrygones. For the young Latin-American practitioner who arrives with two suitcases, a couple of cents, and a diploma under his arm, the road will involve competing with European lawyers, many of them with master's degrees and exchanges, hoping someone will notice him and will accept to process for him the so-longed French work permit. It is not uncommon that the Latin-American scholar, who perhaps has already worked in his home country, has to start as an intern in an open space with seven or eight peers eager to be "the lucky one" (rarely there were two) who receives an offer at the end of the internship. You have to accept that every pyramid has a lower base, and the lower base will be you, and you will carry all its weight.

§40.02 WORK, WORK, AND WORK

Second, a common denominator of associates in Dechert is their unrestricted commitment to work. Especially in the early years, it will be difficult to balance personal life with the harsh demands of work. The path of international arbitration—in Dechert and in other large firms—will involve hard sacrifices, but the reward is immense.

§40.03 THE PASSION

The pizza story is not related to passion, but it is not a non sequitur. The third characteristic of an associate in Dechert is everyone has a peculiarity or strangeness that distinguishes them from the normal or ordinary lawyer. Whether it is a black sense of humor, an almost brutal frankness, the shyness of an intellectual, or the hyperactivity of a small child, the truth is all of us in Dechert are kind of freaks. These qualities that we unconsciously seek in job interviews reflect, in a difficult way to explain, the passion of those professionals who love the law and arbitration. It may be my only advice. If you do not feel passion for this career, you better not do it. Like Ulysses, according to Cavafis, when you start your trip to Ithaca, hope that the journey will be long.

§40.04 LEARN AGAIN

Fourth, the Dechert associate must learn to forget and want to learn everything again. We all arrived in Dechert believing we knew how to write. Many had performed in theater, were student representatives, or participated in moot courts, and, therefore, believed they dominated words. We were wrong. I pride myself in admitting the following in writing. Dechert's work has an implicit seal of quality that requires relearning what we thought we already knew. You must find the honesty and humility to learn again. I will never forget the story of one of my best friends in Dechert. One winter day in 2010, this hero without a cape left his resignation letter on the boss' desk. Minutes later, the furious boss returned the letter. "*This is unacceptable,*" he said. The letter was filled with corrections of typos in red, repetitions, and lack of structure. "*If you are going to give me a letter, give me something well written.*" My friend laughed nervously, threw the letter into the garbage bin, and kept working. A couple of years later, he presented his resignation letter. As it was well written this time, our boss accepted it. Today, I consider my friend to be one of the brightest lawyers in international arbitration in France.

§40.05 YOU WILL BE PART OF THE FAMILY

Finally, once you overcome the horrible filter of the internship and first years as an associate, you will begin to feel that you are part of a family. And in families there is love and understanding but much demand. While writing this chapter, I received the sad news that my mother was on the verge of death. The understanding of my family in Dechert left me stunned. I will never forget how my bosses and colleagues reproached me for answering emails or calling to ask if everything was going well. Like the editors of this book, who were very patient with me, the human prevailed over the professional. And it is one of the qualities for which words will never be sufficient. I will never know if the misdeed of the pizza influenced the decision to hire me. But a decade later, and without ever having set foot in another international firm, I dare to say that this ship with its Poseidons, Laestrygones and Cyclops has taken me through all the Ithacas I wanted to visit.

SOBREVIVIENDO EN EL ARBITRAJE INTERNACIONAL

SOBREVIVIENDO EN EL ARBITRAJE INTERNACIONAL

HISTORIAS DE GUERRA Y LECCIONES APRENDIDAS

Edited by

José María de la Jara

Carolina Arroyo

Álvaro Awad

Wolters Kluwer

Published by:
Kluwer Law International B.V.
PO Box 316
2400 AH Alphen aan den Rijn
The Netherlands
E-mail: international-sales@wolterskluwer.com
Website: lrus.wolterskluwer.com

Sold and distributed in North, Central and South America by:
Wolters Kluwer Legal & Regulatory U.S.
7201 McKinney Circle
Frederick, MD 21704
United States of America
Email: customer.service@wolterskluwer.com

Sold and distributed in all other countries by:
Air Business Subscriptions
Rockwood House
Haywards Heath
West Sussex
RH16 3DH
United Kingdom
Email: international-customerservice@wolterskluwer.com

Printed on acid-free paper.

ISBN 978-94-035-1760-5

e-Book: ISBN 978-94-035-1811-4
web-PDF: ISBN 978-94-035-1855-8

Printed in the United Kingdom.

A Alfredo Bullard,
por todas nuestras conversaciones de viernes por la tarde.
José María de la Jara

A Lucas y Sven.
Carolina Arroyo

A mi mentor, Óscar Contreras Blanco,
por confiar en mí desde el comienzo de mi carrera.
Álvaro Awad

SOBRE LOS EDITORES

José María de la Jara es un abogado peruano dedicado al arbitraje que actualmente trabaja como Global Visiting Lawyer en Washington, D.C. Ha actuado como Coordinador de Capacitación en la Iniciativa de Estado de Derecho de la American Bar Association y trabajó durante ocho años como asociado de arbitraje en Bullard Falla Ezcurra en Lima, Perú. Tiene un J.D. de la Pontificia Universidad Católica del Perú y un LL.M. de la Facultad de Derecho de la Universidad de Columbia. Es embajador de Arbitrator Intelligence, fundó PsychoLAWgy y es autor de más de 50 artículos en la intersección de resolución de disputas, ciencias del comportamiento y tecnología.

Carolina Arroyo es asociada senior en Andrade Veloz, una firma ecuatoriana de abogados donde dirige el Departamento de Resolución de Disputas y Litigios Complejos. Carolina tiene un LL.M de Bucerius Law School y Otto Beisheim School of Management en Alemania. Es profesora en la Universidad San Francisco de Quito, se desempeña como embajadora de Arbitrator Intelligence y es miembro del Comité de Jóvenes del Instituto Ecuatoriano de Arbitraje. Carolina también actúa como secretaria de tribunales arbitrales en el Centro de Arbitraje y Mediación de la Cámara de Comercio de Quito. Carolina es cofundadora diferentes plataformas de internet en las industrias de la construcción y el arte con presencia en América Latina.

Álvaro Awad es socio de Contreras Velozo, una oficina boutique de resolución de disputas en Santiago de Chile. Es profesor de Derecho Civil, Arbitraje y Litigación Oral en la Pontificia Universidad Católica de Chile, donde obtuvo su J.D. *summa cum laude*. Tiene un LL.M. de la Facultad de Derecho de la Universidad de Chicago, donde estudió como Becario Chile y como Becario Fulbright. Es Fundador de la asociación Santiago Very Young Arbitration Practitioners, se desempeña como embajador de Arbitrator Intelligence en Chile y es Reportero del Boletín de Arbitraje Comercial y de Inversiones en América Latina. Está incluido como Árbitro en el Registro Oficial de la Corte de Apelaciones de Santiago.

LISTA DE AUTORES

Ricardo Ampuero es presidente de la Comisión Especial que representa a la República del Perú en Disputas de Inversión Internacional en el Ministerio de Finanzas y Economía del Perú. LL.M. por la Universidad de Columbia.

Félix Antolín es Director de Litigio Civil y Arbitraje en Albagli Zaliasnik, Santiago, Chile. LL.M. por la Universidad de Nueva York.

Crina Baltag es profesora titular de Arbitraje Internacional en la Universidad de Estocolmo. Ph. D. por la Universidad Queen Mary de Londres.

Gary Born es presidente del Grupo de Arbitraje Internacional en Wilmer Cutler Pickering Hale y Dorr LLP. Presidente del Tribunal de Arbitraje del Centro Internacional de Arbitraje de Singapur (SIAC). Autor del Arbitraje Comercial Internacional (2ª ed. 2014), el tratado preeminente en el campo del arbitraje, así como el Arbitraje Internacional: Derecho y Práctica (2ª ed. 2015) y una serie de otros trabajos notables sobre temas internacionales.

Alfredo Bullard es Socio en Bullard, Falla, Ezcura +, Lima, Perú. LL.M. por Yale School of Law.

María Angélica Burgos es Abogada de la Pontificia Universidad Javeriana, Bogotá, LL.M en Regulación, Litigios y Arbitraje de Negocios Internacionales por la Universidad de Nueva York.

Roque Caivano es Profesor de la Universidad de Buenos Aires. Tiene un doctorado en Ciencias Jurídicas por la Universidad del Salvador. Cofundador del Concurso de Arbitraje Internacional de la UBA-Universidad del Rosario.

Briana Canorio es Abogada por la Universidad de Lima. Se desempeñó como directora de la Dirección de Arbitraje Administrativo del OSCE, Sub Gerente de Contratos de la Gerencia Corporativa Legal de PETROPERÚ S.A. y ex representante del Grupo de Jóvenes Árbitros de ICC YAF para Latinoamérica.

Manuel Casas es abogado del Departamento de Litigios de WilmerHale. Antes de unirse a WilmerHale trabajó como asistente legal (U.T.) en la Corte Internacional de Justicia de La Haya.

Manuel Conthe es árbitro y residente del Consejo Asesor del Periódico Empresarial Español Expansión.

Diana Correa es Fundadora Diana Correa International SAS, Bogotá, Colombia. Ph.D por la Université Panthéon Assas (París II).

Daniel Cuentas es Asociado en Osterling Abogados. Embajador de ArbitratorIntelligence. LL.B. por la Universidad Peruana de Ciencias Aplicadas.

Juliana de Valdenebro es Secretaria de Derecho Extranjero en Hogan Lovells en Miami. LL.M. por la Escuela de Derecho de Harvard.

Christopher R. Drahozal es Profesor de Derecho en la Facultad de Derecho de la Universidad de Kansas; Junta de Directores, ArbitratorIntelligence, Inc.

Mauricio Duarte es Asociado internacional, ASJ Tech Store. LL.M. por la Universidad de St. Thomas.

Valeria Galíndez es Fundadora de Galíndez Arbitragem, árbitro. Obtuvo su J.D. Pontifícia Universidade Católica de Sao Paolo.

Diana Gárate es Gerente Senior deEY Law en Lima, Perú. LL.M. por la Escuela de derecho de Columbia.

José Ignacio García Cueto es consultor legal especial en Clifford Chance en Washington D.C., Estados Unidos.

Francisco González de Cossío es árbitro. Tiene un Doctorado en Derecho y Economía y un LL.M por la Universidad de Chicago. OPM en Finanzas por la Harvard Business School.

Clifford J. Hendel es Fundador del despacho madrileño HENDEL IDR y árbitro.

René Irra es Socio de la práctica de arbitraje internacional de Cuatrecasas, México D.F.LL.M. Université Versailles Saint-Quentint-en-Yvelines.

Rafael Llano es Socio en White & Case LLP. Ciudad de México. Abogado, Universidad Católica de Asunción. LLM Facultad de Derecho de Harvard. Ex Consultor Nacional de la Unidad para la Promoción de la Democracia de la Organización de los Estados Americanos en Asunción, Paraguay.

Edson López es Socio del Despacho Integrum en Guatemala a cargo de la práctica de Arbitraje y Derecho Educativo. CEO del Grupo Latinoamericano de Asesores por la Educación (GLAE).

Lucas Loviscek es Asociado en Quinn Emanuel, Urquhart & Sullivan, LLP. LL.M. por la Universidad de Georgetown.

Juan Felipe Merizalde es Consultor legal especial en la oficina de LLP de Dechert, Washington D.C. LL.M. por la Universidad de Nueva York y Master 1 en Derecho internacional por la Université Paris 2 Panthéon-Assas. l.

Caterina Miró Quesada es Asociada Internacional en White & Case LLP. Abogada por la Universidad de Lima. LL.M. Máster en Derecho con Certificado en Derecho de la Energía.

Francisco Muñoz es Gerente Regional de Resolución de Disputas en Mercado Libre, Buenos Aires, Argentina. LL.M. por la Universidad de Nueva York.

Rachel Ong es abogada por la Universidad de Southampton. LL.M por la Universidad de Columbia. Abogada y Solicitor (Supreme Court of Singapore; Senior Courts of England and Wales).

Arturo Oropeza es Abogado visitante en King & Spalding LLP., Nueva York. Cofundador de practicantes de arbitraje muy jóvenes de la Ciudad de México. LL.B. por el Instituto Autónomo de México. LL.M. por la facultad de Derecho de Standford. Este capítulo no refleja los puntos de vista de King & Spalding, sus clientes y / o sus abogados.

Daniela Páez-Salgado es Asociada, Herbert Smith Freehills, Nueva York. LL.M. por la Escuela de leyes de Harvard.

Frank Ramos Socio Director en Clarke Silverglate, Miami. J.D. Facultad de Derecho de la Universidad de Miami.

Juan M. Rey Asociado en Philippi, Prietocarrizosa & Uría, Santiago, Chile. Representante ICC YAF. LL.M. por la Escuela de derecho de Columbia.

Aníbal Sabater es Socio en Chaffetz Lindsey LLP, Nueva York. Presidente del Comité de Derecho Internacional de la Asociación de Abogados de la Ciudad de Nueva York. Director del Centro de Arbitraje Internacional de Nueva York.

Cristóbal Sarralde es Asociado principal, Garrigues, Santiago, Chile. LL.M. por laUniversidad de California, Berkley School of Law.

Robert H. Smit es Profesor Adjunto de la Facultad de Derecho de la Universidad de Columbia.

Cedric Soule es Asociado Senior en King & Spalding LLP en Nueva York. LL.B. en la Universidad McGill, y un M.A. (Oxon) en Filosofía, Política y Economía, St. Hugh's College, Universidad de Oxford, Reino Unido.

Clovis Trevino es Special Counsel en el departamento de arbitraje internacional de Covington & Burling.

Luis Miguel Velarde es Asociado Senior en el Departamento de Arbitraje Internacional de Dechert (París) LLP. LL.B. por la Pontificia Universidad Católica del Perú (PUCP) y un LL.M. por la Escuela de Derecho de Harvard.

Patricia Vera es Directora del Centro de Arbitraje y Mediación de la Cámara de Comercio Ecuaoriano-Americana, Quito, Ecuador. LL.M. por la Universidad San Francisco de Quito.

Shoschana Zusman es Profesora Titular, Facultad de Derecho de la Pontificia Universidad Católica del Perú (PUCP). Socio en Estudio Zusman, Lima Perú. Miembro del Tribunal Administrativo del Banco Interamericano de Desarrollo.

Las opiniones expresadas son de los autores y no reflejan necesariamente las opiniones de otros abogados de las firmas ni las de sus clientes.

Resumen de Contenidos

PRÓLOGO

Sobreviviendo en el Arbitraje Internacional: Historias de Guerra y Lecciones Aprendidas es una extraordinaria compilación sobre los entretelones del mercado del arbitraje internacional.

El libro, publicado desde el comienzo en una conveniente edición bilingüe inglés-español, analiza desde una refrescante perspectiva pragmática la realidad de litigantes y árbitros.

José María, Carolina y Álvaro, tres muy destacados practicantes jóvenes latinoamericanos, han logrado coordinar en una sola publicación las experiencias y consejos de algunos de los más connotados nombres del arbitraje a nivel mundial. Sus enseñanzas se alternan con otros tantos episodios, más bien personales y hasta tragicómicos, inherentes a la práctica arbitral. Se combinan, así, relatos provenientes de diversas jurisdicciones que dan cuenta de las vivencias en distintas etapas de una carrera en arbitraje, desde los inicios en una oficina de abogados hasta los retos que enfrentan los árbitros.

El texto aconseja con prudencia sobre el trabajo propiamente tal (por ejemplo, cómo trabajar con un co-counsel, cómo participar en una deliberación o cómo redactar un primer laudo) y también sobre el desarrollo personal y profesional de abogados y árbitros (cómo compatibilizar la paternidad con el trabajo, cómo desarrollar una marca personal o a qué conferencias asistir).

En este contexto, adquiere cada vez más importancia en nuestro ámbito dar espacio a quienes propongan las mejores prácticas y, asimismo, hayan experimentado las nuevas problemáticas que afloran en el mercado.

Sin lugar a dudas, esta obra es un aporte fundamental para quien pretenda adentrarse en el mundo del arbitraje. Es probable que, en el corto tiempo, se transforme en un texto de consulta ineludible para quien quiera dedicarse a esta tan interesante área del derecho.

Alexis Mourre
Presidente de la Corte de Arbitraje de la Cámara de Comercio Internacional
París, febrero, 2020

PRESENTACIÓN

¿Qué podría hacer para ser un mejor practicante de arbitraje? ¿Cómo podría convertirme en un árbitro respetado? ¿Cómo es trabajar en una empresa internacional? ¿Cómo debo conducirme en un equipo? ¿Qué tan importantes son los eventos sociales para mi carrera en el arbitraje? ¿Se recompensa la creatividad en el arbitraje? ¿Cómo puedo conseguir clientes? ¿Y cómo debo tratarlos? ¿Cómo me transfiero de un área corporativa a la de arbitraje? ¿Puedo prosperar en el arbitraje si también me gusta la academia?

Este libro tiene como objetivo involucrar a su audiencia con confesiones divertidas de leer, lecciones útiles y reflexiones sobre la vida como practicante de arbitraje. Esperamos que este trabajo se convierta en la guía para prosperar en el mercado. Cuenta con practicantes de arbitraje y sus historias íntimas sobre temas críticos como su primer alegato oral, discutiendo temas candentes como la discriminación y brindando experiencia práctica en litigios arbitrales, toma de decisiones y trabajo académico.

Debían formularse preguntas difíciles, como enfrentar la "carrera de ratas" dentro de las oficinas de abogados, el agotamiento y la intimidación y reflexionar sobre el equilibrio entre el trabajo y la vida.

Sobrevivir en el Campo del Arbitraje Internacional: Historias de Guerra y Lecciones Aprendidas presenta a contribuyentes selectos que provienen de diferentes jurisdicciones y tocan temas muy diferentes y creativos.

Ya era hora de recopilar, en un libro, las experiencias y consejos de algunos de los principales participantes en este complejo mercado.

LISTA DE ABREVIATURAS

AAA	Asociación Americana de Arbitraje
ABA	Colegio de Abogados de Estados Unidos de América
BIT's	Tratados Bilaterales de Inversión
IBA	Colegio Internacional de Abogados
CCI	Cámara de Comercio Internacional
CEA	Club Español del Arbitraje
CIADI	Centro Internacional de Arreglo de Diferencias Relativas a Inversiones
CIAR	Centro Iberoamericano de Arbitraje
CNUDMI	Comisión de las Naciones Unidas para el Derecho Mercantil Internacional
CONSUCODE	Consejo Superior de Contrataciones y Adquisiciones del Estado
DNA	Ácido desoxirribonucleico
FODA	Análisis de Fortalezas, Oportunidades, Debilidades y Amenazas
HKIAC	Centro de Arbitraje Internacional de Hong Kong
ICCA	Concejo Internacional de Arbitraje Comercial
ICC YAF	Foro de Árbitros Jóvenes de la Cámara de Comercio International
ICT's	Tecnologías de información y comunicación
ICDR	Centro Internacional para la Resolución de Disputas
INTA	Asociación Internacional de Marcas
ISDS	Solución de controversias inversor-estado
LOI	Carta de Intención
MOU	Memorandum de Entendimiento
NDA	Acuerdo de Confidencialidad

ONG	Organización no Gubernamental
OSCE	Dirección de Arbitraje Administrativo del Organismo Supervisor de las Contrataciones del Estado
SIAC	Centro de Arbitraje Internacional de Singapur
SPA	Acuerdo de Compraventa
SHA	Acuerdo de Accionistas
US	Estados Unidos de Améric
VCLT	Convención de Viena sobre el Derecho de los Tratados
WWA	Women Way in Arbitration

HISTORIAS DE GUERRA Y LECCIONES SOBRE EL TRABAJO COMO ABOGADO DE PARTE

CAPÍTULO 1

¿Qué hace a un excelente abogado de arbitraje internacional?

Gary Born & Manuel Casas

Este capítulo trata sobre cómo ser un excelente abogado de arbitraje internacional. Específicamente, se enfoca en cuatro características que son esenciales para ello. Estas son las características que distinguen a los *excelentes* abogados de arbitraje internacional de aquellos que son simplemente *buenos* o incluso *muy buenos*.

Estas cuatro características son simultáneamente obvias y contraintuitivas. Son obvias porque son el tipo de consejo que te podría dar una abuela sabia; sin embargo, son contraintuitivas porque no son las características típicas que se asocian con un abogado litigante. A continuación, describimos estas características y mencionamos algunos ejemplos de su aplicación en la práctica.

La primera característica es trabajar duro, muy duro, muy, muy duro. La excelencia requiere esfuerzo. No hay atajos ni recetas mágicas que sustituyan una buena dosis de sudor. Ni siquiera los genios están exentos de trabajar duro. De hecho, un verdadero genio afirmó que la genialidad es 99% trabajo duro y sólo 1% talento. Esto también aplica al arbitraje internacional. De hecho, la naturaleza del trabajo es tal que no es inusual que un abogado de talentos medios, pero trabajador, pueda derrotar a un oponente más talentoso, pero flojo.

Todos los aspectos del ejercicio profesional requieren trabajo duro *todo* el tiempo. No basta con trabajar duro las dos semanas antes del vencimiento de un plazo, o unos días antes de una audiencia. Los excelentes abogados de arbitraje internacional trabajan duro en todas las etapas de un caso y, en general, en todas las facetas de su ejercicio profesional. Esto suele implicar dedicar más tiempo del estrictamente necesario para cada tarea, por ejemplo: editar un escrito un par de veces más o dedicar un tiempo adicional para ajustar una presentación.

El trabajo duro también implica estar preparado de más, ya sea para un interrogatorio testimonial, una reunión con un cliente o una audiencia procesal. El exceso de preparación suele dar réditos ya que el esfuerzo-cuando es canalizado adecuadamente-tiende a reflejarse en el producto. Por ejemplo, un escrito redactado en 200 horas suele ser de mejor calidad que el redactado en 20 horas. Pero este exceso de preparación también ayuda a desarrollar habilidades, pues enseña cómo ser un mejor abogado de arbitraje en casos futuros.

La segunda característica es saber escuchar. Escuchar, en vez de hablar, es quizá la habilidad más infravalorada de un abogado litigante. Esto quizá se deba a que, para muchos, la cualidad principal de un abogado litigante es la elocuencia, por lo cual el énfasis suele estar en cómo el abogado habla y qué dice en vez de en *cómo* escucha y *qué* escucha.

Sin embargo, la tarea principal del abogado litigante es persuadir a alguien (en este caso, al árbitro único o a quien preside el tribunal) de que hagan algo. Para lograr esto, el abogado debe entender qué es importante para las personas a las que está tratando de persuadir y con base en ello determinar qué puntos plantear y cómo. Esto es particularmente cierto para los abogados de arbitraje internacional, quienes frecuentemente deben persuadir a personas de distintas culturas y tradiciones jurídicas que, por lo general, tienden a abordar los casos desde distintos ángulos. Los excelentes abogados de arbitraje internacional deben ser capaces de identificar esos ángulos y ajustar su estrategia acordemente. Para ello, es crucial entender qué preocupa al tribunal: ¿qué puntos les interesan a los árbitros? ¿Qué partes del caso les están generando problemas? ¿Qué argumentos están dando buenos resultados? La única manera de contestar estas preguntas es escuchando al tribunal.

Acá, escuchar debe entenderse de manera amplia. No se trata solamente de escuchar las preguntas de los árbitros -aunque esto probablemente sea el mejor lugar para comenzar. Escuchar también incluye observar y analizar la actitud del tribunal (incluyendo su lenguaje corporal y sus interacciones) a lo largo del caso. Al discutir un punto en particular ¿los árbitros parecen interesados, atentos e inmersos en la discusión? ¿O están distraídos, dispersos y desinteresados? ¿Acaso están viendo sus teléfonos o computador o, como (raramente) ocurre, tomando una siesta?

Saber escuchar no es una habilidad restringida a la sala de audiencias. Escuchar a los clientes también es fundamental. El excelente abogado de arbitraje internacional también debe entender las prioridades que su cliente tiene en un caso y saber si hay implicaciones comerciales que, aunque tal vez no sean relevantes desde un punto de vista jurídico, sean cruciales desde el punto de vista del cliente. De nuevo, suele ser imposible determinar estos factores sin haber escuchado al cliente con atención.

Asimismo, también es importante escuchar a los otros integrantes del equipo. En casos grandes suele ser difícil, por no decir imposible, manejar todos los aspectos del caso con un alto nivel de detalle. Por ende, es inevitable que haya personas en el equipo que tendrán un mejor conocimiento de algunos aspectos del caso, ya sea una categoría de documentos o un testigo experto, y que pueden tener cosas útiles que aportar.

La tercera característica es siempre ser sincero con uno mismo. Esto implica varias cosas. Principalmente, el excelente abogado de arbitraje internacional es humilde: no se engaña a sí mismo y, en cambio, admite cuando no sabe algo. Esto se dice fácil. Suele haber una expectativa, a veces muy afianzada a nivel cultural, de que un abogado litigante debe siempre dar la impresión de estar extremadamente seguro tanto de sí mismo como de todo lo que dice. Esta actitud se ve representada por el comentario de un célebre profesor de derecho que se jactaba de 'errar frecuentemente, pero de nunca dudar'. Esta actitud de presunta infalibilidad no es sólo un cliché; también suele ser un obstáculo para hacer el mejor trabajo posible. Es mucho más productivo admitir que no se entiende algo -y tomar las medidas necesarias para resolver esa situación- que continuar con la actitud de sabelotodo y persistir en un error.

La práctica profesional ofrece muchas oportunidades para el autoengaño. Por ejemplo, es común pensar que hemos encontrado el argumento perfecto, el que automáticamente va a ganar el caso, sin antes haber considerado, críticamente, si ese argumento es compatible con los demás que hemos formulado a lo largo del caso, o si tiene algún sustento con base en las pruebas disponibles. Esta actitud no ayuda a ganar casos. En cambio, abordar un caso desde una perspectiva de humildad, sí, pues esto ayuda a detectar los puntos débiles e identificar los aspectos que requieren mejoras.

La cuarta característica es desarrollar excelentes habilidades de comunicación, tanto escritas como orales. Esta es la otra cara de saber escuchar. Ser capaz de detectar con precisión qué argumentos persuadirían al tribunal es insuficiente si luego no es posible comunicarlos con efectividad. Estas habilidades comunicacionales deben ser exhibidas a lo largo de todo el arbitraje. Un memorial impecable pierde credibilidad si la correspondencia procesal anterior es mediocre; o una elocuente presentación en la audiencia se ve menoscabada si los escritos en el caso son deficientes. En efecto, un excelente abogado de arbitraje internacional debe ver cada interacción con el tribunal como una oportunidad de persuadir -y debe abordarlas como tales.

En el caso de los abogados latinoamericanos, también es necesario desarrollar estas habilidades en inglés, sin duda un reto importante para quienes no son hablantes nativos de ese idioma. No obstante, dado el carácter de *lingua franca* que tiene el inglés en el comercio internacional, desarrollar esas habilidades es indispensable. Esto aplica incluso para quienes piensan hacer su carrera entera en América Latina. El aspecto internacional de nuestra área de práctica implica que lo más probable es que un número importante de arbitrajes tengan, por lo menos, *algún* elemento en inglés. Quizá el idioma del arbitraje siga siendo español (o portugués), pero lo más probable es que algún cliente, testigo o experto sólo hable inglés, o que algunos documentos esenciales estén en ese idioma. A final de cuentas, las comunicaciones entre una compañía China invirtiendo en una empresa de infraestructura en Brasil con financiamiento de un banco francés probablemente serán en inglés.

Hacer una lista de las características a las que deben aspirar quienes se están iniciando como abogados de arbitraje internacional es difícil. En definitiva, como cualquier decisión que implique una atribución de cualidad, hay un grado inherente de subjetividad. El litigio es más arte que ciencia y las preferencias personales juegan un rol importante; y aún más en el arbitraje internacional, dada la confluencia de personas formadas en distintas tradiciones jurídicas. La expansión del arbitraje internacional ha contribuido al desarrollo de un estilo de abogacía con un marcado carácter *internacional*. Sin embargo, hay quienes todavía prefieren la asertividad de algunos litigantes de estilo norteamericano, mientras que otros prefieren la colegialidad adoptada por algunos litigantes formados en sistemas de derecho civil.

Al proponer estas cuatro características no pretendemos responder categóricamente qué constituye la excelencia en el arbitraje internacional. Nuestro objetivo es más modesto: compartir una serie de observaciones, desarrolladas a lo largo de los años, que puedan ayudar a aquellos que están comenzando sus carreras a enfocarse en desarrollar habilidades que suelan ser infravaloradas pero que pueden ser útiles en su camino hacia la excelencia en el arbitraje internacional.

CAPÍTULO 2

El Decálogo para trabajar con un co-counsel

Aníbal Sabater[1]

En el arbitraje internacional es frecuente que una parte esté representada por dos o más firmas. A veces ambas firmas tienen perfiles y experiencia parecidos. En otras ocasiones la relación de las firmas es de complementariedad: una firma aporta conocimiento que la otra no tiene sobre una ley o una industria específica. El decálogo que aparece a continuación es una guía para ayudar a las firmas a trabajar de forma eficiente en la representación del cliente. Aunque parte de su contenido pueda aplicarse por analogía, el decálogo no está pensado para aquellas situaciones en las que el cliente comparece representado por una sola firma, pero existe otra asesorándole 'en la sombra'.

Primer Mandamiento:	Los equipos de ambas firmas harán lo posible para conocerse pronto en persona o, en su defecto, por videoconferencia o teléfono. Incluso si los abogados ya se conocían con anterioridad a trabajar en el caso, organizarán un nuevo encuentro tan pronto como les sea posible.
Segundo Mandamiento:	Los equipos de ambas firmas acordarán de antemano —y en especial sin esperar a que surjan crisis o emergencias— en qué áreas sustantivas y procesales del caso trabajará cada una de las firmas.

1. Las opiniones expresadas en este documento son las del autor y no reflejan necesariamente las de otros abogados en su firma o los clientes de la firma.

	El cliente deberá saber en cada momento qué firma es responsable de qué área. Ejemplo: dependiendo de las circunstancias del caso, una firma puede ser responsable del análisis y preparación de los argumentos del caso sujetos a derecho local, mientras que otra firma puede ser responsable del resto de la estrategia.
Tercer Mandamiento:	Los equipos de ambas firmas se familiarizarán rápidamente con sus respectivas áreas de trabajo en el caso e intercambiarán lealmente información sobre ellas.
Cuarto Mandamiento:	Los equipos de ambas firmas acordarán de antemano —y en especial sin esperar a que surjan crisis o emergencias— cómo se le reportará al cliente: en cuestiones en que ambas firmas puedan y deban opinar, ¿tratarán ambas de consensuar su recomendación al cliente de antemano u opinará cada una directamente al cliente con copia a la otra firma? ¿Cuál será el protocolo que se seguirá cuando las firmas no estén de acuerdo en qué recomendación darle al cliente?
Quinto Mandamiento:	Los equipos de ambas firmas trabajarán conjuntamente desde el comienzo del caso para identificar testigos y expertos que puedan apoyar la posición del cliente y se coordinarán para contactarlos, entrevistarlos y trabajar con ellos.
Sexto Mandamiento:	Tan pronto como haya un calendario procesal establecido, las firmas acordarán el procedimiento, los plazos y la división de tareas que seguirán para la preparación de escritos. Los plazos que acuerden las firmas deberán ser lo suficientemente amplios como para darle tiempo al cliente de repasar borradores sin premuras y para evitar retrasos en la presentación de escritos.
Séptimo Mandamiento:	Con la debida antelación, las firmas acordarán qué papel tendrá cada una en las audiencias y en su preparación. Esto incluye determinar: (1) qué firma y, en concreto, qué abogado liderará la representación del cliente en la audiencia; (2) qué firma preparará a cada testigo y experto para la audiencia; (3) qué firma(s) intervendrá(n) en los alegatos orales iniciales y finales (y en caso de que sean varias firmas, qué temas abordará cada una); y (4) qué firma examinará a cada testigo o experto.
Octavo Mandamiento:	Los equipos de ambas firmas serán respetuosos y corteses entre sí, y conscientes de que pertenecen a organizaciones distintas. Sus culturas legales, su experiencia y su papel en el litigio probablemente sean diferentes; pero de ambas se espera que aporten su trabajo intenso en pro del caso.

Noveno Mandamiento:	Los equipos de ambas firmas serán conscientes de que trabajan en un caso en concreto, pero se comportarán como si tuvieran que seguir trabajando por muchos más años. Por eso mismo, si la relación es fluida, tratarán de encontrar más casos en lo que trabajar juntos.
Décimo Mandamiento:	Todo se hará por, para y en consulta con el cliente. Cualquiera de los mandamientos anteriores cede ante una instrucción del cliente disponiendo otra cosa.

CAPÍTULO 3

Manual para armar una segunda silla

Cedric Soule[1] *& Arturo Oropeza*[2]

§3.01 DESCRIPCIÓN INICIAL DEL PRODUCTO

Empecemos por la terminología (intentaremos evitar los anglicismos, así que no hablaremos de *secondchair*): ¿qué es una segunda silla? Un número ordinal y después un sustantivo. Si esta no fuera una guía para abogados podría ser un catálogo de muebles. Hemos mirado en el Diccionario de la Real Academia Española y la búsqueda no arroja resultados, ni siquiera en la sección de "consultas lingüísticas". Ni hablar.

Si es segunda es porque le antecede la primera. Primera causa de nuestra segunda silla. Lógica impecable, cartesiana. ¿Pero quién le antecede? Los anglosajones definen la primera silla en sus diccionarios como el abogado principal ante el tribunal. Después, definen a la segunda silla como el abogado que ayuda a la primera silla. Es decir, nuestro personaje parece haber nacido relegado entre las sombras de un estudio, despacho, bufete u otra palabra que designe el lugar donde se reúnen los personajes que componen el gremio. Les suplicamos no decir "firma", aunque reconocemos que a estas alturas de la globalización es casi imposible. Por otro lado, nuestro personaje tiene un rol secundario dentro de un procedimiento que contempla cierta presentación oral ante un juez.

El arbitraje, como en otras ocasiones, toma prestado este término y lo adapta a su propia configuración. La segunda silla es el abogado que se sienta usualmente al costado del abogado que hace la presentación de alegatos ante el tribunal arbitral durante una audiencia. A su vez, la segunda silla en el arbitraje suele ser más flexible. No es extraño observar una mayor intervención de las segundas sillas, sobre todo si la dimensión y complejidad ameritan la participación de diversos colegas.

1. Este capítulo no refleja los puntos de vista de King & Spalding, sus clientes y / o sus abogados.
2. Este capítulo no refleja los puntos de vista de King & Spalding, sus clientes y / o sus abogados.

Quizás en castellano le podríamos nombrar con más ingenio, aun cuando tenemos prohibido formar sustantivos compuestos o usar guiones para ligar palabras. Ensayemos: el tomador de apuntes (ilegibles) o el increpador de testigos (con la mirada). Conocedor de los confines del índice o porteador de plumas y hechos. Todas ellas le hacen más justicia que el término en inglés, aun cuando muchas veces estas tareas se pierdan en el anonimato de una sala de audiencia o en los murmullos nerviosos de una transcripción estenográfica.

Más allá de las definiciones, lo que es claro es que la segunda silla vive apartada del protagonismo. El reconocimiento, se entiende, será pleno para la primera silla. La ovación y los elogios serán para el abogado que lidera el caso. Seguramente todos en la firma (se los advertimos) hablarán de su oratoria y estructura. De cómo el tribunal le dio la razón con un gesto o cómo un testigo sucumbió ante el filo de sus preguntas. Nuestra segunda silla pasará más bien desapercibida. Tal vez alguna socia le dé una palmada en la espalda o un asociado le invite una copa. Poco más.

La historia ha sabido mantener al margen a los segundos. Sancho no es Don Quijote. El fútbol -hilo evangelizador de la cultura hispana aún más que Cervantes- ofrece ejemplos más claros. Un cinco o un ocho jamás serán un nueve ni un diez. Pero hoy debemos ser más bondadosos con los actores secundarios. Sería injusto desestimar la importancia de su participación. Así como una cocina queda a la deriva sin la supervisión de un buen *sous chef*, cualquier abogado que ha estado en una audiencia sabe que el éxito no depende de una sola persona. El camino al laudo a favor pasa por las voces de diversos actores y no solamente la de un buen orador. Sin un *aide-de-camp* confiable y diligente, el trabajo de años puede desmoronarse y comprometer el resultado del caso.

§3.02 INSTRUCCIONES DE ARMADO

Una audiencia arbitral es un fenómeno complejo donde se desenvuelven cientos de elementos intercalados y simultáneos. Los alegatos orales son la colisión no solamente de argumentos jurídicos sino de personalidades, psicologías y estrategias. Ante este escenario complejo, la mejor respuesta reside en el esfuerzo eficiente y coordinado de un grupo de personas. La segunda silla gravita en el centro de este fenómeno en un tono pasivo, latente pero fundamental. Las mayores habilidades para desempeñar su papel son el conocimiento del caso, el manejo de la comunicación y una organización meticulosa.

No es posible enfatizar con suficiencia los beneficios de dominar el caso. Esto implica conocer todo el expediente, incluyendo los escritos, anexos, pruebas y todos los materiales que sean de relevancia general. La tarea no se limita en ser un procesador bibliográfico. Se debe saber identificar las fortalezas y debilidades de la postura y determinar en qué momento es conveniente transmitir un mensaje a la primera silla o requerir una nota a otro miembro del equipo. La segunda silla también debe conocer las virtudes y falencias de la contraparte, seguir sus líneas argumentativas y esperar cualquier tropiezo o digresión. Anticipar posibles puntos contenciosos y preguntas del tribunal arbitral también está dentro de la orden del día.

Todo llegará a buen puerto en tanto el caso se haya estudiado rigurosa e inteligentemente. Cuando se conoce el caso a plenitud se acota el lugar de lo imprevisible.

La comunicación con el abogado que figurará como primera silla también es esencial. Semanas antes se debe hablar de las expectativas, los modos y las sinergias. De la delimitación de tareas y obligaciones para evitar los temidos errores de coordinación. En este aspecto, la dupla debe funcionar con la precisión de las manecillas de un minutero. Esto será posible mientras mejor se conozca a su pareja en la audiencia y se entable una relación de engranaje y complementación. Aun así, la segunda silla no solamente debe estar al tanto de esta relación primordial sino también de la coordinación constante con otros miembros del equipo, los árbitros, los demás participantes en la audiencia (estenógrafos, intérpretes, etc.) y los funcionarios de la institución arbitral. Con la contraparte se espera un trato diplomático y cortés, sin dejar de percatarse, claro, en sus reacciones, errores y deslices.

No omitimos subrayar el talento en la organización, es decir, en discernir el orden y prioridad de todos los componentes de la audiencia. En ello, la segunda silla debe saber comandar y dirigir al resto del equipo, tomar el control y posicionarse como mariscal en el campo de los alegatos. Parte de esta labor incluye saber despachar tareas y funciones para después filtrar la información y ponerla a disposición de la primera silla. La categorización se convierte en parte esencial del rol para tomar ventaja de las fortalezas y solventar cualquier obstáculo de forma eficiente.

En cualquier caso y a pesar de esta lista de responsabilidades, ser una segunda silla también tiene sus ventajas. La mayor recompensa es quizás el aprendizaje. Observar en proximidad los miles de patrones y pormenores de una audiencia es una de las experiencias más valiosas que un abogado arbitralista puede tener. Cada tribunal, cada alegato y cada intervención tienen su propio ritmo y cadencia. Y, como en cualquier oficio, la habilidad se moldea con el transcurso del tiempo. Ser segunda silla permite, de primera mano, presenciar y asimilar este cúmulo de vivencias.

§3.03 HERRAMIENTAS NECESARIAS

No queremos dejar a un lado la practicidad. Al final del día esta es una guía de sobrevivencia profesional. A continuación, recopilamos una serie de consejos producto de buenos y también de malos días. Estos consejos son consecuencia de reprimendas, celebraciones y emociones encontradas en el universo profesional que habitamos. No pretendemos ser exhaustivos, pero sí articular una lista que pueda ayudar al neófito y no iniciado. Esperamos que los lectores tengan la bondad de la perspectiva y la consideración de la subjetividad.

[A] Estudio, estudio y, al terminar con ello, más estudio

Mientras mejor conozcas el caso mayor será tu tranquilidad y tu confianza; dos elementos fundamentales en la audiencia. Por otro lado, nunca apuestes por los conocimientos de otra persona, en particular de la primera silla. Jamás se debe pensar que la primera silla conoce mejor el caso. Esto en pocas ocasiones es cierto.

[B] La segunda silla debe saber tomar decisiones respecto al caso y delegar tareas a otros miembros del equipo

Con ello se permitirá que la primera silla se concentre en la forma y sustancia de los alegatos.

[C] La segunda silla nunca debe perder el sentido de orientación y pertenencia

Hay que ser claros: la segunda silla no es ni debe ser la primera silla. No se pueden tomar decisiones de fondo sin consulta, no se deben perder los modos y la paciencia con el resto del equipo. Al final de cuentas la segunda silla no deja de ser, en general, un asociado. El ejercicio del liderazgo debe ser más sutil, es decir, se debe dirigir con tacto y consenso.

[D] La segunda silla debe estar preparada para lo inesperado

Incluso estar lista para intervenir y tomar un rol más protagónico en caso de ser requerida. El conocimiento del caso, aparejado a la tranquilidad y la confianza, ayudarán a sortear dichas ocasiones.

[E] Y, por supuesto, sonreír en todo momento

Es importante que la contraparte no perciba lo que puedes estar pensando o sintiendo durante la audiencia. Por otro lado, nunca olvidar que esto es solamente una audiencia (con los histriones que conlleva). Al final de cuentas, todos sabemos que un arbitraje es mucho más que una audiencia, y que el escrito presentado después de la audiencia puede ser tan o incluso más importante que la propia audiencia.

Y terminamos, claro, con una consigna. En todo escalafón hay una voluntad de progreso y superación. La elección de una segunda silla generalmente involucra la valoración del talento y asegura una estela de proyección. Nuestras segundas sillas deberán convertirse gradualmente en primeras con el transcurso del tiempo. Pero la espera no deberá ser inmerecidamente larga. Queremos más asociados jóvenes sentados en la primera silla; más mujeres y más minorías. Como profirió algún prócer carpintero que hoy ignoramos su nombre: "La silla es de quien la trabaja".

CAPÍTULO 4

Mi primer alegato

Rafael Llano

Las audiencias, especialmente las audiencias de fondo, son el momento cumbre del arbitraje. En este momento, las partes ya han intercambiado escritos con sus posiciones. Es aquí cuando el argumento oral toma especial importancia, ya que nos permite por primera vez explicar verbalmente el caso de nuestros clientes al tribunal arbitral. De igual forma, es una oportunidad para poner a prueba los argumentos de nuestra contraparte.

Mi primer argumento oral fue en los alegatos de apertura en una audiencia de fondo en un caso del Centro Internacional de Arreglo de Diferencias Relativas a Inversiones (CIADI) contra un Estado latinoamericano, cuando aún era asociado. Recuerdo que cuando el socio a cargo del asunto me dijo que me encargaría de exponer una parte de la sección de hechos del argumento oral, me sentí emocionado y nervioso a la vez. Había pasado mucho tiempo observando a los socios con los que trabajaba hacer presentaciones orales y mi turno había llegado. Cuando uno se prepara para su primer alegato, es usual querer imitar lo que ha visto antes. Ese fue mi caso. Tomé las cosas buenas que había visto de los socios con los que trabajaba y así empecé mi preparación.

Como punto de partida, imprimí los escritos que había presentado la parte que representaba y a mano resalté e hice notas de los puntos principales que quería hacer en mi presentación. Conforme iba leyendo los argumentos que se habían hecho, fui imaginando cuál sería la mejor manera de presentarlos. Así, fui enumerando diapositivas a lo largo del escrito; poniendo números al lado de los distintos temas e incluyendo referencias a normas legales, documentos y declaraciones de testigos. Ese fue mi primer boceto de esquema, el cual aún conservo como recuerdo.

Una vez que tenía listas las diapositivas que presentaría, me enfoqué en preparar mi presentación oral frente al tribunal. Una vez más, recordé los ejemplos más efectivos que había visto en audiencias previas. Hasta ese momento, tenía catalogados a tres tipos de oradores.

El primero fue al que he llamado el "maestro de la preparación". Esta persona pasa muchas semanas antes de la audiencia preparando su alegato. Lo escribe y practica sin cesar. De hecho, organiza reuniones con el equipo y practica su argumento para ver la reacción de sus colegas. De esta forma pule y mejora paulatinamente su presentación. La repite tantas veces que, al momento de exponer sus argumentos en la audiencia, parece que estuviera improvisando, aunque en realidad tiene su presentación prácticamente memorizada.

Al segundo tipo de presentador lo he llamado el "maestro de la improvisación". Este abogado se prepara antes de la audiencia, y domina los hechos y el derecho del caso, pero al momento de la misma improvisa en gran medida sus argumentos orales, dependiendo de las reacciones y preguntas del tribunal. De esta forma, moldea sus argumentos para hablar sobre los puntos que preocupan al tribunal y que son claves para la posición de su cliente.

Por último, el tercer tipo de presentador es al que llamo el "maestro de la oratoria". Esta persona tiene preparado un libreto, en el cual cada palabra ha sido cuidadosamente elegida. Usa diapositivas para guiar su presentación, pero éstas únicamente contienen referencias generales de los temas que trata. La oratoria es el elemento central, más que las diapositivas.

Al preparar mi primer argumento oral, decidí tomar lo mejor de cada uno de ellos. Preparé diapositivas que contenían los argumentos principales que quería transmitir. Memoricé casi por completo lo que quería decir y también tenía textos escritos que leí.

Si bien creo que mi primer argumento oral cumplió con su cometido, en retrospectiva creo que hoy le doy un mayor valor a ser flexible durante la exposición oral. Es natural tener nervios antes de hacer un alegato, incluso si no es el primero, pero creo que la combinación de las técnicas de los diferentes "maestros" no dio el resultado natural que me habría gustado.

Para una exposición oral exitosa es importante encontrar tu propio estilo e ir desarrollándolo con la práctica y en la medida que vas ganando más confianza en ti mismo. Desarrollar las habilidades para un alegato es como un lápiz, al que poco a poco se le va sacando punta. Uno va aprendiendo de la experiencia, y así, se vuelve como el lápiz, más afilado, más preciso y exacto en lo que se quiere decir. Asimismo, uno va aprendiendo a leer al tribunal y va adaptando su argumento oral y su presentación sobre la marcha, dependiendo de sus reacciones. La preparación es clave, pero también lo es la flexibilidad. La preparación tomará semanas, y múltiples rondas de ensayo y ajustes a las diapositivas. La flexibilidad requerirá conocer el expediente, los hechos y los argumentos legales desde todo ángulo.

Al final del día, las cosas pueden salir de maneras inesperadas. Sin embargo, la preparación y la experiencia nos darán las herramientas para saber reaccionar, por ejemplo, ante una pregunta complicada del tribunal, o hasta ante una falla técnica que podría desconcentrarte si uno no está bien preparado o no conoce suficientemente el material de apoyo que se proyecta durante la audiencia.

Hoy, a más de 10 años de mi primer argumento oral, puedo decir que mi estilo ha evolucionado. Sigo pensando que la preparación intensa es clave. Por ello dedico mucho tiempo a pensar y estructurar mis argumentos, aunque confieso que mis esquemas ya no son a mano. Es importante invertir el tiempo necesario en revisar los escritos de ambas partes, los documentos y fuentes legales relevantes, así como las declaraciones testimoniales e informes de expertos. Doy mucha importancia a la estructura y secuencia de los puntos. Y también al balance entre la exhaustividad y la selectividad en lo que vale la pena dedicar parte del tiempo, usualmente limitado, del que se dispone para los argumentos.

Ya no memorizo mis presentaciones y ahora mi estilo es más conversacional. Siempre utilizo diapositivas, pero solo como guía, y no permito que estas anclen mi presentación o impidan la espontaneidad según sea necesaria. Las diapositivas son una herramienta muy útil, ya que permiten transmitir al tribunal documentos, frases o testimonios clave. Procuro que estas contengan gráficos a fin de hacerlas más didácticas y fáciles de seguir. Las líneas de tiempo a veces ayudan a ubicar al oyente en la historia. Las imágenes de los documentos usados ayudan a hacerlos más reales, casi tangibles.

Finalmente, es importante conocer a tu auditorio. Para ello, es clave investigar quiénes son los miembros del tribunal, desde su experiencia relevante para la disputa hasta sus personalidades y preferencias. Escuchar es tan importante como hablar. Hay que saber escuchar lo que dice el tribunal. Muchos errores se cometen por no hacerlo. Al estar tan metidos en el libreto que hemos preparado, no escuchamos atentamente las preguntas o comentarios del tribunal y dejamos escapar oportunidades de ayudarles a recibir la información que piden y necesitan. Las preguntas son como pequeñas ventanas de oportunidad que debemos saber aprovechar. No digas que las responderás más tarde; si tienes la información, responde a la pregunta, y de lo contrario, asegúrate de obtenerla posteriormente y volver al tribunal con una respuesta. El haberte preparado adecuadamente y a la vez tener flexibilidad, te permitirá realizar tu presentación de una manera más efectiva, proporcionándole al tribunal las herramientas que necesita para entender tu caso y tus mejores argumentos y evidencia. De la misma forma, es importante conocer a tu contraparte. Esto te ayudará a prepararte, para poder anticipar contraargumentos o reacciones y que estos no te tomen por sorpresa.

La experiencia de mi primer alegato me dejó muchas lecciones. Como mencioné, me permitió encontrar mi propio estilo y convertirme en la clase de presentador que soy hoy. Sin embargo, no debemos olvidar que, como abogados, al final del día somos la voz de nuestro cliente, y los argumentos orales son clave para adelantar el caso de nuestro cliente, ya que nos brindan la oportunidad de relatar el caso de manera sencilla, reduciendo grandes conceptos a una narrativa simple que requiera de justicia por parte del tribunal.

CAPÍTULO 5
Consejos de escritura para arbitrólogos

Caterina Miró Quesada

Si bien es importante no perder de vista el panorama completo de nuestro caso y lo que queremos transmitir al redactar los documentos, no hay que olvidar que el diablo está en los detalles. Recuerdo que, en una oportunidad al preparar una solicitud de arbitraje basada en un tratado, identifiqué que las versiones en inglés y español no coincidían en información determinante para la notificación de la disputa. Eso me enseñó la importancia de revisar hasta el más mínimo detalle, ya que algo que parece irrelevante puede afectar nuestros escritos y nuestra posición frente al tribunal arbitral.

Dice el dicho que el papel aguanta todo. Sin embargo, esto no es lo más efectivo cuando buscamos ser persuasivos en nuestros memoriales o escritos dirigidos al tribunal. En el arbitraje internacional, no es extraño encontrar escritos llenos de calificativos, cientos de páginas que dicen mucho y nada a la vez o que solo consiguen que el lector termine de leerlos sin obtener una idea clara de qué fue lo que las partes quisieron transmitir. Como abogados de parte, nuestro trabajo consiste en evitar que los árbitros, luego de leer nuestro memorial, piensen "*aún no sé qué pasó*" o "*no me han dado los argumentos que necesito para resolver este caso*".

Antes de empezar a escribir debemos, como un paso previo, idear un plan de acción. El proceso que debemos llevar a cabo antes de trasladar las ideas al papel es clave para la eficacia de nuestros escritos. Estos deben organizarse de tal manera que reflejen exactamente lo que queremos transmitir al tribunal. Para ello, es aconsejable tener en cuenta los siguientes puntos:

§5.01 CONOCE TU CASO

Identifica cuáles son los hechos clave y la teoría legal de tu caso. Solo conociendo todos los detalles podrás empezar a formular tu posición para cada uno de ellos. Pon a prueba tus argumentos, imaginando si estos pasarían la prueba de un contrainterrogatorio o de las preguntas del tribunal y mira cómo estos pueden ser mejorados o aclarados luego de este ejercicio. Además, anticipa cuáles podrían ser los argumentos de tu contraparte para responderlos de antemano. Siempre es mejor anticipar que reaccionar.

§5.02 ¿QUÉ QUIERO TRANSMITIR?

Es importante identificar cuál es la historia que quieres contar. Para ello, debes poder contestar a las siguientes preguntas: (i) ¿Cuál es la idea principal de tu caso?; (ii) ¿Cuáles son los hechos principales del caso?; y (iii) ¿Cuál es tu posición respecto de cada una de tus pretensiones? Con esta información, podrás empezar a desarrollar la teoría de tu caso.

[A] Resumen de tu posición

Piensa en una o dos oraciones que reflejen tu posición en el caso. Es decir, identifica cuál será el hilo conductor en los escritos que te permitirán transmitir de manera clara tu posición al tribunal arbitral.

[B] Sustento documental y legal

Los hechos tienden a ser uno de los puntos más importantes de nuestros escritos. Identifica los documentos que sustentan los hechos de tu posición, así como los testigos y expertos en los que te puedes apoyar. Asimismo, identifica las fuentes legales que apoyan tu posición, y, además, ten en cuenta posiciones contrarias que te ayudarán a anticipar contraargumentos.

[C] Esquema del escrito

Pon de manera general todas las ideas que se te ocurran para cada uno de los puntos que quieres hacer. Para ello, insisto, es fundamental tener claro qué es lo que se quiere transmitir antes de empezar a escribir.

Una vez completados los puntos anteriores, estarás en condiciones de empezar a escribir tu memorial. Escribir no es tarea fácil. Es un arte que se va desarrollando con la práctica. Una buena opción para mejorar, sobre todo cuando uno recién empieza, es observar qué es lo que hacen personas con más experiencia y aprender de ellos y, de la misma forma, descartar lo que no nos parece efectivo. Por ejemplo, el mantener una libreta de apuntes, un archivo en la computadora o hasta una nota en el celular donde escribamos frases que hemos leído, enfoques o estrategias que nos hayan llamado la atención, será útil cuando llegue el momento de escribir. A fin de ser persuasivo, se pueden seguir los siguientes consejos prácticos en la redacción del memorial:

[1] Conoce a tu lector

Investiga quiénes son los miembros del tribunal arbitral, su experiencia en la industria o temas de tu caso, sus capacidades en el idioma de tu caso, etc. Esto podría afectar tu estrategia y enfoque. Por ejemplo, este conocimiento te dirá si hace falta incluir un capítulo que introduzca de manera básica alguna materia técnica que se va a tocar a lo largo del escrito.

[2] Escribe de manera clara, simple y directa

Al redactar en el idioma español, estamos acostumbrados a utilizar muchas palabras para transmitir nuestras ideas. Sin embargo, debemos evitar esta tentación y escribir nuestros memoriales y escritos de manera clara y simple. Así nos aseguraremos que el tribunal entienda nuestra posición y, de paso, lea todo. Sé directo. Ningún árbitro dirá "*me hubiera encantado que el memorial fuese más largo*".

[3] Cada hecho incluido debe de tener un propósito

Muchas veces olvidamos que el tribunal no tiene el mismo conocimiento de los hechos que nosotros. Cuando uno lee un recuento de hechos por primera vez, no distingue a ciencia cierta qué detalle es importante y cuál no. Por ello, es importante que los hechos que se incluyan sirvan un propósito y sean parte de la historia que se quiere contar. El incluir detalles innecesarios o hechos que no tienen que ver con tus argumentos solo logrará confundir al lector y hará que pierdan la idea que se quería trasmitir. Pero, al mismo tiempo, a veces hay que detenerse a explicar los antecedentes con detalle para evitar que se pierda el punto que queremos transmitir.

[4] No evadas hechos desfavorables

Es mejor que el tribunal escuche tu posición de ti y no de tu contraparte. El esconder hechos no es una buena idea. Muy probablemente estos se darán a conocer en un momento u otro del arbitraje y ahí será más complicado lidiar con ellos. En este sentido, una decisión muy importante es qué hacer con documentos desfavorables, sobre todo cuando es muy posible que deban ser entregados en una fase de exhibición (o intercambio) de documentos en el arbitraje. Podría ser útil poner estos documentos sobre la mesa desde el inicio para controlar el mensaje. Esto, además, ayudará en tu credibilidad frente al tribunal.

[5] Evita ser repetitivo o agresivo

No por presentar la misma idea una y otra vez, esta se vuelve más cierta. Lo mismo sucede con los adjetivos agresivos. Deja que los hechos y tus argumentos hablen por sí solos.

[6] Introducción

Incluye una introducción que le dé al lector una idea clara de qué es lo que leerá en el memorial y cuál será la conclusión. Esta es una buena oportunidad para resaltar los puntos clave de tu posición de la manera más favorable.

[7] Incluye títulos persuasivos y divide el escrito en secciones

Divide tu memorial en secciones que sigan un orden lógico y que sigan tu teoría del caso. En el primer párrafo de cada sección incluye un párrafo introductorio donde expliques de qué tratará la sección, ya que así proporcionarás un contexto de lo que viene. Asimismo, es especialmente importante tomarse un tiempo para pensar en títulos persuasivos para cada una de las secciones; éstos deben reflejar adecuadamente el contenido de las secciones.

[8] Soporte probatorio

Asegúrate que cada afirmación fáctica tenga un soporte documental o testimonial, usando siempre que corresponda un pie de página para indicar la fuente probatoria correspondiente. Desde luego, lo mismo es cierto de los argumentos legales. Es frustrante leer un escrito que no ayude al lector a encontrar el documento u otra prueba en el que se basan sus afirmaciones. Esta práctica te ayudará además a asegurarte que no estás exagerando o subvaluando el peso probatorio de cada pieza de evidencia.

[9] Edición

Finalmente, revisa y corrige el documento. De preferencia, imprímelo. Muchas veces. Los errores en la pantalla pasan desapercibidos. Es importante que tu memorial esté libre de errores tipográficos.

El seguir estos consejos prácticos ayudará a que encuentres tu propio estilo al momento de escribir y, a la vez, identifiques qué cosas te funcionan y cuáles no. Además, te ayudan a aprender de tus errores. La buena escritura es un arte que se va desarrollando con el tiempo.

CAPÍTULO 6

¿Cómo arbitrar desde el Estado?

Ricardo Ampuero

Tuve la oportunidad de participar en un conversatorio que tenía por finalidad presentar diferentes perspectivas del arbitraje internacional y pude compartir la perspectiva de trabajar en la defensa de un Estado en controversias internacionales de inversión.

Uno de los asistentes preguntó qué era lo que disfrutaba más de mi trabajo. Mi respuesta, definida desde el primer día que empecé a trabajar para el Estado, fue la satisfacción y el orgullo que me genera el poder defender y representar a mi país en un fuero internacional. Con mucha sinceridad puedo afirmar que es algo que considero un verdadero privilegio y un honor.

Creo, sin temor a equivocarme, que el punto de partida esencial para abordar lo que significa trabajar en temas de arbitraje desde el Estado es la vocación de servicio. Un verdadero sentido de servicio público genera un nivel de compromiso indispensable para avanzar en los objetivos de la política pública de un país. Un adecuado sistema de coordinación y respuesta del Estado en controversias internacionales de inversión forma parte importante de cualquier política seria de atracción de inversión extranjera directa.

Un abogado que litiga para el Estado debe vivir su caso y comprometerse a realizar el mejor trabajo posible para su cliente. A riesgo de sonar romántico, ese cliente son todos los ciudadanos del país, pues el encargo implica la cautela del tesoro público y la defensa de decisiones soberanas. Por ello, aunque gratificante, es una tarea que conlleva una responsabilidad muy grande de la cual es preciso ser consciente.

El ritmo del trabajo puede ser distinto al que se tiene en una firma de abogados o en el departamento legal de una empresa, pero esto no significa que sea menos intenso. Se debe lidiar con ciertos aspectos que seguramente no están presentes en el sector privado y existen elementos a tener en especial consideración como, por ejemplo, los asuntos relacionados a la responsabilidad internacional del Estado.

En las disputas entre Estados y empresas puede suceder que la empresa que realiza una inversión cambie su personería jurídica en el transcurso de sus operaciones. Asimismo, puede ser disuelta, fusionarse, ser absorbida por otra empresa o puedenocurrir otros movimientos en su estructura societaria. De la misma forma, aunque el número de arbitrajes de inversión mantiene un ritmo de crecimiento sostenido en los últimos años, no todas las empresas que realizan una inversión extranjera directa inician, en relación a cada proyecto, un proceso de arbitraje internacional de inversiones. Un Estado, por el contrario, tiene vocación de permanencia en el tiempo y, considerando el aumento del flujo de inversión extranjera directa, la apertura de mercados y la globalización, puede enfrentar varios arbitrajes internacionales de inversión, generándose la necesidad de precautelar la consistencia y coherencia en sus posiciones a lo largo del tiempo.

El Estado es grande y complejo. En él confluyen distintas agencias y subdivisiones políticas de diferente nivel, cada una con sus propios objetivos, responsabilidades y mandatos legales. Sus actuaciones y decisiones pueden generar reclamos que involucran la responsabilidad internacional del Estado.

Una adecuada coordinación entre las entidades públicas vinculadas a una controversia internacional es crucial para el desarrollo ordenado del caso y para presentar con la mayor solidez posible la posición soberana, pues permitirá la centralización de todos los documentos relevantes, evitar declaraciones públicas que luego puedan ser usadas en contra del propio Estado y, en general, la articulación eficiente del trabajo a desarrollar.

Esto es un reto significativo porque esta coordinación debe estar presente cuando el arbitraje inicia y debe mantenerse a lo largo de todo el proceso. En ese sentido, las agencias estatales deberán interiorizar adecuadamente las contingencias que enfrenta el Estado, establecer cuál será su rol en ese contexto y, dentro del marco de sus propios objetivos y prioridades, encontrar la manera de trabajar de forma armoniosa entre ellas en pos de una defensa efectiva y organizada.

Dependiendo del sistema implementado por el Estado para enfrentar las controversias internacionales de inversión, otro reto es tener un adecuado manejo y supervisión de los estudios jurídicos internacionales que se contratan para cada caso. Cada uno puede tener equipos, estilos y prácticas muy diferentes y es importante velar por que, en cada caso, la prioridad sea la defensa contundente de los intereses del Estado de una forma que se encuentre alineada con los objetivos trazados.

En el caso del Perú, desde que enfrentó su primer proceso de arbitraje internacional de inversiones en el año 2003 (un primer caso en 1998 culminó en un acuerdo que puso fin a la controversia) se identificaron algunos elementos que resultan cruciales para una adecuada defensa de los intereses del Estado. A partir de esas oportunidades de mejora y en línea con su política de atracción de inversión extranjera directa, se creó en el 2006 el Sistema de Coordinación y Repuesta del Estado en Controversias Internacionales de Inversión.

Como parte del Sistema, se creó la Comisión Especial que representa al Estado en Controversias Internacionales de Inversión. Es el órgano colegiado interinstitucional que tiene por objeto la representación del Estado en todas las etapas de la controversia. Es importante resaltar que la Comisión Especial tiene miembros permanentes y miembros no permanentes. Como parte de estos últimos se encuentra cada entidad pública involucrada en la controversia específica, que puede ser más de una entidad.

De esta forma, el sistema se basa en una composición *ad hoc* a cada caso, asegurando que todos los *stakeholders* necesarios participen de la deliberación y adopción de las principales decisiones del caso.

A la Comisión Especial le compete, entre otras responsabilidades, evaluar las posibilidades de negociación en la fase de trato directo y llevar adelante esta etapa de acuerdo a la estrategia adoptada, solicitar informes técnicos a las entidades involucradas en una controversia respecto de las materias vinculadas a la misma, proponer la contratación de abogados y demás profesionales que sean necesarios, lo que incluye a los expertos a ser presentados en cada caso, efectuar la designación de árbitros, determinar la responsabilidad de la Entidad Pública involucrada en la controversia así como coadyuvar en general a la labor de los abogados contratados para el patrocinio del Estado.

De esta forma, existe un involucramiento permanente por parte de los funcionarios del Estado, a través de la Comisión Especial, en el desarrollo e implementación de la estrategia legal. Esto incluye la participación de funcionarios públicos en la identificación de documentos relevantes del caso, en la preparación de testigos, así como la participación en las mismas audiencias. A partir de esta experiencia acumulada de varios casos, el Estado peruano ha manejado con éxito el diseño e implementación de estrategias destinadas a lograr la solución negociada de algunos reclamos, evitando la necesidad de pasar por un proceso arbitral.

Para arbitrar de manera exitosa desde el Estado, resulta crucial, como paso previo, implementar políticas de prevención de disputas. Esto puede abarcar desde mecanismos de alerta temprana que permitan identificar oportunamente potenciales controversias, a fin de evitar que estas situaciones escalen a un litigio, hasta capacitaciones dirigidas a funcionarios públicos, con la finalidad de sensibilizar e informar de la existencia de los compromisos de protección de inversiones que ha asumido el Estado y brindar las herramientas para los procesos de toma de decisiones y la evaluación de los riesgos que implican determinadas medidas.

Una de las lecciones más importantes, que puede ser difícil de asimilar, particularmente si se incursiona en el arbitraje de inversión desde el lado del Estado, cuando se ha tenido una práctica en el sector privado, es aprender a lidiar con la burocracia. Aunque se asocia a un componente frustrante, la burocracia *per se* no es algo negativo. Los procedimientos administrativos responden a una estructura jerárquica y organizada, que divide encargos dentro del Estado. Por ello son necesarios en la administración pública.

En ese sentido, otro elemento a considerar es la responsabilidad a la que están sujetos los funcionarios públicos y su relación con los órganos de control. Bajo el principio de legalidad, los funcionarios públicos solo están habilitados a realizar las acciones que las normas que regulan su actuación permiten y sus decisiones deben estar debidamente motivadas; es decir, deben contar con un soporte razonado y sustentado.

Asimismo, se debe incorporar en la planificación y organización del trabajo el hecho inevitable que, generalmente, el Estado no tiene una capacidad de reacción tan ágil como la podría tener una entidad privada. Esto es así, no solo porque existen procedimientos, revisiones, autorizaciones previas y acciones de control cuyo cumplimiento debe observarse en las decisiones que se toman, incluso en el contexto de la defensa legal en una controversia internacional de inversión, sino también porque la centralización de documentos e identificación de los antecedentes relevantes, dependiendo de la complejidad de los hechos y el número de entidades públicas involucradas, puede ser una tarea ardua que requiere tiempo.

Es importante recordar que en el sistema de solución de controversias de inversión el Estado suele ser la parte demandada, lo que se traduce en que los Estados enfrentan diversos tipos de contingencias. Principalmente están las contingencias económicas, ya que generalmente se discuten pretensiones de indemnización que son millonarias. Esto puede tener un impacto directo en el manejo de las finanzas públicas y la estructuración del presupuesto de las entidades involucradas. Sin embargo, una decisión adversa también puede traer consigo otro tipo de contingencias. Algunas decisiones pueden generar discusiones en la prensa, por parte de actores políticos y en la opinión pública, por lo que será importante coordinar y manejar un plan de comunicación eficiente. Existen casos en que los Estados buscan proteger cierto aspecto del marco jurídico, o dejar sentada determinada posición en algún sector regulado, por lo que un laudo desfavorable puede representar un precedente negativo. De esta forma, son muchos aspectos los que están en juego cuando se activa un arbitraje y el Estado debe atender la demanda que pesa en su contra.

Que los Estados sean generalmente la parte demandada, significa que en muchas ocasiones un soberano solo empieza a organizar su defensa cuando recibe la notificación del inicio de la disputa, la misma que desencadena el cómputo de ciertos plazos procesales. Esto difiere mucho del proceso por el que pasa un demandante, ya que precisamente por ser la parte actora, suele tener control del momento en el que presenta la notificación correspondiente y da inicio al caso. Esta circunstancia puede brindarle la oportunidad de tener un manejo más holgado de la recopilación de documentos y antecedentes relevantes, el desarrollo de la estrategia legal e incluso la organización del trabajo con los expertos y testigos que va a presentar en el arbitraje.

Las controversias internacionales de inversión, por la naturaleza misma de la disputa, pueden involucrar aspectos sensibles para un Estado y, en muchos casos, con implicancias políticas. Las altas autoridades a quien se debe reportar sobre estos asuntos usualmente disponen de un tiempo limitado para dedicar a un solo tema por el número de responsabilidades que ostentan. Por ello resulta fundamental poder identificar cuál es la información indispensable en un determinado asunto y ser capaz de elaborar documentos ejecutivos o transmitir tal información con eficiencia en un periodo muy corto de tiempo.

Existe una metáfora popular para ejemplificar la capacidad de síntesis que se debe tener en estas situaciones. Esto se conoce como la prueba del ascensor. Es decir, se debe ser capaz de sintetizar en lo que dura un viaje en ascensor, digamos menos de un minuto, lo que en otras circunstancias requeriría convocar a una reunión para explicar y discutir el tema. Mi versión de esto es lo que he denominado la prueba de Desamparados.

En una ocasión, a fin de participar en una reunión en el Palacio de Gobierno de Perú, fui convocado por la alta dirección del Ministerio de Economía y Finanzas para explicar, con anterioridad a una reunión, lo que sería abordado más tarde en la cita principal. Preparé una corta presentación con diapositivas que abordaban los antecedentes relevantes, los principales puntos en discusión e incluso posibles escenarios a futuro, considerando ciertas variables en la toma de decisiones.

Llegué al encuentro repasando mentalmente los puntos más importantes y pensando en que había sido un reto resumir tanta información en una presentación tan corta. Conforme pasaban los minutos de espera, en mi cabeza iba recortando cada vez más la presentación, calculando qué información alcanzaría a discutir con el tiempo que quedaba disponible.

Una circunstancia imprevista había demandado extender una cita previa. Este cambio de último minuto, que no es algo inusual, terminó por consumir casi todo el tiempo separado. Me vi entonces en la necesidad de sintetizar los puntos esenciales de la presentación en el tiempo que nos tomó caminar desde la puerta del Ministerio al Palacio de Gobierno[1]. Esta no fue la única vez que una situación similar ocurrió y, desde entonces, no considero que estoy listo para una reunión si el tema a tratar no pasa la prueba de Desamparados.

La coordinación de temas de arbitraje desde el Estado presenta muchos retos, pero también viene con una satisfacción que considero que es difícil encontrar en otro trabajo. A veces, sólo cuando se litiga un caso desde cierta perspectiva, es posible dimensionar algunos intangibles. Se trata de una posición que difícilmente caerá en la monotonía, pues abarca situaciones, regulaciones y decisiones muy distintas una de otra, en sectores e industrias variadas, involucrando agencias de todo nivel. La amplitud y profundidad de temas hacen que sea una experiencia realmente única. Es, finalmente, una labor enriquecedora y gratificante que permite a un abogado entender con mayor claridad los desafíos que deben enfrentar los Estados cuando toman decisiones y que puede generar un cambio de la perspectiva y enfoque bajo los cuales se aborda el sistema de solución de controversias inversionista-Estado.

1. La llamo prueba de Desamparados por el camino que debimos seguir en esa ocasión. La distancia entre el Palacio de Gobierno de Perú y el Ministerio de Economía y Finanzas es corta: requiere subir una cuadra por el Jirón Lampa hasta la Iglesia de San Francisco de Asís y luego girar a la izquierda e ir una cuadra más, por la vía peatonal del Jirón Ancash, hasta la Estación de Desamparados -una antigua estación de trenes en Lima, que hoy hace las veces de la Casa de la Literatura- para finalmente girar nuevamente a la izquierda y avanzar unos metros hasta el ingreso a la Casa de Pizarro.

CAPÍTULO 7

Una embarazosa entrevista *ex parte* a un árbitro

Robert H. Smit

Era principios de la década de 1990, y yo era un asociado de litigio de nivel medio en una gran firma de abogados internacional con sede en Nueva York. El arbitraje comercial internacional todavía era relativamente joven en los Estados Unidos. Había realizado prácticas en la Corte Internacional de Arbitraje de la Cámara de Comercio internacional (CCI) y esperaba ayudar a mi bufete de abogados a desarrollar una práctica de arbitraje internacional. Así que me emocioné cuando un socio principal en el departamento de litigios de la firma me dijo que uno de los clientes más antiguos de la oficina nos había contratado para representarlo en un gran arbitraje de la CCI en el que el cliente había sido demandado. El socio principal me dijo que quería que trabajara con él en el arbitraje porque yo era el único abogado de la firma que sabía algo sobre lo que él llamó arbitraje "Ick"[1].

El contrato que originó la disputa requería que el arbitraje fuera llevado a cabo por un tribunal de tres miembros, con cada una de las partes designando a un miembro del tribunal y los dos árbitros nominados por las partes eligiendo a un presidente. El demandante ya había nominado a un respetado profesor de derecho internacional en una importante escuela de derecho de los Estados Unidos como su árbitro. Sin buscar mi opinión, el socio principal me dijo que quería nombrar a un ex juez de los EE. UU., y que ya había invitado a lo que describió como "el candidato perfecto" —un exjuez federal que conocía muy bien— a nuestras oficinas para una entrevista. Nunca había oído hablar del candidato, que no era conocido en los círculos de arbitraje internacional, aunque se había desempeñado como árbitro en algunos arbitrajes de seguros internos desde que se había retirado como juez.

1. Por sus siglas en inglés: ICC.

En la mañana de la entrevista, el socio principal me indicó que llevara los archivos del caso a la sala de conferencias donde la entrevista debía comenzar a las 10 AM, que organizara el almuerzo para seis personas (el candidato, el socio principal, el representante del cliente, dos asociados junior y yo) y que fuera servido en la sala de conferencias, y hacer reservas para cenar en un restaurante cercano en caso de que fuera a agradar al candidato. *¿Por qué necesitamos tanto tiempo con el candidato solo para confirmar su idoneidad y disponibilidad para servir como árbitro?*, pensé para mis adentros, después de haber leído la guía de la International Bar Association (IBA) pertinente y otras pautas sobre entrevistas *ex parte* permitidas con posibles árbitros designados por una parte. *¿Y una cena?*

La entrevista comenzó inocentemente con las habituales presentaciones y saludos. Luego, el candidato preguntó de qué se trataba el caso, y el socio principal procedió a contárselo. Describió los hechos de fondo clave del caso, los principales problemas que podrían surgir y las posiciones respectivas de las partes sobre esos asuntos. Me preocupé: *¿era esta una "descripción general de la disputa" que las directrices relevantes dicen que es apropiada, o una descripción de "hechos y posiciones que dieron lugar a la disputa" que identifican como inapropiados?* Las pautas no me resultaban claras, pero rápidamente me estaba incomodando.

"¿Por qué no le echa un vistazo a estos para entender mejor el caso?", le dijo el socio principal al candidato, pasándole una copia de la solicitud de arbitraje del demandante y la respuesta de nuestro cliente. Mientras él leía los documentos, pensé: *¿está bien? ¿Hemos acordado con el abogado del demandante compartir los alegatos con los posibles candidatos a árbitros?* Por un lado, los alegatos de las partes claramente involucraban el fondo de la disputa, donde se supone que las comunicaciones ex parte no deben ir. Por otro lado, no había riesgo de que el candidato aprendiera algo de los alegatos que los tres árbitros no aprenderían a su debido tiempo, ya que a ellos también se les proporcionarían esos mismos escritos, mostrando al candidato que los alegatos no deberían infectar la integridad de los procedimientos. Pero mi nivel de incomodidad aumentó.

Después de nuestro almuerzo, el socio principal le preguntó al candidato: "*Entonces, ahora que ha leído los alegatos iniciales de las partes, ¿hay alguna razón para que nuestro cliente dude en nominarlo como su árbitro?*". *¿Qué acaba de preguntar?* No preguntó directamente si el candidato fallaría a favor de nuestro cliente, pero sonó como una pregunta con "guiño" incluido. Luego, el cliente habló por primera vez y le preguntó al candidato: "*Nuestro caso es sólido, ¿no le parece?*"

¡Oh no, eso claramente cruzó la línea! ¿Qué debo hacer? Este era un caso del socio principal, su responsabilidad principal, no la mía, y él, el candidato y el cliente estaban claramente cómodos con lo que se decía. El socio principal y el cliente obviamente querían ganar el caso, y la elección de un árbitro favorable designado por la parte era clave para ese objetivo. No sabía lo que pensaba el candidato, pero estaba acostumbrado a los arbitrajes de seguros al estilo estadounidense, donde se espera que los árbitros designados por las partes tomen partido y las comunicaciones ex parte no son inusuales. Tampoco quería decir nada -expresar cualquier objeción- que pudiera molestar o alienar al socio principal y al cliente de quienes dependía mi futuro en la firma. Y no creía que nada de lo dicho durante esta entrevista previa a la nominación

realmente importara una vez que el tribunal arbitral fuera designado, y el arbitraje estuviera en marcha.

Pero no se sentía bien sentarse allí y no decir nada. Mi silencio me hizo cómplice en comunicaciones *ex parte* que sentí que eran inadecuadas en el arbitraje internacional. Quería construir una carrera en arbitraje internacional, y participar en esta entrevista sin objeciones me pareció una mala manera de comenzar esa carrera. Tenía que hacer algo, y tenía que hacerlo rápidamente antes de que el candidato respondiera a la pregunta del cliente sobre la solidez de nuestro caso.

Así que me excusé de la sala de conferencias para ir al baño. Luego le envié un correo electrónico al socio principal diciendo que no me sentía bien y que no volvería a la reunión. No es mi momento de mayor orgullo.

CAPÍTULO 8

Mi primer interrogatorio cruzado

Cristóbal Sarralde

No es lo mismo participar en un arbitraje internacional que en un litigio o en un arbitraje doméstico. Diversas culturas y sistemas jurídicos se ven envueltos, la antelación con la que se conoce la prueba a rendir por las partes y la flexibilidad en la forma de aportarla, así como el tiempo que estas y el tribunal arbitral tienen para preparar las audiencias hacen del arbitraje internacional una experiencia distinta. Esta diversidad de tradiciones es lo primero que se debe tener presente al momento de enfrentarse a un interrogatorio de testigos y/o de expertos, y más aún, si se trata de un interrogatorio cruzado o *cross examination*, sobre todo, si consideramos que muchos asociados que se dedican al arbitraje internacional han tenido su iniciación laboral en el arbitraje doméstico o, derechamente, en litigación. Asimismo, se debe tener en cuenta que en Latinoamérica los asociados no se encuentran tan familiarizados con el interrogatorio cruzado, ya que no es tan común en el sistema del derecho civil, a diferencia de lo que ocurre en el sistema del *common law*. Se trata de algo que precisamente me ocurrió cuando tuve que enfrentarme a mi primer arbitraje internacional.

En efecto, mis inicios estuvieron vinculados más a la litigación y, luego, al arbitraje doméstico, por lo que cuando tuve que enfrentar mi primer arbitraje internacional y, en particular, el primer interrogatorio cruzado, me di cuenta personalmente que la preparación y la forma de enfrentarlo diferían significativamente de lo que era mi experiencia previa. Afortunadamente, formaba parte de un equipo con experiencia en arbitraje internacional lo que me permitió tomar nota de una serie de cosas prácticas que desconocía. Adicionalmente, el haber tenido una contraparte que no tenía tanta claridad de cómo debía manejar un arbitraje internacional y un interrogatorio cruzado me enseñó reconocer con mayor precisión qué es lo que no se debe hacer en estas circunstancias. Es parte de esta primera experiencia y de lo que fui viviendo a través de los años, lo que intento plasmar a continuación.

Para enfrentar un interrogatorio y, especialmente, uno cruzado, ya sea como parte del equipo encargado de los documentos relevantes, de las preguntas o, directamente, de conducir el interrogatorio mismo, se requiere de una serie de habilidades que, a estas alturas, se encuentran sistematizadas, pueden enseñarse y aprenderse, sin perjuicio que —probablemente— el mejor aprendizaje lo sigue entregando la experiencia misma, la observación, el ensayo y el error.

Lo mejor es comenzar a asistir a interrogatorios cruzados lo antes posible, aunque sea, en una primera instancia, como el asociado encargado de los documentos relevantes y de entregarlos a los testigos y al tribunal. En efecto, cuando se está a cargo de dirigir el *cross examination*, se agradece el haber presenciado audiencias y conocer en vivo y de primera mano la dinámica que se genera.

Sin ánimo de ser exhaustivo, a modo de introducción al primer interrogatorio cruzado que podría enfrentar un asociado en un arbitraje internacional, me gustaría centrarme en cuatro aspectos que, a mi juicio, son cruciales para enfrentarlo exitosamente, y que he concluido como una consecuencia de la experiencia, a saber: (1) la preparación, (2) la claridad en el objetivo, (3) la flexibilidad y (4) la credibilidad. Desde ya hago presente que estos aspectos podrían ser absolutamente aplicables a otro tipo de arbitrajes y litigios. Sin embargo, existen elementos particulares del arbitraje internacional que los impregnan. A continuación, me enfocaré en cada uno de ellos.

§8.01 LA PREPARACIÓN

Sin este elemento, no existe interrogatorio cruzado exitoso. Es el elemento que probablemente engloba y se relaciona más con el resto. En principio, no puede ni debe haber espacio para la mera improvisación. A diferencia de lo que muchas veces ocurre en un litigio local o un arbitraje doméstico, cuando se llega a la audiencia de un arbitraje internacional en la que se realizará el interrogatorio cruzado de los testigos, las partes no solo ya han expuesto todos sus argumentos y fundamentos de hecho y de derecho, sino que, además, han presentado la prueba con la que intentan sustentar sus posiciones. Si a esto sumamos que la fecha de la audiencia se encuentra fijada con mucha antelación, tanto el tribunal arbitral como las partes tendrán un tiempo razonable para conocer muy bien lo que se discute y, especialmente, los hechos y los aspectos más técnicos sobre los que se litiga, por ejemplo, cuando hay informes de expertos que también podrán ser interrogados cruzadamente.

En primer lugar, quien enfrentará un *cross examination* debe conocer a profundidad y con lujo de detalles los hechos que forman parte de la disputa. Asimismo, las presentaciones de las partes y la prueba producida, lo que incluye -evidentemente- las declaraciones escritas de testigos de hechos y de expertos, así como los informes emitidos por estos últimos. Si no se conocen los hechos en detalle, será muy difícil para el abogado que está interrogando pasar fluidamente de un tema a otro para ir persuadiendo con dicha interrogación al tribunal; así como tampoco podrá tener la sensibilidad suficiente para darse cuenta, al escuchar la respuesta del testigo, del momento preciso en que debe detenerse en un tema particular y ahondar en él, porque puede ser crucial para sustentar la posición de su parte, o de suspender la línea de interrogatorio.

En segundo lugar, la preparación también debe considerar la audiencia a la que se enfrentará el abogado que llevará a cabo el interrogatorio cruzado. Esto es, debe tener la mayor cantidad de información respecto del árbitro o del tribunal arbitral, su *background*, estilo y forma de aproximarse a los casos. Lo mismo respecto de los abogados de la contraparte, así como de los testigos de hechos o expertos a quienes se interrogará.

En tercer lugar, la preparación también implicará necesariamente evaluar y decidir qué testigos de hechos o expertos de la contraria vale la pena citar para ser interrogados. Evidentemente, un testigo que de antemano se sabe que es muy sólido podría ser un gran riesgo para la parte que lo cita. Sin embargo, también podría ser mal visto por el tribunal arbitral y una mala táctica no citar a un testigo de la parte contraria que es crucial o clave.

Por último, una adecuada preparación requiere tener claridad acerca de qué preguntas específicas para restarle credibilidad a los testigos se pueden formular, sobre qué asuntos determinados se les va a interrogar cruzadamente, lo que puede incluir las preguntas concretas que se formularán; y, finalmente, respecto de los documentos en los que participaron o que son relevantes para confrontar con los testigos.

§8.02 CLARIDAD EN EL OBJETIVO

El asociado que tiene claridad respecto del resultado que pretende con una interrogación cruzada será capaz de conducir el interrogatorio hacia el punto que pueda sustentar la posición de su parte o desvirtuar o restar credibilidad/razonabilidad a la examinación de la parte contraria.

El punto de partida para determinar el referido objetivo va a ser la declaración o el informe del testigo, dependiendo de si se trata de un testigo de hechos o de un experto. Sin embargo, el interrogador no necesariamente debe sentirse limitado por ello. En efecto, por una parte, el asociado puede tener información adicional sobre hechos en los que participó el testigo y que no se encuentran contenidos en la declaración o en el informe en cuestión; y, por otra, hay que tener presente que, en general, los tribunales arbitrales son proclives a no circunscribir las preguntas del interrogatorio cruzado únicamente al contenido de los *statements* o del informe respectivo, sobre todo si se trata de cuestiones de relevancia en el caso y dependiendo de las reglas aplicables o que hubieren podido acordar las partes.

En segundo término, vale la pena tratar de determinar de la manera más específica posible cuál es el objetivo al interrogar al testigo en cuestión. Probablemente, si se fijan muchos objetivos diversos, si se trata de un objetivo muy genérico o si se intenta confirmar la posición completa de la parte con la *cross examination* del testigo, el interrogatorio va a perder su foco y, con ello, perderá también su fuerza y la atención del tribunal arbitral.

En tercer término, teniendo claro el objetivo del interrogatorio cruzado de un testigo determinado será más fácil utilizar en forma eficiente el poco tiempo con el que generalmente se cuenta para hacer la *cross examination*. No tiene sentido alguno y, por el contrario, puede ser contraproducente, intentar pasear al testigo por diversos hechos que se encuentran lo suficientemente determinados en el arbitraje o que han sido confirmados por otros testigos, o pedirles que identifiquen o intenten explicar una serie de documentos que pueden no tener relevancia o en los cuales el testigo no participó directamente. Por ello, lo recomendable es enfocar el interrogatorio cruzado únicamente en aquello que tiene relación con el objetivo preciso y particular determinado en forma previa, respecto de ese testigo específico, así como en los documentos que se refieren a aquello y en los que efectivamente haya tenido participación el testigo. De este modo, llevar en forma fluida al resultado querido por quien está conduciendo la respectiva *crossexamination* será más fácil.

§8.03 FLEXIBILIDAD

Si bien es relevante enfocarse en el objetivo de la respectiva *cross examination*, también resulta de extrema importancia que quien dirige el interrogatorio cruzado sea capaz de adaptarse al curso que va tomando el mismo o a la audiencia en particular, dependiendo de las respuestas recibidas. Podría pensarse que esto se opone a la preparación y se acerca más a la improvisación, pero no es así. Por el contrario, cuanto más preparado está quien conduce el interrogatorio cruzado, más fácil le resultará flexibilizar su enfoque y adaptarse al curso de la audiencia y a las respuestas del testigo.

Así, una primera sugerencia es preparar los temas sobre los que se interrogará cruzadamente al testigo, más que preguntas específicas. Tener definidos los temas sobre los que recaerá la *cross examination* otorgará mayor holgura a quien conduce el interrogatorio para hacer las preguntas que se requieran, de conformidad con lo que vaya respondiendo el testigo. Sin perjuicio de lo anterior, también pueden prepararse algunas preguntas por temas, particularmente cuando se está interrogando en un idioma distinto al nativo.

Una segunda sugerencia es no preguntar a un testigo sobre todos los temas, ni formular todas las preguntas que se tenían preparadas. El conducir una *crossexamination* no se trata de cubrir todos los temas que se tenían previstos respecto de un testigo, ni hacerle todas las preguntas preparadas. Muchas veces, menos es más. Puede que un hecho que sustenta la posición de la parte de quien conduce el interrogatorio haya quedado bastante confirmado en virtud de la respuesta a una pregunta y que no sea necesario solicitar mayores explicaciones o razones sobre lo mismo al testigo. Esto podría inclusive hacer peligrar el punto ya establecido. De la misma manera, si un testigo está declarando en forma extremadamente perjudicial para la parte que conduce la *cross examination*, tal vez sea mejor no permitir que el testigo continúe fortaleciendo la posición de la parte contraria y, consecuentemente, poner fin tempranamente al interrogatorio.

Finalmente, quien interroga cruzadamente también tendrá que adaptarse a la forma en que se ha aproximado a los hechos o al testigo el tribunal arbitral, así como la contraparte. En efecto, es posible que el tribunal arbitral le haya dado mucha importancia a un hecho en particular, ya sea durante la audiencia previamente al interrogatorio, o durante dicho interrogatorio, en cuyo caso, podría ser deseable introducir ese tema en la *cross examination*, si el testigo pudiera tener algo que decir al respecto. Por el contrario, si el tribunal arbitral ha mostrado que existe cierto hecho al que no le ha dado relevancia alguna, podría ser preferible omitir ciertas preguntas. Lo mismo ocurre en el caso que la parte contraria se oponga a ciertas preguntas o intente restarles relevancia, por cuanto podría ser aquello una señal grave de la importancia del punto o de que el testigo podría responder de manera contraria a su posición, lo que debería motivar a quien conduce la interrogación a reenfocarla hacia ese hecho.

§8.04 CREDIBILIDAD

Por último, jamás hay que olvidar que el ejercicio de interrogar cruzadamente no sólo permitirá al tribunal arbitral hacerse una idea de qué testigo es creíble y cuál no, y, consecuentemente con ello, qué posición y parte debería prevalecer sobre la otra. También le permitirá al árbitro hacerse una idea de los abogados que representan a cada una de las partes y si estos se ven creíbles y serios en su posición.

El interrogatorio cruzado constituye una oportunidad esencial para persuadir al tribunal arbitral. Si el interrogatorio es dirigido con claridad, de forma ordenada, lógica, eficiente y se logran establecer los puntos que sirven de sustento para la posición de la parte representada por quien efectúa el interrogatorio, le otorgará un mayor crédito frente al tribunal arbitral.

En el mismo sentido, si el testigo de la parte contraria se ha mostrado confuso, dubitativo, contradictorio o derechamente ha perdido credibilidad frente al tribunal arbitral, es probable que la posición de la parte que ha sido exitosa en su interrogatorio cruzado gane la apreciación del tribunal arbitral.

Por lo anterior, es recomendable evitar situaciones de hostilidad frente a los testigos o entrar en discusiones irrelevantes con el tribunal arbitral, insistir en preguntas que no tienen un claro objetivo, o que se refieren a hechos sin mayores consecuencias en la decisión a la que tendrá que arribar el tribunal en su laudo.

Como ya señalé y, considerando todos los elementos descritos anteriormente, puede que en la *cross examination* no se validen ni se confirmen todos los puntos relevantes de la posición de una de las partes. Sin embargo, si se consigue validar o confirmar algunos de ellos y lo anterior permite otorgar plausibilidad a dicha posición, puede que —en definitiva— ello constituya una herramienta inclusive más eficaz que cientos de documentos y alegaciones formuladas en los memoriales intercambiados por las partes. Por el contrario, una *cross examination* mal conducida, sin preparación, sin claridad en el objetivo, sin flexibilidad ni credibilidad frente al tribunal podría no sólo tener repercusiones fatales en la posición de la parte a la que se representa, sino también repercusiones en las costas del arbitraje.

CAPÍTULO 9

Arbitrando conforme al Acuerdo de Bangladesh

Clovis Trevino[*]

En 2015, las federaciones sindicales mundiales IndustriALL Global Union y UNI Global Union contrataron a la firma en la que trabajo, Covington & Burling, para representarlas en posibles arbitrajes en virtud del Acuerdo de Bangladesh sobre Incendios y Seguridad en la Construcción.

"¿Qué es el Acuerdo de Bangladesh?" Yo estaba intrigada.

Pronto supe que después del colapso del edificio Rana Plaza 2013 —el desastre más mortal de la industria de la confección en la historia moderna— las Uniones y aproximadamente 200 marcas de ropa de más de 20 países firmaron un acuerdo legal de cinco años para construir fábricas de prendas de vestir en Bangladesh que fueran lugares de trabajo seguros.

En un modelo de responsabilidad sin precedentes, el Acuerdo estableció sistemas independientes de inspección y capacitación en seguridad que cubren más de 1.600 fábricas de ropa y dos millones de trabajadores en Bangladesh. Las marcas firmantes acordaron exigir a sus fábricas proveedoras que implementen acciones correctivas para salvar vidas de manera oportuna y garantizar la viabilidad financiera de la implementación de estas acciones correctivas por parte de su proveedor.

En lo que fue un desarrollo decisivo para las empresas y los derechos humanos, el Acuerdo de Bangladesh establece que una parte puede "apelar" las decisiones del órgano rector interno del Acuerdo en un arbitraje vinculante. La idea de que los sindicatos internacionales y una gran cantidad de marcas mundiales de moda estarían de acuerdo en arbitrar disputas sobre compromisos de derechos humanos relacionados con las empresas fue innovadora. Destacó la promesa de arbitraje como un medio para hacer cumplir las obligaciones de derechos humanos y mejorar las condiciones de vida

[*] Las opiniones expresadas en este capítulo por la autora no reflejan necesariamente las opiniones de Covington & Burling o de sus clientes.

de miles de trabajadores de la confección de Bangladesh. Estaba emocionada de ser parte de esto.

En julio y octubre de 2016, los sindicatos activaron el innovador mecanismo de resolución de disputas del Acuerdo al iniciar un arbitraje contra dos marcas mundiales de moda. En nombre de los sindicatos, llevamos el caso a la Corte Permanente de Arbitraje de La Haya, argumentando que las marcas no habían exigido de manera oportuna a sus fábricas proveedoras que remediaran los riesgos de seguridad en el lugar de trabajo —dejando a miles de trabajadores en riesgo— ni asegurado la viabilidad financiera de dicha remediación, en violación de sus compromisos del Acuerdo.

Los riesgos no podrían haber sido mayores. Los riesgos de seguridad no corregidos iban desde sistemas de alarma contra incendios defectuosos, sistemas de detección de humo, falta de rociadores, puertas de salida, señales de salida y otros riesgos de incendio, eléctricos y estructurales que aumentaron el peligro de otro colapso del edificio como Rana Plaza. Los arbitrajes del Acuerdo de Bangladesh me dieron una rara oportunidad de contribuir a la protección de miles de trabajadores de la confección como terceros beneficiarios del Acuerdo.

En septiembre de 2017, tuvimos nuestra primera victoria. Un tribunal arbitral con sede en La Haya determinó que las reclamaciones de los sindicatos eran admisibles y estaban bajo su jurisdicción, allanando el camino para los primeros arbitrajes en virtud de un acuerdo comercial y de derechos humanos. En su decisión, el tribunal reconoció la naturaleza única e híbrida del Acuerdo de Bangladesh, ubicado en algún lugar entre el derecho público, el derecho privado y el derecho laboral. El tribunal también reconoció "la naturaleza pública del Acuerdo" y el "interés público" en juego en su interpretación y ejecución.

El tribunal logró un equilibrio en materia de confidencialidad. Aunque los nombres de las marcas no se revelarían y los procedimientos se celebrarían en privado para proteger la reputación de las marcas, el tribunal ordenó que ciertos documentos del caso se divulgaran en forma anonimizada en reconocimiento del interés público en la disputa.

Los sindicatos conciliaron el primer arbitraje en diciembre de 2017, llegando a un acuerdo que garantizaría que las fábricas proveedoras asociadas con la marca de moda demandada fueran remediadas y que hubieren fondos sustanciales disponibles para ese trabajo de remediación, de conformidad con el Acuerdo de Bangladesh.

El segundo arbitraje se resolvió a fines de enero de 2018, cuando ayudamos a asegurar uno de los pagos más grandes realizados por una marca para remediar los peligros en el lugar de trabajo en su cadena de suministro, lo que garantizaría la remediación de más de 150 fábricas proveedoras. Como parte del acuerdo, la marca de moda también acordó contribuir económicamente al Fondo de Apoyo a los Trabajadores de la Cadena de Suministro conjunto de los Sindicatos, establecido para apoyar el trabajo de los sindicatos para mejorar los salarios y las condiciones de los trabajadores en las cadenas de suministro mundiales.

Más importante aún, la amenaza de arbitraje bajo el Acuerdo de Bangladesh desencadenó un cambio en toda la industria, con empresas signatarias que intensificaron sus esfuerzos para que sus fábricas proveedoras cumplan con las obligaciones del Acuerdo.

Más allá de la industria de la confección en Bangladesh, los arbitrajes del Acuerdo de Bangladesh suponen una nueva frontera para la resolución de disputas comerciales y de derechos humanos, con una participación significativa y más amplia de las partes interesadas públicas y privadas interesadas en la creación y aplicación de normas empresariales y de derechos humanos que atraviesan fronteras nacionales.

Estoy orgullosa de haber estado a la vanguardia de esta nueva frontera en el arbitraje como medio para proteger y hacer cumplir los derechos humanos.

HISTORIAS DE GUERRA Y LECCIONES SOBRE EL TRABAJO COMO ÁRBITRO

CAPÍTULO 10
Conversación incómoda con tres árbitros

Roque Caivano, Valeria Galíndez & Francisco González de Cossío

§10.01 CARRERA COMO ÁRBITRO

[A] ¿Cuál ha sido el episodio más desagradable en su carrera como árbitro?

Roque: En este aspecto podría mencionar dos: (1) haber sido recusado por la misma parte que me había designado, y por un tema que conocía perfectamente desde el primer día; y (2) Haber tenido que lidiar, siendo presidente de un tribunal, con un árbitro ostensiblemente parcial, que con bastante descaro (y algo de ignorancia) ni siquiera cuidaba las apariencias.

[B] ¿Cuál ha sido el momento de mayor satisfacción en su carrera como árbitro?

Valeria: Sin lugar a dudas, fue al final de una audiencia de una semana en un arbitraje en que era árbitro único, cuando ambas partes y sus abogados aplaudieron y me felicitaron por la conducción. La opinión de las partes, que son los verdaderos usuarios del arbitraje, es finalmente la más importante.

§10.02 ARREPENTIMIENTOS

[A] ¿Si pudiera cambiar algo en su carrera, que cambiaría?

Roque: No demasiado. Quizá seleccionaría un poco más las actividades en que me inmiscuyo, porque en ocasiones me encuentro haciendo cosas que probablemente no debería haber aceptado.

[B] ¿Se arrepiente de uno o más laudos que haya dictado?

Valeria: No. Todos han sido fruto de un análisis atento de todos los argumentos y pruebas y fieles a mi convicción. Por fortuna, hasta el día de hoy no he experimentado situación alguna de disidencia entre los miembros del tribunal o situaciones complicadas en la deliberación. Algunos laudos han sido, evidentemente, más difíciles que otros, ya fuera por la complejidad del caso o por dudas durante la formación de mi convencimiento. Sin embargo, en esos casos siempre tuve la suerte de trabajar con árbitros con mucha experiencia, con quienes el intercambio de opiniones se dio de la forma más abierta posible. Eso me permitió no solo aprender, sino también estar tranquila con la decisión tomada al final.

[C] ¿Se arrepiente de uno o más casos que haya asumido?

Francisco: No. He tenido algunos casos que me han quitado el sueño, o en que he visto cosas muy lamentables, pero no me arrepiento: dicho sentimiento me surge cuando considero que erré, y no detecto que haya sido el caso.

§10.03 VIDA PERSONAL

[A] ¿Considera que es fácil hacer amigos en el mundo del arbitraje?

Roque: No es fácil. El mundo del arbitraje es un ambiente muy competitivo, donde abundan las vanidades y en las que no siempre se actúa sinceramente. De todas maneras, he cosechado muchos y muy buenos amigos en mi carrera.

[B] ¿Cuál es su hobby? ¿Cuánto tiempo dedica a actividades distintas al derecho o al arbitraje?

Valeria: Volví hace poco a practicar el ballet clásico. Fui bailarina de los seis a los 15 años, cuando dejé de practicarlo. Ahora trato de dedicarle dos horas a la semana. No siempre puedo por los viajes y audiencias, pero, como siempre me ha gustado ejercitarme, trato de hacer algo (incluso en gimnasios de hoteles) por lo menos tres veces a la semana. Además de eso, me encanta el cine y siempre estoy leyendo algo no relacionado al arbitraje. Me gustan las novelas y busco siempre leer en distintos idiomas.

[C] ¿Considera que ha renunciado a otros aspectos de su vida personal para tener una carrera exitosa como árbitro? ¿A cuáles?

Francisco: Sí, ocio.

§10.04 COMPETENCIA Y MENTORES

[A] ¿Compite consigo mismo o con otros árbitros?

Roque: Definitivamente, soy mi principal crítico y procuro superarme y no defraudar las expectativas. De todas maneras, aunque no busco competir con otros árbitros, en el fondo somos bastantes intentando ganar espacios en un mundo relativamente pequeño.
Valeria: Siempre conmigo misma.
Francisco: Conmigo mismo. El que deja de mejorar, deja de ser bueno.

[B] ¿Quién fue su mentor o su modelo a seguir?

Roque: No tuve un mentor en particular. Pero he arbitrado con muchos colegas de quienes he rescatado muchas cosas buenas y he aprendido mucho (aun de sus errores).
Valeria: Mi mentor y la persona responsable por introducirme al arbitraje fue el profesor brasileño Arnoldo Wald, con quien aprendí derecho, profesionalismo, disciplina y cómo relacionarme con colegas y clientes. Fueron casi diez años de muchísimo trabajo, algunos de los años más interesantes y desafiantes para mí, en una época en la que Brasil recién estaba comenzando en el mundo del arbitraje. También tuve la fortuna de contar con el apoyo y consejos de otros profesionales admirables como José Emilio Nunes Pinto, Juan Fernández-Armesto y Julie Bédard (a quien considero particularmente un modelo de mujer profesional del arbitraje internacional).
Francisco: José Luis Siqueiros y Jan Paulsson.

§10.05 ACTUACIÓN DEL ÁRBITRO

[A] ¿Cuál considera usted que es el mayor reto para un árbitro?

Roque: En una actividad bastante vertiginosa, el mayor desafío es darse el tiempo necesario para poder dedicarle a cada caso la atención que merecen las partes.
Valeria: Nunca olvidarse de cómo es estar del otro lado (actuando como representante de parte).

[B] ¿Qué hace que un árbitro sea bueno?

Roque: Por encima de todas las cosas, honestidad (inclusive intelectual), dedicación y una buena formación jurídica "de base", que le permita captar la esencia de cada controversia y no perderse tanto en los vericuetos o detalles.

[C] ¿Ha rechazado participar como árbitro por problemas de disponibilidad?¿Cuántas veces?

Valeria: Sí, dos veces.

[D] ¿Trabaja activamente para mitigar los sesgos cognitivos a los que puede enfrentarse al momento de decidir?

Francisco: Sí. Mucho. A veces siento que demasiado —en sí, un sesgo cognoscitivo.

[E] ¿Cuántos casos simultáneos se siente en capacidad de manejar?

Francisco: Pregunta imposible de contestar con un simple número pues los casos varían. Hay veces que un solo caso satura las venas de mi equipo. Hay veces que un par de docenas lo hacen. Depende del tamaño, complejidad y sobre todo laboriosidad del caso.

§10.06 RELACIÓN CON OTROS ÁRBITROS

[A] ¿Se ha tenido que enfrentar alguna vez a un presidente tirano?

Roque: No tanto como tirano, pero sí he tenido presidentes poco dispuestos a escuchar. En estos casos, el reto es ganarse el lugar como coárbitro sin confrontar con el presidente. También he tenido presidentes "cómodos" (alguno, inclusive, rayano en la indolencia). Dificultad que pude sortear logrando buena química con el otro coárbitro, para sacar el caso adelante.

[B] ¿Se ha visto alguna vez afectada su relación profesional con otros árbitros por la aproximación a algún caso?

Roque: No de manera directa, pero en algún caso en que se consolidaron varios arbitrajes muy importantes en uno, y los otros tribunales quedaron desafectados, sentí que los otros árbitros no vieron con demasiada simpatía al tribunal que finalmente concentró la totalidad del caso.
Valeria: No.
Francisco: Sí. Lamentablemente la conducta poco ética no es la excepción. Y ello a veces exige confrontación. No tolerar.

[C] ¿Qué cualidades busca en un coárbitro?

Francisco: Abogado técnico (que conozca el Derecho), inteligencia, que trabaje, que tenga mente abierta. Sobre todo, una persona decente.

§10.07 LOS ÁRBITROS JÓVENES

[A] ¿Qué consejo le daría a quien inicia su carrera como árbitro?

Roque: Que se preparen técnicamente para cuando deban actuar, y que busquen hacerse conocidos en el "mercado", de modo que las partes o los coárbitros los tengan en cuenta al momento de necesitar designar árbitros.
Valeria: Tener mucha humildad. No hay peor cosa que creer que uno lo sabe todo. Habrá siempre algo nuevo que aprender.

[B] ¿Qué tipo de casos cree que podrían asumir árbitros jóvenes?

Francisco: Casos sencillos y pequeños. Que *in crescendo* vayan adentrando al joven a las complejidades del proceso, del Derecho y de juzgar. Es peligroso empezar "por arriba": lo que al principio podría parecer en una bendición, acaba siendo una maldición (para la trayectoria del joven). Tengan paciencia: las cosas buenas *a veces* toman tiempo.

§10.08 LAS MUJERES Y EL ARBITRAJE

[A] ¿Percibe alguna diferencia entre equipos de abogados conformados mayoritariamente por hombres que equipos con un número equivalente o superior de mujeres?

Roque: En general, en los casos en que he intervenido con abogadas mujeres he percibido un mayor grado de dedicación al caso y una forma más metódica y prolija (argumentalmente) de presentar el caso.

[B] Como mujer, ¿ha sentido alguna desventaja en la práctica como árbitro? De ser así, ¿cuál o cuáles?

Valeria: Nunca he sentido desventaja por ser mujer. Pero tengo consciencia de que he sido afortunada por ello.

[C] ¿Cuál es su percepción sobre la participación activa de mujeres y minorías en el arbitraje?

Francisco: No sé si entendí bien pero anticipo que tiene que ver con los esfuerzos de género que existen en el medio arbitral internacional. Mi percepción es que el problema existe, pero es menor a lo que con frecuencia se escucha. Cierto, debemos abrir las puertas a mujeres (de hecho, a todos). También cierto, existe una preponderancia masculina. No tan cierto, que deban forzarse cuotas. Ello puede generar problemas (que ya han ocurrido). En mi opinión, las mujeres llevan ya tiempo jugando un papel importante. No son pocas las árbitros prominentes. He compartido tribunales con muchas; y he elegido a muchas. El criterio a seguir no es distinto al de los hombres (abogado técnico que conozca el Derecho), inteligente, que trabaje, que tenga mente abierta. Sobre todo, una persona decente. En mi opinión, esto debe ser el enfoque.

§10.09 OPINIÓN SOBRE LOS ABOGADOS DE PARTE

[A] ¿Qué estilo prefiere en los abogados de parte? ¿Abiertamente agresivos, pasivos, pasivo-agresivos?

Roque: Prefiero a quienes se comportan lealmente y con corrección hacia el tribunal y hacia sus colegas de la contraparte; a quienes, sin detrimento de la vehemencia que puedan poner en la defensa de los intereses de su cliente, evitan efectuar planteos notoriamente inadmisibles o plantear oposiciones carentes de fundamente. Esa forma de comportarse, lejos de significar una desventaja estratégica, representa un beneficio para la parte a quien representa, porque -a los ojos del tribunal- la credibilidad del abogado proyecta credibilidad a la parte.
Valeria: Un buen abogado es el que sabe adaptarse a las situaciones (no solo al cliente). Tiene que saber identificar cuándo debe ser más agresivo y cuándo eso no es conveniente para su caso. La inteligencia emocional es esencial.
Francisco: Inteligente, preparado, decente. Los estilos citados incluyen variables que pueden o no ser necesarias.

[B] ¿Qué actitudes consideran molestosas o inapropiadas de los abogados de parte?

Roque: Las señaladas al responder la pregunta anterior: la multiplicación de incidencias, oposiciones o planteos, muchas veces ostensiblemente inadmisibles.
Valeria: Falta de objetividad e ironía.
Francisco: Grosería. Hacer los problemas personales.

§10.10 LA CONFIDENCIALIDAD Y LA EVALUACIÓN DE LOS ÁRBITROS

[A] ¿Se sentiría incómodo bajo escrutinio si las partes pudieran revelar en cualquier foro su nombre y valorar su manejo del proceso y el laudo dictado, manteniendo la confidencialidad de las partes?

Roque: No me ha pasado, pero seguramente sí me sentiría incómodo. Un "foro" (entendido como un ámbito público) no es el lugar apropiado para ventilar críticas sobre la actuación de un árbitro, dada la imposibilidad de ahondar en los múltiples matices que un caso puede haber tenido. El árbitro explica sus decisiones en el mismo laudo. Y mi forma de tratar ese aspecto es no dejar ninguna decisión sin motivar, a veces hasta de manera sobreabundante. Mucho menos apropiado es ese ámbito si el árbitro aludido no tendrá la oportunidad de refutar las apreciaciones que se hagan sobre él.

§10.11 ANTES DE SER NOMBRADO COMO ÁRBITRO

[A] ¿Se siente cómodo o considera útiles las entrevistas realizadas por las partes de manera previa a un nombramiento?

Roque: Considero que son útiles para las partes, que muchas veces tienen que "convalidar" la sugerencia de su abogado y designar a alguien a quien probablemente no han visto nunca antes. Alguna vez me he sentido incómodo porque la parte no tenía claro el propósito ni los límites de esta entrevista, y pretendió incursionar en los temas del fondo del caso. A partir de esa experiencia, cuando el abogado me contacta para concertar una entrevista con su cliente, le pido que lo advierta de las "reglas de juego" de esta entrevista, y evite situaciones incómodas.
Francisco: Sí. Deben existir lineamientos, sin embargo.

[B] ¿Le generan preocupación las comunicaciones *ex parte*?

Valeria: No, nunca tuve problemas con eso.

§10.12 DECLARACIÓN DE IMPARCIALIDAD E INDEPENDENCIA

[A] Si el árbitro reconoce su imparcialidad e independencia, ¿no es suficiente dicha declaración? ¿Qué objeto tiene revelar información pasada que, a ojos del árbitro, no afecta su capacidad de decidir la controversia de manera imparcial e independiente?

Roque: En mi opinión, la mirada del árbitro sobre su propia independencia e imparcialidad no es del todo relevante. Coincido absolutamente con las reglas que exigen que la revelación se haga tomando en consideración la mirada de las partes. El objeto de revelar información puntual es "nivelar" la información que el árbitro tiene sobre sus posibles conflictos de intereses, y que probablemente la parte no los tenga. Una revelación puntual, detallada y completa genera confianza, y al final de cuentas evita dudas y recusaciones futuras.

[B] ¿Cómo saber hasta qué punto las relaciones presentes o pasadas, directas o indirectas, financieras, profesionales o de cualquier otro tipo con las partes, sus representantes, abogados o partes relacionadas deben ser reveladas?

Valeria: No hay respuesta precisa para eso. En realidad, creo que nunca habrá porque las relaciones y la forma en que las personas se relacionan cambian constantemente con mucha velocidad. La base es el uso del sentido común.

§10.13 NOMBRAMIENTOS REPETITIVOS

[A] ¿Considera que el nombramiento repetitivo de un árbitro genera en sí mismo una duda razonable?

Roque: Depende de las circunstancias: fundamentalmente de la frecuencia con que es nombrado, del lapso de tiempo que media entre nombramiento y nombramiento y del "tamaño del mercado" donde ese arbitraje tiene lugar (entendiéndose por tal la cantidad de casos que tiene esa parte y los que tiene el árbitro).

[B] ¿Rechazaría ser nombrado en más de una ocasión por la misma parte?

Valeria: Todo dependería de la situación concreta. Llevaría en consideración varios elementos antes de decidir aceptar o no, como cuándo fue el primer nombramiento, quiénes son los abogados y cuál es la materia. En todo caso, haría una revelación.

[C] ¿Se siente cómodo o le genera algún tipo de preocupación ser nombrado en repetidas ocasiones por la misma parte?

Francisco: No, pues soy imparcial. Pero nunca me ha pasado.

§10.14 ROL DEL SECRETARIO ARBITRAL

[A] ¿Considera hipócrita la crítica al secretario arbitral que participa en tareas de redacción del laudo?

Roque: Depende del grado de intervención que se permita al secretario. Una cosa es que redacte la "historia procesal" y otra muy distinta es que se inmiscuya en la toma de decisiones, que son propias de los árbitros. Sé que existen, pero en mi experiencia no he conocido personalmente muchos casos de secretarios que suplan el rol de los árbitros o que excedan lo que se espera que un secretario haga.

Valeria: Totalmente. Hay tareas que son perfectamente delegables que no interfieren de manera alguna en el proceso de deliberación de los árbitros.
Francisco: ¡Sí!

§10.15 EL DOUBLE-HATTING

[A] ¿Le ha generado la doble calidad árbitro/abogado de partealgún tipo de conflicto?

Valeria: No.

[B] ¿Es común participar como árbitro y como abogado de parte en el arbitraje internacional?

Roque: Por lo que se ve en la práctica, son mayoría los casos de árbitros de tiempo parcial, que la mayor parte de las veces actúan como abogados de parte y ocasionalmente como árbitros. No es particularmente mi caso, que casi siempre actúo como árbitro y ocasionalmente soy contratado como abogado (y no para "llevar" un caso sino para asistir al abogado que lo lleva). Pero entiendo que situaciones como la mía son las menos.

CAPÍTULO 11

Saltando a la piscina: ¿cómo redactar tu primer laudo arbitral?

Álvaro Awad

Todo árbitro tuvo su *debut*. Gary Born, Gabrielle Kaufmann-Kohler, Yves Derains, Bernardo Cremades y otros tantos maestros del arbitraje se enfrentaron alguna vez al desafío de redactar su primer laudo.

Al respecto, la formación de nuevos árbitros es esencial para diversificar la comunidad arbitral. Es sabido que la concentración excesiva de casos en un puñado de especialistas provoca tardanzas innecesarias en la solución de conflictos a nivel local e internacional. Por lo mismo, la guía de iniciación a quienes tienen la oportunidad de actuar como árbitros por primera vez resulta beneficiosa.

Si bien la sola idea de impartir justicia y zanjar una controversia —en forma prácticamente definitiva— aterra a más de alguno, esa deferencia hacia la labor jurisdiccional es precisamente el primer paso para llegar a ser un excelente árbitro. La preparación de un laudo bien razonado y ejecutable es una gran responsabilidad. Por lo mismo, debe asumirse con seriedad desde el inicio de una carrera en el mundo del arbitraje.

Pues bien, ¿qué mejor que recibir un par de consejos para esa ocasión tan especial?

Aunque seguramente hay muchos —en serio, muchos— árbitros más experimentados que podrían compartir sus estrategias, en este capítulo presento una recopilación de consejos que me hubiera gustado tener a mano cuando redacté (entusiastamente) mi primer laudo arbitral.

Lo primero que hay que saber es que no existe un estándar único. Cada árbitro tiene su estilo propio. Dicho lo anterior, hay ciertas virtudes que son transversales a toda sentencia bien hecha. Características como la claridad, la precisión y la consistencia en los términos utilizados[1] son indispensables en cualquier especie de escritura legal, incluyendo un laudo.

Desde luego, se sugiere titular el documento como laudo, para que no haya dudas respecto a su naturaleza[2]. Si el caso permite varios tipos de laudos ("interinos", "provisionales", "parciales", "finales", etc.) conviene especificar de cuál se trata. El número de páginas dependerá del caso particular, la cantidad de asuntos debatidos y la magnitud de las presentaciones y pruebas de las partes.

Hay que tener en cuenta que el sarcasmo es inapropiado[3] y, en general, una aproximación respetuosa hacia los temas más discutibles hace que el laudo sea más asimilable para todos los involucrados. En lo posible, el uso de un lenguaje simple es preferible al de una terminología jurídica o técnica. Las abreviaturas pueden ser útiles, pero demasiadas pueden complicar el texto.

Por otro lado, deben considerarse en todo momento las normas procedimentales aplicables. Estas se encuentran en el acuerdo de las partes, el reglamento de la institución arbitral respectiva —en caso de un arbitraje institucional[4]— y la ley de la sede del arbitraje. Si se quiere ser exhaustivo, valdría la pena revisar también la legislación del lugar donde probablemente se ejecutará lo resuelto (si aquel fuere distinto a la sede). Dictar un laudo satisfactorio implica incluir toda la información que estas normas requieren. Por ejemplo, señalar la individualización completa de las partes, el lugar del arbitraje y la fecha del laudo. Quizás hay que firmar este último de tal o cual forma.

Un aspecto central en que quisiera detenerme es la estructura del laudo. El documento debe contener tantas secciones como sean necesarias para cumplir el encargo, siguiendo un formato claro y lógico. Por lo demás, dividir el documento en apartados debidamente organizados facilita su lectura y comprensión. De esta manera, luego de contar la historia de la designación del tribunal, el objeto del arbitraje, los eventos procedimentales más relevantes y las cuestiones relativas a la jurisdicción del tribunal, el laudo dará cuenta resumida de las presentaciones principales de las partes, apuntando los hechos, los argumentos y las pretensiones que se sometieron a la decisión del tribunal[5]. Posteriormente, explicitará la prueba rendida y hará los razonamientos que la ley aplicable amerite (o bien, en el caso de un amigable componedor, señalará lo que dicta la equidad). Finalmente, concluirá con una o más decisiones.

Si el caso tiene pocos puntos en discusión, podría ser suficiente indicar todas las pretensiones de una parte antes de pasar a la exposición de las solicitudes de las demás, tal como se estila. En cambio, cuando se está ante casos más complejos (e.g. arbitrajes multi-parte con una infinidad de cuestiones a ser resueltas), una alternativa es separar

1. International Bar Association Arb40 Subcommitee, *Toolkit for Award Writing*, Sección 5 (2016).
2. Chartered Institute of Arbitrators, *International Arbitration Practice Guideline – Drafting Arbitral Awards*, Part I (2016).
3. International Bar Association Arb40 Subcommitee, *Toolkit for Award Writing*, Sección 5.1 (2016).
4. Muchas instituciones, como la Corte Internacional de Arbitraje de la Cámara de Comercio Internacional (CCI), ofrecen listados de verificación (*checklist*) de laudos muy útiles.
5. El laudo resuelve un asunto sustantivo. Si la decisión sólo versa sobre un asunto procedimental, se trata en realidad de una mera orden procesal.

las secciones del laudo por materia, indicando en cada una las pretensiones de cada interviniente respecto a ese punto determinado. Esta segunda opción es conveniente si la determinación de algunos asuntos depende de la decisión sobre otros[6]. Lo anterior, pues servirá de guía para los considerandos y orientará tanto al sentenciador como al futuro lector.

Al momento de hacer consideraciones sobre los hechos es primordial aclarar si los mismos son o no disputados. De igual forma, deberán respetarse las reglas sobre la carga de la prueba. Cada vez que el árbitro dé por acreditado un hecho debe indicar sus fundamentos y referirse a la evidencia en que se apoya. Hay que citar la prueba de la manera más precisa posible, para luego valorarla según el sistema aplicable.

En cada asunto controvertido habrá que señalar de qué manera la ley instruye a decidir sobre la base de los hechos acreditados en el proceso. Explicitar los razonamientos completos del tribunal es, sin lugar a dudas, la mejor garantía de que el laudo sorteará una eventual impugnación por falta de motivación, pues le permitirá al juez escrutiñador entender la posición de los árbitros.

Ocasionalmente, es ventajoso incluir uno o más razonamientos alternativos del siguiente tipo: "*Incluso si…, de todos modos habría que acoger/rechazar la pretensión, puesto que…*". Estas reflexiones se conocen como *obiter dicta*, al ser argumentos complementarios que "se dicen de paso".

En la parte resolutiva, toda declaración debe ser especialmente clara. Se recomienda que dicha sección no incluya términos definidos ni referencias a otros apartados del laudo, sino que sea autosuficiente, para así facilitar su ejecución.

A modo ejemplar, si se condena al pago de una suma de dinero es elemental señalar el monto y la moneda en que se debe pagar, su reajuste e interés, en su caso (con sus parámetros y las fechas desde y hasta la cual se aplican), quién debe pagar a quién y las demás condiciones del pago.

En lo concerniente a los pagos, no hay que olvidar la decisión sobre las costas del proceso, la que debe ser —al menos sucintamente— fundada.

Luego de emitir un pronunciamiento sobre las pretensiones de las partes, se sugiere incluir al final una decisión general del estilo: "*Se rechaza toda otra pretensión sometida al presente arbitraje*"[7], como frase de cierre para no dejar cabos sueltos.

A fin de dictar el laudo oportunamente, se debe reservar siempre espacio suficiente en la agenda. Una de las virtudes del proceso arbitral frente a la litigación estatal es que, por la especialización y compromiso del tribunal, se puede alcanzar una solución más expedita de las controversias. Por lo mismo, es imprescindible que el árbitro —aunque sea principiante— cumpla con esta expectativa de eficiencia, planificando las etapas del caso en que participa.

Una técnica útil es redactar anticipadamente un borrador confidencial del laudo, donde se vaya incluyendo toda la información relativa a las partes, sus alegaciones del período de discusión y las diversas gestiones que vayan teniendo lugar en el procedimiento. Mantener un borrador actualizado facilita la identificación de los asuntos basales que el tribunal deberá zanjar una vez ponderados todos los medios de

---

6. International Bar Association Arb40 Subcommitee, *Toolkit for Award Writing*, Sección 4.8 (2016).
7. Ibíd., Sección 4.11.

prueba. Ello permite pensar con tiempo en las problemáticas envueltas y sus posibles escenarios de solución.

Si se está integrando un tribunal colegiado, resulta capital que el presidente del tribunal establezca un procedimiento de deliberación. Cada coárbitro debe participar en él con libertad para intercambiar ideas y generar un debate enriquecedor[8].

Cuando se traza el borrador, el árbitro debe tener claro quién estudiará el laudo. En otras palabras, ¿a quién le está escribiendo?[9] Por un lado, la parte vencida revisará exhaustivamente los fundamentos de la decisión. En cambio, la parte vencedora necesitará un laudo particularmente claro en su parte resolutiva. Por último, los tribunales ante los cuales se ejecutará o impugnará lo decidido revisarán tanto la parte resolutiva como la historia procedimental y el respeto al debido proceso.

Es importante que un árbitro haga el ejercicio de pensar en las posibles causales de impugnación del laudo, y esto no solo al momento de firmarlo, sino durante toda la conducción del proceso arbitral y hasta su completo término. En tal sentido, y sin llegar a caer en el extremo de la denominada "paranoia del debido proceso", el tribunal debe tener presente que sus conductas a lo largo del juicio podrían repercutir en la posterior invalidación o inejecución de su decisión.

Por ejemplo, si el árbitro impide durante la tramitación del arbitraje que una de las partes pueda presentar sus argumentos, el laudo difícilmente podrá corregir esta infracción a la bilateralidad de la audiencia. En este ámbito, es aconsejable que el árbitro proteja el fallo dejando constancia expresa de la manera en que se constituyó el tribunal, las notificaciones realizadas y las fases del procedimiento en que se refleje que se respetaron las garantías procesales.

Otro ejemplo: si el árbitro en definitiva decide sobre cuestiones no sometidas a su conocimiento o si otorga más de lo pedido, la parte afectada podrá recurrir la sentencia con altas probabilidades de éxito. Una buena recomendación para evadir este riesgo es explicitar el texto completo del acuerdo de arbitraje, la parte petitoria de los escritos fundamentales del proceso, los puntos precisos a ser resueltos por el tribunal y las decisiones que se tomaron a su respecto.

La justicia arbitral, aunque experta, sigue siendo humana. Ello significa que los laudos pueden contener errores de toda clase, desde omisiones hasta ambigüedades. Por lo mismo, el árbitro —especialmente si es novato— debe revisar con esmero el producto de su trabajo, evitando la necesidad de aclarar o rectificar lo resuelto más tarde. Antes de su dictación, se recomienda hacer una verificación doble —e incluso triple— de las referencias y cálculos contenidos en el laudo.

Por último, un tema que se viene discutiendo con fuerza en la comunidad arbitral internacional es la labor que pueden cumplir los secretarios del tribunal[10]. Si bien es improbable que un árbitro joven cuente con un asistente en su primer fallo, sí es importante advertir que el mandato al árbitro es *intuitu personæ*. Esto significa que este no puede delegar en su secretario —ni en nadie más— su deber de decidir el caso.

8. Véase el Capítulo 13: *Franklin, Rubin o de Bono: cómo enfrentar la primera deliberación* (Manuel Conthe).
9. Ibíd., Sección 5.1.
10. Probablemente la mejor escuela para convertirse en árbitro.

Ciertamente podrá pedir su ayuda para que lo asista durante el procedimiento y en la redacción de los aspectos formales del laudo, pero de ningún modo debe un árbitro dejar de resolver por sí mismo los puntos sustantivos de la controversia[11].

En suma, la redacción del primer laudo es un interesante desafío. Como se ha visto, el cargo de árbitro exige minuciosidad y dedicación. Estas pautas pueden ser provechosas para quienes inician su carrera arbitral.

Con el tiempo, la experiencia mejora el método y permite abordar controversias cada vez más complejas, adquiriéndose un estilo propio. Como en todas las cosas, la práctica hace al maestro.

11. Véase el Capítulo 12: *Guía para ser secretario arbitral* (Lucas Loviscek).

CAPÍTULO 12
Guía para ser secretario arbitral

Lucas Loviscek

§12.01 INTRODUCCIÓN

Este capítulo tiene por objeto compartir mi gratificante y fructífera experiencia como secretario de tribunales arbitrales en arbitrajes tanto ad hoc como institucionales, compartir lecciones aprendidas y transmitir algunas recomendaciones, con la esperanza que estas puedan resultar de utilidad a practicantes jóvenes, y no tan jóvenes, que abren su camino en la fascinante práctica del arbitraje y que tienen interés en desempeñarse como secretarios arbitrales.

A tal efecto, resulta necesario primero entender el rol y la implicancia del secretario[1] en la conducción y desarrollo del procedimiento arbitral. La función principal del secretario es asistir a los árbitros en el cumplimiento de su mandato. El mandato de los árbitros es ponderar los argumentos de las partes y los elementos probatorios y decidir la disputa[2]. El secretario, por lo tanto, no debe suplir, sustituir, o acaparar esas funciones que corresponden al mandato personal de los árbitros[3], pero cumple un rol muy importante en asistir al tribunal en el cumplimiento de dicho mandato para que este pueda conducir el procedimiento y resolver el caso de manera efectiva y eficiente.

---

1. Cuando hago referencia a la figura del "secretario" me refiero indistintamente a secretarias y secretarios
2. Resulta oportuno recordar la célebre frase adjudicada al filósofo griego Sócrates (470 AC-399 AC) sobre las funciones del juez, igualmente descriptivas de las del árbitro en cuanto a sus facultades jurisdiccionales y sin entrar en disquisiciones en cuanto a la naturaleza y prerrogativas de uno y el otro, a saber: "*Cuatro características corresponden al juez: Escuchar cortésmente, responder sabiamente, ponderar prudentemente y decidir imparcialmente*".
3. La elección de los árbitros por las partes es personal en el entendido que se elige a esas personas, y no a otras, para resolver la disputa.

El rol del secretario abarca cuestiones de administración del procedimiento (por ejemplo, organización de documentos y evidencia, preparación de calendarios procesales, manejo de las comunicaciones entre el tribunal y las partes y notificaciones procesales, control de cumplimiento de formalidades, plazos y órdenes procesales por las partes litigantes, etc.) y, dependiendo de la necesidad y directivas del tribunal —y siempre bajo la supervisión de este— puede en algunos casos extenderse a la preparación de borradores de órdenes procesales o hasta de algunas secciones del laudo, al análisis de aspectos legales y a la asistencia en las deliberaciones de los árbitros[4]. Este tipo de funciones dan a quien se desempeña como secretario la experiencia invalorable de: (1) comprender y coordinar las sinergias que existen entre las partes, abogados, peritos, el tribunal y, en su caso, la institución administradora del arbitraje; (2) desarrollar habilidades interpersonales al interactuar con los distintos actores del proceso arbitral y atender sus necesidades; (3) manejar plazos de manera eficiente; (4) manejar y organizar documentos, calendarios, y aspectos procesales importantes para la conducción del proceso; y según el caso y el tribunal arbitral que conozca la disputa, (5) asistir a las deliberaciones y entender cómo piensan los árbitros, identificar evidencia y argumentos relevantes, asistir en la búsqueda de doctrina, jurisprudencia y análisis legal de temas específicos, como así también preparar órdenes procesales y, en algunos casos, borradores de secciones del laudo. Todo ello, claro está, bajo la debida instrucción y supervisión de los árbitros.

Lo expuesto en el párrafo anterior denota las razones por las cuales cada vez más profesionales aspiran a involucrarse como secretarios arbitrales, ya que ello es una oportunidad inmejorable para adentrarse en la práctica del arbitraje y desarrollar las herramientas necesarias ya sea para desempeñarse en dicho rol, o como abogados de parte o incluso, eventualmente, como árbitros. A continuación, algunas lecciones aprendidas y recomendaciones para quienes están formándose en busca de esta posibilidad, o bien se encuentran ya experimentándola.

§12.02 GUÍAS Y RECOMENDACIONES PARA EL DESEMPEÑO DEL SECRETARIO ARBITRAL

Mucho se ha discutido sobre el rol del secretario y, en algunos casos, se ha cuestionado su involucramiento excesivo en lo que se ha catalogado en la comunidad arbitral como la paranoia del "Cuarto Árbitro"[5]. No es el objeto de este capítulo ahondar en esta

4. Cabe aclarar que me refiero aquí a secretarios arbitrales designados en arbitrajes institucionales y ad hoc para el caso concreto y no a secretarios de tribunales arbitrales permanentes o a la Secretaría de instituciones arbitrales. Estos últimos, dependiendo de la jurisdicción, la institución y el reglamento correspondiente, pueden tener funciones más amplias y específicas en lo que respecta a la conducción del procedimiento y dictado de resoluciones interlocutorias propias de un secretario de una corte o juzgado. Como veremos a continuación, la tendencia en la práctica se inclina a otorgar mayores responsabilidades al secretario, pero ello dependerá de cada tribunal, previa consulta con las partes, y de la experiencia que pueda tener el secretario.
5. Al respecto, ver "*The Fourth Arbitrator? The Role of Secretaries to Tribunals in International Arbitration,*" Constantine Partasides, Arbitration International, Vol. 18, No. 2, LCIA, 2002. La discusión se reactivó con el caso *Yukos Universal Limited v. TheRussianFederation* (Caso PCA Nro. AA227), donde Rusia solicitó la nulidad del laudo alegando que en virtud de las horas

última cuestión, pero sí tenerla en cuenta para poder brindar recomendaciones/guías a profesionales que quieran desempeñarse como secretarios arbitrales.

[A] Primera recomendación

Es importante contar con experiencia en litigios y arbitraje o tener formación, o entrenamiento, como secretario de tribunal, para ser considerado y designado para servir en el cargo y para desempeñarlo bien.

En el primer caso en que intervine como secretario arbitral las partes ponderaron que tuviera experiencia en el manejo de litigios y que hubiera actuado como abogado de parte en varios casos, así como también las referencias brindadas por el presidente del tribunal arbitral. En aquella oportunidad yo contaba con tres años de experiencia en litigios y arbitraje; no mucha, por cierto, pero me fue de gran utilidad.

La comunidad arbitral es consciente de la necesidad de contar con secretarios arbitrales bien formados. Esto es así, tanto por el creciente número de procesos arbitrales, como por la complejidad de los casos sometidos a este procedimiento. Usualmente, los procesos arbitrales involucran a una gran cantidad de partes, así como voluminosidad de documentos y evidencia a ser analizados, lo que requiere que los árbitros dicten laudos detallados y minuciosos para evitar nulidades[6].

Existen programas para la formación de secretarios arbitrales que acompañan esta tendencia y que son muy útiles. Uno de ellos es el programa implementado por la Cámara de Comercio Internacional (CCI), que dicta cursos a aspirantes a secretarios en el marco de las conferencias que organiza. Lo interesante también es que aún no existen listas de secretarios, por lo que no es un requisito para ser considerado y nombrado como tal formar parte de alguna lista o someterse a un proceso institucional de selección previo. Es por ello que la formación que tenga el candidato como así también el conocimiento previo que tengan los árbitros o el árbitro presidente del tribunal de su experiencia y forma de trabajar son importantes para ser propuesto y designado como secretario del tribunal.

[B] Segunda recomendación

El CV del candidato debe incluir aptitudes de *case management*, como la capacidad de identificar y organizar documentos relevantes, armar cronología de hechos y de las posiciones de las partes, manejo de plazos y notificaciones, etc. Esto es importante dado que el tribunal suele proponer la utilización de un secretario a las partes y son estas las que deberán prestar su conformidad con el candidato propuesto.

---

trabajadas y los honorarios facturados por el secretario, éste había tenido un rol significativo en las deliberaciones y en la redacción del laudo y que, por lo tanto, los árbitros no cumplieron con su mandato personalmente. Ver más al respectoen, "*The Challenge of the Yukos Award: an Award Written by Someone Else – a Violation of the Trinbunal's Mandate?*" Dmytro Galagan, Kluwer Arbitration Blog, 27 de febrero de 2015.

6. "Young ICCA Guide on Arbitral Secretaries – The ICCA Reports No. 1," International Council for Commercial Arbitration, páginas 1, 26, 27, 43.

Es una práctica común que el tribunal o el presidente del tribunal brinde a las partes copias del CV del candidato y una declaración de su disponibilidad, independencia e imparcialidad antes de nombrarlo como secretario arbitral para que las partes puedan entrevistar al candidato[7] si así lo desean. Este tipo de entrevistas tiene por objeto conocer mejor los antecedentes del candidato y, por supuesto, en ellas no se pueden manifestar opiniones o juicios de valor sobre los temas de fondo de la controversia. Las entrevistas facilitan que el proceso de designación del candidato se realice de forma adecuada y otorgan mayor legitimidad y confianza de las partes a la figura del secretario, lo que coadyuva a la transparencia y eficiencia del procedimiento arbitral.

[C] Tercera recomendación

Es primordial que el secretario responda en todo momento a las instrucciones y supervisión del tribunal o del presidente del tribunal. En las cuestiones sobre las que no exista una instrucción precisa, el secretario debe consultar siempre con el tribunal al respecto. El mandato del árbitro es *intuitu personæ*[8], por lo que no puede delegar las funciones que le son propias y esenciales para el desempeño de su cargo que es ponderar las pretensiones de las partes y decidir la disputa. Si bien le corresponde al árbitro no delegar estas funciones y supervisar y controlar lo que realiza el secretario, el secretario debe a su vez procurar no cruzar los límites de sus funciones al asistir al tribunal en el análisis de las pretensiones de las partes y de la evidencia producida, pues los árbitros generalmente son personas muy ocupadas que enfocarán su atención en las cuestiones legales sustantivas[9].

El secretario debe mantener informado al tribunal en todo momento sobre los avances de su trabajo, así como de los desarrollos procesales del arbitraje, incluyendo el cumplimiento de plazos y de las órdenes procesales. Es fundamental para conservar la transparencia y eficiencia del procedimiento, el manejo apropiado por parte del secretario del calendario procesal y de los calendarios preparados para uso interno del tribunal y del secretario, incluyendo el envío de alertas o recordatorios a los árbitros, como así también que el secretario informe al tribunal (o al presidente, de ser el caso) de cualquier comunicación que las partes o sus abogados tengan con el secretario.

7. La notificación a y la conformidad de las partes en la designación del secretario forma parte de las prácticas y guías propuestas por la mayoría de las instituciones arbitrales. Ver, por ejemplo, *ICC Note on the Appointment, Duties and Remuneration of Administrative Secretaries*, 1 de agosto, 2012, p. 1; *SIAC Practice* Note (PN-01/15), Administered Cases, On the Appointment of Administrative Secretaries, 2 de febrero de 2015; *JAMS Guidelines for Use of Clerks and Tribunal Secretaries in Arbitrations; LCIA Notes for Arbitrators 2017, Section 8.3; Arbitration Institute of the Stockholm Chamber of Commerce, Arbitrator's Guidelines*, enero 2017, p. 6, 7.
8. Este es un principio fundamental del proceso arbitral dado que las partes elijen a los árbitros en base al perfil, experiencia, antecedentes, etc. de ese árbitro en particular y luego de un arduo proceso de *due diligence* para que sea esa persona, y no otra, la que pondere las pretensiones de las partes y decida la disputa.
9. Esto de modo alguno exime, por supuesto, la responsabilidad del árbitro de revisar personalmente las constancias del caso para su decisión, pero el trabajo del secretario lo ayudará a hacer esto de manera más eficiente.

[D] Cuarta recomendación

No dar información del procedimiento a las partes, al margen de aquella que tenga que ver con los plazos y formalidades requeridas y notificadas a las partes por el tribunal, salvo bajo expresa instrucción o autorización por parte de este último para hacerlo.

Como secretario, he vivido situaciones en las que los abogados de parte se han acercado con preguntas unilaterales, por ejemplo, con respecto al orden en que el tribunal resolvería distintas cuestiones pendientes, o sobre el criterio del tribunal con respecto a alguna disposición del reglamento de arbitraje aplicable, o con relación a los tiempos del tribunal para resolver. En estas situaciones, es sumamente importante que el secretario manifieste que no puede responder a esas cuestiones, o de ser el caso, que manifieste que las consultará con el tribunal. Dependiendo del grado de información solicitada, el tribunal puede ordenar al secretario informar o enviar una notificación a las partes con alguna aclaración.

Es recomendable que el secretario discuta con el tribunal sobre sus funciones y el grado de información que puede brindar a las partes de antemano. Por ejemplo, sería razonable que el secretario pudiera contestar preguntas de las partes sobre si un memorial ya está a despacho del tribunal, cuándo estima el tribunal que emitirá una resolución, así como otros aspectos de logística y formalidad en la presentación de memoriales. Si para estas cuestiones, las partes necesitaran hablar directamente con el tribunal, la comunicación entre estas y los árbitros se haría lenta y tediosa. El secretario puede facilitar la comunicación en cuestiones de procedimiento y, de esta manera, hacerlo más ágil y efectivo. Pero de nuevo, en caso de duda, el secretario siempre deberá consultar con el tribunal y este establecer la conducta a seguir.

[E] Quinta recomendación

Conocer bien el reglamento aplicable, las reglas y calendarios fijados por el tribunal en el procedimiento. El secretario debe tener conocimiento cabal de las reglas aplicables al procedimiento, sean estas las de una institución o, si se trata de un arbitraje ad hoc, las reglas CNUDMI o aquellas fijadas por el tribunal. El secretario debe tener también conocimiento y manejar apropiadamente las órdenes procesales que dicte el tribunal y los respectivos calendarios procesales.

Es el secretario quien llevará debida cuenta, con la supervisión del tribunal, de las distintas etapas procesales y los plazos para la presentación de memoriales y resoluciones a dictarse. Es buena práctica que el secretario agende y envíe recordatorios de los plazos al tribunal con la debida antelación (esto generalmente se hace mediante el calendario virtual común creado a tal efecto) y que alerte al tribunal del cumplimiento o no de dichos plazos por las partes. Es buena práctica también que el secretario alerte al tribunal del cumplimiento o no de otras formalidades previstas en las reglas aplicables y órdenes procesales con respecto a la presentación de los memoriales, como el contenido de los mismos, la presentación de anexos y autoridades legales de apoyo, traducciones y límite de páginas, de ser aplicable. Esto también contribuye a la celeridad del proceso, dado que el tribunal puede requerir aclaraciones o requerir enmiendas a las presentaciones sin esperar al momento en que este mismo analizará los argumentos sustantivos. En este sentido, el secretario debe, al igual que el tribunal, cumplir con su cometido de manera imparcial y respetando la igualdad de partes.

Como ejemplo, en un arbitraje comercial bajo las Reglas de la CNUDMI en el que intervine como secretario, el tribunal me había encomendado hacer un escrutinio previo de los plazos y presentaciones y comunicar a los árbitros los resultados de dicho análisis[10]. En aquella oportunidad el escrutinio involucró un análisis previo de la notificación de arbitraje y la contestación, para corroborar que las mismas incluyeran los requisitos dispuestos por las Reglas CNUDMI, y luego el análisis de los alegatos finales que el tribunal arbitral había limitado a 30 páginas. En dicho caso, se pidió clarificación a una de ellas sobre los contratos base del litigio y los documentos correspondientes, en virtud del Artículo 3.d) de las Reglas CNUDMI de 2010[11].

[F] Sexta recomendación

Mantener un registro completo del proceso, para consulta de las partes y el tribunal. Esto, más que una buena práctica, es una obligación del secretario arbitral.

El secretario debe conservar un registro completo y ordenado cronológicamente con todas las actuaciones del proceso, incluyendo las comunicaciones entre las partes y el tribunal, los memoriales y prueba acompañada, las notificaciones, las órdenes procesales y las resoluciones. Hoy es práctica común crear una plataforma virtual a través de medios seguros donde las partes y el tribunal puedan subir, almacenar y descargar las actuaciones y documentos del proceso. Este sistema ordena automáticamente los documentos y sirve de registro o expediente. Es común que en la primera orden procesal se disponga que los memoriales y documentos, además de presentarse vía email, y mediante copias en papel, deban presentarse en la plataforma. De cualquier manera, es práctica recomendable conservar un registro del expediente en papel, el que debe estar a disposición de las partes y del tribunal arbitral.

[G] Séptima recomendación

El secretario debe tener un conocimiento profundo y hacer un manejo eficiente del expediente para mejor asistir al tribunal y, eventualmente, a las partes. La función principal del secretario es asistir al tribunal en resolver la disputa de manera efectiva y eficiente y, en este sentido, como comenté al inicio, dependiendo de cada tribunal y siempre bajo la directiva y supervisión de los árbitros, el rol del secretario puede ir más allá de sus tareas administrativas de procedimiento, incluyendo por ejemplo el análisis

10. Puede ser el caso que esto lo instruya el presidente del tribunal y luego lo comparta con los co-árbitros o bien se le comunique a todos de manera simultánea. Es importante discutir con el presidente la logística de la comunicación con los otros árbitros.
11. Artículo 3.d) de las Reglas CNUDMI de 2010: "La notificación del arbitraje contendrá la siguiente información: d) Una especificación de todo contrato o instrumento jurídico que haya suscitado o al que se refiera el litigio..."

de evidencia para revisión de los árbitros, la búsqueda de jurisprudencia y el análisis legal de temas específicos, la preparación de borradores de órdenes procesales o resoluciones y hasta la preparación de borradores de secciones del laudo[12].

Tuve la oportunidad de ser secretario de un tribunal en un arbitraje CCI donde el presidente del tribunal era quien tenía a su cargo la elaboración de los primeros proyectos de resoluciones, que luego discutía con los otros árbitros. En ese caso, el presidente me encomendó analizar algunos temas y la preparación de borradores de resoluciones. Estos borradores eran revisados por él y luego enviados a los otros miembros del tribunal para su aprobación o comentarios. Tuve también la oportunidad de participar en deliberaciones entre los árbitros. Esta participación se rige por el principio rector en cuanto a que la misma se constriñe a asistir al tribunal, ya que el secretario no puede asumir ninguna función de decisión de la disputa, y no cuenta con ninguna facultad para actuar en representación de alguno de los árbitros. Dados mi participación y conocimiento del procedimiento, el tribunal me encomendó la redacción de borradores de determinadas partes del laudo. Todo esto, sujeto a la supervisión y revisión de los árbitros. Fue una experiencia muy interesante y enriquecedora porque tuve la oportunidad de experimentar el escrutinio que la CCI realiza sobre los laudos, dado que asistí al tribunal también en la preparación de la versión final del laudo, donde los árbitros contemplaron los comentarios de la CCI.

[H] Octava recomendación

Denunciar cualquier posible conflicto de interés. Esta también, más que una recomendación o buena práctica, es una obligación. El secretario debe informar al tribunal arbitral cualquier hecho que pueda afectar su imparcialidad o independencia, o cualquier posible conflicto de interés y el tribunal debe informarlo a las partes. Es responsabilidad del tribunal la selección del secretario adecuado y su supervisión. Es muy difícil que el árbitro pueda identificar cualquier posible conflicto de interés del secretario, con lo cual este último debe estar alerta y reportar cualquier circunstancia al árbitro.

§12.03 CONCLUSIÓN

Actuar como secretario arbitral es sin dudas una ardua tarea. El rol del secretario arbitral es de suma importancia para el manejo eficiente del procedimiento arbitral y para el buen desarrollo del trabajo de los árbitros.

12. La práctica indica que la mayoría de los árbitros delegan funciones de este tipo en los secretarios y la comunidad arbitral y las instituciones arbitrales en su mayoría aceptan esta práctica, sujeto desde ya a la debida instrucción y supervisión del tribunal. En este sentido el *Young ICCA* ha hecho un formidable trabajo realizando encuestas que confirman lo expuesto y elaborando un documento de buenas prácticas para el nombramiento y uso de secretarios arbitrales. Ver "*Young ICCA Guide on Arbitral Secretaries – The ICCA Reports No. 1,*" International Council for Commercial Arbitration, 2014, Annex A, p. 28; Annex B, p. 62; Annex C, p. 76-80; Annex D.

Es también una gran oportunidad para los abogados jóvenes para adentrarse en el mundo y en la práctica del arbitraje internacional, aprender de interactuar con árbitros, abogados de parte e instituciones arbitrales, y desarrollarse en esta práctica junto con facilitar la eficiencia y celeridad del procedimiento arbitral.

El secretario debe ser consciente de los límites, la responsabilidad y lo que se requiere para cumplir cabalmente con dicho rol, para no ejercer funciones que son propias del mandato personal de decisión de la disputa que recae exclusivamente sobre los árbitros, y actuar siempre bajo la consulta, directiva y supervisión de estos. Las recomendaciones brindadas en el presente capítulo propenden a otorgar algunas herramientas para el ejercicio del rol de secretario de un tribunal arbitral, en pos de preservar la legitimidad, integridad y transparencia del proceso arbitral.

CAPÍTULO 13

Franklin, Rubin o de Bono: cómo enfrentar la primera deliberación

Manuel Conthe

Un buen presidente de un tribunal arbitral debe procurar -desde el primer momento- que entre los tres árbitros reine un clima de cordialidad. Así, sus eventuales discrepancias podrán expresarse con libertad, en un ambiente de respeto mutuo, y resolverse de forma amigable, apelando -en caso necesario- a la regla de la mayoría. Para favorecer ese clima, cuando me designan presidente y los tres árbitros todavía no nos conocemos personalmente, suelo invitar a comer a mis colegas, para conocernos, sin abordar todavía ninguna cuestión significativa del arbitraje. Ese temprano encuentro informal será difícil si los árbitros vivimos en lugares distantes, pero convendrá entonces mantener una primera teleconferencia, para evitar la frialdad y los peligros del correo electrónico como medio de comunicación entre desconocidos (especialmente si, en materia de cortesía, alguno de los árbitros no sigue el consejo de Don Quijote de "pasarse mejor de carta de más que de menos").

Creado ese clima de colaboración y respeto, salvo que el tribunal tenga que pronunciarse pronto sobre cuestiones procedimentales de calado (como, por ejemplo, una solicitud de bifurcación del procedimiento, exhibición documental o medidas cautelares), la primera deliberación sustantiva deberá aguardar a que, con la contestación o la dúplica (según el procedimiento elegido), concluya la presentación por las partes de sus escritos rectores.

Durante la audiencia, un buen presidente deberá reservar suficiente tiempo para las preguntas del tribunal, y no poner cortapisas a las de ningún árbitro, pues esas preguntas resultarán útiles no solo a las partes, sino también al presidente del tribunal, para identificar las cuestiones primordiales que preocupan a sus colegas y que deberán ser abordadas en el laudo.

Antes, durante o, normalmente, después de la audiencia, será el momento idóneo para que el tribunal tenga una primera deliberación sustantiva, que en muchos casos le permitirá dirigir a las partes una lista indicativa de preguntas, sobre cuestiones de hecho o de derecho, que querría que las partes aborden en sus escritos de conclusiones. En ocasiones he oído decir que esa lista debe incluir algunas preguntas "para despistar", para que no parezca que el tribunal ha adoptado ya una posición firme sobre las cuestiones capitales del arbitraje. Pero, sinceramente, no creo necesario ese ardid: a esas alturas del arbitraje es natural que los árbitros se hayan formado ya una opinión preliminar; y lo esencial será que las partes tengan la oportunidad de rebatirla y hacerles cambiar de opinión. La mente de los árbitros, aunque no vacía, deberá mantenerse abierta.

Tras los escritos de conclusiones, convendrá que el presidente elabore una lista ordenada y completa de las cuestiones esenciales sobre las que el laudo deberá pronunciarse e invite a sus colegas a que la completen y corrijan.

Identificadas esas cuestiones, llegará el momento de sondear la posición preliminar de los árbitros sobre cada una. Será el trance más delicado, porque los seres humanos somos renuentes a cambiar de opinión una vez que la hemos manifestado (especialmente si lo hemos hecho por escrito). ¿Quién debe ser, pues, el primero en "descubrir sus cartas" y manifestar su opinión?

En mi experiencia, muchos presidentes invitan a los coárbitros a ser los primeros en manifestar su criterio, para reservarse el papel dirimente de *umpire* en caso de discrepancias. Sin embargo, eso pondrá a veces a los coárbitros en un brete, pues tenderán naturalmente a compartir muchos de los puntos de vista de las partes que les designó -esas "predisposiciones doctrinales" pudieron ser precisamente las que motivaron su designación-, pero no les gustará dar pábulo a la asentada creencia de que no son imparciales. De ahí su frecuente reticencia a expresarse con claridad y sus usuales circunloquios y ambigüedades, que no facilitarán una deliberación eficaz.

Por eso, me parece más productivo que sea el presidente quien, libre de esa sospecha o presunción de parcialidad que sobrevolará inevitablemente sobre los coárbitros, sea el primero en "lanzarse al ruedo" y manifestarse. Antes de dar su opinión, podrá seguir el método para resolver casos difíciles que Benjamin Franklin describió en su célebre carta al científico y teólogo británico Joseph Priestley: dividir una hoja de papel en dos columnas, emparejar los argumentos a favor y en contra sobre cada cuestión y ponderar su peso antes de llegar a la decisión final. Siga o no ese procedimiento comparativo, deberá poner énfasis en que, con amplitud de miras, hará suyo cualquier punto de vista distinto pero mejor fundado que el suyo propio. Eso dará pie a que el coárbitro que discrepe de alguna de las opiniones preliminares del presidente exponga las razones de su discrepancia.

Si surgen tales discrepancias, un buen presidente no deberá acallarlas o rebatirlas prematuramente, sino, por el contrario, seguir el método que Robert Rubin, Secretario del Tesoro en la Administración Clinton, describe en sus memorias sobre aquellos años ("*In anuncertainworld*", 2003):

> "*Las reuniones* [en el Tesoro] *producían los mejores resultados cuando aquellos que discrepaban de la opinión dominante era animados a expresarse. Por eso, si en una reunión estaba emergiendo un consenso, yo insistía en que hablaran aquellos que disentían. Manifestarse en desacuerdo conmigo estaba socialmente bien visto y no era desalentado. Si nadie discrepaba, yo le pedía a alguien que hiciera de abogado*

del diablo. Yo decía, por ejemplo: "Estamos llegando a esta conclusión, pero necesitamos saber el punto de vista contrario, para poder analizarlo". Y entonces, yo mismo u otra persona, defendíamos ese punto de vista".

Ese "método Rubin" para evitar decisiones o consensos prematuros guarda cierta relación con el "método de los gorros" o del "pensamiento paralelo" que, años antes, en 1985, propuso Edward de Bono, el célebre consultor maltés. Ese método exige que el presidente de un comité, en vez de dejar que sus miembros se expresen a su libre albedrío, estructure el debate en fases, caracterizadas cada una simbólicamente por el color de un sombrero imaginario: el blanco o la fría constatación de hechos; el negro o la actitud crítica y pesimista; el amarillo o la actitud positiva y optimista; el rojo o la actitud visceral o pasional; el verde o la actitud innovadora, creativa e iconoclasta; y el azul o la organización del debate y la obtención de conclusiones. En cada fase todos los miembros deberán intervenir en la dirección marcada por el presidente. Así, si este les ha pedido que "se pongan el gorro negro", deberán todos esforzarse por descubrir los puntos débiles o los riesgos de la idea que se debate, sin que nadie pueda salir en su defensa, cosa que todos sin excepción deberán hacer cuando el presidente ordene que "se pongan el gorro amarillo". El sistema, al exigir que todos los miembros piensen de forma paralela, evitará los antagonismos personales y los duelos dialécticos. Al obligar a todos a ponerse los distintos gorros, les impedirá encastillarse en posiciones parciales y les forzará a analizar el asunto desde diversas perspectivas. Y, a la postre, permitirá al grupo realizar un concienzudo análisis del asunto en un tiempo razonable.

Confieso que nunca he visto que un tribunal aplique el método de Bono, y ni siquiera yo mismo lo he intentado como presidente. Suelo conformarme con el enfoque de Rubin de tratar de entender bien las razones del discrepante y, cuando no están claras, pedirle que las aclare. Eso permitirá a la eventual mayoría explicar en el laudo por qué no ha acogido el punto de vista del discrepante y hará que la opinión de este, si actúa de buena fe, pueda ser muy breve y sosegada, sin ninguna sorpresa ni afirmación nueva que el laudo no haya ponderado.

Siga o no los consejos de Franklin, de Rubin o de Bono, en mi opinión un buen presidente no debe empezar a escribir una sola palabra de los fundamentos jurídicos del laudo antes de consensuar la lista de cuestiones que deberá abordar y discernir el sentir mayoritario del tribunal sobre cada una de ellas.

CAPÍTULO 14
Votos disidentes en el arbitraje comercial

Clifford J. Hendel

§14.01 INTRODUCCIÓN

El arbitraje comercial internacional es un área de práctica en la que existe una abundancia de literatura (por no decir un exceso de literatura) que cubre una infinidad de temas. Siendo objetivo, algunos de los temas que suelen ser tratados en esta literatura no son especialmente interesantes o importantes; otros, en cambio, sí podrían considerarse interesantes e importantes, pero todo o prácticamente todo lo que se diga o escriba sobre los mismos ya ha sido previamente dicho o escrito.

El resultado es que la literatura, dirían algunos, está compuesta en su gran mayoría bien por discusiones sobre temas de limitada relevancia (la reciente avalancha de artículos y conferencias sobre las Reglas de Praga podría ser un buen ejemplo de ello) o bien por la repetición sin gran novedad de temas más relevantes.

A veces, sin embargo, uno encuentra un tema que parece realmente interesante y sobre el cual poco ha sido escrito o dicho.

La cuestión de votos particulares (o, en algunas jurisdicciones, votos disidentes) -me refiero no sólo al voto minoritario en sí sino a la plasmación del mismo en un escrito, la *dissenting opinion*- en el arbitraje comercial internacional podría ser un ejemplo de ello[1]. En el área del arbitraje de inversión se plantean cuestiones diferentes, por la relevancia en este campo de asuntos de política normativa y precedentes, que

1. El artículo clásico en este campo es de Alan Redfern, "*Dissenting Opinions in International Commercial Arbitration: the Good, the Bad and the Ugly*", *Arbitration International*, Vol. 20, No. 3, LCIA, 2004, pp. 223-242. Otros artículos más recientes incluyen el de Peter Rees y Patrick Rohn, "*Dissenting Opinions: Can They Fulfil a Beneficial Role?*", *Arbitration International*, Vol. 25, No. 3, LCIA, 2009, pp. 329-346 y el de Mark Baker y Lucy Greenwood "*Dissent -But Only if you REALLY Feel You Must: Why Dissenting Opinions in International Commercial Arbitration Should Only Appear in Exceptional Circumstances*"; *Dispute Resolution International*, Vol. 7, No. 1, 2013, pp. 31-40.

son de poca o nula relevancia en el campo de arbitraje comercial; la literatura sobre votos particulares en el campo de arbitraje de inversión es a la vez abundante y animada[2].

§14.02 EL ORIGEN DE MI INTERÉS POR ESTA ÁREA

Hace ya unos quince años que me dedico al arbitraje comercial internacional.

En todos estos años y tras participar en decenas de casos como árbitro, sólo en dos ocasiones surgió la posibilidad de redactar un voto particular. Esta posibilidad se materializó en una de ellas. Tanto en un caso como en el otro, hurgué en la literatura y reflexioné sobre las ventajas y los inconvenientes de emitir votos particulares, y sobre la forma correcta y la incorrecta de hacerlo.

El primero fue un caso en el cual actuaba de presidente. Discrepaba de mis coárbitros sobre la resolución adecuada de una cuestión esencial, pues consideraba que era una cuestión de principio. Después de una serie de sesiones deliberativas, y el intercambio de memoranda y borradores de laudo tratando el tema, nos vimos en un callejón sin salida.

La situación estuvo lejos de ser óptima. Por un lado, me dejaba a mi como presidente en la postura rarísima de tener que considerar la emisión de un voto particular para apartarme de la postura mayoritaria del panel, lo que podría poner en duda mi eficacia como presidente. Por otro lado, mi discrepancia con la mayoría (bien sea incluida en una opinión particular o disidente, bien sea solo por mi voto minoritario) revelaría que uno de los coárbitros se había alineado con la postura de la "otra" parte, lo cual le habría dejado quizás en una posición delicada con la parte que lo había nombrado.

Al final, conseguimos encontrar una solución. Nos pusimos de acuerdo de forma unánime respecto de otra cuestión dispositiva, dejando la cuestión delicada (en la cual, al final, también logramos unanimidad) relegada a mero *obiter dictum* a la luz de nuestra resolución de la otra cuestión.

Por lo que, en definitiva, no hubo ni opinión disidente ni voto minoritario.

En mi segunda experiencia, fui nombrado coárbitro por la institución administradora debido a la ausencia de nombramiento de un árbitro por la demandada dentro del plazo establecido para ello. Este caso dio lugar a la emisión de mi primer y único voto particular/opinión disidente.

Una vez más, una cuestión de principios me obligaba a tomar esta decisión. Mis obligaciones hacia las partes y la institución que me nombró me obligaron no solo a votar en contra del parecer mayoritario, sino a plasmar en unas pocas hojas el porqué

2. Ver, e.g., Jan A. Van Den Berg, "*Dissenting Opinions by Party-Appointed Arbitrators in Investments Arbitration,*" in *Looking to the Future: Essays on International Law in Honor of W: Michael Reisman*, MartinusNijhoff Publishers, 2011, pps. 821-843, y Charlie Brower and Chip Rosenberg, "*The Death of the Two-Headed Nightingale: Why the Paulsson-Van den Berg Presumption that Party-Appointed Arbitrators are Untrustworthy is Wrongheaded*", *Arbitration International*, Vol. 29, No. 1, LCIA, 2013, pp 7-44, y la contestación del Professor Van den Bergen "*Charlie Brower's problem with 100 per cent-dissenting opinions by party-appointed arbitrators in investment arbitration*", *Arbitration International*, Vol 31, No. 3, LCIA, 2015, pp. 381-391.

de mi discrepancia. Aquí también consulté la literatura mencionada e intenté seguir los buenos consejos que contenía.

§14.03 LECCIONES APRENDIDAS

Retrospectivamente, no tengo remordimiento alguno sobre mi actuación en ninguno de estos casos.

Evidentemente, llegar a una decisión unánime -aunque basada en una serie de compromisos "transaccionales" que la podría dejar algo menos del 100% cohesiva- es y tiene que ser un objetivo fundamental para cualquier tribunal y presidente que se respecte. Tardamos semanas en encontrar una solución que gozaría de apoyo unánime en el primer caso, pero me alegró y me alegra que lo lográsemos.

En el segundo caso, la unanimidad no fue posible, pero creía firmemente que la cuestión que dividía el panel era una de principio, por lo que logré redactar una corta y respetuosa opinión disidente. Aquí también, he dormido tranquilo, seguramente más tranquilo que si hubiera resistido la tentación de plasmar mi parecer disidente por escrito.

¿Cuáles son las lecciones, pues, que he aprendido de estas experiencias? Diría que la literatura relevante, aunque limitada y escueta, es muy acertada en este campo y proporciona muy buenos consejos tanto sobre el "cuándo" como el "cómo" de los votos particulares en el arbitraje comercial internacional.

Como primera lección, estoy plenamente de acuerdo con Baker y Greenwood en que un árbitro no debería emitir un voto particular en un arbitraje comercial internacional salvo en circunstancias excepcionales:

> *"El derecho fundamental del árbitro a tener una opinión disidente no debe confundirse con el derecho o la responsabilidad de publicar esa opinión disidente. Sería ingrato tratar de prohibir la disidencia, ya que nadie desearía ser visto como alguien que reprime el derecho de expresión de un árbitro, sin embargo su uso debe ser excepcional y publicarse de manera tal que se minimicen lo más posible los impactos negativos que la disidencia podría tener"*[3].

Y en cuanto a lo que constituyen "circunstancias excepcionales", pues que cada árbitro siga su conciencia:

> *"¿Cuáles son, entonces, las circunstancias excepcionales en las que un árbitro podría y debería disentir por escrito? Creemos que esto es una cuestión de conciencia para el árbitro; a saber, en la situación extremadamente rara en la que un árbitro, actuando de manera justa e imparcial respecto de las partes, simplemente no puede permanecer en silencio y no siente que pueda abordar el problema negándose a firmar el laudo. En 20 años de actuar como árbitro en arbitrajes comerciales, uno de los autores solo se sintió obligado a emitir una disidencia por escrito en un caso: en un asunto legal dispositivo, que, en opinión del autor, la mayoría simplemente prefería ignorar en el interés de lograr un resultado "justo". No hay vergüenza en una opinión mayoritaria sin un disenso. Siempre habrá paneles donde no se pueda llegar a un acuerdo. La pregunta es si el desacuerdo debe publicarse o no como*

3. Baker y Greenwood, op. cit., p 40.

disidencia en la mayoría de los casos comerciales internacionales. Nuestra opinión es que la respuesta a esto debería ser no, a menos que el árbitro realmente sienta que ello debe ser así"[4].

Y como segunda lección estoy plenamente de acuerdo con Redfern, quien observa que el árbitro que se encuentra en la postura de tener que emitir un voto particular debe ser muy cuidadoso para que su escrito no sea ni "feo" ni "malo", sino "bueno"; es decir, corto, centrado y respetuoso, y no agresivo e insultante ni, peor aún, que ponga en cuestión el proceso deliberativo y establezca una hoja de ruta para una eventual acción de anulación.

§14.04 CONCLUSIONES

A la luz de estas conclusiones, mi recomendación al árbitro o counsel interesado en el tema del voto particular en el arbitraje comercial internacional sería -en lugar de reinventar la rueda- la de consultar la excelente literatura disponible y citada arriba.

4. Ibíd.

HISTORIAS DE GUERRA Y LECCIONES SOBRE FIRMAS GRANDES Y CAMINOS ALTERNATIVOS AL ARBITRAJE

CAPÍTULO 15
Retos de una práctica global

Juliana de Valdenebro

La palabra "global" es un elemento intrínseco en la práctica de arbitraje internacional. Por definición, nuestro campo incluye a todo el globo, toda nacionalidad, cultura, tradición jurídica y lenguaje, pues no hay cómo limitar el posible componente "internacional" de un arbitraje.

De hecho, este componente se evidencia no sólo en las partes o en la disputa, sino también en los "*players*" o "jugadores" que hacen parte de esta práctica global. Árbitros, abogados de parte, firmas de abogados, socios, asociados, clientes y expertos, juegan en el campo del arbitraje internacional sin que existan líneas de frontera. He ahí donde realmente se consolida una práctica "global", pues son sus jugadores los que la potencializan.

Ello la hace sin duda una práctica interesante y bastante acorde al mundo globalizado en el que ahora vivimos, pero, sin embargo, son esos mismos componentes los que también conllevan grandes retos. Este escrito pretende analizar algunos de los principales desafíos que se derivan de este mundo legal sin fronteras, procurando abarcar aspectos prácticos, que todo asociado de arbitraje internacional debe considerar, y asimismo aspectos teóricos, que deben ser tenidos en cuenta por cualquier jugador en este campo.

Para desarrollar los posibles retos se debe empezar por considerar que, al tratarse de una práctica globalizada, las reglas de este campo de juego las dictan sus propios jugadores, ya que no hay un organismo central que pueda controlar la creación de nuevas reglas. Para analizar este punto es útil acudir a las categorías de "jugadores" de un sistema jurídico definidas por Marc Galanter. Según este autor, los jugadores de un sistema jurídico se dividen entre "repeated players" y "one-shotters." Al definir los "repeated players", Galanter explica que son aquellos que tienen múltiples oportunidades para interactuar en el sistema jurídico, lo cual incluye a todos los usuarios repetitivos y abarca tanto los clientes como los abogados que participan activamente en el mismo[1].

En el caso de arbitraje internacional, los "repeated players" de este sistema jurídico serían todos los usuarios comunes que hacen parte de esta práctica, incluyendo las instituciones, los árbitros, las firmas, los abogados y ahora los "third party funders" (terceros financistas). Todos estos, según Galanter, tienen una ventaja comparativa, pues en su condición de *repeated players* son quienes tienen la capacidad de influenciar la creación y modificación de reglas aplicables a su campo[2].

De esta característica se deriva el primer reto del arbitraje internacional como práctica global. A saber, esta práctica global tiene sus propias reglas y su propio lenguaje. Si no eres un "repeated player", si es la primera vez que entras a este campo de juego, si eres un usuario primerizo o un "one-shotter", debes entender y acogerte a las reglas creadas por otros. Es más, el jugador primerizo no solo debe aprender un nuevo sistema de reglas jurídicas o soft-law que puede definir su participación en el juego, sino también aprender un nuevo lenguaje lleno de palabras que solo cobran sentido para quienes han practicado antes en este campo.

Es decir, ese nuevo jugador debe empezar por entender los componentes legales del sistema, y luego superar la barrera del *slang* que los jugadores repitentes han impuesto. El usuario primerizo debe aprender desde qué es un memorial, una orden procesal, el sistema de "chess-clock", el "cooling off period", los "terms of reference", el semáforo de las listas verdes, naranjas y rojas, el "hot-tubbing" y un "Redfern", entre otros. También debe entender qué es un tribunal arbitral internacional, qué es y que no es un laudo, y qué es una bifurcación. Además, debe descifrar los varios acrónimos que se usan a diario (CCI, ICSID, AAA, ICDR, IBA, CVDT, BITs, ISDS, entre otros). En fin, para entrar a esta práctica global debes aprender y reaprender un nuevo idioma y, como todo lenguaje, solo con la práctica diaria podrás perfeccionarlo. Esta barrera de reglas y lenguaje creados por los jugadores repetitivos es, por ende, el primer reto que impone la práctica global del arbitraje internacional.

Pero los retos no culminan ahí. Siendo que los jugadores de este campo están esparcidos por todo el mundo, una práctica global también implica enfrentarse a una competencia global. A diferencia de las prácticas locales, la práctica global conlleva que pueda existir un competidor que, en iguales condiciones, puede desbancar a otro aún a pesar de que su base o su origen sean de un lugar completamente diferente. Ello es cierto tanto para la búsqueda de clientes como para el ascenso de un asociado en su práctica profesional.

En cuanto a *bussines development*, se deben considerar dos premisas fundamentales: (1) para competir debes cumplir con tener un mínimo componente que todos tus competidores tienen (ser reconocido como un "repeated player" y tener dominio de las reglas y el lenguaje); y (2) simultáneamente, para ganar debes tener un elemento diferenciador. Es decir, como firma de abogados o como árbitro, debes cumplir con un mínimo de experiencia en el campo, ser debidamente reconocido como

1. GALANTER, Marc, 1974-1975, *Why the Haves Come Out Ahead: Speculations on the Limits of Legal Change*. TheLaw and SocietyReview, Vol. 9, pgs. 97, 114
2. Ibid, p. 100.

jugador por tus pares, tener un equipo debidamente formado y una infraestructura que te permita atender las necesidades del caso. Sin embargo, eso no será suficiente, pues todos tus competidores traerán exactamente lo mismo a la mesa, por lo que se requiere un elemento distintivo que, en un mundo global, es cada vez más difícil de tener. Puede ser el dominio de diferentes idiomas, aunque ya casi todos los equipos tienen esta capacidad, pues están conformados por personas de múltiples orígenes y que son multilingües. También podría ser experiencia en un sector concreto, aunque casi todas las firmas globales pueden conformar equipos por *expertise* en ciertos sectores.

Por ello, en una práctica global, el elemento diferenciador o el valor agregado debe ser identificado y preparado a la medida de cada cliente, de la disputa, o del entorno en el que se desarrollará el servicio, pues sólo ahí se podrá ofrecer algo diferente a lo que presentan los demás jugadores del globo. Por ejemplo, hace poco un cliente expresó que, tras haber entrevistado varias firmas pares, optó por escoger aquella que tenía una experiencia concreta en un arbitraje contra quien sería su contraparte. Conocer el *modus operandi* de la eventual contraparte fue entonces lo que decantó al cliente a favor de una firma.

Luego de encontrar el elemento diferenciador, solo queda transmitir al cliente que puede "confiar" en el equipo que se le presenta, hasta el punto que este sienta que traspasa su problema a las manos de expertos. Esa confianza solo se gana en el "cara a cara", pues no hay medio virtual de este mundo tecnológico que reemplace la interacción directa con el cliente. Lo mismo aplica en el caso de árbitros, y es por ello que la entrevista prenominación es fundamental para poder entregar la disputa a ese tercero.

La competencia global, sin embargo, no se da solo entre firmas de abogados al buscar nuevos clientes o casos. Todo abogado joven que trabaje o busque trabajar en este campo se enfrenta a una competencia global. Es por ello que para los abogados jóvenes es cada vez es más difícil tener valores diferenciadores que sirvan para presentarse ante un nuevo equipo. Hoy en día no basta con ser abogado de una sola jurisdicción, ni basta con haber estudiado un solo sistema jurídico. No, en esta práctica global, los abogados jóvenes asumen el reto de ser abogados preparados para resolver disputas bajo cualquier ley, en múltiples idiomas, y con capacidad para identificar un problema jurídico o fáctico independientemente de su país o tradición jurídica de origen.

Ello implica que todo abogado joven compite, al menos, con todos aquellos de su generación y de su región que quieren practicar arbitraje internacional. Basta con haber participado, como entrevistado o entrevistador, en la feria de trabajo de Nueva York que se organiza cada enero para los estudiantes de LL.M. de universidades americanas, para comprobar la verdadera sensación de competir en un mercado globalizado.

En dicha feria, tras superar la sensación de "speed-dating" por las cortas entrevistas de quince minutos, el entrevistado debe vender todo su potencial explicando qué lo hace diferente de todos sus pares. En esta práctica global ese elemento diferenciador es más difícil de identificar, pues muchos ofrecen las mismas capacidades de idiomas, similar experiencia y, normalmente, el mismo entusiasmo por ser parte de una firma multinacional. Por esta razón, en esta práctica global, el reto de un asociado es diferenciarse en sus habilidades como abogado, en el entrenamiento práctico que ha tenido, y en alguna medida, en el conocimiento de las reglas del juego. Así, el abogado joven que se enfrente a esta práctica global debe concentrar sus esfuerzos en adquirir experiencia concreta que lo diferencie de sus pares.

Ahora bien, alguno de quienes han practicado por fuera de su jurisdicción se habrán encontrado que la práctica global tiene límites que aún no se han podido superar. Por ejemplo, en ciertas jurisdicciones pueden encontrarse límites sobre quién puede ejercer la profesión de abogado. A pesar de tratarse de una práctica que no está ligada a un lugar concreto, ciertos asociados aún enfrentan la necesidad de cumplir con requisitos de exámenes de admisión como abogado en dicho lugar o inclusive la necesidad de cursar estudios adicionales. Ello sólo evidencia que, al final, el sistema global de una u otra forma debe enfrentarse a algunos componentes locales.

Es más, en ocasiones, estos componentes locales son necesarios. Siendo que en esta práctica global no hay entidades encargadas de regular o de supervisar, se trata de una práctica "autogobernada", donde como ya hemos visto son los mismos jugadores los que definen las reglas y supervisan su cumplimiento. Pero estos jugadores no tienen poder sancionador, más allá de una posible sanción pública, por lo que técnicamente la práctica no tiene límites para controlar comportamientos antiéticos. De hecho, a pesar de ser una práctica internacional y moderna, aún no hay la debida transparencia que permita conocer las faltas de los jugadores ni sancionar las mismas.

Por ello, otro de los retos de la práctica global es encontrar la definición de mínimos éticos que sean aplicables a todo jugador, y buscar la forma en la que estos sean puestos en práctica. Sin embargo, la realidad es que poco o nada podrá hacerse para sancionar violaciones a esos mínimos hasta que no haya una entidad central, global, que pueda velar por su cumplimiento. He ahí donde el componente local es inevitable, pues al final es el único recurso para garantizar que, de una u otra forma, los jugadores del mundo globalizado estén atados a mínimas reglas de comportamiento y que pueden ser sancionados localmente.

En general, si fuera necesario definir los retos de la práctica global en una sola línea, estos se resumirían al entender que los propios beneficios de falta de fronteras son en sí el reto del arbitraje internacional. Barreras de lenguaje común, competencia global, legados que aún nos atan a ciertas jurisdicciones y la falta de control o sanción sobre éticas cuestionables, son consecuencias directas de una práctica global que poco o nada se pueden mitigar.

Tal vez la clave del éxito, si es que hay alguna, puede estar en navegar entre este mundo sin fronteras sin olvidar que, ante todo, hay que ser primero un excelente e integral abogado. Lo demás, el lenguaje, el valor añadido, y las oportunidades, vendrán por añadidura.

CAPÍTULO 16

¿Cómo ascender en una firma internacional de abogados?

Luis Miguel Velarde

La formación y desarrollo de un abogado con vocación de trabajar en una firma de abogados internacional (que no es el caso de todos) tiene varias etapas. Con ánimo de simplificar, podemos identificar tres etapas *generales*: (1) seguir la carrera de Derecho, (2) conseguir posicionarse en una buena firma de abogados internacional (lo que puede tomar un tiempo en vista de la gran cantidad de competencia que existe hoy en día) y (3) desarrollarse como abogado (a nivel académico y profesional).

La idea de "ascender en una firma de abogados internacional" hace parte del punto (3). Contratado por una firma de abogados internacional, el abogado buscará asentarse en su posición y, con el paso del tiempo, ir ascendiendo. Este proceso no es fácil. Requiere mucho trabajo así como el desarrollo de una serie de habilidades (*softskills*) que, lamentablemente, no se aprenden en la Facultad de Derecho.

En este capítulo voy a comentar tres habilidades que, en mi opinión, son fundamentales para ascender en una firma de abogados internacional. Algunas de estas habilidades son generales y, por ende, también necesarias para ascender en una firma de abogados local. Otras son específicas (o, en todo caso, más aplicables) a las firmas de abogados internacionales. Las tres habilidades que trataré son: (1) delegar trabajo y dar comentarios acerca del trabajo realizado *(feedback)*, (2) trabajar en equipo y mantener una buena relación con el mismo, y (3) desarrollar la marca personal y vender el negocio.

§16.01 DELEGAR TRABAJO Y DAR COMENTARIOS ACERCA DEL TRABAJO REALIZADO

Aprender a delegar trabajo es fundamental para ascender en una firma de abogados. Esta habilidad es especialmente importante para los abogados *mid-level* o *senior*, cuyas tarifas horarias son más elevadas y a quienes se les exige, progresivamente, trabajar en más casos y de manera más eficiente.

Un abogado que no delega trabajo termina haciendo el trabajo por sí mismo. Esto es más caro para la firma (la tarifa horaria del abogado *mid-level* o *senior* es mayor que la del abogado *junior* que podría hacer parte del trabajo) y puede terminar siendo problemático (en grandes arbitrajes comerciales o de inversión, el cliente muchas veces requerirá que la firma de abogados fije un "*cap*" (límite) en sus honorarios, el cual podría ser excedido, con los problemas internos que eso puede generar, si un abogado *mid-level* o *senior* pasa demasiadas horas trabajando en el caso). Además, un abogado que factura demasiado tiempo en un mismo caso puede ser visto como ineficiente y ser criticado por ello (por ejemplo, en las evaluaciones periódicas que haga la firma), y puede incluso generar reticencia de otros abogados *senior* o socios de la firma para trabajar con él. Como responsables del caso, dichos abogados preferirán no tener que dar explicaciones, más adelante, sobre por qué el número de horas trabajadas en el caso excedió los honorarios pactados con el cliente.

Un abogado *mid-level* o *senior* que delega tiene más tiempo para realizar otras actividades que se esperan de su jerarquía, tales como actividades académicas (por ejemplo, escribir y/o participar en conferencias) y de *business development* (participar en visitas de negocios, organizar talleres de formación en temas relevantes para el arbitraje internacional, etc.). También puede organizar capacitaciones dentro de su firma en beneficio de sus coasociados (por ejemplo, en los temas más técnicos/económicos que surgen en los arbitrajes -algo que, en lo personal, me interesa mucho).

Una adecuada delegación requiere (1) saber en quién delegar y (2) dar comentarios sobre el trabajo realizado (*feedback*).

Saber a quién delegar requiere reflexión. Hay que tomar en cuenta la complejidad de la tarea para decidir quién puede realizarla. Algunas tareas pueden ser delegadas a pasantes, otras a abogados *junior* y otras *no* pueden ser delegadas. Por ello, la delegación de una tarea supone hacer un análisis previo. Esto, a su vez, permitirá dar instrucciones claras y precisas sobre el producto de trabajo esperado.

Una vez que la tarea delegada ha sido realizada, el abogado "delegante" debe darse el tiempo para dar comentarios acerca del trabajo realizado. Estos comentarios son necesarios por una sencilla razón: al dar comentarios, el abogado "delegante" se asegura de transmitir lo que estuvo bien hecho y lo que no estuvo tan bien hecho, así como de indicar los puntos de mejora para la próxima vez. Esto permitirá que, en la siguiente delegación, la calidad del trabajo sea mejor y más cercana a las expectativas del abogado "delegante". Un abogado "delegante" que no da comentarios sobre el trabajo realizado deja al abogado que realizó la tarea en la oscuridad, quien puede pensar que la hizo bien y que no hay nada que mejorar. En este caso, la próxima vez que se le delegue una tarea, es altamente probable que el resultado sea el mismo (y, de existir problemas, no será por culpa suya).

El abogado "delegante" que no comenta la calidad del trabajo recibido merma el fin mismo de la delegación. Si alguien hace mal el trabajo y no se le dan comentarios y recomendaciones (*feedback*)sobre cómo mejorar, esa persona cometerá los mismos errores en el futuro. El trabajo tendrá que ser corregido (si no re-hecho) por el abogado "delegante", lo que incrementará su facturación en el caso y, con ello, el riesgo de que sea visto como ineficiente.

Dar dichos comentarios y recomendaciones es, además, justo. Así como el abogado *mid-level* o *senior* ha sido formado para convertirse en el abogado que es y ocupar la posición que ostenta, él tiene el deber de formar a aquellos abogados más jóvenes con quienes trabaja para que también puedan desarrollarse profesionalmente.

Más allá de las buenas intenciones, quien da comentarios acerca del desempeño de otros abogados debe ser siempre consciente de las diferencias culturales. Los mismos comentarios pueden ser recibidos de forma muy distinta por un abogado europeo o asiático que por un abogado latinoamericano. Es difícil hacer generalizaciones, pero uno debe, en general, ser cuidadoso y tener mucho tino en la forma en que comenta el trabajo de otro. Una regla de oro es siempre comenzar por lo positivo y hacer que quien recibe los comentarios entienda por qué son importantes para él (contribuye a su aprendizaje y desarrollo profesional, permite alinear las expectativas, etc.).

Aunque todo esto puede parecer evidente, en mi experiencia, un problema en algunas firmas de abogados internacionales es que, muchas veces, los abogados "delegantes" no tienen tiempo para dar comentarios sobre el trabajo recibido. Si la calidad del trabajo recibido no les gusta, simplemente intentan trabajar con otro abogado que ya sepa cómo trabajar y no requiera mucho entrenamiento. Esta es, en mi opinión, una mala práctica que, por lo demás, puede ser frustrante para el pasante o abogado junior.

§16.02 TRABAJAR EN EQUIPO Y MANTENER UNA BUENA RELACIÓN CON EL MISMO

Una segunda habilidad que, en mi opinión, es fundamental desarrollar para ascender en una firma de abogados internacional, es trabajar en equipo. Trabajar en equipo es fundamental para hacer un buen trabajo y ser eficiente.

Los equipos están compuestos por personas, cada una con personalidades, intereses, niveles de tolerancia, etc., diferentes. Es normal que nos llevemos mejor con quienes tenemos más cosas en común que con quienes no tenemos mucho en común.

Ahora bien, más allá de estas diferencias, uno debe aprender a integrarse al "grupo" (al menos, en el contexto profesional). Más o menos iguales, todos forman, finalmente, parte del mismo equipo y sus objetivos apuntan en la misma dirección.

Conforme pasa el tiempo y se va ganando en madurez, uno va aprendiendo la importancia de tener una buena relación con los miembros del equipo. Una buena relación no supone ser mejores amigos. Por el contrario, supone ser respetuoso de las ideas de los demás, saber llevar una conversación a pesar de tener puntos de vista distintos, saber reconocer las virtudes de los demás y el buen trabajo realizado, entre otros. Esto es fundamental para que haya respeto mutuo y una buena relación.

Un abogado *mid-level* que no tiene una buena relación con sus pares o colegas más junior tendrá problemas para trabajar con ellos en equipo. Esta puede ser una traba para ascender en una firma de abogados internacional.

En el campo del arbitraje, estas firmas normalmente llevan grandes arbitrajes comerciales internacionales y/o de inversión, los cuales requieren que exista un contacto continuo y fluido entre los diversos miembros del equipo trabajando en el caso. Este contacto continuo incentiva la fluidez de ideas y argumentos, la circulación de evidencia relevante, la adecuada coordinación entre las diversas secciones del escrito en que cada miembro del equipo trabaja, etc., todo lo cual resulta en un mejor producto final.

Un abogado que no tiene una buena relación con su equipo puede sentirse limitado para levantar el teléfono y llamar a hacer una consulta, para proponer tener una reunión interna de *brainstorming* o de simple coordinación, etc., lo que puede llevarlo a trabajar en aislamiento. Esto tendrá un impacto negativo en su trabajo y puede obligarlo, al final de cuentas, a tener que trabajar más, lo que incrementará su facturación en el caso y podría mostrarlo como ineficiente (además de poco hábil en las relaciones interpersonales).

Para poder trabajar en equipo es, pues, fundamental tener una buena relación con los miembros del equipo.

Esta buena relación con los miembros del equipo es también muy importante para las evaluaciones periódicas que hace la firma (que van marcando el progreso del abogado y son determinantes para su ascenso en una firma de abogados internacional). Más allá de la tradicional *downward review* (donde el socio/asociado *senior* evalúa a los abogados más jóvenes), muchas firmas de abogados internacionales también tienen procesos de *upward review* (donde los abogados más junior evalúan a los más *senior*). Una mala relación con el equipo seguramente se verá reflejada en la *upward review*, con el consiguiente perjuicio para el abogado que intenta ascender en la firma.

§16.03 DESARROLLAR LA MARCA PERSONAL Y VENDER EL NEGOCIO

Además de ser capaz y responsable, para ascender en una firma de abogados internacional un abogado debe desarrollar su marca personal y aprender a vender el negocio.

Algunas veces he escuchado la frase "*a ese nadie lo conoce*" o "*¿a quién le ha ganado?*". Más allá de lo reprochable (¿o no?) de estas frases, ellas llaman la atención sobre un punto importante: el abogado debe hacerse una reputación en el mercado.

Existen varias actividades que deberían ser naturales para un abogado y que permiten desarrollar la marca personal. Estas incluyen ser profesor de alguna materia, realizar publicaciones, dar conferencias y/o capacitaciones, etc. Estas actividades son importantes para el desarrollo de la marca personal y son de interés para la firma de abogados por cuanto le dan buena publicidad. Estas actividades, además, permiten al abogado *mid-level* o *senior* tener mayor confianza en sí y hablar con mayor propiedad y seguridad de temas sobre los que, de otra manera, tal vez no se animaría a hablar.

Es fundamental que un abogado *mid-level* se dé tiempo para realizar estas actividades y que las publicite (pero sin exagerar). Mientras mayor sea su (buena) reputación en el mercado, más chances tendrá de ascender en su firma.

Además de desarrollar su marca personal, un abogado *mid-level* y, sobre todo, un abogado *senior*, debe aprender a vender el negocio. Esta habilidad es para el abogado, sin duda, menos natural que las anteriores, aunque es igual o más importante. Para poder vender el negocio, el abogado debe -primero- aprender a relacionarse de manera natural con los demás y a tener conversaciones fluidas. Ser simpático(a) es un gran plus. No todos tienen la misma facilidad para esto. A nivel más sustantivo, además de conocer muy bien el negocio, el abogado debe tener claridad en sus ideas y poder anticipar un criterio legal de manera clara y sencilla (sin entrar en formulaciones complejas que ahuyenten al potencial cliente). Un abogado percibido como simpático, capaz y conocedor en la materia genera la confianza que busca el cliente (el cliente contratará a aquella persona que le inspire confianza para llevar su caso y con quien se lleve bien). Vender el negocio requiere, pues, desarrollar habilidades distintas.

La mejor forma de aprender a vender el negocio es viendo cómo lo hacen otros abogados más experimentados. Esto se consigue participando, por ejemplo, en cenas de negocios, en reuniones de presentación de servicios a potenciales clientes, en reuniones de trabajo con estos últimos y/o sus equipos, etc. Otra forma de aprender (aunque menos eficaz en mi opinión) es participando en capacitaciones sobre la materia.

CAPÍTULO 17
Carrera de ratas en un despacho de abogados

Manuel Casas

No es un secreto que los estudios jurídicos son sitios competitivos, ni que los departamentos de litigio suelen ser los sitios más competitivos dentro de ellos, pues el litigio es una competencia y a los litigantes suele gustarles ganar. Tampoco es un secreto que la carrera profesional en un estudio jurídico suele ser un juego de suma cero: hay un número fijo o limitado de beneficios, como ser parte de la sociedad o rendir una audiencia, y conceder estos beneficios a una persona implica haberlos negado a otra.

Esto pareciera ser la receta perfecta para un ambiente de trabajo tóxico. Y, lamentablemente, a veces lo es. Cuando eso ocurre, es probable que las relaciones entre asociados sean patológicamente negativas; la mentalidad suele ser de guerra a muerte, en la que cualquier diferencia debe ser resuelta a puñaladas y cualquier oportunidad de hacer quedar mal a alguien debe ser aprovechada. En fin, hay prácticas que viven inmersas en una suerte de estado de la naturaleza hobbesiano, donde la regla pareciera ser *advocatus advocato lupus*.

Mi recomendación sobre cómo lidiar con la competencia interna en este tipo de sitios es sencilla: ¡huid! Lo digo en serio. Cuando uno está atrapado en un sitio de trabajo hostil y tóxico, generalmente lo mejor que se puede hacer es buscar otro empleo. Los beneficios en términos de satisfacción profesional, ni hablar de salud física y mental, son invaluables. Salir de un sitio tóxico no es cobardía, es sentido común.

En este tipo de lugar de trabajo no suele ser posible cambiar las cosas desde adentro. De hecho, me atrevo a decir que en buena parte de ellos no hay un deseo de que las cosas cambien, ya sea porque quienes lideran la práctica son, en sí, personas tóxicas, y el ambiente hostil es simplemente un reflejo de sus personalidades, o por una completamente errada –y medianamente estúpida– creencia de que recrear las condiciones de *Los juegos del hambre*[1] saca lo mejor de las personas y lleva a ganar más casos.

Sin embargo, no creo que esto sea representativo de la mayoría de los estudios jurídicos. El resto de este capítulo se enfoca en lo que considero el estudio jurídico medio, es decir, un sitio sólo *medianamente* disfuncional, con personalidades fuertes, trabajando bajo mucho estrés. En otras palabras, un sitio donde, si bien no todo el mundo es un villano, puede que haya uno o dos; donde, si bien nadie estaría dispuesto a perjudicarte gratis, sí hay quienes podrían hacerlo para quedar bien parados; y donde, si bien quizá no te apuñalen por la espalda, quizá sí te lancen un codazo en la mandíbula.

Mi mejor recomendación sobre cómo lidiar con la competencia interna en este tipo de sitios también es sencilla: leer, memorizar y aplicar todos los consejos del libro "*Oráculo manual y arte de prudencia*" de Baltasar Gracián. En mi opinión, no existe una mejor guía para lidiar con las complejidades de la práctica jurídica moderna que esta colección de aforismos escritos por un Jesuita hace casi cuatrocientos años.

A continuación, para demostrar la relevancia del *Oráculo manual* para situaciones actuales, busco aplicar dos de sus aforismos al manejo de la competencia interna en la práctica de arbitraje internacional en un estudio jurídico.

El primer aforismo es probablemente el más importante:

> *"Tener juego limpio. El prudente puede estar obligado a luchar, pero no con juego sucio: cada uno debe actuar como quien es y no como le obligan. En la competición es plausible la galantería: se debe pelear no sólo para vencer con el poder, sino también con la decencia... El hombre de bien nunca utiliza las armas prohibidas"*[2].

Es inevitable que en un estudio jurídico haya competencia. A menos que haya un cambio drástico en la forma en la que se ejerce el derecho, esta es sencillamente la naturaleza de la práctica profesional. Pero el hecho de que exista competencia no quiere decir que esta debería ser ruin o que quienes compiten deberían dejar de lado cualquier tipo de consideración ética. Por el contrario, el triunfo o la derrota, en buena lid, se disfruta más y molesta menos.

Hay dos razones fundamentales para tener juego limpio: una es ética; la otra, pragmática. La primera razón no requiere mucha explicación. Jugar limpio es lo correcto. La ética personal o, a lo sumo, la integridad profesional, deberían ser suficiente motivación para tratar de no ser un canalla.

La segunda razón -pragmática o utilitaria- en realidad tampoco requiere muchas explicaciones. Los beneficios prácticos de no jugar sucio son evidentes. Sin embargo, estos beneficios son incluso mayores para quienes practican arbitraje internacional.

Por un lado, si bien en todo ámbito profesional siempre existe la posibilidad de que el rival de hoy se encuentre en el futuro en una posición de poder, esa posibilidad es incluso más elevada en el arbitraje internacional. En pocas otras disciplinas hay un

1. En la trilogía de *Los juegos del hambre* veinticuatro personas participan en una competencia televisada en la que deben luchar entre sí hasta la muerte. La persona que resulta ganadora, es decir, la única que no murió, luego disfruta de una vida de lujo y riqueza.
2. Baltasar Gracián, *Oráculo manual y el arte de la prudencia*, (J. Ignacio Díez ed.) (2014), aforismo 165.

riesgo tan alto que un antiguo rival se encuentre en posición de decidir nuestro caso como árbitro. Claro está que ningún árbitro que tome en serio sus responsabilidades profesionales sería capaz de alterar la decisión de un caso sólo para desquitarse por una afrenta pasada. Sin embargo, somos humanos y estamos sujetos a una serie de sesgos cognitivos y prejuicios, y una experiencia previa puede predisponer negativamente.

Por otro lado, el mundillo del arbitraje internacional es pequeño y, dado su carácter global, suele estar más interconectado que el de otras áreas de práctica. La gente se conoce (y la gente habla). Por ello, las consecuencias negativas de jugar sucio son más severas. Una mala jugada contra un rival no solo convierte al rival en enemigo, sino probablemente también a sus amistades cercanas.

Aún si la mala jugada es leve, puede tener consecuencias negativas. Es mucho más fácil perder oportunidades que conseguirlas. Por ejemplo, suele bastar que cuando se esté discutiendo la composición de un panel en una conferencia, la lista de candidatos para un tribunal arbitral, o posibles abogados para manejar un caso, alguien diga algo como "*esta persona no me convence*" para que tal persona sea descartada. Jugar sucio aumenta exponencialmente la posibilidad de ser *esa* persona que no convence.

Visto de otro modo, jugar sucio para "ganar" en una competencia (posiblemente irrelevante o de poca monta) es un error característico de pensamiento cortoplacista. Es mejor ampliar la perspectiva y recordar que quien hoy es rival, mañana puede ser el presidente del tribunal, el consultor jurídico de un potencial cliente, o el ministro de justicia. O, siendo menos cínico, quizá una persona profesionalmente irrelevante pero personalmente excepcional. No vale la pena echar esas posibles relaciones por la borda por intentar ganar jugando sucio.

El segundo aforismo es de corte más defensivo:

> "*Atención a quién viene con segunda intención. El hombre astuto se da maña para engañar la voluntad ajena antes de atacarla... Hay que estar atentos a las desveladas intenciones y si se quieren ocultar con segundas, la atención debe ser la primera en descifrarlas. Con cautela se debe advertir la estratagema y seguir las vueltas que da la segunda intención antes de llegar a lo que realmente se quiere: dice una cosa pero quiere otra*"[3].

Aunque se trate de jugar limpio, hay que entender que no todo el mundo lo hará. En algún momento probablemente todos tengamos que lidiar con algún rival que no sea sincero, cuyas verdaderas intenciones difieran diametralmente de las aparentes. Un poco de malicia de litigante puede ser útil para descifrarlas y así evitar caer en una posible trampa.

Sin embargo, el problema con las segundas intenciones es precisamente que son difíciles de descifrar. Consideremos una situación hipotética: un miembro del equipo o un supervisor sugiere que tú seas quien informe al cliente sobre algo "*porque fuiste quien más trabajó en el tema y quien mejor lo conoce*". A primera vista, esto parece algo positivo, pues recompensa el esfuerzo y permite tener visibilidad ante el cliente. Quizá

3. Baltasar Gracián, *Oráculo manual y el arte de la prudencia*, (J. Ignacio Díez ed.) (2014), aforismo 215.

esa es la razón y la sugerencia fue hecha de buena fe. En ese caso, excelente. Pero conviene preguntarse si hay algún trasfondo. Por ejemplo, si lo más probable es que la información sea negativa, y el cliente probablemente se moleste al escucharla, hay que plantearse si la verdadera intención de quien hizo la sugerencia no es evitar ser responsable de ese disgusto y achacarlo a otra persona.

O, consideremos el escenario en que durante una reunión de equipo alguien propone que tú te encargues de resolver el aspecto X de un caso. El aspecto X, por supuesto, es casi irresoluble, pues no solo es incomprensible, sino que no hay ningún precedente ni ningún libro o artículo que lo trate. De nuevo, quizá la propuesta podría haber sido hecha en buena fe por alguien que admira tu intelecto y habilidad jurídica. Pero también es posible que quien propuso que te encargaras del aspecto X haya captado que este es casi imposible de resolver, o que su solución puede traer problemas y esté intentando abonar el terreno para tu fracaso.

No obstante, hay que ser muy cauto al tratar de detectar segundas intenciones. Hay una línea fina entre la prudencia y la paranoia. Sobre todo, hay que manejar con mucho tacto las situaciones en las que se considera que alguien está actuando con segunda intención. La mejor respuesta es quizá indirecta, pues es preferible evitar la trampa dando un paso a un lado que acusar a un colega de querer conducirnos a ella. Eso implicaría acusar a alguien de ser deshonesto, lo que no solo es una declaración formal de guerra, sino que también es una acusación que por lo general no suele funcionar, sobre todo si quien tendió la trampa es hábil, pues la trampa, más que una mentira completa, probablemente sea una media verdad.

En conclusión, la competencia y rivalidad interna dentro de un estudio jurídico probablemente sea inevitable. Ese es un factor que está fuera de nuestro control. La *actitud* con la que se asume esa competencia, por el contrario, sí está bajo nuestro control. De ello depende si esta será una competencia sana o tóxica; de las que nos motiva a esforzarnos para ser mejores abogados o, por el contrario, mejores conspiradores.

Los dos aforismos citados indican el inicio de la ruta para lograr que sea la primera opción. En situaciones potencialmente complicadas, la mezcla de ética y prudencia permite sortear las dificultades. Quizá hay una opción más fácil: conseguir buenos colegas. De los que colaboran más que compiten y están más enfocados en ganar el caso que en ganarte a ti. Esa ha sido la experiencia del autor, por la cual está muy agradecido.

CAPÍTULO 18
Bullying y otros retos de convivencia en los despachos legales

Edson López

Durante mi carrera profesional he conocido socios y asociados de distinto nivel de múltiples despachos -bufetes o estudios, según la cultura propia de cada país- de toda América, Europa y Asia, quienes amablemente me han compartido experiencias personales y de sus organizaciones, lo que me permitió conocer la dinámica de muchos de esos despachos, en cuanto a su modelo de organización, estructura de compensación, plan de carrera y estrategia de expansión, entre otros. Luego de muchas conversaciones en diferentes contextos, concluyo sin temor a equivocarme que -de una u otra forma- todos los abogados enfrentamos prácticamente los mismos retos a mayor o menor escala, independientemente de nuestra nacionalidad, el lugar donde ejerzamos nuestra práctica o la cultura en la que hayamos sido formados personal y profesionalmente.

He tenido la oportunidad de conocer desde despachos con una visión netamente empresarial y otros, por ejemplo, que basan su estrategia comercial en la academia. Pero sin duda alguna, a mi entender todos los Despachos -consciente o inconscientemente- tienen una visión propia de su quehacer y cuentan con una dinámica interna única, independientemente de su tamaño o áreas de práctica a las que se dediquen, entre otros factores.

Como dice Jaime Fernandez Madero[1], las firmas de servicios profesionales -dentro de las que se encuentran los abogados y los auditores- tienen como principal activo el talento humano conformado por trabajadores del conocimiento que funcionan *"en una dinámica de trabajo resistente a los modelos tradicionales"* y en la que *"su trabajo se basa en que pueda aplicar sus conocimientos de manera creativa y sin controles o reglas estrictas"*.

1. J. Fernández Madero, *Organizando Firmas de Servicios Profesionales. El Caso de los Abogados*, p. 31.

Es precisamente por eso que la conformación de un equipo eficiente, de alta calidad técnica y con una gran capacidad de interacción se ha vuelto cada vez más crucial en los despachos que operan en la era de las tecnologías de información y comunicación (TICs).

No es un secreto que las organizaciones empresariales más exitosas que tienen como principal activo su capital humano adaptado o moldeado a su propia cultura, han sabido identificar los grandes retos que enfrentan, implementando tempranamente las acciones que les permiten convertir esos retos en grandes oportunidades. Sin duda alguna, esas organizaciones tienen algo que les dan una ventaja respecto a sus competidores: visión.

Como lo explicaré en detalle más adelante, tampoco es un secreto para nadie que uno de los retos más grandes que actualmente enfrentan las firmas de servicios profesionales es el choque entre las generaciones de socios senior y asociados con dos o tres décadas menos, respecto a la forma de ver la profesión, la forma de hacer las cosas, el uso de la tecnología y, desde mi perspectiva uno de los puntos de mayor conflicto, la tan criticada incapacidad de los *millenials*-que hoy son el grueso del mundo de los Asociados a nivel mundial[2]- de esperar largos períodos de tiempo para escalar posiciones hasta convertirse en socios.

En múltiples foros de organizaciones regionales o globales de abogados, he visto discusiones a veces acaloradas, a veces poco profundas y otras tantas ciertamente desesperadas sobre los retos que implica para un despacho trabajar con los *millenials*. El común denominador de la gran mayoría de estos foros -y a mi muy particular punto de vista un craso error- es partir de la base que trabajar con la generación *millenial* es un "problema", lo que claramente denota una absoluta incomprensión de la necesidad de romper paradigmas y adaptarse al mundo actual, que es uno globalizado, tecnológico y en el que predomina una generación con características muy propias y conductas aprendidas a lo largo de sus vidas, que en buena medida fueron propiciadas por las generaciones anteriores que los educaron en sus hogares, escuelas y en otros ámbitos. Es decir, quienes "crearon" la generación de los *millenials* no son más que los padres y educadores, que hoy tanto se quejan de ellos.

§18.01 LA HIPERPATERNIDAD Y EL BULLYING

Como una premisa general, con sus excepciones por supuesto, los padres de los hijos *millenials* se enfocaron en que sus hijos "no sufrieran lo mismo que ellos sufrieron", en proveerles de "mejores cosas de las que ellos tuvieron a su edad" y de "hacerles la vida más fácil". Cuando esto se llevó a un nivel exacerbado -como en la gran mayoría de casos- y se perdió o simplemente no se tuvo conciencia de lo que se estaba haciendo, se generó un fenómeno que la experta Eva Millet llamó *Hiperpaternidad*[3].

2. Según el Informe anual de Deloitte *MillenialSurvey* de 2014, los millenials representarán el 75% de la fuerza laboral mundial en 2025.
3. E. Millet, *Hiperpaternidad. Del modelo mueble al modelo altar*, Barcelona, Plataforma Editorial, 2015, p. 5.

En síntesis, la *Hiperpaternidad* no es más que una sobreprotección y sobreinvolucramiento de los padres en las vidas de sus hijos, que en algunos casos llegaba a ser insensato e irracional. Este nuevo modelo de paternidad generó *Hipohijos*[4] a quienes sus padres les "manejaban" la vida en muchos sentidos -incluyendo el emocional- convirtiéndolos en buena medida en seres humanos egoístas y con menor respeto y temor reverencial hacia la autoridad. Además, este fenómeno ocurre en el boom de las TICs, lo que además les permitió un acceso rápido e ilimitado a la información, que los proveyó de herramientas para poder debatir frente a la autoridad sobre los dogmas que se consideraban como ciertos y, por si fuera poco, abrió un universo paralelo, que aún sigue siendo en buena medida desconocido para las generaciones anteriores: el mundo virtual.

¿Qué pasó cuando estos *Hipohijos* formados por los *Hiperpadres* empezaron a convivir en la sociedad? Muchas cosas y de todo tipo. Se crearon nuevos mercados basados en la tecnología, cambiando radicalmente y para siempre el mundo -algo que a veces se ignora o minimiza de la generación de los *millenials*- pero además se acentuaron y potenciaron conductas que hasta hace algunas generaciones eran incipientes o irrelevantes, como por ejemplo el bullying o matoneo escolar.

De acuerdo al Departamento de Salud y Servicios Humanos de los Estados Unidos, el bullying es *"un comportamiento agresivo y no deseado entre niños en edad escolar que involucra un desequilibrio de poder real o percibido. El comportamiento se repite o tiende a repetirse con el tiempo. Tanto los niños que son acosados como los que acosan pueden padecer problemas graves y duraderos"*[5].

El bullying es un flagelo que consiste en conductas aprendidas tanto para el acosador, quien lo ve como algo normal; para el acosado, quien se acostumbra a sufrirlo sin saber cómo manejarlo; y para los testigos, que asumen una posición pasiva de no denunciar lo que ven. Estas conductas aprendidas en época escolar, cuando están muy arraigadas en la persona, continúan en distintas etapas de su vida y por ende se trasladan a los ambientes laborales, incluyendo despachos legales, aunque los abogados a veces nos creamos una "especie humana superior" al resto de las profesiones. Aun cuando los términos correctos para este tipo de conductas en el ámbito laboral se conocen como *mobbing*[6]-cuando la conducta usualmente se genera entre pares- o *bossing*[7]-cuando la conducta se genera por acoso de los jefes , para

4. E. Millet, *Hiperniños ¿Hijos perfectos o hipohijos?*, Barcelona, Plataforma Editorial, 2018, p. 28.
5. Stopbullying.org. Disponible en: https://espanol.stopbullying.gov/qu%C3%A9-es-el acoso/346 k/%C3%ADndice.html
6. *"Es tanto la acción de un hostigador o varios hostigadores conducente a producir miedo, terror, desprecio o desánimo en el trabajador afectado hacia su trabajo, como el efecto o la enfermedad que produce en el trabajado"*. Disponible en https://es.wikipedia.org/wiki/Acoso_laboral
7. *"Ataque, atropello u hostigamiento de un empleado susceptible de producir secuelas físicas o psíquicas, constitutivas de lesiones calificadas como derivadas de accidentes de trabajo, que pueden posibilitar la extinción de la relación laboral por voluntad del trabajador. También llamado mobbing, aunque en el bossing la conducta es siempre imputable a un superior. Se consideran actos de bossing, por ejemplo, los comportamientos consistentes en limitar la posibilidad de comunicarse, cuestionar sistemáticamente las decisiones del trabajador, atacar su vida privada, las agresiones verbales, la difusión de rumores y críticas, etc."*. Disponible en https://dej.rae.es/lema/bossing

efectos del presente capítulo me continuaré refiriendo a este tipo de conducta laboral como *bullying* en general.

Este fenómeno está presente prácticamente en todos los centros educativos de nivel primario, secundario o inclusive superior a nivel mundial, en distintos grados, salvo excepciones muy puntuales en países como Finlandia y Suecia, quienes han implementado métodos anti-bullying muy exitosos. Lo mismo ocurre en muchas empresas a nivel global y más aún en las firmas de servicios profesionales, cuya fuente primaria de producción son los individuos que la conforman y deben trabajar en conjunto y a pesar de ello también compiten entre sí, a veces de forma desleal.

Entre otras consecuencias, para la generación de los *millenials* a quienes les causa estrés tener que esperar el mismo proceso de crecimiento profesional que las generaciones que los antecedieron, la competencia por crecer más rápidamente que sus pares los puede llevar a realizar ciertas prácticas relacionadas con conductas aprendidas en su época escolar, tales como el *bullying*, con los consecuentes efectos que esto genera para todos los involucrados y además para la organización a la que pertenecen. Estas prácticas también pueden generarse por sus jefes, pertenecientes a generaciones anteriores, que al sentirse o verse desplazados reaccionan acosando a sus "sustitutos".

Dicho de otra manera, el bullying está presente en los despachos legales y lo podemos equiparar con un cáncer que poco a poco puede ir matando órganos vitales de un equipo de trabajo, y que naturalmente afecta negativamente el funcionamiento global de todo el cuerpo, que es la organización empresarial a la que pertenecen.

§18.02 ¿REALIDAD O FICCIÓN?

Actualmente, en los Estados Unidos de América la mayoría de los estados poseen algún programa de asistencia confidencial para abogados, jueces y estudiantes que diariamente luchan contra el estrés, la ansiedad, la depresión, el abuso de sustancias y las adicciones ocasionadas o relacionadas con el ejercicio de su carrera.

La Comisión de Programas de Asistencia para Abogados de la *American Bar Association (ABA)* es una comisión específicamente constituida para velar por el desarrollo de los programas que brindan ese tipo de asistencia. Esta busca mejorar los servicios que el sistema provee, capacita personal, difunde información y crea plataformas de comunicación entre los abogados, los usuarios del programa y los voluntarios, profesionales dispuestos a ayudar a reducir la problemática (sí, esta problemática es una realidad en nuestro gremio)[8].

Como resultado de la labor de investigación sobre la incidencia del alcohol, abuso de sustancias y enfermedades mentales en abogados y estudiantes de derecho que la Comisión realizó en el año 2016 y 2017, se determinó que los estudiantes estaban reacios a buscar apoyo, debido a preocupaciones acerca de cómo la búsqueda de ayuda y reconocimiento de problemas, podrían afectar su admisión e inserción en el mercado

8. American Bar Association. Disponible en: https://www.americanbar.org/groups/lawyer_assistance.

laboral...Como si se tratara de un control de calidad de productos en el que una falla desecha el producto por completo, sin solución o posibilidad de mejora.

La Comisión y la Fundación *Hazelden Betty Ford* condujeron una investigación, cuyos resultados se incluyeron en el artículo "*The Prevalence of Substance Use and Other Mental Health Concerns Among American Attorneys*"[9]publicado en el *Journal o fAddiction Medicine* en el año 2016. El estudió concluyó que los niveles de depresión, ansiedad y estrés en los abogados, principalmente entre los más jóvenes, era significativo, con un 28%, 19%, y 23% experimentando síntomas de depresión, ansiedad y estrés, respectivamente.

Para aquellos abogados que litigamos y especialmente nos dedicamos al arbitraje, sabemos que la ansiedad y el estrés forman parte inherente del trabajo que realizamos. La preparación de una audiencia o algún imprevisto durante la misma, la presentación de un filling, efectuar un cross-examination de un testigo adverso, son situaciones que por su naturaleza causan estrés, sobre todo porque en todos los casos estamos en una constante lucha contra el reloj para cumplir una fecha fatal que de no cumplirla puede cambiar por completo el rumbo del caso.

Esto es confirmado por otros colegas que contribuyen con detalles específicos:

> *"International arbitration can be very stressful. The stress can be increased as a result of working for difficult clients and difficult bosses. It is also easy to overload yourself, particularly if you are too focused or too ambitious. But if your health is affected you must change things"*[10] (Ben Giarreta)
>
> *"I was given responsibility and tasks that were more akin to mid-level associates in more established groups. For example, I got to do my first cross examination in international arbitration in my second month as a second-year associate. While I initially felt like I was drowning, I would not have wanted it any other way"*[11] *(Nora Fredstie)*

Dos años después, en el año 2018, la revista *Iberian Lawyer* realizó una encuesta a abogados de grandes despachos en España y Portugal. El resultado indicó que la ansiedad y el estrés son los síntomas más repetidos, seguidos de la depresión y el consumo de alcohol. Un 80% consideró que las soluciones deben partir de la propia profesión[12].

Año a año más personas de diversas disciplinas se unen a estos proyectos, generando instituciones como el Instituto de Salud Mental de la Abogacía, la Fundación Dave Nee (que se originó luego del suicidio de Dave Nee, recién graduado que estudiaba para sus exámenes de la *ABA*), el *Treatment Advocacy Center* y muchas otras. ¡Miles de psicólogos, terapeutas médicos, etc. involucrados con un objetivo! Mejorar la calidad de vida y el bienestar de los profesionales que ejercen la profesión de abogado.

9. US National Library of Medicine. Disponible en: https://www.ncbi.nlm.nih.gov/pmc/articles/PMC4736291.
10. https://www.linkedin.com/pulse/how-succeed-international-arbitration-associate-ben-giaretta
11. http://www.youngicca-blog.com/tips-from-the-top-young-icca-interviews-nora-fredstie/
12. IberianLawyer. Disponible en: http://www.iberianlawyer.com/news/news-focus/7698-the-secret-terror.

Lo anterior nos lleva de manera irremediable a plantearnos de nuevo la pregunta ¿Bullying en los estudios de abogados? Como si no existieran ya suficientes factores adversos.

Nuestra materia prima es un cofre que contiene los valores más preciados de nuestros clientes. Su libertad, patrimonio, salud, proyectos, familia, aspiraciones e incluso su vida depende muchas veces de nuestro intelecto, capacidades, destrezas y voluntad.

Los abogados solucionamos problemas, resolvemos situaciones con base en análisis de precedentes, experiencias de éxito o fracaso y conocimientos en diversas disciplinas. Tomamos los errores del pasado y los convertimos en medidas de prevención o medidas de corrección de situaciones futuras o presentes.

Siendo un gremio tan grande que comparte los mismos desafíos, problemas y el mismo sentido de aspiración por una sociedad capaz de resolver conflictos -y por lo tanto capaz de enfocarse en la creación, emprendimiento y desarrollo- ¿Qué es lo que nos divide? ¿Por qué estamos compitiendo?

Como lo indiqué con anterioridad, la estructura típica de un despacho de abogados se organiza con varios socios senior, socios junior, asociados senior y junior, asistentes o *paralegals*. Los asociados junior -de generación *millenial*-son los que en la mayoría de los casos sufren o provocan el bullying.

La edad promedio de los socios junior y senior de un estudio de abogados es de 35 a 60 años respectivamente, por lo que son pertenecientes a la generación X o *Baby Boomers*. Los *Baby Boomers* se caracterizan por dedicar su vida al trabajo, por su compromiso con las tareas o proyectos que inician y en muchos casos la falta de flexibilidad ante un plan trazado, razones por las cuales, con el origen de esta generación, se elevó la tasa de divorcios, ya que la prioridad número uno fue siempre el trabajo.

La generación X, los hijos de los *Baby Boomers*, se caracterizan por su capacidad de organización y administración, independencia, individualidad, valoran la libertad y la responsabilidad. La mayoría de las personas pertenecientes a la generación X se negaron a replicar la falta de atención a la familia que los *Baby Boomers* realizaron, por lo que se dedicaron más calidad y cantidad de tiempo a sus hijos, la generación *millenial*.

La edad promedio de un asociado junior, por su parte, es entre los 23 y los 30 años, lo cual significa que, en su mayoría, los asociados de una firma pertenecen a la generación *millenial*, que se identifican por tener una variedad de características tales como la necesidad de reconocimiento, el trabajo colaborativo, la visión global, la necesidad de gratificación instantánea, la búsqueda de sentido, el uso de su trabajo para hacer una diferencia en el mundo, la ruptura de estructuras jerárquicas tradicionales y, muchas veces, la falta de motivación al no tener alguno de estos elementos.

Como resultado de lo anterior, las firmas de abogados se enfrentan a un choque de generaciones en el que la generación *millenial* busca sobresalir, cumplir sus metas, ganar mucho dinero, tener experiencias fuera de lo tradicional y dejar una huella en su estudio, mientras que la generación X y los *Baby Boomers* luchan por mantener la estructura tradicional de un despacho de abogados, con estructuras rígidas de jerarquía, promoción y atención al cliente, que han tenido éxito en preservar el sistema financiero de sus firmas durante años.

§18.03 ¿POR QUÉ EXISTE BULLYING? ¿QUÉ HACER?

Aventurado e irresponsable sería decir que existe una sola causa del bullying en los despachos legales y además que hay un solo culpable o grupo de culpables. Nada más para ilustrar algunas de las situaciones que se pueden generar, a guisa de ejemplo, además de identificar que se puede generar por la competencia desleal entre los propios asociados para crecer profesionalmente más rápido que sus pares, esta situación también puede originarse debido a que existen socios junior y senior que no desean ser superados por los asociados, por lo que atacan verbal, física o psicológicamente a los mismos para disminuir su autoestima ya sea dándoles tareas para las que no están preparados o saturándolos de trabajo de forma irracional -más allá de lo que las noches o incluso semanas de desvelo que un caso normalmente amerita-, aplicando el concepto etimológico del bullying -bull-, no precisamente por su fuerza física sino por el poder que su jerarquía les otorga. Esto se encuentra íntimamente relacionado con la edad y las generaciones correspondientes a cada uno, ya que la generación *millenial* a la que pertenecen los asociados generalmente se encuentra más capacitada y con más estudios que la generación X o los *Baby Boomers*, no obstante estos últimos poseen más capacidad práctica de aplicación de los conocimientos que poseen[13].

Adicional a las características personales o generacionales, existen muchos factores del medio que nos rodea, como la excesiva carga de trabajo, los plazos urgentes inherentes al quehacer del arbitraje internacional, la desorganización del lugar de trabajo, el sistema jurídico o político adverso, la necesidad de verificar todos los detalles en un caso, la imposibilidad de cometer errores que provoquen consecuencias desfavorables para el cliente y el manejo constante y repetitivo de temas, que involucran situaciones difíciles de manejar emocionalmente, entre muchos otros que añade estrés y crean enojo u hostilidad.

El bullying en los estudios de abogados por lo tanto, es un problema influenciado por factores tanto internos como externos, que necesita la aplicación de una solución integral.

Solucionamos problemas, nuestro nombre y reputación hace que nuestros clientes nos busquen para que resolvamos sus conflictos. Es por ello que el primer paso para solucionar el bullying es aceptar que, ser la persona que soluciona los problemas de los demás, no quiere decir que no necesitemos ayuda.

El segundo paso es reconocer que existe un problema e identificar si el problema se origina en la persona que sufre el bullying o en la otra persona, el que lo provoca. Los programas de asistencia para abogados que existen alrededor del mundo, son confidenciales. Los abogados y estudiantes prefieren la confidencialidad, ya que aceptar que tienen un problema (ya sea como víctima o victimario) puede afectar su posicionamiento social y percepción en el trabajo.

13. MP McQueen, *The American Lawyer. Here Come the Big Law Millennials, 2016.*

Enfrentar que no somos perfectos, a pesar que buscamos la perfección en los casos en que representamos a nuestros clientes, y que estamos siendo molestados o que estamos molestando a otras personas por situaciones que nos incomodan puede causar sentimientos de vergüenza y pena frente aquellos que nos miran como un gran jefe, un excelente padre o madre de familia, un amigo que soluciona todas nuestras dudas o un abogado infalible.

El tercer paso es establecer canales de comunicación oficiales a los cuales los abogados puedan acudir en caso posean un problema. Esta tarea es un tanto más difícil, ya que al tratarse de convivencia entre adultos se reduce la probabilidad de denunciar la situación, pues puede darse el caso que la persona que naturalmente deba recibir esta información no posea las cualidades suficientes, forme parte del grupo de *bullies* o estos sean sus amigos cercanos.

El bullying es una realidad y es por ello que no basta con comunicar que cualquier situación relacionada con esta problemática puede ser reportada, por ejemplo, al administrador del despacho legal, sino que se debe crear un clima de confianza entre todos los miembros, en especial entre jefes y subordinados, para que existan diversas alternativas de comunicación y solución de problemas.

En agosto del año 2017, la *National Task Force on Lawyer Well-Being* de Estados Unidos elaboró un reporte denominado *The Path toLawyerWell-Being: Practical Recommendations for Positive Change,* el cual contiene herramientas prácticas para manejar los problemas relacionados con el bienestar de los abogados. Según el reporte, el bienestar incluye la dimensión emocional, ocupacional, intelectual, social, física y espiritual del ser humano.

Lo anterior reafirma la importancia de tratar esta problemática desde lo interno del ser humano, buscando la mejora del nivel de vida general de los abogados, ya que -de no hacerlo- esto terminará impactando no solo en el clima laboral de los estudios, sino en la permanencia y satisfacción de los clientes.

A finales del siglo veinte surge el concepto de aprendizaje colaborativo, el cual consiste en la adquisición de destrezas y actitudes que ocurren como resultado de la interacción en grupo, es decir que se aprende en conjunto, a través de la cooperación de los miembros de un equipo.

Para lograr el aprendizaje colaborativo se requiere que el grupo posea simetría de conocimientos, una meta común y una división apropiada del trabajo. Es recomendable revisar cada uno de los factores mencionados, ya que los conflictos y acciones como el *bullying* pueden ser producto de una mala gestión o desbalance en alguno de ellos.

Hasta mediados del siglo veinte las teorías del aprendizaje se enfocaron en el conocimiento individual sobre el conocimiento social. No obstante, la revolución tecnológica, el aprendizaje en línea y la prevalencia del interés social sobre el particular, modificaron los paradigmas de la educación.

Si podemos actuar de forma colectiva para recaudar *likes*, aumentar las vistas de un video o hacer viral una moda, ¿qué estamos esperando para poner esfuerzos en común y resaltar nuestras fortalezas y no nuestras debilidades?

El bullying en los despachos de abogados existe, los afecta grandemente, les cuesta productividad, salud emocional y finalmente dinero y reputación. Quien quiera ser consciente de esta realidad y de la importancia que tiene una buena convivencia entre los equipos que manejan los casos de nuestros clientes en las distintas áreas a las que nos dediquemos -algo que se vuelve crítico en los equipos que representan clientes en un arbitraje por muy pequeño o grande que sea, pero que deben funcionar cual reloj suizo para realizar bien sus funciones-, pero sobre todo que trabaje para cambiarla, tendrá una ventaja frente a sus competidores y desde mi perspectiva tendrá a su vez más chance de obtener éxito y aprendizaje positivo en los casos que maneje. Quien no lo haga vivirá con un costo oculto que no sabrá cuán grande es, hasta que sea demasiado tarde.

CAPÍTULO 19
Balance trabajo-vida: arbitraje, ego y golf

René Irra

Recortas y moldeas tu pelo, pero casi siempre olvidas recortar y moldear al Ego.

Albert Einstein

El balance trabajo-vida personal es uno de los mayores dilemas de nuestra sociedad, particularmente en el ámbito de quienes nos dedicamos al arbitraje internacional. Algunas de las razones que nos llevan a dedicar casi la vida entera a esta actividad incluyen la cantidad de horas de estudio para entender, preparar y plantear un caso, las mayores exigencias que nos impone un mercado cada vez más competitivo y, a partir de un cierto momento, la necesidad de asistir a audiencias, conferencias y actividades de *business development* en otras ciudades y países.

Aunque no podemos plantear propiamente un equilibrio (lo que significaría descansar una hora por cada hora de trabajo), la pregunta que nos asalta a todos es cómo evitar que nuestro trabajo afecte otras áreas de nuestra vida (que en realidad son las más importantes) o, por lo menos, cómo encontrar mecanismos para mitigar ese impacto.

El exceso de trabajo puede tener como motivación la falsa ilusión de que, con ese nivel de dedicación, nos volvemos más productivos y, por tanto, más exitosos y apreciados en nuestro entorno profesional. Todo ello en nuestra búsqueda de una vida exitosa, posiblemente con buenos satisfactores materiales y, en consecuencia, con la posibilidad de alcanzar la felicidad. No obstante, pasa todo lo contrario.

Ese régimen a largo plazo es insostenible. Lo único que conseguimos con el trabajo excesivo es ser cada vez más improductivos, corriendo el riesgo de fallar gravemente en nuestra actividad, por decir lo menos. Claramente, las afectaciones más importantes son el daño que nos generamos a nosotros mismos en términos de salud y el que generamos en nuestro entorno afectivo.

En un análisis más reflexivo, nos damos cuenta de que *el exceso de trabajo no es el verdadero problema, sino el síntoma de un problema más profundo y que tiene que ver con el origen de esta conducta.* El punto neurálgico gira en torno a la *verdadera intención con la que hacemos las cosas, lo cual resulta ser el problema de fondo.*

Para encontrar la verdadera intención de nuestra conducta, eso que constituye el motor que nos motiva a decidir incurrir o no en cualquier tipo de excesos, es necesario hacer un ejercicio de rigurosa honestidad personal y determinar el verdadero "por qué" de mi "abuso del trabajo".

Aunque seguramente hay más de una respuesta, sólo me centraré en las dos que me parecen las más relevantes para este breve comentario.

En una primera reflexión, podemos entender el trabajo no como un fin en sí mismo, sino como un medio para alcanzar otros objetivos superiores dentro de nuestra escala personal de prioridades. Así, el trabajo podrá entenderse como aquello que nos permitirá garantizar los satisfactores materiales en beneficio personal y/o de nuestra familia, permitiéndonos tener los medios para hacer lo que nos resulta esencial en la vida. En esta concepción, el trabajo sólo sirve para alcanzar algo superior, no más que eso. Si entendemos el trabajo sólo como un vehículo, será menos complicado auto fijarnos los límites necesarios para no afectar aquello que entendemos como prioritario y no negociable en nuestra vida, ya sea tiempo para uno mismo, para nuestra familia, diversión, descanso, pasatiempos o cualquier otra actividad que nos represente bienestar.

A pesar de que esta reflexión puede ser la respuesta que comúnmente daríamos a la pregunta sobre la intención con la que trabajamos, a varios nos resulta necesario hacer un ejercicio de honestidad aún mayor. Una segunda reflexión más profunda nos puede llevar a descubrir que la intención de fondo con la que nos desempeñamos lleva una carga muy importante de satisfacción de nuestro propio ego descontrolado. Este ego descontrolado es el mecanismo que solemos utilizar para compensar nuestras carencias emocionales, como son la baja autoestima, la necesidad continua de aceptación y reconocimiento o, en general, el reforzamiento constante de nuestra valía frente al mundo que nos rodea.

Aquí, nos damos cuenta de que *la verdadera intención de nuestro actuar es obtener la auto gratificación del aplauso y el reconocimiento público*, que se traduce en ser el que más trabaja, el que más reconocimientos tiene, el destacar en todos los rankings o el ser la estrella de nuestro equipo/práctica/despacho/país/mundo/ universo.

Nos lleva a una actitud protagónica constante y a una conducta que busca el perfeccionismo. Un ejemplo de lo perverso que puede llegar a ser el ego descontrolado se nos presenta en cada memorial o audiencia que preparamos con un perfeccionismo desmedido. Es diferente (1) hacer nuestro máximo esfuerzo a fin de que nuestra *submission* tenga la solidez suficiente para defender exitosamente los intereses de nuestro cliente como se espera de un profesional a (2) pretender que nuestra *submission* sea perfecta con el ánimo de que todo el que lo lea se dé cuenta de lo extraordinariamente brillantes que somos.

Esta conducta desmedida nos llevará indefectiblemente a desatender lo que es realmente importante en la vida. Considero que, en este análisis, es esencial entender que los estímulos externos (poder, posición económica, reconocimiento, éxito profesional) no pueden compensar jamás necesidades internas (felicidad, paz espiritual, vida útil y servicial). Si pretendemos satisfacer nuestras necesidades internas a través de estímulos externos, nos daremos cuenta que nuestras necesidades nunca estarán realmente satisfechas, la búsqueda de satisfactores nunca tendrá límites y esta última será, por tanto, infinita. Aquí nos encontraremos trabajando sin parar nuestra vida entera para saldar la verdadera intención que subyace a nuestra conducta, despilfarrando nuestra vida por lograr un éxito que resultará ser una ilusión.

Una de las reflexiones que me ha dado más luz sobre este tema habla de la búsqueda del oro falso: "*la soberbia es la fuente primordial de dificultades para los seres humanos y el obstáculo principal a todo progreso. La soberbia nos induce a imponernos a nosotros, o a los demás, exigencias que no pueden cumplirse sin violentar o abusar de nuestros instintos. Cuando la satisfacción de nuestros instintos de seguridad y de sociedad se convierte en el objetivo primordial de nuestras vidas, aparece el orgullo para justificar nuestros excesos*"[1].

Son muchas las lecciones que he aprendido después de estas reflexiones y, sobre todo, después de varios descalabros muy importantes. Mi resumen de estas lecciones es el siguiente:

- El éxito profesional nunca subsanará las carencias emocionales de autoestima y amor propio.
- Todo en esta vida es temporal, incluyendo la vida misma. La posición profesional que podamos tener terminará un día y dejaremos de estar en el *spot*. Por ello es muy peligroso destinar nuestras energías enteras en fijar nuestro valor personal a la posición profesional que podamos alcanzar.
- Nada es lo suficientemente importante como para que valga el costo de nuestra propia vida.
- Nada que tenga como intención el ego descontrolado nos llevará a un resultado positivo.
- El entendimiento de estas lecciones nos dará más herramientas para poner nuestros propios límites. Nadie los pondrá por nosotros.

Con estas reflexiones no pretendo incentivar el desatender nuestra obligación profesional, dejar la oficina para ir al campo de golf en este momento y vivir la *dolce vita*. Lo único que planteo es que el descubrimiento de la verdadera intención con la que desarrollamos nuestro trabajo nos permitirá, en primer lugar, definir una escala de prioridades correcta. En segundo lugar, tendremos mayor claridad para establecer con firmeza los límites que sean convenientes a cada uno y podremos, así, aspirar a vivir una vida útil y feliz.

Y para no dejar de lado el golf, que se lleva muy bien con el arbitraje, me quedo con una frase que se le atribuye al golfista profesional discípulo de Ben Hogan, Gardner Dickinson: "*Dicen que el golf es como la vida, pero no les creas, el golf es mucho más complicado*".

1. GRAPEVINE, W. Bill, junio de 1961.

CAPÍTULO 20

Liderazgo empático para asociados en grandes firmas

Daniela Páez-Salgado

La empatía es la habilidad de comprender las emociones y sentimientos de otras personas como si fueran propias. Básicamente, es la capacidad de ponerse "en los zapatos" del otro. La empatía permite entender las frustraciones y reacciones de los demás y -yendo un paso más allá- ayudar a su desarrollo personal y profesional. La empatía, combinada con un deseo de motivar el crecimiento de los miembros de un equipo de trabajo, compone el "liderazgo empático" del que trata esta nota.

Ser "empático" o tener la habilidad de entender, en cualquier grado, a los demás, no suele ser una de las características que generalmente los futuros asociados buscan publicitar en una entrevista de trabajo (tal vez ni siquiera le han dedicado más de unos minutos a su estudio a lo largo de su preparación universitaria). De hecho, parecería que al comenzar a trabajar en *"biglaw"* la empatía no es parte de las destrezas relevantes para los candidatos dentro del ambiente laboral. Las preocupaciones se suelen concentrar en la calidad y sofisticación del trabajo, las horas facturables y el compromiso con los casos en los que se trabajará, entre otros rubros "duros" o ponderables.

En mi caso, por ejemplo, mi práctica internacional comenzó en un equipo que acababa de formarse en la oficina de Nueva York de Herbert Smith Freehills, y en el que trabajaba junto con dos asociadas senior. Por el tamaño del grupo no se me asignó -al menos formalmente- un "mentor" o alguien que haga sus veces. Esto hacía que al principio tuviera cierto recelo de hacer las naturales consultas que a todo nuevo asociado le surgen sobre asuntos del día a día, por no parecer impertinente o interrumpir el trabajo del resto de los abogados.

Esta experiencia, aunque enriquecedora, hizo que desarrollara mucha empatía por los colegas que se fueron uniendo a nuestro equipo (ahora conformado por más de quince asociados). No tiene precio saber que se puede contar con alguien que está dispuesto a detener su propio trabajo para responder preguntas -por mundanas que estas sean- en un ambiente de total seguridad y confianza. En esta profesión todos empezamos por lo básico y debemos aprender a preparar memorándums, a tratar con clientes exigentes y a comunicarle al equipo que cometiste un error.

La práctica del arbitraje internacional es cada vez más sofisticada y requiere de la participación de grupos de personas en los que sus miembros se sientan cómodos de levantar la voz y sabiendo que serán escuchados por todos. A medida que el tiempo va pasando, entiendo que, por un lado, esa habilidad para comprender las emociones y reacciones de las personas es una consecuencia natural de haber vivido situaciones similares a las que se enfrentan mis colegas. Esas experiencias pasadas son las que generan auténtica empatía, pues uno entiende, debido a que sintió "en carne propia", lo que el otro está experimentando.

En cuanto al liderazgo, pienso que para desarrollarse profesionalmente y destacarse en el mundo de *"biglaw"* no es suficiente haber tenido buenas notas, títulos de maestría o un doctorado, ni muchos años de experiencia local o internacional. Otras son las habilidades que se deberían desarrollar desde el inicio de la carrera profesional. Por ello, este capítulo va más allá de cualquier cualificación intelectual y se refiere a habilidades que se definen en la práctica. Por ejemplo, la calidad de líder no sólo queda reservada a los socios, pues el liderazgo se practica desde el inicio de la carrera profesional en una firma. Se trata más bien de una actitud y forma de afrontar los retos laborales que se va cimentando a medida que la persona va creciendo profesionalmente y conforme las tareas y responsabilidades se vuelven más trascendentes para el equipo.

Después de cuatro años trabajando para Herbert Smith Freehills, les comparto mis perspectivas sobre las cualidades y responsabilidades de un "líder empático" en un equipo de arbitraje internacional.

§20.01 COMUNICACIÓN ABIERTA

Uno de los errores más comunes que he visto en mis años de práctica se refiere a que los asociados no tienen la confianza para comunicar que existe un problema, ya sea porque piensan que tendrán que asumir personalmente la responsabilidad, no desean sumar una problemática al caso o temen ser una molestia, sabiendo que todo el equipo está ocupado.

Mi recomendación es que siempre es mejor conversar y buscar vías para solucionar cualquier inconveniente antes que dejarlo en *stand-by*o esperar a que con el tiempo se resuelva. Inclusive si parte del problema ha sido un error del asociado, es fundamental levantar el punto a tiempo.

Por otro lado, asumir que "el socio es quien debe darse cuenta del problema" es fatal. Nuestra realidad es una en que los socios están muy ocupados, manejando sus equipos de trabajo, tratando con clientes, consiguiendo nuevos clientes, además de sus asuntos personales. Por ello, si es que existe un problema o alguna situación que merezca ser compartida, es el asociado quien tiene que informar al resto y no esperar a que de "alguna forma" ello suceda. No hacerlo podría llevar a situaciones de incomodidad extendidas en el tiempo (y algunas veces, irremediables para el caso) que podrían haberse solucionado con una simple conversación con el equipo. No debemos asumir que el socio "se da cuenta de todo", pues ello no es así.

Por ejemplo, supongamos que un asociado está encargado de conducir la revisión de documentos para la preparación de un memorándum sobre las posibilidades de éxito de un caso. Si el asociado se da cuenta de que la tarea le está tomando más tiempo del previsto y no podrá cumplir con el plazo asignado, tiene la obligación de informar inmediatamente al resto del equipo. Es posible que su primera inclinación sea no levantar el punto para que los demás no piensen que es ineficiente. Sin embargo, la realidad es que se ha generado un problema y es fundamental que exista la confianza para poder encender las alertas. A veces, la cantidad de trabajo es desproporcional al tiempo otorgado y esto no necesariamente significa que un asociado no ha cumplido con sus funciones. Tal vez, simplemente, hay que hacer una reevaluación de los plazos, pero es importante que haya la confianza para levantar el punto a tiempo.

Por otro lado, es comprensible que una persona que recién comienza a trabajar sienta miedo de hacer preguntas porque no quiere que parezca que carece de conocimiento o habilidades para el cargo que tiene. En esos casos, siempre es bueno que el asociado que lo supervisa se tome el tiempo de preguntar si existen dudas o si hay la necesidad de volver a analizar las tareas asignadas. Al final del día, esta práctica seguramente le podrá ahorrar al asociado algunas horas en corrección de borradores, que se pudieron haber solventado con una conversación *ex ante*.

Finalmente, otra estrategia para cuando se trabaja en equipo es conversar con sus miembros sobre un problema antes de ir al socio. Así, se puede pensar una solución común que se le puede ofrecer al socio y llegar a una solución eficiente del problema. Todo ello es posible cuando se fomenta un canal de comunicación abierta.

§20.02 FEEDBACK

El *feedback* o retroalimentación es el factor relacionado a la comunicación abierta que debe existir en el sitio de trabajo, pero que le concierne al socio y asociado que supervisa el trabajo de otro. El *feedback* es muy importante para entrenar nuevos asociados y asegurarse de que las expectativas de trabajo se conozcan, comprendan y, eventualmente, se alcancen. Usualmente existe una evaluación *anual* sobre el desempeño de un asociado que se realiza recopilando el *feedback* del equipo de trabajo y del socio. Sin embargo, puede que éste no sea suficiente debido a que el tiempo hace que ciertas situaciones se olviden o se pierda todo un año para que un asociado empiece a mejorar su desempeño.

En Herbert Smith Freehills, por ejemplo, tenemos sesiones de *feedback* cada vez que hemos terminado un *filing*, un proyecto académico o una audiencia. En estas reuniones se evalúa con total honestidad qué se hizo bien y qué se puede mejorar. Además, nos aseguramos de que todos los miembros del equipo conozcan cómo está siendo percibido su desempeño y que entiendan qué tiene que mejorar y qué están haciendo bien.

Timing: Cuando las cosas no salen como se esperaba, no es recomendable brindar *feedback* inmediatamente, ya que en esos momentos de mayor estrés o presión puede ser contraproducente. Esperar a que las aguas se calmen puede ayudar a que la retroalimentación sea objetiva y procesada de mejor manera. Así, esperar (una o dos semanas, por ejemplo), ayuda a que las dos partes puedan transmitir sus opiniones de forma más concreta y objetiva. Asimismo, ayuda a mejorar la percepción del asociado que recibe el *feedback*: de un jefe de equipo calmado, objetivo y no influenciado por la situación que acaba de ocurrir.

§20.03 PROFILE RAISING- ¡NO TODO SON LAS HORAS FACTURABLES!

Una de las metas más importantes de todo asociado es alcanzar, o superar, el mínimo de horas facturables que le requiere su firma. A veces la preocupación por demostrar que somos "rentables" hace que se dejen de lado las actividades de *business development* y *profile raising*, que son fundamentales para el desarrollo profesional en arbitraje internacional. Participar en estas actividades mejora el espíritu de equipo y motiva al resto para involucrarse con personas u organizaciones interesadas en arbitraje internacional.

¿Cómo hacerlo?

El mundo del arbitraje internacional está lleno de eventos para practicantes jóvenes y de conferencias impartidas por abogados y árbitros de muy alto nivel. Es común que a muchos de estos eventos asistan potenciales clientes, con quienes se puede entablar conversaciones informativas sobre la firma, la práctica y el equipo. De ninguna manera, el *business development* está reservado a los socios. Por otro lado, siempre es bueno apoyar con la organización de eventos de uno de tus colegas o de la firma para demostrar interés por colaborar en actividades que finalmente benefician al equipo.

Segundo, proponer y escribir publicaciones. Las publicaciones conjuntas tienen la ventaja de que ayudan a cultivar las relaciones interpersonales por ser proyectos en los que, como autores, las personas se involucran de forma más personal en el contenido del artículo de su autoría. Por ejemplo, si se ha trabajado en un caso que requirió una investigación extensa que merece la pena ser compartida, los miembros del equipo pueden preparar un documento público, que además de ayudar al *profile raising*, permite la interacción directa con colegas en un ambiente diferente al del "trabajo facturable".

Para los socios y equipos de *business development* en la firma, siempre debería ser una prioridad que sus asociados sean activos en elevar su perfil en su medio, inculcando a su vez la responsabilidad como *business developer*. ¡Ello no tiene que ser aburrido! Lo cierto es que los asociados no somos máquinas de trabajo que deben estar investigando, encerrados en una oficina, y tipeando en una computadora todo el tiempo. Una parte importante del desarrollo profesional es poder desarrollar tu perfil desde el inicio, sin importar que seas un asociado que recién comienza. El compartir este tipo de actividades con los miembros del equipo puede cambiar la perspectiva y el rol que un asociado tiene en una firma e incluso le motiva a continuar su desarrollo profesional a futuro.

§20.04 DISPONIBILIDAD Y ACCESIBILIDAD

Presentarse como una persona que está abierta a escuchar, compartir y tiene interés en lo que el resto está haciendo es importante para mantener al equipo motivado. A veces, los niveles de trabajo y estrés pueden hacer que se nos olvide que trabajamos con otras "personas" y que una práctica crece gracias al esfuerzo de cada uno de los miembros del equipo. Mi recomendación es evitar ser esa persona a la que la gente tiene miedo de acercarse o preguntarle algo. Sé abierto e intenta inspirar confianza en el resto.

Además de la disponibilidad -que siempre dependerá de los compromisos laborales y personales- ser accesible a las personas de tu equipo es importante. En otras palabras, saber cómo están, cómo se sienten o en qué casos están trabajando son cosas pequeñas pero que contribuyen a un buen ambiente en el trabajo. En este sentido, participar en los eventos y programas que organiza la firma (desde un almuerzo hasta una charla o un evento externo) no solo ayuda a que te conozcan, sino que es una oportunidad para conocer a los demás. Ello demuestra que te importa lo que sucede en la organización y te interesas por lo que hacen tus colegas. Adicionalmente, estos eventos, que en general son más "relajados", permiten mejorar la relación del día a día que usualmente involucra lidiar con cuestiones relacionadas al trabajo únicamente (¡y mucho estrés!).

§20.05 CONTROL, ORGANIZACIÓN Y DISCIPLINA

El liderazgo conlleva responsabilidad sobre el resto y ello implica control, supervisión y organización. Esta ha sido una de las más importantes misiones que he tenido en Herbert Smith Freehills. Es crucial para el asociado que está liderando un caso saber exactamente cuál es el estatus de cada flujo de trabajo asignado y su coordinación con el responsable, a lo largo del desarrollo de todo el arbitraje. Para ello, usualmente, utilizamos un *case management tracker* donde identificamos las tareas, las responsabilidades cada persona, el estatus y mantenemos al socio a cargo al tanto del avance global del caso.

Por ejemplo:

Tarea	Responsable	Estatus	Deadline

Esta es la mejor forma para identificar las tareas que se están llevando a cabo y poder hacer un seguimiento en cada fase del caso. Asimismo, permite mantener a todo el equipo informado. La frecuencia de la preparación y envío del *case management tracker* ciertamente dependerá del caso particular, pero, en términos generales, una vez a la semana es ideal.

La organización del trabajo no es una habilidad que necesariamente se aprende en la universidad, sino que se desarrolla y adapta en la práctica. Ello es particularmente importante en arbitrajes complejos donde suele haber varios asociados involucrados, diversos testigos y peritos, múltiples partes y pretensiones, documentación voluminosa o procesos judiciales paralelos. La coordinación de todos estos elementos puede volverse una tarea difícil, por lo que es vital mantener una organización detallada de todos los flujos de trabajo.

Este tipo de método también es de utilidad cuando el asociado está encargado de coordinar asuntos con un *local counsel,* o peritos designados para el arbitraje. Para ambos casos, es vital tener un récord de las comunicaciones, solicitudes de información y documentación enviada que han circulado entre las partes. Por ejemplo, en la preparación de un informe pericial, siempre existirán muchísimos documentos que el perito requiere del cliente y es usualmente la responsabilidad del asociado asegurarse que exista un récord de toda esa documentación. De igual forma con el *local counsel,* siempre es bueno proponer *deadlines*, y explicar las expectativas de lo que se espera recibir en términos de trabajo requerido.

Finalmente, nadie debería sentirse avergonzado o nervioso al dar seguimiento a las tareas de cada miembro del equipo y/o peritos o *local counsel*. A veces podría parecer "intenso" o "repetitivo" pero ello es vital para el buen manejo del caso. Lo cierto es que los clientes esperan que, al acudir a cualquiera de los miembros del equipo, estos puedan brindarle una respuesta acerca de las tareas pendientes, su estatus y plazos. Ciertamente, estas son las expectativas de un cliente cuando acude a una firma internacional para su representación en un arbitraje. Por ejemplo, si el socio a cargo está viajando o en una audiencia y no puede atender personalmente al cliente y el cliente quiere conocer el estatus de la propuesta financiera que el experto de daños debía presentar para su consideración, el asociado puede acudir al *tracker* y darle una respuesta precisa y rápida al cliente.

Definitivamente, algo que genera empatía y "buena vibra" en el equipo es el buen humor. Divertirse con los casos en los que estás trabajando, disfrutar de una buena relación con el cliente o los peritos y compartir fuera de la oficina con tu equipo ayuda a disfrutar de la profesión y hacer más ligeras las largas horas de trabajo a las que estamos acostumbrados los abogados que nos dedicamos al arbitraje internacional.

CAPÍTULO 21

Empezando una carrera en arbitraje: el caso de una abogado in-house en una empresa pública

Briana Canorio

Como voy a escribir sobre mi experiencia personal, voy a hacerlo como si estuviera escribiendo en "mi diario". Es ahí donde se empezaron a escribir algunos de los logros que he alcanzado, tanto a nivel personal y profesional, con el apoyo de mi familia (especialmente con la guía de mi madre que intercede por mí desde el cielo), como por el buen consejo de algunas personas que la vida se encargó de poner en mi camino, entre ellos, algunos profesores y abogados que me acompañaron durante mi etapa universitaria y profesional.

Estaba por terminar mis estudios secundarios y una de las cosas que anhelaba era estudiar en una Universidad que no solo me brindara una formación académica sólida para llegar a ser una buena profesional, sino que complementara y fortaleciera la formación de principios y valores éticos que había recibido de mis padres.

¡Y ese deseo se hizo realidad! En la Universidad de Lima no solo me brindaron los conocimientos que uno necesita para desenvolverse en el ámbito profesional, sino que me ofrecieron la oportunidad de conocer excelentes profesionales que desempeñaban sus cargos o funciones con un alto grado de responsabilidad, compromiso, principios y valores éticos. A los profesionales que conocí a lo largo de mi carrera universitaria y que todavía me acompañan (dándome consejos y brindándome todo su apoyo) solo me queda agradecerles[1].

He aprendido que la gratitud es un sentimiento del más alto valor y que debemos ser especialmente agradecidos con quienes de manera desinteresada comparten sus conocimientos y experiencias con nosotros para ser mejores personas y profesionales.

1. Entre ellas, mi agradecimiento especial para Elvira Martínez Coco y Roxana Jiménez Vargas-Machuca.

Para contarles cómo fueron mis inicios en el arbitraje, voy a retroceder el tiempo y situarlos en mi penúltimo año de la carrera de Derecho.

En una de las tantas conversaciones que tuve ese año con el Director Académico, el doctor César Augusto Mansilla Novella[2], me dejó la tarea de pensar en siempre dar una cuota de conocimiento para el servicio de mi país. El doctor Mansilla, persona maravillosa por sus cualidades intelectuales y su conocida y enorme generosidad, pensaba que los profesionales más destacados de las Universidades deberían trabajar para su país, desempeñándose en cargos públicos o siendo líderes políticos; es decir, trabajando para beneficio de la sociedad, actuando con profesionalismo, responsabilidad, prudencia, respeto y generosidad.

Esa tarea no fue nada fácil porque ese año debía decidir si continuaba haciendo mis prácticas en el Estudio Muñiz, donde tenía la posibilidad de quedarme al término de la carrera, o hacer el Servicio Civil de Graduados (SECIGRA). El SECIGRA es un programa administrado por el Ministerio de Justicia de Perú, creado para que los estudiantes de Derecho puedan realizar una práctica jurídica en una entidad o institución del Estado por el periodo de un año.

Al término de ese año académico, visité al doctor Mansilla para decirle que había pensado hacer el SECIGRA y que adoptar esa decisión estaba resultando difícil de aceptar. De esa conversación aprendí que a veces es necesario renunciar a algunas seguridades para seguir avanzando, pues siempre hay mucho por aprender en todo lugar, y si en este nuevo lugar se tiene la posibilidad de aportar con conocimientos, nuestra permanencia sería tanto más significativa. Esta fue una de las primeras decisiones que más adelante marcarían la pauta de mi carrera profesional.

Decidí postular a Petróleos del Perú (PETROPERÚ S.A., empresa de hidrocarburos de propiedad del Estado peruano). En el último año de la carrera de Derecho realicé mis prácticas preprofesionales en dicha empresa, cuya experiencia puedo resumir en dos palabras: enriquecedora y gratificante.

Considero que fue enriquecedora porque tuve la oportunidad de introducirme en los conocimientos del sector de hidrocarburos (*oil&gas*), conocer las normas de contratación pública estatal y otros temas bastante especializados que se enseñan en cursos de postgrado. También fue una experiencia gratificante porque en los asuntos o casos que me asignaron pude contribuir con los conocimientos adquiridos en la Universidad y en las prácticas preprofesionales. De ese modo, arriesgué y renuncié a eventuales seguridades por seguir avanzando en el camino del aprendizaje.

2. En mi opinión, el doctor César Augusto Mansilla Novella fue un brillante catedrático de la Facultad de Derecho de la Universidad de Lima, excelente profesional, magistrado y jurista del país.

   Para aquellos que no tuvieron la suerte de conocerlo, los invito a buscarlo en internet y leer los artículos que escribió sobre diversos temas de derecho procesal y otros; asimismo, podrán encontrar hermosas semblanzas que muchos destacados abogados peruanos escribieron respecto de él, y varios de ellos concluyen que fue un juez sobresaliente, jurista noble y maravillosa persona.

   Ahora que lo recuerdo, el doctor Mansilla fue uno de los primeros árbitros a quien conocí en mi carrera universitaria, porque después de haberse dedicado a la carrera judicial se dedicó a la carrera arbitral y académica.

En PETROPERÚ S.A. debía apoyar en los casos arbitrales que se encontraban en el Centro de Arbitraje de la Cámara de Comercio de Lima y en la Dirección de Arbitraje del Organismo Supervisor de las Contrataciones del Estado (OSCE).

¡Una vez más, un deseo anhelado se estaba haciendo realidad! Cuando llevaba la asignatura "Solución de Controversias" en la Universidad surgieron la inquietud y las ganas de saber más acerca del funcionamiento de la jurisdicción arbitral de la que tanto hablaba el profesor. Esa jurisdicción que se caracterizaba por administrar justicia de forma rápida, eficiente y en la cual se resolvían temas muy especializados. No habían transcurrido dos años de haber llevado esa asignatura y ya estaba poniendo mis conocimientos en práctica y participando en la jurisdicción arbitral.

Mientras me encontraba terminando el año de SECIGRA en PETROPERÚ S.A., recibí la propuesta de continuar trabajando en esa empresa. Así empezó mi carrera profesional en el mundo empresarial.

Durante los tres primeros años trabajando como abogada en PETROPERÚ S.A. brindé asesoría legal a nivel corporativo. Otro abogado y yo nos encargábamos de la defensa de los procesos arbitrales que tenía la empresa. Fueron intensos años de trabajo. Por un lado, me encantaba asesorar y resolver los asuntos legales de las diferentes operaciones de la empresa, dedicando a ello una buena cantidad de horas de trabajo al día y, por otro lado, debía llevar los casos arbitrales que tenía la empresa. El tiempo adicional de mi vida personal que invertí en esos casos arbitrales tuvieron una recompensa al final del proceso cuando recibí los primeros laudos que acogían nuestras posiciones y pretensiones. Ello, como resultado del trabajo conjunto desempeñado con las áreas técnicas de la empresa. No puedo negar que también hubo casos en los que, aun pese a todo el esfuerzo dedicado, la finalidad de la defensa era evitar que la otra parte pudiera obtener más de lo que realmente le correspondía.

El recuerdo del primer caso arbitral ganado (el mío fue uno en arbitraje de contratación pública) siempre permanecerá en la memoria de cada uno, en el cual se recordará que todo lo que hizo y se dio en ese caso no fue en vano. Ese caso será el que nos motivará cada vez que asumamos un nuevo proceso arbitral y así seguiremos sumando más casos y obteniendo mayor experiencia.

Esos años también fueron de mucho aprendizaje respecto de diversos temas técnicos del sector de hidrocarburos. Aprendí sobre los usos y costumbres del mercado internacional de hidrocarburos de los que tanto hablaban los técnicos de la empresa, y empecé a hablar su lenguaje para entenderlos y así poder construir una buena defensa de los casos arbitrales.

Antes de iniciar el cuarto año en PETROPERÚ S.A., recibí la propuesta para trabajar en la Jefatura de la Oficina de Conciliación y Arbitraje Administrativo del Consejo Superior de Contrataciones y Adquisiciones del Estado (CONSUCODE), institución que más tarde se denominó Dirección de Arbitraje Administrativo del OSCE[3]. Acepté la propuesta porque quería conocer más sobre arbitraje en contratación pública y seguir avanzando en mi formación profesional. En esta oportunidad el

3. La Dirección de Arbitraje Administrativo del Organismo Supervisor de las Contrataciones del Estado (OSCE) se encarga de organizar y administrar los procesos arbitrales (institucionales bajo el Sistema Nacional de Arbitraje y procesos ad hoc) que surgen de los contratos que suscribe el

contexto estaba más claro, mi único propósito era conocer cómo funciona una "institución arbitral" que administraba en ese momento alrededor de 500 expedientes arbitrales (entre institucionales y ad hoc). Fue una experiencia gratificante por todo lo que pude aprender de la administración pública.

Durante el periodo que tuve a mi cargo la Dirección de Arbitraje Administrativo del OSCE pude conocer más de cerca el trabajo de los árbitros y comprobé personalmente esa frase de que "el arbitraje vale lo que vale el árbitro". Efectivamente pude observar el trabajo responsable y dedicado de algunos árbitros muy destacados y aprender muchísimo de ellos. Después de año y medio tratando de efectuar algunos cambios para mejorar el sistema arbitral de contratación pública, vi que algunos de esos cambios no podían realizarse debido a las limitaciones del sector público. Antes de que dicha situación originara en mí una frustración, decidí renunciar. A finales del año 2009, empecé a ser designada como secretaria arbitral por dos árbitros muy destacados (los doctores Fernando Cantuarias y Elvira Martínez Coco), a quienes agradezco la confianza y oportunidad que me brindaron para trabajar y aprender de ellos.

Habían pasado solo algunos meses de haber iniciado mi experiencia como secretaria arbitral, cuando recibí una nueva propuesta de PETROPERÚ S.A. para apoyar e integrar el equipo de especialistas que evaluaría uno de los proyectos más importantes de la empresa y del país. Nuevamente, la decisión que debía adoptar no iba a ser nada fácil. El factor preponderante para mi decisión fue que saber que ese proyecto se realizaría una vez en la historia de PETROPERÚ S.A. y quería ser parte del mismo.

Han pasado casi nueve años desde que regresé a PETROPERÚ S.A. y en este periodo de tiempo he tenido la oportunidad de seguir avanzando y aprendiendo, asesorando en temas corporativos trascendentales para la empresa y el país y, además, en algunos casos he tenido la oportunidad de trabajar conjuntamente con despachos de abogados muy reconocidos a nivel internacional. Varios de los temas corporativos en los que trabajé en estos últimos años estuvieron muy vinculados al proyecto por el cual decidí regresar a PETROPERÚ S.A. y en el cual algunos de los logros alcanzados fueron muy satisfactorios: la emisión de bonos en el mercado financiero internacional que recibió el premio del *Project &Infrastructure Finance Awards* 2018 en la Categoría *Best Oil& Gas Financing*, concedido por la revista Latin Finance y en la operación del préstamo sindicado de US$ 1.300 millones con garantía de CESCE que recientemente recibió el Premio *Latin American DowstreamOil& Gas Transaction of the Year* otorgado por IJ Global Project Finance & Infrastructure Journal.

Este periodo fue muy interesante y enriquecedor para mi experiencia arbitral porque tuvimos nuestros primeros casos arbitrales administrados conforme al Reglamento de Arbitraje de la Cámara de Comercio Internacional. En estos casos pude apreciar la actuación responsable y prudente de la Corte y de su Secretaría. En los casos arbitrales complejos y especializados, nos apoyábamos en los despachos de abogados internacionales, con quienes trabajamos conjuntamente con nuestros técnicos como

---

Estado (a través de sus diversas entidades públicas u organismos, programas, etc.) con proveedores locales e internacionales, en el marco de las normas de contratación pública estatal.

un solo equipo de trabajo, uniendo sinergias, aportando conocimientos y experiencias para el caso.

Todo lo que pude observar, aprender y obtener como parte de mi experiencia como abogada *in house* en el trabajo que realicé conjuntamente con los despachos de abogados que contratábamos para la defensa de algunos casos pude compartirlo en el panel *"Experiencia en Arbitrajes Internacionales entre abogados externos y abogados internos"* en la XIV Conferencia Anual de la Cámara de Comercio Internacional (ICC), en el año 2016, cuyo evento se realiza anualmente en Miami y congrega a todos los abogados latinoamericanos dedicados a la práctica arbitral internacional. Asimismo, fui invitada por la Corte de Arbitraje de la Cámara de Comercio Internacional a exponer sobre mi experiencia en *"Arbitrajes en Empresas del Estado"* para la Reunión del Grupo Latinoamericano de los Comités Nacionales de la Cámara de Comercio Internacional en el año 2017.

¡Nuevamente, un deseo se había realizado! Siempre he pensado que lo poco o mucho que uno obtiene de conocimientos y que pueda ayudar a otros debe ser compartido. Es una experiencia gratificante compartir los conocimientos y la experiencia adquirida con los alumnos en las aulas, toda vez que ello alienta a las nuevas generaciones para atreverse a seguir nuevos caminos, innovar y que los ayude a alcanzar sus propias metas. Tuve la oportunidad de ser docente a tiempo parcial de las asignaturas de Acto Jurídico y Contratos en la Universidad que me formó. Posteriormente, enseñé las asignaturas de mecanismos de solución de controversias (conciliación y arbitraje) en temas de contratación pública, gracias a la experiencia que había adquirido en el OSCE. Actualmente como árbitro de la Cámara de Comercio de Lima y del Centro de Análisis y Resolución de Conflictos de la Pontificia Universidad Católica del Perú participo como ponente en eventos de arbitraje nacional e internacional.

Y como todo en la vida, si uno dedica esfuerzo y es perseverante en algo que lo apasiona, los resultados que obtendrá serán maravillosos y sumamente gratificantes. Esos pequeños momentos de satisfacción que ocurrieron en mis inicios de la carrera arbitral me motivaron a postular para ser representante del Grupo de Jóvenes Árbitros de la Cámara de Comercio Internacional *(ICC YAF)*. En el periodo 2017-2019, como representante de ICC YAF para Latinoamérica, puedo decir que conocí a personas maravillosas y talentosas, jóvenes abogados que al igual que yo continúan avanzando en la carrera arbitral.

Finalmente, quisiera concluir diciendo que la perseverancia es la aliada perfecta para alcanzar nuestras metas. Eso sí, mantengamos la curiosidad eterna y la inquietud por siempre aprender algo más, ya sea actualizándonos o consultando a los árbitros que tienen mayor experiencia y que admiramos, para que en el momento que tengamos la oportunidad, nos encontremos preparados y podamos desenvolvernos en esa práctica arbitral que tanto nos apasiona.

CAPÍTULO 22

Sé irremplazable: caminos alternativos en el mercado arbitral

José María de la Jara[*]

§22.01 EL VIRUS DEL DERECHO VERSUS LAS MÁQUINAS DIABÓLICAS

En 1945, dos granjeros se presentaron a la Corte Suprema de Estados Unidos. Estaban realmente molestos por la masificación de una nueva tecnología. Cuando este aparato diabólico, conocido como el avión, cruzaba el cielo, sus gallinas intentaban seguirlo y acababan estrellándose contra las paredes de la granja.

Para sustentar su reclamo, los astutos granjeros se valieron de una noción del derecho de propiedad hasta ese momento incuestionable. "*Desde los tiempos de Lord Blackstone*", argumentaron, "*el derecho de propiedad se extiende hacia abajo, hasta el centro de la tierra, y hacia arriba, hasta donde llegue la vista*".[1] En base a esto concluyeron que los aviones debían solicitarles permiso para volar encima de su granja, o de lo contrario estarían invadiendo su propiedad.

El ejemplo anterior es utilizado por Larry Lessig para explicar cómo el Derecho puede ser utilizado para ahogar la creatividad. Los departamentos de arbitraje no se salvan de esta caracterización.

En primer lugar, los equipos de arbitraje suelen utilizar el sistema de hora facturable. Este impide que los asociados jóvenes tengan el tiempo necesario para aprender otros "lenguajes", como *legal design*, *Project management*, economía o psicología. Un asociado que debe invertir 30 horas revisando miles de documentos en un discovery prefiere canjear su tiempo por horas facturables. No tiene ningún estímulo para detenerse a pensar en una herramienta que en el mediano plazo ayude

* Las opiniones expresadas son del autor y no reflejan necesariamente las opiniones de otros abogados de su firma ni las de sus clientes.
1. Lessig, L. *Free culture*. Disponible en: https://www.researchgate.net/publication/28802969_Free_Culture/link/00b7d5187a44bd9f38000000/download

a automatizar el proceso y reducir ineficiencias. Este modelo perpetúa el ciclo de ignorancia y desincentiva la innovación.

En segundo lugar, la gran mayoría de departamentos de arbitraje siguen la estructura del modelo Cravath. Son los socios quienes toman las decisiones y la remuneración de los asociados no depende de qué tan eficiente sea su productividad (*lockstep*).. A un socio mayor no le parece atractivo invertir tiempo y energía en convencer a los demás que es necesario repensar el modelo de negocio. La opción más fácil es seguir brindando los servicios de la misma manera, hasta que el modelo aguante. La innovación se ve ahogada por mantener "business as usual".

Más grave aún, la cultura de litigio sofoca la colaboración y la creatividad para innovar. El asociado ve rápidamente cómo este virus ataca su capacidad de comunicación, aumentando el uso de frases cargadas de adverbios ("ha quedado claramente probado") y complejas construcciones lingüísticas para protegerse ("tengo entendido que"). Resulta más difícil innovar sin comunicación clara. El virus luego afecta al oído. El asociado cree que puede interrumpir al cliente, que debe terminar sus oraciones y que es aceptable que salte directamente a las conclusiones. La flexibilidad cognitiva también se ve comprometida. Rápidamente nota que concentrarse en problemas por sobre soluciones es premiado. Paga asumir siempre lo peor y no dar el beneficio de la duda. Esto mina la colaboración. Finalmente, el sistema inmunológico del asociado se ve comprometido, llevando al portador del virus a actuar siempre a la defensiva, a rechazar críticas y a no reponerse de desilusiones (resiliencia baja).

Estos síntomas explican por qué el derecho en general y los departamentos de arbitraje en particular son reacios a la innovación.

§22.02 EL MUNDO YA CAMBIÓ, AUNQUE LOS ABOGADOS NO QUIERAN DARSE CUENTA

Hace 300.000 años, el Homo Sapiens descubrió el fuego. Esta nueva tecnología marcó un hito para nuestra sobrevivencia. Permitió cocinar la comida y utilizar el fuego para ahuyentar a depredadores. Pero también se convirtió en el espacio predilecto para contar historias. A pesar de que la única evidencia era el recuerdo sesgado de los protagonistas, esas historias tuvieron un beneficio adaptativo y permitieron organizar la cooperación de la tribu[2].

En el año 2020 es difícil encontrar un tribunal arbitral que se sienta cómodo con un alegato de apertura contado al lado de una fogata. Por eso los abogados han optado por otro tipo de tecnología para (1) comunicarse con la contraparte y el tribunal, (2) recopilar, analizar y producir la evidencia, y (3) y persuadir al tribunal.

Estas innovaciones van desde los clásicos Skype y Zoom para tener video-conferencias con el tribunal, hasta programas como Everlaw y Nextpoint para agilizar la producción de documentos en el discovery, pasando por la contratación de consultores como A2L para la preparación de ambientes de realidad virtual.

2. Smith, D., Schlaepfer, P., Major, K. *et al. Cooperation and the evolution of hunter-gatherer storytelling. Nat Commun* 8, 1853 (2017).

Además, hemos cambiado nuestra forma de trabajar. Utilizamos sistemas de *task management* como Trello y almacenamos documentos en repositorios compartidos en la nube como Google Drive. Incluso algunas firmas de abogados se han atrevido a llevar estos cambios digitales al campo físico, optando por mudar sus oficinas a espacios *co-working* con una política de puertas abiertas. El objetivo de estos cambios no es solo estético y de apariencia frente al cliente. Responde a una demanda por mayor flexibilidad y colaboración[3].

Este proceso de eliminación de barreras físicas y digitales ha revelado las diferencias entre baby boomers, generación X y millenials[4]. Comparados con otras generaciones, los millenials demandan marcadamente mayor flexibilidad. Prefieren centros laborales que permitan el tele-trabajo otorguen licencia parental pagada[5] y son la generación que por lejos está más dispuesta a hacer sacrificios para encontrar un balance entre el trabajo y la familia[6].

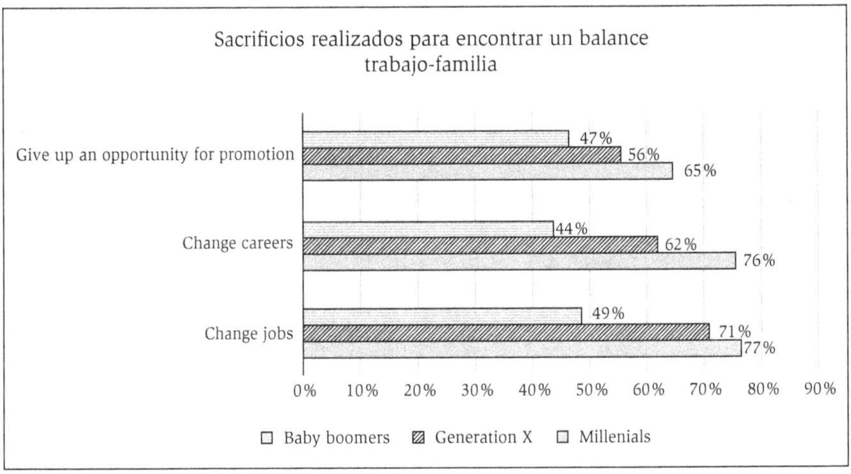

Fuente: EY, *Global generations: a global study on work-life challenges across generations*.

Los resultados del Reporte EY coinciden con lo que Carolina, Álvaro y yo encontramos al encuestar a 35 de los jóvenes profesionales del arbitraje más reconocidos de Latinoamérica. En concreto, encontramos que el 53.6% de encuestados tuvo que perderse un evento familiar realmente importante debido al trabajo, que el 37% dedica menos de cinco horas semanales al ocio, que el 34.3% quiere fundar su

3. DeStefano, M. *Legal Upheaval: A Guide to Creativity, Collaboration, and Innovation in Law*. Chicago: American Bar Association (2018).
4. Se suele identificar a los baby boomers como aquellos nacidos entre 1946 y 1964; a los de la generación X, entre 1967 entre 1980; y a los millenials, entre 1981 y 1996.
5. EY. *Global generations: a global study on work-life challenges across generations*. Disponible en: https://www.ey.com/Publication/vwLUAssets/Global_generations_study/$FILE/EY-global-generations-a-global-study-on-work-life-challenges-across-generations.pdf
6. Ibid., p. 15.

propia firma y que el 46.9% estaría dispuesto a recibir menos dinero por más tiempo libre[7].

Los jugadores del mercado también han cambiado. Esto incluye al reconocimiento internacional de firmas boutique como Chaffetz Lindsey y Three Crowns, la incursión de las Big Four, el protagonismo creciente de los financistas de disputas y el potenciamiento de centros arbitrales distintos como SIAC y HKIAC[8].Aun queda por ver si las firmas latinoamericanas pueden convencer a los clientes que el hecho de que sean más económicas no las hace menos sofisticadas.

Finalmente, desde la crisis económica del 2008 los clientes han tomado control del mercado. Ellos están enfocados en encontrar mayor valor en su gasto en representación legal; es decir, mayor predictibilidad y eficiencia sin comprometer la calidad de los servicios. La encuesta de 2018 de Queen Mary lo confirma. Los costos siguen ocupando el primer lugar en las peores características del arbitraje (67%), y la falta de velocidad tiene el cuarto lugar (34%). La falta de información respecto a la eficiencia de los árbitros, la selección de árbitro por parte de los centros arbitrales, y la propia eficiencia de dichas instituciones también son consideradas (30%, 15% y 11%, respectivamente)[9].

El mundo ya cambió. Y como dice Jordan Furlong, es inútil pensar en el futuro. Solo existe el presente y cada día que una firma de abogados espera que llegue "el futuro" es un día adicional en el que se queda por detrás mientras sus competidores siguen avanzando[10].

§22.03 EL MODELO DELTA

El modelo Delta se centra en tres áreas cruciales para el éxito de un abogado en el siglo 21: el Derecho, Negocios & Operaciones y Habilidades de Efectividad Personal. Este modelo destaca la importancia del conocimiento de herramientas tecnológicas y de la atención en el cliente al momento de brindar servicios legales.

7. De la Jara, J.M., Arroyo, C., Awad, A. *¿Cómo sobreviven los asociados de arbitraje en Latinoamérica?*
8. *2018 International Arbitration Survey: The Evolution of International Arbitration*, EY (May 28, 2020), https://www.ey.com/Publication/vwLUAssets/Global_generations_study/$FILE/EY-global-generations-a-global-study-on-work-life-challenges-across-generations.pdf
9. 2018 International Arbitration Survey: *The Evolution of International Arbitration*, p. 8.
10. HighQ. *SmartLaw 2.0: expert insights for the future of law*, p. 9.

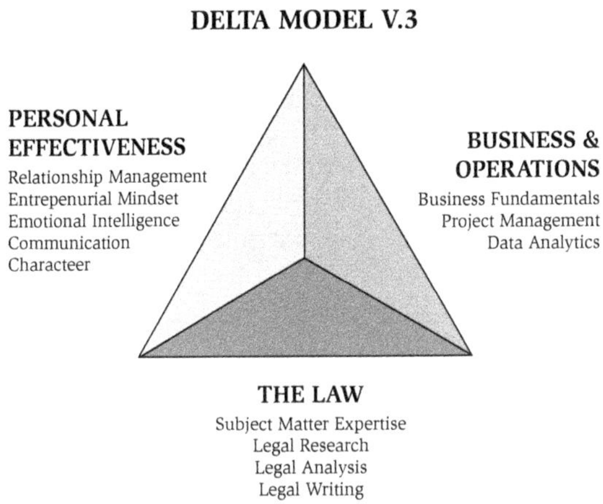

Fuente: Natalie Runyon y Alyson Carre: *Adapting for 21st century success: the Delta Lawyer Competency Model*[11]

Estos son algunos de los nuevos roles que han surgido en el mercado arbitral y que dan cuenta de la importancia del modelo Delta.

[A] *Knowledge attorney*

Al momento de preparar un memorial de demanda o escribir un informe no es necesario reinventar la rueda. Probablemente la firma donde trabajas tiene un modelo que puedes utilizar. Mientras más grande es la oficina, sin embargo, hay mayores posibilidades que el conocimiento se pierda en una carpeta virtual de la que nadie sabe. Por ello el rol del *knowledge attorney* se concentra en crear contenido, automatizar precedentes, liderar entrenamientos, desarrollar plataformas amigables que permitan al equipo acceder al conocimiento e incentivar una cultura de colaboración y basada en datos.

[B] *Discovery specialist*

El discovery es un procedimiento costoso, en dinero para el cliente y en tiempo y energía para los abogados. A pesar de lo anterior, solo el 8% de los encuestados por Berwin Leighton Paisner indicó que la producción de documentos había contribuido significativamente a un resultado favorable[12]. Además, los costos de un procedimiento de producción de documentos se dividen aproximadamente en 8% en la recolección de datos, 19% en el procesamiento y un gigantesco 73% en la revisión de los

11. N. Runyon y A. Carre. *Adapting for 21st century success: the Delta Lawyer Competency Model*, (May 28, 2020, https://legal.thomsonreuters.com/content/dam/ewp-m/documents/legal/en/pdf/white-papers/delta-lawyer-competency.pdf
12. *Berwin Leighton Paisner International Arbitration researched report on the perception of document production in the arbitration process.*

documentos[13]. Dichos costos pueden reducirse dramáticamente con la utilización de software como eDiscovery Point, acompañado por el outsourcing a un especialista en discovery. Éste nuevo rol se encarga de identificar, preservar, recolectar, procesar, revisar y producir información relevante para las disputas. El *Discovery specialist* suele contar con educación en ciencias de la información y en derecho. Así, su conocimiento del lenguaje tecnológico y legal lo convierte en un recurso valiosísimo para abogados sin aptitudes técnicas o aquellos que comprensiblemente prefieren invertir su tiempo en tareas más creativas.

[C] *Trial advocacy consultant*

El litigio arbitral es cada vez más sofisticado. Sin embargo, la mayoría de los litigantes opera de espaldas a la ciencia de la persuasión. Este espacio ha sido ocupado por los consultores de disputas, profesionales dotados de conocimientos legales y psicológicos que trabajan de la mano con el equipo para incrementar sus posibilidades de ganar el caso. Su trabajo se concentra en desarrollar una narrativa persuasiva del caso que incluya técnicas de *storytelling*, dirigir simulaciones de alegatos de apertura y clausura para detectar puntos de mejora, diseñar gráficos, animaciones y maquetas que ayuden a los árbitros a entender el caso y facilitar el proceso de persuasión, así como proveer la ayuda técnica durante la audiencia.

§22.04 ¿Y AHORA QUÉ?

Como indica David Halliwell, los pronósticos para los abogados parecen siempre obvios. Aprende a programar en código de computación. Conviértete en un *designthinker*. Construye una aplicación. Utiliza las redes sociales. Aprende un nuevo lenguaje. Sé consciente. Toca la flauta[14].

En definitiva, ya no es suficiente con ser solo abogado. Utiliza el modelo Delta para encontrar tu propio camino, sin necesidad de abarcar todos los campos. Concéntrate en lo que te apasiona y tiene utilidad para tu carrera. Encuentra un grupo humano guiado por empatía –una tribu. Hazla crecer. Conéctate con un mentor. Arriésgate. Utiliza la tecnología para customizar tu vida pero no dejes que te prive de tener conversaciones significativas. Explota cerebros. Sé irremplazable.

13. N. Pace y L. Zakaras. *Where the money goes. Understand litigant expenditures for producing electronic discovery*, (May 28, 2020), https://www.rand.org/content/dam/rand/pubs/monographs/2012/RAND_MG1208.pdf
14. HighQ. *SmartLaw 2.0: expert insights for the future of law*, p. 16.

CAPÍTULO 23

¡Desafío aceptado! Del mundo corporativo al mundo arbitral

Diana Gárate

Por casi diez años había enfocado mi desarrollo profesional en el ámbito corporativo, particularmente en *Project finance* e infraestructura. En mi día a día trabajaba en licitaciones, contratos de *jointventures*, consorcios, préstamos y un poco de *SPAs, SHAs, NDAs, LOIs, MOUs,* y todos los acrónimos anglosajones que uno se pueda imaginar. Sin embargo, de un momento a otro, descubrí la adrenalina y la pasión por el arbitraje, y mi carrera dio un giro inesperado.

Para ese entonces, ya había cursado un LL.M. con especialización en derecho financiero y corporativo en Nueva YorK. Creía que, a esa altura, cambiar de rumbo no era lo más conveniente. Temía que fuera muy tarde y no sabía cómo ni por dónde empezar. Parecía un riesgo muy grande el que iba a tomar y con mucho que perder. Gracias al consejo de jefes y de mi mentor, decidí estudiar y ejercer arbitraje, e involucrarme en la comunidad arbitral.

Si en este momento estás pensando en tomar la decisión de hacer este cambio, o de aprender más sobre arbitraje, ¡arriésgate! Cuando uno descubre realmente su pasión no hay más vuelta que darle. Yo tomé valor, me arriesgué a empezar de cero en una disciplina nueva para mí, y me dije ¡*challenge accepted*!

Sin embargo, no fue un camino fácil y aún sigo aprendiendo mucho. Para mi buena suerte, me encontré en el camino con muchos colegas y amigos que me ayudaron en esta transición. Es por esta razón que cuando me invitaron a escribir este capítulo, pensé en enfocarlo en los *tips* y consejos que recibí al inicio de mi carrera en arbitraje, y en lo que sigo aprendiendo hasta el momento. ¡Espero les sea de utilidad!

§23.01 EN SUS MARCAS, LISTOS, ¡FUERA!

Mi primer contacto con el arbitraje fue hace cinco años, en un estudio internacional (biglaw) en Nueva York. Era mi primer día de trabajo en el área de financiamiento de proyectos (*project finance*). El socio del área de arbitraje internacional me llamó para preguntarme si alguna vez había visto un arbitraje. "*Nunca he visto un caso ni judicial ni arbitral*", respondí. El socio me contestó: "*Bueno Diana, este será tu primer caso, ¡éxitos!*".

Acto seguido (un día después), me encontraba en un avión rumbo a Perú a tomar declaraciones testimoniales y a recabar medios probatorios para uno de los arbitrajes más importantes contra una entidad estatal peruana en aquel entonces.

Pese a las largas horas de trabajo y a la necesidad de "aprender sobre la marcha", la experiencia fue muy gratificante. El primer caso que vi estaba relacionado a una concesión peruana. "*¡Es mi especialidad!*" pensé, y eso coadyuvó a que realmente pudiera involucrarme y aportar en el caso, pues el fondo de la controversia era mi *expertise*. Sin embargo, debo reconocer que en ese momento no tenía mucho conocimiento teórico sobre el proceso arbitral ni tampoco las habilidades de un litigante.

En ese momento de mi carrera, en el que pasaba largas noches leyendo artículos y libros de Jan Paulsson y Gary Born por primera vez, pensaba que era muy tarde para dedicarme al arbitraje y estuve a punto de desertar. Sin embargo (y felizmente) un muy buen amigo me dio un excelente consejo: "*Diana, no tienes que dejar de lado tu experiencia en proyectos, infraestructura y corporativo, y tampoco tienes que dejar de lado el arbitraje si es que te gusta mucho, ¿por qué no fusionas ambas especialidades?*".

La mayoría de los arbitrajes en Latinoamérica derivan de disputas relacionadas a infraestructura pública o proyectos privados, ya sea de construcción u operación, o de controversias sobre el financiamiento de un proyecto, o disputas entre inversionistas y los Estados. Para ese entonces yo ya me sentía cómoda y contaba con experiencia en dichos asuntos. El reto, sin embargo, era que este tipo de controversias solían -y suelen- ser derivadas a un abogado especialista en arbitraje. Pensé, entonces, ¿por qué, en vez de derivar las disputas de mis clientes de proyectos & infraestructura, no las trabajo con mi equipo, junto con especialistas en arbitraje y litigación? Si conocemos y manejamos el tema de fondo de la controversia, podemos -con un equipo conformado por especialistas en arbitraje y litigación- tomar el caso; y así fue como decidí embarcarme en el mundo arbitral sin dejar de lado mi experiencia transaccional/corporativa.

Como comenté, este camino no fue fácil, y por eso quisiera compartir con ustedes consejos que hicieron más fácil mi transición del mundo corporativo al arbitraje.

[A] ¿Ganar/Ganar?

Una de las situaciones que más me costó es aprender a perder un caso. No es tan fácil, más aún cuando te involucras en un caso que trabajaste por largas horas (e incluso años). Para mí, no había sensación más triste que perder.

Hubiera querido que alguien me explicara cómo es esa sensación. Nunca la tuve en el mundo corporativo, pues en las transacciones corporativas difícilmente hay un "perdedor". Si dos partes cierran la compraventa de una empresa, ambas ganaron. Aunque una parte esté vendiendo la empresa porque se encuentra en quiebra (ejemplo extremo), de todos modos no resulta una pérdida, sino que al menos está recuperando parte de su inversión, o al menos obteniendo los recursos para liquidar su negocio (pagar a trabajadores, pagar impuestos, etc.). En un financiamiento, ambas partes ganan: una consigue los recursos que necesita para desarrollar su proyecto y la otra parte gana intereses, comisiones, etc. como consecuencia del desembolso efectuado, entre otros.

Por el contrario, en un arbitraje es difícil que haya dos partes igualmente contentas; usualmente habrá un ganador y un perdedor en mayor o menor medida. ¿Qué pasa si las partes transan durante el arbitraje? ¿Resulta ser este un escenario *win-win*? Es posible que una de las partes prefiera ahorrarse el costo del tiempo y dinero que implica ir a arbitraje, aun cuando el resultado no sea el mejor. Todas estas preguntas empezaron a surgir durante mi práctica en el arbitraje, mientras lidiaba con la sensación de angustia de que no podía perder un caso, pues no quería afrontar esa sensación de derrota.

Es importante tener en cuenta que esta situación ganador-perdedor es esperable en el arbitraje, y es mejor estar preparado a veces para la derrota, más aún cuando sabes que tienes frente a ti un caso débil. Lo importante además es sacar lo mejor de cada una de ellas y ser un buen perdedor, y tomarlo así: como parte del aprendizaje.

[B] "Es un mundo de hombres"

Otra sorpresa fue descubrir que, a diferencia del mundo del derecho corporativo, existe una mayoritaria presencia de hombres en la comunidad arbitral, no sólo como practicantes y litigantes, sino principalmente en los tribunales arbitrales.

Como mujer, he tenido que presentar mi caso frente a tribunales conformados únicamente por hombres, o tener como contraparte a un equipo de abogados hombres, en las que en ciertas ocasiones he experimentado una valoración profesional distinta por el hecho de ser una mujer joven.

Por esta razón empecé a indagar más sobre temas de diversidad de género e inclusión y descubrí la ONG *Arbitral Women*, una organización internacional que fomenta la mayor participación de las mujeres en la resolución de disputas en todo el mundo.

La ONG busca la mayor visibilidad de las mujeres en el campo de resolución de disputas a través de eventos, reuniones sociales, mentorías y patrocinando a estudiantes de derecho en moots. Inmediatamente me enamoré de esta iniciativa y me convertí en un miembro activo.

Ser una mujer joven proveniente de Latinoamérica (y de un país pequeño) me trajo algunas oportunidades, pero también varios obstáculos en la comunidad de arbitraje nacional e internacional. La mentoría de Arbitral Women y la excelente red de contactos que brinda, ayuda a las mujeres jóvenes a abordar los desafíos que surgen durante los primeros años de su práctica profesional.

[C] Algunos *tips* y sugerencias

Para concluir, quisiera compartir algunos tips y sugerencias útiles para compatibilizar la práctica arbitral con una práctica previa (en corporativo o cualquier otra área del derecho), así como para efectuar una transición *smooth* al mundo arbitral:

- No abandones o cambies tu especialización transaccional y corporativa, más bien compleméntala con el arbitraje.
- Siempre mantente actualizado de las últimas noticias del mundo arbitral y de los casos y laudos importantes (puedes suscribirte a Wolters Kluwer, al Global Arbitration Review, a CIAR Global, leer las noticias de la CCI, el CIADI, periódicos nacionales, etc.)
- Forma parte de una asociación de arbitraje de jóvenes (ICC YAF, asociaciones young por país, CEA under 40, Young ITA, Young ICCA, Arbitral Women, WWL, etc.), y sé un miembro activo y proactivo.
- Crea tu propio nicho en el mundo arbitral. Elige un tema académico, o una especialidad dentro del arbitraje y enfócate y prepárate en ello.
- Lleva cursos de litigación y persuasión y de *advocacy skills*, adicionalmente a cursos teóricos. Es recomendable además llevar cursos de psicología y teatro, ¡te serán de mucha utilidad para aprender a persuadir al tribunal!
- Aplica tus habilidades y tu nuevo "chip" de litigante en el ámbito de tu especialidad: por ejemplo, si también te dedicas al derecho corporativo, al momento de redactar un contrato, o una carta, o cualquier documento en el marco de una transacción corporativa, siempre redáctalo como si fuera a ser leído eventualmente por un tribunal arbitral, o dale un enfoque de prevención del potencial conflicto. Esto significa darle un valor agregado a tu cliente corporativo y a tu asesoría como abogado.
- Tip comercial: aplica el *cross-selling*. Si cuentas con clientes de tu práctica corporativa, ellos serán tus primeros clientes para tu práctica arbitral. No te preocupes en un primer momento por "salir a captar clientes"; primero aproxímate a los que ya tienes en cartera.

Y por último, solo me queda decir, anímate al cambio y *¡Enjoy the ride!*

CAPÍTULO 24
Investigación legal empírica y asociados de arbitraje

Christopher R. Drahozal

§24.01 INTRODUCCIÓN

La investigación empírica, en términos generales, es la investigación "que se origina o se basa en la observación o la experiencia"[1]. Según esa definición, gran parte de la investigación legal es empírica, a diferencia de la teórica, porque se basa en la observación o la experiencia de lo que sucede en el sistema legal. Sin embargo, en el uso común, la investigación empírica se refiere al estudio que recopila información basada en la observación o la experiencia utilizando alguna metodología sistemática. Bajo esta definición más restringida, una investigación que examine un solo caso judicial o arbitral no sería empírico, pero sí lo sería un estudio que examine datos de una muestra de casos similares.

Si bien la investigación empírica es concebida a menudo y efectivamente termina siendo de naturaleza cuantitativa, también puede ser cualitativa. Hay que tener en cuenta por ello que "los métodos de investigación cuantitativa implican la recopilación y el análisis de datos numéricos, mientras que los métodos cualitativos implican la recopilación y el análisis de datos no numéricos"[2]. Uno de los estudios empíricos más conocidos sobre el arbitraje internacional es cualitativo: *Dealing in Virtue* por Yves Dezalay y Bryant Garth[3]. Debido a que mi experiencia es con estudios empíricos

1. *Empirical,* Meriam-Webster Dictionary, https://www.merriam-webster.com/dictionary/empirical (visitado por última vez el 22 de febrero de 2019).
2. Christopher R. Drahozal& Richard W. Naimark (editores), *Towards a Science of International Arbitration: Collected Empirical Research 4* (2005).
3. Yves Dezalay & Bryant G. Garth, *Dealing in Virtue: International Commercial Arbitration and the Construction of a Transnational Legal Order* (1996).

cuantitativos en lugar de cualitativos, el resto de este capítulo se centrará en la investigación empírica cuantitativa.

§24.02 TIPOS DE INVESTIGACIÓN EMPÍRICA CUANTITATIVA

Lee Epstein y Gary King describen los tres objetivos de la investigación empírica como "acumular datos para el uso del investigador u otros; resumir datos para que sean más fáciles de comprender; y hacer inferencias descriptivas o causales, lo que implica el uso de datos que hemos observado para aprender sobre los datos que nos gustaría recopilar"[4]. Los métodos más comunes que utilizan los investigadores empíricos para recopilar datos son las encuestas, los estudios de observación y los experimentos.

Las encuestas, incluidas las entrevistas, recopilan datos haciendo preguntas a las personas. Estas son la que la mayoría de personas relaciona con una investigación empírica. Los estudios de observación recopilan datos mediante el estudio de casos reales, contratos y similares, examinando lo que las personas realmente hacen en lugar de lo que dicen que hacen. Los experimentos recopilan datos al hacer que los participantes en el estudio respondan o analicen situaciones hipotéticas (los experimentos de ciencias sociales obviamente son diferentes de los experimentos en ciencias naturales).

El creciente cuerpo de investigación empírica sobre arbitraje internacional utiliza todas estas metodologías. Este breve capítulo, por supuesto, no es el lugar para una descripción detallada o análisis de esos estudios. Basta decir que los estudios empíricos examinan, al menos en cierto grado, todos los aspectos del proceso de arbitraje internacional, desde el uso de cláusulas de arbitraje en contratos internacionales hasta los procedimientos en arbitrajes internacionales (incluyendo su costo y duración, el nombramiento y la recusación de árbitros, medidas cautelares y árbitros de emergencia, procedimientos multi-parte y mediación), hasta la demografía del árbitro y la toma de decisiones sobre los resultados de los procesos y la ejecución de laudos arbitrales internacionales[5].

§24.03 BENEFICIOS DE LA INVESTIGACIÓN EMPÍRICA

La investigación empírica puede beneficiar a los asociados de arbitraje al proporcionar una perspectiva más amplia sobre cómo es y funciona el mundo legal.

Por ejemplo, un abogado que redacta un convenio arbitral a menudo comienza con una cláusula de un contrato anterior que él o ella preparó o una cláusula de formulario redactada por otra persona (otro abogado de la firma, una cláusula modelo de institución arbitral o un libro de formularios publicado). Quizás el abogado haya leído un artículo sobre redacción de cláusulas por un experto en el tema o haya asistido a una clase al respecto. Un estudio empírico que examina las disposiciones de las

4. Lee Epstein & Gary King, *The Rules of Inference*, 69 U. Chi. L. Rev. 1, 19-20 (2002).
5. Véaseen general Christopher R. Drahozal, *Empirical Findings on International Arbitration: An Overview*, en *Oxford Handbook on International Arbitration* (2019).

cláusulas de arbitraje internacional proporciona información adicional y más sistemática sobre cómo otros abogados las redactan. El estudio puede resaltar problemas o enfoques identificados por otros redactores, lo que permite al asociado de arbitraje aprender no solo de su propia experiencia, sino también de la experiencia (o al menos el comportamiento) de muchos otros.

Además, la investigación empírica puede ayudar a los abogados a elaborar argumentos de políticas públicas dirigidos a quienes toman decisiones legales: jueces, árbitros, reguladores o legisladores. A menudo, los abogados conocerán las prácticas de sus clientes o los hechos del caso en disputa. Pero el caso individual o la disposición del contrato es simplemente una anécdota. Puede no ser típico de todos los casos o contratos. Un estudio empírico bien construido proporciona una perspectiva más amplia y representativa, y puede revelar que el caso aparentemente atroz es, o no, particularmente común.

Finalmente, la investigación empírica puede proporcionar información sobre aspectos del proceso de·arbitraje que de otro modo serían difíciles de observar. Por ejemplo, una investigación experimental reciente sugiere que los árbitros usan la misma heurística decisional y son susceptibles a los mismos sesgos en la toma de decisiones que el resto de nosotros[6]. Este tipo de aportes psicológicos puede ayudar a los abogados a presentar argumentos ante el tribunal o predecir los resultados de los casos. Además, la creciente disponibilidad de *legal analytics* -como *Arbitrator Intelligence*, que está recopilando y pondrá a disposición datos sobre las prácticas de gestión de casos y la toma de decisiones del árbitro[7]- también ayudará a evaluar los casos y seleccionar a los tomadores de decisiones.

La investigación empírica no es en modo alguno la solución a todos los desafíos que enfrentan los asociados de arbitraje. Pero comprender y usar la investigación empírica es otra herramienta que un buen abogado puede usar para representar a los clientes de manera efectiva.

§24.04 LÍMITES DE LA INVESTIGACIÓN EMPÍRICA

Todos los métodos de investigación empírica tienen límites[8]. Comprender esos límites es esencial para ser un usuario diestro en investigación empírica.

Por ejemplo, los resultados de una encuesta proporcionan información sobre cómo los entrevistados respondieron a las preguntas formuladas. Pero los encuestados, ya sea consciente o inconscientemente, podrían proporcionar respuestas que reflejen lo que los encuestados desearían haber hecho en lugar de lo que realmente hacen. Además, la administración de las encuestas plantea cuestiones de representatividad:

6. Véase Susan D. Franck *et al.*, *Inside the Arbitrator's Mind*, 66 Emory L.J. 1115 (2017); Rebecca Helm *et al.*, *Are Arbitrators Human?*, 13 J. Emp. Legal Stud. 666 (2016).
7. Para más información sobre *ArbitratorIntelligence*, véase el sitio www.arbitratorintelligence.org.
8. Véase, e.g., Christopher R. Drahozal, *Arbitration Innumeracy*, YB. on Arb. & Med. 89 (2012); Drahozal& Naimark, *Towards a Science of International Arbitration: Collected Empirical Research* 4 (2005), 8-11. Véase en general Lee Epstein & Andrew D. Martin, *An Introduction to Empirical Legal Research* (2014) en *Oxford Handbook of Empirical Legal Research* (Peter Cane & Herbert M. Kritzer, editores, 2012).

¿son los encuestados representativos de toda la población (de, por ejemplo, abogados de arbitraje) o los resultados de la encuesta están sesgados por una representación excesiva o insuficiente de una parte de la población?

Los estudios observacionales plantean preocupaciones similares sobre la representatividad. Un estudio que examina una muestra de laudos arbitrales, por ejemplo, debe tener en cuenta que muchos casos se concilian antes de que se emita un laudo. Hay muchas razones para creer que los casos conciliados difieren sistemáticamente de los casos resueltos por un laudo (el hecho de que los casos fueron conciliados es un indicador bastante bueno, por lo menos). Como resultado, la solución de casos puede enmascarar (o embellecer) el efecto en el que está interesado el investigador. Un punto relacionado es que es difícil controlar la solidez del caso de un demandante en estudios de resultados judiciales o arbitrales. A menos que el investigador pueda evaluar objetivamente la credibilidad del testimonio de los testigos, por ejemplo, es extremadamente difícil concluir que los resultados difieren, y ello se debe, por ejemplo, al foro, en lugar de las diferencias en los méritos del reclamo.

Los estudios experimentales proporcionan una posible forma de disminuir o evitar ese problema porque utilizan casos hipotéticos o escenarios que mantienen constante la fuerza de la afirmación. Pero extrapolar los resultados de los experimentos de laboratorio a entornos reales es difícil. Los casos hipotéticos implican necesariamente hechos simplificados (sino muy simplificados) con poco o ningún dinero real en juego. Los sujetos podrían ser estudiantes universitarios que estudian psicología, o jueces o árbitros en conferencias que podrían no tomar el experimento tan en serio como lo harían con un caso real. Entonces, si bien los experimentos evitan algunas de las limitaciones de la investigación empírica, vienen con limitaciones propias.

§24.05 CONCLUSIONES

Concluyo con algunos comentarios generales para el asociado de arbitraje sobre el uso de la investigación empírica:

- Los estudios empíricos pueden proporcionar información importante y útil sobre las prácticas del mundo real, yendo más allá de las meras anécdotas a datos más sistemáticos.
- Todos los estudios empíricos tienen limitaciones. Los buenos estudios empíricos identifican y discuten esas limitaciones.
- Tenga en cuenta la publicidad pop y la pseudociencia. No confíe solo en comunicados de prensa e informes de los medios sobre estudios empíricos. Dichos informes pueden ayudarlo a descubrir la existencia de investigaciones empíricas, pero no deberían ser la única fuente en la que confíe.
- No solo lea los resultados de un estudio empírico. Asegúrese de leer también la sección de metodología del estudio. No puede comprender lo que encontró el estudio sin comprender lo que hizo el estudio.

CAPÍTULO 25

Innovación disruptiva en el arbitraje

Mauricio Duarte

Si en la primera mitad de los noventa nos hubiesen preguntado sobre los posibles impactos del internet en el ejercicio del arbitraje, muchos de nosotros no habríamos podido responder a la pregunta. Ahora nos presentamos ante la misma pregunta, pero con tecnologías con una capacidad disruptiva aún mayor y con la capacidad de transformar completamente el mundo.

Aún recuerdo cuando mi profesor en las clases de "*Innovación Disruptiva*" y "*Codificación en Blockchain para Abogados*" afirmaba constantemente:

> "*Estamos viviendo la cuarta revolución industrial impulsada por los cambios acelerados de la tecnología. Ustedes serán testigos que el rol del abogado tradicional empezará a cambiar. El abogado deberá innovar y evolucionar con la tecnología*".

Era imposible no dedicarle la atención que ameritaba a un profesor graduado de la Universidad de Chicago, quien todos recocían como el catedrático que generaba debates en el Foro Económico Mundial con relación al impacto de*blockchain* en la Economía y el Derecho.

La curiosidad y complejidad del tema me llevó a indagar, inicialmente, sobre la tecnología conocida como "*blockchain*" y sus posibles impactos en el Derecho. Fue así como me encontré con mi primer libro sobre el tema, escrito por Dan Tapscott. En el libro encontré una frase fascinante:

> "*La primera generación de la revolución digital nos trajo el Internet de la información. La segunda generación, impulsada por la tecnología blockchain, nos trae el Internet de valor: una nueva plataforma para reformar el mundo de los negocios y transformar para siempre el viejo orden de los asuntos humanos*".[1]

1. Tapscott, D., & Tapscott, A. (2016). *Blockchain revolution: How the technology behind Bitcoin is changing money, business and the world.* Toronto: Portfolio/Penguin. Traducción Libre: "*The first generation of the digital revolution brought us the Internet of information. The second*

Esa afirmación me llevó a cuestionarme la forma en la que los abogados podemos evolucionar, paralelamente, con la tecnología.

Aún recuerdo mis días sentado frente a una computadora antes de escribir en mi blog individual de LinkedIn. Sin mayores plataformas para escribir, pasaba horas cuestionándome sobre la posible innovación disruptiva en el arbitraje. Al inicio, solo escribía pequeños artículos que compartía con unos cuantos conocidos. Llegaba al extremo de preguntarle a mi novia, con estudios en ingeniería eléctrica, si le gustaba el tema.

A pesar de unos comienzos humildes, en el proceso fui aprendiendo como la inteligencia artificial, los contratos inteligentes ("*smartcontracts*"), *blockchain* y los protocolos de ciberseguridad tienen el potencial de simplificar todas las fases del arbitraje.

Debo admitir que cada artículo no mayor a 1.000 palabras podría tomarme entre una a dos semanas. No obstante, entendí que no existe prisa para explorar nuevas ideas. La imaginación y creatividad, sin perder de vista los fundamentos técnicos (de la tecnología) y académicos (del arbitraje), me llevaron a explorar ideas inauditas (para algunos) e increíbles (para otros).

Debo reconocer, como todos, que no soy infalible y he sido criticado por las ideas sobre la relación entre el arbitraje y la tecnología. Aún recuerdo una conversación con un abogado quién me insistía que dejara de "*gastar mi tiempo en temas de ciencia ficción*". Otros colegas fueron enfáticos en mencionar que mis ideas no podían prosperar en el sistema arbitral actual. Claro, en ocasiones consideré dejar de escribir sobre tecnología y limitarme a criticar los reglamentos arbitrales existentes, la normativa arbitral en Guatemala, o algún laudo sobresaliente.

Sin embargo, ideas como: (1) el uso de *blockchain* para eficientizar los procesos de reconocimientos y ejecución de laudos de conformidad con la Convención de Nueva York[2]; y (2) el uso de mecanismos de criptoseguridad en arbitraje[3], eran nociones

generation -powered by blockchain technology- is bringing us the Internet of value: a new platform to reshape the world of business and transform the old order of human affairs for the better".

2. Uno de los objetivos centrales de la Convención de Nueva York era eliminar el "*doble exequátur*", lo que significaba que el laudo necesitaba el reconocimiento en lugar del arbitraje antes de que pudiera ser reconocido en otra jurisdicción. Antes, el reconocimiento y la ejecución de laudos arbitrales era difícil y poco confiable. La Convención de Nueva York eliminó el requisito de *doble exequátur*, con el objetivo de fomentar la eficiencia en el reconocimiento y ejecución de los laudos. Sin embargo ¿puede *blockchain*, la tecnología detrás de Bitcoin, proporcionar otra solución eficiente? *Blockchain*puede describirse como una plataforma digital distribuida e inmutable que almacena datos y registros, conocidos como bloques. Los bloques pueden almacenar diversos tipos de información. En el caso de Bitcoin, los bloques almacenan información sobre transacciones financieras. Estos bloques, que colectivamente forman una "cadena de bloques", se almacenan en varios nodos ("computadoras"), lo que garantiza que ninguna persona o entidad pueda manipular la plataforma digital. Una característica importante de *blockchain*, que la distingue de las tradicionales bases de datos, es la integridad y transparencia del sistema. En otras palabras, sería prácticamente imposible cambiar un dato o registro, pues sería necesario alterar los datos en todas las computadoras. Ahora, con *blockchain* es posible almacenar un laudo debidamente emitido en un procedimiento arbitral. Al tener la información en un protocolo de *blockchain*, la autoridad competente (i.e. juez) podría verificar la existencia del laudo y evitar costos adicionales, procedimientos judiciales y el método tradicional de reconocer los laudos. Ver másen: Duarte, M. (15 de marzo de 2018). *Could Blockchain Help the*

atractivas, apasionantes e interesantes. Finalmente tenía ideas que podía explorar junto con programadores de computación, "*geeks*" de la tecnología y futuristas[4].

A pesar de mi emoción, comprendí que los practicantes del Derecho, especialmente los practicantes del arbitraje, hemos sido renuentes a la incorporación de nuevas tecnologías en la práctica. Esto, pues históricamente los abogados solemos mantener una posición conservadora con respecto al ejercicio de la profesión. Además, la resistencia a la adopción de nuevas tecnologías persiste, en parte, por una preocupación profunda que la tecnología puede alterar el "rol" tradicional del abogado[5]. Por ejemplo, Dana Remus, profesora de la Facultad de Derecho de la Universidad de Carolina del Norte, realizó un estudio sobre la amenaza de la automatización digital en el trabajo de los abogados[6]. El informe concluía que la implementación de nuevas tecnologías daría lugar a una disminución del 13 por ciento en las horas facturables de los abogados.

Al vislumbrar que yo era parte del problema, pero también de la solución, empecé a impulsar mi visión de una relación mutuamente favorable entre el arbitraje y las nuevas tecnologías.

---

*Recognition of International Arbitration Awards?*Recuperado de: http://arbitrationblog.kluwerarbitration.com/2018/04/20/blockchain-help-recognition-international-arbitration-awards

3. El Instituto Nacional de Estándares y Tecnología de los Estados Unidos ("NIST") emitió un Marco para Mejorar la Seguridad Cibernética. El Marco definió objetivos de alto nivel de cualquier programa de gestión de riesgos de seguridad cibernética. Identificar, proteger, detectar, responder y recuperar son los cinco objetivos principales de cualquier programa exitoso de seguridad cibernética que se pueden adoptar y emular en el arbitraje internacional. En 2018, la ICCA, el Colegio de Abogados de Nueva York y el Instituto Internacional para la Prevención y Resolución de Conflictos publicaron un borrador del Protocolo de Ciberseguridad para el Arbitraje Internacional ("Protocolo de Ciberseguridad"). El Protocolo de Ciberseguridad se originó como un reconocimiento, de la comunidad arbitral, que los procedimientos de arbitraje no son inmunes a los ataques cibernéticos. Este primer esfuerzo enfatizó que la atención a la seguridad cibernética es necesaria y esencial para garantizar que el arbitraje internacional mantenga la confidencialidad del proceso. En una era digital, hay una variedad de factores a considerar al adoptar protocolos de seguridad para la transferencia de información sensible. Sin embargo, con el nuevo Protocolo de Ciberseguridad, las instituciones arbitrales y los árbitros tendrán pautas para Identificar, Proteger, Detectar, Responder y Recuperar datos ante cualquier clase de incidente de seguridad cibernética que surja en el transcurso de los procedimientos arbitrales. Ver más en: Duarte, M. (6 de febrero de 2019). *EssentialTipsonCybersecurityforArbitrators: Identify, Protect, Detect, Respond and Recover*. Recuperado de:http://arbitrationblog.kluwerarbitration.com/2019/02/06/essential-tips-on-cybersecurity-for-arbitrators-identify-protect-detect-respond-and-recover/
4. Duarte., M., (22 de noviembre de 2018). High Technology Arbitration, *Legal Business World*, Recuperado de: https://www.legalbusinessworld.com/single-post/2018/11/22/High-Technology-Arbitration
5. Jones, R., & Moore, R. (2013). *Information Technology and Traditional Legal Concepts*. London: Taylor and Francis.
6. Remus, Dana, Levy, & S., F. (2015, December 11). *Can Robots Be Lawyers? Computers, Lawyers, and the Practice of Law*. Recuperado de: https://papers.ssrn.com/sol3/Papers.cfm?abstract_id=2701092

§25.01 CONSEJOS DE "MILLENIAL"

Hoy en día, cualquier practicante interesado en la tecnología puede observar una docena de plataformas que buscan generar mecanismos digitales para la resolución de controversias. Por ejemplo, JUR[7], Jury Online[8], Confideal[9] y Kleros[10] buscan generar la automatización en la resolución de controversias en *Blockchain*.

Las nuevas tecnologías pueden mejorar la eficiencia, transparencia y reducir los costos en los procedimientos arbitrales. Sin embargo, el arbitraje debe innovar aún más y convertirse en un mecanismo confiable para resolver un nuevo tipo de disputas: todas las disputas relacionadas con un ecosistema digital.

Si son conscientes de los desafíos en el arbitraje, pero con la convicción de los beneficios de la tecnología para resolver muchos de los desafíos, les comparto algunos "*tips*" para formar parte de la generación "*millenial*" del mundo arbitral.

[A] #Curiosidad

Todo comienza con ser curioso, informado y crítico sobre las tendencias tecnológicas actuales. Un participante activo, debe involucrarse con la "doctrina" tecnológica. Hay que leer, estudiar, cuestionar y participar en temas tecnológicos para construir nuevas ideas.

En el mundo digital, una de las mejores fuentes de información son otras personas (especialmente técnicos de programación e ingenieros de software). Por ejemplo, discutir con colegas y desconocidos, que he contactado por medio de las redes sociales, ha impulsado mi conocimiento en temas de tecnología.

A todos los interesados, los invito a tener discusiones activas en Medium[11] con abogados, economistas y técnicos sobre las limitaciones de *blockchain* o la Inteligencia Artificial, utilizando un proceso creativo de discusión y aprendizaje.

[B] #DesarolloPráctico

Además de aprender y ser curioso, se necesita *"ejercitar"* el conocimiento con otras personas para desarrollar e implementar ideas en la práctica. Es decir, necesitamos "espacios" con otros profesionales para que la creatividad florezca.

Maniobrar en sociedad siempre ha sido esencial para todos los aspectos del trabajo y la vida. Pero ahora el enfoque está en establecer asociaciones "improbables" y colaboraciones multidisciplinarias que nos permitan crear y mejorar una idea. En una era digital, debemos trabajar con programadores de computación, *nerds*, economistas, matemáticos y otros profesionales para implementar ideas en un ecosistema digital.

7. https://jur.io/
8. https://jury.online/
9. https://confideal.io/
10. https://kleros.io/
11. https://medium.com/

Solo con un desarrollo práctico se puede obtener una “idea desarrollada” para implementar nuevos productos, servicios y estrategias.

[C] #SolucionesParaProblemasComplejos

El silogismo jurídico implica la resolución creativa de problemas con patrones de hechos altamente complejos. Ese proceso requiere pensamiento crítico, análisis y aplicación. Los abogados estamos capacitados para pensar con conceptos sofisticados, y esta es una habilidad importante para resolver los desafíos desconocidos del futuro.

Luego de tener una “idea desarollada” hay que buscar que la misma resuelva problemas altamente complejos. La diversidad en el nombramiento de árbitros, la transparencia de los procedimientos y la reducción de costos en los procesos arbitrales son temas “altamente complejos” que pueden resolverse, en parte, con la tecnología.

Por eso, el abogado es necesario para identificar problemas y adecuar las soluciones (legales) que son compatibles con las herramientas digitales. Es decir, los abogados seremos cruciales en “*dar forma a una nueva arquitectura global para la 4ta Revolución Industrial*” (para referirse al tema de 2019 en el Foro Económico Mundial). Piensen en soluciones a temas complejos. No se limiten a innovar comprando una nueva impresora EPSON 2019 para su despacho.

[D] #ConstrucciónyAplicación

No debemos tratar de predecir y prepararnos para el futuro. Debemos diseñarlo y construirlo. Sin embargo, primero debemos cambiar nuestra forma de pensar sobre el rol del abogado en el futuro.

Los abogados se convertirán en socios importantes para los desarrolladores y programadores de tecnología. Los abogados se convertirán en actores para la construcción de una arquitectura digital descentralizada.

A pesar de lo anterior, los abogados tendremos que aprender, informarnos y entender los fundamentos de la tecnología para construir e implementar soluciones digitales. Para este objetivo, el abogado no deberá trabajar solo. El abogado deberá trabajar con programadores, técnicos de software y especialistas en inteligencia artificial.

Por ejemplo, la oficina Clifford Chance[12] ha implementado la iniciativa *Tech Academy* para que los socios y asociados aprendan a utilizar Inteligencia Artificial, *blockchain* y contratos inteligentes. *TechAcademy* es la primera muestra que, a medida que la tecnología logre una adopción masiva, la demanda de servicios legales aumentará.

12. Cifford Chance. (2018), *Clifford Chance launches Tech Academy,* Recuperado de: https://www.cliffordchance.com/news/news/2018/04/clifford-chance-launches-tech-academy.html

[E] #Perseverancia

Cuando las personas hablan de los "millennials", muchos consideran que son parte de una generación que desea resultados inmediatos. Desafortunadamente, no es así cómo funciona el mundo. Los resultados no son inmediatos. No creo que ser un "millennial" esté relacionado con la edad o la ambición por resultados inmediatos. Ser "millennial" representa una mentalidad o actitud abierta a una era digital.

La perseverancia, junto con la capacidad de adaptarse, son las cualidades críticas que todos necesitamos para seguir siendo relevantes. Si una idea no funciona, es tiempo de pensar en otra. Si una solución tiene fallas, es tiempo de cuestionar el análisis. Reinventar nociones, ideas y soluciones no es sinónimo de fracaso. Está bien celebrar el éxito, pero es más importante prestar atención a las lecciones del fracaso.

Como abogados, indistintamente de la generación, debemos fomentar una cultura de libertad, autoexpresión y emprendimiento socialmente responsable con las herramientas que provee la tecnología. Solo necesitamos tener una mente abierta, ambiciosa y creativa.

[F] #PermanezcanAventureros

No sean complacientes con los procesos y procedimientos existentes. Muy a menudo, son los procedimientos preexistentes los que frenan la evolución de las industrias. Por ejemplo, Blockbuster desapareció al no innovar y considerar, erróneamente, que nadie estaría dispuesto a obtener su contenido digital de Netflix.

En el mismo sentido, los practicantes del arbitraje debemos pensar, crear e implementar ideas innovadoras para el arbitraje. Debemos ser el impulso para una nueva generación arbitral. Ser "millenial" y joven, crea un ímpetu de energía inigualable. Sin embargo, para adentrarnos en una nueva era, necesitamos más "millennials" de mente abierta, ambiciosos y creativos para generar innovaciones para el arbitraje.

[G] #SeanAuténticos

Todos los pasos descritos serán inútiles si no tienen una convicción personal sobre los posibles impactos de la tecnología en el arbitraje. Únicamente siendo auténticos podrán adquirir una pasión genuina por el tema. Esa pasión los llevará a expresarse y pensar creativamente. Muchas veces, recibo el comentario "*ahí viene el tipo blockchain*". Al principio, era en sentido de broma. Ahora, no es una simple broma, sino un adjetivo para alguien que está consciente que la tecnología es una realidad que nos pisa los talones.

§25.02 CONSTRUYAN EL FUTURO DIGITAL

Muchos de nosotros hemos escuchado el mismo regaño que utilizaba mi madre: "¡*Las tecnologías digitales distraen*! ¡*Estás matando tu privacidad*! ¡*La tecnología es adictiva*!

¡*Esas pantallas te van a dejar ciego*!". Sin embargo, la tecnología, como cualquier herramienta, puede ser útil si recapacitamos en los usos positivos que puede tener para resolver problemas complejos.

Estamos adentrándonos en una era digital que nos permite obedecer a nuestra curiosidad. Especialmente para todos los amantes del arbitraje, estamos ante la posibilidad de plantear y construir nuevas soluciones para preservar la excelencia del arbitraje. No obstante, para construir el futuro, debemos encontrar aquello por lo que realmente sentimos pasión.

No importa tanto a cuántas personas sigamos en Twitter, ni el número de seguidores que tengamos en Instagram. Para ser exitoso en un futuro digital, debemos cuestionar, innovar y construir las soluciones del futuro. Pensemos constantemente cómo mejorar el arbitraje (incluya o no a la tecnología). La mayoría de ideas emprendedoras, en su momento, sonaron precipitadas, estúpidas y poco rentables.

Si nosotros entendemos la tecnología, nos atreveremos a soñar. Nosotros seremos parte de la nueva generación que construirá el futuro.Recordemos que, en un futuro, los servicios legales tendrán que ser compatibles con el mundo digital.

A mí me interesa el futuro del arbitraje y espero que a ustedes también. El futuro del arbitraje le pertenece a todos los que estamos dispuestos a incorporar una "tradición de innovación". Veamos más allá de los problemas y construyamos el futuro. Una máquina automatizada puede hacer el trabajo de muchas personas, pero ninguna tecnología puede hacer el trabajo de personas extraordinarias dispuestas a construir nuevas ideas en beneficio del arbitraje.

HISTORIAS DE GUERRA Y LECCIONES SOBRE EL MERCADO DEL ARBITRAJE

CAPÍTULO 26

Preparando una entrevista de trabajo

Frank Ramos

¿Tienes una entrevista de trabajo? Felicidades. Muchos estudiantes de derecho y jóvenes abogados luchan por conseguir entrevistas. Si deseas más entrevistas, dedica tiempo a establecer contactos y a reunirte y desarrollar relaciones con quienes están en condiciones de contratar, o con aquellos que conocen a personas que pueden contratarte. El adagio "no importa qué sabes, sino a quién conoces" aplica a conseguir un trabajo. Y no tienes que venir de una familia con conexiones para conseguir un buen trabajo. Puedes hacer tus propios vínculos haciendo *networking* en asociaciones de abogados voluntarias o sin fines de lucro, donde podrías conocer a abogados que algún día pueden ser tu jefe.

Una vez que consigas la entrevista, haz lo siguiente:

- Estudia el sitio web de la oficina de abogados y los perfiles de los abogados con los que te encontrarás y posiblemente te reunirás.
- Estudia la misión, la visión y los valores de la empresa. Piensa cómo puedes apoyar la misión y la visión de la empresa y cómo tus valores reflejan los de la empresa.
- Revisa las publicaciones en redes sociales y la presencia en línea de la empresa.
- Investiga la empresa y lee todo lo que puedas sobre la empresa que es de dominio público.
- Vístete de manera conservadora y profesional.
- Trabaja en tu lenguaje corporal. Transmite confianza manteniendo contacto visual, mirando hacia arriba, teniendo una buena postura, estirando los hombros, dando un firme apretón de manos sostenido durante unos cuantos segundos, proyectando tu voz y ocupando espacio con tu cuerpo. Sé dueño de tu espacio.

- Comprueba tus nervios en la puerta. Las empresas no contratarán candidatos ansiosos. Sí, sé que necesitas el trabajo. Sí, realmente lo necesitas. Pero la desesperación tiene un aroma y es repelente. Ve a algunas entrevistas simuladas con abogados que conozcas o con otros profesionales que conozcas para que te sientas cómodo al sentarte con alguien y responder sus preguntas.
- Ten listas las respuestas a las preguntas comunes de la entrevista. ¿Por qué te convertiste en abogado? ¿Por qué quiere trabajar aquí? ¿Por qué quieres dejar tu trabajo actual? ¿Qué puedes hacer por nosotros? ¿Dónde te ves en 10 años? Hay docenas de preguntas de entrevista comunes. Prepárate con respuestas reflexivas.
- Prepárate para discutir cómo puedes servir a la empresa. La empresa te está entrevistando porque está evaluando si puedes ayudarlos, no si ellos pueden ayudarte a ti. Enfócate en cómo tus habilidades, intereses y pasiones pueden servir a la empresa y a sus objetivos.
- Presta atención a los diferentes estilos de entrevista. Algunos entrevistadores serán serios, otros intentarán ponerte a prueba y otros solo querrán pasar el rato. Sigue el ejemplo de la entrevistadora y comunícate con ella en sus términos.

El día de la entrevista:

- Llega temprano. Siempre puede esperar en tu automóvil si llegas demasiado temprano. Llegar tarde, incluso un minuto tarde, es imperdonable. El mal tráfico no es una excusa. No puedo decir cuántos candidatos han sido ignorados por llegar tarde.
- Lleva copias adicionales de tu currículum y muestras de escritura.
- Trata a todos con cortesía y respeto. Ya sea la recepcionista o un guardia de seguridad o un asistente legal, trata a todos de la misma manera que tratarías al socio gerente de la empresa.
- Mantén tus respuestas enfocadas y, cuando sea apropiado, breves.
- Escucha y contesta las preguntas formuladas.
- No hables mal de tu firma actual o de firmas anteriores.
- No hables mal de otros abogados o jueces.
- No muerdas el anzuelo para contar chismes.
- Todo lo que haces y dices, todo, está siendo observado, diseccionado y evaluado. Estás bajo un microscopio. Muestra tu mejor comportamiento en todo momento.
- Intenta programar entrevistas por la tarde para que no te preocupe volver a la oficina.
- No preguntes por el salario. Si están interesados, te devolverán la llamada y te informarán de qué se trata.
- A veces recibirás preguntas inapropiadas. Explica amablemente que no te sientes cómodo respondiendo la pregunta y cambia de tema.
- Si te reúnes con diferentes personas, es probable que recibas las mismas preguntas. Prepárate para dar las mismas respuestas varias veces.

Después de la entrevista, haz lo siguiente:

- Envía notas de agradecimiento escritas a mano a todos los que te entrevistaron.
- Espera, y si no escuchas nada, haz un seguimiento.
- Lavar, enjuagar y repetir. Sigue así hasta que encuentres el trabajo que deseas. La mejor de las suertes.

CAPÍTULO 27

Rankings de árbitros/litigantes: ¿importan?

Francisco Muñoz

Se me ha encargado la tarea de analizar si los diversos rankings y encuestas que observamos hoy en día sobre abogados practicantes de arbitraje y árbitros son útiles y si de verdad importan.

La realidad es que sí.

Los rankings y opiniones de revistas o publicaciones tienen relevancia en la actividad profesional tanto a la hora de captar clientes para ser abogado de parte como a la hora de ser designado como árbitro en un caso.

Para abordar este tema, haremos unas precisiones preliminares. En primer lugar, hablaremos de los rankings y opiniones de publicaciones de carácter internacional, de cierto renombre y credibilidad. En segundo lugar, analizaremos la importancia de estos rankings tanto para actividades académicas como para actividades profesionales. Finalmente, las explicaciones las daremos desde una faz empírica, aunque sin poder contar con datos estadísticos de cuál es el nivel real de influencia en los resultados mencionados.

Efectuadas las mentadas precisiones, consideramos que la utilidad de estos rankings es cierta, aunque no necesariamente imprescindible para el ejercicio académico o práctico de la profesión.

La carrera y el éxito de un abogado, dentro de cualquier rama o profesión, pero más especialmente en el arbitraje, deben nutrirse principalmente de la seriedad, conducta, rigurosidad y comportamiento del abogado. La credibilidad del abogado/árbitro juega un rol preponderante. Los rankings no necesariamente son el reflejo de ello.

§27.01 LOS RANKINGS MÁS RELEVANTES EN EL ARBITRAJE INTERNACIONAL

Las revistas y publicaciones especializadas han creado diversos rankings o secciones de opinión sobre abogados practicantes del arbitraje, árbitros y despachos de abogados que participan en esta área.

A modo de ejemplo pueden nombrarse diversos rankings, a saber: (1) Global Arbitration Review (GAR)[1]; (2) The Legal 500 Arbitration[2]; y (3) secciones de Chambers & Partners de Resolución de Disputas y Arbitraje[3], entre otros.

Los rankings de estas prestigiosas publicaciones se caracterizan por contar con la opinión de especialistas en el área y clientes seleccionados. Es decir, los rankings no se sustentan solamente en apreciaciones personales o modalidades de pago. El trabajo que realizan los editores de las publicaciones es esencial para la credibilidad de estos rankings.

Los editores contactan a especialistas o referentes en el área para conocer acerca de los *rankeados* o potenciales *rankeados*. Además, los editores investigan a los seleccionados y consultan con los principales clientes referidos por el estudio jurídico, para saber cómo es el comportamiento del candidato.

Las clasificaciones de los abogados se realizan considerando el arbitraje de manera genérica, aunque algunas publicaciones clasifican a los profesionales de acuerdo a la materia, ya sea arbitraje comercial o de inversión (incluso, algunos se dividen por industrias específicas) y también a sus cualidades como abogado de parte o como árbitro. Estos rankings más especializados -como el de GAR-permiten obtener información con mayor precisión respecto de la calidad del profesional y su verdadera área de experiencia.

Asimismo, estas publicaciones también evalúan y *rankean* a los distintos despachos jurídicos realizando, en su mayoría, una clasificación por “bandas”. Los despachos jurídicos más destacados, por la magnitud de los casos y los profesionales que los integran parte, estarán clasificados como “banda 1” y así sucesivamente, por lo general hasta la banda 4.

Como ya se adelantó, la credibilidad de estas publicaciones está dada principalmente por el trabajo de investigación que realizan. Ya que, pese a iniciarse en muchas ocasiones por la postulación directa o a través del estudio jurídico, si una persona no cuenta con los méritos como para ser seleccionada, no termina siendo *rankeada*.

En consecuencia, el prestigio de la publicación garantiza la fidelidad de los datos. El prestigio de la publicación se mantiene con la investigación que realizan los editores, que se focaliza en la experiencia de la persona clasificada durante el año, según sus pares y clientes. Esto permitiría considerar que el resultado sería imparcial.

1. https://globalarbitrationreview.com/
2. https://www.legal500.com/
3. https://chambers.com/

§27.02 ¿EXISTEN REALMENTE BENEFICIOS POR ESTAR RANKEADO?

Explicado que fuera brevemente cómo funcionan los rankings más prestigiosos, corresponde analizar cuáles son los beneficios, si es que existen, que se desprenden de los mismos.

Partimos de la base de que el estar *rankeado* importa porque trae más beneficios que costos para los abogados que forman parte de esos rankings. Además, los rankings también son beneficiosos para compañías en búsqueda de abogados o árbitros.

[A] Los profesionales son tal vez los principales beneficiados de estar *rankeados* en prestigiosas publicaciones

Tanto los abogados de parte como los árbitros *rankeados* obtienen grandes beneficios por estar presente en estos rankings.

A nuestro entender, los principales beneficiados son los asociados o socios jóvenes, y los árbitros que dan sus primeros pasos como tales. Lo anterior, ya que los rankings les permiten ser más conocidos. Los socios de renombre y los árbitros con experiencia generalmente no obtienen grandes beneficios ya que cuentan con un nombre propio y reputación que hace que sean conocidos de por sí en el mercado.

Consideramos que los beneficios que trae aparejados estar *rankeado* son: (1) el prestigio académico; (2) el reconocimiento profesional; y (3) el conocimiento que puede adquirir un potencial cliente.

En primer lugar, mencionamos el prestigio académico como beneficio para el *rankeado*. Ello, porque el abogado que está incluido en el ranking generalmente es considerado como un especialista en la materia, con sólidos conocimientos del arbitraje.

Esto hace que el *rankeado* eleve su perfil académico, y se le abra la posibilidad de participar como orador en cursos, congresos o eventos. Asimismo, le brinda al *rankeado* contactos y oportunidades académicas de distinto tipo. Los organizadores de eventos o directores de carreras o libros buscan esta clase de perfiles para que participen en las actividades a organizarse.

En segundo lugar, el *rankeado* se ve beneficiado por el reconocimiento profesional que trae aparejado estar nombrado en esta clase de publicaciones. El reconocimiento profesional de los pares y de los clientes que lo eligieron demuestra las bondades como abogado o árbitro de la persona *rankeada* y hace a la solvencia del profesional.

En tercer lugar, el *rankeado* se ve beneficiado por la "publicidad" que trae el ranking. Es sabido que potenciales clientes, en particular grandes compañías o multinacionales, tienden a observar los rankings más prestigiosos para tener un conocimiento previo de los potenciales abogados a contratar o árbitros a seleccionar.

[B] Los rankings también benefician a clientes

En primer lugar, el ranking, en estos casos, sirve muchas veces como carta de presentación de los abogados. Potenciales clientes pueden ver cuál es la opinión de los pares, colegas o qué tipo de clientes asesora. También pueden ver en qué tipo de casos usualmente participa. Finalmente, los clientes pueden buscar, a través de estos rankings, abogados en países donde tal vez no tengan gran experiencia o contactos.

Todo ello con la finalidad de saber si es conveniente contratar a un determinado profesional y si dicho profesional será el adecuado para asistirlos.

En segundo lugar, el ranking le es útil a los clientes para conocer qué clase de árbitro podrán llegar a nombrar o bien quién es el árbitro que ya está entendiendo un caso del cual son parte. La experiencia, los casos en los que participó y el conocimiento que tiene, son fundamentales a la hora de nombrar a un árbitro.

Los rankings permiten darse cuenta de si un árbitro está muy atareado o si verdaderamente está con tiempo suficiente para dedicarle al caso concreto. Ello ya que en los rankings generalmente figuran los últimos casos o temas en los que participó.

§27.03 COROLARIO

A modo de síntesis, creemos que los rankings son una buena herramienta para los asociados y socios jóvenes, como así también para los árbitros que recién comienzan como tales. Los rankings son útiles como publicidad ya que demuestran lo destacado de las personas incluidas. Los rankings traen como beneficio el nombramiento en actividades académicas, como abogado de parte y como árbitro. Existe una relación bastante probada entre los nuevos nombramientos como abogados de parte o árbitros y la figuración en los rankings.

Los abogados y árbitros de renombre, que en su gran mayoría figuran en esos rankings, no obtienen grandes beneficios por figurar en los mismos, ya que son conocidos tanto por clientes como por organizaciones y despachos de abogados. Con lo cual, son nombrados por su peso propio.

CAPÍTULO 28

Eventos: cuándo, dónde, cómo y por qué

Félix Antolín

Ciertamente la vida de los asociados jóvenes que se dedican al arbitraje internacional no es nada de fácil, y transcurre la mayor parte del tiempo *dentro* de las oficinas en que trabajan. Desde análisis de *case law*, fotocopias y redacción de memoriales, las tareas son variadas y a los practicantes jóvenes nos toca aprender, aunque sea a la fuerza, cómo desarrollar habilidades de *multitasking* exitoso sin morir en el intento.

Sin embargo, a los asociados que están iniciando su camino nadie les explica que existe un mundo *fuera* de sus oficinas, y que, más temprano que tarde, salir a ese mundo se convierte en una tarea indispensable para avanzar en el camino del arbitraje internacional. Es justamente aquí donde es necesario detenerse a observar el fenómeno de los *eventos*.

Los eventos en la industria legal corresponden a una figura compleja y de múltiples variables. Si estuviéramos hablando del reino animal, los eventos serían como un ornitorrinco, porque tienen partes y funcionalidades de distintos animales, sin contar con una característica realmente propia y definida. En otras palabras, los eventos pueden moldearse a gusto del consumidor, y en consecuencia es clave conocer qué objetivos pretendemos cumplir participando en un evento. Esta breve contribución pretende ser una guía que permita a los jóvenes practicantes dominar los eventos de arbitraje internacional para obtener de ellos lo que fueron a buscar, y no asistir como meros espectadores o pasajeros.

§28.01 ¿CUÁNDO ASISTIR A EVENTOS?

Esta pregunta, para ser respondida cabalmente, debe mirarse desde dos perspectivas: primero, en qué momento de la carrera profesional es conveniente asistir a eventos; y segundo, en qué oportunidades o períodos de un año calendario debería elegirse participar en ellos.

Con respecto a lo primero, y como en todas las cosas, lo mejor es aprender desde pequeño. Sin duda que el roce y la exposición temprana a los eventos permitirá ir progresivamente obteniendo más beneficios de ellos. En este sentido, y aunque parezca contra intuitivo para las oficinas de abogados, la inversión en enviar a sus practicantes jóvenes a eventos les traerá mayores retornos futuros que mandar por primera vez a asociados que, por años, no han salido de sus despachos. Como veremos más adelante, un factor esencial para enriquecerse de los eventos es la constancia en la participación. En todo caso, esta circunstancia de ninguna manera impide que asociados de mayor experiencia comiencen a participar en eventos, no solo por el valor agregado que igualmente pueden obtener, sino porque además estos pueden plantearse objetivos diversos, como tomarse un *break* del trabajo cotidiano para refrescar y afinar sus habilidades y conocimientos ("*Sharpen the Saw*").[1]

En cuanto a lo segundo, si bien no es posible definir exactamente en qué momentos del año es más conveniente asistir a eventos, sí existen ciertas pautas a tener en consideración. Un buen criterio es estar mirando el mercado, para definir a qué conferencias están asistiendo las personas con quien se pretende interactuar. Otro parámetro es elegir rangos de fechas en que varios eventos, o una conferencia grande y diversos *sid eevents*, están ocurriendo simultáneamente en el mismo lugar. De esta manera es posible maximizar los recursos que implica asistir a un evento y así hacerlo más rentable a los ojos propios y, especialmente, de los jefes.

§28.02 ¿DÓNDE ASISTIR A EVENTOS?

El lugar en que los distintos eventos ocurren claramente es relevante desde varias perspectivas. Por un lado, la zona geográfica en que se encuentre la ciudad del evento respectivo debe ser considerada en atención a las áreas de influencia que tiene, o busca tener, la oficina de abogados en que el practicante trabaja. En otras palabras, por más que un evento en Sofía, Rumania, suene muy interesante, lo cierto es que no tiene tanto sentido asistir desde una oficina de abogados en Bogotá, cuya cartera de clientes es mayormente latinoamericana. Por otro lado, las consideraciones logísticas también son muy importantes a la hora de elegir eventos. No parece buena idea, por ejemplo, emprender un viaje de más de cuarenta y ocho horas a una ciudad, con tres escalas, para asistir a un evento cuya duración no excede de una mañana.

Finalmente en este punto, la importancia que una determinada ciudad tiene para el arbitraje internacional, ya sea como sede o desde el punto de vista de los practicantes que allí ejercen, también puede hacer atractivo asistir a eventos allí[2]. No debemos olvidar que un evento no solo tiene valor en sí mismo, sino que también en cuanto a las distintas actividades que puedan desarrollarse en torno a este. Volveremos sobre esta idea más adelante.

1. *12 reasons you should attend conferences* (Mayo 28, 2020).
2. Así por ejemplo, la Cámara de Comercio Internacional destaca la relevancia de la ciudad de Miami en el material promocional relativo a la *ICC Miami Conferenceon International Arbitration*: https://iccwbo.org/media-wall/news-speeches/12-highlights-to-get-geared-up-for-icc-miami-conference/.

§28.03 ¿CÓMO ASISTIR A EVENTOS?

Esta pregunta dice relación con dos tópicos prácticos muy relevantes: financiamiento para asistir a un evento, y la preparación previa al mismo. En lo que respecta al financiamiento, es innegable que el apoyo de las oficinas a sus asociados es importante. Sin embargo, es tarea de los practicantes jóvenes explicar -o derechamente *persuadir*- a sus jefes de las bondades y beneficios que su participación en un determinado evento traerá a su oficina. Usualmente un plan coherente y responsable, en línea con la práctica de arbitraje que tenga la oficina, permitirá a los practicantes jóvenes abrir puertas en este sentido. Adicionalmente, el financiamiento por parte de las oficinas no es la única opción para asistir a un evento. Varias conferencias cuentan con becas para abogados jóvenes que pueden ser atractivas y, en último término, una inversión directa del practicante puede tener externalidades positivas, como demostrar internamente en su oficina la determinación e interés que tiene por desarrollar su carrera.

En lo relativo a la preparación para un evento, se trata este de un elemento que los practicantes jóvenes no pueden dejar al azar. Asistir a una conferencia sin preparación puede incluso asemejarse a simplemente no haber asistido. Para estos efectos, es muy relevante revisar la lista de *attendees* correspondiente al evento (no tengan miedo de pedirla si no se ha publicado) y contactar previamente a practicantes con quienes puede ser útil reunirse o conocer. Siempre debemos recordar que los demás asistentes a un evento probablemente estén haciendo lo mismo, y no se van a sorprender ni molestar si un desconocido les envía un correo electrónico. En el mismo sentido, también es útil contactar a oficinas de abogados que se encuentren en la ciudad del evento para agendar reuniones, aun cuando dichos abogados no asistan al evento en cuestión. El tiempo es oro y, mientras más se pueda aprovechar el viaje, mejor. Con esta finalidad, mi sugerencia es informar en las respectivas oficinas que se participará en un determinado evento, para obtener *feedback* y datos de los demás abogados que trabajan en ella -lo que, además, siempre genera publicidad interna útil. Por último sobre el particular, es conveniente también tener disponible material promocional de la oficina en que se trabaja (hoy en formato digital es más que suficiente) y, lo más importante, ¡nunca pero nunca olvidar llevar tarjetas de presentación!

§28.04 ¿POR QUÉ ASISTIR A EVENTOS?

Guardando lo mejor para el final, llegamos posiblemente a la pregunta más importante de todas: qué razones o motivos justifican asistir a un evento de arbitraje internacional.

Lo cierto es que existen múltiples razones para asistir a un evento. En la industria legal comúnmente se plantean una serie de beneficios generales que pueden obtenerse de los eventos, así como de utilidades y ganancias específicas que determinados eventos otorgan, dentro de ciertas áreas de la práctica jurídica. Por ejemplo, en el mundo de la Propiedad Intelectual la conferencia anual de la Asociación Internacional de Marcas (INTA, por su sigla en inglés) es masiva y concita la atención de casi toda la industria. En este sentido, se realizó una encuesta respecto a esta conferencia en específico. Un noventa y cinco por ciento de los encuestados señaló que era "*muy probable*" que durante la conferencia tendría reuniones con clientes o contactos conocidos. Un ochenta y uno por ciento indicó que era "*muy probable*" que en la conferencia sostendría reuniones con potenciales clientes o contactos. Finalmente, un ochenta y siente afirmó que era "*muy probable*" que asistiría a recepciones y reuniones sociales organizadas por oficinas de abogados y empresas.[3] Asimismo, los beneficios comúnmente reportados en distintas publicaciones dicen relación con el "*networking*"[4] con la posibilidad de tener acceso a expertos en los campos sobre que trata la respectiva conferencia;[5] adquirir conocimiento sobre los últimos avances tecnológicos en la materia objeto del evento;[6] y derechamente pasar un buen rato.[7]

En este sentido, los eventos que se ofrecen en la industria del arbitraje internacional también comparten los beneficios arriba señalados, aunque con ciertas particularidades. En primer lugar, en los eventos de esta práctica la relación abogado-cliente es mucho más escasa. Salvo contadas excepciones[8], ir a buscar clientes a un evento de arbitraje internacional puede ser un error. La participación de los *in-house counsel* en estas instancias no solo es infrecuente, sino que, además, cuando asisten tienen roles protagónicos (como panelistas por ejemplo), siendo difícilmente alcanzables por asociados jóvenes. En este sentido, la atracción de clientes sí puede producirse de manera indirecta, por la visibilidad que las oficinas de abogados ganan participando en los eventos.

En segundo lugar, por el contrario, los eventos de arbitraje internacional son una gran oportunidad para la reunión de abogados con distintos prestadores de servicios y actores que, no siendo necesariamente abogados, juegan un papel esencial en los procedimientos arbitrales. Me refiero, entre otros, a *court reporters*, estenógrafos y especialmente a expertos. Es muy frecuente ver la participación de peritos, pertenecientes a distintas industrias, en conferencias de arbitraje internacional. En estos casos son ellos quienes están vendiendo sus servicios, y los asociados pueden volver a casa con interesantes datos de profesionales que pueden ser extremadamente útiles para la presentación de sus casos, por ejemplo, elaborando informes de daños o similares.

En tercer lugar, las conferencias de arbitraje internacional también pueden ser instancias sumamente útiles para adquirir conocimientos y estar al día en las últimas tendencias y prácticas de la industria. Debemos recordar que, a pesar de ser

3. Michael Loney, *Survey: the truth about conferences* (Mayo 28, 2020), http://www.managingip.com/Article/3719378/Survey-The-truth-about-conferences.html.
4. *So ... why do you attend the IBA Conference?* (Mayo 28, 2020), https://www.tamimi.com/law-update-articles/so-why-do-you-attend-the-iba-conference/.
5. Lisa Pansini, *5 benefits of attending legal conferences* (Mayo 28, 2020), https://www.rocketmatter.com/general/5-benefits-attending-legal-conference-infographic/.
6. *5 reasons why every attorney should attend legal conferences* (May 28, 2020), https://www.google.com/amp/s/www.practicepanther.com/blog/top-five-reasons-every-attorney-attend-legal-conferences/.
7. Michael Loney, *Survey: the truth about conferences* (Mayo 28, 2020), https://www.takeflyte.com/reasons-to-attend-conferences#.
8. Como las conferencias organizadas por el *CorporateCounsel International ArbitrationGroup*.

fuertemente globalizada, la comunidad de arbitraje internacional sigue siendo relativamente pequeña, lo que ayuda a la participación constante de los *big players* en distintas conferencias, otorgando importantes oportunidades de aprendizaje.

Por último, y sin pretender realizar una enumeración exhaustiva (seguramente a otros practicantes más avezados se le deben venir a la cabeza otras ventajas no mencionadas aquí), los eventos de arbitraje internacional, en general, convocan a practicantes diversos y de distintas generaciones. Es así como, en una misma conferencia, conviven los principales litigantes y árbitros que hoy lideran la industria, con jóvenes asociados que probablemente "llevarán la batuta" el día de mañana. Esta circunstancia presenta una oportunidad única, porque permite a los practicantes que se están iniciando a desarrollar relaciones de largo plazo con sus *pares*. En efecto, en mi experiencia, la búsqueda de brillar frente a un abogado consolidado en un evento suele ser bastante difícil, y en ocasiones hasta inútil, porque el joven y el experimentado, en todo orden de cosas, suelen no compartir los mismos objetivos ni intereses. Al contrario, la confluencia de jóvenes de distintos lugares y *backgrounds*, pero con objetivos similares, permite a los asociados relacionarse entre ellos y tender redes que les serán extremadamente útiles hoy y sobre todo a futuro, además de forjar lindas amistades que perduran en el tiempo.

Así las cosas, y luego de haber intentado explicar las principales pautas para poder navegar en el mundo de los eventos con cierta eficacia, me gustaría cerrar esta contribución con un recordatorio a los asociados y practicantes jóvenes del arbitraje internacional. Al final del día, lo más relevante al momento de asistir a una conferencia o evento similar, dice relación con saber de antemano cuáles son los objetivos que se quieren lograr con dicha participación a corto, mediano y largo plazo, a fin de intentar ejecutar ese plan y ser uno mismo quien pueda moldear el evento a sus necesidades. Con tiempo, paciencia y motivación, cada uno sabrá exactamente cuándo, dónde, cómo y por qué debe participar en un evento de arbitraje internacional.

CAPÍTULO 29

El caos de la Covid Tocando a mi Puerta

Rachel Ong Yue Qing

Esta es mi historia de guerra sobre cómo una pandemia de salud global irrumpió mi planeamiento del Columbia Arbitration Day (CAD). CAD es la conferencia internacional anual de arbitraje internacional de la Facultad de Derecho de Columbia. Como un evento emblemático de la universidad, y definitivamente una conferencia de arbitraje de primera, a través de los años ha reunido con éxito a académicos, profesionales y estudiantes de distintas jurisdicciones para participar en debates enérgicos sobre los desafíos que enfrenta la comunidad internacional de arbitraje. Para septiembre del 2019, este año no parecía muy distinto y el comité de planificación tenía grandes esperanzas para la conferencia. De hecho, incluso decidimos cubrir más terreno al aumentar el número de mesas redondas.

Como una de las co-presidentas, me encargaron armar un panel de discusión sobre resolución de disputas que surgió de la iniciativa One Belt One Road (OBOR). Naturalmente, los practicantes en Hong Kong y China, que estaban familiarizados con la jurisdicción, fueron los principales candidatos para esta discusión A mediados de enero, habíamos asegurado la asistencia de nuestros oradores. Me las arreglé para asegurar la asistencia de algunos oradores de China, un socio en Beijing que solía ser subdirector de la Comisión de Arbitraje Comercial y Económico Internacional de China (CIETAC) antes de pasar a la práctica privada, y otro que se desempeñó como juez en China, entre otros. En Hong Kong, logré asegurar a un expositor que solía servir como Secretario General de una importante institución de arbitraje y actualmente trabaja como árbitro independiente y es miembro de la Comisión de OBOR. En Nueva York, aseguramos la asistencia de un profesor de derecho especializado en jurisdicciones CIS que podría proporcionar una perspectiva única y, en Londres, confirmamos la asistencia del moderador que había participado en múltiples paneles de discusión sobre One Belt and Road Initiative. En este punto, las perspectivas parecían prometedoras y optimistas. Por desgracia, todo estaba a punto de ir cuesta abajo desde allí.

En algún momento de inicios de enero, escuché informes de noticias de una nueva y misteriosa cepa de coronavirus que emanaba de Wuhan y la provincia de Hubei en China que ya había llegado a las costas de Hong Kong, Taiwán y Singapur. Como muchos otros en ese momento, no pensé que tendría un impacto significativo en los Estados Unidos, mucho menos en una conerencia universitaria, y creí que este virus estaría limitado por la geografía. Aproximadamente una semana después, recibí noticias de que el gobierno chino había cerrado la provincia de Hubei para que nadie pudiera entrar y nadie pudiera irse. Los aeropuertos, trenes y carreteras fueron cerrados y fuertemente vigilados para garantizar que nadie se fuera. Medidas tan draconianas atrajeron igual número de alabos y críticas. Sin embargo, yo seguía pensando que la pandemia no tendría impacto alguno en CAD, ya que los oradores que había convocado estaban ubicados en la capital relativamente indemne de Beijing. Sin embargo, varios medios noticiosos comenzaron a informar el impacto inmediato de la Covid-19, como un sistema de salud sobrecargado y desmoronado y largas filas de colas fuera de los hospitales por personas que esperan recibir tratamiento. Los gobiernos de todo el mundo estaban alquilando vuelos para transportar a sus ciudadanos fuera de la ciudad cerrada de Wuhan. Menos de diez días después, el gobierno de Trump, el 31 de enero de 2020, anunció que los extranjeros que habían estado en China continental (excluyendo Hong Kong y Macao) durante los últimos catorce días no podrían ingresar a los EE. UU. Esta prohibición dio un golpe devastador al panel OBOR ya que a la mitad de nuestros oradores no se les permitiría ingresar a los EE. UU.

Los propios expositores afectados no estaban estaban seguros de cuándo se levantaría la prohibición de viajar y qué tan prolongado sería el caos de la Covid-19. Me encontraba en un dilema pues era difícil determinar si la prohibición se levantaría a fines de febrero, de modo que los tres oradores pudieran participar en CAD o si debería comenzar a buscar presentadores fuera de China. Si comenzábamos a buscar participantes fuera de China y la prohibición de viajar se levantaba antes de CAD, podríamos tener un panel de ocho a nueve personas. A medida que pasaban los días, quedó claro que la Covid-19 se estaba extendiendo cada vez más con el cierre de varias ciudades de China y la fuerza laboral que trabajaba desde casa. Otros países cercanos como Singapur y Hong Kong estaban intensificando las medidas y el pánico público se extendía por estos países. Se hizo evidente que la esperanza de que la prohibición de viaje se levantara parecía más idealista que realista.

En este punto, el comité de planificación tuvo que decidir si deberíamos buscar oradores ubicados fuera de China y que también pudieran discutir este tema, o elegir el panel por completo. Si elegíamos la primera opción, ¿íbamos a poner una fecha límite a esta búsqueda? ¿Sería prudente continuar invitando a oradores de Asia a la luz de la prohibición? Si no podíamos llenar el panel antes de la fecha límite, ¿íbamos a reasignar a nuestros tres presentadores restantes en los otros paneles? Si es así, necesitarían tiempo para prepararse para discutir otro tema. Estas fueron algunas de las consideraciones que pasaron por mi mente.

Se decidió que ya no esperaríamos un levantamiento de la prohibición de viajar, y comenzaríamos a buscar oradores fuera de China que también pudieran discutir este tema. Me di una fecha límite de mediados de febrero y todos los plazos se aceleraron a partir de entonces. Si bien los oradores generalmente tendrían dos semanas para responder antes de que les enviáramos un correo electrónico cortés de recordatorio, los oradores potenciales ahora solo tendrían dos días para responder. Durante estas dos semanas, recibimos un puñado de rechazos por varias razones, pero también logramos asegurar la asistencia de dos presentadores con base en Nueva York. A mediados de febrero, se restableció el equilibrio en el panel OBOR y CAD se estaba reafirmando. Se anunciaron volantes de LinkedIn de los respectivos paneles, se diseñó el folleto, se imprimió nuestro horario CAD confirmado, se vendieron boletos, se confirmaron los menús de almuerzo y recepción nocturna.

Sin embargo, esta calma fue de corta duración y, mientras tanto, Covid-19 arrasó Asia y Europa. En este momento, varios eventos importantes de arbitraje internacional se pospusieron y las firmas de abogados emitieron advertencias contra viajes no esenciales. Una semana antes de CAD, mi oradora con sede en Hong Kong escribió para preguntar si la Universidad tenía alguna inquietud con respecto a su asistencia a CAD, ya que quería ser sensible a los sentimientos de los asistentes hacia un orador que venía de una región afectada por Covid-19. En este momento, algunos de mis otros colegas en el comité de planificación estaban recibiendo consultas de los oradores con sede en Europa en sus respectivos paneles sobre si CAD todavía seguía en pie, mientras que otros recibían un aviso de profesionales que, después de sopesar los pros y los contras de viajar, decidieron que no asistirían a CAD. En este momento, la Universidad que estaba al tanto del próximo CAD no expresó ninguna inquietud sobre el evento y consideramos que el CAD procedería según lo planeado. El comité de planificación procedió a confirmar el evento por correo electrónico con todos los oradores involucrados. A lo largo de la semana, hubo una considerable cantidad de movimiento y reorganización en casi todos los cinco paneles restantes, pero ya habíamos previsto esto y, por lo tanto, estábamos mentalmente preparados para que la configuración de los paneles cambiara inevitablemente. La semana de CAD también fue muy ocupada ya que la Asociación Internacional de Arbitraje de Columbia (CIAA) anunciaría CAD en la Facultad. Nos las arreglamos para conseguir una pequeña mesa en el vestíbulo de la Facultad de Derecho y presentar nuestro horario CAD que incluía a todos los oradores confirmados. Los miembros de la junta de la CIAA se turnaban para ocupar la mesa y anunciar CAD al cuerpo estudiantil.

En la mañana del 3 de marzo (tres días antes del evento), la Decana de Servicios Estudiantiles informó verbalmente a los organizadores que la expositora de Hong Kong no podría hablar en el campus, y mucho menos asistir. Aparentemente, se nos comunicó que cualquier persona que llegara de China (incluyendo Hong Kong), Corea del Sur e Italia no estaría permitida en la universidad. Inmediatamente le escribí a la Decana de Servicios Estudiantiles para solicitar una reunión, solo para recibir una respuesta indicando que su primer espacio disponible era el jueves, un día antes de CAD. Dado que la expositora en cuestión estaba a punto de abordar un vuelo de veinte horas en menos de veiticuatro horas, sentí que era justo compartir el último desarrollo con ella. Dada la patente incertidumbre en ese momento, acordamos que no sería sensato viajar una distancia tan sustancial hasta Nueva York solo para que no se le permita ingresar al evento. Solo puedo seguir agradecido de que ella fuera tan comprensiva y amable en esas circunstancias. Sin embargo, yo no estaba lista para excluir su participación por completo, ya que tenía una visión invaluable sobre el tema y su exclusión habría interrumpido el flujo acordado de la discusión. La siguiente opción era lograr que ingrese por Skype en la discusión. Sin embargo, una decepción llevó a otra, y el equipo de IT me informó que no habría un lugar disponible con el equipo apropiado para soportar videoconferencias.

Llamé a los oradores restantes a la mañana siguiente para explicar lo que había sucedido y buscar su opinión sobre si confiaban en llevar la discusión por su cuenta. Sin embargo, fue casi unánime que el panel de discusión se veía gravemente perjudicado sin la participación de nuestra oradora con sede en Hong Kong. También salió a la luz que otro orador con sede en Nueva York acababa de regresar de Singapur esa misma mañana y se había topado con una nueva política firme de autocuarentena, lo que también significaba que no podría asistir a CAD. Esta última noticia dio el golpe mortal al panel. No era posible que la mesa de discusión continuara con solo tres oradores, y tampoco era factible asegurar la asistencia de presentadores de reemplazo dos días antes del CAD. Finalmente, se tomó la dolorosa decisión de cancelarlo.

Hasta hoy, estoy segura de que las preguntas relacionadas con la resolución de disputas que surgen de One Belt One Road siguen siendo un tema emocionante que vale la pena discutir. Mientras que los economistas han acogido con beneplácito la iniciativa One Belt One Road como un paso importante hacia el crecimiento del comercio mundial y los politólogos lo ven como una sólida ancla contra el sentimiento antiglobalización, los miembros de la profesión legal se han mostrado más dubitativos, reflexionando sobre la capacidad de la ley en todos los niveles, nacional, transnacional e internacional, para facilitar la resolución de disputas comerciales entre empresas que puedan surgir en el curso de la implementación de la iniciativa OBOR. ¿Qué opciones de resolución de disputas tienen las partes contratantes cuando sus transacciones transfronterizas se vuelven agrias? ¿Y cuál de estas opciones garantiza mejor que la parte ganadora recupere su dinero?

De hecho, es irónico que la razón detrás de los cambios de último minuto en el panel OBOR haya hecho que esta discusión sea aún más relevante. La Covid-19 ha acuñado un nuevo término: "Ruta de la Seda de la Salud", que es una extensión de la iniciativa de comercio e infraestructura One Belt and Road. Se ha informado ampliamente que China ha estado extendiendo la ayuda médica a múltiples países europeos, incluyendo Italia, España, Francia, Bulgaria y Eslovenia. Con el entrelazamiento de la economía global y una mayor cooperación con China por un número cada vez mayor de países, One Belt One Road adquiere una dimensión ampliada y las características de resolución de disputas se destacan aún más.

CAPÍTULO 30

Sobreviviendo conversaciones difíciles: ¿Cómo asociarte a una firma y formar una familia sin morir en el intento?

Daniel Cuentas

A veces tu vida personal y tu vida laboral se mueven en frecuencias diferentes. Es común que aspectos familiares o personales rocen o hasta colisionen con obligaciones laborales. Para resolver este percance es posible que debas recurrir a conversaciones difíciles.

Puede pasar que tus gastos personales se hayan incrementado y requieras un aumento. O quizás necesites más tiempo para dedicarte a proyectos extralaborales y requieras de un cambio en las condiciones de tu trabajo e incluso un nuevo trabajo. Quizás simplemente necesitas de un permiso o tiempo libre. Estas situaciones representan ejemplos cotidianos que te llevan a tener una conversación difícil.

En mi caso, tras trabajar mucho tiempo en una institución arbitral, mi vida profesional necesitaba un cambio. Luego de una ronda de negociaciones mi incorporación a una firma de abogados era inminente. Acto seguido, tenía que presentar mi renuncia en el centro de arbitraje. Sabía que ello impactaría en la carga de trabajo de mis colegas y que dejaría de formar parte de los planes a futuro. Simultáneamente, mi vida personal también estaba a punto de atravesar por cambios radicales, me iba a casar y tenía la noticia de que también me convertiría en padre.

En ese punto, y luego de la difícil conversación de renunciar a un trabajo donde estaba cómodo, tenía que comunicar al socio de la firma a la que me estaba incorporando que necesitaría algún tiempo para atender mi nuevo *status* civil y familiar. Naturalmente, fue difícil decirle al *senior partner* que su más reciente asociado tenía planes que lo podrían alejar temporalmente de su escritorio. ¡Acababa de incorporarme! ¿Qué pensarían sobre mi compromiso con el trabajo, sobre mi grado de atención y sobre mi productividad? Estos cuestionamientos pasaron inmediatamente por mi cabeza. Creía que la revelación de estos asuntos personales podría hacer que se arrepintiera de su decisión de haberme contratado; y es que finalmente el líder de una firma de abogados espera que sus asociados —especialmente los nuevos— se conviertan en verdaderos *terminators,* sabuesos listos para salir a la caza (o, por lo menos, es lo que yo esperaría).

Como ya podrán advertir, era necesario entrar en conversaciones con mi nuevo empleador y cada vez que uno tiene que afrontar una conversación difícil llega con muchos sesgos sobre qué piensa la persona con la que conversará y sobre lo que piensas de ti mismo. Esto es a lo que Douglas Stone y Bruce Patton llaman *feelings conversation* e *Identity Conversation.*[1]

§30.01 ¿CÓMO AFRONTAR UNA CONVERSACIÓN DIFÍCIL?

Lo que hace que una conversación, sobre cualquier asunto, se torne difícil, es el temor de que el resultado no sea el esperado, o que incluso sea peor que el esperado. En otras palabras, una conversación difícil es aquella cuyas consecuencias no puedes anticipar con certeza y en la que pones en juego tus propias expectativas sobre el resultado o inclusive la relación con la persona que será tu interlocutora.

Una conversación difícil deja dos caminos muy claros: evadirla o afrontarla. Evadir una conversación difícil a veces puede ser tentador. A primera vista puede ser un camino práctico que te ahorrará algunos problemas. Sin embargo, a mi modo de ver, esta opción deja a una persona con la eterna sensación del *what if.*

Por otro lado, un camino más difícil pero que puede procurarte más satisfacciones —si sabes cómo abordarlo— es afrontar la conversación.

Desde mi experiencia hay, al menos, cinco puntos que debes tener en cuenta para afrontar exitosamente una conversación difícil.

A continuación, cinco *hints* que ayudarán a afrontar una conversación difícil.

[A] El "no" ya lo tienes

Puede ser que te dividas en el dilema de afrontar o no una conversación complicada, ya sea que pienses que quizás no sea buena idea pedir un aumento aún y esto puede llegar por sí solo luego, o que no es un buen momento en la empresa para atender temas que para ti son urgentes también. Sin embargo, en todas estas situaciones evitar la conversación solo te deja en la misma posición de haber recibido un "no" por respuesta.

Siendo así, objetivamente, lo peor que te podría ocurrir es que, en efecto, recibas un "no". En ese caso te encontrarías en casi la misma situación en la que te encontrabas antes de iniciar la conversación. Por otro lado, si afrontas la conversación y si las sabes plantear, las cosas pueden salir tremendamente bien. Entonces, puedes decidir quedarte con un "no" que ya tienes anticipadamente o puedes plantear inteligentemente tu conversación y quizás conseguir los resultados que esperas. Me

1. Douglas Stone, Bruce Patton and Sheila Heen. *Difficult conversations: How to discuss what matters most* (Penguin Books, 2000).

parece que un escenario de tener la conversación siempre tendrá mayores beneficios que evitarla.

Es normal pensar que en caso de recibir un "no" por respuesta tu interlocutor tendrá una percepción equivocada de ti. En los casos que planteamos, por ejemplo, que tu jefe piense que no estás contento con el sueldo que recibes o que no estás comprometido con los intereses de la empresa. Todo depende de cómo se plantee la situación y a continuación algunos consejos que pueden ayudarte a evitar dejar las percepciones que temes causar.

[B] No improvises, a menos que sea absolutamente necesario

A ningún abogado se le ocurriría ir a una audiencia de alegatos de apertura o clausura sin haber preparado cuidadosamente lo que va a decir. Lo mismo ocurre cuando se afronta una conversación difícil.

Las conversaciones difíciles, aunque parezca paradójico, empiezan mucho antes de que empieces a hablar. La conversación difícil primero tiene lugar en el fuero interno, en lo que imaginas que dirás y en lo que imaginas que ocurrirá cuando lo digas. Por esta razón, debes pensar muy bien cuáles son las ideas que quieres comunicar y evitar los rodeos. No se trata de diseñar un guion y actuarlo como si fuese una obra de teatro, se trata de establecer claramente cuáles serán las ideas centrales sobre las que debe girar tu conversación y cuáles son los objetivos que quieres lograr.

Como toda regla, hay una excepción. No siempre podemos predecir el curso de una conversación o evento y, sobre este punto, la teoría de la probabilidad explica que en toda situación existen al menos cuatro escenarios: lo que solo tú sabes que puede ocurrir, lo que solo otros saben que ocurrirá, lo que todos (tú incluido) saben y, finalmente, lo que nadie sabe, lo incierto. Este último escenario, que representa el 25 % de cualquier situación, es el que los filósofos llaman destino o suerte[2]. Solo cuando te encuentres en este último escenario, donde la conversación se disparó hacia donde nadie pudo anticipar, tienes permitido improvisar, pero siempre teniendo en cuenta tus objetivos previamente establecidos.

[C] *Keepit real*

A veces al prepararnos para una conversación difícil podemos caer en falacias argumentativas o en llevar a la mesa información que no necesariamente nos consta o peor aún, que no es cierta. Por ejemplo, al pedir un aumento de sueldo podrías verte tentado a decir que los abogados en otras compañías o en otras firmas perciben un mayor sueldo que tú, cuando esta información no te consta o no tienes datos específicos sobre ello. En la misma situación, para conseguir ese aumento podrías verte tentado a maquillar la verdad sobre las razones para pedir dicho aumento, armando historias que puedan volver tu argumento más "dramático".

2. Keynes, J. M. *A treatise on probability,* Nueva York, Harper and Row, 1921.

Si tu interlocutor será tu jefe o socio, lo que implica que probablemente sea una persona con más *seniority* o experiencia que tú, quizás no sea muy estratégico abordarlo con información que no tienes como acreditar o no has verificado. Si acaso esta persona llega a descubrir que la información con la que pretendes fundamentar las razones de tu aumento no es exacta o ha sido inventada sobre la marcha, tu pedido perderá legitimidad y todo esfuerzo habría sido en vano. Menos aconsejable aún es mentir para darle fuerza a tu pedido de aumento, pues las consecuencias de una mentira detectada conllevan a una inmediata pérdida de confianza.

Similar situación puede ocurrir en el escenario de una renuncia. Puedes querer evitar la confrontación y no revelar las razones por las que dejas un trabajo, pero en algunos casos ello puede llevar a que tu ex empleador se imagine cuáles fueron las motivaciones que te hicieron renunciar, lo que puede darle una idea equivocada de ti. Mientras que, siendo sincero, podrías permitirle tomar acciones para que recursos valiosos no se sientan en la necesidad de dejar sus trabajos.

En cualquier caso, ser sincero con las razones que motivan tu decisión de pedir un aumento, renunciar a un trabajo o cualquier otra circunstancia, resulta una herramienta útil pues evita que tu interlocutor llegue a conclusiones equivocadas acerca de ti y tus motivaciones. Ahora bien, la sinceridad en una conversación difícil es bien apreciada cuando se sabe abordar el tema con sentido común y respeto, por lo que es necesario desarrollar esta habilidad para que la conversación no se torne incómoda.

[D] Empatía y *timing*

La empatía es una habilidad muy importante, pues implica colocarse en el lugar de la otra persona. Aunque nunca puedas saber todo lo que la otra persona piensa o siente en relación a un tema específico, ciertamente puedes anticipar algunos escenarios.

En este contexto, ser empático implica que antes de iniciar una conversación difícil o en el curso de esta, te hagas la siguiente pregunta ¿qué haría yo si las cosas fueran al revés? Quizás resulte evidente una pregunta así, pero esta sola pregunta puede ayudar a anticipar algunos escenarios y evitar llevar la conversación por callejones sin salida.

Por otro lado, el *timing* es un elemento que puede ir de la mano con la empatía en algunas ocasiones. Por ejemplo, comunicarle a tu jefe que vas a renunciar cuando acaba de darte un encargo importante o ascenderte, o pedir un aumento cuando clientes estratégicos acaban de dejar la firma, o, peor aún, pretender iniciar una conversación difícil cuando tu interlocutor acaba de tener una reunión muy tensa por otro asunto, son situaciones que pueden evidenciar una falta absoluta de criterio y lo más probable es que, sin importar tus motivaciones, tu conversación no resulte exitosa, además de generar una percepción negativa sobre ti.

En mi experiencia, buenas oportunidades para tener una conversación difícil son a primera hora del día o a última hora. En cualquiera de estos momentos las personas están en mejor disposición para escuchar e intercambiar ideas.

[E] Estar dispuesto a oír un "no"

Como se advirtió, una conversación no necesariamente tiene que terminar favorablemente para nosotros. Es posible que el aumento solicitado sea negado o que los permisos no sean concedidos. En otras palabras, recibir una respuesta negativa o una respuesta que no satisfaga nuestras expectativas es un escenario perfectamente posible y, por tanto, no debe dejarse de lado.

En las negociaciones, y qué duda cabe que estas también son conversaciones difíciles, se suele utilizar el término MAAN *(Mejor Alternativa a un Acuerdo Negociado)*, que no es otra cosa que un Plan B o un *back-up plan.* La necesidad de contar con un plan B es que, a veces, pese a habernos arriesgado a tener una conversación difícil, preparar nuestros mejores argumentos, ser sinceros, empáticos y elegir el mejor momento para afrontar esta conversación; no se pueda obtener el resultado esperado. En ese caso, será importante conocer cuáles son nuestras opciones para que la situación no produzca más ansiedad de la necesaria.

Entonces, iniciar una conversación difícil debe contener como posible escenario el "NO" que inicialmente pensamos que ya teníamos. Si finalmente este temor se confirma, se puede activar un plan B que cada uno haya diseñado o simplemente puede abordarse el tema en una futura conversación, que probablemente será aún más incómoda y que requerirá una nueva preparación, según las pautas antes indicadas.

§30.02 CONCLUSIÓN

Una conversación difícil se puede dar a todo nivel y se torna más difícil aún si tu interlocutor es alguien con un cargo jerárquico superior al tuyo. En cualquier circunstancia una conversación difícil permite dos escenarios: evadir o afrontar. En este breve capítulo se ha resumido por qué es mejor afrontar que evadir y cuáles son técnicas que pueden contribuir a lidiar con una conversación difícil de manera exitosa. En suma, si ante la inminencia de una conversación difícil has decidido afrontarla, sin improvisar, hablando sobre lo cierto, de forma empática y oportuna, asumiendo que puedes obtener una respuesta negativa; es muy probable que puedas lidiar con ella y, eventualmente, conseguir un buen resultado.

En mi caso, la historia con la que empecé estas líneas tuvo un desenlace afortunado. Pude finalmente renunciar a mi anterior trabajo en muy buenos términos, conseguí que mi nuevo jefe accediera a brindarme el tiempo que necesitaba para casarme y recibir a mi hija. Actualmente, sigo siendo asociado de la firma de abogados que me recibió en el medio de estos cambios y puedo mantener el balance del trabajo con mi nueva familia. Naturalmente, todos estos resultados no hubieran sido posibles si mi elección hubiera sido evadir conversaciones difíciles o hubiera afrontado estas sin tener en cuenta los cinco aspectos claves aquí comentados.

CAPÍTULO 31

Cómo crear y desarrollar tu marca personal en arbitraje internacional: de peón a alfil

José Ignacio García Cueto

§31.01 INTRODUCCIÓN: CONCEPTO, CARACTERÍSTICAS E IMPORTANCIA DE LA MARCA PROPIA

No basta con ser bueno. Para ser encontrado, tienes que ser encontrable[1].

El *currículum vitae* ha muerto. La marca personal es el nuevo *currículum vitae*. Tiene múltiples características.

Es *única*. Nos identifica y diferencia del resto. Permite a un abogado destacar en un entorno homogéneo y competitivo[2]. Es algo propio que uno desarrolla y, como su sombra, lo va a acompañar a lo largo de su carrera profesional. Va a definir la percepción que la mayoría de la gente tiene de nosotros en el mercado.

Evoluciona. La marca personal va evolucionando con el paso del tiempo, por lo que la estrategia de desarrollo debe ir adaptándose al perfil del abogado.

Es *frágil*. Tardamos años en construirla, pero segundos en destruirla[3].

Es *compleja*. El nivel de competitividad y especialización en nuestra profesión es cada vez mayor, lo que conlleva que cada vez tener una marca "propia" sea más difícil.

Es *complementaria*. La marca personal propia es compatible con la marca del lugar en el que trabajamos. Ambas marcas pueden ser desarrolladas en paralelo, pero

1. La autoría de la frase es atribuida al Dr. Austin Kleon.
2. Ver Artículo *Lo Necesario Para una Marca Personal*, disponible en:http://forbes.es/business/35717/necesario-una-marca-personal/
3. Warren Buffet dijo una vez que "[i]*t takes 20 years to build a reputation and five minutes to ruin it. Ifyouthinkaboutthat, you'll do thingsdifferently.*"

la propia permite una proyección interna -dentro de nuestro lugar de trabajo- y externa -de cara a nuestros clientes y colegas.

Suele estar olvidada en un cajón. Pese a ser un activo propio tan importante, es un gran olvidado en el sector de la abogacía. Los abogados se centran más en su relación interna con los clientes que en la externa con el mercado.

En conclusión, la marca personal es una de las piedras angulares del éxito de un abogado moderno[4]. No hay una fórmula única para crear y desarrollar la marca personal en el sector de la abogacía. Cada persona aplica o ha aplicado la que ha considerado más idónea. En este caso, expongo la metodología que apliqué para desarrollar la propia por su simpleza. El proceso consta de dos simples pasos y está basada en un método de análisis económico.

§31.02 ¿CÓMO PASO DE PEÓN A ALFIL?: PASOS PARA CREAR Y DESARROLLAR TU PROPIA MARCA

La creación y desarrollo de la marca personal se debe afrontar como cualquier otra decisión de negocio. En los negocios queremos vender un producto. En este caso, queremos vendernos a nosotros a través de nuestra marca personal. Por ello, la creación y desarrollo de la marca debe seguir una visión estratégica de negocio. Para ello, el letrado debe analizar la viabilidad y estrategia a llevar a cabo mediante un análisis "FODA" de Fortalezas, Oportunidades, Debilidades y Amenazas de uno mismo y del mercado en el que opera[5]. La finalidad del análisis FODA es poder determinar mediante un análisis objetivo las ventajas y desventajas competitivas del perfil del abogado y el mercado relevante para determinar la estrategia óptima para la creación y desarrollo de la marca.

El análisis FODA se divide en dos, un análisis *interno* (del abogado) y otro *externo* (de mercado). Las fortalezas y debilidades forman parte del *análisis interno*. Las oportunidades y amenazas forman parte del *análisisexterno.*

	Positivos	Negativos
Internos	Fortalezas	Debilidades
Externos	Oportunidades	Amenazas

El éxito de este análisis depende de lo honesto que sea el análisis interno y del conocimiento que el abogado tenga del mercado en el que opera.

4. Otras, como es evidente, son el conocimiento del derecho de fondo y la capacidad de solucionar problemas en el menor periodo de tiempo posible.
5. El FODA es la traducción al español del anglicismo SWOT (*strengths, weaknesses, opportunities and threats*). La técnica fue originalmente propuesta por el doctor Albert S. Humphrey de Stanford.

[A] El análisis interno: ¿Cuál es tu marca?

El análisis interno debe partir de una premisa: honestidad y objetividad sobre qué fortalezas y debilidades tiene el abogado objeto de análisis. Para ello, un buen punto de partida puede ser responder a las siguientes dos preguntas: (1) ¿por qué yo? y (2) ¿en qué necesito mejorar respecto a mi competencia?

[1] Fortalezas: ¿Por qué yo? Qué puedes ofrecer que te distingue o cómo puedes mejorar para ofrecerlo

En primer lugar, resulta indispensable identificar cuáles son tus ventajas competitivas, qué puedes ofrecer o aportar que te diferencie o haga más interesante que tus colegas del rubro. Algunos parámetros que un abogado debería tener en cuenta son: (1) la experiencia en temas previos relacionados con la materia[6]; (2) los títulos de grado y posgrado que posea[7]; (3) la *expertise* en un área del derecho o en un sector de la industria determinado; (4) los idiomas que domine; (5) la disponibilidad y flexibilidad que tenga, y la facilidad para comunicarse con colegas y terceros; o (6) el precio que puede ofrecerse por los temas frente al precio fijado por el mercado[8].

Una vez que sabes en qué eres bueno y qué puedes aportar, puedes definir qué ofreces y comenzar a posicionarte como un referente en ello[9].

[2] Debilidades: ¿Qué no tienes o en qué es tu competencia mejor que tú?

En segundo lugar, debe realizarse un análisis honesto de las debilidades para poder conocer las ventajas-desventajas competitivas.

Son debilidades aquello que no tenemos o aquello en lo cual otros son mejores que nosotros. En este ejercicio típicamente hay una “lucha de titanes” entre el ego del abogado y la realidad. Sin embargo, no debemos olvidar que esto es una decisión de negocio por lo que los sentimientos no tienen cabida en este análisis. Las variables que hay que considerar para este ejercicio son mayormente las mismas que para las fortalezas, pero “a la inversa”. La falta de experiencia en el sector, títulos, idiomas, etc. pueden resultar debilidades dependiendo de cuáles sean los objetivos que nos hayamos propuesto y quiénes conformen el mercado en el que buscamos insertarnos o desarrollarnos.

---

6. Por ejemplo, si se quiere vender en el mercado de la construcción, sería idóneo haber trabajado previamente en el sector como ingeniero o en otros temas legales relacionados con la construcción.
7. Por ejemplo, si nuevamente se quiere tratar el tema de construcción, tener una licenciatura en ingeniería o un curso de disputas de construcción puede ayudar.
8. El tema del precio es sensible dado que cobrar barato puede abrir muchas puertas y a corto plazo puede ser una buena estrategia. Sin embargo, a largo plazo puede ser terrible dado que, cuando el mercado te reconozca, es muy probable que a los clientes con los que empezaste no puedas cobrarles lo que realmente vales. Como reza la frase popular “lo barato puede salir muy caro”.
9. Ver Artículo *8 Pasos para Crear tu Propia Marca*, disponible en:https://www.pqs.pe/actualidad/noticias/8-pasos-para-crear-tu-propia-marca-personal

Es fundamental en este análisis la experiencia y *expertise*en el mercado relevante. Una persona sin experiencia y/o *expertise*, por inexperiencia o porque es un nuevo operador en el mercado, está en clara desventaja respecto a los otros operadores y tendrá que buscar cómo compensar esas falencias. Sin embargo, pese a contar con experiencia y/o *expertise*puede tenerse debilidades en un mercado relevante. Por ejemplo, puede darse el caso que nuestros competidores tengan mayor *expertise*. En este sentido, puede aplicarse la máxima de Campana de Gauss: *somos tan buenos o malos como lo son nuestros competidores*.

Otros aspectos que podrían ser considerados como debilidades son (1) nuestra ubicación geográfica; (2) no contar con una marca personal establecida en un mercado ya maduro, como la abogacía; (3) un precio más elevado que el de nuestros competidores; o (4) un mercado muy reducido en el cual no tenemos contactos.

[B] El análisis externo: Ahora que ya sé que valgo, cómo desarrollo la marca personal

Una vez realizado el análisis interno para saber qué fortalezas y debilidades tenemos, es momento de realizar un análisis externo de oportunidades y amenazas que presenta el mercado relevante y saber así cómo desarrollar tu marca personal.

[1] Oportunidades: Cuál es tu mercado, qué oportunidades te presenta y cómo crecer y desarrollarte en el mercado

En tercer lugar, debemos definir cuál es nuestro mercado relevante y nuestra audiencia o *pool* de clientes prospectivos. El desarrollo de una marca va dirigido típicamente a poder "venderle" a alguien servicios. En este caso, servicios de asesoría legal.

Conocer quién es tu audiencia y saber por qué puede interesarse en ti, te ayudará a determinar el contenido y la manera en la que te comunicarás con ella[10]. Si, por el contrario, no defines tu mercado e intentas atraer a todos, lo que terminarás logrando es el efecto contrario: no atraer a nadie[11].

Para ello, primero debes definir en qué área jurídica y geográfica quieres penetrar o posicionarte mejor. Una vez definido, debes analizar a profundidad las características básicas del mercado (1) quiénes son los clientes prospectivos; (2) quiénes son tus competidores; (3) cuál es el precio estándar del mercado por los servicios[12], etc. Eso te permitirá identificar dónde están las oportunidades del mercado y optimizar las chances de que tu marca se posicione correctamente y con la audiencia relevante.

10. Ver Artículo *Cómo Construir Tu Propia Marca Personal*, disponible en:https://www.emprendedores.es/gestion/a79283/como-construir-una-buena-marca-personal/
11. Ver Artículo *Personal Branding Guide*, disponible en: https://www.thinkific.com/blog/personal-branding-guide/
12. Es probable que si optas por desarrollarte en un área jurídica nueva o en la que exista una "barrera de entrada natural" (como, por ejemplo, tener conocimiento técnico de la materia) ello pueda significar una oportunidad para tu desarrollo profesional. Asimismo, la selección del área geográfica también resulta relevante, pues existen buenas oportunidades al insertarse en áreas geográficas en crecimiento o con menor competencia.

Una forma efectiva de hacerlo es, una vez que conoces y tienes definidos el mercado y las necesidades, expandir tu red de contactos. Para ello, hay muchas maneras desde (1) solicitar reuniones; (2) dar a conocer tus ideas a través de publicaciones o impartiendo conferencias[13]; (3) participar en redes sociales especializadas; (4) crear o incorporarse a grupos o asociaciones especializadas del rubro[14]; y (5) tener una buena relación con tu competencia y/o otros operadores del mercado[15]. Lo anterior te dará mayor exposición frente a terceros y te ayudará a crear tu marca a través de la opinión de terceros[16].

Importancia especial tienen hoy en día en este ejercicio las redes sociales u otros medios de comunicación como instrumentos para construir una marca personal. Vivimos en un mundo digitalizado, en el que las redes sociales y los medios de comunicación ocupan una parte importante de nuestras vidas: muchos empleadores realizan sus búsquedas laborales por medio de internet, colegas se informan a través de plataformas digitales y clientes buscan información, ya sea sobre temas que les preocupen o sobre sus abogados, por medio de internet.

Estar disponibles y visibles en la red, para que aquellos que quieran conocernos o comunicarse con nosotros puedan hacerlo con facilidad, podrá exponernos a nuevas oportunidades[17].

[2] Amenazas: ¿Qué amenazas presenta el mercado?

Definido el mercado que nos interesa, debemos analizar qué amenazas al desarrollo de la marca existen en el mismo y para poder planear cómo evitar que nos impacten o, de no ser posible evitarlas, mitigar su impacto disruptivo.

Típicamente, las mayores amenazas en cuanto al mercado relevante son (1) precio; (2) fuerte competencia; (3) mercado "comoditizado" en el cual el tipo de servicio no requiere mucha experiencia o *expertise*; o (4) mercado "hiper-populado".

§31.03 EL OUTPUT DEL FODA

El ejercicio anterior permitirá al abogado tener las variables para optimizar su marca e irla desarrollando. El ejercicio debería realizarse cada dos o tres años dado que "todo fluye, nada permanece": el perfil del abogado y el mercado y sus operadores evolucionan con el paso del tiempo. Las variables que típicamente estarán (en un

13. Repetir ideas de otros no ayuda a desarrollar una marca propia. Es primordial que las ideas sean frescas y nuevas.
14. Estas asociaciones podrán brindarte la posibilidad no solo de ampliar tu red de contactos, sino también de continuar tu formación, de impartir cursos, organizar y participar de conferencias u otros eventos de interés relacionados con tu área de especialización.
15. No debe desestimarse la cantidad de casos que a uno le pueden llegar desde la competencia por temas de conflictos de interés.
16. Ver Artículo *Creating and GrowingYour Personal Brand*, disponible en: https://www.thebalancesmb.com/creating-and-growing-personal-brand-2295814
17. Ver Artículo *5 Ways to Build a Powerful Personal Brand*, disponible en https://www.forbes.com/sites/shelcyvjoseph/2018/04/30/5-ways-to-build-a-powerful-personal-brand/#787bf5b9549e

cuadro u otro) en el resultado son las siguientes:

Variables internas	***Variables Externas***
Fortalezas. • Experiencia en temas previos • *Expertise* en un sector determinado • Titulaciones • Disponibilidad • Idiomas • Facilidad para comunicarme con terceros/colegas • Precio competitivo	*Oportunidades* • Áreas jurídicas nuevas • Áreas en que exista una "barrera de entrada natural" (e.g. conocimiento técnico de la materia) • Áreas geográficas en crecimiento • Áreas geográficas con poca competencia
Debilidades. • Menor experiencia o *expertise* que otros competidores • Ubicación geográfica no local • Inexistencia de una marca personal establecida en un mercado maduro	*Amenazas* • Competencia en el mercado: cada vez más un mercado que considera los servicios legales como un "commodity" • Precio de competidores (calidad/precio) • Demasiados competidores

§31.04 CONCLUSIÓN

Es prioritario crear una marca personal pronto e ir trabajando en su desarrollo de forma constante: tener una buena marca no es suficiente si el mercado no la conoce o no sabe encontrarte. Por ello, la creación y desarrollo de la marca debe considerar cuál es la ventaja competitiva de la misma y cómo hacer que esa diferenciación sea advertida en el mercado. Algunos ejemplos de exposición pueden ser dar conferencias, escribir artículos o participar en grupos especializados. La marca crecerá o morirá en función en las decisiones que cada uno vaya adoptando, por lo que es fundamental -para conservarla- aplicar estrategias a largo plazo y no cortoplacistas. Por último, el ejercicio debe realizarse al menos una vez cada tres años ya que los mercados, competencia y operadores cambian.

CAPÍTULO 32
Maternidad y arbitraje internacional

Diana Correa

"Si yo fuera un hombre". Este ha sido un cuestionamiento recurrente durante mis últimos años, que cada vez se presenta con menor frecuencia, pero que volvió fuertemente a rondar mi cabeza cuando me pidieron escribir este capítulo sobre el tema de la maternidad y el arbitraje internacional. Ahora, ha llegado la hora de hacer catarsis.

No voy a hablar del "si yo fuera hombre" inicial de mi primer embarazo, cuando todo esto de la maternidad y hacer carrera en arbitraje internacional era nuevo para mí, en el que criticaba sin cese la que yo creía era la posición "fácil" del hombre que no sufre ni cambios físicos, ni psicológicos, ni hormonales (y aquí explico mi versión del cambio hormonal que se ubica en un terreno gris entre lo físico y lo psicológico), que no da a luz y acto seguido tampoco debe no solo sanar su propio cuerpo sino cuidar el de alguien más completamente dependiente, que no vuelve a dormir profundamente y queda en una especie de sueño ligero con estado de vigilia (al menos durante los primeros días de nacido su bebé), que no está conectado de una manera extraña e inexplicable con ese pequeño ser que ha cobrado vida (porque en realidad el cordón umbilical una vez cortado físicamente se transforma en uno más fuerte que desafía la ciencia).

No. No hablaré de ese "si yo fuera hombre" porque, entre otras, el tiempo me ha demostrado que no todo lo que pensaba a la época era cierto y, si lo es, al menos en parte, los hombres también viven sus propias experiencias con la paternidad y sus carreras en arbitraje. De esto, también se debería hablar más.

Me concentraré mejor en la versión de "si yo fuera hombre" evolucionada y catártica a la que he llegado hoy. "Si yo fuera hombre", pues simple y llanamente me perdería de la maravilla que les describiré a continuación.

Me llamo Diana Correa, soy jurista especialista en derecho internacional, profesora universitaria, árbitro, abogada de parte y madre de tres niñas: Eva de cinco años, Victoria de tres años y Olivia de un año y medio al momento de escribir este capítulo. Parecen muchos títulos al mismo tiempo, irreconciliables para algunos y, al menos, complicados de administrar para otros. Pues bien, es mi realidad (como la de muchas otras mujeres) y aunque el camino no ha sido fácil, puedo decir que sí se puede y aquí les contaré cómo lo he logrado.

§32.01 ¿MAMÁ YO? ¿PARA QUÉ? ¿Y MI CARRERA? ¡SI SOY LA MEJOR TÍA DEL MUNDO!

Esa era mi posición antes de convertirme en mamá. Y es que tenía muchas razones: el mundo está súper poblado, mejor adopto un perro, gasto el dinero en mí misma, viajo, salgo, consiento a mis sobrinos, los de sangre y los de mis amigos (pues me hago llamar por todos ellos "tía" sin verdaderamente serlo) y, sobre todo, persigo mi carrera en arbitraje internacional que amo tanto.

Esta posición me duró tanto que "casi me deja el tren" biológico para ser mamá. Siempre pensé que la maternidad mutilaría drásticamente mi carrera, por lo que había que escoger entre ella (la carrera) y ellos (los hijos). [1] Pensar en un balance entre una vida familiar con hijos y una vida profesional en arbitraje internacional parecía imposible. [2]

---

1. "Even if minority women only faced the same obstacles as white women, they would still confront a number of daunting barriers to success ranging from disproportionate responsibility for child care (not to mention sole responsibility for childbirth), to exclusion from the "old boys club," to sexual harassment." David Wilkins, Diversity in Law Firms in the Legal Profession, Diversity and Inclusion Speaker Series, Inaugural Event, Center on Race, Law and Justice, 21 de febrero de 2018, p. 13, disponible enhttps://www.fordham.edu/download/downloads/id/10095/course_materials.pdf. Ver también: "The generally accepted issue is the choice many women face between partnership —on call 24/7 and under pressure to generate business— or starting a family. [...] For example, partners looking to build a team to work on a deal may assume a mother will not want a demanding client calling at 2am, or to travel frequently for work. These assumptions are not made about fathers. Firms seeking to improve diversity at the top need to make alterations to their processes, says Ms Bi. The problem is exacerbated by pressure to bring work into the firm, says Sarah Chilton, a partner at CM Murray, which specialises in partnership and employment law."Madison Darbyshire y Barney Thompson, Can You Be a Mother and a Senior Law Firm Partner?, Work and Carriers, Financial Times, 16 de abril de 2019, p. 1, disponible enhttps://www.ft.com/content/8e70eb40-5a12-11e9-9dde-7aedca0a081a. Ver también: "Perceptions about motherhood and its compatibility with the life of a professional also seem to inhibit mobility. There seems to be an expectation that women will drop back or drop out after bearing children, and not be as professionally committed once they have family obligations. But-because they often unconsciously accept stereotypical views of themselves-many women lawyers do not ask for, or insist on, the treatment and assistance that would make them truly equal to men at all stages of professional development. Women lawyers themselves share that expectation and many simply assume that they will not be accepted as full professional colleagues after they have children. There is a perception on the part of women with children that they are not getting the same work opportunities they enjoyed B.C. (Before Children).", Cynthia Fuchs Epstein, Robert Sauté, Bonnie Oglensky y Martha Gever, Glass Ceilings and Open Doors: Women's Advancement in the Legal Profession, Fordham Law Review, Vol. 64, Issue 2, 1995, p. 298, disponible enhttps://ir.lawnet.fordham.edu/cgi/viewcontent.cgi?referer=https://www.google.com/&httpsredir=1&article=3203&context=flr.
2. En una encuesta realizada en Estados Unidos, con una muestra de 222 firmas de abogados, sin que la cuestión de la maternidad estuviera consultada directamente, se demostró cierto pesimismo entre las mujeres para poder lograr una vida balanceada entre su carrera y su vida personal (familiar), lo que lleva, aparentemente a las mujeres a querer ser promovidas en sus

Claramente, para ese entonces, la decisión estaba hecha: "*Quiero tener éxito profesional y, para ello, solo tengo tiempo para trabajar*". Y todo esto me duró hasta que, como ya lo he hecho público en varias conferencias, me pasó lo que tanto temía en aquella época y me convertí en mamá. Y digo me pasó, porque no estaba en mis planes, así que solo por eso me autoproclamo una afortunada del destino, la suerte, el alea o como lo quieran llamar.

Bueno, pues bastante equivocada estaba yo sobre la supuesta irreconciliable vida maternal y profesional que se había convertido en mi credo durante años, con lo que tampoco estoy admitiendo que sea fácil. Lo que sí admito, sin ningún escrúpulo, es que si fuera hombre no estaría aquí narrando estas experiencias que, aunque duras, son las mejores de mi vida.

§32.02 CUANDO LOS MITOS SON SOLO ESO: MITOS, Y LA MATERNIDAD NO TE IMPIDE TENER UNA CARRERA EN ARBITRAJE INTERNACIONAL

La maternidad me volvió increíblemente fuerte y sé que a muchas otras mujeres también, por lo que uno tras otro, los mitos en torno a la pérdida de capacidad para llevar a cabo una carrera arbitral siendo mamá se fueron cayendo como al mejor efecto dominó. [3]

[A] Mito sobre la pérdida de trabajo cuando se es mamá

Cuando quedé embarazada de mi primera hija, trabajaba en una firma de abogados dedicada a la práctica del arbitraje internacional. A pesar de que tardé un poco más de tres meses en contarle a mi jefe principal de mi estado por temor a que me despidiera, o por lo menos a que me dejara de tener en cuenta para involucrarme en nuevos casos,

---

carreras pero no hasta ser socias, así: "Only 44 percentofwomenbelievethatthey can haveboth, comparedwith 60 percentofmenwho do (versus 61 percentofwomen and 67 percentofmenacrosstheoverallsample) (Exhibit 4). Almost half of female attorneys call prioritizing work–life balance one of the greatest challenges to their professional success, on par with undermining peers. The difficulty of balancing work and family is the number-one reason that women do not want to make partner (61 percent), followed by inadequate benefits for the personal costs (54 percent) as the number two cited reason. Men cite the same top two reasons, but in reverse order, ranking the personal costs first (56 percent) and the difficulty of balance second (51 percent).", Marc Brodherso, Laura McGee y Mariana Pires dos Reis, Women in Law Firms, octubre de 2017, pp. 5-6, disponible enhttps://www.mckinsey.com/~/media/mckinsey/featured%20insights/gender%20equality/women%20in%20law%20firms/women-in-law-firms-final-103017.ashx.

3. Quisiera aquí resaltar que esta afirmación de carácter general se basa únicamente en mi propia experiencia y en la de algunas mujeres madres y trabajadoras que conozco, lo que no significa que así sea en todas partes, en todas las industrias y todos los trabajos. Por ejemplo, el mito de la pérdida de trabajo por el estado de embarazo lamentablemente parece ser aún real, lo que ha generado que en Estados Unidos se esté adelantando un proyecto de ley para proteger la mujer gestante y su trabajo. Dicho proyecto se llama el "PregnantWorkersFairnessAct", consultable en https://www.congress.gov/bill/116th-congress/house-bill/2694?q=%7B%22search%22%3A%5B%22Pregnant+Workers+Fairness+Act%22%5D%7D&s=1&r=1

esto nunca ocurrió. Todo siguió igual. La confianza nunca se perdió. Seguí conociendo los mismos casos y más, a medida que iban llegando a la oficina.

Esto hizo que rápidamente ganara toda la confianza en mí misma que las náuseas, los temores y los prejuicios me habían hecho perder.

[B] Mito sobre la pérdida de interés profesional en una madre

Después del trabajo que tenía en la firma de abogados cuando mi primera hija nació, no solo cambié de país, sino que cambié de trabajo y de costumbres. A mi regreso a Colombia, que se debió a razones estrictamente personales y familiares, no solo encontré mi trabajo como profesora en derecho internacional, sino que disfruté de la confianza de mis pares y de las instituciones arbitrales, de suerte que he podido desarrollar mi carrera como árbitro y como abogada de parte en arbitrajes internacionales, sin que el hecho de ser mamá me haya afectado en lo más mínimo.

De hecho, las firmas de dos contratos importantes en mi vida profesional llegaron con vientres pronunciadamente inflados de un segundo y un tercer embarazo, respectivamente. Ni el estado de gravidez ni el hecho de ser mamá, inclusive de tres niñas, ha hecho que pierda credibilidad y profesionalismo ante los ojos de mis colegas y de mis clientes.

[C] Mito sobre la falta de tiempo para trabajar de las mamás

El mito hace que se piense que la maternidad es un trabajo a tiempo completo que se vuelve incompatible con cualquier otro trabajo. Este mito además se complementa de un elemento histórico por el cual, por siglos, el rol de la mujer de "ama de casa" hace que sea ella quien se ocupe en exclusiva de los hijos, mientras que el hombre "proveedor" de las necesidades materiales familiares ha asumido el rol de "trabajador". No obstante, desde hace ya algunas décadas esta organización social comienza a verse desafiada por miles de mujeres trabajadoras[4] y por cientos de hombres amos de casa o, simplemente, por padres y madres que trabajamos en nuestras profesiones sin descuidar las actividades asociadas a los hijos. Mi situación actual encaja en la realidad contemporánea de compartir los placeres y las dificultades de la maternidad con el padre de mis hijas quien, a su vez y tanto como yo, debe conciliar las dichas y los tropezones de la paternidad con su trabajo; la diferencia es que el cuestionamiento social se le hace a la mujer, y no al hombre por meros estigmas sociales que no tienen espacio en el mundo de hoy en el que la tecnología, la

---

4. Aquí aclaro que cuando digo "trabajadoras" me refiero a las madres que trabajan en contraprestación a un salario por un trabajo que no consiste en cuidar de sus hijos y del hogar, lo que no significa para nada que no crea que el trabajo de la casa, que entre otras no es remunerado, no sea un trabajo. A propósito de esto, un estudio en 2011 indicaba que el trabajo de la madre que se ocupa del hogar debería ser pagado en $115.000 dólares de Estados Unidos de América por año. "According to a new survey by Salary.com, a division of human resources consultant Kenexa, moms should be charging $115,000 per year for their work", Jenna Goudreau, Forbes, mayo 2 de 2011, disponible enhttps://www.forbes.com/sites/jennagoudreau/2011/05/02/why-stay-at-home-moms-should-earn-a-115000-salary/#5220854b75f4

especialidad, la eficiencia y la igualdad marca la vida profesional de aquellas personas, hombres o mujeres, preparados y capacitados.

Ahora bien, claramente el tiempo se reduce porque hay que distribuirlo en más actividades. Sin embargo, a medida que las actividades se multiplican, también y proporcionalmente se instala una nueva organización de trabajo más eficiente. Lo que se pierde es el tiempo del ocio, de la pausa para el café, de la película de la noche, de procrastinar delante de tu computador todas las mañanas mientras agarras el ritmo de trabajo, de tomar largas pausas de almuerzo, pues sabes que todo eso significa que tendrás que quitarles tiempo a tus hijos y trabajar hasta altas horas de la noche o de la madrugada para cumplir con tu trabajo.

Dicho esto, es completamente falso que las madres no tengamos tiempo de trabajar y, por el contrario, las encuestas muestran que las madres solemos ser mucho más eficientes que cualquier otro tipo de trabajador, llegando a sugerirse, inclusive, que entre más hijos se tengan, más productivas somos las madres. [5]

[D] Mito sobre las pocas ganas de trabajar de las mamás

Bueno, este mito tiene algo de verdad, tanto para las mujeres como para los hombres, pero tampoco mucho. Cuando los hijos nacen, al menos en una gran parte de mujeres, se crea un vínculo fusional que hace que se quiera pasar mucho tiempo con esas pequeñas criaturas indefensas, dependientes e inocentes que te despiertan los sentimientos más nobles, puros y encantadores.

Sin embargo, con el pasar de las semanas, uno se da cuenta que es necesario instaurar la independencia, que ser madre no es sinónimo de esclavitud hacia el hijo, que es necesario y satisfactorio volver a la vida profesional, a arbitrar, a escribir los memoriales y participar en las audiencias porque eso da también sentido a tu vida profesional y personal, aparte de ser fuente de ingresos.

Ahora bien, tampoco hay que confundir ganas de seguir trabajando con ganas y aspiración de ascender en la carrera arbitral, hágase dónde se haga. En efecto, algunos estudios sugieren que no todas las mujeres (incluyendo madres y no madres) trabajadoras de la industria legal, incluyendo practicantes del arbitraje internacional, tendrían como aspiración profesional llegar a ocupar las posiciones más altas en sus respectivas carreras: socias en sus firmas de abogados, directoras de las empresas privadas o de las entidades públicas donde son juristas *in-house*, profesoras universitarias, etc.[6]

---

5. "Mothers of at least two children are, on average, more productive than mothers of only one child, and mothers in general are more productive than childless women." Matthias Krapf, Heinrich W. Ursprung y Christian Zimmermann, Parenthood and Productivity of Highly Skilled Labor: Evidence from the Groves of Academe, Working Paper 2014-001A, Research Division Working Paper Series, Federal Reserve Bank of St. Louis, p. 15, disponible enhttps://s3.amazonaws.com/real.stlouisfed.org/wp/2014/2014-001.pdf
6. Cynthia Fuchs Epstein, Robert Sauté, Bonnie Oglensky y Martha Gever, *Supra.*, p. 359 y ss., disponible enhttps://ir.lawnet.fordham.edu/cgi/viewcontent.cgi?referer=https://www.google.com/&httpsredir=1&article=3203&context=flr

Al parecer, y según dichos estudios, muchas de las mujeres que son madres, sobre todo de niños pequeños, desean por lo general ganar más tiempo con sus hijos para disfrutar más de su rol de madres, por lo que no les interesa realmente ascender en sus respectivas carreras, sino conservar sus cargos en posiciones intermediarias sin arriesgarse a tener un nuevo rol que les demande mayor tiempo y responsabilidad. [7] Es más, quienes no son madres, e incluso algunos hombres, también parecen disfrutar tener más tiempo de ocio y de vida personal y familiar. [8] Esto dicho, es claro de todas maneras que no se trata de una pérdida de interés en seguir trabajando, sino de la honestidad de no querer hacer extra esfuerzos en el ascenso de una carrera, porque se prefiere utilizar el tiempo de dichos esfuerzos profesionales en la familia. Esto obedece a una legítima necesidad que experimentan ciertas mujeres en equilibrar más sus respectivos roles de practicantes de arbitraje internacional y madres.

Si todas estas creencias, y más, que se puedan tener en torno a la maternidad y al arbitraje internacional son, en su gran mayoría, mitos, el ejercicio de ambas actividades sí que requiere organización y disciplina para evitar que esos mitos se conviertan en realidades.

§32.03 EL DÍA A DÍA DE LA PRÁCTICA ARBITRAL INTERNACIONAL Y LA MATERNIDAD

El mensaje que quiero dejar con este capítulo es claramente positivo, porque corresponde genuinamente a lo que siento y a lo que vivo. Sin embargo, y tristemente, ello no significa que todos los practicantes del arbitraje internacional vean en los embarazos y en los hijos algo muy positivo, por lo que los mitos de más arriba pueden seguir difundiéndose. Como la otra cara de la moneda, esto significa que debe haber mujeres que sientan presión y culpabilidad por ser madres, así que sus aspiraciones de carrera se ven frustradas.

Pareciera, en efecto, que las estadísticas no ayudan y, en todo caso, para una mujer (más siendo mamá) convertirse en socia de una firma de abogados es una misión verdaderamente épica. Eso lleva a algunas personas a proponer un sistema de cuotas para incrementar el número de mujeres (madres) que puedan llegar a la posición de socias. [9]

7. "As expected, women associates were more likely to express negative feelings regarding partnership, citing the conflict between firm and family responsibilities. One female associate, who placed herself off-track, suggested that the work and life-style of partnership did not fit into her future: It was just that I didn't want to be involved in the bureaucracy of a large firm. I didn't want the stress. There's so much stress, and pressure, and emphasis on hours, and when you're a partner getting clients and doing huge deals, and I just didn't want that kind of pressure on my life. I ... really enjoy being with family and friends and pursuing outside interests, and I just didn't want that to be 80% of my life. Even if I didn't have children, I would have wanted some sort of balance where it was more of a ... nine to six, nine to seven sort of job, and I didn't have to work weekends, and I had my nights free, and I could just enjoy my life." Ibíd. p. 360.
8. Ibíd. p. 359.
9. "Ms Chilton agrees. ""The statistics are so awful that quotas are not a bad thing," she says. "Having quotaswould encourage firms to make sure females have achieved what they need to achieve to make partnership." Targets of 20%-25% are "depressing", adds Ms Chilton. "If you

Es por esta razón que quiero terminar este capítulo con mi día a día en mi doble rol de mamá y de practicante del arbitraje internacional. De esta manera (1) me uno a las voces que ya han comenzado a hablar del tema, (2) transmito una voz de aliento y de ánimo a aquellas mujeres que dudan y piensan mucho la posibilidad de ser mamás por temores con sus carreras, y (3) intento persuadir a aquellos y aquellas que ven en la maternidad un impedimento para hacer carrera en arbitraje internacional y prefieren contratar a hombres o a mujeres con hijos grandes o sin interés o posibilidad de tener hijos, de que no hay realmente nada que temer.

Con excepción de los malos momentos que son normales en cualquier persona, puedo decir que mi día a día cuando no viajo y estoy en casa es realmente maravilloso, pues me organizo de manera tal que pueda avanzar en mi trabajo mientras veo a mis hijas tanto como puedo. Pero todo esto depende de cómo administre mi tiempo, por lo que aprender y volverse experta en esta fina técnica es vital para poder cumplir con todos los frentes familiares y profesionales.

Aquí van mis consejos:

[A] Trabajo desde casa y tengo flexibilidad en la distribución de mis horas de trabajo

Sé que no es para todo el mundo, y mucha gente, con o sin hijos, no logra trabajar en casa. Sin embargo, ser independiente, tener mi propia estructura y equipo de trabajo en la "nube", sin horarios, sin transporte, sin mala circulación, ha sido clave para poder conciliarlo todo. Cuando digo trabajar desde casa, tampoco significa que me ocupo todo el tiempo de mis hijas, pues primero ellas van a sus colegios y jardines infantiles respectivos, y además no solo mi esposo también trabaja desde casa, sino que dispongo del apoyo de una niñera. Esto significa, simplemente, que el tiempo que le dedicaría al transporte se lo consagro a mis hijas y con ello logro desayunar con ellas, prepararlas para el colegio, recibirlas después del colegio y poder cenar con ellas y prepararlas para la cama.

El tiempo que gano no es solo el del transporte. Es también el tiempo de instalarse, saludar y compartir con los colegas y amigos un rato, un café, salir a almorzar, responder al teléfono, etc. No niego que, a excepción de contestar el teléfono, me siento privada de estos momentos agradables en una oficina, pero como se trata de encontrar un equilibrio así implique hacer sacrificios, pues debo admitir que, en este momento de mi vida, con niñas pequeñas, me hace mucho más feliz y me da más tranquilidad estar pendientes de ellas que de tomar pausas e ir a almorzar todos los días con mis colegas.

---

only have a target of 25 per cent, you're never going to exceed it, and it is so out of kilter with the number of associates." Most leading firms have a roughly 50:50 gender split at associate level, or a slight female majority. That makes the partnership statistics all the more shocking." Madison Darbyshire y Barney Thompson, Can You Be a Mother and a Senior Law Firm Partner?, Work and Carriers, Financial Times, 16 de abril de 2019, p. 1, disponible enhttps://www.ft.com/content/8e70eb40-5a12-11e9-9dde-7aedca0a081a

Es increíble y, aunque suene exagerado, la cantidad de tiempo que se gana al no ir a una oficina todos los días. Esto puede oscilar entre una y tres horas dependiendo de los días. Ustedes mismos pueden hacer los cálculos en sus mentes.

Para quienes trabajen en oficinas, si estas son de abogados, mucho he venido escuchando que cada vez más las grandes estructuras permiten a las madres tele-trabajar. Tal vez no todos los días, pero sí varios. Si se es abogado *in-house*, tal vez esto del tele-trabajo sea más difícil, pero he escuchado algunas colegas que logran llegar muy temprano a la oficina, sacrifican las pausas de café y la hora del almuerzo (donde comen algo rápido) para así salir más temprano de la oficina y poder compartir tiempo con los hijos al regresar a casa. El trabajo universitario, seguido, permite también manejar un poco mejor sus tiempos.

Si tomamos el ejemplo de las firmas de abogados, los estudios demuestran que estas hacen cada vez más esfuerzos para facilitar el logro del balance entre la vida familiar y la vida profesional, como por ejemplo promover el trabajo en casa o reducir los horarios de trabajo[10], y, aunque estos logros aún no son completamente significativos, deben ser fuertemente reconocidos, agradecidos y promovidos para que continúen hasta lograr un equilibrio natural entre la vida personal y familiar, de un lado, y la vida profesional, de otro lado, así[11]:

10. "On the whole, part-time schedules and flex-time arrangements have been implemented to accommodate the needs of mothers. As we have seen, the formal policy at one firm explicitly limits part-time arrangements to women seeking a temporary solution to the conflicts between work and child care responsibilities. [...] Fax machines, cellular telephones, computer networks, and other forms of new communications technology are frequently cited as instruments that enable decentralized approaches to work. Attorneys seeking greater scheduling flexibility might benefit from these developments. Surprisingly few of those interviewed, however, described taking full advantage of communications technology, although several acknowledged that firms should explore this solution to the workhome conflict. Indeed, a former associate at one of the firms in the sample recommended this solution as one way the firms could remove whatever "glass ceiling" is imposed on working mothers by traditional work structures." Cynthia Fuchs Epstein, Robert Sauté, Bonnie Oglensky y Martha Gever, *Supra.*, pp. 409-410 y 412, disponible en https://ir.lawnet.fordham.edu/cgi/viewcontent.cgi?referer=https://www.google.com/&httpsredir=1&article=3203&context=flr

11. "All the law firms surveyed offer the option of working part-time or on a reduced schedule (versus 77 percent across the overall sample) (Exhibit 7). Most law firms allow telecommuting (versus 75 percent across the overall sample). Most law firms (91 percent) offer maternity leave that exceeds government requirements, and most (83 percent) offer paternity leave that also exceeds those requirements (versus 63 percent and 56 percent across the overall sample). All of the law firms surveyed provide emergency backup childcare services (versus 40 percent across the overall sample). But only 22 percent of law firms have on-site childcare, and none subsidize regular childcare (versus 15 percent and 18 percent of organizations across the overall sample)", Marc Brodherson, Laura McGee y Mariana Pires dos Reis, Women in Law Firms, octubre de 2017, p. 10, disponible enhttps://www.mckinsey.com/~/media/mckinsey/featured%20insights/gender%20equality/women%20in%20law%20firms/women-in-law-firms-final-103017.ashx.

Fig. 1: Lo que oficinas de abogados y compañías dicen ofrecer

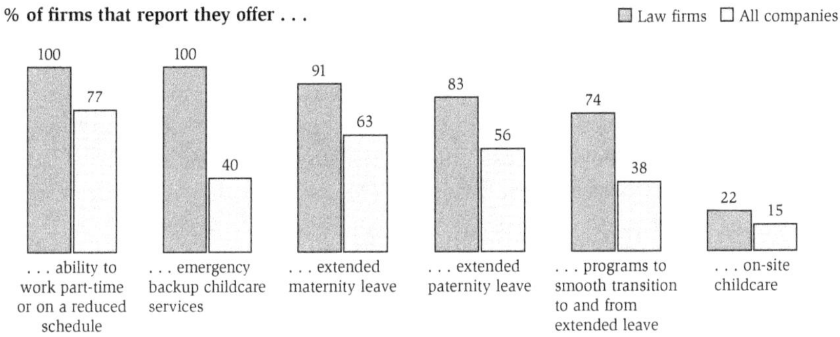

En todo caso, sea cual sea el modelo que cada una quiera o pueda adoptar, lo que es cierto es que muchas veces, estas mujeres, incluyéndome, después de poner los niños en la cama, volvemos a prender el computador, no para ver DesperateHousewives (cosa que personalmente me encantaría) sino para seguir escribiendo laudos, memoriales o artículos.

[B] Trabajo más eficientemente

Como sé que cada segundo mal empleado significa 10 segundos menos con mis hijas, pues sencillamente el tiempo es precioso y trato de no derrocharlo. Esto significa que tengo una rutina casi militar de trabajo, con mini pausas de descanso activo para estirar los músculos y descansar los ojos, trato de ir directo al grano de los asuntos y, sinceramente, el tiempo y la experiencia hace que se desarrollen habilidades para potencializar el trabajo al máximo.

Muchas veces, cuando estoy muy cansada o con poca concentración, en vez de procrastinar en el amplio mundo del internet donde uno se puede perder por horas, voy a ver diez minutos a mis hijas o me pongo a organizar los papeles que nunca quiero ver (particularmente, las facturas para preparar la contabilidad) y esas cortas pausas me llevan de nuevo hacia el camino de la concentración y, si a pesar de esto el cansancio y la falta de concentración continúan, trato de hacer siestas de quince minutos que son realmente efectivas.

[C] Trabajo tratando de tener una mejor higiene de vida

Sin ningún ánimo de entrar en estereotipos o de condenar cualquier práctica, ¿quién no recuerda las largas y sedentarias noches de pre-filing, de pre-audiencia o de audiencia ordenando piza o hamburguesas, comiendo snacks toda la noche con mucho café y sodas? Creo que muchas y muchos, en algún momento de nuestras vidas, vivimos esto. Aunque desde que el sushi se puso de moda, hay que reconocer que uno se siente comiendo más saludablemente.

Pues bien, definitivamente la frase no es de cajón y sí es cierto que "mente sana en cuerpo sano". Inclusive yo diría que va en el sentido opuesto y "cuerpo sano en mente sana" porque se requiere haber comprendido la importancia del cuerpo en la realización de todo, incluyendo sus aspiraciones profesionales. Aunque yo he faltado muchas veces a esta verdad, hago todos mis mejores esfuerzos por integrar una correcta higiene de vida a mi día a día, porque definitivamente es cierto que un cuerpo sano y saludable trabaja mejor que uno enfermo y cansado, pero además para poder cumplir con mis aspiraciones profesionales y mis sueños familiares debo estar bien. Esto implica muchas cosas materiales: dormir y comer lo mejor que se pueda sin olvidar practicar un deporte.

Dormir, para muchos, es un placer, pero en todo caso es una necesidad. Algunos necesitan dormir mucho, otros poco y otros la media. Esto depende de cada persona. En mi caso, reconozco que duermo un poco menos de la media, pero mis horas de sueño son profundas y es justo lo que mi cuerpo necesita. Anecdóticamente, trabajar un poco durante la noche o la madrugada cuando se es mamá (sobre todo de niños pequeños) comporta finalmente beneficios para todos. En efecto, si estás trabajando hasta tarde y tus niños lloran, estarás despierta para ir a su consuelo, dormirlos más rápidamente sin cortar tu ciclo de sueño porque igual ya estás despierta, y volver a tu trabajo después de una pausa; mientras todo esto ocurre, tu esposo podrá seguir durmiendo y lo apreciará tanto, que cuando sea tu momento de dormir, será él quien vaya a consolar a los hijos, de suerte que tus horas de sueño terminan siendo muy efectivas y, sobre todo, ininterrumpidas.

Comer también es un placer para muchos, y para todos es una necesidad. Claramente no estoy en ninguna posición legítima de dar lecciones a este nivel, pero sí he entendido desde hace poco la importancia de comer bien y saludable, por lo que mi solo consejo es el de consultar un médico especialista que te ayude a adoptar mejores hábitos alimenticios. Para esto, debo reconocer que el hecho de ser mamá me obligó a cambiar positivamente este aspecto de mi vida, pues siempre quieres que tus hijos coman lo mejor posible y eso te recuerda que tú también debes hacerlo.

Practicar un deporte, en mi opinión, es lo mejor no solo para el cuerpo, sino para la mente, pues es un momento en el que finalmente me encuentro sola conmigo misma y tanto el arbitraje como las hijas salen de mis pensamientos. En efecto, entre dos y tres veces por semana intento hacer algo de deporte y, a diario, practico cortas pausas activas. El deporte toma tiempo, pero paradójicamente es una gran inversión de tiempo, porque un cuerpo activo trabaja hasta dos y tres veces más rápido que uno cansado y sedentario. De nuevo, ser mamá de niñas pequeñas me ha entrenado físicamente y puedo decir que mi condición física es inclusive mejor que la que tenía cuando no era mamá y solo trabajaba en arbitraje internacional. Ya no solo corro detrás de los aviones para no perder mis vuelos, ahora también corro detrás de mis hijas para estar tan presente como pueda en sus vidas mientras les evito caer.

[D] Trabajo más feliz

No es que antes no lo fuera, pero honestamente, el hecho de ser mamá me ha convertido en un ser más bueno, más empático y más feliz. Siempre he creído que la gente feliz trabaja mejor y de eso he logrado hacer prueba.

Pegar todos los dibujos de mis hijas en el muro al frente de mi escritorio, utilizar los separadores de libros coloridos y originales que ellas me fabrican y encontrar sus carticas llenas de corazones, estrellas y unicornios en mi escritorio son, todos y más, recuerdos que me sirven de válvula de escape a las dificultades propias de la profesión, que siempre me sacan una sonrisa para afrontarlas con el extra escudo de la felicidad familiar. Además, pensar en mis hijas y en su futuro, me hace creer que todo es posible y que vale la pena esforzarme por conseguir los mejores resultados profesionales posibles.

[E] Trabajo con un grupo de apoyo

Todos lo saben y esto sí que no es un mito: la práctica del arbitraje internacional es tan excitante como exigente y la ausencia de urgencias no es lo que caracteriza esta área del derecho. También es bien conocido y esto tampoco es un mito: los niños de por sí demandan mucho tiempo, sin hablar de los imprevistos como caídas o enfermedades, así que las urgencias tampoco faltan. Para no encontrarse atrapado en medio de esas dos situaciones, y asumiendo que profesionalmente se cuenta con los colegas como plan B, lo mejor es tener siempre un grupo de apoyo para atender las urgencias familiares mientras logras llegar a casa o atenderlas.

El mío lo encabeza mi propio esposo, un hombre liberal y completamente solidario, que cree en mi carrera y la impulsa inclusive, algunas veces (muchas veces), por encima de la suya propia. Con él compartimos en igualdad de condiciones el cuidado de nuestras hijas. También me apoyo en mi niñera de cabecera y tengo, al menos, una persona más que potencialmente está lista a ayudarme. Esto sin contar con el apoyo de la familia que para algunos serán sus propios padres, sus suegros, sus hermanos o hermanas, sobrinas o sobrinos, tías o tíos y hasta los buenos vecinos. Para mí, son mis amadas sobrinas, ellas mismas abogadas, pero siempre con una gran disposición de colaborar, así como mis fabulosas amigas del colegio, ellas también en su mayoría madres, todas trabajadoras y empresarias del más alto nivel y, sobre todo, absolutamente solidarias.

[F] Trabajo sin vergüenza de decir que soy mamá

La vergüenza o, al menos, el sentimiento de sentirse "poco profesional" y "poco competitiva" por ser madre, por tomar opciones para extender el período de maternidad, por trabajar desde casa, o por tomar cualquier otro beneficio que las firmas de abogados o las empresas ofrecen a sus empleados padres (mujeres y hombres), lleva a que muchas personas, tanto madres como padres, no lo hagan y se sientan mal de hacerlo, por lo que prefieren seguir sacrificando su balance personal (familiar) y profesional. [12] Venciendo el temor de enfrentar el competitivo mundo del arbitraje, aún dominado por figuras mayores y masculinas, he aprendido que estar embarazada y tener hijos no es para nada símbolo de vergüenza.

Yo hablo de mis hijas, enseño fotos de ellas y si tengo la opción de reprogramar una reunión por motivos familiares, lo hago sin mentir ni inventar excusas. Ser mamá tampoco me impide atender urgencias o seguir el día a día profesional. En efecto, ya he contestado correos electrónicos en salas de parto; ya he participado en audiencias donde mi esposo me ha llevado mi bebé a unas pocas semanas de nacida para que la pueda alimentar durante las pausas; ya he tenido reuniones de equipo con un cargador y mi bebé a cuestas; ya he corregido tesis de maestría y leído tesis doctorales en mis licencias de maternidad; ya he organizado y llevado a cabo eventos de arbitraje con embarazos que están muy cerca de sus términos; y ya he dictado clase con mi hija mayor coloreando en silencio en uno de los pupitres del salón al lado de mis estudiantes. En el otro sentido, aunque no siempre lo logro -de donde la importancia de tener un grupo de apoyo-, ya he llevado a una de mis hijas un martes a las 3 PM a su clase de ballet; a la otra a su clase de taekwondo un viernes a las 2 PM; y a la otra a su terapia física para estimular su desarrollo un lunes a las 11 AM; ya he llevado a mis hijas al jardín a las 9 AM; y ya las he llevado a todas al pediatra, en cualquier momento del día.

Nada de esto me hace menos mamá ni menos profesional. Tampoco me hace una mujer con súper poderes. Esto tan solo da cuenta de una mujer con mucho coraje y organización, apasionada por su vida familiar y profesional, que solo trata de ser lo más presente como madre, sin descuidar en lo más mínimo su profesión.

[G] Trabajo y creo en la educación

Mi alma de profesora me ha llevado, finalmente, a educar a mis hijas, desde sus más tempranas edades, en los valores del trabajo, del esfuerzo propio, del amor por lo que se hace, de la satisfacción del deber cumplido y, en consecuencia, del dinero bien ganado. Ellas saben que cuando mamá trabaja, la puerta del estudio (que es la habitación en mi casa que me sirve de oficina) no se abre. Con el tiempo, ellas se han inventado toda suerte de excusas para intentar penetrar el lugar que solo es reservado para mamá cuando me dicen: "mamá tenemos que trabajar también" y llegan proveídas de libros de colorear y la caja de colores. A veces, las instalo en mesas de trabajo al lado de la mía y cada una hace lo propio, a veces la puerta del estudio se queda cerrada.

12. "While most law firms offer flexible- work programs, many attorneys still fear that participating in these programs will damage their careers. More needs to be done to make these a viable option.", Marc Brodherson, Laura McGee y Mariana Pires dos Reis, Supra., disponible enhttps: //www.mckinsey.com/~/media/mckinsey/featured%20insights/gender%20equality/women%20in%20law%20firms/women-in-law-firms-final-103017.ashx.

§32.04 CONCLUSIONES

Estas son mis experiencias más relevantes sobre cómo logro conciliar mi vida profesional en la práctica del arbitraje internacional con mi vida familiar como madre de tres pequeñas. No es una fórmula mágica, no es un modelo a seguir, pero es la que a mí me funciona. De hecho, hace pocos días almorzaba con una colega (ella sí muy famosa en el mundo arbitral internacional) y yo le preguntaba lo que a mí a veces me preguntan: "y tú, ¿cómo haces para lograrlo todo?", a lo que ella me respondía: "a mis hijos muy poco los veo entre semana, pero los fines de semana se los dedico casi en exclusiva". Es completamente válido, cada una encuentra su fórmula[13], como también lo es el hecho de no querer tener hijos y así permanecer intacta en dicha decisión de vida.

De todo esto, es importante recordar que ser madre, tanto como ser padre, no debería frustrar los sueños de carrera de las practicantes del arbitraje internacional como, tampoco, debería continuar siendo percibido como algo negativo por el resto de los practicantes. La pregunta para la industria del arbitraje internacional que contrata servicios jurídicos es: ¿merece la pena contratar a una mujer, hacerla socia o darle un cargo directivo, para tener que entender la compatibilidad entre su capacidad y brillantez profesional con sus responsabilidades de madre, o sencillamente se elige a un hombre que puede hacer lo mismo "sin" esta responsabilidad? La respuesta a esta pregunta debe basarse en una premisa fundamental consistente en que las responsabilidades de familia son de todos, tanto de hombres como de mujeres, y en esta generación y las que seguirán será insostenible y arcaico pensarlo de otra manera, así que claro que merece la pena contratar a esa mujer tanto como a ese hombre sin que el hecho de tener hijos sea una inquietud siquiera menor.

Sobrevivirán las empresas y estructuras que vean en el hombre y la mujer una igualdad tanto profesional como familiar y, así, adapten las condiciones profesionales para una inclusión por convicción en la cual la diversidad, la igualdad de género, la maternidad y la paternidad sean elementos clave en la ecuación del éxito empresarial. En el mundo legal este proceso ha sido más lento que en otros sectores. Puede ser porque la industria legal, en particular del arbitraje, fue de hombres por mucho tiempo[14]; sin embargo, es importante dejar de presente que la evolución hacia la inclusión de las mujeres (madres o no), en el mundo arbitral es real y cada vez mayor.

13. "Further, there are many different styles of mothering and variation in the use of surrogate care, as well as participation of fathers and other family members. Women also differ with regard to their ability to handle multiple roles that include motherhood, their relative interest in their various roles, and how they allocate their priorities." Cynthia Fuchs Epstein, Robert Sauté, Bonnie Oglensky y Martha Gever, Supra., pp. 409-410, 412, disponible en https://ir.lawnet.fordham.edu/cgi/viewcontent.cgi?referer=https://www.google.com/&httpsredir=1&article=3203&context=flr

14. En esto también hay que recordar que las mujeres, madres o no, hemos venido labrando un camino largo en el mundo del arbitraje datando de muchas décadas atrás. Cómo olvidar así las palabras de Jean McKelvey quien contaba esta historia sobre su primer arbitraje cuando entró en la sala y solo habían hombres, a lo que uno de ellos le preguntó y ella contestó: "'Oh, you're the secretary' and I said, 'No, I'm the arbitrator'", Jean McKelvey, Cornell University Memorial Statement, disponible en https://www.ilr.cornell.edu/about-ilr/founding-faculty/jean-mckelvey.

Ojalá que pronto la diversidad, la equidad de género, la maternidad y la paternidad sean tan normales en el mercado profesional arbitral que de todo esto no haya necesidad de hablar más.

CAPÍTULO 33

Lo que desearía haber sabido antes de comenzar una carrera en arbitraje

Crina Baltag

Lo que desearía haber sabido es que cada controversia tiene su mecanismo de resolución de disputas apropiado.

Mirando hacia atrás, hacia el comienzo de mi carrera en resolución de disputas, la información disponible para abogados y usuarios era escasa. Sin lugar a dudas, existían materiales sobre mecanismos de resolución de disputas distintos al litigio judicial y al arbitraje, pero hace dieciséis años[1], pocos de nosotros hubiéramos entendido, por ejemplo, cómo funciona la mediación, que la información divulgada en el proceso es privilegiada y confidencial[2], o que los tribunales pueden, de hecho, sancionar a la parte que se negaba injustificadamente a participar en el proceso[3]. Además de esto, los usuarios no eran tan conscientes como lo son hoy en día, ya que los abogados *in-house* apenas participaban en el proceso y, a menudo, se limitaban a reunir las pruebas del caso.

Hoy en día, la información está fácilmente disponible para los abogados, así como para los usuarios, por lo que se ha vuelto mucho más fácil evaluar la idoneidad de un mecanismo particular de resolución de disputas para una controversia en particular. Además, con el mayor rol de los abogados *in-house* en la gestión de casos[4], los abogados externos y los abogados de empresa están en una mejor posición para

1. Especialmente en un país de Europa del Este.
2. *Unilever PLC v. Proctor and Gamble* [2000] 1 WLR 2436. Ver también: *Brown v. Patel* [2007]EWHC 625 (Ch) and *Cattley and another v. Pollard [2006] EWHC 3130 (Ch)*.
3. *Halsey v. Milton Keynes General NHS Trust* [2004] 1 WLR 3002.
4. Ugo Draetta, *The Role of In-House Counsel in International Arbitration*, 75 *Arbitration* (2009) 470; Philippe Cavalieros [2014], *In-House Counsel Costs and Other internal Party Costs in International Commercial Arbitration*, 30(1) Arbitration International 201; Jean-Claude Najar, *A* Pro Domo *Pleading: Of In-House Counsel, and their Necessary Participation in International Commercial Arbitration*, 25 Journal of International Arbitration 2008, 623.

determinar si, en el contexto del negocio específico y de la relación subyacente, un mecanismo sugerido de resolución de disputas es la alternativa más conveniente.

Una multitud de procesos se presentan frente a nosotros: negociación, adjudicación[5], evaluación neutral temprana[6], mediación, arbitraje, litigio judicial, etc. Todos estos están aquí para resolver la controversia y servir a los usuarios. Ciertamente, algunos mecanismos tendrán características distintas que, para la disputa en cuestión, serían preferibles a otros. En general, se hace una distinción entre los mecanismos de adjudicación, cuando se solicita a un tercero, ya sea un juez o un árbitro, que decida la disputa, y los mecanismos de no-adjudicación, donde las partes tienen el control total y deciden la mejor solución. Los mecanismos de adjudicación ponen fin a la disputa y resultan más adecuados para disputas complejas. Además, confiar la decisión a un tercero podría acelerar la resolución de la disputa. Al mismo tiempo, es posible que los mecanismos de adjudicación no proporcionen el mejor resultado para las partes. Los intereses reales de las partes rara vez se descubren en los procesos de adjudicación, ya que generalmente se limitan a lo que la ley aplicable establece para la relación jurídica específica y, por lo tanto, aquellos se centran en las posiciones.

En general, se considera que los mecanismos de adjudicación, al no abordar los intereses reales de las partes, no alientan a estas últimas a mantener su relación comercial, e incluso tienden a escalar la disputa, dada su naturaleza confrontacional. Los mecanismos no adjudicativos, como la mediación y la negociación, a menudo proporcionan resultados superiores a las disputas entre las partes, ya que estas retienen el control del proceso. Al favorecer sus reales intereses, las partes son alentadas a explorar la mejor solución, sin limitarse a lo que proporciona la ley.Sin embargo, el mecanismo de no adjudicación no puede emplearse sin el consentimiento de las partes en disputa[7].Incluso cuando son obligatorios por ley, la efectividad de estos mecanismos no es posible si las partes no están realmente involucradas en el proceso[8].

La discusión no carece de relevancia cuando se considera el papel y los deberes de los abogados hacia sus clientes en el contexto de la resolución de disputas. En su trabajo seminal sobre transformación de disputas, Felstiner, Abel y Sarat destacan que:

> *"Los críticos de los profesionales sostienen que 'crean' al menos algunas de las necesidades que satisfacen... Los abogados ejercen un poder considerable sobre sus clientes. Mantienen el control sobre el curso de los litigios... y desalientan a los clientes a buscar una segunda opinión o llevar su negocio a otro lugar... Existe*

5. The Scheme for Construction Contracts (England and Wales) Regulations 1998 (SI 1998/649).
6. UK Civil Procedure Rules and Direction, Rule 3.1(2)(m) and Civil Procedure Rules and Practice Direction - Pre-Action Conduct and Protocols, para. 1.10(c).
7. Con el borrador de la Convención de las Naciones Unidas sobre los Acuerdos de Liquidación Internacionales resultantes de la Mediación (también conocido como la Convención de Singapur), la exigibilidad de los acuerdos de solución mediada ya no debería verse como una desventaja de la mediación: disponible en https://www.uncitral.org/pdf/english/commissionsessions/51st-session/Annex_I.pdf (visitado por última vez el 22 de abril del 2019)
8. Ver la posición de la Corte de Justicia de la Unión Europea sobre la mediación obligatoria en el Caso C-75/16, *Livio Menini, Maria Antonia Rampanelli v Banco Popolare — Società Cooperativa*, Decisión del 14 de junio de 2017.

evidencia de que los abogados a menudo dan forma a las disputas para ajustarse a sus propios intereses en lugar de los de sus clientes"[9].

Ante esta crítica, la relevancia de una elección adecuada de un mecanismo de resolución de disputas, como resultado de un intercambio de información entre abogado y cliente, es evidente. Felstiner Abel y Sarat reconocen que:

> *"Los abogados también producen transformaciones sobre las cuales podemos ser más entusiastas. Proporcionan información sobre opciones y consecuencias desconocidas para los clientes; ofrecen un foro para probar la realidad de la perspectiva del cliente; ayudan a los clientes a identificar, explorar, organizar y negociar sus problemas, y brindan apoyo emocional y social a clientes que no están seguros de sí mismos o de sus objetivos"*[10].

Además, los abogados también tienen la obligación ética de presentar todas estas opciones al cliente. Por ejemplo, el Manual 2018 de la Autoridad de Regulación de Abogados de Inglaterra y Gales (SRA, por sus siglas en inglés) enumera para los abogados las siguientes obligaciones: respetar el estado de derecho y la adecuada administración de justicia, actuar con integridad y en el mejor interés de cada cliente, proporcionar un estándar de servicio adecuado a los clientes, proteger el dinero y los activos de los clientes, etc[11]. El Código de Conducta de SRA 2011 establece en el Capítulo 1 que se debe lograr un estándar de servicio adecuado y esto "*toma en cuenta las necesidades y circunstancias individuales de cada cliente. Esto incluye proporcionar a los clientes la información que necesitan para tomar decisiones informadas sobre los servicios que necesitan, cómo se prestarán y cuánto costarán*"[12]. Para hacerlo, se deben lograr los siguientes resultados: O(1.12): "*los clientes están en condiciones de tomar decisiones informadas sobre los servicios que necesitan, cómo se manejará su asunto y las opciones disponibles para ellos*"; y O (1.13): "*los clientes reciben la mejor información posible, tanto en el momento del compromiso como cuando es apropiado a medida que avanza su asunto, sobre el costo total probable de su asunto*".

Al seleccionar el mecanismo de resolución de disputas apropiado, Sander y Rozdeiczer sugieren que los abogados y los usuarios respondan a las siguientes tres preguntas: (1) ¿Cuáles son mis objetivos? Esta es una forma de aconsejar a los clientes que se centren en sus intereses, en lugar de en sus posiciones; (2) ¿Qué proceso

9. William L. F. Felstiner; Richard L. Abel; Austin Sarat, *The Emergence and Transformation of Disputes: Naming, Blaming, Claiming ...*, 15 Law and Society Review. (1980) 631, 646.
10. William L. F. Felstiner; Richard L. Abel y Austin Sarat, *Supra*, p. 646. Véase también, Robert H. Mnookin; Lewis Kornhauser, Bargaining in the Shadow oftheLaw: The Case ofDivorce, 88 Yale Law Journal (1979) 950, p. 985: "*Los abogados pueden proporcionar la información básica sobre la dotación de negociación de cada cónyuge, las normas legales aplicables y el resultado probable en la corte si el caso es litigado. De hecho, como se señaló anteriormente, la imprecisión en las normas legales aplicables aumenta la necesidad de asesoramiento legal. Un cliente racional querrá una evaluación precisa de los posibles costos de modos alternativos de solución de controversias. Los abogados también son una fuente importante de información sobre los costos de transacción, un elemento importante de los cuales serán los honorarios legales*".
11. Disponible en https://www.sra.org.uk/solicitors/handbook/code/content.page (visitado por última vez el 22 de abril del 2019).
12. Disponible en https://www.sra.org.uk/solicitors/handbook/code/content.page (visitado por última vez el 22 de abril del 2019).

aprovechará las mejores características de la disputa? Como se mencionó anteriormente, cada mecanismo de resolución de disputas viene con ventajas y desventajas que se hacen más evidentes en el contexto de una disputa específica; (3) ¿Qué proceso superará mejor las barreras para la resolución? Algunas disputas, mencionan los autores, podrían estar en desacuerdo sobre la ley aplicable a los méritos del caso, en cuyo caso, un juez o tribunal arbitral puede ser la opción preferida[13].

Al entrar en la era de la Inteligencia Artificial, confío en que mis colegas estarán en una mejor posición para evaluar los mejores intereses de sus clientes y para elegir el proceso adecuado para la resolución de disputas.

13. Frank E. A. Sander and Lukasz Rozdeiczer, *Selecting an Appropriate Dispute Resolution Procedure: Detailed Analysis and Simplified Solution*, in Michael L. Moffitt and Robert C. Bordone (eds.), *The Handbook of Dispute Resolution*, (Jossey-Bass, 2005), 386.

CAPÍTULO 34

El poder propio y el poder derivado

Alfredo Bullard

Es muy fácil recurrir a los otros.
Es muy difícil depender de la obra de uno mismo.

Ayn Rand, El Manantial

§34.01 PODER PROPIO Y PODER DERIVADO

Quienes tienen poder propio confían en su capacidad para hacer lo que se tiene que hacer. Hacen lo que creen y son consistentes con esa creencia. No solo definen lo que tienen que hacer, sino que además lo hacen. Su convicción es la fuente de su conducta. No esperan obtener poder de otros. Son la fuente de su propio poder.

En contraste, los poderes derivados deciden en función a lo que otros piensan que hay que hacer. Para avanzar deciden hacer lo que otros quieren que hagan. Toman prestada, según la situación en la que se encuentran, la convicción de otros. Dicho de otra manera, derivan su poder de los demás. Y cuando el otro al que siguen pierde poder o deja de derivárselos, ellos también lo pierden.

Muchos políticos son poderes derivados. Actúan no en base a lo que creen sino a lo que un grupo de votantes quieren que haga. No importa si creen que dar ciertas regulaciones es malo. Si tienen que darlas para obtener votos las apoyan. Quien tiene poder propio, en cambio, apoya lo que cree, así le cueste no ser reelegido.

Muchas personas son poderes derivados en su trabajo. Proponen o hacen no necesariamente lo que es mejor para su función o deber, sino lo que sus jefes creen que es mejor. Esos ni siquiera plantean la alternativa. El que la decisión sea de un superior (un socio del estudio frente a un asociado) no es excusa para no hacerle notar que ese superior puede estar equivocado.

Imaginemos que un abogado tiene que decidir qué estrategia debe seguir un potencial cliente en un posible caso. Escucha los hechos que le plantea el cliente y llega a la convicción que la estrategia adecuada incluye pedir la terminación del contrato por incumplimiento y los daños y perjuicios. Su conclusión se deriva de su conocimiento, experiencia y convicciones para determinar lo que es bueno para el caso.

Pero el cliente le propone una estrategia distinta. No solo incluye la nulidad del contrato y los daños y perjuicios. Quiere incluir en su demanda la responsabilidad de los gerentes de la contraparte. Quiere vengarse de las personas que tomaron ciertas decisiones que lo perjudicaron.

El abogado cree que demandar a los gerentes no es jurídicamente correcto y que además le hace perder credibilidad al caso. Su disyuntiva está entre lo que considera adecuado o lo que su cliente cree que es adecuado. Sabe que plantear lo que piensa pone en riesgo de que decida dejarlo y contratar a otro abogado. Si el abogado tiene poder propio defiende su posición. El poder derivado asume la del cliente sin discutir, para evitar que se vaya con su caso a otra parte.

Un poder propio actúa por su propia convicción. Le diría al cliente que la estrategia que está proponiendo no es la mejor. Un poder derivado cambiaría su forma de actuar para derivar poder de su cliente, siguiendo no su convicción sino la ajena. Todos queremos derivar poder de nuestros clientes. Es difícil a veces renunciar a hacerlo. Pero tener poder propio a veces implica hacerlo.

Imagina ahora que un potencial cliente llama al abogado a una reunión para explicarle un caso para que formule una oferta para el patrocinio de un arbitraje. Le dice que está compitiendo con otros dos estudios de abogados.

El potencial cliente no tiene jurídicamente un mal caso. La mayoría de sus pretensiones tienen una muy buena base. El resto es muy discutible. Pero viendo el monto total en discusión no es claro que se justifique incurrir en los costos de arbitrar la controversia. El abogado lo descubre rápidamente. Tiene la convicción que lo mejor es transar por lo que le habían ofrecido al cliente. Su disyuntiva es si se lo dice al cliente (indicándole finalmente que es mejor que no lo contraten) o si calla y formula su oferta para que lo contraten.

Decide decir lo que piensa. A las pocas semanas (y sin haber recibido ni un centavo de honorarios), el potencial cliente le manda un correo agradeciéndole el consejo pues gracias al mismo decidió transar. Le agradece la honestidad y claridad en el consejo. El abogado perdió obtener un caso, pero ganó el respeto del cliente. Ese respeto puede generar confianza para que lo busquen en el futuro. Pero eso no es lo realmente importante. Lo importante es que actuó ejerciendo su propio poder, así ello signifique asumir un costo.

Eres un árbitro joven. Es tu primer caso. Has sido nombrado por un estudio prestigioso con muchos arbitrajes. Tienes que laudar. Si el estudio se queda contento con el laudo quizás te vuelvan a nombrar. Pero decides que tu convicción debe ser la fuente de tu poder y no la transmisión de poder a partir de nuevos nombramientos. Laudas lo que tu convicción te indica y desechas seguir las convicciones o deseos de quienes te nombraron.

Es difícil tener poder propio porque el camino del poder derivado es más atractivo y fácil. Finalmente, el poder ya está allí. Hay que salir a tomarlo. En cambio, el poder propio hay que construirlo. Y cuando eres joven el poder propio se ve como lejano y poco asible. En cambio, usar poder derivado está al alcance de tu mano.

Construir poder propio es difícil. Implica sacrificar el corto plazo para apostar por el largo. Implica frustración al ver que otros, quizás con menos méritos, obtienen poder derivado rápidamente y pueden escalar más rápidamente. Para consolidar el poder propio se requiere paciencia. Implica aceptar el fracaso inicial siendo consecuente con hacer lo que uno cree tiene que hacer.

No quiero, sin embargo, que se me malinterprete. No estoy diciendo que los poderes propios actúan siempre de manera correcta y los derivados de manera incorrecta. El poder propio puede ser muy mal utilizado. Los líderes de bandas criminales suelen tener poder propio. En cambio, un poder derivado, si sigue a las personas correctas, puede estar actuando correctamente.

Tener poder propio no tiene que ver necesariamente con la corrección de la conducta. Tiene que ver con la convicción con la que se actúa. Tiene que ver con el motor de la acción y el camino que se sigue para crecer y posicionarse en el mundo.

Y tampoco uso el término "poder derivado" de manera peyorativa. Es legítimo elegir ser un poder derivado. Se puede ser un excelente abogado. Es un éxito distinto. Es diferente al del poder propio. Pero no significa que serás un mal abogado. Es solo que quizás has renunciado a ser uno aún mejor.

Eso sí. Uno está en riesgo de derivar poder de quien no actúa correctamente. Entonces serás vulnerable al error ajeno que se convertirá en error propio. Al menos el poder propio asume las consecuencias de sus propios errores y también las consecuencias de sus aciertos.

Piensa en una persona de cualquier actividad que admires. O más precisamente, en un abogado o árbitro. Descubrirás que usualmente es un poder propio. Ello no significa que todas las personas famosas o destacadas tengan poder propio. Pero usualmente lo que admiramos en una persona es su capacidad de lograr lo que alcanzó a lograr por su propia convicción.

Usualmente un poder propio es auténtico (auténticamente malo o auténticamente bueno). Es lo que es por sus decisiones. La actuación consistente y coherente con su convicción lo hace predecible y confiable. A algunos no les gustará. A otros sí. Pero los poderes propios no actúan para gustar a los demás, sino para hacer lo que consideran que tienen que hacer.

§34.02 EMPATÍA

Poder propio no significa alejarse de los otros. Al contrario. Significa entenderlos y colocarte en su lugar. Trabajamos siempre para otros: los abogados para sus clientes, los árbitros para las partes o los profesores para sus estudiantes. Si quieres hacer las cosas bien tienes que entenderlos y colocarte en el lugar de ellos. Ello no significa necesariamente hacer lo que ellos quieren que hagas. Es hacer lo que según tu convicción es mejor para ellos, incluso cuando eso no les guste.

Para ello tienes que ser claro y directo. No crear falsas expectativas. No vender lo que no tienes ni hacerle creer que su caso es distinto a lo que es. El poder propio, para ser consistente, habla con coherencia y explica con detalle su convicción.

Es un error alejarte de los demás para hacer las cosas bien. Finalmente, uno hace bien las cosas para que otros alcancen sus objetivos. Si no piensas en ellos te alejarás de lo que quieres buscar.

Pero la empatía no se limita a ellos. Incluye a tus coárbitros, a tu contraparte, a tu equipo de trabajo. El poder propio puede (y debe) necesitar de los demás. Tener poder propio no es vivir en una burbuja. Si bien implica definir tu individualidad, es una individualidad abierta a los demás. No puedes desarrollar tu propio poder si no confías y ayudas a desarrollar el de los demás. A diferencia del poder derivado que proviene de otros, el poder propio construye con otros.

Un abogado no empático no va a ser persuasivo con un tribunal. Un árbitro no empático se alejará de sus colegas en el tribunal.

§34.03 HACER LAS COSAS BIEN

La meta de un poder propio no es ganar sino hacer las cosas bien. No es lo mismo. Son cosas distintas. Quien hace las cosas bien tendrá mayores posibilidades de ganar. Pero muchas veces querer ganar no nos deja hacer las cosas bien.

Hay que perder el miedo a perder. Y para ello tu objetivo no debe ser ganar. Cuesta mucho entenderlo y ejecutarlo. La tentación de buscar ganar dejando de hacer lo que consideras debes hacer es un distractivo importante. El cliente o tu jefe posiblemente no lo entienda y te pida otras cosas. Por eso lo debes tener claro. De perder se aprende más que de ganar. Querer ganar te puede alejar de tu objetivo.

Hay muchas formas de ganar haciendo las cosas mal.

Hacer las cosas bien es preparar tu caso, estudiarlo, usar tu inteligencia, ser leal. Puedes mejorar las posibilidades de ganar teniendo comunicaciones *ex parte* con los árbitros. O tergiversando los hechos. O destrozando a un testigo en un interrogatorio sin justificación. Pero no estarás haciendo las cosas bien.

Y no me refiero solo a actuar éticamente. Me refiero a hacer bien tu trabajo.

Si haces las cosas bien no te distraerás de lo que tienes que hacer. La línea para hacer bien las cosas es más fácil de identificar, pero más difícil de seguir. La mejor manera de no llegar a tu objetivo es tomar atajos. Los atajos reflejan dudas sobre tu capacidad de hacer las cosas bien.

Cuando he entrenado equipos de Moot en competencias de arbitraje los integrantes de un equipo están autorizados por las reglas a entrar a otras audiencias para escuchar los argumentos de otros equipos y así poderlos incorporar en sus propios argumentos en audiencias siguientes. Hacerlo no es antiético. Está permitido.

Pero en el mundo real del litigio arbitral uno no puede hacer eso porque la posibilidad no existe. No hay audiencias parecidas para ir a cazar argumentos para tu caso. El equipo que entrenaba decidió no hacerlo. Parece una desventaja. Pero en realidad te fuerza a desarrollar tus propia investigación y argumentos de manera similar a como ocurre en el mundo real. Esa capacidad contribuye a hacer las cosas mejor sin tomar atajos.

Quizás un argumento escuchado en alguna audiencia te ayude a ganar. Pero restringe el desarrollo de tu capacidad de hacer las cosas bien. Y es que en el fondo escuchar a otros equipos es una forma de poder derivado. Confías más en lo que otros hacen que en lo que tu equipo puede hacer. Confía en que tienes el poder de desarrollar tus propias capacidades.

Alcanzar poder propio significa precisamente no buscar atajos.

De la misma manera, un árbitro con poder propio no busca obtener nombramientos tomando atajos. Lo que busca es ser un buen árbitro: independiente, imparcial, trabajador, estudioso, inteligente, empático. Un buen árbitro no se deja atrapar por la desidia. Sabe que su autoridad depende de las partes y se debe a ambas. Si hace las cosas bien es posible que lo nombren más veces, aunque quizás le tome más tiempo lograrlo a si escoge el atajo de favorecer a quien lo nombra. No debe nunca renunciar a hacer las cosas bien.

Un buen indicador de que estás haciendo las cosas bien es que te comiencen a nombrar en más casos para presidir un tribunal. Puede ser un buen síntoma que estás desarrollando poder propio.

§34.04 NO HAY EXCELENCIA SIN HUMILDAD

La excelencia, sin humildad, no brilla. El poder propio se diluye fácilmente si lo lastras con soberbia. Para actuar con convicción hay que ser consciente de nuestras limitaciones. Y la humildad es un signo claro de empatía.

Es importante no confundir la humildad con pasividad o falta de convicción. El poder propio no es medroso con sus ideas. Dice lo que piensa y lo sostiene con decisión. Pero a su vez escucha. No hay que confundir convicción con terquedad. La convicción está abierta al cambio. En eso el poder propio muestra humildad.

Si un abogado en una audiencia estructura un alegato solo para demostrar que sabe y no para persuadir al tribunal de que su cliente tiene la razón, se aleja de hacer las cosas bien. La humildad nos permite ver más claramente cómo lograr un objetivo, porque elimina como herramienta de acción a la arrogancia, que suele oscurecer tu objetivo y sustituirlo con darte visibilidad. La arrogancia siempre esconde algo de inseguridad.

Curiosamente un poder propio no busca demostrar quién es. Busca demostrar consistencia en su conducta haciendo las cosas bien.

Ello no significa no creer en ti mismo. Justo porque crees en ti mismo, no tienes que demostrar a los demás quién eres. Hacerlo es precisamente una característica del poder derivado porque estás buscando el aprecio y admiración de otros para sentirte bien. Es más fácil hacerlo no luciendo lo que eres sino demostrando lo que haces.

Por ejemplo, algunos abogados creen que citar mucha doctrina o muchos casos es muestra de erudición y sabiduría. Lo ven como una forma de lucimiento. Pero como dice Dyke, "*La erudición es piratería redimida por las notas a pie de página*". Y la piratería es una forma de poder derivado.

Eso no significa que no se deba citar a otros. Solo significa que citas para reforzar el fin que persigues para hacer las cosas bien, y no para demostrar cuánto sabes. Por eso las citas deben ayudar a tu caso, a tu laudo o a que se entienda el artículo que has escrito. La mejor forma de lograr admiración es no organizar su conducta para buscar tal admiración. La gente no admira al que busca lucirse sino al que hace bien las cosas.

El poder propio no significa desconocer la experiencia y capacidades de quienes posiblemente sepan más que nosotros. El tener convicciones no significa dejar de escuchar a los demás para formarlas o reconocer su superioridad intelectual o su conocimiento. El respeto a la experiencia de otros es esencial para ser empático. La soberbia, en cambio, es el obstáculo más importante al aprendizaje. Y la humildad puede finamente definirse como la mejor manera de abrirse a aprender.

§34.05 LA FUERZA DE LA AUTOESTIMA

El poder propio se construye sobre autoestima. No se puede sentir el poder que tenemos si no generamos fe en nosotros mismos. Ser humilde no significa no confiar en uno mismo. Es todo lo contrario. La autoestima significa que no se necesita de reconocimiento ajeno para saber lo que podemos hacer. Y por tanto no debemos focalizarnos en generar reconocimiento de otros, sino reconocernos a nosotros mismos. El reconocimiento ajeno posiblemente sea una consecuencia de nuestra capacidad de creer en nosotros mismos. El reconocimiento es bueno, pero no es tu objetivo. Tu objetivo es hacer las cosas bien.

La autoestima genera seguridad. Y la seguridad transmite profesionalismo y capacidad de persuadir. Uno debe saber que está focalizado en hacer las cosas bien y que tiene las capacidades para hacerlo.

He visto a muchos abogados jóvenes dando sus primeros pasos en el arbitraje. Los he visto en sus primeras participaciones en audiencias. Debo decir que lo que más importa para hacer la diferencia no suele ser el conocimiento, la preparación o la inteligencia (que son también importantes). Lo que más hace destacar a una persona es la autoestima con la que se desenvuelve.

A veces he visto abogados jóvenes sentir que tienen que hacer todo lo posible para ganar. Y por ello toman riesgos innecesarios o se desenfocan de lo que tienen que hacer.

El temor a perder es muy mal consejero. Por eso si uno se concentra en hacer las cosas bien, por definición, está pensando en su capacidad para hacerlas y ello es la base para construir su autoestima. El poder propio no le teme a perder. Su valor viene de saberse con capacidad de conseguir su objetivo: hacer las cosas bien.

En un árbitro la autoestima le brinda la seguridad que las partes buscan. El árbitro debe transmitir que está en capacidad de manejar el caso. Sin la autoestima de los integrantes del tribunal las partes se sienten confundidas y se llenan de dudas. Y las partes miran a los árbitros jóvenes con particular suspicacia. Uno no puede cambiar su edad, pero sí la percepción de seguridad que transmite. Una autoestima empática les da a las partes la sensación que el tribunal sabe lo que está haciendo. Transmite madurez y seguridad.

§34.06 Y, FINALMENTE, QUIERE LO QUE HACES

Difícilmente podrás desarrollar poder propio en algo si no disfrutas lo que estás haciendo. Si por las mañanas, cuando te levantas, vas contento a tu trabajo o a la audiencia que te toca, estás marcado un paso importante en tu felicidad. Si no es así, hay algo que tienes que cambiar: tu trabajo, tu profesión, tu jefe o quizás la forma como haces las cosas. Si no disfrutas lo que haces difícilmente podrás hacer las cosas bien.

De todos los elementos necesarios para hacer las cosas bien el más importante es el emocional. Sin equilibrio en las emociones todo lo demás se desarticula. Si tu trabajo te desequilibra emocionalmente entonces estás en el trabajo equivocado.

Ello no significa que no haya malos momentos o que no pases por situaciones de mucho estrés. Pero ese no puede ser el estado constante en el que vives. Como alguna vez me dijo Guido Calabresi, la felicidad depende de dos cosas. La primera es tener un trabajo en el que te pagan por hacer algo que pagarías por hacer. El segundo es tener alguien con quien disfrutes pasar el resto de tu vida. Sin ese equilibrio tu poder propio no fluirá. Cuidar tu vida familiar y amical te dará más estabilidad en el trabajo. Y la estabilidad en el trabajo te dará una mejor vida familiar y amical.

Y recuerda siempre que lo que haces se define a partir de ti mismo y de tu capacidad para lograr lo que te propones. No se puede querer lo que haces si no te quieres a ti mismo.

Como decía Ayn Rand, *"Para decir: 'Yo te quiero', uno debe saber primero como pronunciar 'yo'"*.

CAPÍTULO 35

Si hubiera sido abogado

Shoschana Zusman

No sé si soy feminista, antifeminista o, simplemente, una indiferente más. Al menos, nunca me detuve a pensar en la discriminación a la mujer mientras trataba de hacerme un espacio más o menos digno en la profesión de abogado. Pensaba, incluso, que yo nunca había sido discriminada y que, para ser exitosa en la profesión, era suficiente con estudiar mucho y trabajar duro. Yo creía firmemente en la meritocracia y todo intento explícito de cambiar las cosas me parecía innecesario.

Ahora que lo pienso, mi relativamente pacífica experiencia como profesora de Derecho en los 80's, me impidió ver lo que ya era claro para los demás o, mejor dicho, para "las demás" (con el permiso a la Real Academia). La abogada en ejercicio era una profesional siempre de segundo nivel, relegada generalmente al área de Derecho de Familia u obligada a trabajar de oscura burócrata en un oscuro Ministerio. No tenía contacto con el Derecho patrimonial, ni posibilidad de integrarse a la firma de abogados como socia (y sin aspiración de hacerlo). La abogada tenía un salario bastante inferior que el de sus colegas hombres. Carecía de liderazgo. Se encontraba siempre a la sombra de un abogado-hombre, que era quien, en audiencias, presentaciones o negociaciones, tenía la palabra. La mujer se limitaba a hablarle al oído.

Para mí, ese rol era el que correspondía. Así era y así debía ser. Y —lo más importante—no me incumbía, porque, total, yo era académica y no abogada.

Tiempo después, impulsada por los desastrosos efectos económicos de un divorcio (mal negociado), decidí incursionar en la profesión. Eran tiempos en que los estudios de abogados comenzaban a levantar el veto al ingreso de mujeres a su *staff* profesional —regla no escrita, pero estándar durante la década de los 70— aunque el acceso no era fácil. Los estudios preferían hombres por la misma razón por las que un ilustrísimo profesor de Letras decía que era mejor restringir el ingreso de mujeres a la Universidad: creían que era un desperdicio de tiempo y de dinero entrenar a una mujer, que pronto abandonaría la profesión para dedicarse a sus hijos.

Y, para mí —repito— eso era lo normal y no procedía cuestionar —como se cuestiona hoy— esa marcada desigualdad. Era la ética de la "reserva", de la "femeneidad", de la "delicadeza" y de la "discreción", tan característica de esos años y que hoy ha sido superada.

En la actualidad, el incremento de mujeres en todas las áreas de la profesión legal es notoria. No fue así ni en mi época de alumna de Derecho de la Pontificia Universidad Católica, donde las mujeres éramos una minoría (10 mujeres y 80 hombres) ni cuando decidí incursionar en la profesión, donde —repito— persistía cierta resistencia. Intenté incorporarme a un par de estudios, pero me cerraron amablemente las puertas. Mi perfil no despertaba interés, cosa que sigo sin comprender, pese a que hoy no cambiaría mi independencia por nada.

Debo reconocer el ingenio de las mujeres para hacerse un lugar en la profesión. Incursionaron en temas "exóticos" en los años 90, como por ejemplo regulación, que a los abogados no les interesaba porque el desarrollo del área era todavía incipiente y —sobre todo— porque había que conocer el funcionamiento de las industrias reguladas, incluyendo tediosos (o, mejor dicho, odiosos) aspectos técnicos, muy difíciles de entender. Era pues, un mercado todavía no explorado y casi lo único en lo que las mujeres podían incursionar y, a veces, destacar. Hoy, por supuesto, la regulación es un tema que despierta el mismo interés en abogados de ambos sexos.

Pues bien, como soy incapaz de teorizar sobre un tema sobre el cual mucho se ha escrito y discutido, esta pequeña contribuciones un recuento de algunos incidentes en los que —hoy me percato— el machismo "brilló por su presencia" y donde la pregunta que corresponde hacer es si habría ocurrido lo mismo si yo hubiera sido hombre. He elegido diez anécdotas absolutamente triviales que, por ello, no encierran una reflexión, sino una invitación a reflexionar sobre eso que se llama "machismo" y que, sin duda, subsiste en el ejercicio de la profesión legal.

§35.01 "AYUDE AL SECRETARIO"

En un caso arbitral concluido hace ya varios años, percibí que, en una audiencia, el presidente del tribunal parecía incómodo —no sé por qué— por mi activa participación en encontrar la solución a un problema procesal menor. Terminado el asunto, el presidente me dice, en voz alta y con un discreto toque de ironía:

> *"Doctora, ya que usted ha sido tan activa en buscar la solución al problema, hágame el favor de dictarle el texto al secretario, tal como ha sido corregido".*

Era como si él, por ser presidente —pero, sobre todo, hombre—fuera jerárquicamente superior a mí. Pues, pese a haber percibido el intento de denigración, me acerqué obedientemente al secretario a dictarle el texto. Y lo hice para no crear fricciones, ya que el caso venía "cargado". Pregunta: ¿habría actuado igual el presidente con un árbitro-hombre? No lo creo.

§35.02 YO SOLO HABLO CON CABALLEROS

En un caso arbitral, también concluido hace años, me percaté que el árbitro designado por la otra parte no me dirigía la palabra. De hecho, a veces ni me saludaba. Hablaba exclusivamente con el presidente del tribunal y siempre en voz baja.

Yo atribuí esa actitud a que el árbitro en cuestión, no sé con qué fines, pensaba que lo mejor era ignorarme, convirtiendo la decisión en una "cuestión de hombres". Pues, "saqué garra" y hablé con el presidente del tribunal, manifestándole mi incomodidad por ese inentendible maltrato. Pese a que el presidente le pidió "tolerancia", las cosas no cambiaron. En ese momento, no me expliqué su actitud como una manifestación de machismo pura y dura, sino como una conducta manipuladora. Pero, ahora que lo pienso, el machismo no es incompatible con la manipulación. Al contrario, es una estrategia. El árbitro que solo se comunicaba con caballeros, no consiguió imponerse. Pregunta: ¿hubiera ese curioso árbitro tratado igual a un colega hombre? No lo creo.

§35.03 LA IMPORTANCIA DEL BUEN VESTIR

No puedo negar que tuve épocas de rebeldía contra el así llamado *establishment*, sobre todo en lo referido al "buen vestir", sumamente exigente en el ambiente jurídico de la década de los 70.

Comencé a dictar clases en la Facultad de Derecho vestida informalmente, cuando eso no se estilaba. Ninguna autoridad de la Facultad reprochó mi vestimenta. Tiempo después, fui invitada a una reunión de profesores que habían trabajado en la elaboración del proyecto de Código Civil de 1984 y no se me ocurrió nada mejor que aparecerme en *jeans*. Al verme así vestida, se me acercó un profesor de Derecho Civil y en tono de reproche y con desfachatez, me dijo que *"esa no era manera de vestirse"*. Pregunto: ¿se lo habría dicho a un hombre? Posiblemente sí, si se hubiera tratado de un abogado joven. Pero, hacerle esa observación a un abogado de su generación, como era mi caso, ¡imposible!

§35.04 LOS GRITOS DE CRISTÓBAL

En el difícil camino de asesorar a un cliente a punto de ser declarado en quiebra, decidí que no asistiría a una reunión convocada para llegar a una transacción. Ello porque -lo recuerdo con nitidez- mi inseguridad era muy grande y estaba dominada por el miedo de quedar mal.

Horas después, recibí una llamada telefónica del abogado de la otra parte -el tal Cristóbal- quien, a gritos, me dijo que no había asistido a la reunión con la intención de frustrar el arreglo (que, según él, a mi cliente le convenía). Me dijo de todo, desde mentirosa, tramposa e irresponsable, hasta persona de mala fe y de conducta dudosa. ¡Y yo que no había asistido por falta de confianza en mí misma!

Lo interesante es que ninguna explicación fue suficiente y los alaridos no cesaban. Curioso caso de histeria masculina. Hoy, por supuesto, lo pondría en su lugar.

Pero en ese momento no tuve el coraje de hacerlo. La pregunta es, nuevamente, ¿habría Cristóbal tratado igual a un hombre? Sinceramente, no lo creo.

§35.05 LA CUOTA

Años atrás, cuando algunos organismos internacionales estaban intentando introducir el arbitraje en el Perú, me invitaron a un conversatorio con árbitros extranjeros. Asistí. Un funcionario -peruano y supuestamente amigo mío- me dijo sin titubear que yo estaba en esa reunión porque tenían que cubrir la cuota de mujeres, que dichos organismos propiciaban.

¡Y yo que creía que era un reconocimiento a mi trabajo y no a mi género! ¡Qué equivocada estaba! Pregunto: ¿hubiera hecho ese funcionario el mismo ponzoñoso comentario a un colega hombre, parte de una minoría discriminada? No lo creo.

§35.06 ¡REGRESEN A LA UNIVERSIDAD!

En un arbitraje, en el que yo era árbitro de parte y la presidenta una mujer, discutimos el caso con el tercer árbitro. Hombre por supuesto. Las dos árbitras coincidimos en el sentido que debía tener el laudo y él estuvo en contra. En nuestra reunión de intercambio de pareceres, noté que el buen señor se iba sulfurando cada vez más, hasta que en un momento nos dijo: *"¡ustedes dos tienen que regresar a la Universidad, porque no saben de lo que están hablando!"*

Pregunta: ¿y si yo hubiera sido hombre? ¿Y si el tribunal hubiera estado presidido por un hombre? ¿Lo habría mandado de regreso a la Universidad? Francamente no lo creo. Mujer aguanta todo. Tiempo después, me percaté que el árbitro en cuestión me había quitado el saludo. Espero que se le pase.

§35.07 NO PUEDO VER SUFRIR A UNA DAMA

Este es uno de los pocos casos -si no el único- en que agradecí haber nacido mujer. Cuando estaba iniciándome como abogada, tuve que ir a hablar con el asesor legal de un Ministerio, quien me comunicó que su informe legal sería contrario a los intereses de mi cliente.

Yo, sorprendida y frustrada, solo atiné decirle, "*ay doctor, eso no puede ser*". Y, para mi sorpresa me dijo lo siguiente: "*doctora, voy a cambiar el sentido de mi opinión, porque no puedo ver sufrir a una dama*". Pregunta: ¿hubiera tenido la misma reacción si el "sufrido" era hombre? Es claro que no.

§35.08 EL VETO

Como miembro de un tribunal administrativo y debido a la costumbre de rotación del cargo de presidente, ese año me correspondía ejercer dicho cargo. Pues, se propuso mi nombre y, para mi sorpresa, uno de los miembros del tribunal se opuso ferozmente a mi designación, sin dar una sola explicación mínimamente convincente.

Sus argumentos eran que "no le parecía", que yo "no estaba preparada para representar al tribunal", que "en todo caso fuera Juan" y generalidades semejantes que escondían sus verdaderas razones que -hoy entiendo- eran su incomodidad de "someterse" a una presidenta mujer.

A lo que yo respondí que, si él no estaba de acuerdo, yo declinaba, pero no porque no mereciera el cargo, sino porque siempre he huido de presidencias y de representaciones semejantes, porque añaden una carga burocrática al ya difícil trabajo de análisis y redacción, que prefiero no asumir. Pregunta: ¿se habría opuesto si el propuesto era un hombre? Definitivamente no, porque terminamos eligiendo a un hombre como presidente con su total anuencia.

§35.09 PARA MACHISTAS, LAS MUJERES

Lo que a continuación describo no corresponde a una situación concreta, sino a la observación de la conducta de algunas abogadas, tanto en arbitrajes como en negociaciones y reuniones con clientes. Por ejemplo, abogadas inseguras creen que interrumpiendo lo que dice otra (no otro) van a ganar puntos en una audiencia básicamente formada por hombres. Esa actitud es un error porque frustra la posibilidad de llegar a una solución, cualquiera que ella sea. Guardar respetuoso silencio es lo correcto. No por ello una abogada es menos.

Esa anécdota me recuerda que, en una oportunidad, discutiendo un caso con una joven abogada, ella ponía la cabeza entre sus manos y me decía: "bueno, otra vez, te lo voy a volver a explicar, ¡a ver si ahora entiendes lo que estoy diciendo!" Y yo entendía lo que ella postulaba, solo que estaba equivocada.

Otra conducta frecuente en mujeres machistas es la de explotar el "feminismo", convirtiéndolo, no en un derecho a ser escuchada por igual, sino en un privilegio del cual no gozan los hombres. Para eso, la estrategia es señalar que el abogado de la contraparte le está faltando el respeto como mujer, incentivando con ello a los demás a llamar la atención al abogado "faltoso". Gran error. Igualdad de oportunidades no es lo mismo que privilegio y, mientras no se entienda eso, las mujeres seremos las peores cómplices del machismo.

Finalmente, la actitud de algunas abogadas de no saludarme o de no despedirse o de mirarme con odio (si soy su contraparte o miembro de un tribunal) es francamente inentendible. Son ellas las que incrementan la discriminación.

§35.10 ¡MIRA MAMITA!

Un abogado ya mayor y muy querido, con quien compartí más de un tribunal arbitral, utilizaba las siguientes frases al dirigirse a mí: *¡mira mamita! ¡mira hijita! ¡tú no entiendes lo que las partes quieren decir! ¡lo que pasa es que no captas bien, amor! ¡yo te voy a explicar! ¡es que te falta "calle"!* No me lo imagino dando un trato tan "afectuoso" a un hombre, ¡aunque podría ser que sí!

CAPÍTULO 36

¿Cómo generar un impacto significativo a través de una carrera en resolución de controversias?

María Angélica Burgos

La denominada generación de los *millenials* irrumpió y desafió a las empresas y a la cultura profesional. En el caso del mercado legal, las firmas de abogados se siguen preguntando cuáles son las estrategias adecuadas para retenerlos, dado que parecen ser una generación difícil de satisfacer. En la mayoría de los casos, las estrategias son en vano, porque al final del ejercicio los abogados *millenials* continúan abandonando sus trabajos corporativos.

Dentro de los desafíos propuestos por los *millenials* queda un interrogante sobre la mesa que toca el ADN de nuestra profesión: ¿cómo generamos un impacto positivo y significativo a través del ejercicio del Derecho? Y ¿qué entendemos precisamente por *impacto positivo?*

Según una reciente encuesta de Deloitte, la generación de los "*millenials*" busca que su empresa no solo se enfoque en la generación de ingresos, sino que incentive objetivos balanceados, que incluyan: (1) generar impacto positivo en la sociedad y el medio ambiente; (2) crear ideas, productos y servicios innovadores; (3) crear empleos, desarrollar carreras y mejorar la vida de las personas y (4) impulsar la diversidad y la inclusión en el trabajo. [1] Estas aspiraciones parecen ser concretas y realizables en el día a día profesional, sin embargo, las personas entrevistadas notaron que sus empresas no priorizaban estas áreas, sino que enfocaban su atención en la generación de ingresos, en la eficiencia y en los aspectos comerciales. [2] En el caso de los abogados, Susan Smith

1. Deloitte. Deloitte 2018 *Millenial Survey. MillenialsDissapointed in business, unprepared for industry 4.0*. Disponible en: https://www2.deloitte.com/co/es/pages/about-deloitte/articles/millennialsurvey2018.html
2. Ibíd.

Blakely observó recientemente que los más jóvenes buscan un propósito y un sentido en su trabajo que vaya más allá de la generación de dinero y que además quieren sentir que con su trabajo están haciendo una diferencia. [3]

El deseo de contribuir a la sociedad y de generar un impacto positivo no es un anhelo exclusivo de los abogados *millenials*. Todo lo contrario. Parecería que aquellos que han escogido una profesión que sirve a la justicia y al imperio del derecho, se inclinan por la realización de unos valores colectivos que en definitiva redundan en una mejoría para toda su sociedad. Se puede afirmar que todos los abogados, en mayor o menor medida, tenemos interés en generar impacto en nuestra sociedad.

Y este es, sin lugar a dudas, el caso de los abogados que practicamos en el área de resolución de controversias, pues al solucionar diferencias por vía de la adjudicación y no de las armas, estamos anteponiendo el imperativo de la justicia y del derecho por encima del de la fuerza. No en vano, hace poco una colega que admiro profundamente me comentó que por esta razón creía que teníamos el mejor trabajo del mundo. El derecho, tan imperfecto como es, nos brinda una solución que —por lo menos en teoría— está disponible para todas las personas en igualdad de condiciones. No me cabe duda que, a través de la realización de este objetivo, los abogados generamos un impacto significativo en nuestras sociedades.

Sin embargo, este es un ideal que puede parecer intangible y distante de las actividades que realizamos a diario en nuestras oficinas. En el contexto de un mundo legal que evoluciona rápidamente, que es exigente, que nos enfrenta a una competencia agresiva y que encara desafíos gigantes como los cambios en el mercado, la tecnología y la liberalización de la profesión,[4] parecería muy lejano —sino ingenuo— que pudiéramos avocarnos a la generación de impacto positivo y al mismo tiempo ser exitosos profesionales. Me resisto a creer que la única posibilidad sea abandonar nuestros trabajos corporativos para buscar una profesión en el sector sin ánimo de lucro o en el sector público.

Entonces la pregunta que nos queda es ¿cómo generar impacto positivo significativo en nuestra sociedad y en nuestro entorno, desde nuestro trabajo dentro de un equipo de arbitraje? ¿Cómo logramos aquello que tan articuladamente describieron los *millenials:* generar impacto positivo, innovar, crear carreras y mejorar la vida de las personas e impulsar la diversidad y la inclusión en el trabajo?

En mi opinión, podemos generar impacto positivo en varios frentes: en nuestra sociedad y en nuestra comunidad, en las organizaciones legales a las que pertenecemos, en nuestra profesión, en nuestros equipos de trabajo y en las personas con las que nos relacionamos. En todos estos frentes, el impacto puede implicar la creación de bienestar, la innovación, el crecimiento y la diversidad e inclusión en el campo laboral. También podemos generar impacto positivo de manera individual o de manera colectiva, bien sea como equipos de trabajo o como organizaciones legales.

Y, en la práctica, ¿cómo lo hacemos?

---

3. Susan Smith Blakely, *What Millenial Lawyers Want*, Wolters Kluwer, 2019 (Kindle Edition).
4. Richard Susskind, *Tomorrow's Lawyers. An Introduction to Your Future*, Second Edition. Oxford UniversityPress, 2017, (Kindle Edition).

A continuación, resumo algunas ideas sobre las formas en las que como abogados de resolución de controversias podemos generar este impacto, bien sea desde nuestro actuar individual o colectivo. Naturalmente, estas ideas no pretenden ser exhaustivas ni comprehensivas.

§36.01 PRIMERO, REAFIRMANDO NUESTRO COMPROMISO ÉTICO

Los abogados que trabajamos en la resolución de controversias tenemos un compromiso superlativo con la ética. Nuestra profesión exige estándares de comportamiento que generen confianza en las labores que realizamos, no sólo por la calidad del trabajo que hagamos sino también porque actuemos de manera correcta. Específicamente, en materia de ética contamos con varios derroteros tanto en la ley doméstica como en instrumentos de *softlaw* internacionales. En mi opinión, este compromiso supone no solo seguir estrictamente nuestros deberes éticos y profesionales, sino también requerir que estos sean cumplidos por nuestros colegas y rechazar las malas prácticas. Solo de esta manera contribuimos a que se genere una cultura de ética en la práctica del arbitraje.

§36.02 SEGUNDO, RESPETANDO LOS DERECHOS HUMANOS

Las organizaciones de abogados, como empresas, tienen la responsabilidad de respetar los derechos humanos, indistintamente del tamaño que éstas tengan. [5] Esto se traduce en cuatro acciones principales, que surgen de los Principios Rectores sobre las Empresas y los Derechos Humanos, adoptados por el Consejo de Derechos Humanos en el año 2011: (1) adoptar compromisos políticos de asumir su responsabilidad de respetar los derechos humanos; (2) abstenerse de infringir los derechos humanos de terceros; (3) hacer frente a las consecuencias adversas que generan sus actividades o en las que tengan alguna participación, incluyendo la reparación, cuando quiera que esta proceda; y (4) realizar procesos de debida diligencia que les permitan identificar, prevenir, mitigar y rendir cuentas sobre su impacto en materia de derechos humanos. [6] La Guía Práctica de la *International Bar Association* (IBA) sobre Empresas y Derechos Humanos para Abogados Mercantiles aclaró que la responsabilidad de respetar los derechos humanos de los bufetes es aplicable a los aspectos de su negocio que no sea la prestación de servicios jurídicos, pues estos deben prestarse de manera independiente.[7] Así, una manera en la que podemos generar impacto es entendiendo estas responsabilidades e incorporándolas dentro de nuestras prácticas.

En el caso de las organizaciones legales, hay retos importantes en derechos humanos, por ejemplo, en materia de discriminación y acoso. Recientemente, una

5. Principios Rectores sobre las Empresas y los Derechos Humanos: puesta en práctica del marco de las Naciones Unidas para "proteger, respetar y remediar", adoptados por el Consejo de Derechos Humanos mediante Resolución 17/4 del 16 de junio de 2011. Principio Rector 14.
6. Ibíd., Principios Rectores 11-24.
7. Guía Práctica de la IBA sobre Empresas y Derechos Humanos para Abogados Mercantiles, adoptada por una resolución del Consejo de la IBA, 28 de mayo de 2016, p.36

encuesta de la IBA en la profesión legal encontró que un porcentaje significativo de hombres y mujeres habían sufrido *bullying* e intimidación en el transcurso de sus carreras.[8] Además, esta encuesta encontró que hay niveles de discriminación por género y prácticas de acoso que son preocupantes. [9]

Como abogados tenemos la posibilidad de promover la discusión sobre estas problemáticas en nuestras organizaciones y de ser gestores de su solución. Existen varias maneras de hacerlo, incluyendo la creación y participación en grupos de discusión dentro de la organización, creando consciencia de la existencia de estas dificultades, buscando alternativas para combatirlas y promoviendo conversaciones directas respecto a estos desafíos. Cambiar nuestra actitud colectiva frente a estos desafíos y trabajar en nuestras percepciones inconscientes (*unconscious bias*), nos llevará a construir firmas de abogados más incluyentes y diversas, que presten servicios legales a las expectativas del mundo actual. También es importante que aquellas personas que hacen parte del liderazgo de las firmas generen la capacidad de escuchar y de ser autocríticos frente a los aspectos en donde hay trabajo por adelantar, y se atrevan a propiciar los cambios necesarios para que las organizaciones realmente progresen en estos aspectos.

§36.03 TERCERO, APOYANDO A NUESTROS CLIENTES EN COMPRENDER SUS RESPONSABILIDADES EN MATERIA DE DERECHOS HUMANOS

Al igual que las empresas legales, las empresas que son nuestros clientes tienen responsabilidades en materia de derechos humanos. Como sus asesores, tenemos el deber de ofrecer nuestro consejo independiente y de cumplir con los estándares éticos que regulan nuestra profesión. Sin embargo, estamos en una posición privilegiada para apoyar a nuestros clientes en el entendimiento de sus responsabilidades en materia de derechos humanos. La Guía Práctica de la IBA ha denominado este rol como el del asesor de confianza, el cual se logra con diferentes medidas que permitirían al abogado convertirse en un asesor especializado en cuestiones empresariales y de derechos humanos, a saber: ofrecer capacitaciones sobre empresas y derechos humanos a los clientes, proporcionar asesoramiento sobre una base probono, realizar sesiones informativas para los clientes, entre otras[10]. Estimo que como abogados de resolución de controversias podríamos cumplir este rol para nuestros clientes, sin exceder el mandato que nos fue conferido.

---

8. "*The findings of our survey include responses that suggest that some lawyers experience alarming levels of bullying and intimidation. These findings suggest that significant percentages of both women and men —women almost 50 percent and men 30 per cent—have been subject to bullying and intimidating conduct during the course of their careers.*" IBA Legal Policy and Research Unit, *Women in Commercial Legal Practice*, Diciembre de 2017. p. 16 Disponible en: https://www.ibanet.org/LPRU/Women-business-Lawyers-Initiative-Front-page.aspx
9. IBA Legal Policy and Research Unit, *Women in Commercial Legal Practice*, Diciembre de 2017. P. 34 Disponible en: https://www.ibanet.org/LPRU/Women-business-Lawyers-Initiative-Front-page.aspx
10. Guía Práctica de la IBA sobre Empresas y Derechos Humanos para Abogados Mercantiles, adoptada por una resolución del Consejo de la IBA, 28 de mayo de 2016, p.41

§36.04 CUARTO, COMPROMETIÉNDONOS CON VALORES

Los abogados podemos comprometernos de manera voluntaria con los valores en los que creemos. En los últimos años han surgido una serie de iniciativas que invitan a los abogados a dar un paso adelante en la auto-regulación y a comprometerse a tomar acciones puntuales en pro de valores específicos, como los son la inclusión, la diversidad, la transparencia, la no-discriminación y el buen trato. En algunos casos, el compromiso con valores puede interrelacionarse con los compromisos políticos que pueden adoptar las organizaciones legales en materia de derechos humanos. Un ejemplo de esto es el *Equal Representation in Arbitration Pledge*, que a la fecha ha sido firmada por alrededor de 3.500 organizaciones y personas naturales[11]. A través del Pledge, como se la ha llamado, los firmantes se comprometen a tomar medidas razonables que estén a su alcance para mejorar el perfil y la representación de las mujeres en el arbitraje. El Pledge ha impactado el campo del arbitraje, e incluso, fue reconocido por Global Arbitration Review, como uno de los desarrollos más destacados del arbitraje. Existen además otras iniciativas importantes que propenden por mayor diversidad en el campo de la resolución de controversias internacionales como el *Alliance for Equality in Dispute Resolution*.

Tratándose del compromiso con valores, hay que recordar que los esfuerzos también deben orientarse a las acciones, puesto que los compromisos públicos que quedan inactivos no generan el impacto pretendido. Debemos generar una visión colectiva que nos permita exigir el cumplimiento de esos valores a quienes se comprometen con ellos y ser autocríticos en aquellas situaciones en que dichos compromisos no están siendo suficientes.

Por ejemplo, en materia de diversidad, la última encuesta de Arbitraje Internacional de Queen Mary University y de White & Case, reconoce que, si bien no hay consenso en el nexo causal entre diversidad y la calidad de las decisiones, la mayoría de los entrevistados coincidieron en que la diversidad debía promoverse[12]. Este estudio mostró que en materia de las designaciones de árbitros hay una percepción muy positiva entre los usuarios del arbitraje sobre el avance en diversidad de género, pero al tiempo resaltó que se debe ampliar la discusión sobre diversidad para incluir a grupos étnicos y culturales, incrementar la diversidad geográfica e incluir otras generaciones[13]. Esto nos muestra que se ha logrado un impacto significativo en poner sobre la mesa la discusión de género, pero al tiempo nos invita a considerar la diversidad de manera más holística y global. Al apostarle a la diversidad como valor, debemos ser conscientes de que no basta con compromisos políticos y acciones para incrementar la participación de las mujeres en el arbitraje, pues existen otros grupos minoritarios cuya participación en la resolución de controversias contribuiría enormemente.

11. Véase: http://www.arbitrationpledge.com/ (Consultada por última vez el 29 de marzo de 2019).
12. Queen Mary University, White & Case, *2018 International Arbitration Survey: The Evolution of International Arbitration*, p. 17.
13. Ibíd., pp. 17-18.

§36.05 QUINTO, PRESTANDO SERVICIOS LEGALES PROBONO

La prestación de servicios legales probono es una de las maneras más claras de generar un impacto legal positivo y significativo.

Los servicios probono pueden adoptar diferentes modalidades: desde la atención de casos individuales pasando por asesorías en litigios de alto impacto o de interés social, hasta en investigaciones que permitan desarrollar algún tema específico para instituciones civiles, culturales o educativas. Como lo dispone la Declaración de Trabajo Pro-Bono para el Continente Americano, el trabajo probono es gratuito, pero debe prestarse con la misma calidad y estándares profesionales (y éticos) con los que se prestan los servicios legales remunerados. [14] Se trata de un compromiso concreto de los abogados con la realización de uno de los valores de nuestra profesión: el acceso a asesoría legal y a la justicia en general.

Los proyectos probono son una excelente oportunidad para prestar el conocimiento y la experiencia que tenemos al servicio de una causa con impacto. Conozco varios abogados de resolución de controversias que han participado en proyectos probono de litigios de alto impacto, en representación de partes en foros internacionales de derechos humanos y en la conciliación de diferencias entre dos pequeños empresarios, usando las habilidades adquiridas en sus quehaceres diarios.

El trabajo probono también nos permite innovar en el derecho y perseguir intereses distintos a los del área de práctica en la que estemos involucrados. En mi experiencia, he podido participar en investigaciones jurídicas de cuestiones de interés público para asociaciones civiles y en la atención de casos particulares que generaron un cambio significativo en la vida de las personas. Recuerdo con mucho aprecio el caso de una madre que acudió a los servicios pro-bono porque a su hija se le negaba la prestación de servicios de salud por un error en el registro civil, y que gracias a esa asesoría pudo normalizar la situación.

Estoy convencida que el impacto positivo no se genera exclusivamente en los grandes actos ni en los más visibles. Tampoco se mide en resultados, puestos en rankings, comisiones de éxito, estadísticas ni notas de prensa. El impacto positivo se causa con pequeñas acciones que hacen que la vida de los otros sea mejor y que generen sentimientos de bienestar y de progreso. Este impacto es tan importante cuando se despliega sobre nuestros compañeros de trabajo, nuestros colegas y nuestras organizaciones legales, como cuando impulsa a una comunidad específica o a uno de nuestros clientes. También dejamos una huella definitiva cuando trabajamos bajo los estándares éticos más altos, de manera decorosa y defendiendo el derecho por encima de la fuerza, la deshonestidad y la trampa.

En su charla TED *"Being Young and Generating Impact"* ("Ser Joven y Generar Impacto"), Natalie Warne cuenta la historia de una organización social que, con el apoyo de un gran número de pasantes y voluntarios, logró impulsar la aprobación de un proyecto de ley en Estados Unidos para tomar acción frente al reclutamiento de menores por Joseph Kony. En esa charla, la joven describió a los "anonymous

14. Declaración de Trabajo Pro Bono para el Continente Americano.

extraordinaires" como aquellas personas que impulsan los movimientos y que trabajan de manera desinteresada y vigorosa por aquellas causas en las que creen. Al cerrar, Natalie resaltó: *"In the small anonymous monotonous every single day acts, I have to remind myself to be extraordinary."*[15] Creo que esta es la filosofía que los abogados de arbitraje podemos adoptar para generar impacto positivo: ser anónimos extraordinarios en nuestras tareas y actividades diarias.

15. *"En los actos diarios monótonos, anónimos y pequeños, debo recordarme a mí misma el ser extraordinaria"*. Natalie Warne, *"Being Young and making an impact"*, Ted Talk, Abril 2011, Disponible en: https://www.ted.com/talks/natalie_warne_being_young_and_making_an_impact#t-757429

CAPÍTULO 37
¿Qué quieren las mujeres en el arbitraje?

Carolina Arroyo Aguirre[*]

En la película *What Women Want*, Nick Marshall, el personaje interpretado por el actor Mel Gibson, adquiere un poder sobrenatural para escuchar lo que, según el guion de la película, son los deseos, pensamientos, sentimientos y anhelos de las mujeres. Marshall, un hombre machista de mediana edad que creía conocerlo todo sobre las *mujeres*, descubre un estereotipo muy básico sobre las mismas: ellas -aparentemente- no siempre dicen lo que piensan, ni necesariamente piensan todo lo que dicen.

En el ámbito del derecho, mucho se ha escrito sobre cuál es el estado de la profesión legal para las mujeres, qué obstáculos enfrentan al momento de ascender y cuáles son las iniciativas de diversidad, necesarias para una mayor y más activa participación de las mujeres en el arbitraje. Sin embargo, no se ha profundizado sobre cómo viven su profesión las mujeres jóvenes, cuáles son sus anhelos o si estos difieren de lo que aspiran los hombres.

En este capítulo intentaré examinar las experiencias y aspiraciones de las mujeres jóvenes que litigan en arbitraje, sobre algunos aspectos de su profesión. ¿Es verdad que las mujeres litigantes prefieren su desarrollo profesional al del ámbito familiar? ¿Son los hombres litigantes más ambiciosos o menos emocionales que las mujeres? ¿Están las mujeres más dispuestas a renunciar al dinero por más tiempo de ocio?

A continuación, trataré de responder estas y otras preguntas, con base en una encuesta[1] enviada por correo electrónico a los asociados de firmas con prácticas de arbitraje que fue respondida de manera anónima. La muestra está compuesta por treinta y cinco practicantes de arbitraje internacional, residentes en veintiún países del

* Las opiniones expresadas son de la autora y no reflejan necesariamente las opiniones de otros abogados de su firma ni las de sus clientes.

1. La encuesta fue desarrollada por José María de la Jara, Carolina Arroyo y Álvaro Awad, editores de este libro y consta en el Apéndice I.

mundo, con una edad comprendida entre los 24 y 40 años. En esta muestra, el 31,4% de los encuestados fueron mujeres.[2]

La encuesta tenía diferentes secciones con preguntas direccionadas a conocer la siguiente información sobre los participantes: (1) datos demográficos; (2) experiencia como litigante; (3) experiencia como árbitro o secretario administrativo; (4) balance trabajo-vida; (5) expectativas sobre su futuro profesional; y (6) experiencias y otros.

Este capítulo está escrito con base en un análisis cualitativo y cuantitativo general de las respuestas, sin que se haya realizado un estudio estadístico profundo y pormenorizado, debido al tamaño de la muestra. Nos enfocaremos en ciertas preguntas cuyas respuestas consideramos más relevantes para conocer qué tan ciertos podrían ser algunos estereotipos sobre los pensamientos y expectativas de las mujeres jóvenes y su profesión: (1) cómo se valoran a sí mismas en el ámbito laboral; (2) qué tan preparadas se sienten para asumir grandes retos profesionales; (3) cuáles son sus expectativas a futuro; y (4) cómo perciben los beneficios del trabajo, entre otros.

A continuación, me referiré a las respuestas de algunas de las preguntas de la encuesta y lo que sugieren estos resultados:

§37.01 ¿TE SIENTES UN MIEMBRO IMPORTANTE EN TU TRABAJO?

Esta pregunta estaba encaminada a conocer cómo se perciben o se sienten valorados los participantes en sus trabajos; específicamente, si creen que son miembros importantes de su equipo. De los veinte y cuatro hombres encuestados, el 42% respondió estar "totalmente de acuerdo" con dicha afirmación, mientras que el 37% dijo estar "de acuerdo". Es decir, un porcentaje del 79% se consideró un miembro importante de su equipo. Tan solo un porcentaje del 17% dijo no estar de acuerdo ni en desacuerdo, mientras que un porcentaje residual del 4% contestó estar en "desacuerdo" o, lo que es lo mismo, no sentirse un miembro importante de su equipo. En el caso de las mujeres, el 45% de las encuestadas dijo estar "totalmente de acuerdo", mientras que el 55% dijo estar "de acuerdo" con la afirmación.

Si bien los datos parecerían sugerir que no existen diferencias relevantes entre las respuestas de hombres y mujeres, llama la atención que, en el caso de los hombres, un 4% haya respondido que no se siente un miembro importante de su equipo de trabajo, mientras que ninguna mujer haya contestado lo mismo. Las respuestas podrían indicar que las mujeres no permanecen en trabajos en los que no se sienten importantes o que los hombres permanecen en equipos pese a no sentirse importantes en las tareas que desempeñan.

§37.02 ¿QUÉ TAN PREPARADO TE SIENTES PARA PARTICIPAR EN UN CASO COMO ÁRBITRO ÚNICO?

En esta pregunta el 50% de los hombres dijo sentirse suficientemente preparado para asumir un caso como árbitro único, mientras que el 8% dijo no encontrarse para nada

2. Los resultados de la encuesta constan en el Apéndice II.

preparado. Un total del 29% reconoció que todavía le hace falta preparación y tan solo un 13% dijo que se siente "sobradamente preparado"; es decir, que sus habilidades están por encima de las que se requieren para manejar un caso como árbitro único. Por el contrario, en el caso de las mujeres encuestadas, el 46% afirmó que le faltaba preparación requerida para asumir un caso sola, el 18% dijo no sentirse "nada preparada", el 27% dijo estar "suficientemente preparada", dejando un 9% que contestó que se encuentra "sobradamente preparada".

Estas respuestas sugieren que las mujeres parecerían ser más cautas al momento de valorar su preparación para enfrentar nuevos retos como árbitros. En el caso de los hombres, la mayoría contestó sentirse suficientemente preparado, mientras que, en el caso de las mujeres, la mayoría contestó que le hacía falta preparación para actuar como una árbitro única. Las respuestas a esta pregunta podrían sugerir que los hombres se sienten más seguros sobre sus habilidades al momento de enfrentar un nuevo reto profesional, mientras que las mujeres parecerían evaluarse de manera más crítica.

§37.03 ¿QUÉ ESPERAS LOGRAR EN LOS PRÓXIMOS 10 AÑOS?

En este caso, la mayoría de hombres y mujeres encuestados establecieron que su objetivo principal para los próximos diez años era convertirse en socios de las firmas en las que actualmente trabajan. Por lo tanto, no parecería existir una diferencia evidente entre los practicantes de arbitraje, según su género, respecto de sus expectativas a futuro.

Es interesante, sin embargo, que el 16% de los hombres y el 45% de las mujeres de la muestra quieren dedicarse a ser árbitro, pero consideran otras opciones también, como dedicarse a la academia, a su familia, o a hacer un doctorado. Por otro lado, el 18.18% de las mujeres y el 8.33% de los hombres esperan dedicarse exclusivamente a ser árbitro y el 16.67% de los hombres y 9.09% de las mujeres quieren fundar su propia firma.

§37.04 EN EL SUPUESTO QUE BUSCARAS UN NUEVO TRABAJO, BUSCARÍAS UN LUGAR QUE OFREZCA...

A los encuestados se les solicitó que escogieran una o varias alternativas sobre lo que buscarían en su próximo trabajo. Entre las alternativas se incluyeron las siguientes: un sueldo más alto, más tiempo libre, mayor exposición (en el mercado), más oportunidades de aprendizaje, mayor reconocimiento de sus logros y más trabajo probono.

La mayoría de los hombres, el 58.33%, buscaría un sueldo más alto, en ciertos casos acompañado de más oportunidades de aprendizaje, mayor exposición y mayor reconocimiento de sus logros. Por el contrario, tan solo el 27.27% de las mujeres buscaría un sueldo más alto, acompañado de más oportunidades de aprendizaje y trabajo probono.

La mayoría de las mujeres, el 36.36% y el 20.83% de los hombres reconoció que buscaría un trabajo que ofrezca más tiempo libre, al igual más oportunidades de aprendizaje, mayor exposición y mayor reconocimiento de sus logros.

Finalmente, tan solo 12.5% de los hombres y el 27.27% de las mujeres encuestadas buscarían en un nuevo empleo más oportunidades de aprendizaje, mayor exposición y mayor reconocimiento de sus logros, sin considerar un sueldo más alto.

§37.05 ¿CREES QUE ES POSIBLE TENER EL MISMO SUELDO Y PRESTIGIO CON MENOS HORAS DE TRABAJO?

Un total del 59% de los hombres y el 80% de las mujeres encuestadas considera que es posible tener el mismo sueldo y prestigio con menos horas de trabajo. Si evaluamos esta respuesta junto a lo respondido anteriormente por las mujeres, parecería que ellas piensan que es posible trabajar menos y tener los mismos beneficios y que, de cualquier manera, preferirían un trabajo que les dé más tiempo libre que uno con un sueldo más alto.

Por otro lado, en la encuesta también se incluyeron afirmaciones sobre ciertas circunstancias que podrían haberse presentado en la vida de los participantes, con el fin de conocer cuál es el estado de bienestar como asociados en firmas de arbitraje. Las afirmaciones tratan sobre salud mental, física, entra otras. En los siguientes párrafos analizaremos las respuestas de los participantes.

§37.06 HE ASISTIDO A UNA CONSULTA MÉDICA POR SUFRIR DE ANSIEDAD VINCULADA AL TRABAJO

El 25% de los hombres y el 36% de las mujeres reconocieron que han asistido a una consulta médica por sufrir de ansiedad vinculada al trabajo al menos una vez. Estos resultados sugieren que las mujeres parecerían sufrir más ansiedad o que, en todo caso, buscarían más ayuda que los hombres para enfrentar los problemas de ansiedad relacionados al trabajo.

§37.07 HE LLORADO POR ASUNTOS VINCULADOS AL TRABAJO

El 82% de las mujeres y 25% de los hombres afirmó haber llorado al menos una vez por asuntos vinculados al trabajo. Estos resultados sugieren que las mujeres exteriorizan más que los hombres sus emociones respecto de asuntos laborales o que los asuntos laborales las afectan más a ellas a nivel personal.

§37.08 ME HE PERDIDO ALGÚN EVENTO FAMILIAR REALMENTE IMPORTANTE POR CUMPLIR CON COMPROMISOS LABORALES

El 75% de los hombres encuestados y el 73% de las mujeres respondieron que se han perdido al menos un evento familiar realmente importante por compromisos de trabajo. Esta respuesta sugiere que hombres y mujeres mantienen, en principio, el mismo nivel de compromiso con sus actividades laborales, incluso si esto afecta su ámbito familiar. Estos datos muestran que, contrario a lo afirmado con frecuencia, las mujeres no priorizan el ámbito familiar más que los hombres en el grupo demográfico de la muestra.

§37.09 HE SENTIDO PÁNICO POR ENFRENTAR A MI JEFE POR ALGO EN LO QUE NO ESTÁBAMOS DE ACUERDO

El 25% de los hombres y el 45% de las mujeres afirmó haber sentido "pánico" por enfrentar a su jefe por algo en lo que no estaban de acuerdo. Según esta respuesta, las mujeres parecerían sufrir más emocionalmente al momento de enfrentarse a sus superiores. No conocemos si esta respuesta habría variado dependiendo de si el "jefe" es del mismo sexo o no.

§37.10 HE TEMIDO SERIAMENTE PERDER MI TRABAJO

El 64% de las mujeres y el 50% de los hombres nunca ha temido perder su trabajo. Llama la atención que, pese a que las mujeres parecerían sufrir más por las confrontaciones propias del trabajo, temen perder su trabajo en menor medida que los hombres.

§37.11 HE MANTENIDO UNA ENEMISTAD VISIBLE CON ALGUIEN EN EL TRABAJO

El 45% de las mujeres y el 33% de los hombres contó que ha mantenido una enemistad visible con alguien en el trabajo. Pese a que es imposible conocer las diferentes razones para enemistades en el ámbito laboral, es interesante conocer que las mujeres exteriorizan sus emociones respecto a sus colegas más que los hombres.

§37.12 HE SENTIDO ENVIDIA PROFUNDA POR EL LOGRO DE UN COMPAÑERO DEL TRABAJO

El 83% de los hombres y el 73% de las mujeres nunca ha sentido envidia profunda por el logro de un compañero del trabajo. Estos resultados sugieren que, en los equipos de arbitraje, aparentemente no se experimentan muchos casos de envidia o de emociones negativas entre colegas.

§37.13 HE SENTIDO FELICIDAD AUTÉNTICA POR EL ÉXITO DE UN COMPAÑERO DEL TRABAJO

El 82% de las mujeres y el 92% de los hombres ha sentido al menos una vez felicidad auténtica por el éxito de un compañero, lo que sugiere que las relaciones entre colegas y asociados en la práctica arbitral es saludable.

§37.14 ¿CUÁL ES EL NÚMERO DE HORAS QUE TRABAJAS EN PROMEDIO A LA SEMANA? Y ¿CUÁNTO TIEMPO DEDICAS A ACTIVIDADES DE OCIO?

El 38% de los hombres y el 18% de las mujeres trabajan entre cincuenta y cinco y sesenta y cinco horas semanales en promedio; es decir, entre once y trece horas diarias, sin considerar los fines de semana. El 55% de las mujeres y el 33% de los hombres trabajan entre cuarenta y cinco y cincuenta y cinco horas semanales en promedio, o entre nueve y once diarias en una semana laboral. Estos datos sugieren que los hombres trabajan más horas.

Sin embargo, es interesante que, pese a que las mujeres parecerían dedicar menos horas al trabajo que los hombres, el 73% de las mujeres dedica menos de cinco horas al ocio durante la semana, con respecto al 42% de los hombres que tiene ese tiempo de ocio. Esto sugiere que, si bien las mujeres dedican menos horas a la semana que los hombres al trabajo, esas horas no se destinan necesariamente al ocio. Lamentablemente, en la encuesta no se incluyeron preguntas que permitan conocer a qué otras actividades dedican las mujeres su tiempo adicional, ya que no es al trabajo o al ocio.

§37.15 ¿ESTARÍAS DISPUESTO A RECIBIR MENOS DINERO POR MÁS TIEMPO LIBRE?

El 73% de las mujeres y el 29% de los hombres estarían dispuestos a recibir menos dinero por más tiempo libre. Esta es quizás una de las principales diferencias encontradas entre las aspiraciones de hombres y mujeres que trabajan como asociados en firmas de arbitraje.

La mayoría de las mujeres estarían dispuestas a renunciar al dinero por mayor tiempo libre, mientras que la mayoría de los hombres no estarían dispuestos a hacerlo.

§37.16 ¿ESTÁS SATISFECHO CON EL SUELDO QUE RECIBES?

El 54% de los hombres y el 73% de las mujeres están satisfechos con el sueldo que reciben por su trabajo. No obstante, es interesante conocer que, en la muestra, el 29% de los hombres dijo no estar de acuerdo con el salario que recibe, pero ninguna mujer contestó lo mismo. Estos resultados podrían significar que las mujeres no permanecen en un lugar de trabajo si no se encuentran satisfechas con las condiciones laborales, a diferencia de un porcentaje de los hombres encuestados, o que para las mujeres el salario no es el principal criterio para evaluar el bienestar de su trabajo.

§37.17 ¿ESTÁS SATISFECHO CON LOS ESFUERZOS DE TU TRABAJO POR GENERAR UN BALANCE TRABAJO-VIDA?

Finalmente, en la encuesta se preguntó a los participantes si se encontraban satisfechos con los esfuerzos realizados por sus firmas de abogados para generar un balance entre el trabajo y vida personal. El 73 % de las mujeres y el 54 % de los hombres respondieron que están de acuerdo con los esfuerzos de sus firmas para alcanzar este balance, mientras que el 29 % de los hombres dijo no estar de acuerdo con dichos esfuerzos.

Las respuestas a la encuesta permiten conocer de manera general ciertas diferencias entre las aspiraciones y experiencias de asociados, hombres y mujeres, en la práctica arbitral. Los hombres parecerían sentirse más preparados que las mujeres para enfrentar nuevos retos profesionales, como, por ejemplo, ser árbitros únicos en un caso.

Una de las diferencias que más llaman la atención es la disponibilidad de las mujeres a renunciar a parte de su sueldo por más horas libres. Sorprende que, pese a que un porcentaje relevante de los hombres encuestados no se encuentra de acuerdo con los esfuerzos de sus firmas para generar un balance adecuado entre el trabajo y su vida personal, y trabaja en promedio más horas por semana que las mujeres, la mayoría de ellos no renunciaría a parte de su sueldo por más tiempo libre.

En definitiva, parecería que las mujeres son más críticas consigo mismas al valorar sus habilidades, se sienten miembros importantes de sus equipos en mayor medida que los hombres, pero tienen más miedos a confrontar a sus jefes, lo que no incrementa el temor a perder su trabajo. Asimismo, ellas lloran más que los hombres por razones laborales y acuden a consulta en mayor medida que los hombres por problemas de ansiedad relacionada al trabajo. Los hombres, por su parte, parecerían tener mayor autoestima al valorar sus habilidades, sentir menos miedo de enfrentar a sus jefes, pero, al contrario que las mujeres, parecen experimentar en mayor medida el miedo a perder su trabajo.

Debo reconocer que, al experimentar la maternidad mientras escribía este capítulo y me esforzaba por sacar este y otros proyectos adelante, descubrí que algunas de mis respuestas a la encuesta habrían cambiado, de haber participado en ella después de convertirme en madre. Ahora sé que las necesidades y expectativas cambian con la llegada de un hijo, por lo que, en términos generales, resulta muy difícil conocer exactamente qué quieren las mujeres en el arbitraje, si no se tienen en cuenta otros aspectos relevantes de su vida.

Si bien mi apreciación sobre mis capacidades no se ha visto modificada, mis aspiraciones y necesidades en términos prácticos sí se han visto alteradas. Todavía aspiro a que en diez años ya me habré convertido en socia de la firma en la que trabajo actualmente, pero ahora sé que no estaría dispuesta a perderme un evento familiar importante por asuntos de trabajo.

Este capítulo pretendía dar a conocer lo que quieren las mujeres en el arbitraje. No sé si lo ha hecho, o si esto realmente sea posible. Lo que sé es que, al menos en mi caso, escribir esta pieza me permitió visualizar con claridad lo que yo como mujer aspiro de una carrera en el arbitraje: tener la posibilidad de cuidar de mi familia, dedicarle el tiempo y la atención que quiero darle, sin que esto impida el desarrollo de mi profesión al máximo de mis posibilidades.

APÉNDICE I ¿CÓMO SOBREVIVIMOS LOS ASOCIADOS DE ARBITRAJE?

IDENTIFICACIÓN

1. Descripción (opcional)
2. Género
   - Mujer
   - Hombre
   - Otro
   - Prefiero no decirlo
3. País de residencia
4. Edad

EXPERIENCIA COMO LITIGANTE

5. ¿Hace cuánto te encuentras en tu actual trabajo?
   - 1-2 años
   - 3-5 años
   - 5-7 años
   - 8-10 años
   - Más de 10 años
   - Otro
6. ¿Te sientes un miembro importante en tu trabajo?
   - Totalmente de acuerdo
   - De acuerdo
   - Ni de acuerdo ni en desacuerdo
   - En desacuerdo
   - Totalmente en desacuerdo
   - No lo sé
7. ¿Invirtió tu centro de trabajo en entrenarte en las habilidades necesarias en audiencia?
   - Totalmente en desacuerdo
   - En desacuerdo
   - Ni de acuerdo ni en desacuerdo
   - De acuerdo
   - Totalmente de acuerdo
   - No lo sé
8. En los últimos dos años, ¿has tenido alguna de las siguientes responsabilidades? Puedes marcar más de una:
   - Asistir a otro abogado en la ejecución de un interrogatorio
   - Estar en control de la evidencia que se va a mostrar en los alegatos/al testigo
   - Ser responsable de la presentación Power Point
   - Alegato de apertura

- Interrogatorio directo de un testigo.
- Interrogatorio cruzado de un testigo.
- Interrogatorio directo de un experto legal.
- Interrogatorio cruzado de un experto legal.
- Interrogatorio directo de un perito.
- Interrogatorio cruzado de un perito.
- Alegato de clausura.
- Hasta el momento no me ha tocado ejecutar directamente ninguna de dichas actividades

9. Cuéntanos una historia de terror que hayas presenciado o sufrido en una audiencia

ÁRBITRO, ACADEMIA Y RANKING

10. En los últimos dos años, ¿has sido designado como árbitro?
    - Sí
    - No
11. En los últimos dos años, ¿has sido designado como secretario administrativo de un tribunal?
    - Sí
    - No
12. ¿Qué tan preparado te sientes para participar en un caso como árbitro único?
    - Sobradamente preparado
    - Suficientemente preparado
    - Aún me falta preparación
    - Para nada preparado
13. ¿Cuántos papers o artículos publicaste en el 2018?
    - Ninguno
    - 1
    - 2
    - 3
    - 4
    - 5 o más
14. ¿En cuántas conferencias expusiste en el 2018?
    - Ninguna
    - 1
    - 2
    - 3
    - 4
    - 5
    - 6
    - 7
    - 8
    - 9

- 10 o más

15. ¿Has sido destacado en alguna guía como Chambers / Partners?
    - No
    - Sí
16. ¿Crees que ya deberías haber sido destacado?
    - Sí
    - No
17. ¿Cuál es tu posición actual?
    - Asociado en una firma de abogados
    - Asociado senior en una firma de abogados
    - Socio en una firma de abogados
    - Of counsel en una firma de abogados
    - Fundadora de mi propia firma
    - Abogado del Gobierno
    - Abogado in-house de una compañía
    - Gerente legal de una compañía
    - Otra

TU FUTURO

18. ¿Qué esperas lograr en los próximos 10 años?
    - Ser socio de la firma en la que trabajo actualmente
    - Fundar mi propia firma/negocio/consultora
    - Trabajar en el Estado
    - Dedicar la mayoría de mi tiempo a ser árbitro
    - Dedicarme a la academia
    - Dedicarme a mi familia
    - Otra
19. ¿Cuál es el principal reto para alcanzar el futuro profesional que deseas?
    - Lograr la aprobación de los socios de la firma en que trabajo.
    - Ser más notado en el mercado (arbitral)
    - Encontrar tiempo para realizar más publicaciones
    - Lograr una relación más directa con los clientes
    - Mayor capacitación y educación
    - Que haya cultura de mayor flexibilidad
    - Conseguir clientes
    - Encontrar balance
    - Otra
20. En el supuesto que buscaras un nuevo trabajo, buscarías un lugar que ofrezca...
    - Un sueldo más alto
    - Más tiempo libre
    - Más trabajo probono
    - Más oportunidades de aprendizaje

- Mayor exposición
- Mayor reconocimiento de los logros

21. ¿Crees que es posible tener el mismo sueldo y prestigio, con menos horas de trabajo?
    - Sí
    - No
22. Piensa en los asociados de los próximos 5 años. ¿Qué tan importante crees que les resultarán las siguientes habilidades y conocimientos?

	Muy importante	Importante	Neutral	Poco importante	No es importante
Escribir un libro					
Conocimiento sobre techlaw					
Entender lenguaje de programación					
Poder programar código					
Especializarse en una rama del derecho					
Manejo de técnicas de diseño y design thinking					
Realizar un PhD					
Enseñar en una universidad					
Aprender a deliberar y persuadir					
Networking					
Escribir un buen laudo					
Trabajo probono					

BALANCE TRABAJO-VIDA

23. ¿Cómo calificarías el ambiente en tu centro de trabajo

Muy relajado	1	2	3	4	5	6	7 Muy estresante

24. En toda mi carrera como asociado...

	Sí	Sí, más de una vez	No
He asistido a una consulta médica por sufrir de ansiedad vinculada al trabajo.			
He llorado por asuntos vinculados al trabajo.			
Me he enojado injustamente con un compañero de trabajo.			
Me he perdido algún evento familiar realmente importante por cumplir con compromisos laborales.			
He sentido pánico por enfrentar a mi jefe por algo en lo que no estábamos de acuerdo.			
He temido seriamente perder mi trabajo.			
He mantenido una enemistad visible con alguien en el trabajo.			
He sentido envidia profunda por el logro de un compañero del trabajo			
Me he sentido frustrado por mi desempeño en una audiencia			
He sentido felicidad auténtica por el éxito de un compañero del trabajo			

25. ¿Quién es el principal responsable de la situación en la que se encuentra tu ambiente de trabajo?
    - Los socios
    - Los asociados
    - Los practicantes o asistentes legales
    - La administración
    - Los clientes
    - Yo mismo
26. ¿Cuál es el número de horas que trabajas en promedio a la semana?
    - Menos de 35 horas semanales
    - Entre 35 y 45 horas semanales
    - Entre 35 y 55 horas semanales
    - Entre 55 y 65 horas semanales
    - Más de 65 horas semanales
27. En una semana laborable (lunes-viernes), ¿cuánto tiempo dedicas a actividades de ocio?
    - Menos de 5 horas
    - 5-8 horas
    - 8-10 horas
    - 11-14 horas
    - 15-20 horas

- Más de 20 horas

28. ¿Haces deporte? ¿Cuántas horas a la semana?
    - No hago deporte
    - 1
    - 2
    - 3
    - 4
    - 5
    - 6
    - 7
    - 8
    - 9
    - 10 o más
29. ¿Estarías dispuesto a recibir menos dinero por más tiempo libre?
    - Sí
    - No
30. Actualmente, ¿dónde te ubicas en la siguiente escala dinero-tiempo libre?

Máxima remuneraciónMínimo tiempo libre	1	2	3	4	5	6	7	Máximo tiempo libre, mínimo de remuneración

31. ¿Cuántas tazas de café tomas al día?
    - No tomo café
    - 1 taza
    - 2 tazas
    - 3 tazas
    - 4 tazas
    - 5 o más tazas
32. ¿Dedicarte al arbitraje te ha llevado a una vida poco saludable?
    - Sí
    - No
33. En los últimos 12 meses, ¿has consumido...

	Sí	No
Tabaco		
Alcohol		
Marihuana		
Adderal, modafinilo u otra “smartdrug”.		
Antidepresivos.		
Ansiolíticos.		
MDMA u otra “partydrug”.		
Cocaína.		

34. ¿Estás satisfecho con...

	Totalmente de acuerdo	De acuerdo	Ni de acuerdo ni en desacuerdo	En desacuerdo	Totalmente en desacuerdo
El sueldo que recibes					
La relación con tu jefe directo					
la relación con los socios de tu área					
la relación con los asociados de tu área					
Tu oportunidad de realizar trabajo probono					
La libertad para tratar con clientes					
La libertad para administrar procesos					
Tu capacidad de atraer clientes					
Los esfuerzos de tu trabajo por generar un balance trabajo-vida					
Tu desarrollo profesional					

35. En tu opinión, ¿cuál es la mayor virtud de los abogados de 50 70 años de tu país?
36. ¿Y el mayor defecto?

TRIBU Y MENTORÍA

37. ¿Te parece importante...

	Totalmente de acuerdo	De acuerdo	Ni de acuerdo ni en desacuerdo	En desacuerdo	Totalmente en desacuerdo
Tener a alguien con quien puedo hablar de problemas laborales					
Tener a un mentor que me puede guiar					
Tener a un grupo de soporte emocional					

38. ¿Admiras a algún joven profesional del arbitraje latinoamericano? Cuéntanos quién es
39. ¿Tienes a un mentor comprensivo que te ayuda a evolucionar profesionalmente?
40. Si te provoca, cuéntanos quien es tu mentor y algo que admiras de él/ella.
41. Muchísimas gracias por tu apoyo. ¿Quieres aparecer en la lista de personas que respondió esta encuesta?
    - Sí
    - No

APÉNDICE II RESULTADOS DE LA ENCUESTA

42. ¿Te sientes un miembro importante en tu trabajo?
    - Totalmente de acuerdo
    - De acuerdo
    - Ni de acuerdo ni en desacuerdo
    - En desacuerdo
    - Totalmente en desacuerdo
    - No lo sé

Hombres

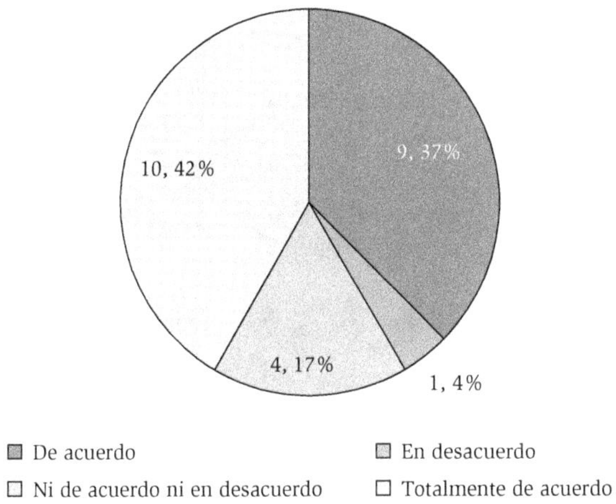

Mujeres

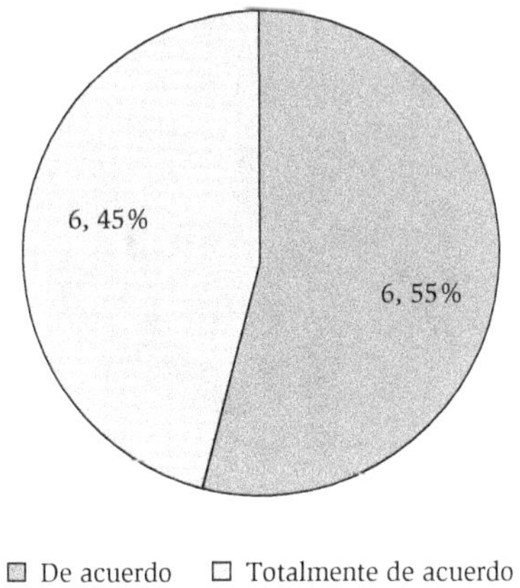

43. ¿Qué tan preparado te sientes para participar en un caso como árbitro único?
    - Sobradamente preparado
    - Suficientemente preparado
    - Aún me falta preparación
    - Para nada preparado

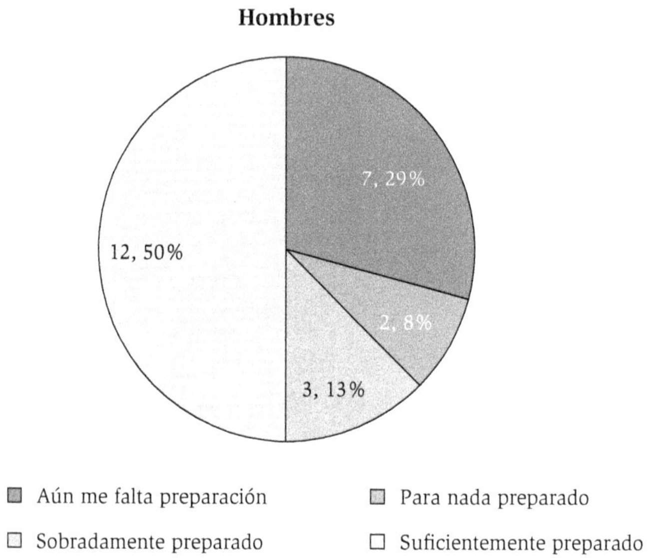

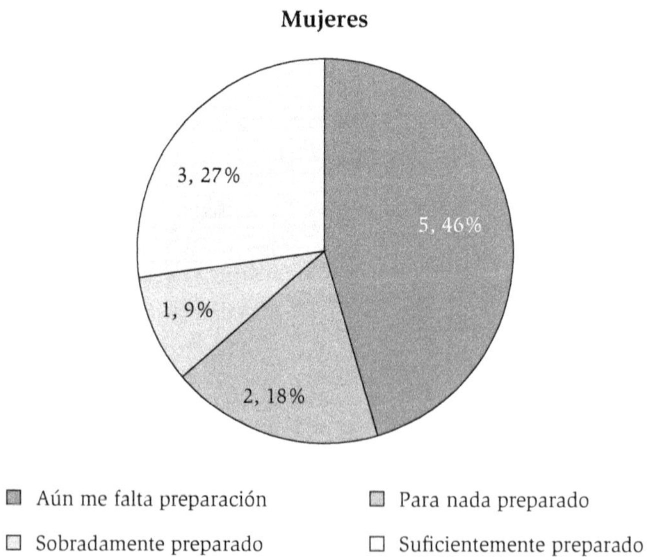

44. ¿Qué esperas lograr en los próximos 10 años?
    - Ser socio de la firma en la que trabajo actualmente
    - Fundar mi propia firma/negocio/consultora
    - Trabajar en el Estado
    - Dedicar la mayoría de mi tiempo a ser árbitro
    - Dedicarme a la academia
    - Dedicarme a mi familia
    - Otra

Hombres

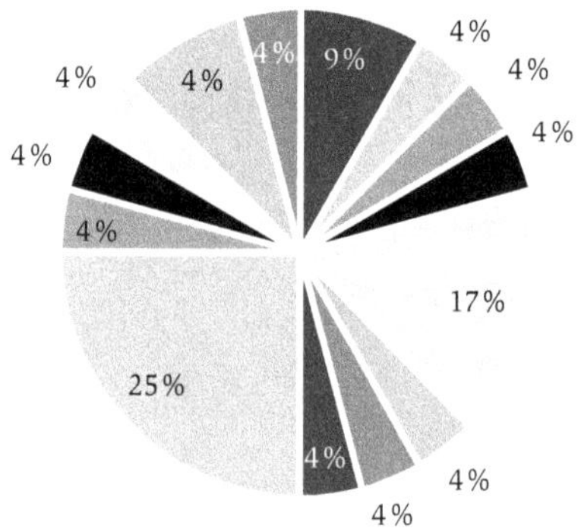

- Dedicar la mayoría de mi tiempo a ser árbitro.
- Dedicar la mayoría de mi tiempo a ser árbitro. Dedicarme a la academia. Dedicarme a mi familia.
- Dedicar la mayoría de mi tiempo a ser árbitro. Dedicarme a la academia. Doctorado en un tercer idioma
- Dedicarme a la academia.
- Fundar mi propia firma/negocio/consultora.
- Fundar mi propia firma/negocio/consultora. Dedicarme a la academia. Dedicarme a mi familia.
- Fundar mi propia firma/negocio/consultora. Dedicarme a mi familia.
- Fundar mi propia firma/negocio/consultora. Trabajar en el Estado.
- Ser socio de la firma en la que trabajo actualmente.
- Ser socio de la firma en la que trabajo actualmente. Dedicar la mayoría de mi tiempo a ser árbitro. Dedicarme a la academia.
- Ser socio de la firma en la que trabajo actualmente. Dedicarme a la academia.
- Ser socio de la firma en la que trabajo actualmente. Dedicarme a mi familia.
- Ser socio de la firma en la que trabajo actualmente. Fundar mi propia firma / negocio / consultora.
- Ser socio de la firma en la que trabajo actualmente. Ser la referencia principal del arbitraje internacional en mi país.

Mujeres

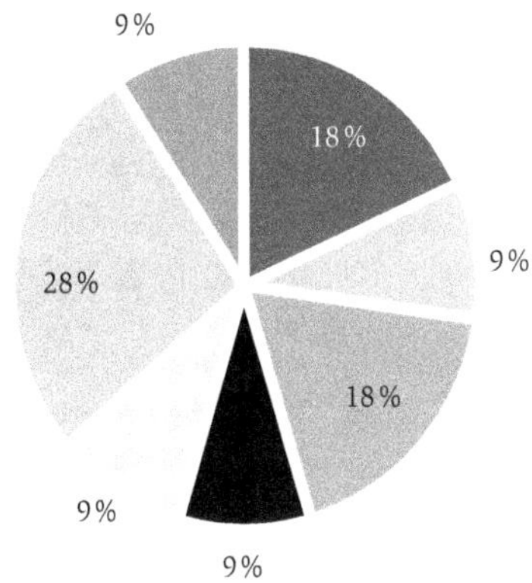

- Dedicar la mayoría de mi tiempo a ser árbitro.
- Dedicar la mayoría de mi tiempo a ser árbitro. Dedicarme a la academia.
- Dedicar la mayoría de mi tiempo a ser árbitro. Dedicarme a la academia. Dedicarme a mi familia.
- Fundar mi propia firma/negocio/consultora.
- Fundar mi propia firma/negocio/consultora. Dedicar la mayoría de mi tiempo a ser árbitro. Dedicarme a la academia.
- Ser socio de la firma en la que trabajo actualmente.
- Ser socio de la firma en la que trabajo actualmente. Fundar mi propia firma/negocio/consultora. Dedicar la mayoría de mi tiempo a ser árbitro.

45. En el supuesto que buscaras un nuevo trabajo, buscarías un lugar que ofrezca...
    - Un sueldo más alto
    - Más tiempo libre
    - Más trabajo probono
    - Más oportunidades de aprendizaje
    - Mayor exposición
    - Mayor reconocimiento de los logros

Hombres

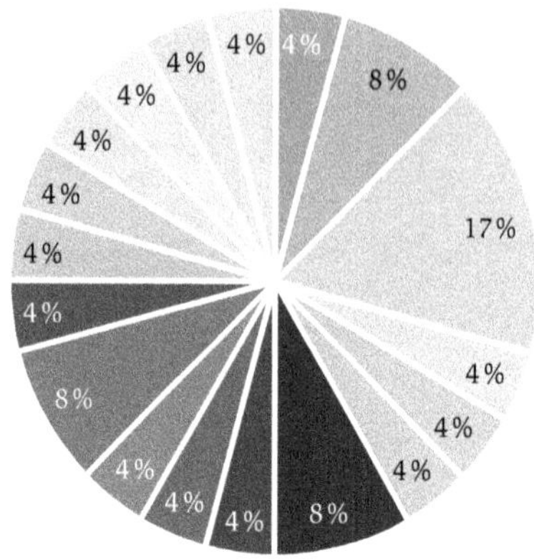

- Más oportunidades de aprendizaje
- Más oportunidades de aprendizaje, Mayor exposición
- Más tiempo libre
- Más tiempo libre, Más oportunidades de aprendizaje
- Mayor exposición
- Mayor exposición, Mayor reconocimiento de los logros
- Un sueldo más alto
- Un sueldo más alto, Más oportunidades de aprendizaje
- Un sueldo más alto, Más oportunidades de aprendizaje, Mayor exposición
- Un sueldo más alto, Más oportunidades de aprendizaje, Mayor exposición, Mayor reconocimiento de los logros
- Un sueldo más alto, Más tiempo libre
- Un sueldo más alto, Más tiempo libre, Más oportunidades de aprendizaje, Mayor exposición
- Un sueldo más alto, Más tiempo libre, Más trabajo pro bono, Mayor exposición, Mayor reconocimiento de los logros
- Un sueldo más alto, Más tiempo libre, Mayor exposición
- Un sueldo más alto, Más tiempo libre, Mayor reconocimiento de los logros
- Un sueldo más alto, Mayor exposición
- Un sueldo más alto, Mayor exposición, Mayor reconocimiento de los logros
- Un sueldo más alto, Mayor reconocimiento de los logros

Mujeres

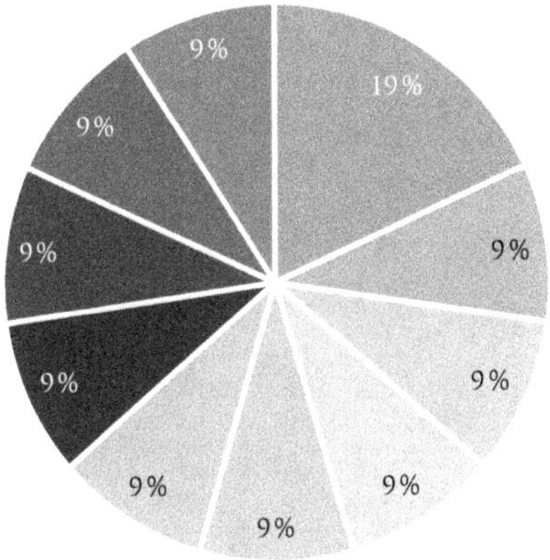

- Más oportunidades de aprendizaje
- Más oportunidades de aprendizaje, Mayor exposición, Mayor reconocimiento de los logros
- Más tiempo libre
- Más tiempo libre, Mayor exposición
- Más tiempo libre, Mayor exposición, Mayor reconocimiento de los logros
- Más tiempo libre, Mayor reconocimiento de los logros
- Mayor exposición, Mayor reconocimiento de los logros
- Un sueldo más alto, Más oportunidades de aprendizaje
- Un sueldo más alto, Más tiempo libre, Más oportunidades de aprendizaje
- Un sueldo más alto, Más tiempo libre, Más trabajo pro bono, Más oportunidades de aprendizaje

46. ¿Crees que es posible tener el mismo sueldo y prestigio, con menos horas de trabajo?
    - Sí
    - No

Hombres

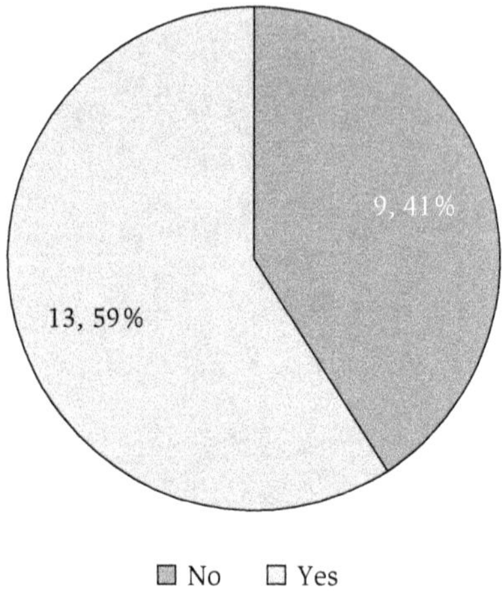

Mujeres

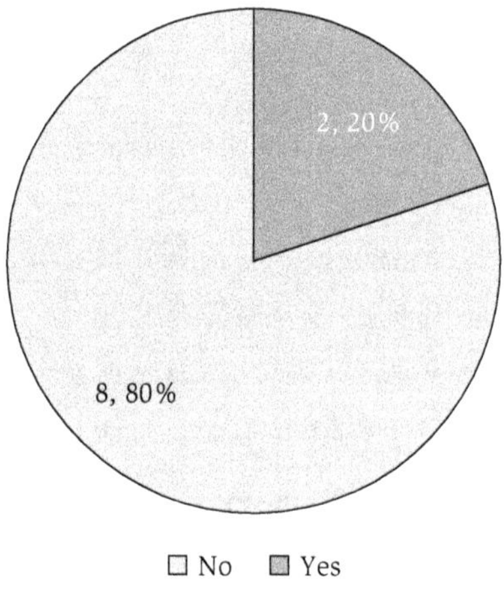

47. En toda mi carrera como asociado...

	Sí	Sí, más de una vez	No
He asistido a una consulta médica por sufrir de ansiedad vinculada al trabajo.			
He llorado por asuntos vinculados al trabajo.			

	Sí	Sí, más de una vez	No
Me he perdido algún evento familiar realmente importante por cumplir con compromisos laborales.			
He sentido pánico por enfrentar a mi jefe por algo en lo que no estábamos de acuerdo.			
He temido seriamente perder mi trabajo.			
He mantenido una enemistad visible con alguien en el trabajo.			
He sentido envidia profunda por el logro de un compañero del trabajo.			
Me he sentido frustrado por mi desempeño en una audiencia.			
He sentido felicidad auténtica por el éxito de un compañero del trabajo.			

He asistido a una consulta médica por sufrir de ansiedad vinculada al trabajo.

Hombres

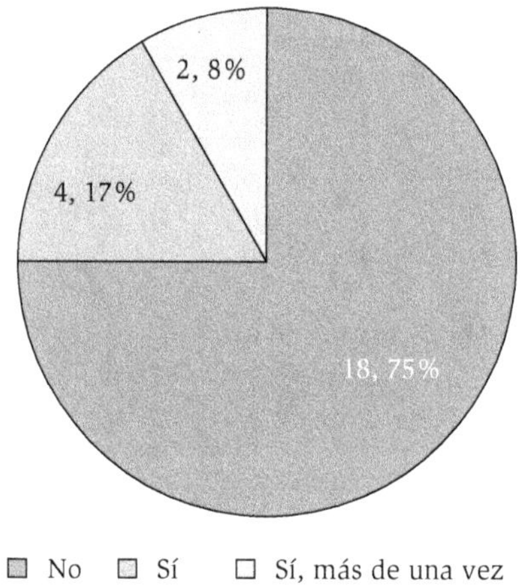

Mujeres

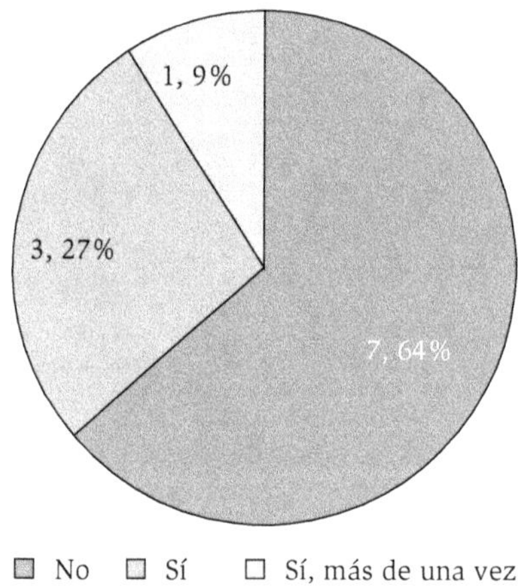

He llorado por asuntos vinculados al trabajo.

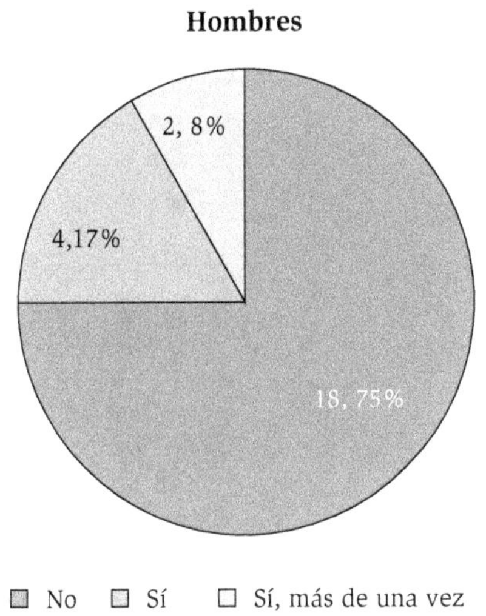

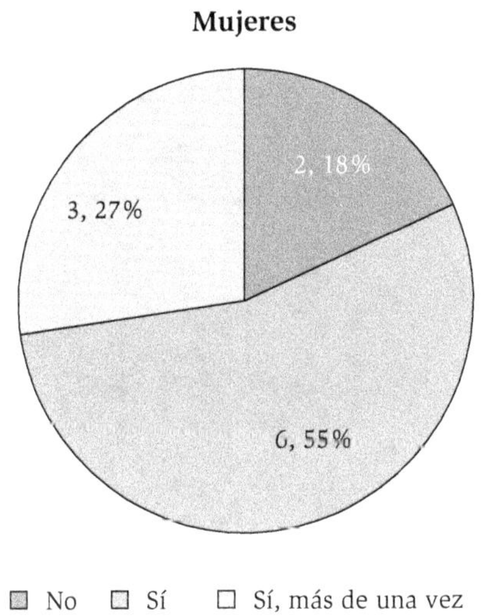

Me he perdido algún evento familiar realmente importante por cumplir con compromisos laborales.

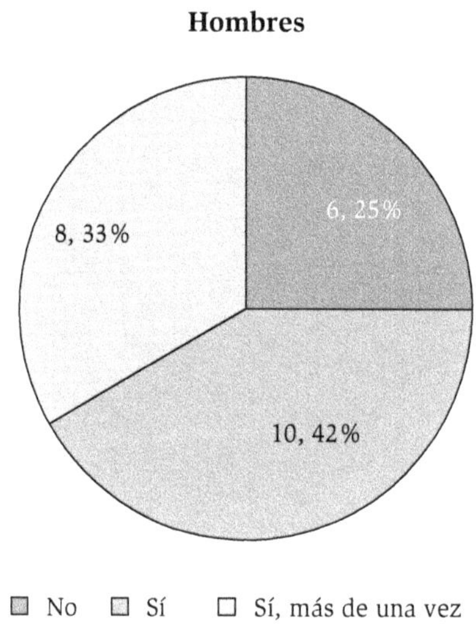

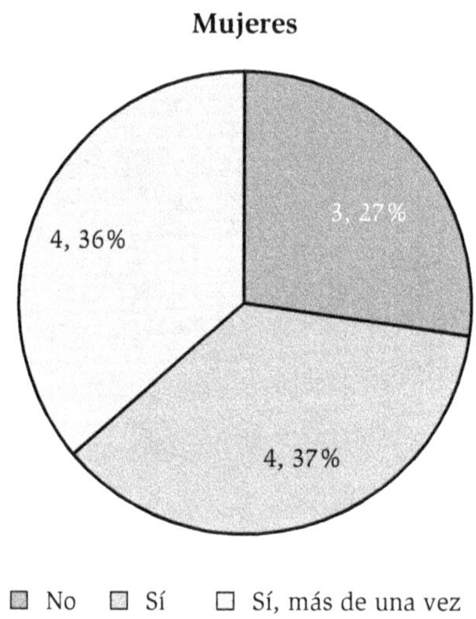

He sentido pánico por enfrentar a mi jefe por algo en lo que no estábamos de acuerdo.

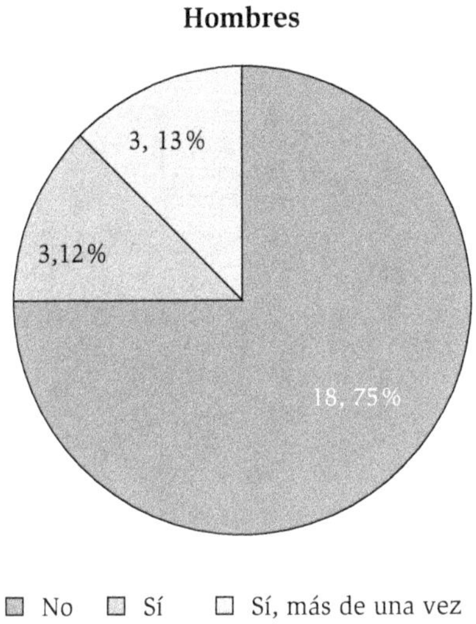

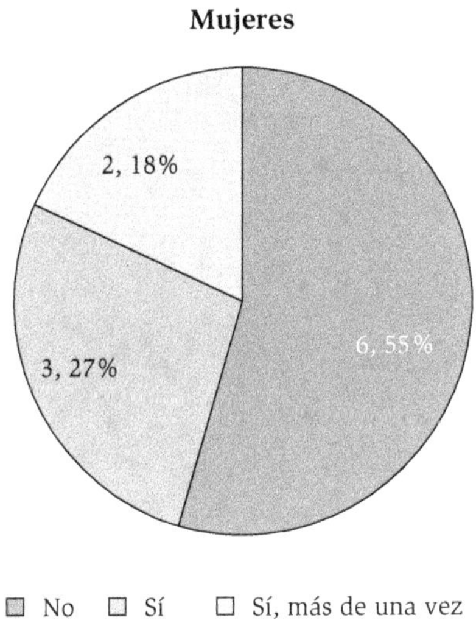

He temido seriamente perder mi trabajo.

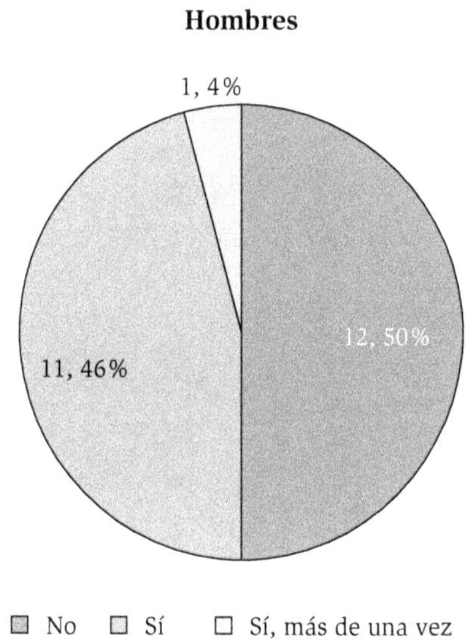

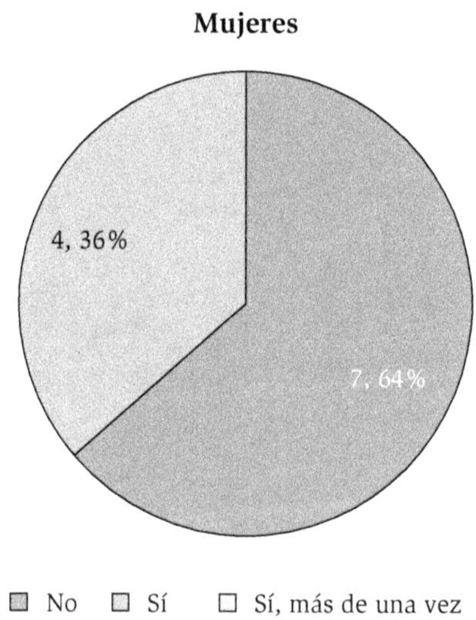

He mantenido una enemistad visible con alguien en el trabajo.

Hombres

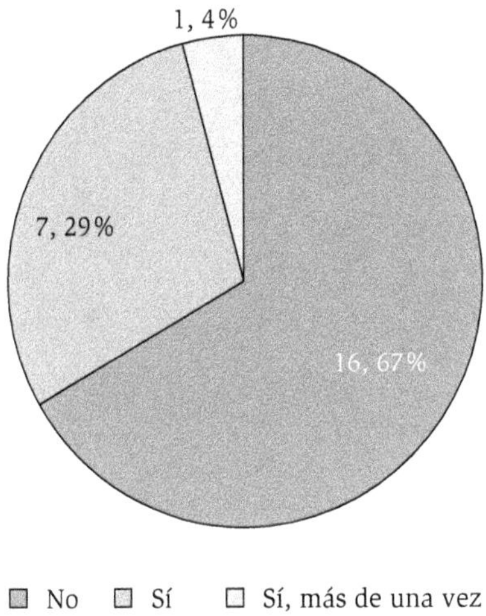

Mujeres

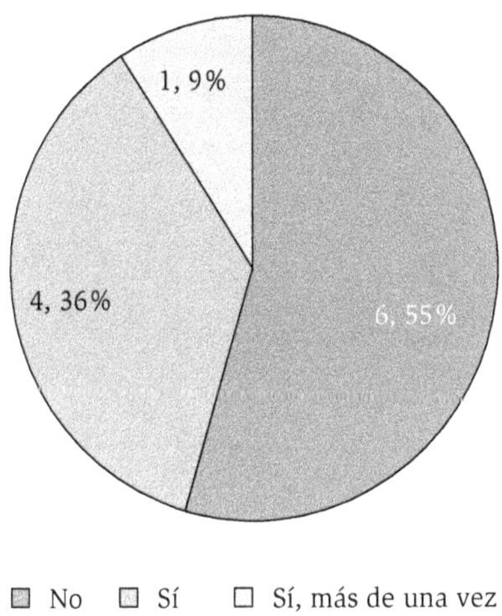

He sentido envidia profunda por el logro de un compañero del trabajo.

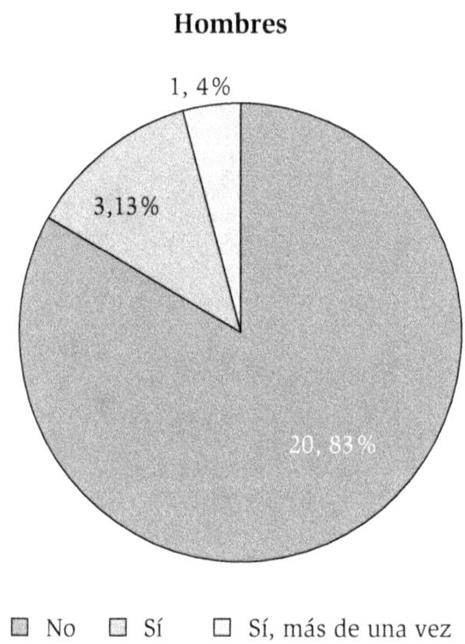

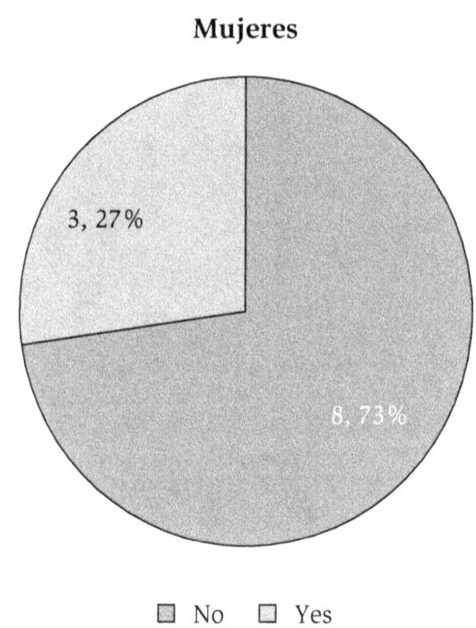

He sentido felicidad auténtica por el éxito de un compañero del trabajo.

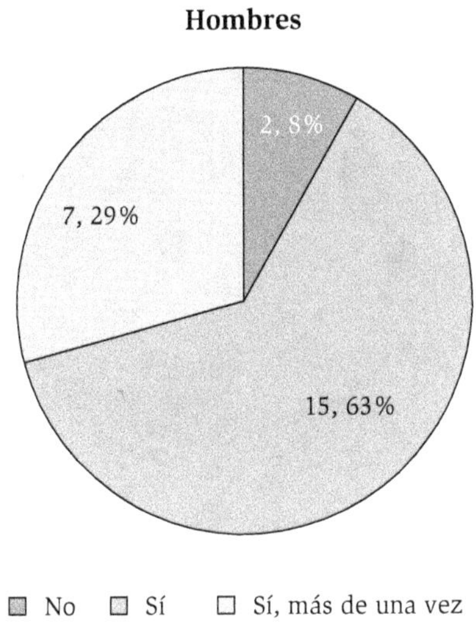

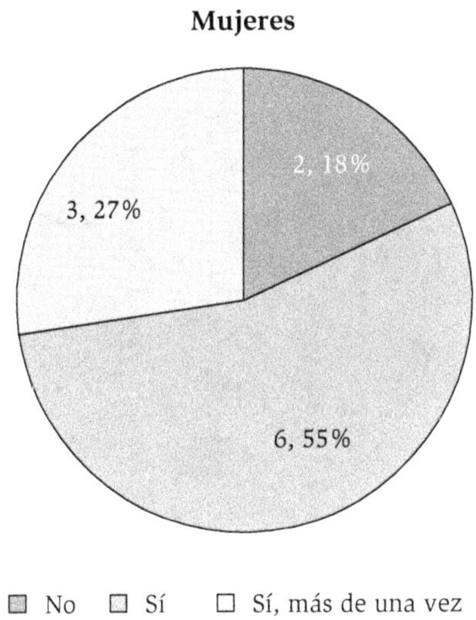

48. ¿Cuál es el número de horas que trabajas en promedio a la semana?
    - Menos de 35 horas semanales
    - Entre 35 y 45 horas semanales
    - Entre 35 y 55 horas semanales
    - Entre 55 y 65 horas semanales
    - Más de 65 horas semanales

Hombres

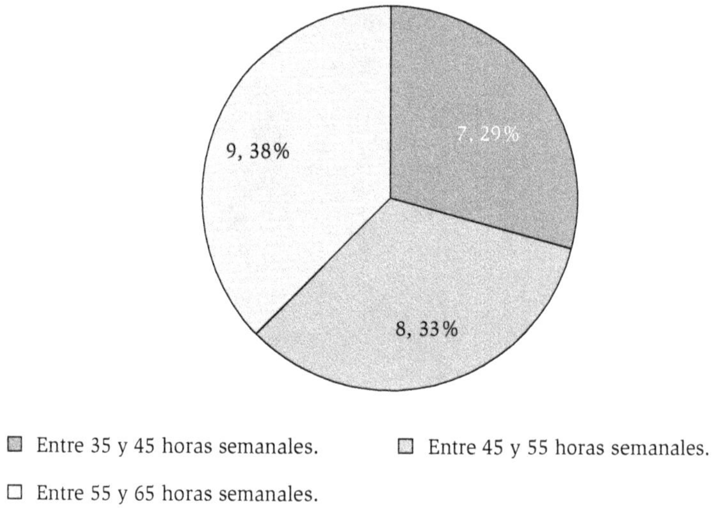

Mujeres

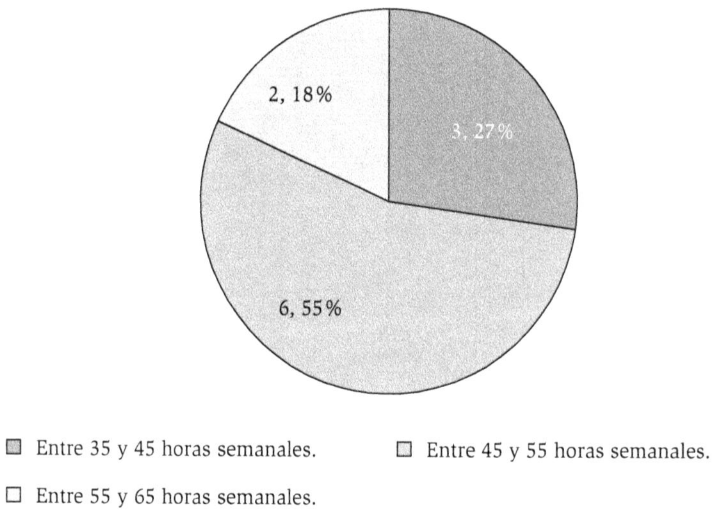

49. En una semana laborable (lunes-viernes), ¿cuánto tiempo dedicas a actividades de ocio?
    - Menos de 5 horas
    - 5-8 horas
    - 8-10 horas

- 11-14 horas
- 15-20 horas
- Más de 20 horas

Hombres

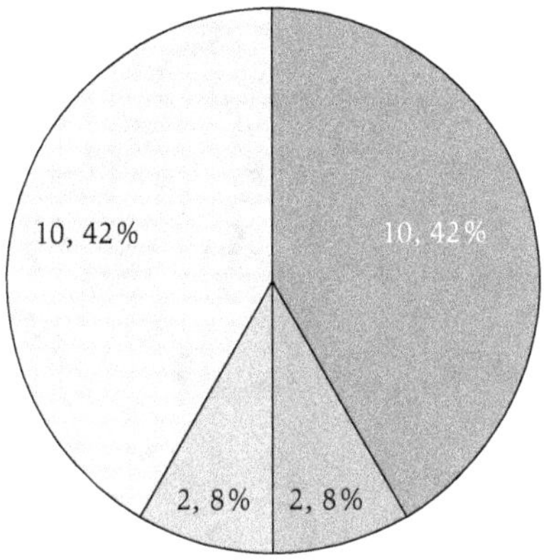

5-8 horas. Más de 20 horas. 8-10 horas. Menos de 5 horas.

Mujeres

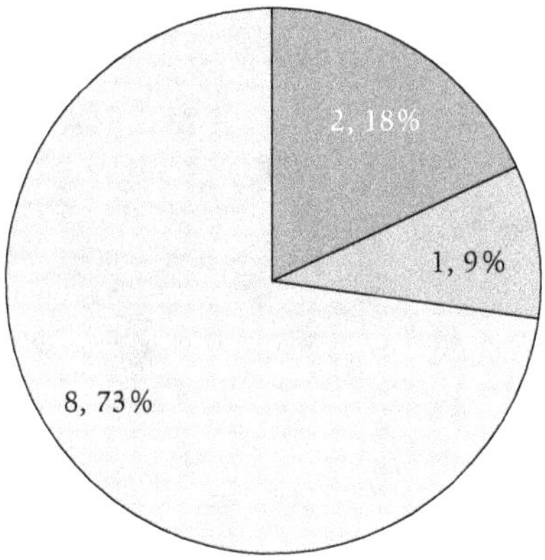

5-8 hours. 8-10 hours. Less than 5 hours.

50. ¿Estarías dispuesto a recibir menos dinero por más tiempo libre?
- Sí
- No

Hombres

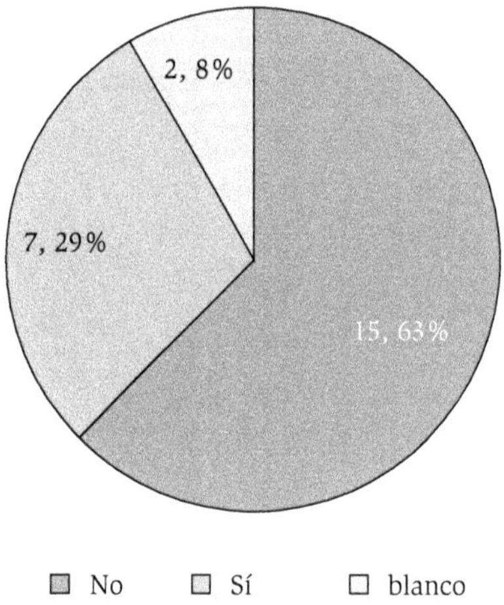

Mujeres

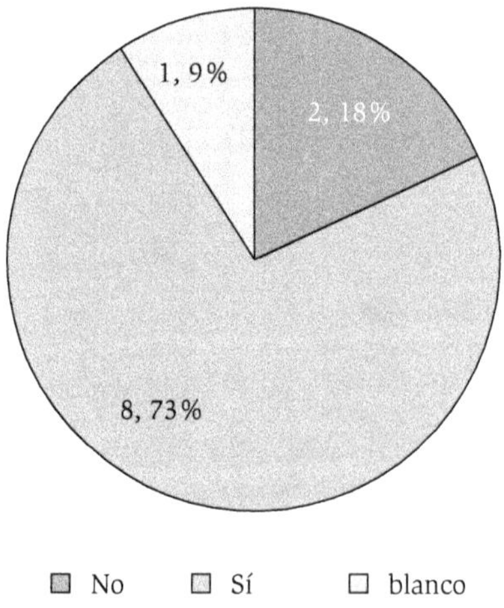

51. ¿Estás satisfecho con...

	Totalmente de acuerdo	De acuerdo	Ni de acuerdo ni en desacuerdo	En desacuerdo	Totalmente en desacuerdo
El sueldo que recibes.					
Los esfuerzos de tu trabajo por generar un balance trabajo-vida.					

El sueldo que recibes.

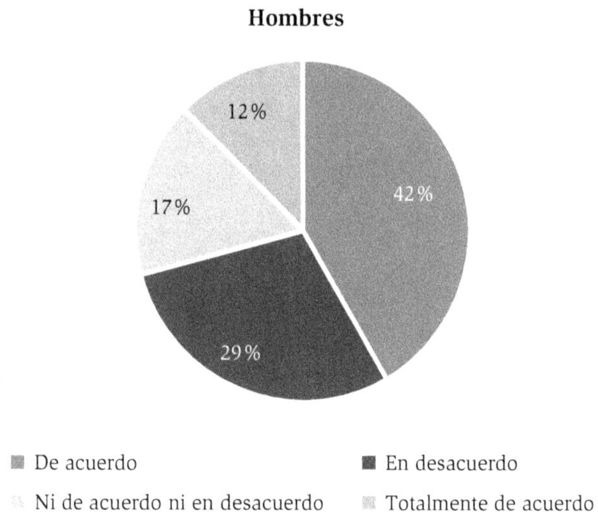

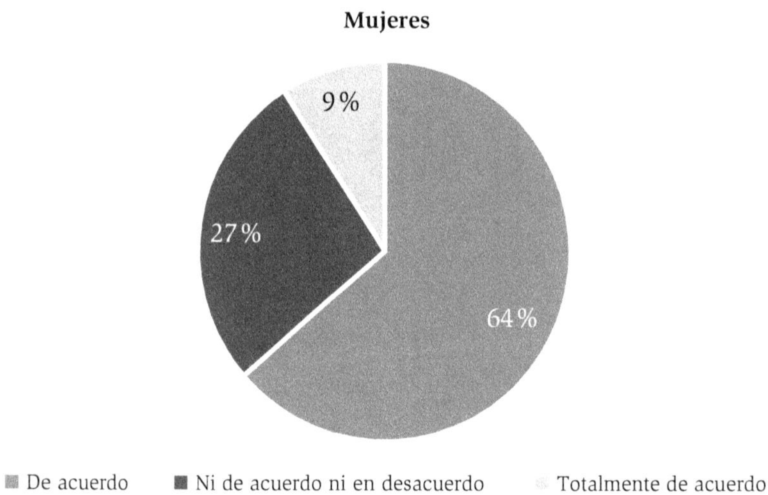

Los esfuerzos de tu trabajo por generar un balance trabajo-vida.

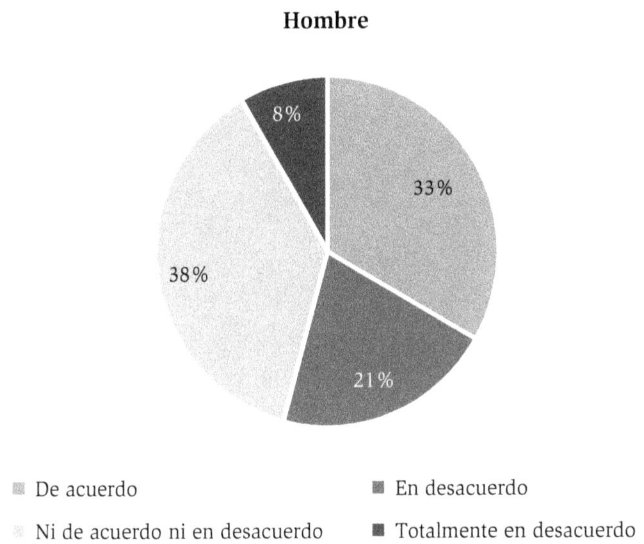

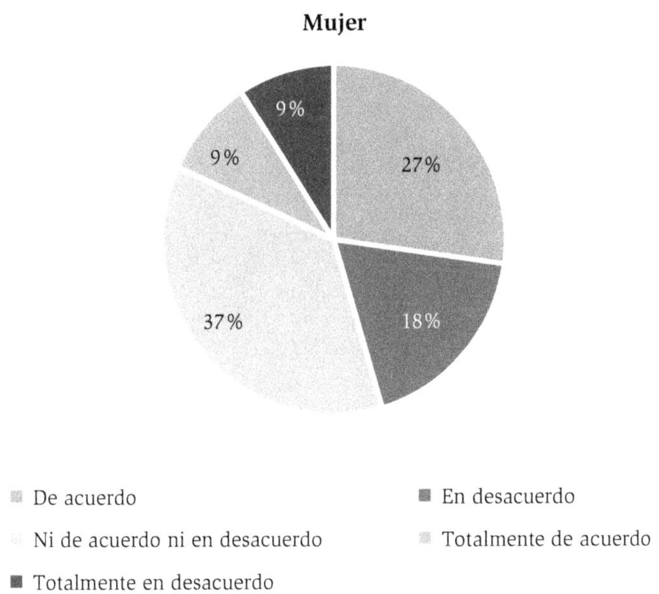

CAPÍTULO 38

Diversidad en el arbitraje

Patricia Vera

Sin duda alguna, las ventajas del arbitraje, entre ellas la confidencialidad de los procedimientos y el poder escoger a los árbitros que resolverán la controversia, lo han hecho un sistema más atractivo y confiable. Sin embargo, pese a que los conflictos que se someten a arbitraje cada vez son cada vez más diversos, la participación de mujeres sigue siendo limitada y se encuentra dentro de porcentajes bajos de participación en distintas instituciones arbitrales, especialmente en calidad de árbitros.

Este tema ha sido tratado en varios artículos y análisis estadísticos por parte de algunas instituciones arbitrales mediante sus reportes anuales. En ellos llama la atención que, pese al crecimiento del arbitraje a nivel internacional, y además de la importante participación activa de mujeres abogadas, exista un mayor número de casos en los que las partes o los demás miembros del tribunal arbitral designen más a hombres que a mujeres. Lo anterior, no obstante que la participación de mujeres en el arbitraje ha contribuido a la creación de grupos que tienen por objeto promover la paridad de designaciones en casos de arbitraje y generar una amplia red de contactos con una participación activa de mujeres.

Los datos e información recogida por las diferentes instituciones arbitrales a nivel mundial demuestran un porcentaje bajo de participación de mujeres. Según la CCI, solo el 16.7% de árbitros son mujeres, con un promedio de participación de mujeres en el año 2017 del 18%. Asimismo, el Instituto de Arbitraje de la Cámara de Comercio de Estocolmo, que maneja un alto número de arbitrajes, cuenta con un promedio de 18% de participación de árbitros mujeres. Esto no se distancia de la realidad en el caso de Ecuador, donde la participación de mujeres en calidad de árbitros también es muy reducida, por lo que, actualmente, las instituciones arbitrales trabajan por incrementar el número de árbitros mujeres en sus listas.

Llama mucho la atención y surge la necesidad de entender las razones por las que el porcentaje de participación de mujeres en el arbitraje como árbitros es tan baja con relación a la actividad arbitral y el número de casos. En un artículo escrito por Caroline dos Santos, denominado *Diversity in International Arbitration: a No-Woman's Land?*[1] la autora hace un interesante análisis sobre los sesgos inconscientes que se tienen al momento de designar árbitros. Sesgos que vienen con nosotros a lo largo del tiempo y que, implícitamente, llevan a nombrar árbitros de la siguiente categoría: hombres blancos, de edad mayor y con canas en el cabello.

Los sesgos se remontan a la costumbre y tradiciones que de manera inconsciente nos llevan a tener ciertas inclinaciones o crear estereotipos. A inicios de mi carrera en derecho, la primera imagen que se me venía a la mente cuando pensaba en un juez era la de un hombre de edad avanzada, representando la figura masculina de respeto y reconocimiento.

La participación de las mujeres en las designaciones como árbitros en la actualidad sigue siendo baja, con relación a las designaciones efectuadas a árbitros hombres. A ello se suma la poca participación de mujeres jóvenes en calidad de árbitros, debido a las varias limitaciones que el propio sistema ha ido generando.

Hoy por hoy, las mujeres con las designaciones más importantes y además grandes representantes del género femenino son dos: Brigitte Stern y Gabrielle Kaufmann-Kohler. Ambas han marcado la diferencia en la historia de designaciones femeninas como árbitros por su reconocida trayectoria y excelencia profesional.

Es importante destacar que el incremento de la participación de mujeres en tribunales arbitrales, al igual que las designaciones recaídas sobre los árbitros hombres, debe hacerse en consideración de las cualidades profesionales y humanas de cada persona. Bajo ningún concepto se debería designar a mujeres solo por el hecho de ser mujer o por cumplir con una cuota preestablecida. Por el contrario, se debería brindar igualdad de oportunidades en función de sus méritos y esfuerzos.

El tener consciencia de la existencia de sesgos y patrones que culturalmente venimos repitiendo, como todo, tiene un lado negativo y un lado positivo. El lado negativo es, quizás, darnos cuenta que a pesar del desarrollo y crecimiento del arbitraje a nivel internacional, actualmente exista una gran diferencia en el número de designaciones de árbitros hombres y mujeres. Sin embargo, el lado positivo sería el haber despertado el interés de las mismas mujeres por cambiar una realidad que inconscientemente venía generándoles límites. Asimismo, el tener consciencia de que los cambios tienen que ser generados desde las mismas mujeres ha motivado a que muchas profesionales se preparen más y formen parte de los nuevos espacios que buscan fortalecer una red internacional de mujeres profesionales; y que, desde sus distintos roles en la comunidad arbitral, fomenten la participación de mujeres en tribunales arbitrales, la academia y como oradoras en conferencias de arbitraje.

Varias organizaciones y grupos han surgido con el afán de crear espacios en los que las mujeres profesionales interesadas en el arbitraje puedan generar contactos y tengan un punto de partida. Entre las organizaciones más relevantes con este fin están *Arbitral Women* desde 1993, *The Pledge* desde el 2015 y *CEA Mujeres* del Club Español del Arbitraje desde el 2017.

1. Caroline dos Santos, *Diversity in International Arbitration: a No-Woman's Land*, mayo de 2006. Disponible en https://www.lalive.law/wp-content/uploads/2018/12/Diversity-in-international-arbitration_dos-Santos.pdf..

Una manera de difundir y fomentar la participación de mujeres en el arbitraje desde las propias mujeres ha sido compartiendo sus experiencias y conocimientos profesionales, los retos a los que se han enfrentado a lo largo de sus carreras y la forma en que fueron escalando en su vida profesional. Esas experiencias motivan a otras jóvenes abogadas que, en muchas ocasiones, quieren incursionar en el mundo arbitral pero no saben de qué manera hacerlo.

Actualmente, existen también programas de mentoría para mujeres que desean conocer más acerca de arbitraje y que les permite tener contacto de manera personalizada con un mentor o mentora que pueda guiarlas según sus expectativas y los retos que deseen enfrentar.

El conocimiento sobre el bajo porcentaje de participación de mujeres en el arbitraje ha generado mucho interés en la comunidad arbitral internacional y ha despertado la conciencia al momento de escoger a un árbitro, invitar a una conferencista o sugerir algún nombre de una mujer.

Un importante paso para incrementar la participación de mujeres en el arbitraje viene también del lado de las instituciones arbitrales, ya que han comenzado a incluir en sus listas a reconocidas y destacadas mujeres, con experiencia y trayectoria profesional. La mayoría de los centros o cortes de arbitraje realizan un minucioso análisis al momento de incluir a un árbitro dentro de sus listas, por lo que el ser parte de una de ellas genera gran respaldo y confianza en quienes acuden a un proceso arbitral. Hace poco una de las más reconocidas cortes de arbitraje europeas, la Corte de Arbitraje de Madrid, alcanzó la paridad en designaciones de árbitros.[2]

Finalmente, los verdaderos cambios en materia de diversidad se verán en la medida que cada uno de los distintos actores tenga conciencia y se comprometa a considerar y designar a más mujeres como árbitros. Lo anterior, en función de su experiencia y capacidades y no simplemente por el hecho de ser mujer, dejando prejuicios o sesgos de lado, que inconscientemente acompañan a la humanidad desde hace mucho tiempo.

2. http://www.arbitramadrid.com/documents/20181/26618/180907+Nota+de+prensa.pdf/36b86733-4eac-4e81-ae45-4d0a897c2e72

CAPÍTULO 39

Tres mentores, tres lecciones[1]

Juan M. Rey

Litigar, a veces, es un oficio. Como el carpintero que empieza su carrera como aprendiz hasta llegar con los años a ser maestro, los litigantes solemos empezar como procuradores hasta llegar al ansiado *first chair*. La experiencia importa.

Porque está muy bien lo que leemos en los libros. Es necesario y un requisito para ser un buen litigante. Pero la experiencia, las "canas", pesan. En la experiencia, la repetición, hay un valor. No tan relevante como lo académico, sin duda. Pero los litigantes no trabajamos -todavía- convenciendo robots. Trabajamos convenciendo humanos. Seres con su propia historia, emociones y trasfondo. Y eso, se aprende en gran medida en la cancha.

En el mundo del arbitraje, nadie obtiene esa experiencia gratis. Debido al atractivo intelectual de la materia y un mal comprendido "glamour" en los papeles de lo que hacemos en arbitraje[2], la experiencia literalmente se paga. Abundan las pasantías gratuitas y los puestos de pasante a los que aplican graduados de las mejores maestrías y doctorados dispuestos a trabajar "por el pancho y la coca"[3].

Para navegar las traicioneras aguas del arbitraje y adquirir las canas relevantes, es importante tener un buen mentor que nos ayude. Quisiera utilizar tres ejemplos de mentores que fui adquiriendo por los años -anonimizados por supuesto- en la esperanza que anime a quien lea esta reseña a conseguirse los propios.

---

1. En este capítulo hablo de mentores profesionales, no de mentores personales. Para los segundos, me guardo para mí esas historias.
2. Cualquier persona que haya sido un asociado trabajando en una audiencia en París, Nueva York o cualquier otro lugar "glamoroso" sabe que (i) la pizza de Domino's (único sustento del asociado junior) sabe igual en todas las ciudades, con independencia de qué tan glamurosa sea la ciudad; (ii) cuando uno pasa tres o más días sin dormir, el suelo de un war room es mejor descanso que la mejor cama del Hotel Plaza de turno; y (iii) al final de una audiencia, lo único que se quiere es encerrarse en el hotel a dormir. Los únicos que disfrutan los lugares de audiencia suelen ser los árbitros, socios y los clientes (dicho esto con un poco de envidia sana, y otro poco de la otra).
3. Frase tomada de mi Mentor Argentino, según se define a continuación.

A mi primer mentor lo llamaremos el "Mentor Uruguayo". De mi Mentor Uruguayo, aprendí a litigar.

Mi Mentor Uruguayo es el socio encargado del área contenciosa en el primer estudio donde trabajé. Por esos motivos desconocidos de la vida, este socio que peina varias canas encima me tomó estima y me dejó ser su sombra por un buen tiempo[4]. En efecto, consciente que el proceso de *mentoring* de los grandes estudios es una linda historia que no siempre se plasma en los hechos, este socio prefirió entrenarme al mostrarme —en vivo y en directo— cómo destruía mis escritos uno por uno.

Así, como procurador[5] y luego como abogado de primer y segundo año, este socio me pedía trabajos directos constantemente y yo le mandaba mis mejores esfuerzos. Luego de enviar los escritos, en la noche, me sentaba detrás de su silla y veía cómo me corregía. Y el Mentor Uruguayo realmente corregía. Escritos enteros hechos con el más florido de los lenguajes terminaban reducidos a un gran manchón rojo de control de cambios.

No aprendí escribiendo sino viendo cómo escribía mi Mentor Uruguayo. Podría decirse que aprendí a escribir, leyendo.

A mi segundo mentor lo llamaremos el "Mentor Argentino". De mi Mentor Argentino, aprendí a confiar en mí mismo.

Salí del L.L.M. con 25 años, y un trabajo en Washington D.C. Todavía me acuerdo de mi primer día de trabajo en esa firma. No tenía ni idea de qué iba a hacer, cómo iba a hacerlo y cuánto me costaría hacer lo que me iban a pedir. [6] Llegué un lunes 2 de junio. No tenía casa, porque me habían pedido empezar antes. Llegué a un hotel mientras encontraba lugar para vivir. Al primer día la Asociada Senior del despacho —a quien le debo la vida, y la cordura— me avisó que a fin de mes teníamos un vencimiento de una dúplica de un arbitraje CNUDMI. Luego, a fin de julio, debíamos presentar un escrito en un proceso cautelar ante el CIADI, y debíamos celebrar una audiencia. Todo en dos meses.

Como siempre, uno sobrevive a estos embates de trabajo. Mi bautismo de fuego había sido un tanto acelerado (dos *filings* y una audiencia en los primeros dos meses) pero había salido airoso. Sin embargo, al tiempo, la Asociada Senior que me había protegido al comienzo decidió cambiar de trabajo. Ahí quedamos mi compañero y yo, dos recién llegados[7], trabajando directamente con nuestro jefe, quien en su juventud había sido el abogado a cargo de litigar -a los 30 años- los casos más relevantes de la primera década del s. XXI en arbitraje de inversión. Y yo sentía que apenas me sabía atar los cordones.

4. Mi Mentor Uruguayo mide cerca de dos metros. Yo claramente no. Demás está decir que caminando detrás suyo por las calles de ciudad vieja en mi querida Montevideo llevando carpetas de audiencia, más de una persona nos comparó con Don Quijote y Sancho Panza.
5. Dependiendo del país, procurador significa paralegal, interno, practicante o pasante.
6. Por supuesto que tampoco le había preguntado qué se esperaba de mí a quien sería mi jefe, porque entre los exámenes de calificación a la firma y los nervios de la situación, en mi entrevista hablamos del Real Hervido —un equipo amateur de Fray Bentos, en el departamento de Río Negro, Uruguay— en lugar de hacerle las preguntas que debía.
7. En la guerra se forjan lazos de hermandad. Siendo asociado de primer año forjas lazos aún más fuertes.

Nunca había visto a alguien trabajar como mi Mentor Argentino. Si mi compañero y yo pasábamos sin dormir, él pasaba sin dormir. En Audiencia preparaba el contrainterrogatorio y luego lo ejecutaba sin haber *pegado un ojo*. Todo lo que le mandábamos resultaba mejorado —hasta modificado íntegramente— luego de su corrección. Todo sin perder la fe en el arbitraje. Y en ese marco de admiración' nos dio a mi compañero y a mí, a los 26 y 28 años respectivamente, nuestros primeros interrogatorios. [8]

Yo no lo podía creer. Este socio de un estudio internacional que había litigado los casos que uno lee en los libros confiaba en mí, un chico de 26 o 27 años para ejecutar en audiencia contrainterrogatorios. Ese hecho —menor en su opinión, que hasta el día de hoy se enoja cuando yo le digo que le debo mi pequeña carrera porque él "*no quier*[e] *ser mentor de nadie*" — me dio más confianza en mí mismo que la mejor nota en el examen más difícil de cualquier universidad. Esa confianza me acompaña hasta hoy. Y hasta el día de hoy lo llamo para consultarle mis decisiones profesionales.

A mi tercer mentor lo llamaremos el "Mentor Chileno". De mi Mentor Chileno, estoy aprendiendo a vivir del arbitraje, sin morir en el intento.

Llegué de Washington D.C. a Santiago de Chile en pleno invierno sureño. Los primeros días en mi nueva oficina almorzaba a las 12.00 del mediodía —puntual— en mi escritorio trabajando. Al sexto día un socio de la oficina pasó a ver si estaba bien y para animarme a que salga a almorzar. "*Mira que no estás más en D.C.*". Este aterrizaje luego de varios años en Estados Unidos a una cultura muy parecida a la mía sin llegar a ser mía fue un aprendizaje en sí mismo. Quería todo ya. No entendía cómo alguien podía *subirse a una call* cuatro minutos tarde. Me desesperaba ante reuniones que pudieron haber sido un mail de equipo. Estaba viviendo un proceso de adaptación.

"*Tranquilo Gordo, que cada día tiene su afán*". Mi Mentor Chileno más que mentor fue un psicólogo de nuestra vuelta a América Latina. Así, es muy difícil seguir nervioso por un resultado cuando tu jefe —un tipo que a los 31 ya era árbitro CCI— está muy tranquilo y confiando en el proceso.

Es que litigar tiene un requisito práctico de sentido común que -creo- te lo dan principalmente las canas. Precisamente, cuando alguien -como mi Mentor Chileno- ha visto decenas de *filings* anuales por quince años ininterrumpidos, es que puede decirle a su asociado senior que no se preocupe por un *filing* ante un evento relevante de salud. "*Gordo, nadie es imprescindible, la salud está primero*".

En la vorágine de un caso, a veces se pierde de vista el bosque. Evidentemente si hay que trabajar toda la noche se trabaja toda la noche. Pero mi Mentor Chileno me enseñó que un excelente abogado exhausto es un mal abogado. Que, a veces, la búsqueda de la perfección es enemiga de los resultados. Que cuando vienen los hijos, los cumpleaños perdidos no tienen repetición. Que ser feliz y ser *Banda 1 de Chambers* es compatible.

8. Recuerdo el mío hasta el día de hoy. Fue un directo y re directo breve, en una audiencia bajo las reglas CNUDMI en París. El abogado de la contraparte que hacía el contrainterrogatorio era uno de esos abogados del que uno lee sus artículos y admira profundamente. Objeté dos veces a su contrainterrogatorio, y una la gané. Llamé a mi novia (ahora esposa) a contarle que había ganado una objeción. Ella estaba feliz por mí, pero me confesó que no terminaba de entender mi emoción.

CAPÍTULO 40

Como sobrevivir una década en Dechert

Juan Felipe Merizalde

"*Me van a echar...*", pensé, mientras bajaba por la Rue des Courcelles, en dirección a la esquina con la Avenue de Messine. Eran las 11:45 PM y el último recorrido del bus 80 -con dirección a Jules Joffrin- pasaría en cualquier momento. "*¿Cómo se me ocurrió hacer eso?*", "*¿Con qué pagaré el arriendo a fin de mes?*", seguí pensando. Los 1800 euros mensuales que me pagaban en 2008 alcanzaban, en el mejor de los casos, para los gastos del mes, un par de salidas, y un ahorro de 100 o 200 euros para viajar en diciembre a ver a mi madre. Pero esa fría noche de invierno era distinta de las cuatro o cinco noches por semana en las que tenía que correr para alcanzar el último bus. Ese día, jamás lo olvidaré, Eduardo -mi jefe, mi mentor, y no obstante ello, mi amigo- descubrió que yo era el responsable de una fechoría que podía y debía representar el fin de mis días en el mundo arbitral.

Veníamos de terminar la audiencia de daños en el caso Oxy. Oxy fue un unicornio para muchos. El último día, con una mezcla de cansancio, orgullo y satisfacción, pedimos pizza para todos; expertos, testigos, abogados y clientes. Tras un rato de diversión recordando anécdotas de la audiencia, uno de ellos sugirió el plan que marcaría mi futuro: "*Guardemos las cajas vacías de la pizza y cuando Eduardo venga en su* scooter, *las pegamos en su parte trasera* (la de la moto, no la de Eduardo) *para que tenga que repartirlas*". El plan era perfecto. Sin embargo, nadie imaginó que el olor de la pizza se escaparía del armario y, mezclada con el olor de dos jóvenes que llevaban tantas noches en un espacio de ocho metros cuadrados, nos delataría.

Once años más tarde, mientras reflexionaba sobre esta amable invitación a escribir sobre el difícil tema de sobrevivir una década en Dechert, pensé que esta historia lo resumiría todo. Y al menos cinco circunstancias dan cuenta de ello:

§40.01 DESDE ABAJO CRECERÁS

Primero, porque en Dechert, al igual que en muchas otras firmas en París, el camino de entrada será largo y lleno de lestrigones. Para el joven latinoamericano que llega con dos maletas, un par de centavos y un diploma bajo el brazo, el camino implicará competir con abogados europeos, muchos de ellos con maestrías e intercambios, con la esperanza de que se fijen en ti y acepten tramitarte el tan anhelado permiso de trabajo francés. No es raro, entonces, que el estudioso latinoamericano, que quizás ya había trabajado en su país de origen, deba comenzar como pasante en un *open space* con siete u ocho pares deseosos de ser "el afortunado" (en raras ocasiones eran dos) que reciben una oferta al final de la pasantía. Hay que aceptar que toda pirámide tiene una base inferior y esa base serás tú y cargarás todo ese peso.

§40.02 TRABAJAR, TRABAJAR Y TRABAJAR

Segundo, un común denominador de los asociados en Dechert es su entrega irrestricta al trabajo. En especial en los primeros años, será difícil capotear la vida personal con las duras exigencias del trabajo. El camino del arbitraje internacional —en Dechert y en las demás firmas grandes—implicará duros sacrificios. Pero la recompensa es inmensa.

§40.03 LA PASIÓN

La historia de la pizza no guarda relación con la pasión. Pero esto no es un *non sequitur*. La tercera característica del asociado en Dechert es que cada cual tiene una particularidad o rareza que lo distingue del abogado normal u ordinario. Ya sea el sentido negro del humor, una franqueza casi brutal, la timidez del intelectual o la hiperactividad de un niño pequeño, la verdad es que todos en Dechert somos un poco *freaks*. Y estas cualidades que inconscientemente buscamos en las entrevistas de trabajo reflejan, de una forma difícil de explicar, la pasión del que ama el derecho y el arbitraje. Y este quizás será mi único consejo: si no sientes pasión por esta carrera, es mejor que no lo hagas. Como Ulises, según Cavafis, cuando emprendas tu viaje a Ítaca, pide que el camino sea largo.

§40.04 APRENDER DE NUEVO

Cuarto, el asociado de Dechert debe aprender a olvidar y querer aprenderlo todo de nuevo. Todos llegamos a Dechert creyendo que sabíamos escribir. Muchos habían actuado en teatro, fueron representantes estudiantiles o participaron en *moots*, por lo que creían dominar la palabra. Nos equivocamos. El trabajo de Dechert, me precio en afirmarlo por escrito, tiene un sello implícito de calidad que requiere re-aprender lo que creíamos ya sabido. Hay que encontrar la honestidad y humildad de aprender de nuevo. Nunca olvidaré la historia de uno de los mejores amigos que tuve en Dechert. Un día de invierno en 2010, este héroe sin capa dejó su carta de renuncia sobre el escritorio del jefe. Minutos más tarde, este vino furioso y le devolvió la carta. "*Esto es inaceptable*". La carta estaba llena de correcciones en rojo, repeticiones insulsas y falta de estructura. "*Si va a darme una carta, deme algo bien hecho*". Mi amigo se rio nerviosamente, tiró la carta a la papelera y siguió trabajando. Un par de años más tarde, presentó su carta de renuncia, esta vez bien escrita. El jefe la aceptó y mi amigo es hoy por hoy uno de los abogados más brillantes del arbitraje internacional en Francia.

§40.05 SERÁS PARTE DE LA FAMILIA

Finalmente, una vez que sobrepases el horrible filtro de la pasantía y los primeros años de ser asociado, comenzarás a sentir que haces parte de una familia. Y en las familias hay cariño y comprensión, pero mucha exigencia. Durante la redacción de este capítulo, tuve la triste noticia de que mi madre estuvo al borde de la muerte. La comprensión de mi familia en Dechert me dejó atónito. Jamás olvidaré cómo mis jefes y colegas me recriminaron por responder correos o llamar a preguntar si todo andaba bien. Al igual que los editores de este libro, que tuvieron mucha paciencia conmigo, lo humano primó sobre lo profesional. Y esta es una de las calidades para las que las palabras siempre serán cortas. Nunca sabré si la fechoría de la pizza influyó en la decisión de contratarme. Pero una década más tarde, y sin haber nunca pisado otra firma internacional, me atrevo a decir que este barco con sus poseidones, lestrigones y cíclopes me ha llevado por todas las Ítacas que quise visitar.

www.ingramcontent.com/pod-product-compliance
Lightning Source LLC
LaVergne TN
LVHW020003031026
849161LV00023B/858
* 9 7 8 9 4 0 3 5 1 7 6 0 5 *